VISITING COLLEGE CAMPUSES

THE PRINCETON REVIEW

VISITING COLLEGE CAMPUSES

Seventh Edition

BY JANET SPENCER AND SANDRA MALESON

RANDOM HOUSE, INC.
NEW YORK
www.PrincetonReview.com

Princeton Review Publishing, L. L. C.
2315 Broadway
New York, NY 10024
Email: bookeditor@review.com

This book was originally published by Citadel Press Books, an imprint of Carol Publishing Group, New York, and was originally titled The Complete Guide to College Visits.

ISBN 0-375-76400-3
ISSN 1016-1437

Editorial Director: Robert Franek
Editor: Erik Olson
Production Editor: Vivian Gomez
Production Coordinator: Greta Blau

Manufactured in the United States of America

9   8   7   6   5   4   3   2   1

Seventh Edition

Dedicated to Leonard Maleson, in loving memory.

ACKNOWLEDGMENTS

Our special thanks to the Admissions Office staff members at each of the colleges and universities included in our guidebook. To our own research staff, Jennifer McCormick, Judy Farbman, Mickey Aronskind, Gabrielle Vitellio, and C.J. Rinaldi, we express our particular appreciation. Their thoroughness and persistence provided the details that will be so useful to our readers. We would like to thank the folks at The Princeton Review—Jennifer Fallon, Amy Kinney, Kevin McDonough, Julie Mandelbaum, Michael Palumbo, Nicole Kontolefa, Robert Franek, and Greta Englert— for their production, design, and editorial skills, and for keeping the book current. Thanks, too, to the many college alumni and students who gave us the student's perspective on schools included in this work and to the many parents, particularly Joan Powell and Helen Pomeroy, whose understanding of our mission and unstinting support and encouragement sustained us. We also thank college guidance counselors Laura Clark and Debra Ellman for sharing with us their expertise. And thanks to Martin Levin, former president of the Association of American Publishers, Inc., in the absence of whose initial enthusiasm this book would never have gotten off the ground.

Our own families receive our deepest gratitude. Thanks to Paul Maleson and Ron Spencer for their legal advice and moral support. Susannah and Stephen Maleson helped with various chores (physical and mental) and provided Sandy's initial experiences with college visiting. Amanda Spencer's college search and the prospect of George Spencer's college search were the real force that started the whole project.

This book has been fun to put together; we hope you have fun using it.

CONTENTS

INTRODUCTION

PARENTS, READ THIS

Planning the successful college trip can be a logistical nightmare. *Visiting College Campuses* will help you avoid this nightmare by simplifying the planning process. Since all the information you need is provided here in one place, you can concentrate on making the college visiting experience pleasurable for you, your prospective college student, and the whole family. The college visit is a time to be together and to share the common goal of finding the environment in which your college student will thrive academically and socially for the next four (or five, or six) years.

If you are at all involved in your child's college application process, you will probably play a major role in planning these college visits. While you know they are supposed to be enjoyable, uplifting, and informative experiences, you may be overwhelmed by the prospect of making them happen. Even the seasoned college visitor can feel this way because each child has his or her own personalized list of possible colleges. What's more, even if you're visiting some schools for the second time, the information you gathered the last time around may well be obsolete. Sure, the college is still in the same place, but don't assume the admissions office is.

You may be asking yourself "Where do I start?" or, more plaintively, "Why am I doing this?" Well, relax. We put this book together to help you, and we did so for three reasons. First, we think visiting colleges is important. Each trip will teach you and your child not only about the specific schools you visit, but also about colleges in general. Your child will acquire a basis for comparison and will refine his or her ideas of what to look for in a college. Second, we think college visiting should be a great experience, a sort of mini-vacation. This country contains a wealth of universities and colleges that can stimulate the indifferent scholar and inspire the budding genius. Some of these schools will introduce you to intriguing spots you may not otherwise visit. The third reason is perhaps the most important. Even if your teenager is super-confident, you can't overlook the possibility that he might end up in a "safety" school. Anyone can suffer the disappointment of rejection from the first-choice school, and a visit to other colleges can turn up exciting second choices (and may even lead to a change in first choice). Help your child find these great places—**GO VISITING!**

STUDENTS, READ THIS (PARENTS TOO)

Visiting a college shouldn't be an awful experience, but it can be. Students and their families often optimistically embark on college visits without planning where to stay, what questions to ask, or what to do while they're there. You may be lucky; this seat-of-the-pants approach can sometimes work, but it's always best to have a plan.

That's why we wrote *Visiting College Campuses*. Whatever time you've allowed for visiting Dream College should be spent learning about the life you'll live if you go there, not rushing around looking for the admissions office, the nearest Ramada Inn, or the tour guide who left 15 minutes before you arrived.

SOME THINGS TO THINK ABOUT IN ADVANCE

The college visit, at a minimum, will consist of a tour and, typically, a group information session and/or individual interview. With the proper planning, this can be accomplished in two to three hours. Here are a few reasons for allowing more time.

If you have special interests, by all means, plan to explore what the college has to offer you in these areas. You may want to sit in on a lecture by some well-known professor. If so, you can check the sidebar information in each college entry in this book to see what kind of arrangements you need to make. If you plan on participating in inter-collegiate athletics, an interview with a coach will give you insight into the program offered, the requirements for participation, how your schedule will be affected, and what restrictions (athletes' tables, curfews, etc.) will affect your day-to-day life.

Just remember, you can't see everything in one visit. In fact, if you try, you may have nothing left in your mind but a blur. It's more important for you to see the things that are important to you or that will impact your daily life on campus. If you find that the tour still leaves some of your questions unanswered, by all means, speak up. Ideally, you will have allowed time to spend in the campus social centers, such as the student union. Plan on eating lunch in the cafeteria or having a snack in the coffee shop. If school is in session, you'll be in the right place to get a feel for the students.

If the surrounding environment is important to you, take time to check it out. By exploring the nearby town, or discovering the lack thereof, you will avoid future surprises.

SOME SPECIFICS TO THINK ABOUT WHEN YOU VISIT

When visiting colleges, you will have certain questions in mind. The more colleges you visit, the more these questions will be refined and prioritized. The following list of questions isn't all-inclusive, but it does deal with some of the larger issues that could affect what you look for in a school.

HOW BIG IS THE PLACE?

If your list of college choices includes a mix of large and small schools, you'll want to find out which type of campus is best for you. If you're at a large school, think about whether you will feel overwhelmed. Sure, you'll have a wide choice of courses and professors, but will you enjoy being in a class of 300 or more students? Will you enjoy walking across a large campus? If not, the cozy, friendly feel of a small school might hold more appeal for you. Will you enjoy knowing everyone on campus by your sophomore year, or will you be desperately seeking a new face? Try to talk to the students you see. What do they think about the class size and the size of the student body? How well do they maneuver on campus and access what they need or enjoy?

WHAT IS THE SCHOOL'S CHARACTER?

Some schools are known as party schools, some as bastions of intense intellectualism. Usually the reality is somewhere in between. Talk to the students. Do they know and love their school's reputation, or do their comments paint a different picture? Do the students stay on campus on weekends? What do they do? Are social events campus-wide and do all students participate? What kinds of social events are there? Is the football (lacrosse, basketball) team the main focus of social life? Does one have to belong to a fraternity or sorority to be in the mainstream? As you listen to the students' answers to your questions, or even to their random remarks about life on campus, you will glean something of the school's character.

WHAT ARE THE STUDENTS LIKE?

Once again, talk to the students, and listen to their answers. Are they friendly? Arrogant? Competitive? Where do they come from? Do they like the school? Why? Do their reasons relate to your own concerns? Are the students unified, or is there divisiveness on campus? Does everyone look like you, or not like you? How diverse and inclusive is the campus? Take a look at the bulletin boards and the school newspapers for clues.

A WORD ABOUT TOUR GUIDES . . .

We say "talk to students," but you might only have a chance to talk to the tour guide. By and large, the tour guide will be a wonderful advocate for the college. But, remember, tour guides are not chosen, nor do they volunteer, for the task of leading potential applicants around because they have complaints about the school. So expect their prepared remarks to be positive. They will answer your questions honestly, but you can assume that they will also put a positive gloss on their answers. Hence, our recommendation is that you keep your eyes and ears open and engage other students in conversation whenever possible.

A very important point must be made here. You will have a natural tendency to like or dislike a school based on your feelings about the tour guide. Try to restrain this inclination, especially when you're not impressed by your guide. He might not always be your type of person, but that doesn't mean you won't find other folks on campus who are. Look around.

LIVING V. LIFE

Beware of confusing the living situation with life on campus. You may be horrified when you see four students living in a room intended for two, or see long registration lines, large classes, and crowded cafeterias. This living situation results from a lot of people doing the same thing at the same time.

On the other hand, the life of the campus is defined by how its students interact, and what people do with their time. We've already talked about ways of getting the feel for the college life. If you can't have a great living situation *and* a great student life, consider your priorities.

AFTER YOUR VISIT

Usually, only the odd or wacky things about a visit to a college stick out in your mind, so right after your visit, *write down* your impressions about the school. Many people believe in a grading system from 1 to 10 for categories like food, social life, academics, campus, student body. We think it's more helpful to write down the words that first come to mind after your experience. Describe as fully as you can the range of things that come into your head. Most often, these words will translate to a summary of your experience. Sometimes one word will pop up more than once. Pay attention to what you write; that will give you insight into what you feel about the college.

Remember that a college visit, done properly, can be the most useful tool you have in understanding what it is like to be student at a given school and, eventually, deciding if you want to go there.

THE TEN-STEP PLAN
FOR SUCCESSFUL COLLEGE VISITS

Planning the college visiting trip can be daunting. At a minimum, it involves obtaining information and doing some logistical fancy footwork. This book contains all the information you need to make the planning easy and to ensure that the trip is great fun. Following this step-by-step plan will make your life even easier.

No doubt you already have in mind some colleges you want to visit. Where do you begin, and when? Hint: Your child will get the best feel for a school when students are around—this means visiting during its regular session. Here's how you do this:

STEP 1
Figure out the days your child has off from school beginning in the spring semester of junior year. Obvious times will be spring break and Easter or Passover break. Also, if possible, leave the last week of August as well as early September free for visiting.

STEP 2
Once you have isolated a block of days, target a general geographical area to visit.

STEP 3
Make sure the colleges you are planning to visit in that area will be in session during your proposed trip.

Keep in mind that colleges have spring breaks at different times. Some begin as early as the first week of March, and some as late as the second week of April. Consult the College Calendars in this book or check with the admissions office of the school(s) you wish to see. If some of the schools in your targeted area are in session and some are not (and only one trip is feasible), you will have to make some hard choices. You may choose to plan around the more serious possibilities on your list or, alternatively, around the schools you know least about. Perhaps moving your trip a few days earlier or later will make a difference. Or consider going back to Step 2 for a different geographical area.

Also note that some, but not all, schools start the fall semester in late August rather than after Labor Day. You may wish to use the last days of summer for making an extended trip. (Some schools discourage visits while students are arriving, so double check with the admissions office as to if, and when, your visit might not be appreciated.) Columbus Day weekend is another option for a trip, as some colleges are in session on Monday when your child may be off. Consult the College Calendars in this book.

Saturday visits may be possible if your child is interested in a nearby school. Usually, though not always, the school's admissions office is open on Saturday morning during the regular academic year, and there may be morning classes. Check the entry in this book for the school you are considering visiting on Saturday. The campus will probably be quieter on Saturday than it is during the regular week.

STEP 4

By this point you will have targeted a particular geographical area for your tour and have made a list of the schools you would like to visit. Here's a suggestion: As long as you are in the area, think about expanding your itinerary to include some other colleges in the neighborhood. Get ideas by consulting the maps in this book. Some of these colleges may be unfamiliar to you; check them out with the college guidance counselor or in a college guidebook. You may be in for some pleasant surprises.

STEP 5

You are now going to plot your itinerary. If you are visiting two or more schools in one trip, you will want to prevent backtracking by making a nice, easy loop. This will allow you to spend more time on campuses, and less time en route. Here's how:

Determine the first college you want to visit in the area and how you will get there. Check the entry for car, plane, bus, or train information and maps showing the major cities and their distances from the schools.

Now, in order to plan out your loop, you are going to have to know where your target schools are located in relation to each other. Many of the schools will be in towns you have never heard of. Instead of undertaking serious map work, simply consult the regional and state maps in this book, where this information is provided.

Once you have laid out your loop, establishing the order in which you are going to visit your target schools, you will want to know how long it will take you to get from one school to another. Refer to the Mileage Matrices in this book for the mileage between schools on a state-wide and region-wide basis. With this information, you can estimate how long it will take you to get from one school to another by car.

STEP 6

Now estimate how much time you will spend at the school. This largely depends on what you want to do when you visit. Your options may include some or all of the following: a self-guided tour of the campus using a map supplied by the admissions office, a student-led tour of the campus, an on-campus interview with an admissions office staff member, an information session (a group meeting with a staff member, often in lieu of interviews), a visit to classes, a meeting with a faculty member or athletic coach, an overnight stay. Check the entries in this book for details on availability, schedules and how and when to make arrangements. You can also call the school for additional information.

The basic college visit will include a student-led tour and possibly an interview or information session. For this, you should plan on a minimum of two to three hours per visit and no more than two visits per day.

Once you have determined what you want to do on campus and how long it will take you to get to the next college in your loop, you can identify the optimum time for your campus visit. The accuracy of your calculations here becomes more important, of course, the tighter your schedule.

STEP 7

What about arrangements? If you wish simply to go on a tour, this will require a minimum of advance planning, although some schools request advance notice even for tours—check the entry in this book. Tours are typically conducted according to a schedule and you may want to time your visit accordingly. Check the entries in this book or call the admissions office.

At many colleges, (though not all), your child can be interviewed by a staff member of the admissions office at the time of your visit, even though an application has yet to be filed. If an interview is required as part of the admissions process, consider coordinating the interview with your campus visit.

Now, if you opt for the on-campus interview, you will have to do some advance planning. Call the admissions office far enough in advance so that a convenient time slot is still available (see the entries in this book, since the required amount of advance notice varies from school to school). Hint: your child may be more comfortable touring the school before sitting down for the interview. Be sure to indicate your preference to the admissions office.

You may encounter a logistical hurdle if you are planning a spring trip. Some schools do not interview juniors until late spring (consult the entry in this book for details). In such an event, decide which is more important, seeing the school in session or having an on-campus interview.

Should your child schedule the interview? Some students may be up to this, but for others, merely talking about the interview and the college visit so far in advance will create unnecessary anxiety. It is okay for the parent to schedule the interview. In fact, ad hoc scheduling decisions may have to be made while conferring with the admissions office— decisions which are best made by the primary trip planner: you.

STEP 8

Now that you have the interview scheduled and know when the tour will depart, you can determine the precise time you should arrive at the admissions office. Hint: Plan to get there early so your child can relax before the tour and can look through student yearbooks and other publications.

Don't plan to rush off right after the interview either. During your 20- to 45-minute tour the guide will have taken you through the eating facilities and student union, but you may want to return on your own. Relax over lunch or coffee among the students.

STEP 9

Continue on! Consult your Step 5 itinerary to determine how long it will take to get to your next school. Allowing for adequate travel time, begin the planning process again at Step 6. Repeat this process for additional schools. Visiting more than two schools in one day is not advised.

STEP 10

Where to stay: Many college towns have great character. Why not stay in a local inn that has some special charm? Poke around in the shops or visit some of the local attractions. Or stay at a nearby resort, dude ranch, spa, campground, etc. and bring the whole family. In your free time, you can swim, play tennis, canoe, fish, or hike. Or splurge on a luxury hotel with an indoor pool and health club near shops and other amenities. Investigate what is within walking distance. There might be a delightful bed and breakfast with afternoon tea and homemade muffins in the morning, for example, right up the block. Sometimes the school itself has accommodations available. Check the entries in this book for all of the best, most convenient, and amusing accommodations near the colleges (as well as some budget options).

The key to the college trip is to make it fun and stress-free, as well as worthwhile. Advance planning will make things go smoothly and help you avoid disappointments. Good luck, and happy visiting.

PART I

How This Book Works

Visiting College Campuses helps you make sure you have everything planned in advance. To make it easier to find information about the schools of your choice, we've used the same format for every school. Look at the sample page below:

Office Hours

Page Header

The Blurb

Highlights

Sidebar

The Rest of the Story

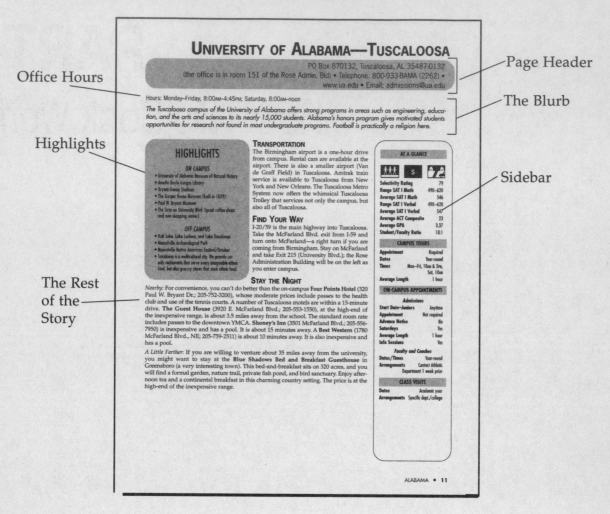

UNIVERSITY OF ALABAMA—TUSCALOOSA

PO Box 870132, Tuscaloosa, AL 35487-0132
(the office is in room 151 of the Rose Admin. Bld) • Telephone: 800-933-BAMA (2262) •
www.ua.edu • Email: admissions@ua.edu

Hours: Monday–Friday, 8:00AM–4:45PM; Saturday, 8:00AM–noon

The Tuscaloosa campus of the University of Alabama offers strong programs in areas such as engineering, education, and the arts and sciences to its nearly 15,000 students. Alabama's honors program gives motivated students opportunities for research not found in most undergraduate programs. Football is practically a religion here.

HIGHLIGHTS

ON CAMPUS
• University of Alabama Museum of Natural History
• Amelia Gayle Gorgas Library
• Bryant-Denny Stadium
• The Gorgas House Museum (built in 1829)
• Paul W. Bryant Museum
• The Strip on University Blvd. (great coffee shops and new shopping center)

OFF CAMPUS
• Hart Lake, Lake Lurleen, and Lake Tuscaloosa
• Moundville Archaeological Park
• Moundville Native American Festival/October
• Tuscaloosa is a multicultural city. We provide not only restaurants that serve every imaginable ethnic food, but also grocery stores that stock ethnic food.

TRANSPORTATION
The Birmingham airport is a one-hour drive from campus. Rental cars are available at the airport. There is also a smaller airport (Van de Graff Field) in Tuscaloosa. Amtrak train service is available to Tuscaloosa from New York and New Orleans. The Tuscaloosa Metro System now offers the whimsical Tuscaloosa Trolley that services not only the campus, but also all of Tuscaloosa.

FIND YOUR WAY
I-20/59 is the main highway into Tuscaloosa. Take the McFarland Blvd. exit from I-59 and turn onto McFarland—a right turn if you are coming from Birmingham. Stay on McFarland and take Exit 215 (University Blvd.); the Rose Administration Building will be on the left as you enter campus.

STAY THE NIGHT
Nearby: For convenience, you can't do better than the on-campus **Four Points Hotel** (320 Paul W. Bryant Dr.; 205-752-3200), whose moderate prices include passes to the health club and use of the tennis courts. A number of Tuscaloosa motels are within a 15-minute drive. **The Guest House** (3920 E. McFarland Blvd.; 205-553-1550), at the high-end of the inexpensive range, is about 3.5 miles away from the school. The standard room rate includes passes to the downtown YMCA. **Shoney's Inn** (3501 McFarland Blvd.; 205-556-7950) is inexpensive and has a pool. It is about 15 minutes away. A **Best Western** (1780 McFarland Blvd., NE; 205-759-2511) is about 10 minutes away. It is also inexpensive and has a pool.

A Little Farther: If you are willing to venture about 35 miles away from the university, you might want to stay at the **Blue Shadows Bed and Breakfast Guesthouse** in Greensboro (a very interesting town). This bed-and-breakfast sits on 320 acres, and you will find a formal garden, nature trail, private fish pond, and bird sanctuary. Enjoy afternoon tea and a continental breakfast in this charming country setting. The price is at the high-end of the inexpensive range.

AT A GLANCE		
Selectivity Rating		79
Range SAT I Math		490–620
Average SAT I Math		546
Range SAT I Verbal		490–620
Average SAT I Verbal		547
Average ACT Composite		23
Average GPA		3.37
Student/Faculty Ratio		18:1

CAMPUS TOURS	
Appointment	Required
Dates	Year-round
Times	Mon–Fri, 10AM & 2PM, Sat, 10AM
Average Length	1 hour

ON-CAMPUS APPOINTMENTS	
Admissions	
Start Date–Juniors	Anytime
Appointment	Not required
Advance Notice	No
Saturdays	Yes
Average Length	1 hour
Info Sessions	Yes
Faculty and Coaches	
Dates/Times	Year-round
Arrangements	Contact Athletic Department 1 week prior

CLASS VISITS	
Dates	Academic year
Arrangements	Specific dept./college

ALABAMA • 11

Here's a rundown of the components you'll find on each page.

PAGE HEADER

The page header contains the college or university's admissions office address as well as the building it's in (which is not always included on the mailing address, but is very important to know once you're on campus). We've also included the admissions office phone number, fax number when possible, Web address, and e-mail address, so you can contact the school.

OFFICE HOURS

The header is followed by the admissions office's hours. Use this information to start planning your college visit. Write or call them (or, even better, do both) to arrange for your information session, tour, etc.

"The Blurb"

The blurb is the *italicized* stuff near the top of each profile. The general idea behind every blurb is to give you some useful and interesting information about the school—where it's located, what students do for fun, school history, amusing trivia, etc.

Sidebar

The At a Glance section that starts each sidebar relates some basic information that, like the blurb, is meant to give you a general sense of the school and the students who go there. The three icons at the top of each sidebar give the school's enrollment, tuition, and environment respectively.

Enrollment:

Large (more than 10,000 undergraduates)

Medium (4,000 to 10,000 undergraduates)

Small (less than 4,000 undergraduates)

Tuition (for in-state students):

Very Expensive (more than $15,000)

Expensive ($10,000 to $15,000)

Moderate (less than $10,000)

Environment:

Urban/City

Suburban

Rural/Small Town

The rest of the sidebar contains all sorts of information about the things you should do to learn about a school when visiting campus. This information will help you plan stuff like interviews (with admissions, faculty, and coaches), tours, information sessions, dorm stays, and class visits.

Highlights

Once you've survived that nerve-wracking interview and the thirty-minute campus tour in the rain (minus your umbrella), why not kick back and see the sights? In the highlights box, we have listed some of the attractions for which each college town is famous as well as some points of interest right on campus. These recommendations run the gamut from museums and art galleries to state parks and waterslides. We hope they make your good visits even more enjoyable, and your bad visits something less than disastrous.

The Rest of the Story

The remainder of the entry is about the part of your trip that happens off campus: how to get to the school and where to stay. You know, the fun stuff. It's divided into the following sections:

Transportation

This section starts out with the transportation available to campus; nothing makes a short couple of days seem like a long, horrible couple of days like getting stuck at the bus station, or taking a train when you could have flown. Once you decide on plane, train, or bus, we tell you the best way to get to campus from the airport, train station, or bus depot.

Find Your Way

If you are looking at schools in your general vicinity, you are probably driving. For you, the driver, we provide directions from the major highways to the front door of the admissions office.

Stay the Night

If you're going to stay overnight, *make reservations*. Do not get to the school and then decide where you are going to stay. Too often this puts you at the mercy of over-priced on-campus motels or last-resort hovels only too happy to take a tourist for a few extra bills. *Visiting College Campuses* gives you tons of choices—hotels, motels, resorts, bed-and-breakfasts—at each college we cover. We also let you know what prices to expect: cheap, moderate, or pricey. We even tell you when a subtle drop of a university's name will get you a special rate.

AND THERE'S MORE

To start off each new state, we provide a detailed road map and mileage matrix for the colleges and large cities in that state, so you know how far it is from, say, Dallas to the University of Texas at Austin, how far it is from school to school within the state, and how far it is from Dallas to San Antonio.

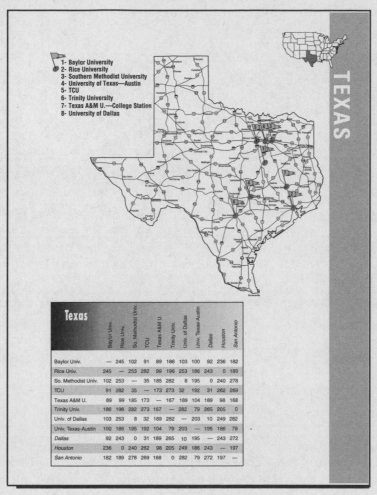

1- Baylor University
2- Rice University
3- Southern Methodist University
4- University of Texas—Austin
5- TCU
6- Trinity University
7- Texas A&M U.—College Station
8- University of Dallas

TEXAS

Texas

	Baylor Univ.	Rice Univ.	So. Methodist Univ.	TCU	Texas A&M U.	Trinity Univ.	Univ. of Dallas	Univ. Texas-Austin	Dallas	Houston	San Antonio
Baylor Univ.	—	245	102	91	89	186	103	100	92	236	182
Rice Univ.	245	—	253	282	99	196	253	186	243	0	189
So. Methodist Univ.	102	253	—	35	185	282	8	195	0	240	278
TCU	91	282	35	—	173	273	32	192	31	262	269
Texas A&M U.	89	99	185	173	—	167	189	104	189	98	168
Trinity Univ.	186	196	282	273	167	—	282	79	265	205	0
Univ. of Dallas	103	253	8	32	189	282	—	203	10	249	282
Univ. Texas-Austin	100	186	195	192	104	79	203	—	195	186	79
Dallas	92	243	0	31	189	265	10	195	—	243	272
Houston	236	0	240	262	98	205	249	186	243	—	197
San Antonio	182	189	278	269	168	0	282	79	272	197	—

The road maps and mileage matrices will help you better plan a group of visits in a single state. Similarly, in Appendix One we have included mileage information for specific regions of the country. So, for example, if you are looking at schools in the South Atlantic region, you can find out how far it is from the University of Miami to the University of Georgia. It's good to know in advance that you'll be driving 717 miles between the two campuses. Florida and Georgia may be adjoining, but Miami and Athens most certainly are not.

Southeast	Bellarmine Univ.	Birmingham	Centre Coll.	Fisk Univ.	Jackson, MS	Louisville	Millsaps Coll.	Rhodes Coll.	Tuskegee Univ.	Univ. Alabama	Univ. Kentucky	Univ. Mississippi	Univ. South	Univ. Tennessee	Vanderbilt Univ.
Bellarmine Univ.	—	365	85	175	587	0	585	376	491	420	77	460	263	245	175
Birmingham	365	—	377	192	245	360	240	249	136	49	402	175	162	257	188
Centre Coll.	85	377	—	194	603	92	604	399	514	435	36	424	241	155	189
Fisk Univ.	175	192	194	—	414	176	412	203	319	247	214	287	93	181	0
Jackson, MS	587	245	603	414	—	586	585	213	287	187	660	157	407	493	414
Louisville	0	360	92	176	586	—	208	378	492	418	74	399	264	247	175
Millsaps Coll.	585	240	604	412	585	208	—	208	286	190	623	167	414	496	411
Rhodes Coll.	376	249	399	203	213	378	208	—	386	238	424	65	260	384	210
Tuskegee Univ.	491	136	514	319	287	492	286	386	—	149	530	312	270	337	325
Univ. Alabama	420	49	435	247	187	418	190	238	149	—	462	163	220	214	246
Univ. Kentucky	77	402	36	214	660	74	623	424	530	462	—	465	277	172	214
Univ. Mississippi	460	175	424	287	157	399	167	65	312	163	465	—	274	468	249
Univ. South	263	162	241	93	407	264	414	260	270	220	277	274	—	161	96
Univ. Tennessee	245	257	155	181	493	247	496	384	337	214	172	468	161	—	180
Vanderbilt Univ.	175	188	189	0	414	175	411	210	325	246	214	249	96	180	—

Appendix Two contains a state-by-state guide to each school's academic calendar. The easy-to-reference format shows you exactly what's going on, month by month, at the schools of your choice. So if you're planning to visit Auburn University in March, you'll know at a glance that exams are scheduled during the second and third weeks, and you can plan your trip accordingly.

School	January	February	March	April	May
Alabama AUBURN UNIVERSITY	Winter session begins 2nd wk. No classes MLK Day.	Classes continue.	Exams 2nd–3rd wks.	Spring break 1st wk.	Exams 2nd wk. Summer session begins 3rd wk.
TUSKEGEE UNIVERSITY	Spring session begins 3rd wk.	Classes continue.	Spring break 2nd wk. Classes resume 3rd wk.	No classes Good Fri. through Easter Mon.	Exams 2nd wk.

PART II

College Entries Arranged by State

ALABAMA

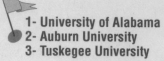

1- University of Alabama
2- Auburn University
3- Tuskegee University

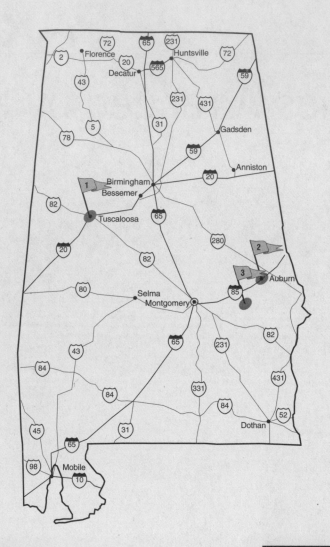

Alabama	Auburn Univ.	Tuskegee Univ.	Univ. of Alabama	Birmingham	Montgomery
Auburn Univ.	—	20	165	117	59
Tuskegee Univ.	20	—	149	136	39
Univ. of Alabama	165	149	—	49	104
Birmingham	117	136	49	—	93
Montgomery	59	39	104	93	—

AUBURN UNIVERSITY

Admissions Office, 202 Martin Hall, Auburn, AL 36849-5149
(Martin Hall is on Thatch Avenue) • Telephone: 800-282-8769 •
Email: admissions@auburn.edu

Hours: Monday–Friday, 8:00AM–4:45PM

Auburn is a cost-effective, conservative school with southern values that offers a ton of majors and is especially strong in the sciences. Every student is required to complete a broad core curriculum during freshman and sophomore year that covers writing skills and all of the major arts and sciences. Much of the social life revolves around athletics; there is plenty of "Auburn spirit," especially for the football team.

HIGHLIGHTS

ON CAMPUS
- University Theater

OFF CAMPUS
- Old Main and Church Street district
- Chewacla State Park

TRANSPORTATION

Hartsfield International Airport in Atlanta, Georgia is approximately 100 miles away from campus. Dixie Excursions (334-887-6295) runs vans for four daily round-trips between the airport and campus. Rental cars are available at the airport. The Columbus, Georgia airport is 40 miles away from campus but is not as accessible as the Atlanta airport.

FIND YOUR WAY

From I-85 (which runs from Atlanta, Georgia to Montgomery, Alabama), take Exit 51 onto U.S. Rte. 29 N. This becomes College St., which borders the campus. The campus is approximately three miles away from I-85.

STAY THE NIGHT

Nearby: Across the street from the university is the **Auburn University Hotel and Conference Center** (241 S. College St.; 334-821-8200 or 800-2-AUBURN), where you can rent a double room at a moderate rate. The hotel has a restaurant, lounge, gift shop, pool, weight room, and tennis court privileges. Also across the street is the inexpensive **Heart of Auburn Motel** (334-887-3462 or 800-843-5634). This large motel offers basic accommodations and has a pool. **The Crenshaw Guest House** (371 N. College St.; 334-821-1131) offers suites at a moderate rate and a carriage house in the garden at an inexpensive rate. It is a few blocks from the university and is on a historic block.

A Little Farther: **The Quality Inn—University Center** (1577 S. College St.; 334-821-7001) is one mile away. It is inexpensive (tell them you're visiting the university), and you can enjoy a pool, game room, restaurant, lounge, and gift shop. Bands play on the premises Friday and Saturday nights. For additional lodging, see www.auburn-opelika.com.

AT A GLANCE

Selectivity Rating		78
Range SAT I Math		510–610
Average SAT I Math		563
Range SAT I Verbal		490–600
Average SAT I Verbal		547
Average ACT Composite		24
Average GPA		3.34
Student/Faculty Ratio		16:1

CAMPUS TOURS

Appointment	Required
Dates	Year-round
Times	Mon–Fri, 8:00AM–4PM
Average Length	1 hour

ON-CAMPUS APPOINTMENTS

Admissions

Start Date–Juniors	Anytime
Appointment	Required
Advance Notice	1 week
Saturdays	No

Faculty and Coaches

Dates/Times	Year-round
Arrangements	Contact faculty directly

CLASS VISITS

Dates	Year-round
Arrangements	Contact Admissions Office

TUSKEGEE UNIVERSITY

Admissions Office, Old Administration Building, Tuskegee Institute, Tuskegee, AL 36088 • Telephone: 800-622-6531 • www.tuskegee.edu • Email: admissions@tusk.edu

Hours: Monday–Friday, 8:00AM–4:30PM

Despite several quality liberal arts departments and a great veterinary program (over 70 percent of all African American veterinarians in the world are trained here), Tuskegee is proudest of its engineering programs, which enroll nearly a quarter of the students. It also produces the most African American military officers—including West Point and the Naval Academy. Alumni of "the Tuskegee Experience" include 1980s pop phenom Lionel Richie.

AT A GLANCE

Selectivity Rating	72
Range SAT I Math	370–550
Average SAT I Math	438
Range SAT I Verbal	340–540
Average SAT I Verbal	441
Average ACT Composite	19
Average GPA	3.2
Student/Faculty Ratio	13:1

CAMPUS TOURS

Appointment	Preferred
Dates	Year-round
Times	7 days a week
Average Length	Varies

ON-CAMPUS APPOINTMENTS

Admissions
Start Date—Juniors	N/A
Appointment	Preferred
Saturdays	Sometimes
Info Sessions	Yes

Faculty and Coaches
Dates/Times	Year-round
Arrangements	Other, 1 week

CLASS VISITS

Arrangements	Contact Visiting Center

TRANSPORTATION

The Montgomery Airport is approximately 40 miles away from campus. Taxi and limousine services are available to take you to campus. You can also take a taxi from the airport to the Montgomery bus station, and then take a bus to the university.

FIND YOUR WAY

Take I-85 or U.S. Rte. 29 to Tuskegee.

STAY THE NIGHT

Nearby: You can't get nearer than the on-campus **Kellogg Conference Center,** a state-of-the-art facility with luxurious hotel accommodations, dining facilities, meeting rooms, and satellite-learning capability. The Conference Center provides a delectable breakfast and luncheon buffet, as well as daily a-la-cart selections.

A Little Farther: Auburn is 20 minutes away from Tuskegee. See the Auburn University entry for places to stay in that area.

HIGHLIGHTS

ON CAMPUS
- George Washington Carver Museum
- Kellogg Conference Center
- Tuskegee Chapel
- Tuskegee Cemetery
- General Daniel "Chappie" James Center

OFF CAMPUS
- Carver Museum
- Tuskegee National Forest

UNIVERSITY OF ALABAMA—TUSCALOOSA

PO Box 870132, Tuscaloosa, AL 35487-0132
(the office is in room 151 of the Rose Admin. Bld) • Telephone: 800-933-BAMA (2262) •
www.ua.edu • Email: admissions@ua.edu

Hours: Monday–Friday, 8:00AM–4:45PM; Saturday, 8:00AM–noon

The Tuscaloosa campus of the University of Alabama offers strong programs in areas such as engineering, education, and the arts and sciences to its nearly 15,000 students. Alabama's honors program gives motivated students opportunities for research not found in most undergraduate programs. Football is practically a religion here.

HIGHLIGHTS

ON CAMPUS
- University of Alabama Museum of Natural History
- Amelia Gayle Gorgas Library
- Bryant-Denny Stadium
- The Gorgas House Museum (built in 1829)
- Paul W. Bryant Museum
- The Strip on University Blvd. (great coffee shops and new shopping center)

OFF CAMPUS
- Holt Lake, Lake Lurleen, and Lake Tuscaloosa
- Moundville Archaeological Park
- Moundville Native American Festival/October
- Tuscaloosa is a multicultural city. We provide not only restaurants that serve every imaginable ethnic food, but also grocery stores that stock ethnic food.

TRANSPORTATION

The Birmingham airport is a one-hour drive from campus. Rental cars are available at the airport. There is also a smaller airport (Van de Graff Field) in Tuscaloosa. Amtrak train service is available to Tuscaloosa from New York and New Orleans. The Tuscaloosa Metro System now offers the whimsical Tuscaloosa Trolley that services not only the campus, but also all of Tuscaloosa.

FIND YOUR WAY

I-20/59 is the main highway into Tuscaloosa. Take the McFarland Blvd. exit from I-59 and turn onto McFarland—a right turn if you are coming from Birmingham. Stay on McFarland and take Exit 215 (University Blvd.); the Rose Administration Building will be on the left as you enter campus.

STAY THE NIGHT

Nearby: For convenience, you can't do better than the on-campus **Four Points Hotel** (320 Paul W. Bryant Dr.; 205-752-3200), whose moderate prices include passes to the health club and use of the tennis courts. A number of Tuscaloosa motels are within a 15-minute drive. **The Guest House** (3920 E. McFarland Blvd.; 205-553-1550), at the high-end of the inexpensive range, is about 3.5 miles away from the school. The standard room rate includes passes to the downtown YMCA. **Shoney's Inn** (3501 McFarland Blvd.; 205-556-7950) is inexpensive and has a pool. It is about 15 minutes away. A **Best Western** (1780 McFarland Blvd., NE; 205-759-2511) is about 10 minutes away. It is also inexpensive and has a pool.

A Little Farther: If you are willing to venture about 35 miles away from the university, you might want to stay at the **Blue Shadows Bed and Breakfast Guesthouse** in Greensboro (a very interesting town). This bed-and-breakfast sits on 320 acres, and you will find a formal garden, nature trail, private fish pond, and bird sanctuary. Enjoy afternoon tea and a continental breakfast in this charming country setting. The price is at the high-end of the inexpensive range.

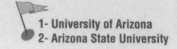

1- University of Arizona
2- Arizona State University

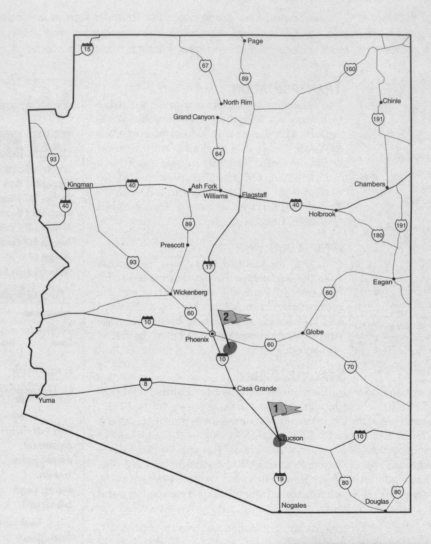

Arizona	Arizona State Univ.	Univ. Arizona	Phoenix	Tucson
Arizona State Univ.	—	103	4	113
Univ. Arizona	103	—	117	0
Phoenix	4	117	—	117
Tucson	113	0	117	—

ARIZONA STATE UNIVERSITY

Undergraduate Admissions Office, PO Box 870112, Tempe, AZ 85287-0112 • Telephone: 480-965-7788 • www.asu.edu • Email: ugradinq@asu.edu

Hours: Monday–Friday, 8:00AM–5:00PM

It's hard not to have a good time at ASU, what with year-round sun, warmth, fantastic sports and recreation facilities, and over 30,000 peers to accompany you as you strut through the streets of Tempe. Although the school basically caters to business students, there are a number of outstanding programs here.

HIGHLIGHTS

ON CAMPUS
• ASU Memorial Union
• Grady Gammage Auditorium
• ASU Art Museum
• Sun Devil Stadium
• Computing Commons Gallery

OFF CAMPUS
• Tempe Town Lake
• Desert Botanical Gardens
• Baseball Spring Training
• Phoenix Zoo
• The Grand Canyon

TRANSPORTATION
Sky Harbor Airport in Phoenix is approximately 15 minutes from campus. Taxis, limousines, and shared rides are available at the airport, or you can call a local taxi company or Super Shuttle (800-331-3565 from outside Arizona, or 602-244-9000 in Arizona). Amtrak train and Greyhound bus service are available to Phoenix. Taxis can take you to campus from the stations. Phoenix Transit System buses also travel between Phoenix and Tempe (call 602-257-8426 for more information).

FIND YOUR WAY
From Sky Harbor Airport, take Highway 202 Loop East to Scottsdale/Rural Rd. Turn right (south) onto Rural Rd. to Apache Blvd. Turn right (west) onto Apache Blvd. to Forest Avenue. Turn right (north) onto Forest Avenue. The Student Services building is located on the corner of Forest Avenue and Lemon Street (southwest corner of campus). Park in Visitor Parking Structure #1.

STAY THE NIGHT
Nearby: You have three convenient choices just across the street from the university. **Twin Palms Hotel** (225 E. Apache Blvd.; 480-967-9431) has moderate rates and a heated outdoor pool. **The Holiday Inn** (915 E. Apache Blvd.; 480-968-3451) is slightly more expensive but still moderately priced. It has a dining room, a heated outdoor pool, and an exercise room. **The Tempe Mission Palms Hotel** (60 E. 5th St.; 480-894-1400) is the priciest of the three, with most rooms in the expensive range; but some rooms are available at a moderate rate. It has an exercise room, a sauna, a Jacuzzi, two tennis courts, a lounge, and a restaurant.

A Little Farther: The area is known for its beautiful resorts and hotels that can accommodate a wide range of interests and needs. For more information call Tempe Chamber of Commerce at 480-967-7891.

AT A GLANCE

Selectivity Rating	76
Range SAT I Math	490–610
Average SAT I Math	551
Range SAT I Verbal	480–590
Average SAT I Verbal	538
Average ACT Composite	23
Average GPA	3.36
Student/Faculty Ratio	22:1

CAMPUS TOURS

Appointment	Preferred
Dates	Year-round
Times	Contact Admissions Office (480-727-7013)
Average Length	1 hour

ON-CAMPUS APPOINTMENTS

Admissions

Start Date—Juniors	Anytime
Appointment	Preferred
Advance Notice	Yes, 3 weeks
Saturdays	No
Average Length	30 min.
Info Sessions	Yes

Faculty and Coaches

Dates/Times	Year-round
Arrangements	Contact coach directly 3 weeks prior

CLASS VISITS

Dates	Academic year
Arrangements	Contact Admissions Office

UNIVERSITY OF ARIZONA

Admissions Office, Robert L. Nugent Building,
Tucson, AZ 85721-0040 • Telephone: 520-621-3237 • www.arizona.edu

Hours: Monday–Friday, 8:00AM–5:00PM

The University of Arizona in Tucson is a comprehensive institution with programs ranging from the liberal arts to technologically advanced engineering studies and about 25,000 highly satisfied and highly tanned students. Famous Chinese dissident and astrophysicist Fang Lizhi continues his groundbreaking research here, and he teaches undergraduate classes.

AT A GLANCE

Selectivity Rating		75
Range SAT I Math		500–620
Average SAT I Math		556
Range SAT I Verbal		490–600
Average SAT I Verbal		543
Average ACT Composite		23
Student/Faculty Ratio		19:1

CAMPUS TOURS

Appointment	Preferred
Dates	Year-round
Times	10AM–2PM
Average Length	1 hour

ON-CAMPUS APPOINTMENTS

Admissions

Start Date–Juniors	Anytime
Appointment	Not required
Advance Notice	Yes, 1 week
Saturdays	No
Average Length	45 min.
Info Sessions	Yes

Faculty and Coaches

Dates/Times	Year-round
Arrangements	Contact Admissions Office 1 week prior

CLASS VISITS

Dates	Year-round
Arrangements	Contact Admissions Office

TRANSPORTATION

Tucson International is 10 miles away from campus. For Stagecoach (van) service to campus, call 520-889-9681 at least 24 hours in advance; taxi service is also available. Amtrak trains and Greyhound/Trailways buses serve Tucson. Sun Tran is the public transportation system and operates buses throughout the area.

FIND YOUR WAY

Take Speedway to Mountain Avenue. Turn right onto Mountain and get on the left-hand lane. At the stop sign on Second Street, turn left. Visitor parking is in the garage to your right.

STAY THE NIGHT

Nearby: **Plaza Hotel and Conference Center** (1900 E. Speedway; 520-327-7341 or 800-843-8052) is direcly across the street from the university and is a full-service, seven-story hotel with an outdoor pool. The rates are highest during January and February. **Marriott University Park Hotel** (880 East Second St.; 520-792-4100 or 800-228-9290) is one block away from the university and is a four-star, full service, nine-story atrium hotel with an outdoor heated pool and Jacuzzi, a fitness center, a business center, and a full service restaurant. The **Lodge on the Desert** (306 N. Alvernon Way; 520-325-3366 or 800-456-5634) is four miles away from campus, and is a moderately-priced choice with rates somewhat higher during the winter season (December to May). The lodge will remind you of a Mexican hacienda. The **Arizona Inn** (2200 E. Elm St.; 520-325-1541), just over one mile away from campus, has all the amenities of a grand hotel, including tennis courts, a swimming pool, and acres of lawns and gardens. Some less expensive choices are more convenient to the campus. **University Inn** (950 N. Stone Ave.; 520-791-7503 or 800-233-8466) has a midtown location close to shopping and to the university, and you can have a double room in a relaxed atmosphere for an inexpensive rate. **La Quinta Motor Inn** (665 N. Freeway; 520-622-6491) is six miles away from campus. One mile away from campus (courtesy car to the campus) is the **Ramada Downtown** (1601 N. Oracle Rd.; 520-884-7422), with double rooms avaialble at moderate rates, a peaceful garden, and a heated pool. **La Posada del Valle** (1640 N. Campbell Ave.; 520-795-3840) has a moderate special rate for university visitors that drop by from June to September. **Peppertree's Bed and Breakfast** (724 E. University Blvd.; 520-622-7167) is a 1905 territorial home offering a full gourmet breakfast and afternoon tea.

A Little Farther: Consider **Tanque Verde** (14301 E. Speedway; 520-296-6275). This is a fabulous ranch offering horseback riding, tennis courts, indoor and outdoor pools, a sauna, and an exercise room. It's a very expensive choice, but the cost includes three full meals. Don't forget that the very expensive **Canyon Ranch Spa** (602-749-9000 or 800-742-9000) is also in Tucson.

HIGHLIGHTS

ON CAMPUS
- Flandrau Science Center
- Center for Creative Photography
- UA Museum of Art
- Athletics Events
- Arizona State Museum

OFF CAMPUS
- Spring Training—Major League Baseball
- AZ/Sonora Desert Museum
- Old Tucson
- Kartchner Caverns
- Sabino Canyon

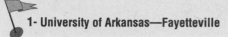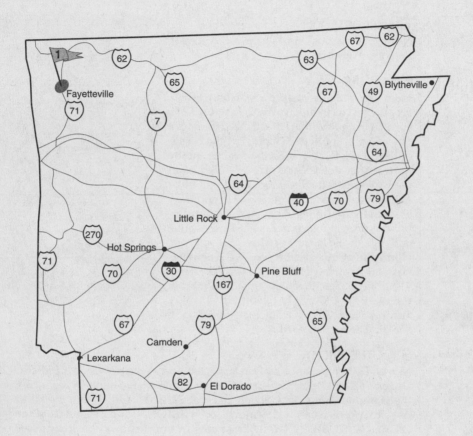

1- University of Arkansas—Fayetteville

ARKANSAS

	Univ. Arkansas-Fay.	Little Rock
Univ. Arkansas-Fay.	—	191
Little Rock	191	—

Arkansas

UNIVERSITY OF ARKANSAS—FAYETTEVILLE

Office of Admissions, 200 Silas Hunt Hall,
Fayetteville, AR 72701 • Telephone: 800-377-8632 • www.uark.edu •
Email: uofa@uark.edu

Hours: Monday–Friday, 8:00AM–5:00PM

The University of Arkansas offers a good learning opportunity (for students focused enough to take advantage of it) at a fraction of the cost charged by smaller, upscale/boutique schools. As at many southern schools, students have a propensity for religion and conservatism.

AT A GLANCE

Selectivity Rating	80
Range SAT I Math	520–650
Average SAT I Math	587
Range SAT I Verbal	510–640
Average SAT I Verbal	576
Average ACT Composite	25
Average GPA	3.57
Student/Faculty Ratio	16:1

CAMPUS TOURS

Appointment	Preferred
Dates	Year-round
Times	10:30AM & 1:30PM
Average Length	1 hour

ON-CAMPUS APPOINTMENTS

Admissions

Appointment	Preferred
Advance Notice	Yes, 1 week
Saturdays	No
Average Length	30 min.
Info Sessions	No

Faculty and Coaches

Dates/Times	Year-round
Arrangements	Contact Admissions Office 1 week prior

CLASS VISITS

Dates	Varies
Arrangements	Contact Admissions Office

TRANSPORTATION

Nearest airport is the Northwest Arkansas Regional Airport.

FIND YOUR WAY

From the south: Take I-40 to I-540 North (exit 7). From I-540 North to Razorback Road (exit 61). Turn right on Razorback Road, heading north. The campus entrance is located at the corner of Razorback Road and Sixth Street. **From the north:** After Bella Vista, take I-540 South all the way to Fayetteville. From I-540, exit Hwy 112 (exit 66). Turn right on Hwy 112 and travel south for two miles until you reach the campus entrance at the corner of Garland Avenue and Cleveland Street. (After crossing the North Street intersection, Hwy 112 becomes Garland Avenue.) **From the east:** Take Hwy 412 to I-540. See directions from north. **From the west:** Take Hwy 412 to east via Cherokee Turnpike from Tulsa, Oklahoma, to I-540 South. See directions from north.

STAY THE NIGHT

Nearby: Lodging near campus includes the **Best Western Windsor Suites** (1122 S. Futrall Dr., exit 62, 800-WESTERN); the **Clarion Inn** (1255 S. Shiloh Dr., Exit 62, 800-223-7275); the **Hampton Inn** (735 S. Shiloh Dr., Exit 62, 800-HAMPTON); the **Hilton** (70 N. East Ave., Exit 62 then east to downtown, 800-HILTONS); and the **Red Roof Inn** (1000 Futrall Dr., Exit 62, 800-RED-ROOF). Please identify yourself as a university guest to be assured of securing their special rates.

A Little Farther: Lodging farther away from campus includes the **Holiday Inn Express** (1251 N. Shiloh Dr., Exit 64, 800-HOLIDAY) and the **Inn at the Mill** (3910 Greathouse Springs Rd., Exit 69, 501-443-1800).

HIGHLIGHTS

ON CAMPUS

- Bud Walton Arena
- Old Main
- Reynolds Razorback Stadium
- Whitaker Equine Facility
- Senior Walk (every graduate has their name engraved here)

• OFF CAMPUS

- Dickson Street
- Boston Mountains
- Devil's Den State Park
- Walton Arts Center
- Farmer's Market on the Square

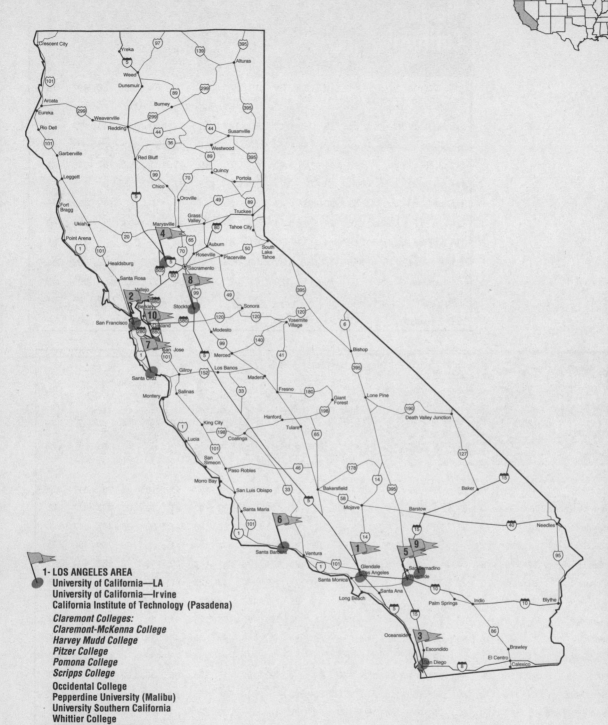

CALIFORNIA

1- **LOS ANGELES AREA**
   University of California—LA
   University of California—Irvine
   California Institute of Technology (Pasadena)

   Claremont Colleges:
   Claremont-McKenna College
   Harvey Mudd College
   Pitzer College
   Pomona College
   Scripps College

   Occidental College
   Pepperdine University (Malibu)
   University Southern California
   Whittier College
2- **SAN FRANCISCO AREA**
   University of California—Berkeley
   Mills College (Oakland)
   University San Francisco (SF)
   Stanford University
   St. Mary's College of California (Moraga)
3- **SAN DIEGO AREA**
   University of California
   University of San Diego
4- **University California—Davis**
5- **University California—Riverside**
6- **University California—Santa Barbara**
7- **University California—Santa Cruz**
8- **University of the Pacific**
9- **University of Redlands**
10- **Santa Clara University**

Northern California

	Mills College	St. Mary's College	Santa Clara Univ.	Stanford University	U.Cal.-Berkeley	U.Cal.-Davis	U.Cal.-Santa Cruz	Univ. San Francisco	Univ. of the Pacific	Los Angeles	Sacramento	San Diego	San Francisco
Mills College	—	10	51	38	10	71	69	16	88	345	88	497	13
St. Mary's College	10	—	49	42	11	64	80	24	74	372	79	491	21
Santa Clara University	51	49	—	12	59	123	35	63	130	326	140	472	5
Stanford University	38	42	12	—	40	103	47	34	77	340	120	482	35
U.Cal.-Berkeley	10	11	59	40	—	70	80	15	81	367	87	513	11
U.Cal.-Davis	71	64	123	103	70	—	135	71	61	365	21	611	67
U.Cal.-Santa Cruz	69	80	35	47	80	135	—	87	110	323	149	484	75
Univ. San Francisco	16	24	63	34	15	71	87	—	94	403	84	516	0
Univ. of the Pacific	88	74	130	77	81	61	110	94	—	312	39	470	85
Los Angeles	345	372	326	340	367	365	323	403	312	—	382	122	384
Sacramento	88	79	140	120	87	21	149	84	39	382	—	509	95
San Diego	497	491	472	482	513	611	484	516	470	122	509	—	504
San Francisco	13	21	53	35	11	67	75	0	85	384	95	504	—

Southern California

	California Tech.	Claremont McKenna	Harvey Mudd Coll.	Occidental College	Pepperdine University	Pitzer College	Pomona College	Scripps College	U.Cal.-Irvine	U.Cal.-Los Angeles	U.Cal.-Riverside	U.Cal.-San Diego	U.Cal.-Santa Barbara	Univ. of Redlands	Univ. of San Diego	USC	Whittier College	Los Angeles	Sacramento	San Diego	San Francisco
California Tech.	—	26	26	6	38	26	26	26	51	23	55	118	116	58	127	15	18	5	387	117	392
Claremont McKenna	26	—	0	32	78	0	0	0	42	51	26	119	160	33	123	41	30	35	447	117	442
Harvey Mudd Coll.	26	0	—	32	78	0	0	0	42	51	26	119	160	33	123	41	30	35	447	117	442
Occidental College	6	32	32	—	34	32	32	32	56	18	64	130	106	67	139	11	26	0	380	130	379
Pepperdine University	38	78	78	34	—	78	78	78	62	18	104	134	78	111	143	32	46	8	368	134	370
Pitzer College	26	0	0	32	78	—	0	0	42	51	26	119	160	33	123	41	30	35	447	117	442
Pomona College	26	0	0	32	78	0	—	0	42	51	26	119	160	33	123	41	30	35	447	117	442
Scripps College	26	0	0	32	78	0	0	—	42	51	26	119	160	33	123	41	30	35	447	117	442
U.Cal.-Irvine	51	42	42	56	62	42	42	42	—	54	50	76	140	67	85	43	38	29	427	75	464
U.Cal.-Los Angeles	23	51	51	18	18	51	51	51	54	—	74	126	94	84	135	15	33	0	358	126	380
U.Cal.-Riverside	55	26	26	64	104	26	26	26	50	74	—	92	192	15	95	58	58	62	436	85	439
U.Cal.-San Diego	118	119	119	130	134	119	119	119	76	126	92	—	212	124	9	122	110	118	509	0	507
U.Cal.-Santa Barbara	116	160	160	106	78	160	160	160	140	96	192	212	—	203	221	101	116	87	371	212	312
Univ. of Redlands	58	33	33	67	111	33	33	33	67	84	15	124	203	—	127	77	61	69	537	117	466
Univ. of San Diego	127	123	123	139	143	123	123	123	85	135	95	9	221	127	—	129	119	127	518	0	516
USC	15	41	41	11	32	41	41	41	43	15	58	122	101	77	129	—	18	0	375	122	423
Whittier College	18	30	30	26	46	30	30	30	38	33	58	110	116	61	119	18	—	18	395	110	402
Los Angeles	5	35	35	0	8	35	35	35	29	0	62	118	87	69	127	0	18	—	382	123	384
Sacramento	387	447	447	380	380	447	447	447	427	358	436	509	371	537	518	375	395	382	—	509	95
San Diego	117	117	117	130	134	117	117	117	75	126	85	0	212	117	0	122	110	122	509	—	504
San Francisco	392	442	442	379	370	442	442	442	464	380	439	507	312	466	516	423	402	284	95	504	—

CALIFORNIA INSTITUTE OF TECHNOLOGY

Office of Undergraduate Admissions, MC 55-63, Pasadena, CA 91125
(The office is at 515 S. Wilson) • Telephone: 800-568-8324 • www.admissions.caltech.edu •
Email: ugadmissions@caltech.edu

Hours: Monday–Friday, 8:00AM–5:00PM

Arguably the best school in the country for science and technology, Caltech is "a weird, wacky, wonderful place." Though some professors "cannot teach at all," the faculty has "enough brainpower to toast bread." So do the "imaginative" and "intense" students who study more than four hours each day thanks to a "suicidal (yet effective) course load."

HIGHLIGHTS

ON CAMPUS
- Palomar Observatory
- Moore Laboratory
- Mead Chemistry Laboratory

OFF CAMPUS
- Santa Monica Pier
- Venice Beach
- Disneyland
- L.A. County Museum of Arts
- Universal Studios

TRANSPORTATION

Los Angeles International Airport is 40 miles away. Shuttle vans, taxis, and rental cars are available at the airport; contact the airport to make arrangements. Burbank Airport is 20 minutes away from Caltech. Amtrak trains and Greyhound/Trailways buses serve Los Angeles.

FIND YOUR WAY

Take the 210 Freeway to the Lake Ave. off-ramp. Turn south on Lake Ave. to Del Mar Blvd., then left on Del Mar to Wilson. Turn right on Wilson to 515 S. Wilson. Use street parking.

STAY THE NIGHT

Nearby: The **Holiday Inn** (303 E. Cordova St.; 818-449-4000) offers a moderate special rate for college visitors and has lighted tennis courts and a heated outdoor pool. You also have two basic inexpensive options within 2.5 miles of Caltech. One is the **Comfort Inn** (2462 E. Colorado Blvd.; 818-405-0811). Let them know you are visiting the college so you can get the special rate. The other option is the **Best Western Colorado Inn** (2156 E. Colorado Blvd.; 818-793-9339), which is even less expensive than the Comfort Inn. Lodgings include continental breakfast and access to a heated pool and a Jacuzzi; the inn is nearby places to eat. A moderate special double rate is available at the **Pasadena Hilton,** located only one mile away from Caltech. **Irish Inn** (119 N. Meredith Ave.; 818-440-0066) offers a moderate rate and includes a gourmet breakfast to college visitors. The inn is in a quiet, residential area and has a country Irish decor. You will find flowers, fruit, and sherry in your room, and the inn can also fix you lunch and dinner.

A Little Farther: See the University of California—Los Angeles entry for accommodations (particularly **Terrace Manor,** which is 20 minutes away).

CLAREMONT MCKENNA COLLEGE

Office of Admission and Financial Aid, 890 Columbia Avenue,
Claremont, CA 91711 • Telephone: 909-621-8088 • www.claremontmckenna.edu/admission •
Email: admission@claremontmckenna.edu

Hours: Monday–Friday, 8:00AM–5:00PM

"If I had a personal talk with God about creating a great school, He would create CMC," says an obviously satisfied student from the truly exceptional Claremont McKenna College in sunny Claremont, California. CMC, one of the five Claremont Colleges, is home to just over 1,000 mostly politically conservative and professionally oriented students.

AT A GLANCE

Selectivity Rating	96
Range SAT I Math	650–730
Average SAT I Math	700
Range SAT I Verbal	630–730
Average SAT I Verbal	690
Average ACT Composite	30
Student/Faculty Ratio	8:1

CAMPUS TOURS

Appointment	Not required
Dates	Year-round
Times	Varies
Average Length	1 hour

ON-CAMPUS APPOINTMENTS

Admissions

Start Date—Juniors	After May 1 Junior year
Appointment	Required
Advance Notice	Yes, 2 weeks
Saturdays	No
Average Length	1 hour
Info Sessions	Yes

Faculty and Coaches

Dates/Times	Year-round
Arrangements	Contact Admissions Office

CLASS VISITS

Dates	Academic year
Arrangements	Contact Admissions Office

TRANSPORTATION

Ontario International Airport is a 15-minute drive from campus. Taxis and limousines are available for the drive to campus from the airport; a shuttle is also available to the Claremont Inn near campus. Greyhound buses serve Claremont; the terminal is just south of I-10.

FIND YOUR WAY

From I-10 (San Bernardino Freeway), exit at Indian Hill Blvd. North. Proceed north to 10th St. and turn right (east). Go approximately half a mile to Columbia Avenue (a dead end). Turn right (south) onto Columbia and proceed to the admissions office on the southeast corner of Columbia and 9th St.

STAY THE NIGHT

Nearby: The Claremont Graduate University, Pomona, Claremont McKenna, Harvey Mudd, Scripps, and Pitzer—known as the Claremont Colleges—are all located in Claremont, California—a charming little town not far from Los Angeles. The following choices are suitable for any of the schools. At **Faculty House** (703 N. College Way; 909-621-8109), on campus, the rates for college visitors are in the inexpensive range and include continental breakfast. Within walking distance, about half a mile from the schools, is **Claremont Inn** (555 W. Foothill Blvd.; 909-626-2411 or 800-854-5733). The moderate rate includes continental breakfast. An inexpensive choice a little farther away (10 minutes) is the **Ramada Inn** (840 S. Indian Hill Blvd.; 909-621-4831). There is a heated pool, a Jacuzzi, lighted tennis courts, and a café with a Japanese-American menu. An even less expensive rate is available at the **Howard Johnson's Motor Hotel** (721 S. Indian Hill Blvd.; 909-628-2431), located only 10 minutes away from the colleges.

HIGHLIGHTS

ON CAMPUS

- Marian Miner Cook Athenaeum
- Aquatics Center
- Emett Student Center/The Hub
- The Research Institutes
- Keck Science Center

OFF CAMPUS

- Disneyland
- Raymond M. Alf Museum
- Rancho Santa Ana Botanic Gardens
- Venice Beach
- Los Angeles County Museum of Arts

HARVEY MUDD COLLEGE

301 East 12th Street, Admissions Office Claremont, CA 91711-5990
(the office is in Kingston Hall) • Telephone: 909-621-8011
www.hmc.edu • Email: admission@hmc.edu

Hours: Monday–Friday, 8:00AM–5:00PM

Students study over four hours a day on average at Harvey Mudd College, the engineering branch of the five Claremont Colleges (Harvey Mudd, Claremont McKenna, Scripps, Pomona, and Pitzer). Outstanding academic programs are available in engineering, biology, chemistry, physics, mathematics, and computer science. The college offers an abundance of tremendous facilities.

HIGHLIGHTS

ON CAMPUS
- Liquidamber Mall
- That Pizza Place
- Linde Activities Center
- The "Quad"

OFF CAMPUS
- Rancho Santa Ana Botanic Gardens
- Mount Baldy
- Angeles National Forest
- Los Angeles County Fairgrounds
- California Speedway
- Disneyland, Universal Studios, the beaches, and many other attractions that are a short driving distance away from campus.

TRANSPORTATION
Ontario International Airport is five miles away from campus. The Claremont Inn (909-626-2411) shuttle takes passengers from the airport to the inn, which is just five blocks away from campus. Taxis are also available at the airport for the ride to campus. Greyhound buses serve Claremont; the terminal is just south of I-10.

FIND YOUR WAY
From I-10, exit onto Indian Hill Blvd. North. Take Indian Hill N. for a few miles to 12th St. Turn right (east) on 12th St. for five blocks to the admissions office at 301 E. 12th (Kingston Hall).

STAY THE NIGHT
Nearby: Call for an appointment in advance. We will help with hotel arrangements for family members; we will also provide one evening in a residence hall and meal passes to students.

AT A GLANCE

Selectivity Rating	94
Range SAT I Math	720–790
Average SAT I Math	750
Range SAT I Verbal	650–750
Average SAT I Verbal	700
Average GPA	3.8
Student/Faculty Ratio	9:1

CAMPUS TOURS

Appointment	Required
Dates	Year-round
Times	Sept–May 11AM,1:30PM, & 3:30PM; Jun–Aug 10AM & 2PM
Average Length	1 hour

ON-CAMPUS APPOINTMENTS

Admissions
Start Date–Juniors	May 15
Appointment	Required
Advance Notice	Yes, 1 week
Saturdays	Sometimes
Average Length	30 min.
Info Sessions	Yes

Faculty and Coaches
Dates/Times	Academic year
Arrangements	Contact Admissions Office 1 week prior

CLASS VISITS

Dates	Academic year
Arrangements	Contact Admissions Office

MILLS COLLEGE

Office of Undergraduate Admission, 5000 MacArthur Blvd., Oakland, CA 94613 (the office is in Mills Hall) • Telephone: 800-876-4557 • www.mills.edu • Email: admission@mills.edu

Hours: Monday–Friday, 8:30AM–5:00PM

Mills College, located in Oakland, California, is a small, women's liberal arts college. Mills boasts a very diverse campus, a stellar Bay Area location, and a wide array of extracurricular and recreational options, ranging from kayaking and horseback riding to rugby and yoga programs.

AT A GLANCE

Selectivity Rating	74
Range SAT I Math	490–590
Range SAT I Verbal	540–670
Average ACT Composite	25
Average GPA	3.52
Student/Faculty Ratio	9:1

CAMPUS TOURS

Appointment	Required
Dates	Year-round
Times	During academic year
	Mon–Fri, 10AM & 2:30PM
Average Length	1 hour

ON-CAMPUS APPOINTMENTS

Admissions

Start Date—Juniors	Anytime
Appointment	Required
Advance Notice	Yes, 1 week
Saturdays	No
Average Length	45 min.
Info Sessions	No

Faculty and Coaches

Dates/Times	Academic year
Arrangements	Contact Admissions
	Office 2 weeks prior

CLASS VISITS

Dates	Academic year
Arrangements	Contact Admissions
	Office

TRANSPORTATION

The Oakland International Airport is a 20-minute drive from campus. Taxis are available at the airport for the drive to campus; no advance arrangements are necessary. The Bayporter shuttle service provides shared van service from the Oakland and San Francisco airports to campus. Public bus service is available at the campus entrance.

FIND YOUR WAY

From San Francisco, take I-80 East (Bay Bridge) to I-580 East (MacArthur Freeway). Take the second MacArthur Blvd. exit (the exit immediately after the exit for High Street), about 8.5 miles away from the bridge. At the end of the ramp, turn right onto MacArthur Blvd.; turn left at the first traffic light into campus. **From the east,** I-580 West to the MacArthur Blvd./High St. exit (just after the Hwy. 13 junction). Turn left at the stop sign and proceed under the overpass. Turn left at the stoplight. The college gates are immediately on the left at the next traffic light. **From the south,** take I-880 North (Nimitz Freeway) to Oakland. Exit at High St. (three miles past the Oakland Airport exit). Turn right onto High St. and continue three miles to MacArthur Blvd. Turn right onto MacArthur, continue under the overpass and bear right. The college gates are immediately ahead on the left. **From the north,** take I-80 South to I-580 East at the Bay Bridge interchange. From there, follow the directions above from San Francisco. Call 510-430-3250 for recorded directions.

STAY THE NIGHT

Nearby: Through the admissions office or by calling directly (510-430-2145), you can book a dormitory-style room at the **Alderwood Conference Center.** Reservations are a must and are particularly difficult to come by during the summer. Bathrooms are dormitory style. Rates are very inexpensive and there are places to dine on campus. Places include the **Oakland Marriott at City Center** (1001 Broadway; 510-451-4000), the **Jack London Inn** (444 Embarcadero West; 510-444-2032), and the **Waterfront Plaza Hotel at Jack London Square** (10 Washington St.; 510-836-3800). The **Washington Inn** (495 10th St.; 510-452-1776), opposite the Oakland Convention Center, is about six minutes away from the college. The rates are moderate (ask for the special college visitors rate) and include a full breakfast and privileges at a nearby health club. A moderately-priced motel about 15 minutes away is the **Best Western Thunderbird Inn** (233 Broadway at 3rd St.; 510-452-4565). It has a heated pool, a sauna, and an adjacent restaurant.

A Little Farther: If a resort appeals to you, the **Claremont Resort Hotel and Tennis Club** (Domingo and Ashby Ave.; 510-843-3000), about 15 minutes from the college, is great. There you will have access to tennis courts, a swimming pool, and an exercise room. Rates run very high. Check the University of California—Berkeley and the University of San Francisco entries for other possibilities.

HIGHLIGHTS

ON CAMPUS

- The Mills Museum
- Trefethen Aquatic Center
- Mills Hall
- Greek Theater
- The Tea Shop

OFF CAMPUS

- Jack London Square
- Lake Merritt
- Paramount Theater
- Pacific Ocean and San Fransico Bay
- San Fransisco

OCCIDENTAL COLLEGE

Admissions Office, 1600 Campus Road, Los Angeles, CA 90041 • Telephone: 800-825-5262 • departments.oxy.edu/admission/ • Email: admission@oxy.edu

Hours: Monday–Friday, 8:00AM–5:00PM; Saturday (only from September–December), 9:00AM–noon

Nearly one-third of Oxy's graduates proceed to professional programs within a year, and just as many go on to academic graduate programs. Oxy's program requires students to complete a demanding two-year core curriculum that includes healthy doses of world culture, math, science, humanities, and at least one foreign language.

HIGHLIGHTS

ON CAMPUS

- Thorne Hall Auditorium
- Keck Theater
- Johnson Student Center
- Patterson Field
- Hillside Amphitheater

OFF CAMPUS

- J. Paul Getty Center
- Dodger Stadium
- Griffith Park Observatory
- Disneyland
- Rose Bowl

TRANSPORTATION

Burbank Airport is 10 miles away from campus. Super Shuttle and taxi service are available from the airport to campus. Los Angeles International Airport is farther from campus, but close enough that buses run from the airport to hotels in the Pasadena area (not too far away from campus). Amtrak trains and Greyhound/Trailways buses serve Los Angeles. Rapid Transit District bus service (public transportation) to campus is available from downtown Los Angeles: take either line 83 (on York Blvd.) or line 84 (on Eagle Rock Blvd.). Call 213-626-4455 for bus information and schedules.

FIND YOUR WAY

From downtown L.A., take I-110 N. (Harbor Freeway). Follow signs for Pasadena. Take I-5 N. (Golden State Freeway) toward Bakersfield. Then take Rte. 2 (Glendale Freeway) going toward Glendale. Exit at Verdugo Rd.; turn left at the end of the off ramp onto Eagle Rock Blvd. Continue on Eagle Rock Blvd. for five traffic lights to Westdale Ave. Turn right onto Westdale and follow it until it ends at Campus Rd. **From the Ventura Freeway (Rte. 134) heading east,** go through Glendale to the Harvey Dr. exit. Turn right at the end of the off ramp and then left at the light onto Broadway. When Broadway merges with Colorado Blvd., continue on Colorado Blvd. to Eagle Rock Blvd. Turn right and continue for four traffic lights to Westdale Ave. Turn left onto Westdale and follow it to Campus Rd. **From the Ventura Freeway (Rte. 134) heading west,** exit at Colorado Blvd. Take Colorado Blvd. to Eagle Rock Blvd. (approximately one mile). Turn left onto Eagle Rock Blvd. and continue four traffic lights to Westdale Ave. Turn left onto Westdale and proceed to Campus Rd.

STAY THE NIGHT

Nearby: In the moderate range, about 15 minutes away, is the **Sheraton Pasadena** (303 East Cordove Street; 626-449-4000). Ask for Occidental College's special rate. This hotel has a pool and exercise room. **Doubletree Hotel** (191 North Los Robles; 626-792-2727) has a full health club, exercise room, pool, and Jacuzzi. The least expensive place is also the closest to campus; the **Welcome Inn** (1840 West Colorado Blvd.; 323-256-1673). The California Institute of Technology entry also has suggestions for accommodations in Pasadena.

AT A GLANCE

Selectivity Rating	87
Range SAT I Math	590–680
Average SAT I Math	630
Range SAT I Verbal	580–670
Average SAT I Verbal	630
Average ACT Composite	27
Average GPA	3.8
Student/Faculty Ratio	11:1

CAMPUS TOURS

Appointment	Not required
Dates	Varies
Times	Contact Admissions Office
Average Length	1 hour

ON-CAMPUS APPOINTMENTS

Admissions

Start Date–Juniors	June 1
Appointment	Required
Advance Notice	Yes, 2 weeks
Saturdays	Sometimes
Average Length	45 min.
Info Sessions	Yes

Faculty and Coaches

Arrangements	Contact Admissions Office 2 weeks prior

CLASS VISITS

Dates	Academic year
Arrangements	Contact Admissions Office

PEPPERDINE UNIVERSITY

Office of Admission, 24255 Pacific Coast Hwy., 2nd Floor of the Thornton Administration Build., Malibu, CA 90263-4392 • Telephone: 310-456-4861 • seaver.pepperdine.edu/admission
Email: admission-seaver@pepperdine.edu

Hours: Monday–Friday, 8:00AM–5:00PM

A stunning beach-front location in idyllic Malibu and a deep-seated affiliation with the Church of Christ set Pepperdine apart from all other colleges and universities. Pepperdine seeks "to pursue the very highest academic standards within a context that celebrates and extends the spiritual and ethical ideals of the Christian faith." A weekly assembly is mandatory, and the core curriculum contains three religion surveys.

AT A GLANCE

Selectivity Rating	85
Range SAT I Math	580–680
Average SAT I Math	628
Range SAT I Verbal	550–660
Average SAT I Verbal	612
Average ACT Composite	26
Average GPA	3.61
Student/Faculty Ratio	12:1

CAMPUS TOURS

Appointment	Preferred
Dates	Year-round
Times	Mon–Fri, 9AM–3PM, on the hour
Average Length	1 hour

ON-CAMPUS APPOINTMENTS

Admissions

Start Date–Juniors	May
	(at the end of junior year)
Appointment	Required
Advance Notice	Yes, 1 week
Saturdays	No
Average Length	30 min.
Info Sessions	Yes

Faculty and Coaches

Dates/Times	Year-round
Arrangements	Contact Athletic Department 2 weeks prior

CLASS VISITS

Dates	Year-round
Arrangements	Contact Admissions Office

TRANSPORTATION

Los Angeles International Airport is 25 miles away from campus. Rental cars, commercial shuttle service, and taxis are available at the airport. For Super Shuttle, call 213-338-1111; for Prime Time Shuttle, call 213-558-1606. Amtrak trains and Greyhound Trailways buses serve Los Angeles.

FIND YOUR WAY

Take **I-10 W. (Santa Monica Freeway)** to the end, where it becomes the Pacific Coast Hwy. (California Rte. 1). Continue for 14 miles, turn right onto Malibu Canyon Rd., then turn left onto Seaver Dr., which is the campus entrance. **From the Ventura Freeway (U.S. Rte. 101)**, take the Las Virgenes exit; turn south onto Las Virgenes, which becomes Malibu Canyon Rd., and follow it through the canyon. Turn right onto Seaver Dr., which is the campus entrance.

STAY THE NIGHT

Nearby: Enjoy sleeping to the sound of the pounding surf at **Casa Malibu** (22752 Pacific Coast Hwy.; 310-456-2219), a relatively small, moderately-priced motel only a mile-and-a-half from campus. The motel has a nice patio overlooking a private beach, and the rooms have refrigerators. **Malibu Beach Inn** (22878 Pacific Coast Hwy.; 310-456-6444) is a little closer at about a mile away, but it's a little more expensive. One budget choice, **Goodnight Inn** (26557 Agora Rd., Calabasas; 818-880-6000), is about 15 minutes away. A heated outdoor pool and Jacuzzi are on the premises, and a restaurant is close by.

A Little Farther: The quaint, inexpensive **Bay Side Hotel** (2001 Ocean Ave.; 310-396-6000) is 25 minutes away in Santa Monica. The hotel has 38 rooms, some with kitchens; the rooms that overlook the ocean are a bit more expensive than those overlooking the courtyard. There is a small additional charge for rooms with kitchens. A French bakery and buffet are nearby. About 30 minutes away, also in Santa Monica, is the large, bustling **Sheraton Miramar** (101 Wilshire Blvd.; 310-576-7777). Rates are very expensive, but it is across the street from the beach. The Sheraton has a heated pool, bike rentals, and a shopping mall adjacent to it. You can have privileges at the Santa Monica Athletic Club and its tennis courts. For more overnight options, you can check with Bed & Breakfast International at 800-872-4500.

HIGHLIGHTS

ON CAMPUS

- Theme Tower
- Smother's Theatre
- The Sandbar
- Payson Library
- Alumni Park

OFF CAMPUS

- J. Paul Getty Museum
- Santa Monica Pier/3rd Street Promenade
- Universal City Walk
- Hollywood
- Dodger Stadium

PITZER COLLEGE

Admissions Office, Broad Hall, Room 101, 1050 North Mills Avenue, Claremont, CA 91711-6101 • Telephone: 800-749-9371 • www.pitzer.edu • Email: admission@pitzer.edu

Hours: Monday–Friday, 8:00AM–5:00PM; Saturday, 9:00AM–noon

Pitzer is a place for individuals and is considered by far the most flexible and liberal of the five Claremont Colleges (Claremont McKenna, Harvey Mudd, Pitzer, Pomona, and Scripps). The "not-exactly-gorgeous" campus is dotted with "student murals and the occasional hammock," but students say the "challenging and stimulating" academic experience provides "the perfect place for thinkers and people who want to learn for their own enrichment."

HIGHLIGHTS

ON CAMPUS

- The Arboretum
- Marquis Library
- Gloria and Peter Gold Student Center
- McConnell Center
- Grove House
- The Claremont Colleges Consortium

OFF CAMPUS

- Universal Studios
- Disneyland
- Raymond M. Alf Museum
- Joshua Tree National Park
- Los Angeles County Museum of Art

TRANSPORTATION

Ontario International is 12 miles east of Claremont on I-10 (the San Bernardino Freeway). Direct or connecting flights are available from all parts of the country. Hotel shuttles (Claremont Inn, Sheraton Fairplex, and Ramada Inn), taxis, and rental cars are available for the ride to campus. Los Angeles International Airport is about 50 miles west of Claremont. Air and ground connections are available from there to Ontario International Airport. Greyhound buses serve Claremont; the terminal is just south of I-10.

FIND YOUR WAY

From any area except Pasadena, take I-10 to Indian Hill Blvd. (Exit 470) and travel north, toward the mountains, for three miles. At 12th St., turn right and continue on until the road ends. Turn right as 12th St. curves into N. Mills Ave. The admissions office is in Broad Hall, the building that faces N. Mills Ave. **From Pasadena and the San Fernando Valley,** take I-210 E. until it terminates at Foothill Blvd. Drive four miles on Foothill Blvd. and turn right on Claremont Blvd. Make the first right onto 9th St., and continue on until the road ends. Turn right onto N. Mills Ave. Broad Hall is on N. Mills Ave.

STAY THE NIGHT

Nearby: Lodgings include the **Shilo Inn Suites Hotel** (Pomona Hilltop, 3101 Temple Ave.; 909-598-7666 or 800-222-2244), the **Sheraton Suites Fairplex** (601 W. McKinley Ave.; 909-622-2220 or 888-627-8074), the **Sheraton Ontario** (429 N. Vineyard Ave.; 909-937-8000 or 800-582-2946), the **Marriott Ontario** (2200 East Holt Blvd.; 909-975-5000 or 800-284-8811), **La Quinta Inn & Suites Ontario** (3555 Inland Empire Blvd.; 909-476-1112), the **Western Inn** (1191 East Foothill Blvd.; 909-949-4800), and the **Country Suites by Ayres** (1945 East Holt Blvd.; 909-390-7778 or 800-248-4661).

AT A GLANCE

Selectivity Rating	82
Range SAT I Math	550–670
Average SAT I Math	610
Range SAT I Verbal	570–670
Average SAT I Verbal	624
Average ACT Composite	25
Average GPA	3.52
Student/Faculty Ratio	12:1

CAMPUS TOURS

Appointment	Preferred
Dates	Year-round
Times	Mon–Fri, and during academic year, Sat mornings
Average Length	1 hour

ON-CAMPUS APPOINTMENTS

Admissions

Start Date—Juniors	May 1
Appointment	Preferred
Advance Notice	Yes, 1 week
Saturdays	Sometimes
Average Length	30 min.
Info Sessions	Yes

Faculty and Coaches

Dates/Times	Academic year
Arrangements	Contact Admissions Office 2 weeks prior

CLASS VISITS

Dates	Academic year
Arrangements	Contact Admissions Office

POMONA COLLEGE

Admissions Office, 333 North College Way, Claremont, CA 91711-6312 • Telephone: 909-621-8134 • www.pomona.edu/admissions • Email: admissions@pomona.edu

Hours: Monday–Friday, 8:00AM–5:00PM; Saturday (in the fall), 10:00AM–2:00PM

The overall environment is very conducive to learning at Pomona College—something of an academic paradise, and the most distinguished school in the Claremont cluster (Claremont McKenna, Harvey Mudd, Pitzer, Pomona, and Scripps). The "involved and caring" administration receives raves for spoiling students with perks like "study-break snacks in the dining halls every night at 10:30 PM" and "a new campus center with a bar."

AT A GLANCE

Selectivity Rating	95
Range SAT I Math	680–750
Average SAT I Math	720
Range SAT I Verbal	690–760
Average SAT I Verbal	730
Average ACT Composite	32
Average GPA	3.9
Student/Faculty Ratio	9:1

CAMPUS TOURS

Appointment	Not required
Dates	Year-round
Times	Varies throughout the year
Average Length	1 hour

ON-CAMPUS APPOINTMENTS

Admissions

Start Date—Juniors	March 1
Appointment	Required
Advance Notice	Yes, 3 weeks
Saturdays	Sometimes
Average Length	30 min.
Info Sessions	Yes

Faculty and Coaches

Dates/Times	Year-round
Arrangements	Contact Admissions Office

CLASS VISITS

Dates	Academic year
Arrangements	Contact Admissions Office

TRANSPORTATION

Ontario International Airport is 10 miles away from campus. Taxi, shuttle service, and rental cars are available at the airport. A 24-hour express shuttle to Claremont is available (for this service, call 800-554-6458; in California, call 909-973-1100 or 310-338-1111). It is also possible to fly into Los Angeles International Airport (LAX), then take a commuter flight to Ontario, rent a car, or take a shuttle van to Claremont. Greyhound buses serve Claremont; the terminal is just south of I-10, approximately a mile-and-a-half from campus. Metro link (train) serves Claremont from downtown L.A.

FIND YOUR WAY

From anywhere except Pasadena and the San Fernando Valley, take I-10 to Indian Hill Blvd. (Exit 47). Drive north approximately one mile to Bonita Ave.; turn right and go four blocks to the Summer Hall parking lot (on the left). **From Pasadena and the San Fernando Valley,** take I-210 (Foothill Freeway) E. and exit Towne Ave. Drive south approximately one mile; turn left on Foothill Blvd. (Rte. 66). Continue east two miles to Indian Hill Blvd.; turn right and proceed south 10 blocks to Bonita Ave. Turn left on Bonita and go four blocks to the Summer Hall parking lot (on the left).

STAY THE NIGHT

Nearby: **The Pomona College Faculty House,** located on campus offers a complimentary breakfast and inexpensive housing (703 North College Way; 909-621-8109). The **Claremont Inn** (555 W. Foothill Blvd.; 909-626-2411) is within walking distance—about a half mile from Pomona. An alternative is the **Sheraton Suites Fairplex** (601 McKinley Avenue; 800-722-4055).

HIGHLIGHTS

ON CAMPUS

- Smith Campus Center
- Sontag Greek Theater
- Rains Center for Sports and Recreation
- Brakett Observatory

OFF CAMPUS

- Los Angeles and Pasadena
- J. Paul Getty Center, Los Angeles County Museum of Art
- Universal Studios, Disneyland
- Joshua Tree National Park, Angeles National Forest
- Lakers, Dodgers, Angels

SAINT MARY'S COLLEGE OF CALIFORNIA

Office of Admissions, PO Box 4800,
Moraga, CA 94575-4800 • Telephone: 800-800-4762 • www.stmarys-ca.edu •
Email: smcadmit@stmarys-ca.edu

Hours: Monday–Friday, 8:30AM–4:30PM; (3:30PM during summer); Saturdays (during academic year), 9:00AM–1:00PM

St. Mary's College "is booming with new buildings, technologies, and media," but academics are firmly planted in history. All St. Mary's College students must complete a core curriculum centered on SMC's discussion-oriented Great Books Seminar Program, which teaches students "how to learn, not what to think." Beyond the core, many students shift their interests toward the pre-professional majors, especially business administration.

HIGHLIGHTS

ON CAMPUS
- J.C. Gatehouse Science Building
- Cassin Student Union
- College Chapel
- Hearst Art Gallery
- Oliver Dining Hall

OFF CAMPUS
- Downtown San Francisco
- Lafayette Reservoir and Mt. Diablo State Park
- Broadway Plaza (shopping, dining, theater, etc.)
- Golden Gate Park—San Francisco
- Downtown Berkeley (Shattuck and Telegraph Ave.)

TRANSPORTATION

Several private shuttle services are available from both San Francisco and Oakland International airports. Please be sure to book your ground transportation prior to arriving at the airport. Listed are several companies that provide this direct service. Prices may vary and round-trip arrangements may be more economical than two one-way passages: Airport Connection (650-401-8300), Bayporter Express (510-864-4000), East Bay Connection (800-675-3278), and Leisure Living Transportation (925-943-1512). Public transportation is availble on BART (Bay Area Rapid Transit Rail System), which operates rail service in San Francisco and the East Bay (www.transitinfo.org/BART. or www.bart.gov).

FIND YOUR WAY

From San Francisco Bay Bridge or San Rafael/Richmond Bridge: Take Highway 580 toward Hayward and then Highway 24 toward Walnut Creek. Once through the Caldecott Tunnel, take the third exit, which is called Orinda/Moraga. Turn right and follow Moraga Way about five miles. Turn left onto Moraga Road, then right onto Saint Mary's Road. The college is about one mile farther on the right. **From Walnut Creek/Highway 680:** Take Highway 24 West (Oakland direction) to the Central Lafayette exit. Keep to your right, go under the freeway, and make a right onto Mt. Diablo Blvd. After one block, make a left onto Moraga Road and stay on it for one-third mile, then make a left onto Saint Mary's Road and stay on it for about four miles; the college will be on the left. **From BART:** Take the S.F./Colma-Pittburg/Bay Point train to either the Orinda or the Lafayette station. From there, take the County Connection bus (Route 106 or 206) to Saint Mary's College. County Connection buses operate to and from the college from approximately 6:00 AM to 6:00 PM, Monday through Saturday. For bus schedules or more information, phone County Connection at 925-676-7500 or visit www.cccta.org.

STAY THE NIGHT

Nearby: There are a number of overnight accomodations near Saint Mary's College campus in Moraga. While we don't endorse any particular establishment, for your convenience, we have listed those most often used by campus visitors. Ask these hotels if they offer a Saint Mary's discount. The **Lafayette Park Hotel** (3287 Mt. Diablo Blvd., 800-368-2468) located in Lafayette is within 15 minutes of the campus.

A Little Farther: The **Embassy Suites Hotel** (1345 Treat Blvd. 800-362-02779), the **Holiday Inn Walnut Creek** (2730 North Main Street 925-932-3332), and the **Marriott Walnut Creek** (2355 North Main Street 925-934-2000) are about 20 minutes away from campus.

AT A GLANCE

Selectivity Rating	78
Range SAT I Math	500–600
Average SAT I Math	552
Range SAT I Verbal	500–600
Average SAT I Verbal	551
Average GPA	3.4
Student/Faculty Ratio	13:1

CAMPUS TOURS

Appointment	Preferred
Dates	Year-round
Times	Email
	smcadmit@stmarys-ca.edu
	for times
Average Length	1 hour

ON-CAMPUS APPOINTMENTS

Admissions

Start Date—Juniors	N/A
Appointment	Preferred
Advance Notice	Yes, 1 week
Saturdays	No
Average Length	30 min.
Info Sessions	Yes

Faculty and Coaches

Dates/Times	Academic year
Arrangements	Contact coach
	directly 2 weeks prior

CLASS VISITS

Dates	Academic year
Arrangements	No Class visits
	during midterms
	finals: Oct 13–17,
	Dec 8–12, &
	May 17–20, 2004

SANTA CLARA UNIVERSITY

Undergraduate Admissions, 500 El Camino Real
Santa Clara, CA 95053 • Telephone: 408-554-4700 • www.scu.edu •

Hours: Monday–Friday, 8:00AM–5:00PM; Saturday, 9:00AM–noon

Academic life at Catholic Santa Clara University is dictated by an academic calendar divided into three fast-paced 10-week sessions that really keep the undergraduates on their toes. Students like the individual attention they receive from their very encouraging and outstanding instructors, claim that levels of discussion are mind-numbing, and they complain that amazing SCU is underrated.

AT A GLANCE

Selectivity Rating	80
Range SAT I Math	560–660
Average SAT I Math	618
Range SAT I Verbal	550–650
Average SAT I Verbal	601
Average ACT Composite	27
Average GPA	3.57
Student/Faculty Ratio	12:1

CAMPUS TOURS

Appointment	Preferred
Dates	Year-round
Times	Mon–Fri, 10:30AM & 2:15PM
Average Length	1 hour

ON-CAMPUS APPOINTMENTS

Admissions

Start Date–Juniors	June 15, between junior and senior year
Appointment	Required
Advance Notice	Yes, 2 weeks
Saturdays	No
Average Length	30 min.
Info Sessions	Yes

Faculty and Coaches

Dates/Times	Academic year
Arrangements	Contact faculty and athletic department directly

CLASS VISITS

Dates	Varies
Arrangements	Contact Admissions Office

TRANSPORTATION

San Jose International Airport is a three mile drive from campus. Rental cars, taxis, and public buses (Valley Transportation Authority #10) are available for the trip from the airport to campus. San Francisco International Airport is 45 miles north of the campus. From there, Airport Connection Shuttles take visitors to the San Jose airport; call 800-AIRPORT (from out of state) or 415-877-0903 (in California) for shuttle timetables and reservations. Amtrak trains serve San Jose; call 800-USA-RAIL for information. From the train station, take bus #81 westbound for the three mile trip to campus. Greyhound buses also serve San Jose. From the bus depot, walk one block north to W. Santa Clara St. and board a westbound bus #22; this bus makes several stops along the perimeter of the campus.

FIND YOUR WAY

From U.S. Rte. 101 (Bayshore Freeway), take the Santa Clara/De La Cruz Blvd. exit. Proceed south two miles. As the road forks, keep to the right and follow the signs to the university. **From I-880,** take the Alameda/Santa Clara exit. Travel north one mile to campus. **From I-280,** proceed to the interchange with I-880. Take I-880 N. toward Oakland and take the Alameda/Santa Clara exit. The university is one mile north of the exit.

STAY THE NIGHT

Nearby: The **Candlewood Suites** (481 El Camino Real, Santa Clara; 408-241-9305) is located directly across the street from the University. **Days Inn Santa Clara** (859 El Camino Real; 408-244-2840) is located five blocks from the university. **Fairmont Hotel,** (170 South Market St., San Jose; 408-998-1900), is a 15-minute drive from campus. **San Jose Hilton and Towers,** (300 Almaden Blvd., San Jose; 408-287-2100), is a 12-minute drive from campus.

A Little Farther: The **Marriott Hotel** (2700 Mission College Blvd.; 408-988-1500) is in Santa Clara, 20 minutes away. Rates range from moderate to very expensive. It has all the usual Marriott amenities, including indoor and outdoor pools and a lighted tennis court. There is also the **Westin Hotel** (5101 Great America Pkwy. Santa Clara, CA; 408-986-0700), which has a 5,000-square-foot pool deck and pool. Plus, Paramount's Great America® theme park and a 72-par championship golf course are right across the street.

HIGHLIGHTS

ON CAMPUS

• Mission Church
• Pat Malley Fitness Center
• Mission Gardens
• Benson Memorial Student Center
• Leavey Activities Center
• At the heart of Santa Clara University is the historic Mission Santa Clara de Asis.

OFF CAMPUS

• Downtown San Jose
• Great America Theme Park
• Santa Cruz
• San Francisco (45 miles away)
• Lake Tahoe (4 hours away)

SCRIPPS COLLEGE

Office of Admissions, 1030 Columbia Avenue, 1030 Columbia Avenue, Claremont, CA 91711 • Telephone: 800-770-1333 • www.scrippscol.edu/admission.html • Email: admission@scrippscollege.edu

Hours: Monday–Friday, 8:00AM–5:00PM, Saturdays (in the fall), 8:00AM–1:00PM

Scripps College is the women's college in the Claremont Colleges cluster (Claremont McKenna, Harvey Mudd, Pitzer, Pomona, and Scripps). Overall, 2,500 courses are available to students, and nearly all classes are very small. Professors are accessible and receive high ratings for their teaching abilities.

HIGHLIGHTS

ON CAMPUS
- Williamson Gallery
- Rare book room, Denison Library
- Margaret Fowler Garden
- Malott Commons
- Graffiti Wall

OFF CAMPUS
- Disneyland
- Beaches
- Hollywood
- Joshua Tree Monument
- Rodeo Drive

TRANSPORTATION

Ontario International Airport is 15 miles away from the campus. Taxis are available for the ride to campus (call from the courtesy phones at the airport). Greyhound buses serve Claremont (the terminal is just south of I-10). The Amtrak station is five miles away from campus.

FIND YOUR WAY

From I-10 (San Bernardino Freeway), take Exit 47 (Indian Hill Blvd.) and proceed north on Indian Hill. Turn right on Tenth St. and proceed east to the corner of Tenth St. and Columbia Ave. **From Pasadena and the San Fernando Valley,** take I-210 E. until it terminates at Foothill Blvd. Drive three miles on Foothill and turn right on Dartmouth Ave., then left on Tenth St. to Columbia Ave.

STAY THE NIGHT

Nearby: Only a two-minute drive to campus, the **Claremont Inn** (555 W. Foothill Blvd.; 909-626-2411) is quite convenient and offers a special college rate. A couple of miles farther and a bit more expensive is the **Sheraton Suites Fairplex** (601 W. McKinley Ave., Pomona; 800-325-3535 or 909-622-2220), which offers pleasant accommodations. Ask for the college rate there, too. There is also the **Marriott Hotel** (2200 E. Holt Blvd., Ontario; 909-986-8811), about 15 minutes away from campus.

AT A GLANCE

Selectivity Rating	83
Range SAT I Math	600–690
Average SAT I Math	641
Range SAT I Verbal	620–720
Average SAT I Verbal	666
Average ACT Composite	28
Average GPA	3.8
Student/Faculty Ratio	11:1

CAMPUS TOURS

Appointment	Preferred
Dates	Year-round
Times	Varies
Average Length	1 hour

ON-CAMPUS APPOINTMENTS

Admissions

Start Date–Juniors	Anytime
Appointment	Required
Advance Notice	Yes, 2 weeks
Saturdays	Sometimes
Average Length	30 min.
Info Sessions	Yes

Faculty and Coaches

Dates/Times	Year-round
Arrangements	Contact Admissions Office 2 weeks prior

CLASS VISITS

Dates	Academic year
Arrangements	Contact Admissions Office

STANFORD UNIVERSITY

Stanford Office of Undergraduate Admission, 520 Lasuen Mall, Old Union 232, Stanford, CA 94305-3005 • Telephone: 650-723-2091 • www.stanford.edu • Email: undergrad.admissions@forsythe.stanford.edu

Hours: Monday–Friday, 8:30AM–5:00PM

Some of the brightest minds in the world are at Stanford University, an Ivy-caliber university with a California atmosphere. The engineering, physical sciences, and liberal arts programs are all nationally renowned, and students say "you get what you pay (a lot) for." Sandra Day O'Connor and John Steinbeck are alums.

AT A GLANCE

Selectivity Rating	98
Range SAT I Math	690–780
Range SAT I Verbal	660–760
Average GPA	3.9
Student/Faculty Ratio	7:1

CAMPUS TOURS

Appointment	Required
Dates	Varies
Times	Admission: June–Dec.; General: year-round
Average Length	1 hour

ON-CAMPUS APPOINTMENTS

Admissions

Start Date—Juniors	N/A

Faculty and Coaches

Dates/Times	N/A
Arrangements	Contact faculty directly

CLASS VISITS

Dates	Academic year
Arrangements	Contact Admissions Office

TRANSPORTATION

San Francisco International Airport is 25 miles away from campus, and San Jose International Airport is 16 miles away from campus. Limousine and van service are available from the airports to campus. For service, call Airport Connection at 800-AIRPORT or 650-363-1500. A Sam Trans Bus (650-871-2200) to campus is available at San Francisco airport's upper level near TWA; take the #7F bus, which leaves every 30 minutes and takes nearly an hour to reach campus. Taxis are also available. Amtrak trains and Greyhound buses serve San Francisco. From San Francisco and San Jose you can take a commuter train, the CAL TRAIN, to Palo Alto and get out at the University Ave. Depot, Palo Alto, and take bus #24, bus #86, or the Marguerite (Stanford's red shuttle bus) to campus. For further information about the CAL TRAIN, call 800-558-8661.

FIND YOUR WAY

From Highway 101 North and South, take the Embarcadero Rd. exit west toward Stanford. At El Camino Real, Embarcadero turns into Galvez Rd. as it enters the university. Stay in the left lane and continue toward the center of campus. Galvez ends at Serra St., where there is metered parking. The visitor information center is in Memorial Hall, which is across from Hoover Tower on Serra St. **From Highway 280 North and South,** exit Sand Hill Rd. east toward Stanford. Continue east, turning right at the traffic light on Santa Cruz Ave. Make an immediate left onto Junipero Serra Blvd. Turn left at the second stoplight, Campus Drive East. Turn left when you reach Serra St. at the gas station. Follow Serra St. until it ends at Galvez St. Turn right onto Galvez and look for the first parking lot on the right. The Visitor Center is in front of Memorial Hall. Please note that parking is monitored Monday to Friday from 8:00AM to 4:00PM.

STAY THE NIGHT

Nearby: Please refer to our website for a list of accommodations and price ranges: www.stanford.edu/dept/uga/visiting/index.html.

HIGHLIGHTS

ON CAMPUS

- Cantor Center for the Visual Arts
- Rodin Sculpture Garden
- Memorial Church
- Observation Deck at Hoover Tower
- New Guinea Sculpture Garden

OFF CAMPUS

- San Francisco
- Great America Theme Park
- Sonoma and Napa Valleys
- Santa Cruz
- Stanford Shopping Center

UNIVERSITY OF CALIFORNIA—BERKELEY

Office of Undergraduate Admissions and Relations with Schools, 110 Sproul Hall, #5800
Berkeley, CA 94720-5800 • Telephone: 510-642-3175 • www.berkeley.edu •
Email: ouars@uclink.berkeley.edu

Hours: January–April: Monday–Friday, 9:00AM–noon and 1:00PM–4:00PM; May–December: 9:00AM–noon

The Berkeley campus of the University of California offers a tremendously diverse education in the liberal arts, natural sciences, and technology. The school enrolls about 22,000 students, many of whom advance to graduate studies. Berkeley is a hotbed for student activism and individual thinking, a cultural paradise, and the campus is home to 23 libraries.

HIGHLIGHTS

ON CAMPUS

- Botanical Gardens
- Lawrence Hall of Science
- Museum of Anthropology
- Museum of Art

OFF CAMPUS

- Berkeley Marina
- Bistro Viola Restaurant

TRANSPORTATION

Oakland International Airport is 20 miles away from campus. The Airporter Shuttle provides transportation from the airport to campus; call 800-AIRPORT at least 24 hours in advance to arrange for it. Public transportation to campus is also available. From the airport, take the shuttle bus to the BART subway system at Richmond, then take the subway to Berkeley. Amtrak trains serve nearby Oakland. Greyhound/Trailways buses also serve the area.

FIND YOUR WAY

The best approaches to the university are from Rte. 24 or from I-80. For more detailed driving instructions, call the Visitor Center (510-642-5215). The Visitor Center is in room 101 of University Hall, on Oxford St., north of Bancroft Way, across from the West Circle entrance to campus.

STAY THE NIGHT

Nearby: You have several choices within walking distance of campus. The least expensive is the **Berkeley Motel** (2001 Bancroft Way; 510-843-4043), a no-frills establishment. Moderately-priced places include the **Shattuck Hotel** (2086 Allston Way; 510-845-7300), one block from the west end of campus, with special rates for college visitors, offering a continental breakfast and parking; and the **Durant Hotel** (2600 Durant Ave.; 510-845-8981), which is two blocks from campus and near the small shops on the main strip. Nearby **Grandma's Rosegarden Inn** (2740 Telegraph Ave.; 510-549-2145) is a real charmer. Rates are moderate and include wine and cheese and a full breakfast. The inn is near restaurants and shops.

A Little Farther: Check the University of San Francisco entry for suggestions across the bay.

AT A GLANCE

Selectivity Rating		94
Range SAT I Math		620–740
Average SAT I Math		671
Range SAT I Verbal		570–700
Average SAT I Verbal		629
Average GPA		4.26
Student/Faculty Ratio		16:1

CAMPUS TOURS

Dates	Year-round
Times	Mon–Sat, 10AM; Sun 1PM
Average Length	2 hours

ON-CAMPUS APPOINTMENTS

Admissions

Start Date–Juniors	N/A
Info Sessions	Year-round for prospective freshmen only

Faculty and Coaches

Dates/Times	Subject to faculty/coach availability
Arrangements	Contact coach directly

CLASS VISITS

Dates	Year-round
Arrangements	Contact faculty directly

UNIVERSITY OF CALIFORNIA—DAVIS

Undergraduate Admissions and Outreach Services, 175 Mark Hall, One Shields Avenue (mailing only) Davis, CA 95616 • Telephone: 530-752-2971 • www.ucdavis.edu • Email: thinkucd@ucdavis.edu

Hours: Monday–Friday, 9:00AM–noon and 1:00PM–4:00PM

The Davis campus of the University of California is located in rural Davis, near Sacramento. The school's programs run the gamut from the arts and sciences to business and education, and students give high marks to the school's technology resources. Campus life is reportedly laid back.

AT A GLANCE

Selectivity Rating	82
Range SAT I Math	560–660
Average SAT I Math	637
Range SAT I Verbal	500–620
Average SAT I Verbal	598
Average ACT Composite	28
Average GPA	3.71
Student/Faculty Ratio	19:1

CAMPUS TOURS

Appointment	Required
Dates	Year-round
Times	Mon–Fri, 10AM & 2PM; Sat–Sun, 11:30AM & 1:30PM
Average Length	2 hours

ON-CAMPUS APPOINTMENTS

Admissions

Start Date–Juniors	N/A
Info Sessions	No personal interviews

Faculty and Coaches

Dates/Times	Subject to faculty/ coach availability
Arrangements	Contact coach directly as soon as possible

CLASS VISITS

Dates	Year-round
Arrangements	Contact Visiting Center

TRANSPORTATION

Sacramento International Airport is 20 miles away from campus. Davis Airporter Limousine Service (530-756-6715) is available to/from the airport; call at least one day in advance. Rental cars are also available at the airport.

FIND YOUR WAY

From Sacramento and from San Francisco, take I-80 to the UC Davis exit, which will lead you right to the campus. **From the north,** take Hwy. 113; exit at either the Russell Blvd. or UC Davis (Hutchison Dr.) exit and go east to campus.

STAY THE NIGHT

Nearby: The 18-room **Davis Bed and Breakfast Inn** (422 A St.; 530-753-9611) is just across the street from the university. The low price includes a full breakfast. **Best Western University Lodge** (123 B St.; 530-756-7890), just two blocks away, is another basic facility. A half block away is **Aggie Inn** (245 1st St.; 530-756-0352), with pretty rooms, spa, sauna, continental breakfast, and moderate rates.

A Little Farther: At the university, you are only about 25 minutes west of Sacramento, where you might prefer to stay. Built in 1912, **Abigail's Bed and Breakfast** (2120 G St.; 530-441-5007) is a colonial revival mansion located in downtown Sacramento. It's within easy reach of many of the attractions of the city. Rates range from moderate to expensive include a delicious breakfast. If you need twin beds, be careful to check in advance. **American Youth Hostel** (900 H St.; 530-443-1692) is a converted 100-year-old mansion within walking distance of Amtrak, Old Sacramento, and the Capitol, and one block away from the Yolo bus to Davis. The hostel is very affordable.

HIGHLIGHTS

ON CAMPUS
- Celeste Turner Wright Hall
- Peter J. Shields Library
- The Recreation Hall
- The Walter A. Buehler Alumni & Visitors' Center

OFF CAMPUS
- Napa Valley
- Old Sacramento
- Sutter's Fort
- Sacramento River

UNIVERSITY OF CALIFORNIA—IRVINE

Office of Admissions and Relations with Schools, 204 Administration Building, Irvine, CA 92697-1075 • Telephone: 949-824-6703 • www.admissions.uci.edu •

Hours: Monday–Friday, 9:00AM–5:00PM

The Irvine campus of the University of California is located about an hour from Los Angeles and provides a research-oriented education in the arts and sciences. Irvine's programs in science are legendary. The campus is a mere five minutes away from the beach and an hour away from mountain skiing resorts.

HIGHLIGHTS

ON CAMPUS

- Anteater Recreation Center
- Bren Events Center
- Anteater Ballpark
- Cross-Cultural Center
- Beall Center for Art & Technology

OFF CAMPUS

- Irvine Spectrum
- The Block At Orange
- Newport Beach
- Disneyland
- South Coast Plaza

TRANSPORTATION

The John Wayne Airport (Orange County) is five miles away from campus. Taxis are available at the airport. The County Bus stops on campus.

FIND YOUR WAY

The campus is one mile south of the I-405 freeway. **From San Diego (south of Irvine),** take I-405 to the Culver Rd. exit and proceed south to Campus Dr. Turn right on Campus Dr. to W. Peltason Dr. (the university entrance). Turn left on W. Peltason Dr. **From Los Angeles (north of Irvine),** take I-405 to the Jamboree exit and proceed south to Campus Dr. Turn left on Campus Dr. and proceed to Bridge Rd. (the university entrance). Turn right on W. Peltason Dr.

STAY THE NIGHT

Nearby: The **Atrium Hotel** (18700 MacArthur Blvd.; 949-833-2770), five minutes away (and close to the airport), has a special moderate double-occupancy rate for university visitors. A shuttle bus will take you to the Irvine Racquet Club, where you can play squash and use the exercise room. The **Holiday Inn—Orange County** (2726 S. Grand Ave., Santa Ana; 949-966-1955) is only 15 minutes away from campus. Ask for the special inexpensive double-occupancy rate for university visitors. The **Ramada** has a fitness room and an outside pool and Jacuzzi. You have a couple of interesting, moderately-priced choices about 10 minutes away from the university. The **Country Inn** (325 S. Bristol St., Costa Mesa; 949-549-0300) is a large hotel with a country inn atmosphere. It is located in a business district and has two pools, Jacuzzis, and exercise facilities, as well as a French restaurant on the premises. Ask for the university rate (moderate) at the **Irvine Hyatt Regency** (17900 Jamboree Blvd.; 949-975-1234), which is 10 minutes away. There are lighted tennis courts, as well as a pool, Jacuzzi, and exercise rooms. At the **Newport Beach Marriott Hotel and Tennis Club** (900 Newport Center Dr., Fashion Island; 949-640-4000) you can enjoy an ocean view in the lounge, lighted tennis courts, exercise rooms, pools, patios, balconies, and a band that plays Top 40 tunes. Golf privileges and a shopping center are an additional plus. For more accommodations, visit www.confserv.uci.edu/hotels.html.

A Little Farther: For something different, consider **Newport Beach,** a 15-minute drive. Prices are on the expensive side (full breakfast included) at the eleven room **Doryman's Inn** (2102 W. Oceanfront, Newport Beach; 949-675-7300), a historical landmark just across from Newport Pier. The inn, housed in a 1920s brick building, provides an elegant atmosphere with views of the Pacific from the roof deck.

AT A GLANCE

Selectivity Rating	77
Range SAT I Math	560–670
Average SAT I Math	610
Range SAT I Verbal	510–620
Average SAT I Verbal	560
Average GPA	3.68
Student/Faculty Ratio	18:1

CAMPUS TOURS

Appointment	Not required
Dates	Year-round
Times	Mon–Fri, noon
Average Length	1 hour

ON-CAMPUS APPOINTMENTS

Admissions

Start Date–Juniors	Anytime
Saturdays	No

Faculty and Coaches

Dates/Times	N/A
Arrangements	N/A

CLASS VISITS

Arrangements	N/A

UNIVERSITY OF CALIFORNIA—LOS ANGELES

Office of Undergraduate Admissions, 405 Hilgard Avenue, 1147 Murphy Hall,
Los Angeles, CA 90095-1436 • Telephone: 310-825-3101 • www.ucla.edu/admissions.html
Email: ugadm@saonet.ucla.edu

Hours: Monday–Friday, 9:00AM–5:00PM

The distinguished Los Angeles campus of the University of California enrolls about 24,000 students and offers a wide range of programs including respected pre-medical programs. The educational and extracurricular opportunities on campus are vast but require student initiative, and the bustling city of Los Angeles does not lack for entertainment options.

AT A GLANCE

Selectivity Rating	92
Range SAT I Math	590–720
Average SAT I Math	653
Range SAT I Verbal	550–670
Average SAT I Verbal	611
Average ACT Composite	26
Average GPA	4.11
Student/Faculty Ratio	17:1

CAMPUS TOURS

Appointment	Required
Dates	Year-round
Times	Varies
Average Length	1 hour

ON-CAMPUS APPOINTMENTS

Admissions

Saturdays	No

Faculty and Coaches

Arrangements	Contact coach directly

CLASS VISITS

Dates	Academic year
Arrangements	Tours Office

TRANSPORTATION

Los Angeles International Airport (LAX) is 20 minutes away from campus. Burbank Airport is 30 minutes away from campus. Call the following numbers to arrange transportation from LAX: 818-556-6600 for Super Shuttle; 800-262-7433 for Prime Time Shuttle. Checker Cab Service (818-956-5959) also runs between campus and LAX. Amtrak trains and Greyhound/Trailways buses provide transportation to Los Angeles.

FIND YOUR WAY

From the I-405 freeway (north or south), take the Wilshire Blvd. exit and follow it east to Westwood Blvd. Turn left onto Westwood Blvd. and drive onto the campus. **From downtown,** take Wilshire Blvd. west and turn right onto Westwood Blvd.

STAY THE NIGHT

Nearby: For the most current visitor information go to the following website:

www.ucla.edu/audience/visitors.html

A Little Farther: For the most current visitor information go to the following website:

www.ucla.edu/audience/visitors.html

HIGHLIGHTS

ON CAMPUS

• The UCLA Library
• UCLA Fowler Museum of Cultural History
• UCLA Book Store
• DeNeve Plaza
• Kerckhoff Coffee House

OFF CAMPUS

• J. Paul Getty Center
• Santa Monica Pier
• UCLA Ocean Discovery Center
• UCLA Geffen Playhouse
• Venice Beach

UNIVERSITY OF CALIFORNIA—RIVERSIDE

Office of Relations with Schools, 1120 Hinderaker Hall, Riverside, CA 92521 • Telephone: 909-787-4531 • www.ucr.edu • Email: discover@pop.ucr.edu

Hours: Monday–Friday, 9:00AM–5:00PM

The Riverside campus of the University of California is located about an hour away from Los Angeles. Riverside offers programs ranging from the liberal arts to business to a fast-track, seven-year MD program. For athletic excellence, check out the men's and women's karate teams, winners of six national championships.

HIGHLIGHTS

ON CAMPUS
- Athletic events
- Student Recreation Center and intramural sports
- Touring music and comedy acts
- University libraries
- the Commons

OFF CAMPUS
- Starbuck's
- University Village shops and theatres
- Galeria at Tyler shopping
- Disneyland
- Sun and snow in nearby desert and mountain resorts

TRANSPORTATION

Ontario International Airport is 20 miles away from campus. Taxis and shuttles are available to and from the airport. The Metrolink runs through Riverside to Orange and Los Angeles counties.

FIND YOUR WAY

From California Rte. 60/215, take the University Ave. exit. At the exit ramp, turn left (east), and proceed one block to the main entrance of the campus. Make a right turn into the kiosk for parking instructions. Parking is $5 per day.

STAY THE NIGHT

Nearby: The **Courtyard by Marriott** (1510 University Ave.; 909-272-1200) is five blocks from campus and charges low rates. The **Comfort Inn** (1590 University Ave.; 909-683-6000) also gives special rates to university visitors. About 10 minutes away is the **Holiday Inn Riverside** (3400 Market St.; 909-784-8000), a multi-story hotel with a heated pool, Jacuzzi, sauna, cafe, entertainment, and the works. Rates vary from high moderate to expensive. The **Historic Mission Inn** (3649 Mission Inn Ave.; 909-784-0300) is located approximately five miles away from the campus.

AT A GLANCE

Selectivity Rating	79
Range SAT I Math	490–620
Average SAT I Math	553
Range SAT I Verbal	440–560
Average SAT I Verbal	504
Average ACT Composite	21
Average GPA	3.46
Student/Faculty Ratio	19:1

CAMPUS TOURS

Appointment	Preferred
Dates	Year-round
Times	Varies
Average Length	1 hour

ON-CAMPUS APPOINTMENTS

Admissions

Start Date—Juniors	N/A

Faculty and Coaches

Dates/Times	Academic year
Arrangements	Contact coach directly 2 weeks prior

CLASS VISITS

Dates	Academic year
Arrangements	HOST Program, (909) 827-6500

UNIVERSITY OF CALIFORNIA—SAN DIEGO

Office of Admissions and Outreach, 9500 Gilman Drive, La Jolla, CA 92093-0021 • Telephone: 858-534-4831 • www.ucsd.edu/admissions • Email: admissionsinfo@ucsd.edu

Hours: Monday–Friday, 8:00AM–4:30PM

The San Diego campus of the University of California is actually located in the quaint community of La Jolla. UCSD offers a solid liberal arts and sciences education, and its engineering and science programs are rated particularly high. For fun, students enjoy surfing and camping on the nearby beach.

AT A GLANCE

Selectivity Rating	83
Range SAT I Math	600–700
Average SAT I Math	646
Range SAT I Verbal	540–650
Average SAT I Verbal	593
Average ACT Composite	25
Average GPA	3.98
Student/Faculty Ratio	19:1

CAMPUS TOURS

Appointment	Preferred
Dates	Year-round
Times	Mon–Sat, 11AM
Average Length	120 min.

ON-CAMPUS APPOINTMENTS

Admissions

Start Date—Juniors	N/A

Faculty and Coaches

Dates/Times	Academic year
Arrangements	Contact coach directly 3 weeks prior

CLASS VISITS

Arrangements	Contact Admissions Office

TRANSPORTATION

San Diego International Airport is 15 miles away from campus. Taxis, shuttles, and public buses are available for the ride to campus from the airport. Amtrak trains and Greyhound/Trailways buses serve downtown San Diego. The San Diego Metropolitan Transit System provides bus service in the area and the San Diego Trolley runs on two lines from the Amtrak depot.

FIND YOUR WAY

From I-5, exit to Gilman Dr. W. Follow it to the information kiosk, where you may get a parking permit, campus map, and directions. Parking is free on weekends.

STAY THE NIGHT

Nearby: The closest hotel to the university is the **Residence Inn by Marriott** (8901 Gilman Dr.; 858-587-1170). Another hotel within walking distance is the **Radisson Hotel of La Jolla** (3299 Holiday Ct.; 858-453-5500).

A Little Farther: **La Jolla Marriott Hotel** (4240 La Jolla Village Dr.; 858-587-1414), the **Hyatt Regency Hotel** (3777 La Jolla Village Dr.; 858-552-1234), and the **Embassy Suites** (4550 La Jolla Village Dr.; 858-453-0400) are all within two miles of campus.

HIGHLIGHTS

ON CAMPUS

- Geisel Library
- Stuart Art Gallery (sculpture)
- Sun God Statue
- Ocean Cliffs
- Stephen Birch Aquarium and Museum

OFF CAMPUS

- San Diego Zoo
- Balboa Park
- Beaches
- Gaslamp Quarter
- Old Town

UNIVERSITY OF CALIFORNIA—SANTA BARBARA

Undergraduate Admissions, 1210 Cheadle Hall,
Santa Barbara, CA 93106 • Telephone: 805-893-2881 • www.admit.ucsb.edu •
Email: appinfo@sa.ucsb.edu

Hours: Monday–Friday, 9:00AM–noon, 1:00PM–5:00PM

The University of California's Santa Barbara's laid-back campus enrolls about 17,000 students in a variety of programs in the liberal arts and sciences, business, and technology. Students claim the Santa Barbara campus has one of the nation's most active social scenes and report that no UCSB experience is complete without a weekend party at the notorious Isla Vista area of student residences.

HIGHLIGHTS

ON CAMPUS
- Storke Tower Plaza/University Center
- University Art Museum
- UCSB Davidson Library
- Recreation Center
- Career and Counseling Services Center

OFF CAMPUS
- Stearns Wharf/Santa Barbara Zoo
- Old Spanish Days and their weekly summer festivals
- Santa Yenz/Solvang Danish Village
- Los Padres National Forest
- Santa Barbara Mission, Museum, and Botanic Gardens

TRANSPORTATION

The Santa Barbara Airport is a five-minute drive from campus. Taxis are available at the airport. Amtrak trains and Greyhound buses serve downtown Santa Barbara. A direct express bus is available from downtown to campus. Taxis are also available for the ride from the stations to campus.

FIND YOUR WAY

From the north, take U.S. Highway 101 south to the Storke Road/Glen Annie Road exit, which is approximately 12 miles north of Santa Barbara. Turn right on Storke Road and proceed two miles to El Colegio Road. Turn left onto El Colegio Road and proceed to the campus entrance. **From the south,** take U.S. Highway 101 north to the Airport/UCSB exit (route 217), which is approximately eight miles north of Santa Barbara, then continue to the campus entrance. The daily parking fee at the campus is $5 per day from Monday to Friday. There is no charge for weekend parking.

STAY THE NIGHT

Nearby: The campus is west of Santa Barbara, in Goleta, with no lodgings within walking distance. Two moderately-priced motels are a short drive away; both have heated pools and complementary van service to and from the airport. The closest (about two miles away) is a **Holiday Inn** (5650 Calle Real, Goleta; 805-964-6241), with a restaurant. About four miles away from campus is the **Ramada Limited** (4770 Calle Real, Santa Barbara; 805-964-3511 or 800-654-1965); rates there are only slightly more expensive than at the Holiday Inn, and the price includes a continental breakfast. Nearby beaches are a plus, and it is close to downtown shopping. If you need even more relaxation, watch the ducks on the freshwater pond.

A Little Farther: Santa Barbara has many small inns. You might consider **The Cheshire Cat** (36 W. Valerio St.; 805-569-1610), which is a 20-minute drive from campus. Prices range from moderate to expensive. All rooms have private baths and telephones. The inn is close to the Mission Santa Barbara and to the shops and restaurants of the town. The price includes a gourmet continental breakfast and afternoon wine. The famous, very expensive **San Ysidro Ranch** (900 San Ysidro Lane; 805-969-5046) is situated in the foothills of the Santa Ynez Mountains. It's 10 miles south of Santa Barbara and 25 minutes from campus. Hiking, swimming, golf, tennis, and an exercise room are available. **Circle Bar B Guest Ranch** is a more down-home guest ranch in Goleta (1800 Refugio Rd.; 805-968-1113), 30 minutes north of the university. This family-run, 1,000-acre ranch has 30 horses, hiking and riding trails, a swimming pool, and a Jacuzzi. While its price is on the expensive side, it does include three meals a day. Comedy theater is presented on weekends. Also try the **Best Western South Coast Inn** (5620 Calle Real, Goleta; 805-967-3200) or the **Super 8** (6021 Hollister Ave, Goleta; 805-967-5591), or check the UCSB website at www.ucsb.edu for other Santa Barbara lodging.

AT A GLANCE

Selectivity Rating	80
Range SAT I Math	550–660
Average SAT I Math	602
Range SAT I Verbal	510–620
Average SAT I Verbal	570
Average ACT Composite	25
Average GPA	3.71
Student/Faculty Ratio	17:1

CAMPUS TOURS

Appointment	Not required
Dates	Year-round
Times	Mon–Fri, 12:00AM, 2:00 PM
Average Length	Varies

ON-CAMPUS APPOINTMENTS

Admissions

Start Date–Juniors	N/A
Appointment	Not required
Advance Notice	No
Saturdays	No
Info Sessions	Yes

Faculty and Coaches

Arrangements	Contact faculty directly

CLASS VISITS

Dates	Academic year
Arrangements	Contact Visiting Center

UNIVERSITY OF CALIFORNIA—SANTA CRUZ

Office of Admissions, Cook House,
Santa Cruz, CA 95064 • Telephone: 831-459-4008 • www.admissions.ucsc.edu •
Email: admissions@ucsc.edu

Hours: Monday–Friday, 9:00AM–5:00PM

The Santa Cruz campus of the University of California enrolls about 10,000 students, the majority of whom have high praise for the school's educational programs, which include the liberal arts and sciences, as well as technology and engineering programs. The school offers a no-grades option, which students say encourages learning instead of GPA worries.

AT A GLANCE

Selectivity Rating	79
Range SAT I Math	520–630
Average SAT I Math	573
Range SAT I Verbal	500–620
Average SAT I Verbal	564
Average ACT Composite	23
Average GPA	3.46
Student/Faculty Ratio	19:1

CAMPUS TOURS

Appointment	Required
Dates	Year-round
Times	Varies
Average Length	120 min.

ON-CAMPUS APPOINTMENTS

Admissions

Saturdays	No

Faculty and Coaches

Dates/Times	Academic year
Arrangements	Contact faculty directly

CLASS VISITS

Arrangements	Contact Admissions Office

TRANSPORTATION

San Jose International Airport is 35 miles away from campus. Rental cars, buses, and limousines are available for the ride to Santa Cruz. Commercial bus service is available to Santa Cruz, and bus transportation within the county is convenient. Amtrak is also a good idea; take it to San Jose and transfer to a bus to Santa Cruz. The Metro Transit Center downtown serves Santa Cruz County; Rte. 1 loops through the campus.

FIND YOUR WAY

From U.S. Rte. 101 S. (from San Francisco), exit to I-880 S. Take I-880 to Rte. 17 S., then take Rte. 17 to Rte. 1 N. (toward Half Moon Bay). From Rte. 1, turn right on Bay St. in Santa Cruz and proceed to campus. **From Rte. 101 N.,** exit to I-880 S., then to Rte. 17 S. Follow the preceding directions from that point.

STAY THE NIGHT

Nearby: You have a variety of choices within a few miles of campus. The least expensive and simplest is the **Ramada Limited** (130 W. Cliff Dr.; 831-423-7737), about two miles away from campus on the boardwalk across from the beach. Some of the units have ocean views and balconies. **Mission Inn** (2250 Mission St., Hwy. 1; 831-425-5455), about one mile away from the university, is also reasonably-priced. It's located in town, close to golf courses, and there is a covered hot tub in the courtyard. Two wonderful inns are within five minutes of the university. Both are moderately-priced and include breakfast. **Darling House** (314 W.Cliff Dr.; 831-458-1958), is an elegant ocean-side mansion set among orchards and palms. Each room has a theme or historical background. Rooms with a view are more expensive (but there's a discount for university visitors). **Babbling Brook Inn** (1025 Laurel St.; 800-866-1131) is in town and has a country French ambience set in landscaped gardens among redwoods. You can stroll through the garden walkways or play tennis and golf nearby. Wine, cheese, tea, and homemade cookies are served in the afternoon. **West Coast Santa Cruz Hotel** (175 W. Cliff Dr.; 831-426-4330) is a beachfront hotel two miles away from the university. Its double rooms range from moderate to very expensive. All the rooms have ocean views and private balconies (and the views from the inn are fabulous). Relax in the heated pool, Jacuzzi, or sauna. Another possibility is the **Henry Cowell State Park Campgrounds,** which will cost you $17 per night plus a reservation fee.

HIGHLIGHTS

ON CAMPUS

- Arboretum
- Farm and Garden
- East Field House
- Bay Tree Bookstore/Grad Student Commons
- Pogonip Open Area Reserve

OFF CAMPUS

- UC Santa Cruz Long Marine Lab
- Boardwalk
- Mystery Spot
- Henry Cowell and Big Basin State Parks
- Natural Bridges and Lighthouse Beach

UNIVERSITY OF REDLANDS

Office of Admissions, PO Box 3080, 1200 E. Colton Ave, Redlands, CA 92373-0999 • Telephone: 800-455-5064 • www.redlands.edu • Email: admissions@redlands.edu

Hours: Monday–Friday, 8:30AM–5:00PM; Saturday, 9:00AM–3:00PM

The primary reason to attend University of Redlands is the innovative and experimental Johnston Center for Integrative Studies, in which students fully customize their own majors in tandem with faculty members and, instead of grades, receive precise narrative evaluations from their collaborating professors. Recent student-designed majors have centered on utopian theory, ethnobotany, and Spanish, ceramics, and anthropology, to name a few.

HIGHLIGHTS

ON CAMPUS
- Armacost Library
- Peppers Art Center
- Currier Gymnasium/Fitness Center
- Chapel
- Post Office

OFF CAMPUS
- Los Angeles/Hollywood
- Palm Springs/Desert Hot Springs
- Mountain Resorts: Forest Falls, Big Bear, Arrowhead
- Beaches
- Downtown Redlands
- There are also several amusement parks (Disneyland, Magic Mountain, Raging Waters, Knotts Berry Farm) within driving distance.

TRANSPORTATION

Ontario International Airport is 28 miles west of the town of Redlands off I-10. It is 27 miles away from campus. Taxi, limousine, bus, and shuttle service are available from the airport to campus. For more information, visit www.lawa.org/ont/ontframe.html.

FIND YOUR WAY

From Los Angeles, take I-10 E. to the University St. exit in Redlands. Turn left and head north on University St. to Colton Ave.; turn right onto campus. **From the east,** take I-10 W. to the Redlands Blvd.-Ford St. exit; turn right (Ford becomes Judson). At Colton Ave., turn left and continue for a quarter of a mile to campus. For more information on ground transportation from LAX, visit www.lawa.org/lax/laxframe.html.

STAY THE NIGHT

Nearby: You have two inexpensive choices within a mile or two of campus. The **Goodnight Inn** (1675 Industrial Park Ave.; 909-793-3723) has a heated pool and spa. The **Best Western Sandman** (1120 W. Colton Ave.; 909-793-7001) is about a mile away from the university. For a small additional charge, you may have a kitchen unit. There is a pool and a Jacuzzi at the latter.

A Little Farther: In San Bernardino, **Inland Empire Hilton** (285 E. Hospitality Lane; 909-889-0133) is about 15 minutes away from Redlands. Rates are at the high end of the moderate range. The motor hotel has a swimming pool, Jacuzzi, and health club; a public golf course is close by. See suggestions in the University of California—Riverside entry, particularly the Sheraton Riverside. It's about 30 minutes from the University of Redlands.

AT A GLANCE

Selectivity Rating	73
Range SAT I Math	520–630
Average SAT I Math	574
Range SAT I Verbal	520–610
Average SAT I Verbal	565
Average ACT Composite	24
Average GPA	3.5
Student/Faculty Ratio	13:1

CAMPUS TOURS

Appointment	Preferred
Dates	Year-round
Times	Mon–Fri, 10AM, 1PM, & 4PM
Average Length	1 hour

ON-CAMPUS APPOINTMENTS

Admissions

Start Date–Juniors	Anytime
Appointment	Required
Advance Notice	Yes, 1 week
Saturdays	Sometimes
Average Length	1 hour
Info Sessions	Yes

Faculty and Coaches

Dates/Times	Year-round
Arrangements	Contact visiting coordinator 1 week prior

CLASS VISITS

Dates	Academic year
Arrangements	Contact visiting coordinator

UNIVERSITY OF SAN DIEGO

Office of Undergraduate Admissions, 5998 Alcala Park,
San Diego, CA 92110-2492 • Telephone: 800-248-4873 • www.sandiego.edu/ugadmiss/ •
Email: admissions@sandiego.edu

Hours: Monday–Friday, 8:30AM–5:00PM; Saturday (during winter), 10:00AM–2:00PM

Class sizes are small, discussion is encouraged, and professors are engaged at this Southern California Catholic institution. USD's 180-acre spread is adorned with lavish white buildings, palm trees, year-round flora, an ever-present grounds crew, and a breathtaking view of Mission Bay's Pacific waters.

AT A GLANCE

Selectivity Rating		74
Range SAT I Math		540–640
Average SAT I Math		590
Range SAT I Verbal		520–620
Average SAT I Verbal		570
Average ACT Composite		26
Average GPA		3.74
Student/Faculty Ratio		15:1

CAMPUS TOURS

Appointment	Preferred
Dates	Year-round
Times	Mon–Fri, 10AM & 2PM
Average Length	120 min.

ON-CAMPUS APPOINTMENTS

Admissions
Start Date–Juniors	N/A

Faculty and Coaches
Arrangements	Contact Athletic Department 2 weeks prior

CLASS VISITS

Dates	Academic year
Arrangements	Contact Admissions Office

TRANSPORTATION

San Diego International Airport is five miles away from campus. Taxi and shuttle services are available for the ride from the airport to campus; advanced arrangements are not necessary. Amtrak trains serve San Diego from Los Angeles. Greyhound/Trailways buses also serve San Diego. The San Diego Metropolitan Transit System provides bus service in the area, and the San Diego Trolley runs throughout San Diego county with shuttles from USD to the Old Town Trolley station.

FIND YOUR WAY

From I-5, exit at Sea World Dr.; turn east and follow the signs to the university. **From I-8,** exit at Morena Blvd. and follow the signs to the university.

STAY THE NIGHT

Nearby: Please consult our website at www.sandiego.edu for a comprehensive list of local hotels in a variety of price ranges.

HIGHLIGHTS

ON CAMPUS
• Donald P. Shiley Center for Science and Technology
• Joan B. Kroc Institute for Peace and Justice
• Jenny Craig Pavilion (Sporting/concert venue)
• Aromas Coffee House
• Copley Library

OFF CAMPUS
• San Diego Zoo
• Sea World
• San Diego Wild Animal Park
• Downtown San Diego's Gaslamp Quarter
• La Jolla

UNIVERSITY OF SAN FRANCISCO

Admissions Office, 2130 Fulton St.,
San Francisco, CA 94117 • Telephone: 800-225-5873 • www.usfca.edu •
Email: admission@usfca.edu

Hours: Monday–Thursay, 8:30AM–6:00PM; Friday, 5:00PM

The Jesuit University of San Francisco is one of the premier private universities in California and offers a wealth of excellent degree programs and a demanding core curriculum. The McLaren School of Business consistently ranks as one of the country's top international business schools, and you just can't beat college life in the heart of San Francisco.

HIGHLIGHTS

ON CAMPUS
- Koret Health and Recreation Center
- War Memorial Gym
- St. Ignatius Church
- Geschke Learning Resourse Center
- Loan Mountain Campus

OFF CAMPUS
- Golden Gate Bridge
- Alcatraz Island
- Union Square (shopping)
- Pacific Bell Park
- Golden Gate Park

TRANSPORTATION

San Francisco International Airport is a 20-minute drive away from campus. Visitors can take shuttle service at the airport without making advanced arrangements. Amtrak trains serve nearby Oakland; Greyhound/Trailways buses bring passengers to San Francisco.

FIND YOUR WAY

If you enter the city from the airport or the Bay Bridge, follow the signs to the Golden Gate Bridge. Exit the Freeway on Fell St. and proceed for approximately three miles. Turn right at Masonic, and then left on Golden Gate Ave. The entrance to the university is on the left. **If you enter the city from the Golden Gate Bridge,** follow Park Presidio to Fulton St. Turn left and the university is at the top of the hill. **From I-280,** follow 9th Ave. for three miles. Go through Golden Gate Park and turn right on Fulton Street.

STAY THE NIGHT

Nearby: The small, 36-room **Stanyan Park Hotel** (750 Stanyan St.; 415-751-1000) is about six blocks away. Rooms are comfortable and romantic, and the moderate rate includes continental breakfast. Joggers will particularly appreciate being across from Golden Gate Park. The **Laurel Motor Inn** (444 Presidio Ave.; 415-567-8467), about eight blocks away, is moderately-priced (including continental breakfast) and convenient.

A Little Farther: Just blocks from Union Square (also 15 minutes from the university), is **The Petite Auberge** (863 Bush St.). This is a French-style country inn decorated with soft colors, antique pieces, and fresh flowers. The rates are on the expensive side and include full breakfast and afternoon tea. Of course, there are some fabulous and very expensive hotels in San Francisco. A few of them are the **Mandarin Oriental** (222 Sansome St.; 415-885-0999 or 800-622-0404), the **Huntington Hotel** (1075 California St.; 415-474-5400 or 800-227-4683), and the **Four Seasons Clift** (495 Geary St.; 415-775-4700 or 800-652-5438).

UNIVERSITY OF SOUTHERN CALIFORNIA

Office of Undergraduate Admissions, 700 Childs Way,
Los Angeles, CA 90089-0911 • Telephone: 213-740-1111 • www.usc.edu/admission/ •
Email: admitusc@usc.edu

Hours: Monday–Friday, 8:30AM–5:00PM

If you are looking for a world-class university with awesome facilities and a strong academic reputation, check out the University of Southern California, which, as an added bonus, is located near glitzy downtown Los Angeles. Among students and alumni, the "Trojan family" mentality is strong, which means thousands of instant and permanent connections for job-hunting graduates.

AT A GLANCE

Selectivity Rating	82
Range SAT I Math	640–720
Average SAT I Math	683
Range SAT I Verbal	600–700
Average SAT I Verbal	652
Average ACT Composite	30
Average GPA	3.96
Student/Faculty Ratio	10:1

CAMPUS TOURS

Appointment	Required
Dates	Year-round
Times	Mon–Fri, 8:35AM–5PM
Average Length	1 hour

ON-CAMPUS APPOINTMENTS

Admissions

Start Date–Juniors	Anytime
Appointment	Required
Advance Notice	Yes, 1 week
Saturdays	No
Average Length	30 min.
Info Sessions	Yes

Faculty and Coaches

Dates/Times	Year-round
Arrangements	Contact faculty or coach directly 1 week prior

CLASS VISITS

Dates	Academic year
Arrangements	Contact academic unit

TRANSPORTATION

Los Angeles International Airport is 15 miles away from campus. Taxis (approximately $28) and the Super Shuttle (approximately $15) are available for the ride from the airport to campus. Taxis can be picked up outside the airport terminal. The Super Shuttle is a minibus that will take you anywhere in Los Angeles and Orange counties; call 310-782-6600 a day or two in advance or when you arrive. Amtrak trains and Greyhound/Trailways buses provide transportation to Los Angeles.

FIND YOUR WAY

From I-110 (Harbor Freeway), exit onto Exposition Blvd. and go one block west. The campus will be on the right. **From I-10 (Santa Monica Freeway),** exit onto Hoover St. and go south approximately one mile to Jefferson Blvd. The campus will be directly ahead. **From the Los Angeles International Airport,** take the Glenn Anderson Freeway (105) east to the Harbor Freeway north (I-110). Exit on Exposition Blvd. and go one block west. The campus will be on your right.

STAY THE NIGHT

Nearby: Across the street is the **Radisson Hotel** (3540 S. Figueroa St.; 213-748-4141), with a special double-occupancy rate available for a moderate price. See the Pepperdine University entry for information about bed-and-breakfasts in the area. Also see suggestions for downtown Los Angeles in the University of California—Los Angeles entry. USC is 2.5 miles south of downtown, right in the city.

HIGHLIGHTS

ON CAMPUS

- Fisher Art Gallery
- School of Cinema—Television
- Leavey Library
- Heritage Hall
- Bing Theater

OFF CAMPUS

- Exposition Park
- Museum of Contemporary Art
- The Staples Center
- Los Angeles Music Center
- Disney Hall

UNIVERSITY OF THE PACIFIC

Planning and Research, Knoles Hall, 3rd Fl, 3601 Pacific Ave, Stockton, CA 95211 • Telephone: 800-959-2867 • www.uop.edu • Email: admissions@pacific.edu

Hours: Monday–Friday, 8:30AM–5:00PM; select Saturdays, 9:00AM–noon

Students at University of the Pacific say they are spoiled with great professors who are not only teachers in class, but also friends on campus. Health sciences are the school's strongest programs (particularly popular with the students is the incredible five-year dental program), although music, engineering, and business-related majors are also well-regarded (and reportedly, excellent).

HIGHLIGHTS

ON CAMPUS
- Brubeck Istitute for Jazz Studies
- John Muir Collection and Center
- Alex Spanos Center
- Reynolds Art Gallery
- Pharmacy and Health Sciences Building

OFF CAMPUS
- Wineries
- Stockton Civic Theater
- San Joaquin Delta Waterways
- Weber Point Events Center
- World Famous Asparagus Festval

TRANSPORTATION

The Sacramento International Airport is one hour away from campus; Oakland International is about one-and-a-half hours away from campus; San Jose International is about one-and-a-half hours from campus; San Francisco International is about two hours away from campus. Limited transportation is available from these airports. For Super Shuttle Service from Sacramento International, call 1-800-BlueVan for a reservation. Greyhound provides direct and frequent service to Stockton. For fare and schedule information, call 1-800-843-2121. The bus station is approximately three miles away from campus; therefore we recommend you take a taxi to campus. Amtrak trains (1-800-USA-RAIL) provide direct service to Stockton from almost everywhere in California. The Amtrak Station is approximately five miles south of campus, and taxi service is available.

FIND YOUR WAY

From I-5, exit at March Lane. Drive east about one-and-a-half miles, and turn right on Pacific Avenue. The main campus entrance is less than one mile south of the intersection of March Lane and Pacific Avenue. Turn right into campus at the traffic light. Guest parking is to your right. Permits are required on weekdays, from 8:00AM to 5:00PM anywhere on campus during the school year. Visitor permits may be obtained at the Office of Admissions or in Burns Tower lobby.

STAY THE NIGHT

Nearby: The university has four guest rooms in residence halls on campus that are incredible bargains. You must book well in advance by calling the Housing Office at 209-946-2331. You can find breakfast on campus at the Summit. The nicest places to stay in Stockton are the **Stockton Radisson Hotel** (2323 Grand Canal Blvd.; 800-333-3333), the **Marriott Courtyard** (3252 March Lane; 888-472-9700), and the **Marriott Residence Inn** (888-472-9801). **La Quinta Inn** (2710 W. March Lane; 800-531-5900) is less expensive. Also less expensive are the **Red Roof Inn** (2654 W. March Lane; 209-478-4300) and the **Super 8 Motel** (209-477-5576). All of the above lodging is within 5 to 10 minutes away from campus. Exit March Lane for all of them.

A Little Farther: Stockton is about 80 miles east of San Francisco. If you wish to stay there, check suggestions in the entry for University of San Francisco, Stanford, or Santa Clara University, to the southwest.

WHITTIER COLLEGE

Office of Admissions, 13406 E. Philadelphia St.,
Whittier, CA 90608 • Telephone: 562-907-4238 • www.whittier.edu •
Email: admission@whittier.edu

Hours: Monday–Friday, 8:00AM–5:00PM

Only one school can claim Richard Nixon as an alumnus, and that school is Whittier College, a solid little liberal arts college not far from Los Angeles, with a rich Quaker heritage and endless academic options. Students must choose between two courses of study: the Liberal Education track (focused on the development of creative and analytical skills) or the Whittier Scholars Program (in which students work with advisors to design their own majors).

AT A GLANCE

Selectivity Rating	74
Range SAT I Math	490–600
Average SAT I Math	539
Range SAT I Verbal	490–590
Average SAT I Verbal	547
Average ACT Composite	23
Average GPA	3.05
Student/Faculty Ratio	11:1

CAMPUS TOURS

Appointment	Preferred
Dates	Year-round
Times	Mon–Fri, 10AM & 2PM
Average Length	1 hour

ON-CAMPUS APPOINTMENTS

Admissions

Start Date—Juniors	Anytime
Appointment	Required
Advance Notice	Yes
Saturdays	No
Average Length	30 min.
Info Sessions	Yes

Faculty and Coaches

Dates/Times	Academic year
Arrangements	Contact Admissions Office 2 weeks prior

CLASS VISITS

Dates	Academic year
Arrangements	Contact Admissions Office

TRANSPORTATION

The Los Angeles and Ontario airports are both 25 miles away from campus. Super Shuttle service is available from both airports to campus; call 818-556-6600. No particular advanced arrangements are necessary for transportation from Los Angeles, but for transportation from Ontario, call 24 hours in advance. Amtrak trains and Greyhound/Trailways bus lines serve Los Angeles. Taxis are available for the ride to campus from the terminals.

FIND YOUR WAY

From the 605 freeway, exit onto Beverly Blvd. East. Proceed east to Painter Blvd. and turn right. Take Painter to Philadelphia St. (the entrance to the college), turn right, and park behind Weingart Hall.

STAY THE NIGHT

Nearby: The **Whittier Hilton Hotel** (7320 Greenleaf Ave.; 562-945-8511) is six blocks away. It has a pool, Jacuzzi, tennis courts, and an exercise room. Rates are moderate, but don't forget to mention Whittier College to receive a special rate. About one mile away, also with an inexpensive rate for visitors (including continental breakfast), is the **Whittier Vagabond Hotel** (14125 E. Whittier Blvd.; 562-698-9701). A wide selection of restaurants is available in nearby Uptown Whittier Village. For bed-and-breakfasts, check the Pepperdine University entry for the bed-and-breakfast referral services.

HIGHLIGHTS

ON CAMPUS

- Wardman Library
- Walter F. Dexter Student Center
- Harris Amphitheater
- Ruth B. Shannon Center for the Performing Arts
- George Allen Fitness Center

OFF CAMPUS

- Chinatown, Little Tokyo
- Los Angeles County Museum of Art
- Disneyland
- Universal Studios
- Joshua Tree National Park

1- **Colorado College**
2- **Colorado School of Mines**
3- **University of Colorado—Boulder**
4- **University of Colorado—Denver**

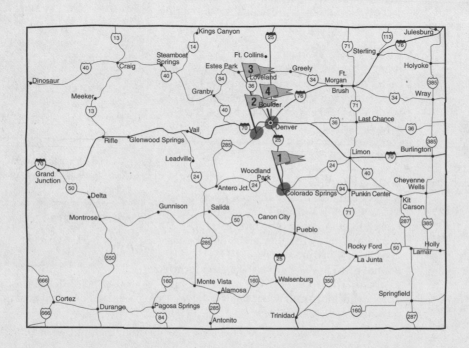

Colorado	Colorado Coll.	Colorado Sch. Mines	U. Colorado-Boulder	U. Colorado-Denver	Denver
Colorado Coll.	—	83	96	70	70
Colorado Sch. Mines	83	—	20	10	10
U.Colorado-Boulder	96	20	—	26	26
U. Colorado-Denver	70	10	26	—	0
Denver	70	10	26	0	—

COLORADO COLLEGE

Admissions office, 14 East Cache La Poudre,Colorado Springs, CO 80903 •
Telephone: 800-542-7214 • www.coloradocollege.edu/admission/ •
Email: admission@coloradocollege.edu

Hours: Monday–Friday, 8:30AM–5:00PM; Saturday (during term), 10:00AM–noon.

This small liberal arts college breaks up its academic year into three-and-a-half-week blocks (the block plan) during which students concentrate on a single course. Courses are intense and the workload can vary widely, but students who stick around love the concept. Outside of class, skiing is big and the nationally-ranked NCAA Division I hockey team enjoys rabid support.

AT A GLANCE

Selectivity Rating	90
Range SAT I Math	590–670
Average SAT I Math	625
Range SAT I Verbal	590–670
Average SAT I Verbal	622
Average ACT Composite	27
Student/Faculty Ratio	9:1

CAMPUS TOURS

Appointment	Preferred
Dates	Year-round
Times	Varies
Average Length	1 hour

ON-CAMPUS APPOINTMENTS

Admissions

Start Date—Juniors	June after junior year
Appointment	Required
Advance Notice	Yes, 2 weeks
Saturdays	Sometimes
Average Length	30 min.
Info Sessions	Yes

Faculty and Coaches

Dates/Times	Academic year
Arrangements	Contact coach directly 2 weeks prior

CLASS VISITS

Dates	Academic year
Arrangements	Contact Admissions Office

TRANSPORTATION

Colorado Springs Airport is 10 miles southeast of campus. Taxis are available for the ride to campus.

FIND YOUR WAY

From I-25, take the Uintah St. exit and turn east. Proceed about one-half mile to Cascade Ave. Turn right and you are on campus. The admissions office is in Cutler Hall on the west side of Cascade Ave., and the second driveway is on your right and about half a block north of Cache La Poudre.

STAY THE NIGHT

Nearby: You have many choices, since the college is just north of the downtown section of Colorado Springs. If you are looking for a vacation with swimming and golf, the very luxurious **Broadmoor** (800-634-7711) is a 15-minute car ride away from the college; **Antlers Adams Mark Hotel** (4 S. Cascade Ave.; 719-955-5600 or 800-528-0444) is in downtown Colorado Springs and about one mile away from campus. For a more complete listing of possible hotels, please see:

www.coloradocollege.edu/Admission/visiting/where.cfm

A Little Farther: For a listing of possible hotels please see:

www.coloradocollege.edu/Admission/visiting/where.cfm

HIGHLIGHTS

ON CAMPUS
• Worner Student Center
• Palmer Hall
• Shove Chapel
• Cutler Hall (admission)
• View of Pikes Peak

OFF CAMPUS
• Garden of the Gods (great hiking)
• Old Colorado City and Manitou Springs
• Pikes Peak
• U.S. Olympic Training Center
• Historic downtown area

COLORADO SCHOOL OF MINES

Admissions Office, CSM Student Center, 1600 Maple Street, 1811 Elm St., Golden, CO 80401-1842 • Telephone: 800-446-9488 • www.mines.edu • Email: admit@mines.edu

Hours: Monday–Friday, 8:00AM–5:00PM

Colorado School of Mines is a small, prestigious, and very difficult engineering school where students often do homework seven days a week. The predominantly introverted students at CSM do math for fun, surf their idle hours away on the Internet, or dream about spending the big bonuses from the high-tech employers who are certain to hire them upon graduation.

HIGHLIGHTS

ON CAMPUS
- Geology Museum
- National Earthquake Center
- Center for Technology and Learning Media
- Barnes & Noble
- Volk Gymnasium

OFF CAMPUS
- Adolph Coors Brewery
- Colorado Railroad Museum
- Buffalo Bill's Grave and Museum
- St. Mary's Glacier
- Ski Resorts: Winter Park, Keystone, Copper Mountain

TRANSPORTATION

Denver International Airport is about 45 miles away from the campus. Buses, taxis, and shuttles are available for the drive from the airport to the campus. For taxi information, call Yellow Cab at 303-777-7777.

FIND YOUR WAY

From the east, take I-70 W. through Denver to Exit 265. Take Colorado Route 58 to Golden. Exit to Highway 93 (Washington Ave.) and head southeast (away from Boulder) to the campus. **From the west,** take I-70 E. past Idaho Springs to U.S. Rte. 6 E. Turn left on 19th St. to the campus.

STAY THE NIGHT

Nearby: Choices include the **Golden Hotel** (800 11th Street; 303-279-0100), the **Table Mountain Inn** (1310 Washington Ave.; 303-277-99-898), and the **Holiday Inn Denver West** (14707 W. Colfax Ave.; 303-279-7611). The Holiday Inn is three miles away from school and offers a special rate for college visitors. It also has an indoor pool, exercise room, ping-pong and pool tables, video games, and a singer during happy hour. The moderately-priced **Denver-Marriott West** (1717 Denver W. Blvd.; 303-279-9100), 10 minutes away from campus, has all the Marriott amenities, including an indoor pool, sauna, whirlpool, game room, exercise room, and a restaurant. An inexpensive rate is available to school visitors at the **Day's Inn West** (15059 W. Colfax Ave.; 303-277-0200), four-and-a-half miles away from campus.

A Little Farther: Please check major hotel listings for the Golden/Lakewood area.

AT A GLANCE

Selectivity Rating	86
Range SAT I Math	610–700
Average SAT I Math	650
Range SAT I Verbal	540–640
Average SAT I Verbal	590
Average ACT Composite	28
Average GPA	3.73
Student/Faculty Ratio	12:1

CAMPUS TOURS

Appointment	Preferred
Dates	Year-round
Times	Mon–Fri, 9AM–3PM
Average Length	1 hour

ON-CAMPUS APPOINTMENTS

Admissions

Start Date—Juniors	Anytime
Appointment	Preferred
Advance Notice	Yes, 1 week
Saturdays	No
Average Length	1 hour
Info Sessions	No

Faculty and Coaches

Dates/Times	Year-round
Arrangements	Contact Athletic Department 1 week prior

CLASS VISITS

Dates	Academic year
Arrangements	Contact Admissions Office

UNIVERSITY OF COLORADO—BOULDER

Admissions Office, 552 UCB,
Boulder, CO 80309-0030 • Telephone: 303-492-6301 • www.colorado.edu •
Email: apply@colorado.edu

Hours: Monday–Friday, 9:00AM–5:00PM

As the beautiful campus of the University of Colorado is situated right beside the Rocky Mountains, people are really into outdoor activities. Academically, CU—Boulder is a big-time research university with nationally renowned programs in music, psychology, and the biological sciences; it also offers a highly-touted entrepreneurship program. Steve Wozniak, the founder of Apple Computers (and one hell of an entrepreneur) is an alum.

AT A GLANCE

Selectivity Rating	83
Range SAT I Math	540–640
Average SAT I Math	590
Range SAT I Verbal	520–620
Average SAT I Verbal	569
Average ACT Composite	25
Average GPA	3.5
Student/Faculty Ratio	16:1

CAMPUS TOURS

Appointment	Required
Dates	Year-round
Times	See www.colorado.edu/visit/
Average Length	120 min.

ON-CAMPUS APPOINTMENTS

Admissions

Start Date–Juniors	N/A
Appointment	Required
Advance Notice	Yes, 2 weeks
Saturdays	No
Average Length	30 min.
Info Sessions	Yes

Faculty and Coaches

Arrangements	Contact Admissions Office

CLASS VISITS

Dates	Varies
Arrangements	Contact Admissions Office

TRANSPORTATION

Denver International Airport is about 40 miles away from the campus. Buses, taxis, and shuttles are available for the drive from the airport to campus. For taxi information, call Yellow Cab at 303-777-7777.

FIND YOUR WAY

From U.S. Rte. 36, take the Baseline Rd. exit and turn left (west) on Baseline. At the second light, turn right (north) on Broadway. At the first light, turn right on Regent Dr. The Regent Administrative Center is on the left side of the street.

STAY THE NIGHT

Nearby: You have several options very close to the University of Colorado. **The Holiday Inn** (800 28th St.; 303-443-3322) is just across the street and has an exercise and game room. The **University Inn Motel** (1632 Broadway; 303-442-3830) is three blocks away from campus. The **Millennium Hotel** (1345 28th Street; 303-443-3850) is within walking distance and has an exercise room, tennis courts, and a pool. Restaurants are nearby, and the downtown mall is only three blocks away. The **Briar Rose** (2151 Arapahoe Ave.; 303-442-3007), half a mile away from the university, includes a deluxe continental breakfast. All 11 rooms have private baths. If you're in the mood for luxury, try the **Pearl Street Inn** (1820 Pearl St.; 303-444-5584), a lovely Victorian inn with a brick-walled inner courtyard. The inn has 7 rooms, all with private baths; the rates are expensive but include a full breakfast. Just a mile away from the school is the **Hotel Boulderado** (2115 13th St.; 303-442-4344), a turn-of-the-century hotel with rooms starting at high-moderate to expensive rates.

HIGHLIGHTS

ON CAMPUS

- Fiske Planetarium
- Heritage Center
- University of Colorado Museum
- The Fine Arts Gallery
- Colorado Shakespeare Festival (summers only)

OFF CAMPUS

- Chataqua (Flatirons hiking trails)
- Pearl Street (art galleries and shopping)
- The Hill (shopping and restuarants)
- Lake Eldora (ski resort)
- Rocky Mountain National Park

University of Colorado—Denver

Office of Admissions, PO Box 173364, Denver, CO 80217 • Telephone: 303-556-3287 • www.cudenver.edu • Email: admissions@carbon.cudenver.edu

Hours: Monday–Friday, 8:00AM–5:00PM

The Denver campus of the University of Colorado educates a largely nontraditional student body of about 8,000 and offers large doses of hands-on, career-oriented education. All students can take advantage of on-campus day care as well as "nooners:" cultural, educational, personal enrichment, or recreational events held each day at noon.

HIGHLIGHTS

ON CAMPUS
- PE/Events Center & Emmanuel Gallery
- The Auraria Library
- Tivoli Student Union
- St. Elizabeth's Church
- Tivoli Movie Theater

OFF CAMPUS
- The Denver Art Museum
- Denver Zoo
- Denver Museum of Nature & Science
- Denver Broncos at Mile High Stadium
- LoDo (Lower Downtown Denver; shopping)

TRANSPORTATION

Denver International Airport is about 35 miles away from Denver. Buses, taxis, and shuttles are available for the drive from the airport to campus. For taxi information, call Yellow Cab at 303-777-7777. Amtrak trains and Greyhound/Trailways buses serve Denver.

FIND YOUR WAY

From I-25/U.S. 87, exit to Speer Blvd. heading toward downtown Denver (southeast). Continue in the same direction when Speer splits for one-way traffic. Turn into the Auraria Campus at Larimer St. and proceed to the Admissions Office.

STAY THE NIGHT

Nearby: You have three great choices within 15 minutes of the university. Built in 1892, the renowned **Brown Palace Hotel** (321 17th St.; 303-297-3111) is listed on the National Register of Historic Places, and is 15 minutes away from the university. Rates are quite expensive. For more familiar accommodations close to school, try the **Comfort Inn** (401 17th St.; 303-296-0400) one mile away, where a double room and continental breakfast can be had for a moderate rate. Also consider the **Ramada Inn Mile-High Stadium** (1975 Bryant St.; 303-433-8331), five minutes from the campus. It's a little bit more expensive than the Comfort Inn, but still has low-to-moderate rates and offers an exercise room, outdoor pool, and rooftop cafe/lounge.

A Little Farther: Golden is only 12 miles to the west. Check the Colorado School of Mines entry for some less urban suggestions.

AT A GLANCE

Selectivity Rating	72
Average SAT I Math	526
Average SAT I Verbal	518
Average ACT Composite	22
Student/Faculty Ratio	14:1

CAMPUS TOURS

Appointment	Required
Dates	Year-round
Times	Mon–Fri, 9AM–5PM
Average Length	1 hour

ON-CAMPUS APPOINTMENTS

Admissions

Start Date–Juniors	N/A
Info Sessions	N/A

Faculty and Coaches

Dates/Times	Year-round
Arrangements	Contact faculty directly

CLASS VISITS

Dates	Year-round
Arrangements	Contact Admissions Office

1- **University of Bridgeport**
2- **Connecticut College**
3- **University of Connecticut**
4- **Fairfield University**
5- **University of Hartford**
   Trinity College
6- **Wesleyan University**
7- **Yale University**

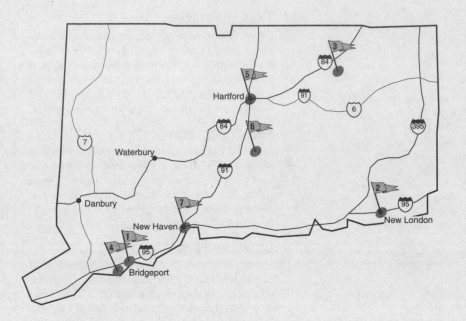

Connecticut	Connecticut Coll.	Fairfield Univ.	Trinity College	Univ. Bridgeport	Univ. Connecticut	Univ. Hartford	Wesleyan Univ.	Yale University	Hartford	New Haven
Connecticut Coll.	0	74	50	71	35	52	42	53	48	52
Fairfield Univ.	74	0	59	5	86	64	47	24	64	25
Trinity College	50	59	0	56	29	4	17	41	0	39
Univ. Bridgeport	71	5	56	0	83	61	43	21	61	20
Univ. Connecticut	35	86	29	83	0	29	38	66	27	64
Univ. Hartford	52	64	4	61	29	0	21	45	0	44
Wesleyan Univ.	42	47	17	43	38	21	0	26	15	25
Yale University	53	24	41	21	66	45	26	0	39	0
Hartford	48	64	0	61	27	0	15	39	0	42
New Haven	52	25	39	20	64	44	25	0	42	0

CONNECTICUT COLLEGE

Office of Admission, 270 Mohegan Avenue, New London, CT 06320 • Telephone: 860-439-2200 • www.conncoll.edu/admissions

Hours: Monday–Friday, 8:30AM–5:00PM; Saturday (fall only), 8:30AM–3:30PM

Fine arts, drama, and dance are tremendous at Connecticut College; the liberal arts are excellent; and several NCAA Division III intercollegiate sports teams (the Camels) are quite competitive. As a result, the student population at this homey little college of about 2,000 students is very diverse, at least in terms of students' interests.

HIGHLIGHTS

ON CAMPUS
- Lyman Allyn Museum
- Connecticut College Arboretum
- Caroline Black Garden (International Peace Garden)
- View of Long Island Sound from the Green
- Harkness Chapel

OFF CAMPUS
- Mystic Seaport
- Mystic Aquarium
- Eugene O'Neill Theatre/Harkness Park
- Local beaches
- Foxwoods Casino Resort

TRANSPORTATION

Bradley International Airport near Hartford, Connecticut, and T. F. Green Airport in Providence, Rhode Island, are about one hour away from campus. The Groton/New London commuter airport is only a 15-minute drive away from campus. Van and limousine services and rental cars are available for the trip from the airports to campus. Amtrak trains and Greyhound buses operate to New London. Taxis are available at the stations for the two-mile ride to campus.

FIND YOUR WAY

From New York and points west, take I-95 North to Exit 83. Turn left at the end of the ramp, and then turn right at the light onto Rte. 32 North. The college entrance is one mile ahead on the left. **From Boston and the east,** take I-95 South to Exit 84 North. From there, take Rte. 32 North; the college entrance is one mile ahead on the left. **From Hartford,** take I-91 South to Rte. 2 South. Exit Rte. 2 at I-395 South; from I-395, take Exit 78 to Rte. 32 South. Proceed on Rte. 32 to the college entrance, which will be on the right.

STAY THE NIGHT

Nearby: Close to the college (about 10 minutes away) is the **Lighthouse Inn** (6 Guthrie Pl.; 860-443-8411), a Victorian country place with 52 rooms and a restaurant. Prices are moderate, and higher during the summer than during the winter. Almost one mile away from campus is the **Queen Anne Inn** (265 Williams St., New London; 860-447-2600). Prices range from inexpensive to expensive; rooms come with private baths, and services include a full breakfast. Guests may use the Waterford Health and Racquet Club. A few minutes away from campus is the **Radisson Hotel** (35 Governor Winthrop Blvd., New London; 860-443-7000) offering moderate prices (and special rates for college visitors), an indoor pool, and lighted tennis courts. Also close by is the **Holiday Inn** (I-95 and Frontage Rd., New London; 860-442-0631); it also offers a special rate for college visitors. The brand new **Spring Hill Suites by Marriott** (North Frontage Road, New London) is only minutes from the college (860-439-0151).

A Little Farther: You can have a seashore vacation while visiting Connecticut College. The **Shore Inne** (54 E. Shore Ave., Groton Long Point; 860-536-1180) is about 15 minutes away from the campus. If you share a bath, it's very cheap. Guests have been coming here since the turn of the century to enjoy the wonderful views, beaches, tennis courts, and nearby fishing dock. The **Old Mystic Inn** (52 Main St., Old Mystic; 860-572-9422) was built in the 1800s when Mystic was a whaling, fishing, and shipbuilding town. The price, including breakfast, is in the moderate-to-expensive range. There is also a **Mystic Hilton** (20 Coogan Blvd.; 860-572-0731) right by Mystic Aquarium and Seaport; the rates are expensive. The **Inn at Mystic** (860-536-9604) is a moderate-to-expensive choice, with lower rates in the winter and early spring and an excellent restaurant.

AT A GLANCE

Selectivity Rating	91
Range SAT I Math	602–682
Average SAT I Math	650
Range SAT I Verbal	612–687
Average SAT I Verbal	660
Average ACT Composite	27
Student/Faculty Ratio	11:1

CAMPUS TOURS

Appointment	Not required
Dates	Year-round
Times	Varies
Average Length	30 min.

ON-CAMPUS APPOINTMENTS

Admissions

Start Date—Juniors	April 1 of junior year
Appointment	Required
Advance Notice	Yes, 3 weeks
Saturdays	Sometimes
Average Length	45 min.
Info Sessions	Yes

Faculty and Coaches

Dates/Times	Year-round
Arrangements	Contact Athletic Department 3 weeks prior

CLASS VISITS

Dates	Academic year
Arrangements	Contact Admissions Office

FAIRFIELD UNIVERSITY

Office of Admissions, 1073 N. Benson Road, Rm. 114,
Fairfield, CT 06824 • Telephone: 203-254-4100 • www.fairfield.edu •
Email: admis@mail.fairfield.edu

Hours: Monday–Friday, 8:30AM–4:30PM; Saturday (during term), 9:00AM–12:30PM

Clear, articulate, and extremely knowledgeable professors are the highlight of this solid Catholic liberal arts school with a strong Jesuit tradition. Campus social life is reportedly excellent, and New Haven and New York City are both close by when students need a change of pace.

AT A GLANCE

Selectivity Rating	79
Range SAT I Math	570–650
Average SAT I Math	610
Range SAT I Verbal	540–630
Average SAT I Verbal	585
Average ACT Composite	28
Average GPA	3.6
Student/Faculty Ratio	13:1

CAMPUS TOURS

Appointment	Preferred
Dates	Year-round
Times	Varies
Average Length	1 hour

ON-CAMPUS APPOINTMENTS

Admissions

Start Date–Juniors	April
Appointment	Required
Advance Notice	Yes, 3 weeks
Saturdays	Sometimes
Average Length	30 min.
Info Sessions	Yes

Faculty and Coaches

Dates/Times	Academic year
Arrangements	Contact coach directly 2 weeks prior

CLASS VISITS

Dates	Academic year
Arrangements	Contact Admissions Office

TRANSPORTATION

La Guardia Airport in New York City is approximately 50 miles (a 75-minute drive) away from campus. Metro-North train service is available to Fairfield from New York City and from New Haven. Taxis are available at the Fairfield train station.

FIND YOUR WAY

From New York on I-95 (Connecticut Tpke.), take Exit 22 and turn left onto Round Hill Rd. Turn right onto Barlow Rd. and then make a left to the university. **From New Haven on I-95,** take Exit 22 and turn right onto North Benson Rd. Turn left on Barlow Rd. and make a right to the university. **From New York Rte. 15 (Merritt Pkwy.),** take Exit 44 heading south, turn left off Exit 44 then right onto Black Rock Tpke. Proceed two miles and turn right on Stillson Rd. At the second light, bear left onto N. Benson Rd. The university entrance is ahead on the right.

STAY THE NIGHT

Nearby: Accommodations in Fairfield are limited, but there are some good places at which to stay. The least expensive is the **Holiday Inn** (1070 Main St.; 203-334-1234), about 15 minutes away in Bridgeport, where a double is available for a moderate rate. A little bit more expensive, in the high-to-moderate range, is the **Westport Motor Inn** (1595 Boston Post Rd. E.; 203-259-5236), about 20 minutes away in Westport. It has a restaurant, fitness room, and heated pool. The **Marriott Hotel** (180 Hawley Ln., Trumbull; 203-378-1400) is 15 minutes away and slightly more expensive. It has a pool, exercise room, and a lounge with music. The **Seagrape Inn** (1160 Reef Road; 203-255-6808) is located in the beach section of Fairfield. For additional suggestions, see the University of Bridgeport entry.

HIGHLIGHTS

ON CAMPUS

- Quick Center for the Arts (includes The Walsh Art Gallery, the Kelley Theatre & the Wien Theatre
- Egan/Loyola Chapel
- Nyselius Library
- Leslie C. Quick, JR Recreation Complex
- Barone Campus Center

OFF CAMPUS

- New York City
- Fairfield Historical Society
- Long Island Sound
- Connecticut Audubon Center
- Harbor Arena and Harboryard

TRINITY COLLEGE (CT)

Admissions Office, 300 Summit Street, Hartford, CT 06016 •
Telephone: 860-297-2180 • www.trincoll.edu/pub/admissio/ •
Email: admissions.office@trincoll.edu

Hours: Monday–Friday, 8:00AM–4:30PM; Saturdays (during fall), 9:00AM–noon

Trinity College is an excellent liberal arts college in Hartford, Connecticut. Beyond academics, students enjoy an active social scene and a campus that is beautiful every season. The library is custodian to Hartford's Mark Twain Memorial, which has an extensive collection of his work including much of his correspondence.

HIGHLIGHTS

ON CAMPUS
- The Learning Corridor
- Library
- The Science/Engineering Labs
- Summit Suites (newest residence hall)
- The Chapel

OFF CAMPUS
- Wadsworth Athenaeum
- Bushnell Theater
- Old State House
- Mark Twain and Harriet Beecher State Houses
- Hartford Civic Center

TRANSPORTATION

Bradley International Airport, north of Hartford, is 15 to 20 minutes away from campus (except during rush hour). Limousine service is available from the airport to downtown hotels. You can take a taxi from the hotels to campus. Amtrak trains and Greyhound buses serve Hartford. Take a taxi to campus from the terminals.

FIND YOUR WAY

From the west, take I-84 E. to exit 48 (Capitol Ave.) At the traffic light at the end of the exit ramp turn left. Go to the first traffic light (Washington St.) and turn right. Proceed through eight traffic lights (1.1 miles). Turn right at the eighth light onto New Britain Ave. Proceed on New Britain Ave. to the traffic light at Summit St. and turn right into the campus. **From the east,** take I-84 W. through Hartford to Exit 48 (Asylum Ave.). Turn left onto Asylum St. and follow the roadway to the right. Bear right through the brownstone arch onto Trinity St. Get in the left lane and proceed to the second traffic light (Washington St.). The Bushnell Memorial Hall will be on the left and the state capitol on the right. Make a left onto Washington St., then follow the above directions to campus. **From the south,** take I-91 N. to I-84 W. Follow the directions listed for those coming from the east. **From the north,** take I-91 S. to I-84 W. Follow the directions listed for those coming from the east.

STAY THE NIGHT

Nearby: The **Hastings Hotel and Conference Center** (85 Sigourney Street; 860-727-4200) offers a college visitor rate (Trinity rate) and is less than five minutes away from the campus and downtown. The **Hilton Hartford** (860-728-5151) offers reasonable rates and is located next to the Civic Center approximately 10 minutes away. The **Crowne Plaza's** (50 Morgan St.; 860-549-2400) rate for a double is pretty expensive, but the hotel is nice and there are no unpleasant surprises. In Glastonbury, 15 minutes away from Hartford, is **Butternut Farm** (1654 Main St.; 860-633-7197), a moderately-priced bed-and-breakfast (full breakfast included), 15 minutes away from Wesleyan and the University of Hartford. Also consider the **Chester Bulkeley House** (184 Main St.; 860-563-4236), a bed-and-breakfast in historic Wethersfield, 10 minutes away from Trinity and The University of Hartford, and 20 minutes from Wesleyan.

A Little Farther: To the east of Hartford, about 25 minutes from Trinity (an easy drive on I-84) are some places with character, including the **Old Babcock Tavern** (484 Mile Hill Rd., Tolland; 860-875-1239), a nice little bed-and-breakfast, and the **Tolland Inn** (63 Tolland Green; 860-872-0800), another quiet place. Moderate prices are the rule. If you are going to visit Sturbridge, keep in mind that it's only another 25 minutes up the road from Tolland.

AT A GLANCE

Selectivity Rating	93
Range SAT I Math	600–690
Average SAT I Math	642
Range SAT I Verbal	590–690
Average SAT I Verbal	630
Average ACT Composite	27
Student/Faculty Ratio	9:1

CAMPUS TOURS

Dates	Year-round
Times	Varies throughout year
Average Length	1 hour

ON-CAMPUS APPOINTMENTS

Admissions

Start Date–Juniors	June 1 at the end of junior year
Appointment	Required
Advance Notice	Other
Saturdays	Yes
Info Sessions	Year-round except as noted above

Faculty and Coaches

Dates/Times	Year-round
Arrangements	Contact Admissions Office 1 week prior

CLASS VISITS

Dates	Academic year
Arrangements	Contact Admissions Office

UNIVERSITY OF BRIDGEPORT

Admissions Office, 126 Park Avenue,
Bridgeport, CT 06601 • Telephone: 800-972-9488 • www.bridgeport.edu •
Email: admit@.bridgeport.edu

Hours: Monday–Friday, 8:30AM–4:30PM

Located in Fairfield, Connecticut, just a short ride from New York City, the small University of Bridgeport combines a liberal arts education with scientific, legal, business, and professional programs. Bridgeport often sponsors trips into area cities and offers the use of a steam bath and sauna at the Wheeler Recreation Center.

AT A GLANCE

Selectivity Rating	65
Range SAT I Math	370–490
Average SAT I Math	438
Range SAT I Verbal	360–500
Average SAT I Verbal	427
Average ACT Composite	16
Average GPA	2.77
Student/Faculty Ratio	11:1

CAMPUS TOURS

Appointment	Preferred
Dates	Year-round
Times	Wed at 10:30AM & 2:30PM; Sat 10:30AM
Average Length	Varies

ON-CAMPUS APPOINTMENTS

Admissions

Start Date–Juniors	Year-round
Appointment	Required
Advance Notice	Yes, 1 week
Saturdays	Sometimes
Average Length	30 min.
Info Sessions	Yes

Faculty and Coaches

Dates/Times	Year-round
Arrangements	Contact Admissions Office 1 week prior

CLASS VISITS

Dates	Year-round
Arrangements	Contact Admissions Office

TRANSPORTATION

Sikorsky Airport in Bridgeport is 15 minutes from campus. Bradley International Airport near Hartford is 75 minutes away from campus. La Guardia Airport and JFK in New York are an hour-and-a-half away from campus. Taxis and limousines are available from these airports to campus. Amtrak and Metro-North trains and Greyhound buses serve Bridgeport. Taxis are available for the ride from the stations to campus. The ferry is available from Port Jefferson, New York.

FIND YOUR WAY

From the north, take I-95 South, take exit 27 and where the exit forks, take the left hand fork marked "University of Bridgeport." You are now on South Avenue, parallel to I-95. Continue on South Avenue to the fourth light. Turn left onto Park Avenue. Proceed South on Park Avenue, approximately half a mile to the campus. **From south,** take I-95 North, and get off at exit 26; at the bottom of the ramp continue straight on Pine Street. Make a right onto Harbor Street and make the next left onto Admiral Street. Make a right onto Iranistan Avenue. Proceed South on Iranistan Avenue to Waldemere Avenue. Make a left onto Waldemere Avenue, travel to Park Avenue (look for the arch). Make a left onto Park Avenue. **From the Merritt Parkway,** take exit 52 (south fork) and bear left to route 8/25 Connector to exit 1 (Prospect Street/Myrtle Avenue). At the bottom of the ramp take a right onto Prospect Street to Park Avenue. Make a left on Park Avenue. Proceed south on Park Avenue, approximately half a mile to the campus.

STAY THE NIGHT

Nearby: Five minutes from the university, the **Bridgeport Holiday Inn** (1070 Main St.; 203-334-1234) has special rates and is relatively affordable. A bit further, the **Hampton Inn in Milford** (129 Plains Rd.; 203-874-4400) is located four miles away from the Sikorsky Airport. The **Stratford Ramada** (225 Lordship Blvd.; 800-2 Ramada) is about 20 minutes away from campus. The **Trumbull Marriott** (180 Hawley Ln.; 800-221-9855), with its indoor pool, up-to-date health club, two restaurants, and two lounges is the most expensive.

HIGHLIGHTS

ON CAMPUS

- Arnold Bernhard Center
- Wheeler Recreation Center
- John J. Cox Student Center
- The University Gallery
- Hubbell Gymnasium

OFF CAMPUS

- Seaside Park
- The Maritime Aquarium
- South Norwalk (SoNo)
- Main St.—Westport
- Wooster Street

University of Connecticut

Lodewick Visitors Center, 115 North Eagleville Road Unit 3225, U88, Storrs, CT 06268-3088 • Telephone: 860-486-3137 • visitors.uconn.edu • Email: beahusky@uconn.edu

Hours: Monday–Friday, 8:00AM–5:00PM

The University of Connecticut is a public school with a well-deserved reputation for quality education in the arts and sciences. The UConn 2000 plan aims to reconstruct school facilities (including the dorms) over the next few years. Until the plan is complete, the UConn campus will definitely look like a work in progress.

HIGHLIGHTS

ON CAMPUS
- State Museum of Art
- Dairy Product Salesroom
- Puppetry Museum
- Green Houses
- Jorgensen Auditorium and Connecticut Repertory Theater

OFF CAMPUS
- Caprilands Herb Farm
- Connecticut State Museum of Natural History
- William Benton Museum of Art

TRANSPORTATION

Bradley International Airport in Windsor Locks, Connecticut (north of Hartford) is approximately 40 miles away from campus. Public transportation from the airport to campus is inconvenient and expensive; you must take a bus or taxi to Hartford, then another bus or taxi to Storrs via Willimantic. A rental car is a better alternative. Private limousine services include the Horizon Airport Shuttle (860-429-8002) and the Airport Shuttle (860-450- 2170). Call for rates and reservations.

FIND YOUR WAY

From the north and south, take I-91 to I-84 in Hartford. Take I-84 northeast to Exit 68, then take Connecticut Rte. 195 S. to Storrs and the campus. Turn right on North Eagleville Rd. and turn left onto North Hillside Rd. Park in the north parking garage (fee charged). Tours begin in the Visitors' Center on the corner of N. Eagleville and N. Hillside Roads. The Admissions Office is located one block past the parking garage on Hillside Road. **From Boston,** take I-84 southwest to Exit 70; then take Connecticut Rte. 32 S. to Connecticut Rte. 195; take Rte. 195 S. to Storrs. **From Providence,** take U.S. 44 W. to Rte. 195, then 195 S. to Storrs.

STAY THE NIGHT

Nearby: Close to the campus (a mile-and-a-half away) is **Altnaveigh Inn** (957 Storrs Rd.; 860-429-4490), a pleasant bed-and-breakfast that has six rooms. **Tolland Inn** is about seven miles away from Storrs (see the Trinity College entry). If you prefer a standard motel, try the **Best Western** (Rtes. 195 and 6; 860-423-8451), 15 minutes away from campus. Here you will find the usual amenities and an adjacent shopping mall. Consider also the **Quality Inn and Conference Center** (51 Hartford Tpke., Vernon; 860-646-5700 or 1-800-228-5151), right off I-84 at Exits 63 and 64.

A Little Farther: See the listings in the University of Hartford and Trinity College entries for other possibilities.

AT A GLANCE

Selectivity Rating	78
Range SAT I Math	530–630
Average SAT I Math	584
Range SAT I Verbal	520–610
Average SAT I Verbal	565
Student/Faculty Ratio	17:1

CAMPUS TOURS

Appointment	Required
Dates	Year-round
Times	Varies
Average Length	120 min.

ON-CAMPUS APPOINTMENTS

Admissions

Start Date—Juniors	January of junior year
Appointment	Required
Advance Notice	Yes, 1 week
Saturdays	No
Average Length	1 hour
Info Sessions	Yes

Faculty and Coaches

Arrangements	Contact Athletic Department

CLASS VISITS

Dates	Academic year
Arrangements	Contact Admissions Office

UNIVERSITY OF HARTFORD

Admissions Office, 200 Bloomfield Ave,
West Hartford, CT 06117 • Telephone: 800-947-4303 • www.hartford.edu •
Email: admissions@mail.hartford.edu

Hours: Monday–Friday, 8:30AM–4:30PM

The University of Hartford is located just two miles away from downtown Hartford and offers a liberal arts education in music, engineering, and nursing, to name just a few. The school's 4,000 largely traditional students can join the ham radio club or play water polo in an inner tube. Singer Dionne Warwick is a University of Hartford alum.

AT A GLANCE

Selectivity Rating	72
Range SAT I Math	480–580
Average SAT I Math	531
Range SAT I Verbal	480–570
Average SAT I Verbal	528
Average ACT Composite	23
Student/Faculty Ratio	12:1

CAMPUS TOURS

Appointment	Preferred
Dates	Year-round
Times	Seasonal; Contact Admissions Office
Average Length	1 hour

ON-CAMPUS APPOINTMENTS

Admissions

Start Date–Juniors	At their convenience
Appointment	Preferred
Advance Notice	Yes, 1 week
Saturdays	Sometimes
Average Length	30 min.
Info Sessions	Yes

Faculty and Coaches

Dates/Times	Year-round
Arrangements	Contact Admissions Office 1 week prior

CLASS VISITS

Dates	Academic year
Arrangements	Contact Admissions Office

TRANSPORTATION

Bradley International Airport, which is north of Hartford, Connecticut, is 20 miles away from campus. Taxis and airport shuttles are available for the trip to campus. Amtrak trains and Greyhound buses serve Hartford. Taxis are available at the stations for the trip to campus.

FIND YOUR WAY

From I-84 W., take Exit 44 and turn right onto Kane St. At the first light, turn left onto Prospect St. Proceed two-and-a-half miles to the end of the street, then turn right onto Albany Ave. Turn left at the first light onto Bloomfield Ave. and proceed half a mile to the university, which is on the right. **From I-84 E.,** take Exit 44. Proceed on Caya Ave. for a very short distance to the light at Prospect Ave. Turn left onto Prospect and follow the preceding directions from that point.

STAY THE NIGHT

Nearby: The most convenient place to stay is probably the **West Hartford Inn** (900 Farmington Ave.; 860-236-3221), about eight minutes away from the campus. This is a typical bare-bones motel, but comfortable enough. The price is moderate.

A Little Farther: The **Goodwin Hotel** (1 Haynes St., Hartford; 860-246-7500 or 800-922-5006) is about 15 minutes away from the campus. Doubles are moderate on weekends, but the rates are expensive during the week. This hotel definitely has character, but unless you have a reason to stay in Hartford, you might find it more enjoyable to head north to Simsbury. The **Simsbury 1820 House** (731 Hop Meadow St.; 860-658-7658 or 800-TRY-1820) is a lovely country inn with 34 rooms, a restaurant, and loads of charm. The rates are at the high end of the moderate range. The inn will help guests arrange golf, skiing, hiking, canoeing, and tubing outings. This is a good choice if you're arriving by plane, since it's only 15 minutes away from Bradley Airport. Also try the **Avon Old Farms Hotel** (Rtes. 10 and 44; 800-677-1651 or 800-836-4000), 25 minutes away from campus. For a moderate-to-expensive rate, you can stay in an attractive country hotel that has an exercise room, sauna, and pool.

HIGHLIGHTS

ON CAMPUS

- Museum of American Political Life
- Art Gallery
- Sports Center
- Java City Coffee House
- Hawk's Nest

OFF CAMPUS

- Hartford Civic Center (concerts)
- Meadows Music Theater (outdoor concert venue)
- Bushnell Theater (Broadway Tours)
- Mark Twain House
- Minor League sports (baseball, hockey)

WESLEYAN UNIVERSITY

The Stewart Reid House, Middletown, CT 06459-0265 •
Telephone: 860-685-3000 • www.wesleyan.edu/admiss/ •
Email: www-admiss@wesleyan.edu

Hours: Monday–Friday, 8:30AM–5:00PM; Saturday (in the fall), 10:00AM–noon.

Students praise the amazing opportunities for personal and intellectual satisfaction and solid academic reputation of Wesleyan University, a school of about 3,000 students that has the resources and facilities of a school twice its size. Outstanding fine arts complement the uniformly strong curricula in the humanities and sciences. Socially, "Diversity University" is a haven for political correctness.

HIGHLIGHTS

ON CAMPUS
- Center for the Arts
- Davison Arts Center
- Zilka Gallery
- Olin Memorial Library
- Van Vuek Observatory

OFF CAMPUS
- Gillette Castle and State Park
- Goodspeed Opera House
- Dinosaur State Park
- Lyman Orchards
- Wadsworth Falls State Park

TRANSPORTATION

Bradley International Airport near Hartford is 20 miles away from campus. Taxi service is available from the airport to campus; the Admissions Office will give you the number to call for this service. Peter Pan and Greyhound bus service are available to Middletown from Boston, Hartford, New Haven, New York, Springfield, and other cities. Amtrak service from New York and Boston stops in Meriden, 10 miles west of Middletown.

FIND YOUR WAY

From the south, take I-91 to Exit 18; from there, follow Rte. 66 into Middletown, turning right onto High St. and right onto Wyllys Ave. **From the north,** take I-91 to Exit 22S; from there, take Rte. 9 to the Wesleyan exit (Washington St.). Follow Washington St. to the fourth light and turn left onto High St. and right onto Wyllys Ave.

STAY THE NIGHT

Nearby: **Radisson Hotel** (100 Berlin Rd., Cromwell; 203-635-2000), five minutes away from the campus, has a special rate for college visitors, a health club, and glass-domed indoor pool. The **Holiday Inn** (4 Sebethe Dr., Cromwell; 203-635-1001) is a little bit farther from campus, but it's much less expensive if you get the college visitor rates. The **Ramada Inn** (275 Research Pkwy., Meriden; 203-238-2380) also offers a special rate for college visitors. The **Hampton Inn** (10 Bee St., Meriden; 203-235-5154), 15 minutes away from campus, is another good low-priced alternative.

A Little Farther: Wesleyan is only about 15 miles away from Hartford, so check the entries for Trinity, University of Hartford, and Yale University.

AT A GLANCE

Selectivity Rating	97
Range SAT I Math	650–730
Average SAT I Math	690
Range SAT I Verbal	640–740
Average SAT I Verbal	700
Average ACT Composite	29
Student/Faculty Ratio	9:1

CAMPUS TOURS

Dates	Year-round
Times	Call for times
Average Length	1 hour

ON-CAMPUS APPOINTMENTS

Admissions

Start Date—Juniors	May at the end of junior year
Appointment	Required
Advance Notice	3 weeks
Saturdays	Sometimes
Info Sessions	Year-round

Faculty and Coaches

Dates/Times	Year-round
Arrangements	Contact Admissions Office 4 weeks prior

CLASS VISITS

Dates	Year-round
Arrangements	Contact faculty directly

YALE UNIVERSITY

Office of Undergraduate Admissions, PO Box 208234,
New Haven, CT 06520-8234 • Telephone: 203-432-9316 • www.yale.edu/admit/ •
Email: undergraduate.admissions@yale.edu

Hours: Monday–Friday, 9:00AM–4:45PM; Saturday–Sunday, 10:00AM–4:00PM

What can you say about uniformly excellent Yale University, truly one of America's great universities? Students say there is a genuine focus on undergraduates, the professors seem to genuinely enjoy teaching, and you really do learn a lot in class. Yale has no core curriculum, and instead requires students to complete a broad range of general prerequisites. Actress Jodie Foster and conservative icon William F. Buckley are alums.

AT A GLANCE

Selectivity Rating	99
Range SAT I Math	680–770
Range SAT I Verbal	680–770
Student/Faculty Ratio	7:1

CAMPUS TOURS

Appointment	Not required
Dates	Year-round
Times	Mon–Fri, 10:30AM & 2PM; Sat–Sun, 1:30PM
Average Length	1 hour

ON-CAMPUS APPOINTMENTS

Admissions

Start Date—Juniors	Juniors: no date; Seniors: July–Dec.
Appointment	Required
Advance Notice	No, 3 weeks
Saturdays	No
Average Length	30 min.
Info Sessions	Yes

Faculty and Coaches

Arrangements	Contact Athletic Department

CLASS VISITS

Dates	Academic year
Arrangements	Contact Admissions Office

TRANSPORTATION

Bradley International Airport, near Hartford, is 50 miles away from campus. Tweed Airport in New Haven has commuter service from most major East Coast cities. Amtrak trains serve New Haven from Boston or Washington, DC via Penn Station in New York. There is hourly Metro-North train service between New Haven and Grand Central Station in New York; call 212-532-4900 for schedule details. Greyhound, Arrow (800-231-2222), and Peter Pan (800-343-9999) provide intercity bus service to New Haven.

FIND YOUR WAY

From I-95, take Exit 47 to reach campus. **From I-91,** take Exit 3. Go past three traffic lights and make the first right onto Hillhouse Avenue, where Yale is located.

STAY THE NIGHT

Nearby: Yale has several hotels and motels within walking distance. **The Colony Inn** (1157 Chapel St.; 203-776-1234) offers special moderate rates for Yale visitors. There are also the **Holiday Inn** (30 Whalley Ave.; 203-777-6221), the **New Haven Hotel** (229 George St.; 800-NH-HOTEL), **Three Chimneys Inn** (1201 Chapel St.; 800-443-1554), and the **OMNI New Haven Hotel** (155 Temple St.; 800-THE-OMNI).

A Little Farther: Inexpensive accommodations can be found at the **Quality Inn** (100 Pond Lily Ave.; 203-387-6651), 15 minutes away from campus, with special rates for Yale visitors. A **Howard Johnson's** (400 Sargent Dr.; 203-562-1111) is 10 minutes away from campus. Also check the **Nutmeg B&B Agency Host** (800-727-7592), which has a wide listing of bed-and-breakfasts in the area.

HIGHLIGHTS

ON CAMPUS

- Old Campus
- Sterling Memorial Library
- Yale British Art Center
- Beinecke Rare Book and Manuscript Library
- Payne-Whitney Gymnasium

OFF CAMPUS

- Long Wharf Theater
- Wooster Square
- Shubert Theater
- Amistad Memorial
- East Rock Park

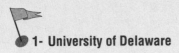

1- University of Delaware

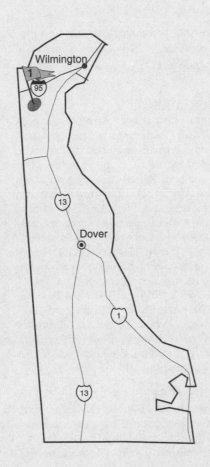

Delaware	Univ. Delaware	Wilmington
Univ. Delaware	—	12
Wilmington	12	—

UNIVERSITY OF DELAWARE

Admissions Office, 116 Hullihen Hall,
Newark, DE 19716-6210 • Telephone: 302-831-8123 • www.udel.edu •
Email: admissions@udel.edu

Hours: Monday–Friday, 8:00AM–5:00PM; Saturday, 9:00AM–2:00PM

State residents and students from all over the Northeast converge on the University of Delaware, a very student-oriented college with easily accessible professors. Lively Main Street runs literally through what students consider absolutely the most gorgeous campus anywhere.

AT A GLANCE

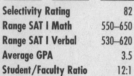

Selectivity Rating	82
Range SAT I Math	550–650
Range SAT I Verbal	530–620
Average GPA	3.5
Student/Faculty Ratio	12:1

CAMPUS TOURS

Appointment	Preferred
Dates	Year-round
Times	Mon–Fri: 10AM, 12PM, 2PM; Sat: 10AM & 12PM
Average Length	Varies

ON-CAMPUS APPOINTMENTS

Admissions

Appointment	Required
Advance Notice	2 weeks
Saturdays	No
Info Sessions	Yes

Faculty and Coaches

Dates/Times	Year-round
Arrangements	Contact departments directly 2 weeks prior

CLASS VISITS

Dates	Academic year
Arrangements	Contact departments directly

TRANSPORTATION

Philadelphia International Airport is a one-hour drive away from campus. Transportation to and from campus is provided by Delaware Express (800-648-5466), Super Shuttle (302-655-8878), or taxi. Rental cars are also available at the airport. Amtrak trains that run between Florida and New England stop in Wilmington, a 20-minute ride away from campus and Newark. Delaware Administration for Regional Transportation (DART) buses transport passengers between Wilmington and Newark; for schedules, contact DART (302-652-DART). SEPIA rail service is available to Newark from Wilmington and Philadelphia. Greyhound buses travel directly to the university from Baltimore, New York City, Philadelphia, and Washington, DC; for schedule information, call 302-655-6111.

FIND YOUR WAY

From the north, take I-95 S. to Delaware Exit 1B, Rte. 896 N. This takes you onto South College Avenue; continue past the stadium and fieldhouse until you reach the main campus. Turn into the Visitor Parking lot #41. **From the south,** take I-95 N. to Delaware Exit 1, then follow directions from the north.

STAY THE NIGHT

Nearby: A **Mariott Courtyard Hotel** will be completed on campus in fall 2003. Details are available online at www.udel.edu/hotel. Off I-95 in Newark, you will find the usual chain motels. A listing is available online at:

www.udel.edu/visit/accommodations.html.

HIGHLIGHTS

ON CAMPUS

• Trabant University Center
• Perkins Student Center
• Memorial Hall
• Morris Library
• Delaware Stadium/Bob Carpenter Center

OFF CAMPUS

• Hagley Museum
• Longwood Gardens

1- **American University**
2- **Catholic University**
3- **Georgetown University**
4- **George Washington University**
5- **Howard University**

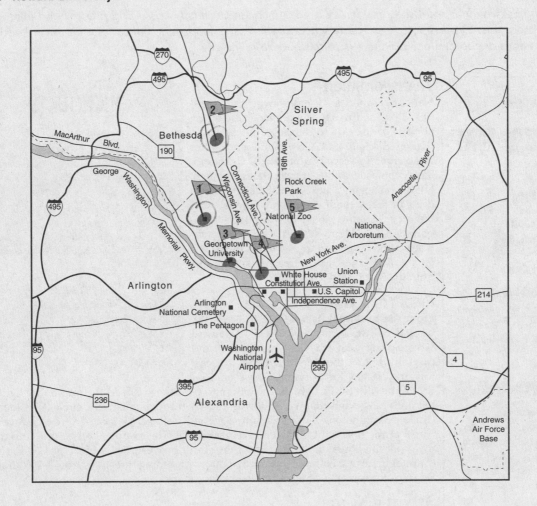

District of Columbia	American Univ.	Catholic Univ.	Geo. Washington U.	Georgetown Univ.	Howard Univ.
American Univ.	—	7	3	2	5
Catholic Univ.	7	—	3	5	2
Geo. Washington U.	3	3	—	1	3
Georgetown Univ.	2	5	1	—	3
Howard Univ.	5	2	3	3	—

AMERICAN UNIVERSITY

Admissions, 4400 Massachusetts Ave. N.W., Washington, DC 20016-8001 •
Telephone: 202-885-6000 • http://admissions.american.edu •
Email: afa@american.edu

Hours: Monday–Friday, 9:00AM–5:00PM; Saturday (September–May), 9:00AM–2:00PM

Just inside the Beltway in a nice, safe, residential area, American University has strong pre-law and international relations programs. Once reputed as a party school, it still has its fun lovers, but campus life is centered completely off campus due to the fact that there is so much to do in the city.

AT A GLANCE

Selectivity Rating	82
Range SAT I Math	550–650
Average SAT I Math	600
Range SAT I Verbal	560–670
Average SAT I Verbal	613
Average ACT Composite	27
Average GPA	3.33
Student/Faculty Ratio	15:1

CAMPUS TOURS

Appointment	Preferred
Dates	Year-round
Times	Mon–Fri, 10AM, 12PM, 1PM, 3PM
Average Length	1 hour

ON-CAMPUS APPOINTMENTS

Admissions

Start Date–Juniors	May
Appointment	Required
Advance Notice	Yes, 2 weeks
Saturdays	Sometimes
Average Length	45 min.
Info Sessions	Yes

Faculty and Coaches

Dates/Times	Year-round
Arrangements	Contact Admissions Office 2 weeks prior

CLASS VISITS

Dates	Academic year
Arrangements	Contact Admissions Office

TRANSPORTATION

National Airport is 10 miles away from campus. Taxis and rental cars are available at the airport for the ride to campus. Amtrak trains (Union Station) and Greyhound and other bus companies serve Washington, D.C. The city has a fantastic public transportation system, but the university advises that it may be best to drive or take a cab if you are not familiar with the area. If you do plan to use public transportation (the Metro system), the Metro subway station nearest campus is Tenleytown/AU on the Red Line. Take a free AU shuttle bus from the Metro stop to campus.

FIND YOUR WAY

From the northeast, take I-95 S. to I-495 (the Capital Beltway); then take I-495 W. toward Silver Spring. Leave the Beltway at Exit 39 and carefully follow the signs for River Rd. east toward Washington. Continue east on River Rd. to the fifth traffic light. Turn right onto Goldsboro Rd. At the first traffic light, turn left onto Massachusetts Ave. Follow it directly through one traffic circle (Westmoreland Circle); continue one more mile into a second traffic circle (Ward Circle). Leave Ward Circle at the first right turn, onto Nebraska Ave. The campus will be on the right; the main parking lot is on the left. **From the south or west,** take I-95 N. or I-66 E. to I-495 (Capital Beltway). Follow I-495 north. Follow preceding directions from I-495 and River Rd. A campus map is at www.american.edu/maps.

STAY THE NIGHT

Nearby: The reasonably priced **Adams Inn** (1744 Lanier Pl. N.W.; 202-745-3600) is a bed-and-breakfast located in Adams Morgan, near the zoo, 10 to 15 minutes away from the university. Shops and restaurants are within walking distance. The **Holiday Inn** (5520 Wisconsin Ave., Chevy Chase, MD; 301-656-1500) has moderate prices that drop on the weekends. Health club privileges are available, and there's good shopping nearby. The **Embassy Suites DC-Downtown** is located in the Chevy Chase Pavilion, an upscale shopping area (at the intersection of Wisconsin Avenue and Military Road, NW; 202-362-9300).

A Little Farther: Two glitzier choices that are about 20 to 25 minutes away are the **Hyatt Regency Bethesda** (7400 Wisconsin Ave., Bethesda, MD; 301-657-1234 or 800-228-9000), with a heated pool, exercise room, and spa; and the **Bethesda Marriott** (5151 Pooks Hill Rd., Bethesda, MD; 301-897-9400), which has an indoor pool, a health spa, lighted tennis courts, and golf privileges. The **Canterbury** (1733 N St. N.W.; 202-393-3000 or 800-424-2950), about a 10 to 20 minute drive (depending on traffic), is elegant, but is very expensive. Health club privileges are available.

HIGHLIGHTS

ON CAMPUS

• Mary Graydon Center (student center)
• Sports Center Complex and Jacobs Fitness Center
• Woods-Brown Outdoor Ampitheatre
• Greenberg Theatre
• Davenport Coffee Lounge
• • Visit the main quad
• See the action from our Quad Cam
http://my.american.edu/content.cfm?load=includes/webc.cfm.

OFF CAMPUS

• Smithsonian Museums and the Mall
• National Zoo
• Kennedy Center for Performing Arts
• MCI Center
• U.S. Capitol

THE CATHOLIC UNIVERSITY OF AMERICA

Office of Undergraduate Admissions, 620 Michigan Ave. N.E., Washington, DC 20064 • Telephone: 800-673-2772 • http://admissions.cua.edu • Email: cua-admissions@cua.edu

Hours: Monday–Friday, 9:00AM–6:00PM; Saturday, 10:00AM–3:00PM

America's only Catholic university with a papal charter is dedicated to all branches of literature and science, both sacred and profane. Though some students complain about the number of compulsory philosophy and religion courses, most agree that CUA's immense and required core curriculum is very beneficial and well structured. CUA's breathtaking basilica, the world's seventh largest church, dominates the Washington, D.C. campus.

HIGHLIGHTS

ON CAMPUS
- Mullen Library
- St. Vincent de Paul Chapel
- Basilica of the National Shrine of the Immaculate Conception

OFF CAMPUS
- National Gallery
- Smithsonian Insitution
- Kennedy Center for the Performing Arts
- Library of Congress
- Washington Zoo

TRANSPORTATION

Washington National Airport is approximately 10 miles (a 30-minute drive) away from campus. Taxis and Metro lines can bring you to campus from the airport; no advanced arrangements are needed. The Metro Red Line Brookland/CUA stop is adjacent to campus. If you fly to Dulles International Airport, you can take the Washington Flyer limousine to many downtown hotels and then reach campus by Metro. Amtrak trains and Greyhound buses serve Washington. Taxis and Metro service can bring you to campus.

FIND YOUR WAY

From I-95 S., exit to the Capital Beltway (I-495 W.). Take the Beltway to the first exit (New Hampshire Ave.); proceed south on New Hampshire to N. Capitol St. Turn left on N. Capitol to Michigan Ave., then turn left on Michigan to the campus. **From I-95 N.,** cross the Beltway to get on I-395 (the Shirley Hwy.). Stay on I-395; cross the bridge over the Potomac River into the District of Columbia, and follow I-395 to New York Ave. Turn right onto New York Ave., then left onto N. Capitol St., and then right onto Michigan Ave. to the campus.

STAY THE NIGHT

Nearby: **Days Inn** (4400 Connecticut Ave.; 202-244-5600) offers easy access to the university by subway, and breakfast is included in the moderate rate. There is an inexpensive supersaver rate that must be booked 30 days in advance by calling 800-325-2525. The **Quality Inn—Capitol Hill** (415 New Jersey Ave. N.W.; 202-638-1616), with a rooftop pool, is a pricier alternative. So is the **Hyatt Regency** (400 New Jersey Ave. N.W.; 202-737-1234). Attention shoppers: The renovated Union Station, with its many stores, is close to both of these places. The **Embassy Inn** (1627 Sixteenth St. N.W.; 202-234-7800) is a small, European, family-style establishment with moderate rates and offers continental breakfast.

AT A GLANCE

Selectivity Rating	85
Range SAT I Math	520–640
Range SAT I Verbal	530–640
Average GPA	3.38
Student/Faculty Ratio	8:1

CAMPUS TOURS

Appointment	Required
Dates	Year-round
Times	Mon, Wed, Fri, 10:30AM & 2PM
Average Length	1 hour

ON-CAMPUS APPOINTMENTS

Admissions

Start Date—Juniors	Anytime
Appointment	Required
Advance Notice	1 week
Saturdays	No
Info Sessions	Year-round

Faculty and Coaches

Dates/Times	Year-round
Arrangements	Contact Admissions Office

CLASS VISITS

Dates	Year-round
Arrangements	Contact Admissions Office

THE GEORGE WASHINGTON UNIVERSITY

Office of Admissions, 2121 I St. N.W., Suite 201,
Washington, DC 20052 • Telephone: 800-447-3765 • www.gwu.edu/admissions.html
Email: gwadm@gwu.edu

Hours: Monday–Friday, 8:30AM-5:00PM

The most unique aspect of George Washington University is that Washington, D.C. becomes your classroom because professors know how to integrate it into their courses. In addition, nearly one-quarter of the students are engaged in international studies and many others pursue government-related majors such as political science, political communication, and criminal justice.

AT A GLANCE

Selectivity Rating	89
Range SAT I Math	590–680
Average SAT I Math	620
Range SAT I Verbal	580–680
Average SAT I Verbal	620
Average ACT Composite	26
Student/Faculty Ratio	13:1

CAMPUS TOURS

Appointment	Required
Dates	Year-round
Times	Varies throughout year; Contact Admissions Office
Average Length	1 hour

ON-CAMPUS APPOINTMENTS

Admissions

Start Date—Juniors	May 1
Appointment	Required
Advance Notice	2 weeks
Saturdays	Yes

Faculty and Coaches

Arrangements	Contact Admissions Office

CLASS VISITS

Dates	Academic year
Arrangements	Contact Visiting Center

TRANSPORTATION

Washington National Airport is five miles away from GW's Visitor Center. Taxis and Metro subways (the Foggy Bottom—GWU Metro station is on campus) can bring you to GWU from the airport. Transportation to Washington is available from the Dulles International and Baltimore International airports. Amtrak trains come into Union Station, only a taxi or Metro ride from campus. Greyhound buses also serve Washington. From the Visitor's Center arrangements can be made to visit both Foggy Bottom and Mount Vernon campuses.

FIND YOUR WAY

From the north, take I-95 S. to I-495 (Capital Beltway) toward Silver Spring/Northern Virginia. Take Exit 33 heading south on Connecticut Ave. for about nine miles. Turn right onto Florida Ave. (just past the Washington Hilton) and turn left immediately onto 21st St. N.W. Turn right on 22nd St. The visitors' entrance to the parking garage is on 22nd Street between M and I Streets. **From the west,** take I-66 or Rte. 50 across the Theodore Roosevelt Bridge and exit at E St., then turn again at Virginia Ave. Bear left, following signs for 23rd St. Turn right on 23rd St. and continue a few blocks to campus. Turn right on H St. and left onto 22nd to the parking garage. **From the south,** take I-395 to the Arlington Memorial Bridge exit. Cross the bridge and bear left at the Lincoln Memorial. Turn left onto 23rd St. N.W., then right on H St. and left onto 22nd St. to the parking garage.

STAY THE NIGHT

Nearby: You have a number of choices within walking distance of GWU's Visitor Center. A popular choice is the **George Washington University Inn** (824 New Hampshire Ave.; 800-426-4466) otherwise known as "The Official GW Hotel!" Other good choices are located on GWU's website at www.gwu.edu.

HIGHLIGHTS

ON CAMPUS
- The Smith Center
- The Hippo
- Media and Public Affairs Building
- Kogan Plaza
- Gelman Library

OFF CAMPUS
- Vietnam Memorial
- Washington Monument
- Freer Gallery of Art
- Kennedy Center
- National Air and Space Museum

GEORGETOWN UNIVERSITY

Admissions Office, 37th and O Sts. N.W.,
Washington, DC 20057 • Telephone: 202-687-3600 • www.georgetown.edu •
Email: @georgetown.edu

Hours: Monday–Friday, 9:00AM–5:00PM; select Saturdays, 9:00AM–1:00PM

Students at Georgetown University enjoy studying. That's a good thing because they study from three to five hours per day. Washington, D.C. offers tons of off-campus cultural and social activities, and internships abound for the many political-minded students on campus. Speaking of politics, would you believe that both Bill Clinton and Pat Buchanan call Georgetown their alma mater?

HIGHLIGHTS

ON CAMPUS
- Yates Field House
- The Leavey Center
- The Observatory
- The Quadrangle
- Healy Hall

OFF CAMPUS
- U.S. Capitol
- Smithsonian Institute
- National Mall and Monuments
- Library of Congress
- Arlington National Cemetery

TRANSPORTATION

Subways (the Rosslyn station on the Metro Blue Line is a 30-minute walk) all travel to campus from the airport. If you fly to Dulles International Airport, you can take the Washington Flyer limousine to many downtown hotels and then reach campus by taxi. (Taxis all the way from Dulles to campus are very expensive.) Amtrak train service arrives at Union Station in Washington; from there, take a taxi or the Metro Red Line to Du Pont Circle and transfer to the G-2 bus to campus (37th and O Sts. N.W.). Greyhound buses also serve Washington.

FIND YOUR WAY

From the north, take I-95 S. and exit to I-495 W. (the Capital Beltway). Follow I-495 W. to the George Washington Memorial Pkwy. Follow the parkway toward Washington and exit onto Key Bridge. Cross the bridge, and turn right on M St.; then turn left on 33rd St., and left again on Prospect St. Prospect ends at the entrance to the university's parking lot.

STAY THE NIGHT

Nearby: A very popular, convenient place is the on-campus **Georgetown University Guesthouse** (3800 Reservoir Rd.; 202-687-3200). Nearby **Georgetown Holiday Inn** (2101 Wisconsin Ave. N.W.; 202-338-4600) has special rates for students and their families (though rooms are not always available). Our choice is the **Georgetown Inn** (1310 Wisconsin Ave. N.W.; 202-333-8900 or 800-424-2979). Within walking distance (six blocks) of campus, this moderately expensive place has a special countrified charm. A glitzy alternative is the **Marriott Key Bridge** (1401 Lee Hwy., Arlington, VA; 703-524-6400). Moderate prices, pool, health club, and views that overlook the Potomac are its finer points. **Kalorama Guesthouse** (1854 Mintwood Pl.; 202-667-6369) is an interesting possibility. Rates range from inexpensive to moderate. The atmosphere is personal, and it's close to the Metro.

A Little Farther: Elegant and expensive **Canterbury** (1733 N St. N.W.; 202-393-3000 or 800-424-2950) is an all-suite hotel with health club privileges available. Charming **Morrison Clark Inn** (11th St. and Massachusetts Ave. N.W.; 202-898-1200 or 800-332-7898) is about 15 minutes away from Georgetown. The rates here range from expensive to very expensive, but continental breakfast is included. The inn is close to the Smithsonian.

AT A GLANCE

Selectivity Rating	98
Range SAT I Math	640–730
Range SAT I Verbal	640–730
Student/Faculty Ratio	11:1

CAMPUS TOURS

Appointment	Not required
Dates	Year-round
Times	Mon–Sat on a varied schedule

ON-CAMPUS APPOINTMENTS

Admissions

Start Date–Juniors	N/A
Info Sessions	Yes

Faculty and Coaches

Dates/Times	Year-round
Arrangements	Contact coach directly

CLASS VISITS

Dates	Academic year
Arrangements	Contact Admissions Office

HOWARD UNIVERSITY

EM/Admission, 2400 6th St NW Suite 111,
Washington, DC 20059 • Telephone: 800-HOWARD-U • www.howard.edu •
Email: admission@howard.edu

Hours: Monday–Friday, 8:30AM–5:00PM

Most of the friendly, seriously ambitious students at traditionally African American Howard University major in pre-professional areas such as international business, legal communications, political science, and pre-med. Howard's hometown of Washington, D.C. provides great opportunities for social activism, internships, and future full-time jobs.

AT A GLANCE

Selectivity Rating		74
Range SAT I Math		430–680
Average SAT I Math		534
Range SAT I Verbal		440–680
Average SAT I Verbal		545
Student/Faculty Ratio		8:1

CAMPUS TOURS

Appointment	Required
Dates	Year-round
Times	Mon–Fri, 10AM–3PM
Average Length	1 hour

ON-CAMPUS APPOINTMENTS

Admissions

Start Date–Juniors	N/A

Faculty and Coaches

Arrangements	Contact Admissions Office 2 weeks prior

CLASS VISITS

Dates	Academic year
Arrangements	Contact Admissions Office

TRANSPORTATION

Washington National Airport is approximately eight miles away from campus. Taxis and subways are available for the trip from the airport to campus. For public transportation information, Amtrak trains, and Greyhound buses, call the Washington Metropolitan Area Transit Authority (202-637-7000) upon arrival.

FIND YOUR WAY

From I-95 S. continue until it becomes the Capital Beltway E. Exit to the Baltimore-Washington Pkwy. South. At the intersection with U.S. Rte. 50, head west (toward the center of Washington). This becomes New York Ave. Turn right (north) on 6th St. until you reach the university. **From I-95 N.**, exit to I-395 N. (Shirley Memorial Hwy.) and cross the Potomac River. Exit to U.S. Rte. 1/50 N., which becomes 6th St. Leave Rte. 1/50 and stay on 6th St. until you reach the university.

STAY THE NIGHT

Nearby: The **Howard Inn** (2225 Georgia Ave.; 800-368-5729) is on campus, but its rates are fairly expensive. A cheaper option is available 10 minutes away at the **Center City Travel Lodge** (1201 13th St. N.W.; 202-682-5300), with a special double rate for college visitors. If you're willing to pay for luxurious surroundings, consider the upscale **Park Terrace Hotel** (1515 Rhode Island Ave. N.W.; 202-232-7000 or 800-424-2461). See other entries for Washington, DC, particularly George Washington and Catholic Universities, which are close Howard. If you want to stay in Georgetown, see the selections in the Georgetown University entry.

HIGHLIGHTS

ON CAMPUS
• Founders Library
• Rankin Chapel

OFF CAMPUS
• Smithsonian Institute
• National Mall and Monuments
• Library of Congress
• Arlington National Cemetery

1- Eckerd College
2- University of Florida
3- Florida Institute of Technical
4- Florida International University
5- Florida Southern College
6- Florida State University
   Florida A&M U. (Tallahassee)
7- University of Miami
8- New College
9- Rollins College
10- University of the South
11- Stetson University

Florida

	Eckerd Coll.	Florida A&M	Florida Inst. Tech.	Florida Int'l	Florida Southern	Florida State Univ	New College	Rollins Coll.	Stetson Univ.	Univ. Florida	Univ. Miami	Univ. So. Florida	Miami	Orlando	St. Petersburg
Eckerd Coll.	—	304	168	258	65	260	40	92	124	166	278	32	253	104	0
Florida A&M	304	—	343	527	277	—	329	266	275	154	522	273	517	261	300
Florida Inst. Tech.	168	343	—	165	106	326	199	72	119	178	185	143	178	60	165
Florida International	258	527	165	—	215	479	216	237	285	343	20	265	0	229	253
Florida Southern	65	277	106	215	—	261	88	76	109	132	230	36	222	54	70
Florida State Univ.	260	—	326	479	261	—	289	300	263	158	494	275	469	254	252
New College	40	329	199	216	88	289	—	152	187	194	256	63	216	132	39
Rollins Coll.	92	266	72	237	76	300	152	—	42	142	257	112	251	0	127
Stetson Univ.	124	275	19	285	109	263	187	42	—	105	294	124	290	31	149
Univ. Florida	166	154	178	343	132	158	194	142	105	—	363	134	333	114	173
Univ. Miami	278	522	185	20	230	494	256	257	294	363	—	267	4	242	256
Univ. So. Florida	32	273	143	265	36	275	63	112	124	134	267	—	260	89	32
Miami	253	517	178	0	222	469	216	251	290	333	4	260	—	221	253
Orlando	104	261	60	229	54	254	132	132	31	114	242	89	221	—	104
St. Petersburg	0	300	165	253	70	252	39	127	149	173	256	32	253	104	—

ECKERD COLLEGE

Admissions Office, 4200 54th Ave. S.,
St. Petersburg, FL 33711 • Telephone: 800-456-9009 • www.eckerd.edu/admissions •
Email: admissions@eckerd.edu

Hours: Monday–Friday, 8:30AM–5:00PM; September–May: Saturdays, 10:00AM–1:00PM

Life's a beach at Eckerd College, a small liberal arts college in St. Petersburg, Florida with a waterfront program that allows students to go sailing, canoeing, or swimming whenever they want, free. Highlights of the excellent academic program include a rigorous core curriculum and phenomenal opportunities for undergraduate research.

AT A GLANCE

Selectivity Rating	78
Range SAT I Math	500–620
Average SAT I Math	564
Range SAT I Verbal	510–620
Average SAT I Verbal	564
Average ACT Composite	25
Average GPA	3.23
Student/Faculty Ratio	14:1

CAMPUS TOURS

Appointment	Required
Dates	Year-round
Times	Arranged around scheduled interviews
Average Length	1 hour

ON-CAMPUS APPOINTMENTS

Admissions

Start Date–Juniors	Fall of junior year
Appointment	Required
Advance Notice	Yes, 2 weeks
Saturdays	Sometimes
Average Length	30 min.

Faculty and Coaches

Dates/Times	Academic year
Arrangements	Contact Admissions Office 2 weeks prior

CLASS VISITS

Dates	Academic year
Arrangements	Contact Admissions Office

TRANSPORTATION

Tampa International Airport is 30 minutes away from the campus by car. Taxi and limousine services are available and can be arranged upon arrival (follow ground transportation signs after retrieving luggage from the baggage claim). Car rentals are also available at the airport. Greyhound and Trailways bus lines serve St. Petersburg. Amtrak trains serve Tampa, and bus service is available from there to St. Petersburg.

FIND YOUR WAY

From the east and north, take I-4 W. or I-75 S. and I-275 S. to Tampa; continue on I-275 across Tampa Bay via the Howard Frankland Bridge to St. Petersburg. Continue south on I-275 (past the downtown St. Petersburg exits) and take Exit 4 (Pinellas Bayway/St. Petersburg Beach). Proceed around traffic circle (bearing left) to the first parking lot on the right, outside Franklin Templeton Hall. Additional parking is available across the street. **From the south,** take I-75 N. to I-275 and the Sunshine Skyway. After crossing the bridge and Tampa Bay, take the Pinellas Bayway-St. Petersburg Beach exit at 54th Ave. South. Proceed west on the Pinellas Bayway (54th Ave. S.) and turn left at the traffic light into the college's main entrance, just before the Bayway tollbooth. Proceed around the traffic circle (bearing left) to the first parking lot on the right, outside Franklin Templeton Hall. Additional parking is available across the street. **From the west (and any other direction by sea),** the college's Waterfront Complex is accessible from Egmont Lighthouse by way of Mullet Key Channel, the Skyway Channel, and Frenchman's Creek. Temporary docking is available for visitors.

STAY THE NIGHT

Nearby: Accommodations may be available on campus at the **Continuing Education Center Lodge** (727-864-8313; $50 single occupancy, $70 double occupancy). St. Pete Beach is approximately four miles away from campus and offers affordable, scenic accommodations. **Howard Johnson's** (727-360-7041; 6100 Gulf Blvd.) and the **Trade Winds Resort** (5500 Gulf Blvd.; 800-237-0707) both offer discounts to college visitors. The **Holiday Inn SunSpree Marina Cove** (6800 Sunshine Skyway Lane; 800-227-8045) is the closest off-campus accommodation. It has a tennis court, two pools, children's playground, and full-service restaurant.

HIGHLIGHTS

ON CAMPUS
- Waterfront Program
- Turley Athletic Complex
- Galbraith Marine Science Lab
- Marine Necropsy Lab
- Hough Campus Center

OFF CAMPUS
- Tampa Bay Devil Rays and Buccaneers
- Salvador Dali Museum
- Florida International Museum
- St. Pete Beach and Ft. DeSoto Park
- Ybor City

FLORIDA A&M UNIVERSITY

Student Union Building, Suite 105, Foote-Hilyer Administration Center, Tallahassee, FL 32307 • Telephone: 850-599-3796 • www.famu.edu • Email: adm@famu.edu

Hours: Monday–Friday, 8:00AM–5:00PM

Fine academic programs at historically African American Florida A&M include pharmacy, architecture, and engineering. Business administration takes the cake, though; over one-third of FAMU graduates opt for career-track jobs in commerce. Socially, Rattlers football, a vigorous Greek system, and the awesome Marching 100–considered by students to be the greatest band in the universe–are the ties that bind FAMU students together.

HIGHLIGHTS

ON CAMPUS

- The Black Archives
- FAMU/FSU College of Engineering
- Athletic Department
- Army/Navy ROTC
- School of Pharmacy

OFF CAMPUS

- The Tallahassee Junior Museum
- The Florida Capitol
- The Governor Square Mall
- Wakulla Spring (with Glass Bottom Boats)
- Over 25 parks and recreation centers

TRANSPORTATION

Taxis and bus shuttles are available to take students between FAMU/FSU/TCC/Malls. The Tallahassee Regional Airport is less than a 10-minute drive to FAMU.

FIND YOUR WAY

From I-10 East/West, from Highway 90 E/W, signs and check points are strategically placed pointing to the direction of the university.

STAY THE NIGHT

Nearby: Most hotels and motels are less than five miles away from the university. The prices range from $37 per night to $120 per night. It all depends on your choice and what payment options you decide to use.

AT A GLANCE

Selectivity Rating	79
Range SAT I Math	450–560
Range SAT I Verbal	450–550
Average ACT Composite	20
Average GPA	3.18
Student/Faculty Ratio	20:1

CAMPUS TOURS

Appointment	Required
Dates	Year-round
Average Length	120 min.

ON-CAMPUS APPOINTMENTS

Admissions

Appointment	Required
Advance Notice	Yes, 2 weeks
Saturdays	Sometimes
Average Length	30 min.
Info Sessions	No

Faculty and Coaches

Dates/Times	Year-round
Arrangements	Contact Athletic Department 2 weeks prior

CLASS VISITS

Dates	Varies
Arrangements	Student Orientation Office

FLORIDA INSTITUTE OF TECHNOLOGY

Admissions Office, 150 West University Blvd.,
Melbourne, FL 32901-6975 • Telephone: 800-888-4348 • www.fit.edu/admission •
Email: admissions@fit.edu

Hours: Monday–Friday, 8:00AM–5:00PM

Originally, Florida Institute of Technology had a limited set of majors and almost exclusively served nearby Cape Canaveral. Although technology is still at the forefront of Florida Tech's classes, the overwhelmingly male student body can also choose to major in business or even psychology. The importance of the space program is still evident on campus.

AT A GLANCE

Selectivity Rating	76
Range SAT I Math	550–650
Average SAT I Math	600
Range SAT I Verbal	500–610
Average SAT I Verbal	555
Average ACT Composite	25
Average GPA	3.6
Student/Faculty Ratio	12:1

CAMPUS TOURS

Appointment	Preferred
Dates	Year-round
Times	Mon–Fri, 10AM & 2PM
Average Length	1 hour

ON-CAMPUS APPOINTMENTS

Admissions

Start Date–Juniors	Anytime
Appointment	Preferred
Advance Notice	2 weeks
Saturdays	No
Average Length	30 min.
Info Sessions	No

Faculty and Coaches

Dates/Times	Year-round
Arrangements	Contact Admissions Office 2 weeks prior

CLASS VISITS

Dates	Academic year
Arrangements	Contact Admissions Office

TRANSPORTATION

Melbourne International Airport is about two miles away from campus. Taxis are available at the airport.

FIND YOUR WAY

From I-95, take Exit 180 (old exit #71, U.S. Rte. 192). Take Rte. 192 E. for five miles to Country Club Rd. Turn right onto Country Club Rd. and proceed for one mile to the campus. Go to www.fit.edu/ugrad/directions.htm for more information.

STAY THE NIGHT

Nearby: For lodgings in the immediate vicinity, you are limited to well-known chains. Close to Florida Tech and Melbourne Airport, the **Ramada Inn** (1881 Palm Bay Rd., NE, Palm Bay, FL; 321-723-8181) and **Hilton Melbourne Airport** (200 Rialto Place; 800-445-8667) are both good options. The **Raddison Suite Hotel Oceanfront** (3101 N Highway A1A, Indialantic; 321-773-9260) is about 15 minutes away and offers oceanfront suites and a swimming pool. The **Holiday Inn Beach Resort** (2605 North A1A, Melbourne; 321-777-4100) is 20 minutes away and has tennis courts, outdoor pools, a location on the beach, and a special rate for Florida Tech visitors. For a complete listing of hotels, see our website at:

www.fit.edu/ugrad/hotels.htm

A Little Farther: Florida Institute of Technology is only about an hour's drive away from Orlando, the home of Disney World. The same hotel chains have other locations conveniently close to Disney World, Sea World, Universal Studios, and all of the major theme parks, as well as vacation packages that include one day at the Kennedy Space Center.

HIGHLIGHTS

ON CAMPUS

- Clemente Center
- Olin Engineering Complex
- Denius Student Center
- Botanical Gardens

OFF CAMPUS

- Kennedy Space Center
- Disney World
- RonJon's Surf Shop at Cocoa Beach
- Orlando Attractions
- Pleasure Island

FLORIDA INTERNATIONAL UNIVERSITY

Admissions Office, University Park Campus, PC 140, Miami, FL 33199 • Telephone: 305-348-2363 • www.fiu.edu • Email: admiss@fiu.edu

Hours: Monday–Friday, 8:00AM–5:00PM (to 7:00PM on Tues. and Thurs.); Saturday (first of the month), 9:00AM–noon

Nearly 25,000 students attend classes on comprehensive, public Florida International University's two separate campuses, both of which are in the Miami area. Distractions include the Everglades, Miami nightlife, beaches, and excursions to the Bahamas; the fact that Miami is a vacation destination makes FIU a plus for hospitality management majors.

HIGHLIGHTS

ON CAMPUS

- The Art Museum
- Wolfsonian-a Museum of Art & Design
- North Campus Library
- Steven & Dorothea Green Library

OFF CAMPUS

- Everglades National Park
- Historical Museum of South Florida
- Villa Viscaya Museum
- Miami Seaquarium
- Parrot Jungle Theme Park

TRANSPORTATION

Miami International Airport is eight miles (a 15-minute drive) away from the University Park campus. Super Shuttles and taxis (305-444-4444 or 305-888-8888) are available for the ride from the airport to the N. Miami and University Park campuses. Amtrak trains and Greyhound/Trailways buses serve Miami. Greyhound has several stations in the Miami area, including one in N. Miami Beach.

FIND YOUR WAY

To reach the University Park Campus **from 826 (Palmetto Expressway)** take 826 north or south to SW 8th St. exit (Tamiami Trail) and head west. Proceed on 8th St. to SW 112th Ave. Turn left. **From I-95** take I-95 north or south to 836 (Dolphin Expressway) and head west. Continue on 836 west to the NW 107th Ave. South exit. Proceed on 107th Ave. to SW 8th St. (Tamiami Trail). Turn right proceed on 8th St. to SW 112th Ave. Turn left. From the Florida Tpke. take the Florida Tpke. to SW 8th St. exit (Tamiami Trail) and head east. Proceed on SW 8th St. to SW 112th Ave. Turn right. To reach North Campus **from Miami** take I-95 north to 135th St. Head east to U.S. 1. Head north to 151st St. Turn right. **From Ft. Lauderdale:** Take I-95 south to 163rd St. Head east to U.S. 1. Head south to 151st St. Turn left.

STAY THE NIGHT

Nearby: Florida International University has two campuses. One is in N. Miami and the other, the University Park campus, is in the southern part of Miami, just southwest of the airport. Since the primary Admissions Office is at the University Park campus, our nearby lodgings are focused there. The **Best Western Miami Airport Inn** (1550 N.W. Lejeune Rd.; 305-871-2345) has special inexpensive rates for college visitors. **Days Inn** (3401 N.W. Lejeune Rd.; 305-871-4221), **Quality Inn Airport** (2373 N.W. 42nd Ave.; 305-871-3230), and **Crossway Inn/Howard Johnson's** (1850 N.W. 42nd Ave.; 305-871-4350), all with special rates for college visitors, are even less expensive. The **Holiday Inn Airport South** (1101 N.W. 57th Ave.; 305-266-0000) has an inexpensive rate if booked three days in advance. Moderate rates are available at the **Sheraton River House** (3900 N.W. 21st St.; 305-871-3800), which has a pool, restaurant, tennis court, sauna, exercise room, jogging course, and golf. Similar amenities and rates can be found at the **Hilton Hotel** (Miami Airport, 5101 Blue Lagoon Dr.; 305-262-1000). If you're looking for bed-and-breakfasts contact the **Bed-and-Breakfast Company Tropical Florida** (PO Box 262, South Miami, 33243; 305-661-3270).

A Little Farther: Coconut Grove is a cosmopolitan area of Miami, only a 25-minute drive away from the campus. Try **Double Tree at Coconut Grove** (2649 S. Bayshore Dr.; 305-858-2500). This is normally an expensive choice, but there are special rates available, depending on the time of year and availability of rooms.

AT A GLANCE

Selectivity Rating	71
Range SAT I Math	480–570
Average SAT I Math	533
Range SAT I Verbal	480–570
Average SAT I Verbal	528
Average ACT Composite	22
Average GPA	3.43
Student/Faculty Ratio	17:1

CAMPUS TOURS

Appointment	Required
Dates	Varies
Times	Mon & Wed 9:30AM; Fri, 3PM
Average Length	1 hour

ON-CAMPUS APPOINTMENTS

Admissions

Start Date–Juniors	Anytime
Appointment	Not required
Advance Notice	Yes, 1 week
Saturdays	No
Info Sessions	Yes

Faculty and Coaches

Dates/Times	N/A
Arrangements	Contact Admissions Office

CLASS VISITS

Arrangements	Contact Admissions Office

FLORIDA SOUTHERN COLLEGE

Office of Admissions, 111 Lake Hollingworth Drive, Lakeland, FL 33801 • Telephone: 800-274-4131 • www.flsouthern.edu • Email: fscadm@flsouthern.edu

Hours: Monday–Friday, 8:00AM–5:00PM

Frank Lloyd Wright quite literally made his mark on this Methodist liberal arts college in Lakeland. Wright designed several campus buildings including the Anne Wright Chapel. Springtime is a treat for baseball lovers thanks to the plethora of spring training baseball sites in the area.

AT A GLANCE

Selectivity Rating	78
Range SAT I Math	460–560
Average SAT I Math	516
Range SAT I Verbal	470–570
Average SAT I Verbal	517
Average ACT Composite	22
Average GPA	3.43
Student/Faculty Ratio	17:1

CAMPUS TOURS

Appointment	Preferred
Dates	Year-round
Times	Varies
Average Length	1 hour

ON-CAMPUS APPOINTMENTS

Admissions

Appointment	Preferred
Advance Notice	Yes
Saturdays	No
Average Length	30 min.

Faculty and Coaches

Dates/Times	Academic year
Arrangements	Contact Admissions Office

CLASS VISITS

Dates	Academic year
Arrangements	Contact Admissions Office

TRANSPORTATION

Orlando International Airport is one hour away from campus and Tampa International Airport is 45 minutes away from campus.

FIND YOUR WAY

From the North: Go eastward and take I-75 southbound. The Sumterville exit is about 25 miles south of Ocala. At the Sumterville Exit, head east (left at the light), and continue until you reach Highway 301; turn left. Almost immediately, you will turn right and head south on Rte. 471 until it ends at U.S. Highway 98; turn left. Remain southbound on 98 until you get into Lakeland. When you reach Memorial Blvd. (look for a Circle K convenience store on your left), make a left. Continue on Memorial Blvd., and then make a right on Ingraham Ave. Stay on Ingraham Ave., and make a right on Lake Hollingsworth Drive (1.8 miles). Make another right on Johnson Ave., turn right. Park in either of the two parking lots on your right. **From the Southeast:** Take the Florida Tpke. north to the Yeehaw Junction Exit (Rte. 60). Follow Rte. 60 west toward Tampa. Once in Bartow, follow the signs for Highway 98 North. Once on 98, proceed into Lakeland. Watch for Grove Park Shopping Plaza on your left. Turn left onto North Crystal Lake Drive (There is a Wendy's at the intersection). Continue on Crystal Lake Drive until it ends and turn right on Lake Hollingsworth Drive. Follow directions from the north. **From the East:** From NE Florida, follow I-95 South to I-4 West. Stay on I-4 to Exit # 19, Turn left. Continue on State Road 33, bearing right just after the overpass (the street name will change to Massachusetts Ave.). Massachusetts will end at Lake Morton Drive. Turn right. Follow the perimeter of the lake until you reach Success Ave. (on your right). Follow Success Ave. until it ends at Lake Hollingsworth Drive. Turn left. Make another left at Johnson Ave. Turn right into the second parking lot. **From the West and Southwest:** Follow I-75, or I-275, follow I-4 East to exit 15A (570E, Polk Pkwy. exit). Proceed approximately 6.1 miles to Exit 7 (South Florida Ave.; toll $0.50). Turn left onto 37N (South Florida Ave.) and proceed approximately 1.5 miles and turn right onto Beacon Road. Proceed to the lake and turn left onto Lake Hollingsworth Drive. Follow the lake around Johnson Ave. and turn left. Proceed up Johnson to the second parking lot.

STAY THE NIGHT

Nearby: The **Holiday Inn South** (3405 South Florida Avenue, 800-833-4902) is approximately three miles away from the college. Only one mile away from campus is the **Terrace Hotel** (329 East Main Street, 888-644-8400). Three-and-a-half miles away from the college are **Four Points Sheraton** (4141 South Florida Avenue, 863-647-3000) and **Marriott Courtyard** (3725 Harden Boulevard, 863-802-9000).

HIGHLIGHTS

ON CAMPUS

- Wellness Center
- New Upper Classmen Dorms
- New Pool
- New Music Building
- Cafeteria

OFF CAMPUS

- Downtown
- Tigertown
- Lakeland Square Mall
- Munn Park

FLORIDA STATE UNIVERSITY

Office of Visitor Services, A2500 University Center, Tallahassee, FL 32306-2400 •
Telephone: 850-644-6200 http://admissions.fsu.edu/ •
Email: admissions@admin.fsu.edu

Hours: Monday–Friday, 8:00AM–5:00PM; Saturday, 9:00AM–noon

Florida State University offers a first-rate education at a bargain-basement price. Oodles of solid majors include business, meteorology, education, hotel/restaurant management, and the performing arts. Social life here is even better. FSU students have an awesome ability to party, and immensely popular sports teams win national championships pretty regularly. Burt Reynolds is an FSU alum.

HIGHLIGHTS

ON CAMPUS
- FSU College of Law
- Strozier Library
- Bobby E. Leach Student Recreation Center
- Doak Campbell Stadium
- National High Magnetic Field Laboratory

OFF CAMPUS
- Maclay State Gardens
- Pebble Hill Plantation
- Nearby Gulf beaches
- Wakulla Springs

TRANSPORTATION

The Tallahassee Airport is five miles away from campus. Taxis and hotel limousines are available at the airport.

FIND YOUR WAY

For directions to specific campus locations from Interstate 75 and other major routes, go to www.fsu.edu/~visitor and click on Directions, or call the Visitor Center at 850-644-3246.

STAY THE NIGHT

Nearby: Nearby are the **Doubletree Hotel** (101 S. Adams St.; 850-224-5000), the **Radisson Hotel** (415 N. Monroe; 800-333-3333), and the **Courtyard by Marriott** (1018 Apalachee Pkwy.; 800-321-2211). Other options include the **Cabot Lodge** (2735 N. Monroe; 850-386-8880 or 1653 Raymond Diehl Rd.; 850-386-7500), the **Ramada Inn** (2980 N. Monroe; 850-386-1027), and the **Shoneys Inn** (2801 N. Monroe; 850-386-8286). For inexpensive accommodations, your options include the **Travelodge Motel** (691 W. Tennessee; 850-224-8161), the **Hampton Inn** (3210 N. Monroe; 850-562-4300), and the **Days Inn** (2800 N. Monroe; 850-385-0136). For a complete listing of hotels and motels in the Tallahassee area, you can also call the Tallahassee Area Convention and Visitors Bureau at 850-413-9200.

A Little Farther: If you are willing to drive 30 minutes south to Wakulla Springs State Park, you will find a fabulous old-fashioned lodge and nature preserve. Built in 1937 in Spanish mission style, the **Wakulla Springs Lodge and Conference Center** (1 Springs Dr., Wakulla Springs; 850-224-5950) features glass-bottom boat rides and nature walks. You may run into conference groups and people on day-long trips during summer weekends.

AT A GLANCE

Selectivity Rating	83
Range SAT I Math	520–620
Average SAT I Math	577
Range SAT I Verbal	520–620
Average SAT I Verbal	569
Average ACT Composite	24
Average GPA	3.8
Student/Faculty Ratio	23:1

CAMPUS TOURS

Appointment	Required
Dates	Varies
Times	Varies
Average Length	1 hour

ON-CAMPUS APPOINTMENTS

Admissions

Start Date–Juniors	N/A
Info Sessions	Yes

Faculty and Coaches

Dates/Times	Year-round
Arrangements	Contact Visitor Center 2 weeks prior

CLASS VISITS

Arrangements	Not recommended

NEW COLLEGE OF FLORIDA

New College of Florida Admissions, 5700 N. Tamiami Trail,
Sarasota, FL 34243-2197 • Telephone: 941-359-4269 • www.ncf.edu •
Email: admissions@ncf.edu

Hours: Monday–Friday, 8:00AM–5:00PM

New College is not your garden variety state school. There aren't any huge, ridiculous introductory classes, or any grades. Instead, under a contract system specific to the school, every class is pass/fail and students receive written evaluations. The academic environment is largely devoid of traditional structure and self-motivation is crucial—but along with the flexibility comes high expectations and rigorous workloads.

AT A GLANCE

Selectivity Rating	95
Range SAT I Math	590–680
Average SAT I Math	637
Range SAT I Verbal	640–730
Average SAT I Verbal	693
Average ACT Composite	27
Average GPA	3.9
Student/Faculty Ratio	11:1

CAMPUS TOURS

Appointment	Required
Dates	Year-round
Times	Mon, 2PM; Tues–Fri 11AM & 2PM
Average Length	1 hour

ON-CAMPUS APPOINTMENTS

Admissions

Start Date–Juniors	Year-round
Appointment	Required
Advance Notice	1 week
Saturdays	No
Info Sessions	Year-round

Faculty and Coaches

Dates/Times	Subject to faculty/coach availability
Arrangements	Contact faculty directly

CLASS VISITS

Dates	Academic year
Arrangements	Contact Admissions Office

TRANSPORTATION

The Sarasota/Bradenton Airport is across the street from campus; taxis and limousines are available for the ride to campus. Taxis are always stationed outside the baggage claim area. Greyhound and Trailways bus lines provide service to Sarasota.

FIND YOUR WAY

From I-75 S., take Exit 40 (University Pkwy.). Head west for about seven miles on University Pkwy. to the end (in front of the Ringling Museum of Art). Turn right onto Bayshore Rd., and proceed approximately $3/10$ of a mile to the pink arch. Turn left through the arch, and continue going straight to the loop in front of College Hall. Park along the drive in the designated areas. The New College Office of Admissions is located on the first floor of College Hall.

HIGHLIGHTS

ON CAMPUS

- The R.V. Heiser Natural Sciences Complex
- The Rhoda and Jack Pritxker Marine Biology Research Center
- The Caples Fine Arts Complex
- Historic bayfront mansions
- Jane Bancroft Cook Library

OFF CAMPUS

- The Ringling Museum of Art
- Mote Marine Laboratory and Marine Mammal Hospital
- Marie Selby Botanical Gardens
- Free public beaches
- Myakka State Park

STAY THE NIGHT

Nearby: You have several inexpensive choices. Within walking distance is the very inexpensive **Knights Inn** (5340 N. Tamiami Trail; 800-843-5644). The **Days Inn** (4900 N. Tamiami Trail; 800-325-2525) is a mere half mile away from the school. Both have outdoor pools. The **Hampton Inn** (5000 W. Tamiami Trail; 800-Hampton), a quarter mile away from the school, offers a continental breakfast and a special rate for college visitors. The Hampton Inn also has an outdoor pool and exercise room. The **Courtyard by Marriott** (850 University Pkwy.; 800-321-2211) is a newer facility directly across from the airport and only a quarter mile away from school. In the moderate to expensive range is the **Hyatt Sarasota** (1000 Blvd. of the Arts; 941-366-9000), a seven-minute drive away from the school. It has a heated pool and the usual Hyatt amenities. About 20 minutes north of the college is the town of Palmetto. The **Five Oaks Inn** (1102 Riverside Dr.; 941-723-1236), overlooking the Manatee River, offers rooms at moderate prices and might provide you with an offbeat and pleasant alternative to the usual chain motels.

A Little Farther: **Colony Beach Resort** (1620 Gulf of Mexico Dr.; 813-383-6464 or 800-237-9443) on Long Boat Key, fairly close to Sarasota, is a great, family-oriented resort with tennis, beach, pool, spa, and activities for children. One- or two-bedroom apartments with kitchens are fairly expensive. The **Long Boat Key Club** (301 Gulf of Mexico Dr.; 813-383-8821 or 800-237-8821), up the road from Colony Beach Resort, is somewhat more formal. Rates are expensive.

ROLLINS COLLEGE

Office of Admissions, 1000 Holt Ave., 2720, Winter Park, FL 32789-4499 • Telephone: 407-646-2161 • Email: admission@rollins.edu

Hours: Monday–Friday, 8:30AM–5:00PM

"Personally, I think Rollins beats the hell out of sitting in a 1,200-student lecture hall," explains one student at Rollins College, a small liberal arts college with a solid academic reputation and connections with graduate schools and companies. Perpetually sunny Winter Park, Florida and a dazzling Spanish-style campus are tough to beat.

HIGHLIGHTS

ON CAMPUS
- Cornell Campus Center
- Alfond Sports Center
- Art Gallery, Cornell Fine Arts Museum
- Olin Library

OFF CAMPUS
- Disney World
- Sea World
- Universal Studios
- Beaches

TRANSPORTATION

Orlando International Airport is 13 miles away from campus. Taxis and limousines are available. Amtrak trains serve Winter Park; the station is on Park Ave. To get to campus, head south on Park Ave. about six blocks.

FIND YOUR WAY

From the north and east, take I-4 W. to Exit 87 (Fairbanks Ave.). Turn left onto Fairbanks. Turn right onto Park Ave. The Office of Admission is in the Marshall and Vera Lea Rinker building, on the corner of Fairbanks and Park. **From the south and west,** take I-4 E. to Exit 87 (Fairbanks Ave.). Turn right onto Fairbanks and travel three miles to the campus.

STAY THE NIGHT

Nearby: You have some nice choices in Winter Park, the home of Rollins, but you have to pay a little more to stay there. Our favorite is the **Park Plaza Hotel** (307 Park Ave. S.; 407-647-1072). This European-style hotel, with antiques, a garden, and a delightful balcony, is a great place to relax after a long day on campus. A mile away is the moderately-priced **Best Western Mount Vernon** (110 S. Orlando Ave.; 407-647-1166). It has a pool and restaurant and most of the rooms have refrigerators. For a change of pace, consider the six-room **Courtyard at Lake Lucerne** (211 N. Lucerne Circle East; 407-648-5188), a short five-minute drive from Rollins in Orlando. This inn, located in an old and picturesque part of Orlando, is the oldest house in town. Other local accommodations include the **Comfort Inn, Comfort Suites, Four Points Orlando—Downtown, Westin Grand Bohemian, Marriott Orlando—Downtown, Marriott Courtyard,** and the **Radisson Plaza Hotel Orlando.**

AT A GLANCE

Selectivity Rating	81
Range SAT I Math	530–630
Average SAT I Math	580
Range SAT I Verbal	530–620
Average SAT I Verbal	576
Average ACT Composite	24
Average GPA	3.4
Student/Faculty Ratio	11:1

CAMPUS TOURS

Appointment	Preferred
Dates	Year-round
Times	Mon–Fri 11AM & 2PM
Average Length	1 hour

ON-CAMPUS APPOINTMENTS

Admissions
Appointment	Preferred
Advance Notice	No
Saturdays	No
Info Sessions	Yes

Faculty and Coaches
Dates/Times	Academic year
Arrangements	For faculty appts, contact Admissions Office 2 weeks prior

CLASS VISITS

Dates	Academic year
Arrangements	Contact Admissions Office

STETSON UNIVERSITY

Admissions Office, 421 North Woodland Blvd., Unit 8378,
DeLand, FL 32723 • Telephone: 800-688-0101 • www.stetson.edu/admissions
Email: admissions@stetson.edu

Hours: Monday–Friday, 8:00AM–5:00PM; September–May: Saturdays, 8:30AM–noon

Students on Stetson University's beautiful and historic palm tree-laden campus enjoy the multitude of majors and great facilities you'd find at a big university and the personal attention you only find at small colleges. The sunny Florida location is obviously a bonus.

AT A GLANCE

Selectivity Rating	79
Range SAT I Math	500–610
Average SAT I Math	557
Range SAT I Verbal	510–620
Average SAT I Verbal	566
Average ACT Composite	24
Average GPA	3.57
Student/Faculty Ratio	11:1

CAMPUS TOURS

Appointment	Preferred
Dates	Year-round
Times	Sept–May: Mon–Fri, 10AM & 2PM
Average Length	1 hour

ON-CAMPUS APPOINTMENTS

Admissions

Start Date–Juniors	Anytime
Appointment	Preferred
Advance Notice	Yes, 1 week
Saturdays	No
Average Length	30 min.
Info Sessions	Yes

Faculty and Coaches

Dates/Times	Academic year
Arrangements	Contact Athletic Department 2 weeks prior

CLASS VISITS

Dates	Academic year
Arrangements	Contact Admissions Office

TRANSPORTATION

The Daytona Beach International Airport is approximately 20 miles away from campus. The Orlando International Airport is approximately 55 miles away from campus. From either airport, DOTS shuttle service is available to campus; call 800-231-1965 (within Florida) or 800-223-1965 (from out of state). Amtrak train service is available to DeLand; take a taxi from the station to campus. Greyhound bus service is available, and the bus depot is within walking distance of campus.

FIND YOUR WAY

From I-4, take Exit 114 to Florida Rte. 472 (it heads in only one direction from the exit); proceed on Rte. 472 for three miles to Rte. 17/92 N. Proceed for five miles to campus. **From I-95,** take Exit 261 to U.S. Rte. 92 W. Proceed for 20 miles to the merger of Routes 92 and 17. Continue south (left) on Rte. 17/92 for one-and-a-half miles to campus. **From the northwest,** take I-75 S. to Exit 352 (Ocala). Take Florida Rte. 40 E. for approximately 45 miles to Barberville. Turn south on U.S. Rte. 17 for 14 miles to campus.

STAY THE NIGHT

Nearby: **University Inn** (644 N. Woodland Blvd.; 904-734-5711) is within walking distance. It offers basic accommodations with a special rate for university visitors. There is a coffee maker in each room and an outdoor pool. The **Holiday Inn DeLand** (350 International Speedway Blvd.; 904-738-5200) is two miles away. For a bed-and-breakfast option, try the **DeLand Country Inn** (228 W. Howry Ave.; 904-736-4244), just a few blocks away from the school. There is also **Clauser's Bed & Breakfast** (201 East Kicklighter Road, Lake Helen; 904-228-0310) and the **Best Western Deltona Inn** (487 Deltona Blvd, Deltona; 904-574-6693).

HIGHLIGHTS

ON CAMPUS

- Lynn Business Center
- DuPont-Ball Library
- Duncan Art Gallery
- Hollis Center
- Gillespie Museum

OFF CAMPUS

- Atlantic Ocean Beaches
- Orlando Attractions
- Blue Springs State Park
- Daytona International Speedway
- St. Augustine Historical Sites

UNIVERSITY OF FLORIDA

Admissions Office, 201 Criser Hall,
Gainesville, FL 32611-4000 • Telephone: 352-392-1365 • www.ufl.edu •

Hours: Monday–Friday, 8:00AM–5:00PM

The University of Florida in very hot and humid Gainesville is the most prestigious public university in the state, and its reputation, coupled with a very low in-state tuition, makes it the first choice of many Florida residents. Socially, football is king and the Greek system is a very prominent mainstay of campus life.

HIGHLIGHTS

ON CAMPUS
- Center for Performing Arts
- Florida Museum of Natural History
- The Harn Museum of Art
- Brains Institute
- Lake Alice Wildlife Reserve

OFF CAMPUS
- Devil's Millhopper
- Gainesville
- State Geological Site

TRANSPORTATION

The Gainesville Regional Airport is approximately seven miles away from campus. Taxis and regional transit services are available at the airport.

FIND YOUR WAY

From I-75, exit to Archer Rd. and proceed east to U.S. Rte. 441 (13th St.). Head north (left turn) on 13th St. to the Admissions Office (at the corner of 13th St. and S.W. 2nd Ave.).

STAY THE NIGHT

Nearby: You have a choice of lodgings quite close by, including a motel on campus, the **Reitz Union** (352-392-1607). A slightly more expensive choice is the **Holiday Inn** (1250 W. University Ave; 352-376-1661), which is one block away from campus. This facility has an indoor pool. Across the street from the college is the **University Centre Hotel** (1535 S.W. Archer Rd.; 352-371-3333), which is more posh and moderately-priced (ask for the special rate). A **Sheraton** (2900 S.W. 13th St.; 352-377-4000) is three miles away from campus and also has a special rate for visitors to the university. It also has an outdoor pool and a nature walk.

A Little Farther: Try the **Herlong Mansion** (PO Box 667, Micanopy; 352-466-3322), eight miles south of Gainesville. The mansion's moderate price includes a deluxe continental breakfast during the week and a full breakfast on the weekends.

AT A GLANCE	
Selectivity Rating	87
Range SAT I Math	580–680
Range SAT I Verbal	550–660
Average GPA	3.8
Student/Faculty Ratio	21:1

CAMPUS TOURS	
Appointment	Preferred
Dates	Year-round
Times	Mon–Fri, 10AM & 2PM
Average Length	1 hour

ON-CAMPUS APPOINTMENTS

Admissions
Start Date–Juniors — No interviews, only info sessions

Faculty and Coaches
Arrangements — Contact coach directly 2 weeks prior

CLASS VISITS

Dates	Academic year
Arrangements	Contact faculty directly

UNIVERSITY OF MIAMI

Office of Admission, PO Box 248025,
Coral Gables, FL 33124-4616 • Telephone: 305-284-4323 • www.miami.edu/admission •
Email: admission@miami.edu

Hours: Monday–Friday, 8:30AM–5:00PM; Saturdays, 9:00AM–noon

Students say the University of Miami—Suntan U.—is what you make of it: "You can receive a first-rate education here if you seek it." Professors receive good marks for their instruction skills and especially for their accessibility, which is rare at a large school. The computer, recreational and athletic, lab, and library facilities are all excellent as well.

AT A GLANCE

Selectivity Rating	85
Range SAT I Math	570–670
Range SAT I Verbal	550–650
Average GPA	4.02
Student/Faculty Ratio	13:1

CAMPUS TOURS

Appointment	Not required
Dates	Year-round
Times	Sept–May: Mon–Fri, 11AM, 1PM, & 3PM. Jun–Aug: Mon–Fri, 11AM
Average Length	1 hour

ON-CAMPUS APPOINTMENTS

Admissions
Start Date–Juniors	N/A

Faculty and Coaches
Arrangements	Contact faculty directly

CLASS VISITS

Dates	Academic year
Arrangements	Contact Admissions Office

TRANSPORTATION

Miami International Airport is located in Coral Gables and is approximately 20 minutes away from campus. Supershuttle (located on the downstairs level outside of baggage claim) and taxis are available for the ride to campus. Supershuttle is approximately $11 per person and taxis cost in the neighborhood of $15 to $20.

FIND YOUR WAY

From the north, take I-95 S. to U.S. 1. Continue south for about five miles. Make a right on Red Rd. (S.W. 57th Ave.) and continue to the second light, which is at Miller Rd. (S.W. 56th St.). Make a right onto Miller Rd. and follow to the end. Make a left onto San Amato Dr. and follow the directory signs to the Ashe Building, then make a right onto Memorial Dr. (the main entrance). Ask the guard for directions to parking and the Office of Admission (located in the Ashe Building, Rm. 132). **From the west,** take I-75 to 826 S. Continue to the Miller Rd. exit. Make a left onto Miller Rd (S.W. 56th St.) and follow to the end. Follow the preceding directions to the Office of Admissions. **From Miami International Airport,** take Le Jeune Rd. south for about five miles through downtown Coral Gables. Make a right onto U.S. 1 and travel for about one-and-a-half miles. Turn right onto Red Rd. (S.W. 57th Ave.) and continue to the second light, which is at Miller Rd. (S.W. 56th St.). Make a right onto Miller Rd. and follow to the end. Follow the above directions to get to the Office of Admissions.

STAY THE NIGHT

Nearby: The **Holiday Inn University of Miami** (1350 S. Dixie Hwy.; 305-667-5611) offers college visitors a special double-occupancy rate. No surprises here, but very convenient (it's across the street from the university). Our choice for a place with character is the **Hotel Place St. Michel** (162 Alcazar Ave.; 305-444-1666), which is less than five minutes away from the university and three blocks away from the Miracle Mile shopping area. A bit farther away (10 minutes), you'll find the moderately-priced **Marriott-Dadeland** (9090 S. Dadeland Dr.; 305-670-1035). Other hotels in the area include the **Biltmore Hotel** (1200 Anastasia Ave.; 305-445-1926); the **Holiday Inn Coral Gables** (2051 Le Jeune Rd.; 305-443-2301); and the **Grand Bay Hotel** (2669 S. Bayshore Dr.; 305-858-9600). Check the **Bed and Breakfast Company Tropical Florida** (PO Box 262, South Miami; 305-661-3270) for bed-and-breakfast accommodations in the area.

A Little Farther: If a resort beckons, **Sonesta Beach Hotel** (350 Ocean Dr.; 305-361-2021), about 25 minutes away from the university in Key Biscayne, might be for you. Sonesta Beach has tennis courts, an Olympic pool, a fitness center, boat rentals, and three restaurants.

HIGHLIGHTS

ON CAMPUS
- Lowe Art Museum
- Jerry Herman Ring Theater
- Convocation Center
- Mark Light Stadium
- Gusman Concert Hall

OFF CAMPUS
- Everglades National Park
- Coconut Grove
- Miami Beach
- South Beach
- Florida Keys

UNIVERSITY OF SOUTH FLORIDA

Office of Admission, SVC 1036, 4202 E. Fowler Ave.,
Tampa, FL 33620-9951 • Telephone: 877-USF-BULL • www.usf.edu •
Email: jglassma@admin.usf.edu

Hours: Monday–Friday, 9:00AM–5:00PM (to 6:00PM on Tuesdays and Wednesdays)

The University of South Florida, which is located 10 miles north of downtown Tampa, is home to botanical gardens, a planetarium, and a weather station for research. There's also a championship golf course, swimming pools, art galleries, and the Sun Dome (which hosts concerts and sporting events).

HIGHLIGHTS

ON CAMPUS
- Center Gallery
- The Tampa Campus Library
- Contemporary Art Museum
- Botanical Garden
- Sun Dome

OFF CAMPUS
- Busch Gardens (theme park)
- The Tampa Museum of Art
- Raymond James Stadium
- International Plaza
- Ybor City

TRANSPORTATION

Tampa International Airport is 15 to 20 miles away from campus. Buses, taxis, shuttles, and rental cars are available at the airport. Central Florida Limousine (813-276-3730) provides limousine service. During peak tourist seasons, you should make car rental reservations. Most hotels provide courtesy vans for airport transportation. Amtrak trains and Greyhound/Trailways buses provide service to Tampa. City and suburban bus service is provided by Hart Line (813-254-4278).

FIND YOUR WAY

I-275, I-75, and I-4 are the principal routes to Tampa. **From I-275,** take the Fowler Ave. exit (not Fletcher); turn east on Fowler to the university entrance, which is just past McKinley Blvd. **From I-75 (north or south),** take the Fowler Ave. exit; turn west to the university entrance. **From the east on I-4,** take the Columbus Dr./50th St. exit and proceed north on 50th for approximately seven miles. (Note that 50th becomes 56th after half a mile.) Turn west on Fowler Ave. to the university entrance. **From other routes U.S. Rte. 41 S., Florida Highway 60 S. and W., U.S. Rte. 92 N. and E.** take 40th or 50th St. or Nebraska or Florida Ave. to Fowler Ave. and the university's main entrance.

STAY THE NIGHT

Nearby: There are a number of hotels located within a five-minute radius of the university that offer special rates to USF visitors, including **La Quinta Inn** (800-687-6667), **Wingate Inn** (813-979-2828), and the **Embassy Suites** (813-977-7066), all located on Fowler Ave. In addition, the **Amerisuites** (813-979-1922) and **Quality Suites** (813-971-8930) are located on Bruce B. Downs Blvd.

AT A GLANCE

Range SAT I Math	480–580
Average SAT I Math	532
Range SAT I Verbal	470–570
Average SAT I Verbal	524
Average ACT Composite	26
Average GPA	3.6
Student/Faculty Ratio	17:1

CAMPUS TOURS

Appointment	Preferred
Dates	Year-round
Times	Mon–Fri, 11AM & 2PM; plus 1st Sat of each month
Average Length	120 min.

ON-CAMPUS APPOINTMENTS

Admissions
Start Date–Juniors	N/A

Faculty and Coaches
Dates/Times	Year-round
Arrangements	Contact Admissions Office

CLASS VISITS

Dates	Year-round
Arrangements	Contact Admissions Office

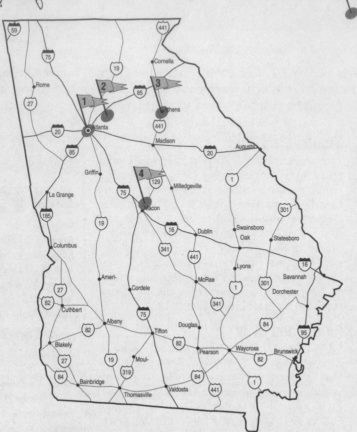

1- **ATLANTA AREA**
   Clark University
   Emory University
   Georgia Institute of Technology
   Morehouse College
   Morris Brown College
   Oglethorpe University
   Spelman College
2- **Agnes Scott College**
3- **University of Georgia**
4- **Mercer U. (Macon)**
   Wesleyan College

Georgia	Agnes Scott Coll.	Clark Atlanta Univ.	Emory Univ.	Georgia Tech.	Mercer U.	Morehouse College	Morris Brown Coll.	Oglethorpe Univ.	Spelman College	Univ. Georgia	Wesleyan Coll.	Athens	Atlanta	Macon
Agnes Scott Coll.	—	9	4	5	85	9	9	14	9	68	78	65	1	91
Clark Atlanta Univ.	9	—	5	1	87	0	0	13	0	80	80	72	0	86
Emory Univ.	4	5	—	3	90	5	5	7	5	64	84	67	1	91
Georgia Tech.	5	1	3	—	85	1	1	9	1	68	78	72	0	87
Mercer Univ.	85	87	90	85	—	86	85	96	85	93	6	93	84	0
Morehouse College	9	0	5	1	86	—	0	13	0	70	81	72	0	86
Morris Brown College	9	0	5	1	85	0	—	13	0	70	79	72	0	86
Oglethorpe Univ.	14	13	7	9	96	13	13	—	13	61	90	67	1	96
Spelman College	9	0	5	1	85	0	0	13	—	70	79	72	0	86
Univ. Georgia	68	70	64	68	93	70	70	61	70	—	98	0	66	90
Wesleyan Coll.	78	80	84	78	6	81	79	90	79	98	—	99	78	0
Athens	65	72	67	72	93	72	72	67	72	0	99	—	66	90
Atlanta	1	0	1	0	84	0	0	1	0	66	78	66	—	82
Macon	91	86	91	87	0	86	86	96	86	90	0	90	82	—

AGNES SCOTT COLLEGE

Office of Admission, 141 E. College Ave.,
Decatur, GA 30030-3797 • Telephone: 800-868-8602 • www.agnesscott.edu/admission •
Email: admission@agnesscott.edu

Hours: Monday–Friday, 8:30AM–4:30PM

Students at this college for women enjoy dorms that resemble palaces and easy access to Atlanta via the rapid transit system a short jaunt away. Scotties laud their incredible, enthusiastic professors and say the education is of the highest caliber. Weekend social life often entails seeking out fraternity parties at nearby Georgia Tech or Emory.

HIGHLIGHTS

ON CAMPUS
- New $36.5 million Science Center
- Alston Campus Center
- Newly renovated Bradley Observatory
- McCain Library

OFF CAMPUS
- CNN
- The Fabulous Fox Theater
- Atlanta History Center
- The High Museum of Art
- Martin Luther King, Jr. National Historic Site

TRANSPORTATION

Hartsfield International Airport in Atlanta is 20 miles away from campus. MARTA trains (public transportation) take to you to campus from the airport: Take the train from the airport to Five Points station, then transfer to an eastbound train to the E6 station in Decatur; either walk, take a taxi, or take the #15 bus for two blocks to campus. Taxi service from the airport is also available. Amtrak trains and Greyhound buses serve Atlanta. MARTA provides buses and rapidrail trains in the metropolitan area.

FIND YOUR WAY

From the north, take I-75 S. past I-285 to I-85 N. Take I-85 N. to the Clairmont Rd. exit. Turn right (signs will point to Decatur) and proceed for several miles until Clairmont ends at the square in Decatur. Turn right onto Ponce de Leon and at the first light (Commerce), turn left. At the second light (Trinity), turn left. At the first light, turn right onto McDonough; cross the train tracks and turn immediately to the left onto E. College Ave. Enter the campus by turning into the first driveway on the right. **From the north on I-85 S.,** pass I-285 and exit to Clairmont Rd. Turn left, then follow the preceding directions from Clairmont Rd. **From the south on I-75/85 N.,** exit to I-285 E. Follow I-285 to 33 (Covington Hwy.). Head west (left) toward Decatur. Covington becomes E. College Ave. The campus is on the left; enter the second driveway past Candler St. **From the east and west,** take I-20 to I-285 N. Follow the preceding directions from that point.

STAY THE NIGHT

Nearby: Seniors are invited to stay overnight with a current student in a residence hall. Please schedule your visit with the Office of Admission two weeks in advance. The **Decatur Holiday Inn and Conference Center** (130 Clairmont Rd.; 404-371-0204) has moderate room rates, an indoor pool, and an exercise room. **University Inn** and the **Emory Conference Center Hotel** are also conveniently located.

AT A GLANCE		
	$$$	

Selectivity Rating	79
Range SAT I Math	540–650
Average SAT I Math	590
Range SAT I Verbal	570–680
Average SAT I Verbal	620
Average ACT Composite	26
Average GPA	3.69
Student/Faculty Ratio	10:1

CAMPUS TOURS

Appointment	Preferred
Dates	Year-round
Times	Mon–Fri, 10AM & 2PM, Sat, 10AM
Average Length	1 hour

ON-CAMPUS APPOINTMENTS

Admissions

Start Date–Juniors	Anytime
Appointment	Required
Advance Notice	Yes, 1 week
Saturdays	Yes
Average Length	30 min.
Info Sessions	Yes

Faculty and Coaches

Dates/Times	Academic year
Arrangements	Contact Admissions Office 2 weeks prior

CLASS VISITS

Dates	Academic year
Arrangements	Other

CLARK ATLANTA UNIVERSITY

Office of Admissions, 223 James P. Brawley Drive, SW
Atlanta, GA 30314 • Telephone: 800-688-3228 • http://admissions.cau.edu •
Email: admissions@panthernet.cau.edu

Hours: Monday–Friday, 9:00AM-5:00PM; select Saturdays

Clark Atlanta University is a historically African-American university of about 5,000 students affiliated with the United Methodist Church. Clark Atlanta offers a diverse and comprehensive liberal arts and sciences education as well as vocational and pre-professional options. It also boasts a rich social life, as the campus is only minutes from downtown Atlanta.

AT A GLANCE

Selectivity Rating	65
Average SAT I Math	444
Average SAT I Verbal	466
Average ACT Composite	19
Average GPA	2.8
Student/Faculty Ratio	15:1

CAMPUS TOURS

Appointment	Required
Dates	Varies
Times	Mon–Fri, 10AM & 2PM
Average Length	1 hour

ON-CAMPUS APPOINTMENTS

Admissions

Start Date–Juniors	September
Appointment	Required
Advance Notice	1 week
Saturdays	No

Faculty and Coaches

Arrangements	Contact Athletic Department 1 week prior

CLASS VISITS

Arrangements	Contact Admissions Office

TRANSPORTATION

Hartsfield International Airport in Atlanta is 12 miles away from campus. Taxis, limousines, and MARTA trains (public transportation) are all available. Amtrak trains and Greyhound buses serve Atlanta. MARTA trains and buses (public transportation) are available for travel throughout the metropolitan area.

FIND YOUR WAY

From I-75/85 (N. and S.), take I-20 W. and exit at Ashby St. Turn right on Ashby and continue to Fair St. Turn right on Fair and continue to James P. Brawley Dr. The campus is on the right; several parking lots are on the left. **From I-20 E.,** exit at Ashby St. and turn left (north) to Fair St. From there follow the preceding directions. **From I-20 W.,** exit at Ashby St. and turn right to Fair St. From there follow the preceding directions. **From downtown,** take Peachtree St. south to Martin Luther King Dr. and turn right. Continue to James P. Brawley Dr. and turn left. Continue to the next traffic light, which is Fair St. The university is ahead on both sides of the street. Brawley Dr. is closed to vehicular traffic at this point; park on either side of the street.

STAY THE NIGHT

Nearby: These suggestions also apply to Morehouse College, Morris Brown College, and Spelman College. Within a 10-minute walk of campus is **Paschal's Motor Hotel** (830 Martin Luther King Dr. S.W.; 404-577-3150), which has a pool and a restaurant. It offers a special inexpensive rate for visitors to any of the above colleges.

HIGHLIGHTS

ON CAMPUS
- Clark Atlanta University Art Galleries
- CAU Radio and Television Station
- Thomas Cole Science Research Center
- Heritage Commons Residence Hall

OFF CAMPUS
- Woodruff Arts Center
- High Museum of Art
- The Atlanta Historical Society
- Stone Mountain Park
- Underground Atlanta

EMORY UNIVERSITY

Office of Admissions, 200 Boisfeuillet Jones Center, Atlanta, GA 30322 • Telephone: 800-727-6036 • www.emory.edu • Email: admiss@emory.edu

Hours: Monday–Friday, 8:00AM–5:00PM

The professors are geniuses, the student body is outstanding, and the resources are unlimited at Emory, one of the South's premier universities. Hometown Atlanta offers many opportunities for volunteering, internships, jobs, and virtually unlimited social options. Emory's alumni list includes Newt Gingrich and reads like a "Who's Who" of the American South.

HIGHLIGHTS

ON CAMPUS
- Michael C. Carlos Museum
- Lullwater Park
- Clifton Health Sciences Corridor
- Top of Woodruff Library
- Dooley's Den at the Depot
- Candler Library Reading Room

OFF CAMPUS
- Carter Center of Emory University
- CNN Center
- Martin Luther King Jr. Center
- Coca-Cola Museum
- Underground Atlanta
- Virginia Highland

TRANSPORTATION

Atlanta's Hartsfield International Airport is approximately 15 miles (a 30- to 40-minute drive) away from campus. Airport limousines, rental cars, and public transportation (a combination of MARTA rapid-rail line and buses) provide transportation from the airport to campus. For public transportation from the airport, take the Northbound MARTA train to the Five Points rapid-rail station in downtown Atlanta. From there, take the train eastbound to the Candler Park station; then take the #6 Emory bus to campus. Amtrak trains and Greyhound/Trailways buses serve Atlanta. The city's MARTA public transportaion system of rapid-rail lines and buses connects Emory to all parts of the city.

FIND YOUR WAY

From I-85, take the Clairmont Road exit (Exit #91). Turn east on Clairmont Rd. and follow it approximately three miles to N. Decatur Rd. Turn right and follow N. Decatur Rd. for approximately one mile to the Emory campus. Turn right in the Emory Village on Dowman Dr. at the main gates of the campus. The Admissions Office is the first building on the left (the B. Jones Center). **From I-20,** take the Moreland Ave. N. exit. Turn north on Moreland Ave. and follow it approximately three miles, at which point it becomes Briarcliff Rd. Continue straight on Briarcliff Rd. approximately one mile. At the large intersection with Oxford Rd., make a soft left onto campus on Dowman Dr., past the main gates of the campus. The Admissions Office is the first building on the left (the B. Jones Center).

STAY THE NIGHT

Nearby: University-owned **Emory Inn** and more expensive **Emory Conference Center Hotel** (1641 Clifton Road NE; 800-933-6679 or 404-712-6700) are convenient and both offer a swimming pool, spa, weight room, restaurant, lounge, as well as a shuttle to the Admission Office. **Holiday Inn Select** (130 Clairemont Avenue; 800-225-6079 or 404-371-0204) in nearby quaint Decatur also offers a shuttle to the Admissions Office. For nearby bed-and-breakfast listings, contact Bed and Breakfast Atlanta at 404-875-0525 or 875-9672.

A Little Farther: The stunning **Ritz-Carlton Buckhead** (3434 Peachtree Road NE; 404-237-2700) faces Atlanta's two best-known shopping centers. Attached to Lenox Square Mall is the **J.W. Marriott** (3300 Lenox Road; 800-228-9290 or 404-262-3344). In midtown, **The Four Seasons** (75 14th Street; 800-332-3442 or 404-8819898) offers luxury near Atlanta's Arts Center. Some less expensive options just a few miles away from campus are the **Courtyard Marriott** (1236 Executive Park Drive; 800-321-2211 or 404-728-0708) and the **Hampton Inn** (1975 North Druid Hills Road; 800-426-7866 or 404-320-6600).

AT A GLANCE

Selectivity Rating	88
Range SAT I Math	660–740
Range SAT I Verbal	640–720
Average GPA	3.8
Student/Faculty Ratio	6:1

CAMPUS TOURS

Appointment	Required
Dates	Varies
Times	Mon–Fri, some Sats
Average Length	1 hour

ON-CAMPUS APPOINTMENTS

Admissions

Info Sessions	Yes

Faculty and Coaches

Dates/Times	Year-round
Arrangements	Contact coach/faculty directly 2 weeks prior

CLASS VISITS

Dates	Academic year
Arrangements	Contact Admissions Office

GEORGIA INSTITUTE OF TECHNOLOGY

Office of Undergraduate Admission, 219 Uncle Heine Way,
Atlanta, GA 30332-0320 • Telephone: 404-894-4154 • www.gatech.edu •
Email: admission@gatech.edu

Hours: Monday–Friday, 8:00AM–4:30PM

This is not a liberal arts school. It is Georgia Tech, a world-class engineering school where a stressful atmosphere and freshman elimination courses ensure that only the strong handle the great all-around academics. Survivors will make lots of money when they graduate from what students insist is the best public school in the state.

AT A GLANCE

Selectivity Rating	89
Range SAT I Math	650–740
Average SAT I Math	689
Range SAT I Verbal	600–690
Average SAT I Verbal	642
Average GPA	3.7
Student/Faculty Ratio	14:1

CAMPUS TOURS

Appointment	Not required
Dates	Year-round
Times	Mon–Fri, 11AM & 2PM
Average Length	1 hour

ON-CAMPUS APPOINTMENTS

Admissions

Start Date—Juniors	N/A

Faculty and Coaches

Dates/Times	Year-round
Arrangements	Contact coach directly

CLASS VISITS

Arrangements	Contact faculty directly

TRANSPORTATION

Hartsfield International Airport in Atlanta is approximately 11 miles away from campus. To get to campus, take the MARTA (public transit) rail line from the airport baggage claim to the North Ave. station (about a 20-minute ride). Walk three blocks west to campus, or transfer to a bus on Route 13. Fare is $1.50 each way, and exact change is required (change machines are available at MARTA stations). At the intersection of North Ave. and Fowler St., ascend the stairs under the archway, and make an immediate right. Follow the path to the Student Success Center (which appears to be attached to the west stands of the football stadium). Amtrak trains and Greyhound/Trailways buses also offer service to Atlanta.

FIND YOUR WAY

From I-75/85 S., take Exit 249 D (North Ave.). Turn right onto North Ave. Cross Techwood Dr. (the first traffic light), and continue on North Ave. approximately one block to Fowler St., which will be immediately before the cement walkway above the street. Turn left onto Fowler St. and park in the first level of the visitors' parking deck. **From I-75/85 N,** take Exit 249 D (Spring St./West Peachtree). Proceed through the first intersection to the next intersection (West Peachtree), and turn left. Continue for one block and turn left on North Ave. Cross over the interstate and Techwood Dr. Continue on North Ave. one block to Fowler St. and park in the first level of the vistiors' parking deck.

STAY THE NIGHT

Nearby: Make reservations and obtain special rates at many local inns and hotels by calling Connections (800-262-9974). **Regency Suites** (975 W. Peachtree St.; 404-876-5003) offers moderate rates, kitchenettes, and continental breakfast. The Regency also has a fitness room and offers pool privileges at an athletic club. The more expensive **Marriott Suites** (35 14th St.; 404-876-8888) offers a great breakfast, an indoor/outdoor pool, and a workout room. The nearby **Holiday Inn Express** (244 North Ave.; 404-881-0881) has moderately-priced rooms and is located within walking distance of the campus.

A Little Farther: Morehouse, Agnes Scott, and Emory are not very far from Georgia Tech. Check the entries for these schools for additional suggestions.

HIGHLIGHTS

ON CAMPUS
- Olympic Aquatic Center/Pool
- Georgia Tech Plaza
- The Hill/Tech Tower
- Bioengineering and Bioscience Building
- Edge Intercollegiate Athletic Center

OFF CAMPUS
- Martin Luther King Jr. Center for Nonviolent Change
- Centennial Olympic Park
- CNN Center
- World of Coca-Cola Museum
- Jimmy Carter Presidential Library

MERCER UNIVERSITY—MACON

Office of Admissions, 1400 Coleman Avenue, Macon, GA 31207-0001 • Telephone: 800-637-2378 • www.mercer.edu • Email: admissions@mercer.edu

Hours: Monday–Friday, 8:00AM–5:00PM; Saturday, 9:30AM–noon

Mercer University's main campus is located in Macon, the hub of central Georgia. Mercer is the second largest Baptist-affiliated institution in the world, and it offers a liberal arts and sciences education with professional and career applications to about 4,500 students, all of whom can enjoy the Recreation Center's adventure trips, primarily outdoor outings.

HIGHLIGHTS

ON CAMPUS
- University Center (to be completed Jan. 2004)
- Connell Student Center
- Greek Village
- McCorkle Music Building
- Jesse Mercer Plaza

OFF CAMPUS
- Macon Mall
- Downtown Macon
- Joshua Cup Coffee House
- Darrell's Pub/Downtown Tavern
- Ingleside Village

TRANSPORTATION
Taxis and shuttle buses are available from Atlanta Airport. Atlanta Airport is 70 miles away. Macon Airport is 10 miles away. Macon bus service is available on campus.

FIND YOUR WAY
From I-75 heading north (from Florida), take I-75 North to Exit #164 (Hardeman Avenue/Forsyth Street). Turn right at the top of the exit ramp. Proceed to the second traffic light, and turn right onto College Street. Follow College Street to the north entrance of the campus. Enter the north entrance, and proceed to the three-way stop. Turn left onto Elm Street. University Welcome Center will be on the right. **From I-75 heading south (from Atlanta),** take I-75 South to Exit #164 (Hardeman Avenue/Forsyth Street). Take the ramp off the interstate, and follow the road to the second light. Turn left at the second light, and proceed to the third traffic light. Follow the directions from the north. **From I-16 heading west (from Savannah),** take I-16 West until it merges with I-75 South. Take I-75 South to Exit #164 (Hardeman Avenue/Forsyth Street). Take the ramp off the interstate, and follow the road to the second light. Turn left at the second light and proceed to the third traffic light. Follow the directions from the north.

STAY THE NIGHT
Nearby: The **1842 Inn** (353 College Street; 478-741-1842 or 800-336-1842) is a historic bed-and-breakfast that offers a Mercer rate for Fridays and Saturdays is $170 to $210 per night for a single room and $220 to $260 per night for a double room; the Mercer rate from Sundays to Thursdays is $139 per night for a single room and $189 per night for a double room. The **Best Inn & Suites** (130 Holiday North Drive, Exit 169 off I-75 at Arkwright Road and Riverside Drive; 478-475-4280 or 800-331-3131) offers a Mercer rate of $79 per night, plus tax, for a one bedroom studio suite and $119 per night, plus tax, for a two bedroom suite. Some other choices include the **Courtyard by Marriott** (3990 Sheraton Drive, Exit #169 off I-75, at Arkwright Road and Riverside Drive; 478-477-8899 or 800-321-2211), the **Crowne Plaza-Macon** (located on the corner of 1st and Spring Streets, Exit #1 off I-16 at Spring Street; 478-746-1461 or 800-227-6963), the **Fairfield Inn** (4011 Sheraton Drive, Exit #169 off I-75, at Arkwright Road and Riverside Drive; 478-738-9007 or 800-228-2800), the **Hampton Inn** (3680 Riverside Drive, Exit #169 off I-75, at Arkwright Road and Riverside Drive; 478-471-0660 or 800-426-7866), the **Hawthorne Inn & Suites** (107 Holiday North Drive, Exit #169 off I-75, at Arkwright Road and Riverside Drive, 478-471-2121 or 800-527-1133), and the **Holiday Inn-Macon Conference Center** (Exit #169 off I-75 and Arkwright Road; 478-474-2610 or 800-465-4329).

AT A GLANCE

Selectivity Rating	75
Range SAT I Math	530–630
Average SAT I Math	580
Range SAT I Verbal	530–630
Average SAT I Verbal	578
Average ACT Composite	25
Average GPA	3.6
Student/Faculty Ratio	15:1

CAMPUS TOURS

Appointment	Preferred
Dates	Year-round
Times	Mon–Fri, 9:00AM, 11:00AM, & 2:00PM
Average Length	1 hour

ON-CAMPUS APPOINTMENTS

Admissions

Start Date–Juniors	Spring of junior year
Appointment	Preferred
Advance Notice	Yes, 1 week
Saturdays	Yes
Average Length	1 hour
Info Sessions	Yes

Faculty and Coaches

Dates/Times	Academic year
Arrangements	Contact Admissions Office 2 weeks prior

CLASS VISITS

Dates	Academic year
Arrangements	Contact Admissions Office

MOREHOUSE COLLEGE

Admissions Office, 830 Westview Dr. S.W.,
Atlanta, GA 30314 • Telephone: 800-851-1254 • www.morehouse.edu/admissions •
Email: admissions@morehouse.edu

Hours: Monday–Friday, 9:00AM–5:00PM.

There is a true spirit of pride that flows through Morehouse College, an all-male, predominately African American liberal arts college in Atlanta with a solid core curriculum and a great national reputation. Half of all recent Morehouse graduates go on to pursue a graduate degree, and Martin Luther King, Jr. and Spike Lee head up a list of notables who received their undergraduate degrees from Morehouse.

AT A GLANCE

Selectivity Rating	85
Range SAT I Math	480–600
Average SAT I Math	550
Range SAT I Verbal	480–590
Average SAT I Verbal	530
Average ACT Composite	23
Average GPA	3.27
Student/Faculty Ratio	15:1

CAMPUS TOURS

Appointment	Required
Dates	Varies
Times	Mon–Fri, 9AM–3PM
Average Length	1 hour

ON-CAMPUS APPOINTMENTS

Admissions

Start Date—Juniors	Last semester of junior year
Appointment	Required
Advance Notice	2 weeks
Saturdays	No
Info Sessions	Yes

Faculty and Coaches

Dates/Times	Academic year
Arrangements	Contact Athletic Department

CLASS VISITS

Dates	Varies
Arrangements	Special Arrangements

TRANSPORTATION

Hartsfield International Airport in Atlanta is 10 miles away from campus. Taxis, airport limousines, and MARTA (public transportation) trains and buses are available for the trip from the airport to campus and throughout the metropolitan area. Amtrak trains and Greyhound buses serve Atlanta.

FIND YOUR WAY

From I-75/85, exit to I-20 W. Exit I-20 W. at Lee St. and turn right for two blocks until you reach campus. **From I-20 E.,** exit to Ashby St., and turn left for three blocks. Turn right on Westview and continue until you hit campus.

STAY THE NIGHT

Nearby: These suggestions also apply to Morris Brown College, Spelman College, and Clark Atlanta University. Within a 10-minute walk of campus is **Castle Berry Inn** (186 Northside Dr. S.W.; 404-893-4663 or 866-499-4852), which has a restaurant. It offers a special inexpensive rate for a nice accommodation.

A Little Farther: The stunning **Ritz-Carlton Buckhead** (3434 Peachtree Rd.; 404-237-2700) is the essence of luxury. The hotel faces Atlanta's two best-known shopping centers. Prices are pretty high. For a complete change of scene, consider the **Evergreen Conference Center and Resort** in Stone Mountain Park (1 Lakeview Dr., Stone Mountain; 770-879-9900). You will find activities galore, including golf, fishing, and boating.

HIGHLIGHTS

ON CAMPUS

- Forbes Arena
- Graves Hall
- Martin Luther King International Chapel
- Technology Tower

OFF CAMPUS

- Woodruff Arts Center
- High Museum of Art
- The Atlanta Historical Society
- Stone Mountain Park
- CNN

MORRIS BROWN COLLEGE

Admissions Office, 643 Martin Luther King Dr. N.W., Atlanta, GA 30314 • Telephone: 404-739-1560 • www.morrisbrown.edu • Email: admission@morrisbrown.edu

Hours: Monday–Friday, 9:00AM–5:00PM

Morris Brown College, home to about 2,100 students, is a historically African-American institution located in Atlanta. The school's programs are career-oriented and range from the liberal arts and sciences to education and psychology. Student recreational options range from a chess club to a baton-twirling team.

HIGHLIGHTS

OFF CAMPUS

- Woodruff Arts Center
- High Museum of Art
- The Atlanta Historical Society
- Stone Mountain Park

TRANSPORTATION

Hartsfield International Airport in Atlanta is a 15-minute drive away from campus. Public transportation (MARTA) trains and buses are available for the ride to campus from the airport; call 404-848-4711 for schedule information. Amtrak trains and Greyhound buses serve Atlanta, and MARTA is available from the stations to campus.

FIND YOUR WAY

From I-75/85, take Exit 93 to I-20 W. Exit I-20 at Exit 19 (West End) and head north on Ashby St. Turn right on Martin Luther King Dr. and proceed to the Admissions Office.

STAY THE NIGHT

Nearby: These suggestions also apply to Morehouse College, Spelman College, and Clark Atlanta University. Within a 10-minute walk of campus is **Paschal's Motor Hotel** (830 Martin Luther King Dr. S.W.; 404-577-3150), which has a pool and a restaurant. It offers a special inexpensive rate for visitors to any of the above colleges.

A Little Farther: The stunning **Ritz-Carlton Buckhead** (3434 Peachtree Rd. N.E.; 404-237-2700) is the essence of luxury. The hotel faces Atlanta's two best-known shopping centers. Prices are pretty high. For a complete change of scene, consider the **Evergreen Conference Center and Resort** in Stone Mountain Park (1 Lakeview Dr., Stone Mountain; 770-879-9900). You will find activities galore, including golf, fishing, and boating.

AT A GLANCE

Range SAT I Math	360–440
Average SAT I Math	396
Range SAT I Verbal	370–450
Average SAT I Verbal	400
Average ACT Composite	16
Average GPA	2.63
Student/Faculty Ratio	18:1

CAMPUS TOURS

Appointment	Preferred
Dates	Year-round
Times	Mon–Fri, 9AM–2PM
Average Length	1 hour

ON-CAMPUS APPOINTMENTS

Admissions

Start Date–Juniors	September
Appointment	Required
Advance Notice	Yes, 2 weeks
Saturdays	No

Faculty and Coaches

Dates/Times	Academic year
Arrangements	Contact Admissions Office 2 weeks prior

CLASS VISITS

Dates	Academic year
Arrangements	Contact Admissions Office

OGLETHORPE UNIVERSITY

Office of Admission, 4484 Peachtree Road, N.E.,
Atlanta, GA 30319 • Telephone: 800-428-4484 • www.oglethorpe.edu/admission •
Email: admission@oglethorpe.edu

Hours: Monday–Friday, 8:30AM–5:00PM; Saturday, 11:00AM–11:30AM

Classes are challenging but rewarding at Oglethorpe University, an unheralded but exceptional liberal arts school with an unusually demanding, broad-based core curriculum. From ultimate frisbee on the Quad to parties on Greek Row to academic discussions at dinner, students say there is something for everyone at this little school on the outskirts of Atlanta.

AT A GLANCE

Selectivity Rating	84
Range SAT I Math	540–650
Average SAT I Math	603
Range SAT I Verbal	560–680
Average SAT I Verbal	617
Average ACT Composite	26
Average GPA	3.7
Student/Faculty Ratio	12:1

CAMPUS TOURS

Appointment	Preferred
Dates	Year-round
Times	Mon–Fri, 11:30AM & 1:30PM; Sat by appt.
Average Length	Varies

ON-CAMPUS APPOINTMENTS

Admissions

Start Date—Juniors	Anytime
Appointment	Preferred
Advance Notice	No
Saturdays	Yes
Average Length	1 hour

Faculty and Coaches

Dates/Times	Academic year
Arrangements	Contact Admissions Office 2 weeks prior

CLASS VISITS

Arrangements	Contact Admissions Office

TRANSPORTATION

Hartsfield International Airport in Atlanta is located about 15 miles away from campus. Rapid rail, airport shuttle, taxi, car rental, and limousine services are available. MARTA is the city's public transportation system and provides bus service in addition to rapid rail service. The Brookhaven/Oglethorpe University MARTA station is located one mile due south of campus on Peachtree Road and is served by the North Doraville MARTA line. Atlanta is also a major hub for both Greyhound buses and Amtrak trains.

FIND YOUR WAY

From I-85/75, take exit 89 (North Druid Hills Road). Proceed north/west on North Druid Hills approximately two-and-a-half miles (make sure to veer right at Roxboro Road, remaining on North Druid Hills) until it ends at Peachtree Road. Turn right (north) onto Peachtree and travel for one mile. The campus is on the left. **From I-285,** take exit 21 (Ashford-Dunwoody Road). Proceed south/east on Ashford-Dunwoody approximately two-and-a-half miles until it ends at Peachtree Road. Turn right (south) onto Peachtree and proceed approximately one block. The campus is on the right.

STAY THE NIGHT

Nearby: Many hotels and inns are located within a five-mile radius of Oglethorpe's campus. One conveniently located place is the **Sierra Suites** (3967 Peachtree Road; 404-237-9100), located directly next to the Brookhaven/Oglethorpe University MARTA station; it provides a discount for Oglethorpe University visitors. Also try the **Holiday Inn Select** (4386 Chamblee-Dunwoody Road; 770-457-6363), which features a weight room, a pool, a resturant, and reasonable prices. The **Red Roof Inn** (1960 North Druid Hills Road; 404-321-4174) offers nice accommodations at economic rates, and the **Swissotel Atlanta** (3391 Peachtree Road; 404-365-5500) is a world-class luxury hotel located in the Lenox/Buckhead area five minutes south of Oglethorpe's campus.

HIGHLIGHTS

ON CAMPUS
- Oglethorpe University Museum
- Phillip Weltner Library
- Conant Performing Arts Center
- Hermance Stadium

OFF CAMPUS
- Lenox Square Mall/Phillips Plaza
- The High Museum of Art
- Stone Mountain Park
- The Fox Theater
- Martin Luther King Jr. Center

SPELMAN COLLEGE

Admissions Office, 350 Spelman Lane, Atlanta, GA 30314 • Telephone: 800-982-2411 • www.spelman.edu • Email: admiss@spelman.edu

Hours: Monday–Friday, 9:00AM–5:00PM

Spelman College is one of only two remaining all-female colleges in the country and one of the nation's preeminent historically African American institutions. "Spelman is a great school for up-and-coming African American females," says one student. "Here, we learn to express ourselves and to stand up for what we believe in."

HIGHLIGHTS

ON CAMPUS

- Sister's Chapel
- The Spelman College Art Museum
- Camille Olivia Hanks-Cosby Academic Center
- Science Center
- The Oval and Alumni Arch

OFF CAMPUS

- Martin Luther King Jr. Center of Non-Violent Change
- Historic Auburn Avenue
- Six Flags
- Stone Mountian Park
- Centennial Olympic Park

TRANSPORTATION

Hartsfield International Airport in Atlanta is a 20-minute drive away from campus. Taxis, airport limousines (to some hotels), and MARTA (public transportation) trains are available for the trip from airport to campus. Amtrak trains and Greyhound buses provide service to Atlanta. MARTA trains and buses provide very good public transportation throughout the metropolitan area. The campus is accessible from #68 Ashby (West End station), #63 Atlanta University Ctr. (Vine City station), or #13 West Fair.

FIND YOUR WAY

From I-75 North and South: Take I-20 West and exit at Lee Street. Turn right onto Lee Street, and continue through the next traffic light (Westview Drive). You will see a large parking lot on the right-hand side. Turn right into the first driveway, and you will approach the gates of Spelman College. **From I-20 West:** Exit Ashby Street. Cross Ashby Street, and continue on Oak Street to the next traffic light. Turn left on to Lee Street, cross the bridge over I-20, and continue through the next two traffic lights. You will see a large parking lot on the right-hand side. Turn right into the first driveway and you will approach the gates of Spelman College. **From I-20 East:** Exit at Lee Street. Turn right on to Lee Street, and continue through the next light (Westview Drive). You will see a large parking lot on the right-hand side. Turn right into the first driveway and you will approach the gates of Spelman College. **From Downtown Atlanta:** Take Peachtree Streets south to Martin Luther King Jr. Drive and turn right. Continue on M.L. King Jr. Drive to Northside and turn left. Continue on Northside through next three traffic lights (passing Burger King on the right). Turn right at the fourth traffic light (Greensfery Avenue). Continue on Greensfery through the stop sign. Turn left into the gate of Spelman College.

STAY THE NIGHT

Nearby: The **Sheraton Atlanta Hotel** is a full-service hotel located in the heart of downtown Atlanta. This is a 765 room hotel with a 24-hour fitness center and an indoor swimming pool. Three onsite restaurants allow for formal or casual dining. This hotel is conveniently located near the major highways and is a seven-minute drive from Spelman's campus. The **Regency Suites** is located in Midtown and is about a 10-minute drive away from campus. There are several other resorts, hotels, and inns in the area. Please contact Connections at 800-262-9974 for information and reservations on these and other properties. Please ask them about the Spelman educational rate offered by many of the hotels.

AT A GLANCE

Selectivity Rating	82
Range SAT I Math	500–599
Average SAT I Math	524
Range SAT I Verbal	500–600
Average SAT I Verbal	549
Average ACT Composite	22
Average GPA	3.1
Student/Faculty Ratio	14:1

CAMPUS TOURS

Appointment	Required
Times	Mon–Fri, 11AM or 2PM

ON-CAMPUS APPOINTMENTS

Admissions

Start Date–Juniors	Anytime
Appointment	Required
Advance Notice	2 weeks
Saturdays	No

Faculty and Coaches

Arrangements	Contact faculty directly

CLASS VISITS

Arrangements	Varies

UNIVERSITY OF GEORGIA

Office of Undergraduate Admissions, Terrell Hall, Athens, GA 30602 • Telephone: 706-542-8776 • www.uga.edu/admissions/ • Email: undergrad@admissions.uga.edu

Hours: Monday–Friday, 9:00AM–4:00PM

The University of Georgia "is a large school with a lot going for it—improving academics, an improving football team, and a diverse student body," explains one student. This school is getting nothing but better, and with admissions getting tougher, it is assured that the trend will continue. Especially rewarding is the excellent and very selective honors program.

AT A GLANCE

Selectivity Rating	84
Range SAT I Math	560–650
Average SAT I Math	611
Range SAT I Verbal	550–650
Average SAT I Verbal	604
Average GPA	3.65
Student/Faculty Ratio	13:1

CAMPUS TOURS

Appointment	Not required
Dates	Year-round
Times	Mon–Fri, 9AM; 1:15PM, & 3PM; Sat, 10:30AM & 2:30PM
Average Length	1 hour

ON-CAMPUS APPOINTMENTS

Admissions

Start Date—Juniors	N/A
Info Sessions	Yes

Faculty and Coaches

Arrangements	Contact faculty directly 2 weeks prior

CLASS VISITS

Arrangements	Contact faculty directly

TRANSPORTATION

Hartsfield International Airport in Atlanta is an hour-and-a-half away from campus. Athens has its own small commuter airport, which is served by USAir.

FIND YOUR WAY

From Atlanta, take I-85 to Highway 316 (University Pkwy.). This connects to the Athens Bypass, which leads to downtown Athens; or call the UGA Visitors' Center at College Station Rd.

STAY THE NIGHT

Nearby: You can stay on campus at the **Center for Continuing Education** (706-548-1311). A double room is inexpensive and you can use the pool and weight room. Across the street, the **Holiday Inn** (Broad and Lumpkin St.; 706-549-4433) has moderate rates, an indoor pool, an exercise room, and a restaurant. A cheaper choice is the **Marriott Court Yard** (166 Finley St.; 706-369-7000), which serves continental breakfast.

A Little Farther: Eight miles away from campus is **Rivendell Bed & Breakfast** (3581 Barnett Shoals, Watkinsville; 706-769-4522) where, for an inexpensive rate, you can enjoy a very pleasant ambience and a full southern breakfast. The house boasts beautiful walking trails and a picnic area and is situated on the river.

HIGHLIGHTS

ON CAMPUS

- The Arch
- Sanford Stadium
- Ramsey Student Center for Physical Activities
- Performing and Visual Arts Complex
- Tate Student Center

OFF CAMPUS

- Downtown Athens
- Classic Center
- Botanical Gardens
- Milledge Avenue
- Bishop Park

WESLEYAN COLLEGE

Office of Admissions, 4760 Forsythe Road, Macon, GA 31210-4462 • Telephone: 800-447-6610 • www.wesleyancollege.edu/admissions/ • Email: admissions@wesleyancollege.edu

Hours: Monday–Friday, 8:30AM–5:00PM; select Saturdays

Wesleyan College is an extremely small, traditional liberal arts school in Macon, Georgia that offers a wonderful, well-rounded education in an all-female environment. Social life on Wesleyan's very pretty campus is filled with wonderful traditions, including Wesleyan's one-of-a-kind class system under which each incoming class has a name, a set of cheers, and a mascot.

HIGHLIGHTS

ON CAMPUS
- Historic Quad of buildings with Georgian brick design
- Equestrian and Fitness Centers
- Lake
- Residence Halls

OFF CAMPUS
- Downtown restaurants and shops
- Georgia Music Hall of Fame
- Georgia Sports Hall of Fame
- Hay House

TRANSPORTATION

Wesleyan is approximately 80 miles away from Atlanta International Airport. Groome shuttle bus is available for trips to and from the airport. Taxis are also available.

FIND YOUR WAY

Wesleyan College is located near Interstate 75 and is easily reachable from any direction. **Traveling south from the Atlanta area or north from Valdosta,** take I-75 to I-475. Take the Zebulon Road exit. Turn right from the south and left from the north onto Zebulon Road. Take Zebulon Road 2.6 miles until it dead ends at Forsyth Road. Turn right. Wesleyan is half a mile away on the right. **Traveling from Savannah or the East Coast,** take I-16 to I-75 south. Exit Hardeman Avenue and turn right. Wesleyan is approximately five miles away on the left. **Traveling west from Alabama and Columbus,** take US 80 to I-475 north. Exit right on Zebulon Road. Take Zebulon Road 2.6 miles until it dead ends at Forsyth Road. Wesleyan is half a mile away on the right.

STAY THE NIGHT

Nearby: You have a range of choices that include the **Jameson Inn** (Plantation Drive 1-475, Zebulon road, Exit #9; 478-474-8004), the **Fairfield Inn by Marriott** (110 Plantation Drive I-475, Xebulon Road, Exit #9; 478-474-9922), the **1842 Inn** (353 College Street; 800-336-1842), the **Holiday Inn** (North-side, I-75, Arkwright Road, Exit #169; 478-474-2610), and the **Hampton Inn** (I-75, Arkwright Road, Exit #169; 478-471-0060).

AT A GLANCE

Selectivity Rating	69
Range SAT I Math	480–610
Average SAT I Math	562
Range SAT I Verbal	500–610
Average SAT I Verbal	574
Average ACT Composite	25
Average GPA	3.53
Student/Faculty Ratio	11:1

CAMPUS TOURS

Appointment	Preferred
Dates	Year-round
Times	Mon–Fri, 8:30AM–5PM; call for other available times
Average Length	1 hour

ON-CAMPUS APPOINTMENTS

Admissions

Start Date—Juniors	Anytime
Appointment	Preferred
Advance Notice	No
Saturdays	Yes
Average Length	30 min.
Info Sessions	Yes

Faculty and Coaches

Dates/Times	Year-round
Arrangements	Contact Admissions Office 1 week prior

CLASS VISITS

Dates	Academic year
Arrangements	Contact Admissions Office

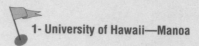
1- University of Hawaii—Manoa

Nihau
Puuwai

Kauai
Hanalei • Kilauea
Waimea •
• Lihue

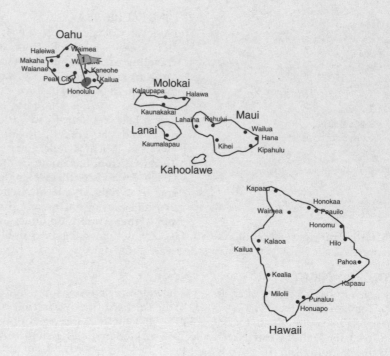

Oahu
Haleiwa • Waimea
Makaha • Wahiawa
Waianae • • Kaneohe
Pearl City • • Kailua
Honolulu

Molokai
Kalaupapa • • Halawa
Kaunakakai
Lahaina • Kahului
Lanai
Kaumalapau •
Kihei
Maui
Wailua
Hana
Kipahulu

Kahoolawe

Kapaau
Waimea • Honokaa • Paauilo
Honomu
Kalaoa • Hilo
Kailua •
Pahoa
Kealia • Kapaau
Milolii •
Punaluu
Honuapo

Hawaii

	Univ. of Hawaii	Honolulu
Hawaii		
Univ. of Hawaii	—	0
Honolulu	0	—

HAWAII

UNIVERSITY OF HAWAII—MANOA

School & College Services, 2600 Campus Road, Rm. 214, SSC Room 001,
Honolulu, HI 96822 • Telephone: 800-823-9771 • www.hawaii.edu/admissions/ •
Email: ar-info@hawaii.edu

Hours: Monday–Friday, 8:00AM–4:00PM

Aloha! The University of Hawaii at Manoa is not only the flagship campus of the University of Hawaii system, but also it is the premier institution of higher learning and research in the Pacific Basin. Also, the campus is totally gorgeous—as you might have guessed. The UH library's Japanese collection is among the tenth largest in the nation.

HIGHLIGHTS

ON CAMPUS

- Campus Center
- Queen Liliu'Okalani Center for Student Services
- Hemenway Hall
- Athletic Complex
- Japanese Garden at the East West Center

OFF CAMPUS

- Waikiki Beach/Diamond Head
- Ala Moana Shopping Center
- Hanauma Bay
- Aloha Tower Market Place
- Polynesian Cultural Center

TRANSPORTATION

Honolulu International Airport is the closest airport. Available transportation includes taxis, shuttles, and rental cars, which are available to take you from the airport to campus. The city bus departs from the second floor of the airport to campus; this is an option if you only have a carry-on bag.

FIND YOUR WAY

From Honolulu International Airport, take H1 East, and exit on University Avenue. Proceed north on University Ave. to the college entrance. The airport is nine miles away from the university, but driving time varies with traffic.

STAY THE NIGHT

Nearby: All hotels in the Waikiki Beach area are within a 10- to 15-minute drive to campus. The outrigger hotels operate 20 hotels in Oahu, with prices ranging from inexpensive to expensive. Contact their reservations agent at 800-442 7302. **Hilton, Sheraton,** and **Marriott Hotels** are also located in the Waikiki area.

AT A GLANCE

Selectivity Rating	80
Range SAT I Math	510–610
Average SAT I Math	563
Range SAT I Verbal	470–570
Average SAT I Verbal	523
Average GPA	3.34
Student/Faculty Ratio	12:1

CAMPUS TOURS

Appointment	Preferred
Dates	Year-round
Times	Tues–Thurs, 1PM–2:30PM, Mon–Wed, & Fri, 9AM–10:30AM
Average Length	Varies

ON-CAMPUS APPOINTMENTS

Admissions

Faculty and Coaches

Dates/Times	N/A
Arrangements	Contact department directly

CLASS VISITS

Dates	Academic year
Arrangements	Contact Visiting Center

1- Idaho State University
2- Albertson College
3- University of Idaho

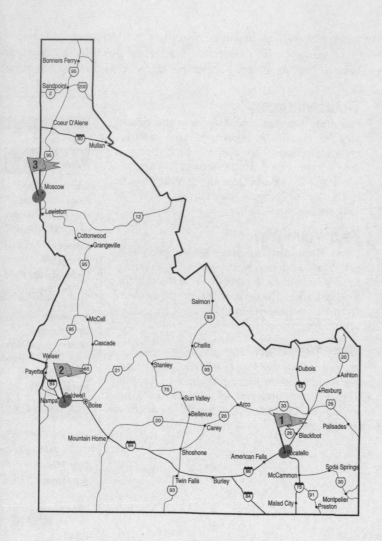

Idaho	Albertson Coll.	Idaho State Univ.	Univ. of Idaho	Boise
Albertson Coll.	—	261	357	27
Idaho State Univ.	261	—	612	234
Univ. of Idaho	357	612	—	299
Boise	27	234	299	—

ALBERTSON COLLEGE

Office of Admissions, 2112 Cleveland Boulevard,
Caldwell, ID 83605 • Telephone: 800-224-3246 • www.albertson.edu •
Email: admission@albertson.edu

Hours: Monday–Friday, 8:00AM–5:00PM

There are plenty of outdoor opportunities like fishing, hiking, and camping at this isolated campus in southwestern Idaho, but not much as far as big city high life goes. Intimate may be an understatement because if you're not in class, professors will usually call you at home and get you out of bed.

HIGHLIGHTS

ON CAMPUS
- J. A. Albertson Activity Center
- McCain Student Center
- Langroise Center for Performing & Fine Arts
- Centennial Amphitheater
- Berger's Bench

OFF CAMPUS
- Downtown Boise
- Boise River (fishing & rafting)
- Boise Foothills (hiking & mountain biking)
- Bogus Basin Ski
- Ste. Chapelle Winey

TRANSPORTATION
Boise airport is 25 miles away from campus. Rides are available from admission staff, taxi, or treasure valley transit.

FIND YOUR WAY
From westbound or eastbound I-84, take the 10th Ave. exit. Turn left onto 10th Ave. Continue on 10th Ave. until you come to the 10th Ave. and Cleveland Blvd. intersection. Turn left onto Cleveland Blvd., and continue on Cleveland for approximately two miles. The campus will be on your right. Turn right onto Indiana. The campus is still on the right. Park at the large parking lot behind the Activity Center.

STAY THE NIGHT
Nearby: Tell the hotel you choose that you are visting the campus to get a special visitors' rate. **Best Western Suites** is two miles away from campus. It's approximately $60 per night. **LaQuinta Inn** is also two miles away from campus. It's also approximately $60 per night.

AT A GLANCE	
Selectivity Rating	80
Range SAT I Math	510–616
Average SAT I Math	563
Range SAT I Verbal	510–630
Average SAT I Verbal	571
Average ACT Composite	24
Average GPA	3.6
Student/Faculty Ratio	12:1

CAMPUS TOURS	
Appointment	Preferred
Dates	Year-round
Times	Upon request
Average Length	1 hour

ON-CAMPUS APPOINTMENTS	
Admissions	
Start Date–Juniors	Upon request
Appointment	Preferred
Advance Notice	Yes, 1 week
Saturdays	Sometimes
Average Length	1 hour
Info Sessions	Yes
Faculty and Coaches	
Dates/Times	Year-round
Arrangements	Contact Admissions Office 2 weeks prior

CLASS VISITS	
Dates	Academic year
Arrangements	Contact Visiting Center

IDAHO STATE UNIVERSITY

Office of Enrollment Planning and Academic Service, PO Box 8054, Pocatello, ID 83209-8270 • Telephone: 208-282-2475 • www.isu.edu • Email: info@isu.edu

Hours: Monday–Friday, 8:00AM–5:00PM; Tuesday 8:00AM–7:00PM

Educating almost 12,000 traditional and nontraditional students, Idaho State provides a wide range of educational options, from traditional liberal arts programs to vocational and career offerings at its main campus location in Pocatello, Idaho. The Craft Shop in the student union offers pottery, weaving, and leatherworking classes.

AT A GLANCE

Average ACT Composite	21
Student/Faculty Ratio	17:1

CAMPUS TOURS

Appointment	Preferred
Dates	Varies
Times	Mon–Fri, by appointment
Average Length	120 min.

ON-CAMPUS APPOINTMENTS

Admissions

Start Date—Juniors	N/A
Appointment	Preferred
Advance Notice	No
Saturdays	No
Average Length	1 hour
Info Sessions	Yes

Faculty and Coaches

Dates/Times	Year-round
Arrangements	Contact Visiting Center 1 week prior

CLASS VISITS

Dates	Year-round
Arrangements	Contact Visiting Center

TRANSPORTATION

Situated approximately 10 miles away from campus is the Pocatello Regional Airport. Call the Office of Enrollment. Taxis are available for transportation from the airport to campus; call 208-232-1115.

FIND YOUR WAY

From I-20, take the Clark St. exit and turn west into town on Clark St. to 8th Ave. Turn left on 8th Ave. and proceed to the stop light at 8th and Martin Luther King Jr. Way, then turn right.

STAY THE NIGHT

Nearby: Accommodations in Pocatello offer convenience and value, but nothing out of the ordinary. Two very basic, quite inexpensive hotels are situated just across the street from the university. Frequented regularly by university visitors, the **Econolodge** (835 S. 5th Ave.; 208-233-0451) offers special rates. If you're craving hustle and bustle, you might try the **Red Lion** (2055 Pocatello Creek; 208-233-2200), a five-minute drive away from campus. It has restaurants, an indoor pool, a weight room, a sauna, and evening entertainment in the lounge. Rooms are only slightly more expensive than the two choices listed above. About five miles away is a **Holiday Inn** (1399 Bench Rd.; 208-237-1400) with an indoor pool, miniature golf, ping pong, whirlpool, sauna, and fitness center privileges. **Ameritel** (1440 Bench Rd.; 208-234-7500) has a 24-hour pool, hot tub, and exercise room. It offers a deluxe continental breakfast and free HBO.

HIGHLIGHTS

ON CAMPUS

• Idaho Museum of Natural History
• Rock Climbing Wall at Reed Gym
• Holt Arena
• Wilderness Center
• Particle Accelerator

OFF CAMPUS

• Ross Park Aquatic Center
• Pocatello Pump at Ross Park
• Mink Creek Recreation Area
• Justice Park Camping and Picnic Area
• Lava Hot Springs

UNIVERSITY OF IDAHO

New Student Services, PO Box 444253,
Moscow, ID 83844-4264 • Telephone: 888-884-3246 • www.students.uidaho.edu •
Email: admappl@uidaho.edu

Hours: Monday–Friday, 8:00AM–5:00PM

A great environmental sciences program and the colleges of agriculture and engineering are the greatest strengths at the relatively small University of Idaho, and over 90 percent of seniors pass the Fundamentals of Engineering Exam on the first try (the national rate is much lower). Also, a nutty tradition at University of Idaho takes place on Hello Walk, a shaded walkway where everyone exchanges hellos whenever they pass each other.

HIGHLIGHTS

ON CAMPUS
- Campus Commons (food and meeting rooms)
- Student Union (Admissions, Registrar, Financial Aid)
- Kibbie Dome (athletics)
- Bookstore
- See our campus live with Web cams at www.uidaho.edu/webcams

OFF CAMPUS
- University Pointe (shops and restaurants
- Salmon, Snake, and Clearwater rivers (recreation)
- Washington State University

TRANSPORTATION
The closest airport is 10 miles away from campus, Pullman-Moscow, Pullman Washington. More extensive service is available at Spokane International, 90 miles away from campus. Shuttle services are also available.

FIND YOUR WAY
On U.S. Highway 95, 85 miles south of Coeur d'Alene Idaho and 300 miles north of Boise Idaho.

STAY THE NIGHT
Nearby: The **Best Western University Inn** (1516 Pullman Rd, Moscow, ID; 208-882-0550) is adjacent to campus.

AT A GLANCE

Selectivity Rating	73
Range SAT I Math	48–47
Average SAT I Math	559
Range SAT I Verbal	47–47
Average SAT I Verbal	549
Average ACT Composite	23
Average GPA	3.4
Student/Faculty Ratio	19:1

CAMPUS TOURS

Appointment	Preferred
Dates	Year-round
Times	Mon–Fri, 9:30AM & 1:30PM
Average Length	1 hour

ON-CAMPUS APPOINTMENTS

Admissions

Start Date–Juniors	Anytime
Appointment	Required
Advance Notice	Yes, 1 week
Saturdays	No
Average Length	45 min.
Info Sessions	Yes

Faculty and Coaches

Dates/Times	Year-round
Arrangements	Other, 2 weeks

CLASS VISITS

Dates	Academic year
Arrangements	New Student Services

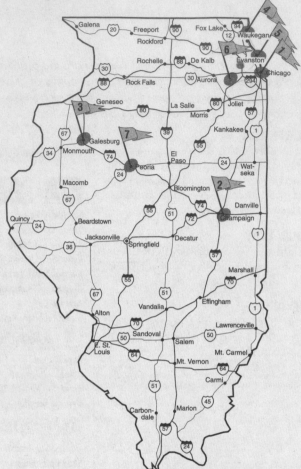

1- University of Chicago
Illinois Institute of Technology
2- University of Illinois—
Champaign-Urbana
3- Knox College
4- Lake Forest College
5- Northwestern University
6- Wheaton College
7- Bradley U.

Illinois

	Bradley	Illinois Inst. Tech.	Knox Coll.	Lake Forest Coll.	Northwestern Univ.	Univ. Chicago	Univ. Illinois-Champ.	Wheaton Coll.	Chicago	Peoria	Springfield
Bradley	—	168	47	191	184	169	94	160	167	—	74
Illinois Inst. Tech.	168	—	198	32	17	3	143	34	0	152	198
Knox Coll.	47	198	—	221	206	196	139	183	184	53	106
Lake Forest Coll.	191	32	221	—	15	34	179	53	20	182	230
Northwestern Univ.	184	17	206	15	—	19	161	38	10	167	215
Univ. Chicago	169	3	196	34	19	—	140	37	0	155	195
Univ. Illinois-Champ.	94	143	139	176	161	140	—	158	135	92	198
Wheaton Coll.	160	34	183	53	38	37	158	—	16	143	182
Chicago	167	0	184	20	10	0	135	16	—	170	202
Peoria	0	152	53	182	167	155	92	143	170	—	202
Springfield	74	198	106	230	215	195	198	182	202	74	—

BRADLEY UNIVERSITY

Office of Admissions, 1501 West Bradley Avenue, Peoria, IL 61625 • Telephone: 800-447-6460 • http://admissions.bradley.edu/ • Email: admissions@bradley.edu

Hours: Monday–Friday, 9:00AM–5:00PM

With approximately 5,000 undergraduate students and a few hundred graduate students, private, comprehensive Bradley University bills itself as the ideal size for living and learning. It's easy to establish one-on-one relationships with BU's knowledgeable professors and it's easy, quick, and convenient to get to and from class on Bradley's beautiful and self-contained campus.

HIGHLIGHTS

ON CAMPUS
- Caterpillar Global Communications Center
- Michel Student Center
- Olin Hall of Science
- Cullom-Davis Library
- Heuser Arts Center

OFF CAMPUS
- Lakeview Museum of Arts and Sciences
- The Peoria Civic Center
- Northwoods Mall
- The Shoppes at Grand Prairie
- The Illinois River Valley River Front

TRANSPORTATION

Peoria is just three hours away by Interstate from Chicago, St. Louis, and Indianapolis. The Greater Peoria Airport is served by airlines with flights to the same cities as well as Denver, Minneapolis, and Atlanta. There is daily bus service from Chicago's O'Hare airport to our student center.

FIND YOUR WAY

Interstate 74 into Peoria and take exit 91 or 91a. Proceed on University Street south through two stoplights, and turn right into the main campus entrance. Parking is available in the first lot for all visitors.

STAY THE NIGHT

Nearby: There are more than a dozen popular locations within three miles of campus for overnight accomodations. Call the Visitors Center for help in making a reservation.

AT A GLANCE

Selectivity Rating	76
Range SAT I Math	550–670
Average SAT I Math	610
Range SAT I Verbal	540–650
Average SAT I Verbal	597
Average ACT Composite	25
Student/Faculty Ratio	14:1

CAMPUS TOURS

Appointment	Preferred
Dates	Year-round
Average Length	Varies

ON-CAMPUS APPOINTMENTS

Admissions

Appointment	Preferred
Advance Notice	Yes, 2 weeks
Saturdays	Sometimes
Average Length	1 hour
Info Sessions	Yes

Faculty and Coaches

Dates/Times	Year-round
Arrangements	Contact Admissions Office 2 weeks prior

CLASS VISITS

Dates	Academic year
Arrangements	Contact Admissions Office

ILLINOIS INSTITUTE OF TECHNOLOGY

Office of Undergraduate Admissions, 10 West 33 Street, Chicago, IL 60616 • Telephone: 800-448-2329 • www.iit.edu/admission/ • Email: admission@iit.edu

Hours: Monday–Friday, 9:00AM–5:00PM; September–May: Saturdays, 9:00AM–3:00PM

This demanding math- and science-oriented school on the south side of Chicago requires students to complete two Interprofessional Projects before graduation. IPROs bring together undergraduates and graduates from different academic disciplines to complete a task as a team. Recent IPROs have ranged from designing a new football stadium for the Chicago Bears to improving automated patient monitoring systems.

AT A GLANCE

Selectivity Rating	83
Range SAT I Math	630–730
Average SAT I Math	681
Range SAT I Verbal	550–650
Average SAT I Verbal	602
Average ACT Composite	28
Average GPA	3.6
Student/Faculty Ratio	12:1

CAMPUS TOURS

Appointment	Preferred
Dates	Year-round
Times	Mon–Fri, 9AM–5PM; Sat, 9AM–2PM
Average Length	1 hour

ON-CAMPUS APPOINTMENTS

Admissions

Start Date–Juniors	Anytime
Appointment	Preferred
Advance Notice	Yes
Saturdays	Yes
Average Length	30 min.
Info Sessions	Yes

Faculty and Coaches

Dates/Times	Year-round
Arrangements	Contact Admissions Office 2 weeks prior

CLASS VISITS

Dates	Academic year
Arrangements	Contact Admissions Office

TRANSPORTATION

Chicago's Midway Airport is 10 miles away from campus; O'Hare International Airport is 25 miles away from campus. CTA/transit/taxis are available at both airports. Take the Blue Line from O'Hare to the Green Line, which then takes you to campus. Take the Orange Line from Midway, transfer to the Green Line, which takes you to campus. Amtrak trains and Greyhound/Trailways buses provide service to Chicago's Loop area. For public transportation within Chicago, use either the CTA north-south subway or the CTA Lake/Dan Ryan rapid transit. On the CTA north-south subway, take the Englewood A train or the Jackson Park B train and get off at the ITT/Bronsville stop. Turn right onto State St. and walk two blocks north to the 33rd St. exit. Turn left onto 33rd St. to Perlstein Hall. On the CTA Lake/Dan Ryan rapid transit, take the A or B train and get off at ITT/Bronsville stop. Proceed north to the 33rd St. exit. Turn right onto 33rd St.

FIND YOUR WAY

From the Dan Ryan Expy./I-90/94, take the 31st St. exit. Go east on 31st about one block to State St. Turn right at State and proceed to 33rd St. and turn right. Perlstein Hall is on the NW corner of 33rd and State Sts. **From Lake Shore Dr.,** exit at 31st St.; turn right onto 31st and proceed west to State St. Turn left (south) on State for two blocks to 33rd St. and turn right to Perlstein Hall. **From Stevenson Expy./I-55 or Eisenhower Expy./I-290,** exit at the Dan Ryan Expy. (Indiana exit) and proceed south to the 31st St. ramp and exit the expressway. Go south to 33rd St. and turn left (east) to Perlstein Hall.

STAY THE NIGHT

Nearby: Located on Chicago's famous Magnificent Mile, in the heart of the city's business and shopping district, the **Hotel Intercontinental** (505 North Michigan Ave.; 312-321-8880) features a full fitness center and a junior Olympic-sized swimming pool. One block off Magnificent Mile, **The Hyatt Regency Chicago** has a whopping 2,019 rooms and is attached to the 83-acre Illinois Center complex containing over 100 stores and 43 restaurants. For considerably less money, The **Days Inn** (644 North Lake Shore Dr.; 312-943-9200 or 800-541-3223 outside 312 and 708 area codes) is only four blocks from Magnificent Mile and offers views of Lake Michigan. There is also the **Best Western Grant Park Hotel** (1100 South Michigan Ave.; 312-922-2900), which offers safe, affordable, no-frills lodging. To obtain a discounted rate at any of the above hotels, mention the Illinois Institute of Technology when making reservations. Also, airport to hotel and hotel to airport transportation can be arranged via **Continental Air Transport**. For schedule information call 312-454-7800; for reservations call 312-454-7799 or 800-654-7871.

HIGHLIGHTS

ON CAMPUS

- S.R. Crown Hall
- McComick Tribune Center
- HUB rec center
- IIT Research Institute
- State Street Village

OFF CAMPUS

- Comiskey Park/U.S. Cellular Field
- Sears Tower
- Hancock Center
- Magnificent Mile
- Oprah Studios

KNOX COLLEGE

Office of Admission, 2 E. South St., Galesburg, IL 61401 • Telephone: 800-678-5669 • www.knox.edu/admission.xml • Email: admission@knox.edu

Hours: Monday–Friday, 8:00AM–4:30PM; Saturday (during term), 9:00AM–noon

Freedom to flourish is the motto of Knox College, a fabulous place to go to school located in the rural reaches of central Illinois. Knox students report receiving extremely generous financial aid packages and they praise the trimester system because it allows students to concentrate more on classes and take advantage of nice, long breaks between sessions.

HIGHLIGHTS

ON CAMPUS

- Old Main—Site of historic Lincoln-Douglas debates
- Old Knox County Jail
- Seymour Library
- Umbeck Science Center
- T. Fleming Fieldhouse

OFF CAMPUS

- Historic Seminary Street Shops and Restaurants
- Carl Sandburg Birthplace and State Historic Site
- Lake Storey Recreational Area
- Galesburg Railroad Museum
- Bishop Hill—National Historic Landmark

TRANSPORTATION

Greater Peoria Airport in Peoria and Quad Cities Airport in Moline are 40 minutes away from campus. The Admissions Office will send a representative to pick up visitors arriving at either airport; call 800-678-KNOX or 309-341-7100, at least one week in advance to make arrangements. Amtrak provides daily train service linking Galesburg to Chicago and to the West Coast. A college representative will pick you up at the station. Call the Admissions Office at least one week in advance to make arrangements.

FIND YOUR WAY

From the north, take I-74 East to Exit 46; take U.S. Rte. 34 W. to the Seminary St. exit. Turn left on Seminary St. and proceed to Main St. Turn left onto Main St. and proceed to Cherry St. Turn left on Cherry St. and cross South St. to the parking lot at the corner of Cherry and Berrien Streets. **From the south,** take I-74 West to Exit 48A (Main St.). Take Main St. to Cherry St. Turn left on Cherry St. and cross South St. to the parking lot at the corner of Cherry and Berrien Streets.

STAY THE NIGHT

Nearby: Galesburg offers a wide range of overnight accommodations, including some wonderful bed-and-breakfast options. **The Seacord House** (624 N. Cherry St.; 309-342-4107) is known for its hospitality and moderate prices. For a more upscale experience in Victorian luxury, try the **Fahnestock House** (591 N. Prairie St.; 309-344-0270) or the **Great House** (501 E. Losey St.; 309-342-8683). More conventional travelers will find comfortable, affordable accommodations with pool, breakfast, and other amenities at the **Country Inn and Suites** (907 W. Carl Sandburg Dr.; 309-344-4444), **Fairfield Inn** (905 W. Carl Sandburg Drive; 309-344-1911), or **Holiday Inn Express** (East Main St. at I-74; 309-343-7100). The **Best Western Prairie Inn** (east Main Street at I-74; 309-343-7151) offers full-service amenities with fine dining, cocktail lounge, pool, and recreational facilities.

AT A GLANCE

Selectivity Rating	81
Range SAT I Math	550–660
Range SAT I Verbal	550–680
Student/Faculty Ratio	12:1

CAMPUS TOURS

Appointment	Required
Dates	Year-round
Times	Weekdays and Saturdays during academic year
Average Length	1 hour

ON-CAMPUS APPOINTMENTS

Admissions

Start Date—Juniors	April 1
Appointment	Required
Advance Notice	Yes, 1 week
Saturdays	Sometimes
Average Length	1 hour
Info Sessions	No

Faculty and Coaches

Dates/Times	Academic year
Arrangements	Contact Admissions Office 1 week prior

CLASS VISITS

Dates	Academic year
Arrangements	Contact Admissions Office

LAKE FOREST COLLEGE

Admissions Office, 555 N. Sheridan Rd., Lake Forest, IL 60045 • Telephone: 800-828-4751 • www.lfc.edu • Email: admissions@lakeforest.edu

Hours: Monday–Friday, 8:30AM–5:00PM; Saturday, 9:00AM–noon

An excellent combination of strongly challenging academics, competitive Division III sports, great financial aid, and a choice location set this small liberal arts college apart from the pack. Lake Forest also boasts a gorgeous campus, good grub, and a safe suburban location on the well-to-do North Shore of Chicago.

AT A GLANCE

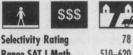

Selectivity Rating	78
Range SAT I Math	510–620
Average SAT I Math	573
Range SAT I Verbal	520–620
Average SAT I Verbal	570
Average ACT Composite	25
Average GPA	3.4
Student/Faculty Ratio	12:1

CAMPUS TOURS

Appointment	Preferred
Dates	Year-round
Times	Mon–Fri, 10AM, 11AM, 1PM & 2PM
Average Length	1 hour

ON-CAMPUS APPOINTMENTS

Admissions

Start Date—Juniors	Anytime
Appointment	Preferred
Advance Notice	Yes, 1 week
Saturdays	Yes
Average Length	45 min.

Faculty and Coaches

Dates/Times	Academic year
Arrangements	Contact Admissions Office 1 week prior

CLASS VISITS

Dates	Academic year
Arrangements	Contact Admissions Office

TRANSPORTATION

O'Hare International Airport (Chicago) is 25 miles away from campus. Bus and limousine service are available from the airport to campus. Call O'Hare Midway Limousine (847-234-4550) and ask for shared ride service. Make arrangements one day in advance. Amtrak trains and Greyhound buses serve Chicago. The METRA/Chicago and North Western North Line commuter railroad serves Lake Forest.

FIND YOUR WAY

From the North, take I-94 S. from Milwaukee. Just past the Wisconsin-Illinois border, stay left to get onto U.S. Rte. 41. Continue south on U.S. 41 to Deerpath in Lake Forest. Exit and turn left (east) on Deerpath toward the town and the college. Proceed east through the Lake Forest business district and cross the railroad tracks. At the second stop sign beyond the tracks, you will be at Sheridan Rd., facing the entrance to the college's North Campus. For Middle Campus and most college offices, turn right (south) onto Sheridan and go one block to College Rd. Turn left (east) into the college. The entrance to South Campus is at Maplewood and Sheridan. **From the West/Southwest,** take I-294 (Tri-State Tollway), which becomes I-94 N. to Illinois Rte. 60 (Town Line Rd.). Exit and turn right (east) on Rte. 60. At the first stop light, turn left (north) on Illinois 43 (Waukegan Rd.). At the first light, turn right (east) on Deerpath toward the town and the college. **From Chicago,** take I-94 N. (the Edens Expy) toward Waukegan. When I-94 splits off toward Milwaukee, stay on the Edens, which becomes U.S. 41. Exit at Deerpath in Lake Forest and turn right (east) on Deerpath toward the town and the college.

STAY THE NIGHT

Nearby: Our first choice for convenience and charm is the English-style **Deer Path Inn** (255 E. Illinois Rd.; 847-234-2280), a 10-minute walk away from the college. Prices are expensive and include a full buffet breakfast. Less costly lodgings may be found at the **Highland Park Courtyard by Marriott** (2005 Lake Cook Rd., Highland Park; 847-831-3338), at the junction of U.S. 41 and I-94. Amenities include an indoor pool and an exercise room, and it's only 20 minutes away from campus.

HIGHLIGHTS

ON CAMPUS
- Donnelley Library & Freeman Library
- Sonnenschein Gallery
- Sports Center
- Dixon Science Center
- Career Advancement Center

OFF CAMPUS
- Bank Lane Bistro
- Chicago Botanic Garden
- Lake Region Historical Society
- Cuneo Museum and Gardens
- The Art Institute of Chicago

NORTHWESTERN UNIVERSITY

1801 Hinman Ave., PO Box 3060, Evanston, IL 60208-3060 • Telephone: 847-491-7271 • www.ugadm.northwestern.edu • Email: ug-admission@northwestern.edu

Hours: Monday–Friday, 8:30AM–5:00PM; Saturday, 9:00AM–12:30PM

Located minutes away from Chicago in Evanston, Illinois, Northwestern University is an academically tremendous school that provides a nationally-respected, comprehensive, liberal arts education for about 8,000 largely traditional students. Each spring, students look forward to Dillo Day, an annual anything goes, day-long event complete with bands, booths, food, and a whole lot of craziness.

HIGHLIGHTS

ON CAMPUS

- Shakespeare Garden
- Dearborn Observatory
- Norris Student Center
- Henry Crown Sports Pavilion and Acquatic Center
- The lakefill on Lake Michigan

OFF CAMPUS

- The Charles Gates Dawes House Museum
- The Mitchell Museum of the American Indian
- Evanston Art Center
- Grosse Point Lighthouse
- Old Orchard Shopping Center (Westgate)

TRANSPORTATION

O'Hare International Airport in Chicago is 18 miles away from campus. Bus service is available from the airport to Northwester's Foster Walker Complex (and to Evanston's Holiday Inn and Omni Orrington Hotel). Amtrak trains and Greyhound/Trailways buses provide service to Chicago. From there, take the CTA rapid-transit system to Howard St. and transfer to the Evanston train. Get off at the Davis St. stop and walk east on Davis St. to Orrington Ave.; walk north on Orrington to Clark St., then east on Clark to Hinman Ave. and the Admissions Office.

FIND YOUR WAY

From I-94 (Edens Expy.), take the Dempster St. east exit. From Dempster, head north on Hinman Ave. to the Admissions Office (at Clark St.).

STAY THE NIGHT

Nearby: There's a range of choices in Evanston. The **Omni Orrington Hotel** (1710 Orrington Ave.; 847-866-8700) is one block away from the southern tip of the university. Its rates are expensive, although on the weekends you may be able to get a moderate rate. The **Hilton Garden Inn** (1818 Maple Avenue; 847-475-6400), is about six blocks away from campus. The **Homestead** (1625 Hinman Ave.; 847-475-3300), just two blocks south of the campus and the lake, has 10 guest rooms and a French restaurant. Another bargain is the **Best Western University Plaza** (1501 Sherman Ave.; 847-491-6400), just four blocks away from campus. Its rates include a breakfast buffet. Other alternatives are the **Hampton Inn and Suites** (Old Orchard Rd.; 847-583-1111—20 minutes away from campus), and the **Doubletree Hotel North Shore** (9599 Skokie Blvd.; 847-679-7000—15 minutes away from campus).

A Little Farther: Check the University of Chicago entry for alternatives a little farther away. Winnetka, covered in the Lake Forest College entry, is not too far north of Evanston, and the Chateau Des Fleurs listed there might interest you.

AT A GLANCE

Selectivity Rating	98
Range SAT I Math	660–750
Average SAT I Math	703
Range SAT I Verbal	640–730
Average SAT I Verbal	675
Average ACT Composite	30
Student/Faculty Ratio	7:1

CAMPUS TOURS

Appointment	Not required
Dates	Year-round
Times	Varies according to time of year
Average Length	120 min.

ON-CAMPUS APPOINTMENTS

Admissions

Appointment	Not required
Advance Notice	Other
Saturdays	Sometimes
Info Sessions	Yes

Faculty and Coaches

Dates/Times	Year-round
Arrangements	Contact coach directly

CLASS VISITS

Dates	Year-round
Arrangements	Contact Admissions Office

UNIVERSITY OF CHICAGO

Admissions Office, 1116 E. 59 St.,
Chicago, IL 60637 • Telephone: 773-702-8650 • www.uchicago.edu •

Hours: Monday–Friday, 8:30am–5:00pm

The storied University of Chicago "is a place that you will love and hate for the same reasons. You have never worked harder, done more, or slept less, but you will never learn as much or be so greatly rewarded," according to a student who seems to share the general sentiment. A rigorous core curriculum consumes about one-third of the total credits required for graduation. Authors Susan Sontag and Kurt Vonnegut, Jr. are alums.

AT A GLANCE

Selectivity Rating	95
Range SAT I Math	650–750
Range SAT I Verbal	660–750
Student/Faculty Ratio	4:1

CAMPUS TOURS

Dates	Year-round
Times	Varies throughout the year
Average Length	1 hour

ON-CAMPUS APPOINTMENTS

Admissions

Start Date—Juniors	June
Appointment	Required
Advance Notice	1 week
Saturdays	Sometimes
Info Sessions	Year-round

Faculty and Coaches

Dates/Times	Year-round
Arrangements	Contact coach directly as soon as possible

CLASS VISITS

Dates	Academic year
Arrangements	Contact faculty directly

TRANSPORTATION

Chicago's Midway Airport is 10 miles away from campus. The C.W. Airport Service Bus (312-493-2700) provides service to Ida Noyes Hall on campus. Taxis also are available for the ride to campus. O'Hare is a one-hour drive from campus. The C.W. Airport Service Bus also regularly travels from O'Hare to campus throughout the day and evening. From Palmer House, take a taxi or an Illinois Central train to campus (see below). Amtrak trains provide service to Chicago's Loop area. From there, take a taxi directly to campus or take the #207 bus or a taxi to a Metra commuter train station on Michigan Ave. Greyhound/Trailways buses also serve the Loop area. From the bus stations, walk east to Michigan Ave. and Van Buren St. The station entrances are on the west side of the street are well marked. Take a southbound train, get off at 59th St., and walk about six blocks west to the Admissions Office.

FIND YOUR WAY

From major routes near Chicago, take an expressway to I-55 N. (the Stevenson Expressway). Take I-55 N. to Lake Shore Dr. S. (U.S. Rte. 41). Follow Lake Shore Dr. S. to the 57th St. exit (Museum of Science and Industry). Follow the curve (Cornell Dr.) to the fourth right turn, the Midway Plaisance. Take the Midway approximately six blocks west to Woodlawn Ave.; turn right on Woodlawn for one block, then turn left on 59th St. at Rockefeller Chapel. Follow 59th St. for a-block-and-a-half to the Admissions Office.

STAY THE NIGHT

Nearby: The **International House** (1414 E. 59th St.; 312-753-2270) has single rooms available in a dorm-style atmosphere on campus at a very inexpensive rate during the summer months (through mid-September). Rooms also may be available later during the academic year. Fairly close to campus is the **Ramada Inn Lake Shore** (4900 S. Lake Shore Dr.; 312-288-5800), with student rates in the moderate range (if available). Two reasonably-priced hotels are located about five miles away from campus. The **Blackstone Hotel** (636 S. Michigan Ave.; 312-427-4300) has an inexpensive student rate that includes a continental breakfast. The **Best Western Grant Park Hotel** (1100 S. Michigan Ave.; 312-922-2900) is within walking distance to most museums and shops. Rates are lower during the week, and package specials are available; check for details.

HIGHLIGHTS

ON CAMPUS

- Joseph Regenstein Library
- David & Alfred Smart Museum of Art
- Bartlett Gymnasium
- Court Theatre

OFF CAMPUS

- Art Institute of Chicago
- Adler Planetarium & Astronomy Museum
- Shedd Aquarium
- Museum of Science & Industry
- Comiskey Park

UNIVERSITY OF ILLINOIS AT URBANA—CHAMPAIGN

Admissions Office, 901 West Illinois, Urbana, IL 61801 • Telephone: 217-333-0302 • www.uiuc.edu • Email: admissions@oar.uiuc.edu

Hours: Monday–Friday, 8:30AM–5:00PM

The University of Illinois is a very big state school with a very big Greek system that is a great bargain for in-state students (which is pretty much everybody). A good education is easily within reach for students who don't need to be led by the hand to find it. Film critic Roger Ebert is an alum.

HIGHLIGHTS

ON CAMPUS
- The Krannert Art Museum
- The Krannert Center for Performing Arts
- Assembly Hall
- The Beckman Institute
- The Japan House

OFF CAMPUS
- Lake of the Woods Park
- The Virginia Theater
- Allerton Park
- Tuscola Outlet Mall
- Jarlings Custard Cup

TRANSPORTATION

Willard Airport, owned and operated by the University, is five miles away from campus. Taxis, limousines, and rental cars are available at the airport for the trip to campus. Amtrak provides daily service to Champaign from Chicago and from the south (through Memphis). The Amtrak station is in downtown Champaign, approximately one mile away from campus. Taxis and city bus services are available from the station. Greyhound/Trailways provide national and regional service to Champaign. The bus station is one mile away from campus.

FIND YOUR WAY

From I-74 (E. and W.), take the Lincoln Ave. exit. Turn south on Lincoln Ave.; after 1.75 miles, turn right onto Illinois St. Proceed for one block to the Campus Visitors' Center on the left in the Levis Faculty Center. **From the north,** head south on I-57 to I-74. Head east on I-74 to the Lincoln Ave. exit; then follow the preceding directions from that point. **From the south,** head north on I-57 to Exit 235, the junction with I-72. Head east; as you arrive in Champaign, I-72 becomes University Ave. Follow University Ave. east through Champaign, into Urbana, to Lincoln Ave. (approximately 3.5 miles). Turn right (south) on Lincoln; after the second light, turn right onto Illinois St. Proceed for one block to the Campus Visitors' Center, which is on the left in the Levis Faculty Center.

STAY THE NIGHT

Nearby: You have two choices right on campus. The **Quality Hotel** (302 John St., Champaign; 217-384-2100) offers a continental breakfast. Its sister hotel, the **Clarion** (2001 Neil St., Champaign; 217-352-7891), about a 10-minute drive from the Admissions Office, has an indoor pool, sauna, whirlpool, and weight room. Also on campus is **Illini Union** (1401 W. Green, Urbana; 217-333-1241), with rooms available at the low end of the moderate range. It's within walking distance of the campus tour and has a bowling alley, eating facilities, and a game room. Several inexpensive choices are within five miles of the school. **Jumer's Castle Lodge** (Lincoln Square, Urbana; 217-384-8800) is less than two miles away from the university and offers an indoor pool, sauna, and Jacuzzi.

AT A GLANCE

Selectivity Rating	85
Range SAT I Math	600–720
Average SAT I Math	660
Range SAT I Verbal	550–670
Average SAT I Verbal	613
Average ACT Composite	27
Student/Faculty Ratio	15:1

CAMPUS TOURS

Appointment	Required
Dates	Year-round
Times	Mon–Fri, 10AM & 1PM
Average Length	1 hour

ON-CAMPUS APPOINTMENTS

Admissions

Start Date–Juniors	N/A
Info Sessions	Year-round

Faculty and Coaches

Dates/Times	Year-round
Arrangements	Contact Admissions Office 2 weeks prior

CLASS VISITS

Dates	Academic year
Arrangements	Contact Visiting Center

WHEATON COLLEGE (IL)

Admissions Office, Student Services Building, Second Floor, North End, Suite 201, 501 E. College Ave., Wheaton, IL 60187 • Telephone: 800-222-2419 • www.wheaton.edu/admissions • Email: admissions@wheaton.edu

Hours: Monday–Friday, 8:00AM–5:00PM; Saturday (select), 8:00AM–noon

Ultra-religious Wheaton College, a strong evangelical and academic school in the far-flung reaches of suburban Chicago, is outwardly devoted to the growth of God's work on earth and also academically well-respected. If the integration of faith and learning is what you want out of college, Wheaton is arguably the best school in the nation with a Christ-based worldview.

AT A GLANCE

Selectivity Rating	91
Range SAT I Math	610–700
Average SAT I Math	658
Range SAT I Verbal	620–710
Average SAT I Verbal	661
Average ACT Composite	28
Average GPA	3.71
Student/Faculty Ratio	11:1

CAMPUS TOURS

Dates	Year-round
Times	Sept–May: Mon–Fri, 3 tours daily
Average Length	1 hour

ON-CAMPUS APPOINTMENTS

Admissions

Start Date–Juniors	Aug 15 before senior year
Appointment	Required
Advance Notice	2 weeks
Saturdays	Sometimes
Info Sessions	Year-round

Faculty and Coaches

Dates/Times	Year-round
Arrangements	Contact Admissions Office 2 weeks prior

CLASS VISITS

Dates	Year-round
Arrangements	Contact Admissions Office

TRANSPORTATION

O'Hare International Airport in Chicago is 20 miles away from campus. Call Airtran O'Hare (800-851-0200) to arrange for transportation from the airport to campus. Amtrak trains and Greyhound/Trailways buses also serve Chicago.

FIND YOUR WAY

From the east, take I-88 W. and exit at Naperville Rd. Go north to Roosevelt Rd. in Wheaton. Turn east and go two blocks to Chase St. Turn north and go nine blocks to 418 Chase. **From the south,** take I-55 N. to I-355 N.; exit I-355 to Roosevelt Rd. (Rte. 38). Proceed west to Chase St. in Wheaton. Turn north and go nine blocks to 418 Chase. **From the west,** take I-88, Rte. 56 (Butterfield Rd.) east to Naperville Rd., then go north to Roosevelt Rd. in Wheaton. Turn east two blocks to Chase St. Turn north to 418 Chase. **From the north,** take the Tri-state Tollway 294 S. to I-88. Go west on I-88 to the Naperville Road exit. Proceed north to Roosevelt Rd. in Wheaton. Turn east and go two blocks to Chase St. Turn north and go nine blocks to 418 Chase.

STAY THE NIGHT

Nearby: The **Wheaton Inn** (301 W. Roosevelt Rd.; 630-690-2600), one mile away from the college, is your closest and most expensive option. (All the rooms have telephones in the bathroom and down duvets.) You will find lower rates (with the special rate for college visitors) about three miles away from the campus at the **Carol Stream Holiday Inn** (200 S. Gary Ave., Carol Stream; 630-665-3000). For a very small additional charge you can obtain a pass to the Wheaton Sports Center. You have several other choices about five miles to the south of campus. Two of these are the moderately-priced **Hilton Inn** (3003 Corporate West Dr., Lyle/Naperville; 630-505-0900 or 800-HILTONS) and the less expensive **Courtyard by Marriott** (1205 E. Diehl Rd., Naperville; 630-505-0550 or 800-321-2211). Both have indoor pools and exercise rooms. A more basic and less expensive option is **Travel Lodge** (1617 N. Naperville-Wheaton Rd., Naperville; 630-505-0200 or 800-255-3050), also five miles away. The inexpensive rate (a special rate for college visitors) includes a continental breakfast.

A Little Farther: The **Harrison House Bed and Breakfast** (26 N. Eagle St., Naperville; 630-355-4665) is within walking distance of shops, restaurants, and the historic Naperville settlement. Harrison House has moderate rates that include a full breakfast. Golf courses and antique stores are in the area. Wheaton is due west of Chicago. If you want more urban alternatives, check the entries for the University of Chicago and Northwestern.

HIGHLIGHTS

ON CAMPUS

- Billy Graham Center
- Wade Center (collection of English authors including C.S. Lewis)

OFF CAMPUS

- Wheaton is 25 miles outside of Chicago
- Ravinia Music Festival
- Art Institute
- Chicago Field Museum
- Sears Tower and Hancock Building

1- DePauw University
2- Earlham College
3- Indiana University
4- University of Notre Dame
5- Purdue University
6- Rose-Hulman Inst. of Tech.
7- Valparaiso Univ.
8- Wabash College

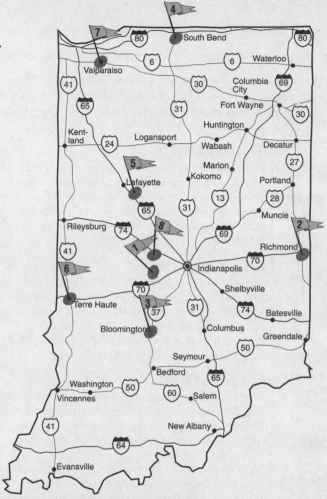

Indiana	DePauw Univ.	Earlham Coll.	Indiana Univ.	Purdue Univ.	Rose-Hulman	Univ. Notre Dame	Valparaiso U.	Wabash Coll.	Fort Wayne	Gary	Indianapolis
DePauw Univ.	—	108	46	59	30	176	153	28	165	145	36
Earlham College	108	—	122	135	147	173	229	120	94	226	73
Indiana Univ.	46	122	—	105	56	198	209	73	174	198	51
Purdue Univ.	59	135	105	—	107	110	98	28	117	90	55
Rose-Hulman	30	147	56	107	—	215	179	57	204	178	74
Univ. Notre Dame	176	173	198	110	215	—	56	177	79	58	140
Valparaiso Univ.	153	229	209	98	179	56	—	119	108	26	158
Wabash Coll.	28	120	73	28	57	177	119	—	163	118	50
Fort Wayne	165	94	174	117	204	79	108	163	—	132	132
Gary	145	226	198	90	178	58	26	118	132	—	153
Indianapolis	36	73	51	55	74	140	158	50	132	153	—

DePauw University

Office of Admission, 101 East Seminary St.,
Greencastle, IN 46135 • Telephone: 800-447-2495 • www.depauw.edu/admission/ •
Email: admission@depauw.edu

Hours: Monday–Friday, 8:00AM–5:00PM; Saturday (September–May), 8:00AM–4:00PM

A Winter Term during which students do things that are not done in the classroom and excellent financial assistance separate this small liberal arts school from the pack (many students say they chose DePauw over the likes of Harvard and Vanderbilt because they couldn't pass up the bargain). A gargantuan Greek system provides most campus social life.

AT A GLANCE

Selectivity Rating	85
Range SAT I Math	570–670
Average SAT I Math	620
Range SAT I Verbal	560–650
Average SAT I Verbal	610
Average ACT Composite	27
Average GPA	3.74
Student/Faculty Ratio	10:1

CAMPUS TOURS

Appointment	Preferred
Dates	Year-round
Times	Varies
Average Length	1 hour

ON-CAMPUS APPOINTMENTS

Admissions

Start Date—Juniors	After April 1
Appointment	Preferred
Advance Notice	Yes, 2 weeks
Saturdays	Sometimes
Average Length	45 min.
Info Sessions	Yes

Faculty and Coaches

Dates/Times	Year-round
Arrangements	Contact Admissions Office 2 weeks prior

CLASS VISITS

Dates	Academic year
Arrangements	Contact Admissions Office

Transportation

Indianapolis International Airport is 45 miles away from campus. The Admissions Office will provide transportation to campus for students traveling alone; call 800-447-2495 ten days to two weeks in advance to arrange for this service.

Find Your Way

From I-70, exit to State Road 231 N. and proceed seven-and-a-half miles into Greencastle. Turn left on Seminary Street. Travel three city blocks. The Admissions Office is located on the north side of the road; visitor parking is located to the east of the building.

Stay the Night

Nearby: The **Walden Inn** (2 Seminary Sq.; 765-653-2761) is a small hotel adjacent to DePauw's campus (within walking distance of the Admissions Office). Prices are moderate. Ask about the Gourmet Get-Away package, which includes dinner and champagne. You will also be able to use the university's athletic facilities, including an indoor swimming pool and tennis courts. The inn's dining room, the Different Drummer, is known throughout the state. Another lovely spot near campus is the **Commercial House Bed & Breakfast,** (765-653-6579). The moderate price includes a full breakfast, full work-out facility, and cable television in each room.

A Little Farther: There are three motels in Cloverdale (eight miles south of Greencastle where I-70 meets Rte. 231), all with inexpensive rooms: the **Best Inn** (R.R. 2; 765-795-3000); the **Dollar Inn** (R.R. 2; 765-795-6900); and the **Holiday Inn Express** (I-70 and Rte. 231; 765-795-5050 or 800-HOLIDAY). The Holiday Inn is a little more expensive than the others, but its price includes a buffet breakfast. **Days Inn** (Rte. 1; 765-795-6400), nine miles south of the university, has very inexpensive rates. Its special rates for DePauw visitors include a continental breakfast.

HIGHLIGHTS

ON CAMPUS

- DePauw University School of Music
- Roy O. West Library, Music Library, and the Prevo Science Library
- Cafe Roy coffee shop
- Memorial Student Union
- Bowman Park

OFF CAMPUS

- Indianapolis
- Cagles Mill Lake
- Turkey Run State Park
- Crawfordsville

EARLHAM COLLEGE

Admissions Office, National Rd. W.,
Richmond, IN 47374 • Telephone: 800-327-5426 • www.earlham.edu •
Email: admission@earlham.edu

Hours: Monday–Friday, 8:00AM–5:00PM; Saturday (select), 9:00AM–noon

Everybody from the president to the professors to the students is on a first name basis at Earlham College, a tiny Quaker-affiliated liberal arts school in Indiana. Earlhamites like the very challenging, but not overwhelming, classes and the fact that their voices carry a lot of weight with the administration. On campus, the atmosphere is one of tolerable weirdness, and activities include a student-run farm and a very popular gospel choir.

HIGHLIGHTS

ON CAMPUS
- Athletics and Wellness Center
- Joseph Moore Natural History Museum
- The Swing
- Trails and Rope Courses
- Equestrian Center

OFF CAMPUS
- Hayes Arboretum
- Wayne County Historic Museum
- Cope Environmental Center
- Whitewater Gorge
- Whitewater State Park

TRANSPORTATION

Dayton International Airport in Ohio is approximately 40 miles away from campus. For unaccompanied visiting students, the college provides complimentary round-trip shuttles between the airport and campus. Call 800-EARLHAM in advance to arrange for this transportation. Greyhound bus service is available to Richmond. The college provides complimentary transportation to and from the bus terminal; contact the Admissions Office to arrange for this service.

FIND YOUR WAY

The usual approach to Richmond is from I-70. Take exit 149A S. to U.S. Rte. 40 W. Turn right at the stoplight; Earlham is on the left, approximately three city blocks after this turn. On-campus signs will direct you to the Admissions Office.

STAY THE NIGHT

Nearby: A lovely bed-and-breakfast, **The Lantz House Inn** is located in Centerville, Indiana just four miles west of Earlham. Call 1-800-495-2689 and ask for the special Earlham rate. **Lee's Inn** (6030 National Rd. E.; 765-966-6559), a 20-minute drive away from the college, is a moderately-priced (breakfast included) lodging. It offers a variety of amenities, including queen-size beds and Jacuzzis. Ask for the special rate for Earlham visitors.

A Little Farther: Richmond is just west of the Ohio border. In Ohio, there are some interesting bed-and-breakfast choices that would make sense if you had reason to be in or near Dayton before or after your Earlham visit. In Dayton, one hour from Earlham, is **Price's Steamboat House Bed-and-Breakfast** (6 Josie St.; 937-223-2444), a 22-room Victorian mansion. Steamboat House is listed on the National Register of Historic Homes and is in a quiet, historical district near downtown Dayton.

AT A GLANCE

Selectivity Rating	79
Range SAT I Math	530–650
Average SAT I Math	590
Range SAT I Verbal	550–690
Average SAT I Verbal	620
Average ACT Composite	26
Average GPA	3.4
Student/Faculty Ratio	11:1

CAMPUS TOURS

Appointment	Required
Dates	Year-round
Times	Mon–Fri, 11AM & 3PM; Sat, 10AM & 11AM
Average Length	1 hour

ON-CAMPUS APPOINTMENTS

Admissions
Start Date–Juniors	Anytime during junior year
Appointment	Required
Advance Notice	Yes, 1 week
Saturdays	Yes
Average Length	1 hour
Info Sessions	Yes

Faculty and Coaches
Dates/Times	Academic year
Arrangements	Contact either Admissions Office or coach 2 weeks prior

CLASS VISITS

Dates	Academic year
Arrangements	Contact Admissions Office

INDIANA UNIVERSITY—BLOOMINGTON

Office of Admissions, 300 N. Jordan Ave.,
Bloomington, IN 47405-1106 • Telephone: 812-855-0661 • www.iub.edu •
Email: iuadmit@indiana.edu

Hours: Monday–Friday, 8:00AM–5:00PM; Saturday, 8:00AM–noon (during academic year)

Bloomington, home of Indiana University, is the perfect college town. It's not a big city, but it's always open to students. The beautiful campus is home to top-notch business and journalism schools as well as a competitive School of Music. Socially, the Greek system and Hoosier basketball are predominant.

AT A GLANCE

Selectivity Rating	74
Range SAT I Math	500–610
Average SAT I Math	556
Range SAT I Verbal	490–600
Average SAT I Verbal	543
Average ACT Composite	24
Student/Faculty Ratio	20:1

CAMPUS TOURS

Appointment	Required
Dates	Academic year
Times	Mon–Fri, 10AM, 1:30PM, & 2:30PM; Sat, 9:00AM & noon
Average Length	1 hour

ON-CAMPUS APPOINTMENTS

Admissions

Start Date—Juniors	Anytime
Appointment	Required
Advance Notice	2 weeks
Saturdays	Sometimes
Info Sessions	Year-round

Faculty and Coaches

Dates/Times	Year-round
Arrangements	Contact Admissions Office 2 weeks prior

CLASS VISITS

Dates	Academic year
Arrangements	Contact Admissions Office

TRANSPORTATION

Indianapolis International Airport is 50 miles away from campus. For transportation between the airport and campus, call either the Bloomington Shuttle Service (1-800-589-6004) or limousine services (1-800-888-4639, 1-812-339-7269, 1-800-589-6004). Greyhound Bus Lines also stop in Bloomington.

FIND YOUR WAY

From the north, take Indiana Rte. 37 S. to the first Bloomington exit (College Ave.), then drive approximately three-and-a-half miles to the second stoplight. Turn left on State Rte. 45/46 and drive a mile to the second stoplight (Indiana State Police Post on the corner) and turn right. Proceed to the next traffic light (approximately half a mile) and turn left onto 17th St. As you reach the crest of the hill, turn right onto Jordan Ave. Proceed on Jordan through two traffic lights; then, proceed through the next stop sign. The Admissions Office is immediately on the left. **From the west and southwest,** take Indiana Rte. 45 or 48; then turn left onto Indiana Rte. 37 bypass. Continue north, then turn right onto the Rte. 46 bypass. At the fourth light (Indiana State Police Post on the right), turn right, and follow the preceding directions from the Indiana State Police Post. **From the east,** follow Indiana Rte. 46, which becomes E. 3rd St. in Bloomington. Follow 3rd St. to Jordan Ave. and turn right on Jordan. The Admissions Office is on the right, just past the circular intersection.

STAY THE NIGHT

Nearby: The only place within walking distance is the on-campus **Indiana Memorial Union** (900 E. Seventh St.; 812-855-2536.). The Union, with approximately 186 guest rooms, is a university-owned facility. Rates are moderate, but bookings are tight. If you are visiting on a football weekend or holiday, be sure to reserve a place early.

A Little Farther: There are several chain hotel/motels in the area and a number of bed-and-breakfast facilities. The Monroe County Convention and Visitors Bureau (1-800-800-0037) can provide up to date information on hotel availability and special event activities. Also, Bloomington is located within 20 to 45 minutes of three state parks (Brown County in Nashville, 812-988-6406; McCormick's Creek in Spencer, 812-829-4881; and Spring Mill in Mitchell, (812-849-4129), which offer lodge facilities.

HIGHLIGHTS

ON CAMPUS

- Indiana Memorial Union
- Art Museum
- Lilly Library
- Assembly Hall
- Student Recreational Sports Center

OFF CAMPUS

- Downtown Square
- Kirkwood Avenue
- Brown County State Park
- Chorten/Tibetan Culture Center
- Lake Monroe

PURDUE UNIVERSITY—WEST LAFAYETTE

Office of Admissions, 1080 Schleman Hall,
West Lafayette, IN 47907 • Telephone: 765-494-1776 • www.purdue.edu/admissions •
Email: admissions@purdue.edu

Hours: Monday–Friday, 8:00AM–5:00PM; Saturdays (during fall and spring semesters), 9:00AM–noon

Purdue University in Indiana is one of the great buys of higher education, especially for Hoosiers, who make up the vast majority of the career-minded, math-oriented student population. Great programs in business and engineering (one in five pursues an engineering degree) and a hopping Greek scene are other highlights. Neil Armstrong, the first person to walk on the moon, is an alum.

HIGHLIGHTS

ON CAMPUS
- Purdue Memorial Union
- Recreational Sports Center
- Fountain areas
- Libraries
- Sporting events

OFF CAMPUS
- Wolf Park
- Wabash Heritage Trail
- Ft. Quiatenon

TRANSPORTATION

Indianapolis International is approximately 65 miles away from campus. The Lafayette Limo Service, which is not affiliated with the university, provides round-trip shuttle service to and from campus for a fee; call 765-497-3828 to make arrangements. Purdue also has its own airport, serviced by commuter flights from Chicago and Indianapolis. Amtrak trains and major bus lines service Lafayette and W. Lafayette.

FIND YOUR WAY

Greater Lafayette can be reached by U.S. Rtes. 52 and 231, I-65, or Indiana Rtes. 25, 26, 38, and 43. The university is near the intersection of Indiana Rte. 26 (State St.) and Grant St. The Visitor Information Center is at 504 Northwestern Ave.

STAY THE NIGHT

Nearby: The inexpensive **Union Club** (765-494-8900) is conveniently located on campus. The **University Inn** (3001 Northwestern Ave.; 765-463-5511) is a mile-and-a-half away. Rates are at the low end of the moderate range, and there is an indoor pool, sauna, Jacuzzi, and exercise room.

A Little Farther: Many chain hotels/motels in the Lafayette/West Lafayette area. Check chain websites for more information.

AT A GLANCE

Selectivity Rating	75
Range SAT I Math	530–660
Average SAT I Math	595
Range SAT I Verbal	500–610
Average SAT I Verbal	555
Average ACT Composite	26
Student/Faculty Ratio	16:1

CAMPUS TOURS

Appointment	Required
Dates	Academic year
Times	Mon–Fri, 9AM, 10AM,1PM, & 2PM; Sat, 9:30am
Average Length	120 min.

ON-CAMPUS APPOINTMENTS

Admissions
Start Date–Juniors	Anytime
Saturdays	Yes

Faculty and Coaches
Dates/Times	Year-round
Arrangements	Contact Athletic Department 2 weeks prior

CLASS VISITS

Dates	Academic year
Arrangements	Contact Admissions Office

ROSE-HULMAN INSTITUTE OF TECHNOLOGY

Office of Admissions, 5500 Wabash Avenue, CM 1, Terre Haute, IN 47803-3999 •
Telephone: 800-552-0725 (IN), 800-248-7448 (outside IN) • www.rose-hulman.edu/admissions •
Email: admis.ofc@rose-hulman.edu

Hours: Monday–Friday, 8:00AM–5:00PM (closed noon–1:00PM

Professors and students alike are "wacky math and science geeks" at tiny Rose-Hulman Institute of Technology in Indiana, the "best undergraduate engineering school in the nation." It's a good thing professors are committed to helping students because they really pile on the work and jack up the difficulty level in the stressful but rewarding courses.

AT A GLANCE

Selectivity Rating	90
Range SAT I Math	640–720
Average SAT I Math	680
Range SAT I Verbal	570–670
Average SAT I Verbal	620
Average ACT Composite	29
Student/Faculty Ratio	13:1

CAMPUS TOURS

Appointment	Required
Dates	Year-round
Times	Mon–Fri, 8:30AM & 1:30PM
Average Length	120 min.

ON-CAMPUS APPOINTMENTS

Admissions

Start Date–Juniors	April 1
Appointment	Required
Advance Notice	Yes, 1 week
Saturdays	No
Average Length	45 min.
Info Sessions	Yes

Faculty and Coaches

Dates/Times	Year-round
Arrangements	Contact Admissions Office 1 week prior

CLASS VISITS

Dates	Academic year
Arrangements	Contact Admissions Office

TRANSPORTATION

Taxis are available. Indianapolis International Airport is the nearest commercial airport to the campus.

FIND YOUR WAY

West of Indianapolis on I-70, exit on Exit 11, go north three miles to U.S. 40. Turn right. The entrance is a quarter mile on the left.

STAY THE NIGHT

Nearby: Your choices include the **Fairfield Inn, Holiday Inn, Knights Inn, Comfort Inn, Drury Inn, Hampton Inn,** and **Days Inn.**

HIGHLIGHTS

ON CAMPUS
• Sports and Recreation Center
• Hatfield Hall

OFF CAMPUS
• Honey Creek Mall
• Indiana State University
• Movie theaters

UNIVERSITY OF NOTRE DAME

Office of Undergraduate Admissions, 220 Main Building, Notre Dame, IN 46556 • Telephone: 574-631-7505 • www.admissions.nd.edu • Email: admissio.1@nd.edu

Hours: Monday–Friday, 8:00AM–5:00PM; Saturday (fall and winter), 8:00AM–noon

The University of Notre Dame is the most famous Catholic university in the country and with good reason: it's a great school with an almost mythical tradition. A definite Catholic core curriculum includes the Freshman Year of Studies program, which prescribes the entire freshman curriculum. Students say it's tough, but after graduation, "Domers get jobs."

HIGHLIGHTS

ON CAMPUS

- Grotto
- The Dome (main building)
- Basilica of the Sacred Heart
- Notre Dame Stadium
- Eck Center

OFF CAMPUS

- College Football Hall of Fame
- Morris Civic Auditorium
- East Race Waterway (whitewater rafting)
- Bendix Woods Park
- Studebaker National Museum

TRANSPORTATION

South Bend Regional Airport in South Bend, Indiana is four miles away from campus. USAir and Northwest Airlines provide direct connecting flights into the airport; United Express and American Eagle Airlines have several daily shuttle flights in from Chicago's O'Hare International Airport. Other airlines fly to South Bend from other Midwestern cities. Taxis are always available at the airport's terminal entrance for the ride to campus. Amtrak and South Shore railroads serve South Bend from Chicago. Taxis are available at the train station for the ride to campus. Bus transportation to the area is provided by Greyhound and United Limo bus lines through their terminals at the South Bend Regional Airport.

FIND YOUR WAY

Approach S. Bend on the Indiana Toll Rd. (I-80/I-90) and exit at Interchange 77. Proceed south on U.S. Rte. 31/33. Turn east on Angela Blvd., and at the next traffic light, turn north on Notre Dame Ave. As you approach the campus, turn right on the drive between the Hesburgh Center and the University Club. Follow the signs to the visitor parking area, which is located to the south of the stadium, near the Alumni-Senior Club.

STAY THE NIGHT

Nearby: The on-campus **Morris Inn** (574-631-2000) has a restaurant and overlooks the golf course. You also enjoy athletic privileges, including racquetball, tennis, and golf. Prices are at the low end of the moderate range. Five minutes away is a small, charmingly decorated hotel, the **Jamison Inn** (1404 N. Ivy Rd.; 574-277-9682). Rates are moderate and include breakfast. For a traditional bed-and-breakfast, consider the **Queen Anne Inn** (420 W. Washington; 574-234-5959), about one mile away from the school. The guest rooms (all with private baths) are named for birds in the area. The moderate price includes a wonderful full breakfast. Simple, inexpensive accommodations may be found at the **Signature Inn Hotel** (220 Dixie Way S.; 574-277-3211), five minutes away from campus. There is an outdoor pool and a free breakfast. A **Marriott Hotel** (123 N. St. Joseph St.; 574-234-2000) is about 10 minutes away from campus in the downtown area.

AT A GLANCE

Selectivity Rating	98
Range SAT I Math	650–730
Average SAT I Math	685
Range SAT I Verbal	620–720
Average SAT I Verbal	665
Average ACT Composite	31
Student/Faculty Ratio	12:1

CAMPUS TOURS

Appointment	Required
Dates	Year-round
Times	Jan–Dec: Mon–Fri, 11AM & 3PM; Sat 10AM & 11AM

ON-CAMPUS APPOINTMENTS

Admissions

Start Date–Juniors	N/A

Faculty and Coaches

Dates/Arrangements	Contact faculty or coach directly

CLASS VISITS

Dates	Academic year
Arrangements	Contact Admissions Office

VALPARAISO UNIVERSITY

Office of Admission, Kretzmann Hall,
Valparaiso, IN 46383-9978 • Telephone: 888-468-2576 • www.valpo.edu/admissions •
Email: undergrad.admissions@valpo.edu

Hours: Monday–Friday, 8:00AM–5:00PM; Saturday (academic term), 9:00AM–noon

Valparaiso University's greatest strength lies in its ability to offer a broad variety of majors across four different colleges (arts and sciences, nursing, business administration, and engineering) while still managing to provide its students with flexibility, small classes, and personal attention. Happy students say Valparaiso is a very prestigious university that offers a fabulous academic experience and the best education money can buy.

AT A GLANCE

Selectivity Rating	79
Range SAT I Math	530–650
Average SAT I Math	596
Range SAT I Verbal	530–630
Average SAT I Verbal	583
Average ACT Composite	26
Student/Faculty Ratio	13:1

CAMPUS TOURS

Appointment	Preferred
Dates	Varies
Times	Varies
Average Length	1 hour

ON-CAMPUS APPOINTMENTS

Admissions

Start Date—Juniors	Anytime
Appointment	Preferred
Advance Notice	Yes, 2 weeks
Saturdays	Sometimes
Average Length	45 min.
Info Sessions	Yes

Faculty and Coaches

Dates/Times	Academic year
Arrangements	Contact Admissions Office 2 weeks prior

CLASS VISITS

Dates	Academic year
Arrangements	Contact Admissions Office

TRANSPORTATION

Midway and Chicago O'Hare airports are the closest to campus. They're accessible by the Tri-State Bus service

FIND YOUR WAY

You can reach Valpo easily by plane, train, bus, or automobile. The campus is just an hour east of Chicago and two-and-a-half hours north of Indianapolis, which allows for convenient access from airports in Chicago (O'Hare or Midway), Gary, South Bend, or Indianapolis. The South Shore Railroad and Tri-State Bus Lines connect with Valparaiso, as do U.S. interstates 65, 80/90, and 94. For directions to campus, contact the Office of Admissions or visit our website at www.valpo.edu/admissions/visit. Please remember to check with the Office of Admissions before making airline reservations, as the office has limited services and hours.

STAY THE NIGHT

Nearby: Area lodging includes the **Courtyard by Marriott** (2301 U.S. 30 & Ind. 49, Valparaiso; 800-321-2211), **Inn at Aberdeen** (South Ind. 2, Valparaiso; 219-465-3753), **Econo Lodge** (713 Plaza Drive, Chesterton; 219-929-4416), **Radisson at Star Plaza** (I-65 & U.S. 30, Merrillville; 219-769-6311), **Fairfield Inn** (2101 U.S. 30 & Ind. 49, Valparaiso; 800-228-2800), **Gray Goose Inn** (350 Indian Boundary Rd., Chesterton; 219-926-5781), **Super 8** (2 Locations on Ind. 49, Valparaiso & Chesterton; 800-800-8000), **Red Roof Inn** (I-65 & U.S. 30, Merrillville; 219-738-2430), **Hampton Inn and Suites** (1451 Silhavy Rd.; 219-531-6424), **Valparaiso University Guild Bed & Breakfast,** contact Ruth Laube (219-462-5873), **Spring House Inn** (303 N. Mineral Springs Rd., Porter; 219-929-4600), **Holiday Inn Express** (U.S. 30 West, Valparaiso; 800-HOLIDAY), and **Indian Oak Resort** (558 Indian Boundary Rd., Chesterton; 219-926-2200).

HIGHLIGHTS

ON CAMPUS
- Chapel of the Resurrection
- Valparaiso University Center for the Arts
- Brauer Art Museum
- Athletic Recreation Center

OFF CAMPUS
- Indiana Dunes (Lake Michigan)
- Chicago
- Merrillville (for shopping, dining, etc.)

WABASH COLLEGE

PO Box 301, 301 W. Wabash Avenue,
Crawfordsville, IN 47933 • Telephone: 800-345-5385 • www.wabash.edu/admissions/ •
Email: admissions@wabash.edu

Hours: Monday–Friday, 8:00AM–4:30PM

All-male Wabash College in rural Indiana is a bit more focused and rigorous than most liberal arts institutions. Students must complete a required liberal arts core, fulfill a major concentration, and pass comprehensive written and oral examinations in order to graduate. Students say this tiny enclave offers a profoundly rewarding academic experience that challenges students to a high degree of competition and self-improvement.

HIGHLIGHTS

ON CAMPUS
- Allen Athletic Center
- Wabash Chapel
- New Science facility under construction
- New Center of Inquiry for Liberal Arts
- Lilly Library

OFF CAMPUS
- Ben-Hur Museum, home of Lew Wallace, author of Ben-Hur
- Lane Place, home of Henry S. Lane, statesman-friend of A. Lincoln
- Shades State Park
- Turkey Run State Park

TRANSPORTATION
Wabash representatives will pick up visitors and return them to the airport. Indianapolis is the nearest airport, it's miles away.

FIND YOUR WAY
From the east: I-74 to exit 39, four miles to Crawfordsville. Turn left on U.S. 231. **From the west:** I-74 to exit 34. Turn south into Crawsfordville (five miles). **From the north:** I-65 to U.S. 231, south to Crawfordsville. Turn west onto W. Wabash Avenue. **From the south:** I-70 to U.S. 231 north to Crawfordsville. Turn west onto W. Wabash Avenue.

STAY THE NIGHT
Nearby: Accommodations in area include the **Holiday Inn, Comfort Inn, Elston Grove Bed Breakfast, Lew Wallace Inn,** and **Days Inn.**

AT A GLANCE

Selectivity Rating	86
Range SAT I Math	560–655
Average SAT I Math	609
Range SAT I Verbal	530–620
Average SAT I Verbal	576
Average ACT Composite	26
Average GPA	3.57
Student/Faculty Ratio	11:1

CAMPUS TOURS

Appointment	Preferred
Dates	Year-round
Times	Varies
Average Length	1 hour

ON-CAMPUS APPOINTMENTS

Admissions

Start Date—Juniors	Anytime
Appointment	Preferred
Advance Notice	Yes, 1 week
Saturdays	Sometimes
Average Length	30 min.
Info Sessions	Yes

Faculty and Coaches

Dates/Times	Academic year
Arrangements	Contact Admissions Office 1 week prior

CLASS VISITS

Dates	Academic year
Arrangements	Contact Admissions Office

1- **Cornell College**
2- **Grinnell College**
3- **University of Iowa**
4- **Iowa State University**

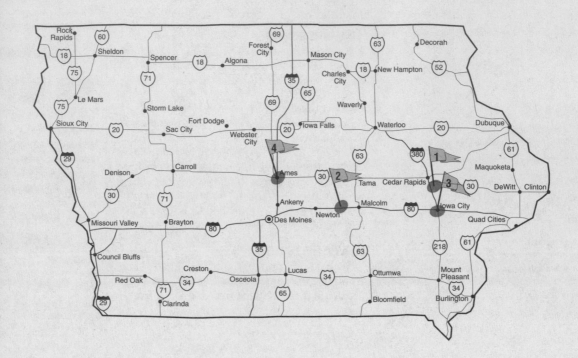

Iowa	Cornell College	Grinnell College	Iowa State Univ.	Univ. Iowa	Des Moines
Cornell College	—	79	113	19	130
Grinnell College	79	—	60	67	55
Iowa State Univ.	113	60	—	137	30
Univ. Iowa	19	67	137	—	112
Des Moines	130	55	30	112	—

CORNELL COLLEGE

Admissions Office, 600 First St. West, Mount Vernon, IA 52314-1098 •
Telephone: 800-747-1112 • www.cornellcollege.edu/admissions/ •
Email: admissions@cornellcollege.edu

Hours: Monday–Friday, 8:00AM–4:30PM; Saturday, by appointment; Summer: Monday–Friday, 8:00AM–4:00PM

Cornell's ultra-flexible One-Course-At-A-Time program offers one class for three-and-a-half weeks, then a four-day block break. There are nine blocks during the academic year and about 60 courses each term. Cornell University has asked Cornell College to change its name in the past, but Cornell College is actually two years older than the Ivy in Ithaca. Perhaps the upstart younger cousin ought to rename itself instead.

HIGHLIGHTS

ON CAMPUS
- Commons-Orange Carpet (student center)
- Cole Library
- Small Multi-Sports Center
- Kimmel Theatre (new state-of-the-art theater)
- McWethy Hall (newly renovated art building)
- King Chapel

OFF CAMPUS
- Ceder Rapids
- Iowa City
- Palisades State Park
- Uptown Mount Vernon
- Amana Colonies

TRANSPORTATION

The Eastern Iowa Airport is 17 miles (a 20-minute drive) away from campus. If you need transportation to campus, a shuttle for a reasonable fee is provided by the airport. The Greyhound and Jefferson Bus lines do connect in Cedar Rapids. The nearest Amtrack Station is 70 miles south in Mount Pleasant.

FIND YOUR WAY

From I-80 at Iowa City, take Iowa Rte. 1 N. for 20 miles; the college is at the intersection of Rte. 1 and U.S. Rte. 30. **From I-380 at Cedar Rapids,** go east on U.S. 30 for 20 miles; the college is at the intersection of U.S. 30 and Iowa Rte. 1.

STAY THE NIGHT

Nearby: The **College Guesthouse, Brackett House,** circa 1877 is an antique-filled stately home that provides modern comfort and convenience at a moderate price (418 Second St. W.; 319-895-4425). There are also other bed-and-breakfasts and hotel accomadations in Mount Vernon. Cedar Rapids is only 20 minutes away from the school, while Iowa City is only 25 minutes away.

A Little Farther: Between Cedar Rapids and Iowa City are the historic Amana Colonies; they are 40 minutes southwest of Mount Vernon.

AT A GLANCE

Selectivity Rating	79
Range SAT I Math	540–640
Average SAT I Math	590
Range SAT I Verbal	540–660
Average SAT I Verbal	599
Average ACT Composite	26
Average GPA	3.53
Student/Faculty Ratio	11:1

CAMPUS TOURS

Appointment	Preferred
Dates	Year-round
Average Length	Varies

ON-CAMPUS APPOINTMENTS

Admissions

Start Date–Juniors	Anytime
Appointment	Preferred
Advance Notice	Yes, 2 weeks
Saturdays	Sometimes
Average Length	1 hour
Info Sessions	Yes

Faculty and Coaches

Dates/Times	Academic year
Arrangements	Contact Admissions
	Office 2 weeks prior

CLASS VISITS

Dates	Academic year
Arrangements	Contact Admissions
	Office

GRINNELL COLLEGE

Office of Admission, John Chrystal Center, 1103 Park Street, Grinnell, IA 50112-1690 • Telephone: 800-247-0113 • www.grinnell.edu/admission • Email: askgrin@grinnell.edu

Hours: Monday–Friday, 8:00AM–5:00PM; Saturday, 8:00AM–noon

Small Grinnell College in Iowa offers an open approach to a liberal arts education and the kinds of learning opportunities that intellectually curious students dream of. Grinnellians are a pretty laid back, smart, liberal, and opinionated bunch—they describe themselves as high school rejects who are cool and weird. On campus, don't be surprised to see people dressed in medieval costumes while jousting.

AT A GLANCE

Selectivity Rating	91
Range SAT I Math	620–710
Average SAT I Math	670
Range SAT I Verbal	630–730
Average SAT I Verbal	682
Average ACT Composite	30
Student/Faculty Ratio	10:1

CAMPUS TOURS

Appointment	Required
Dates	Year-round
Times	Academic year: Mon–Fri, 8AM–5PM, Sat 9AM–noon
Average Length	1 hour

ON-CAMPUS APPOINTMENTS

Admissions

Start Date–Juniors	Anytime
Appointment	Required
Advance Notice	Yes, 2 weeks
Saturdays	Yes
Average Length	1 hour
Info Sessions	Yes

Faculty and Coaches

Dates/Times	Academic year
Arrangements	Contact Admissions Office 2 weeks prior

CLASS VISITS

Dates	Academic year
Arrangements	Contact Admissions Office

TRANSPORTATION

The Des Moines and Cedar Rapids airports are approximately 60 miles away from campus. Transportation is available most days during the academic year, except during breaks, holidays, and exam periods. There is no charge for this service, but reservations must be made at least 10 days in advance. Flights should be arranged to arrive and/or depart between 10:00 AM and 9:00 PM CST.

FIND YOUR WAY

From I-80, take Exit 182; drive north on Highway 146 for three miles to Grinnell. Turn right (east) on 6th Avenue and proceed three blocks. Visitor parking for the Office of Admission, located in the John Chrystal Center, is on the left.

STAY THE NIGHT

Nearby: Prospective students are welcome to spend an evening in the residence halls throughout the academic year. Contact the Admissions Office at least 10 days in advance. Housing on campus is not available for parents or others traveling with you. Within walking distance of campus you'll find the **Carriage House Bed and Breakfast** (641-236-7520), the **Marsh House Bed and Breakfast** (641-236-0132 or 641-236-6782) and The **Guest House Bed and Breakfast** (641-236-5843 or 641-236-6161). Three hotels are located a short distance away from campus on Highway 146, just off I-80: **Country Inn and Suites** (641-236-9600), **Super 8** (800-800-8000), and the **Days Inn** (800-325-2525).

A Little Farther: The city of Newton, 20 miles west of Grinnell, also offers a variety of motels including **Best Western Newton Inn** (800-528-1234), **Holiday Inn Express** (800-HOLIDAY), **Radisson Inn** (800-333-3333) and **La Corsette Maison Inn Bed and Breakfast** (641-792-6833). The Amana Colonies, one of Iowa's most well-known tourist attractions, can be found approximately 40 miles east of Grinnell with overnight accommodations available at the **Comfort Inn** (800-228-5200) or **Holiday Inn** (800-465-4349). The Admissions Office is happy to recommend additional accommodations if desired.

HIGHLIGHTS

ON CAMPUS

- Two building on campus are listed on the National Register of Historic Places: Mears Cottage and Goodnow Hall
- Faulconer Gallery
- Burling Library
- Forum
- Bucksbaum Center for the Arts

OFF CAMPUS

- Downtown Grinnell's restaurants and coffee shops
- Rock Creek State Park
- The Grinnell Historic Museum

IOWA STATE UNIVERSITY

Office of Admissions, 100 Alumni Hall,
Ames, IA 50011-2011 • Telephone: 800-262-3810 • www.iastate.edu •
Email: admissions@iastate.edu

Hours: Monday–Friday, 8:00AM–5:00PM; Saturday (select), 9:00AM–noon

Strong agriculture, science, and engineering programs and an abundance of research resources make Iowa State University a world-class institution. Iowa State makes a big effort to include the large number of older and otherwise nontraditional students on campus.

HIGHLIGHTS

ON CAMPUS
- Union Drive Community Center (dining center)
- Reiman Gardens
- Lied Recreation Center
- Memorial Union
- Campanile
- C6 Virtual Reality Lab (available to visitors on a very limited basis.)

OFF CAMPUS
- CampusTown
- North Grand Mall
- Numerous Parks
- Hickory Park
- Downtown Ames/Main Street

TRANSPORTATION

Des Moines International Airport is 35 minutes away from campus. Car rental, taxis, and commercial buses are available for the trip from the airport to the campus. CyRide, the local bus system, offers an inexpensive shuttle during breaks.

FIND YOUR WAY

Ames is centrally located and well served by ground transportation. North-south Interstate 35 passes Ames on the east, with east-west Highway 30 intersecting to bring visitors to campus. East-west Interstate 80 intersects with Interstate 35 just 25 miles south of Ames. Follow the Iowa State/Ames signs on interstates and Highway 30.

STAY THE NIGHT

Nearby: The **Memorial Union** (2229 Lincoln Way; 520-292-1111), the student union building on campus, can't get any closer to the school than that! The 'MU' has a cafeteria open all day and a bowling alley in the building. There are several available options around the city of Ames. For more information, contact the Ames Convention and Visitors Bureau at 800-288-7470 or visit www.visitames.com.

A Little Farther: There are plenty of hotels in Des Moines and the surrounding areas.

AT A GLANCE

Selectivity Rating	75
Range SAT I Math	550–670
Average SAT I Math	620
Range SAT I Verbal	510–650
Average SAT I Verbal	590
Average ACT Composite	24
Average GPA	3.47
Student/Faculty Ratio	16:1

CAMPUS TOURS

Appointment	Preferred
Dates	Year-round
Times	Mon–Fri, 10AM & 2PM
Average Length	1 hour

ON-CAMPUS APPOINTMENTS

Admissions
Start Date–Juniors	Anytime
Appointment	Preferred
Advance Notice	Yes, 2 weeks
Saturdays	Yes
Average Length	1 hour
Info Sessions	Yes

Faculty and Coaches
Dates/Times	Year-round
Arrangements	Contact Admissions Office 2 weeks prior

CLASS VISITS

Dates	Varies
Arrangements	Available during open house programs only

UNIVERSITY OF IOWA

Admissions Office, 100 Bowman House, Admissions Visitors Center, 230 N. Clinton St., Iowa City, IA 52242 • Telephone: 800-553-4692 • www.uiowa.edu/admissions • Email: admissions@uiowa.edu

Hours: Monday–Friday, 8:00AM–4:30PM; selected Saturdays, 9:00AM–11:00AM

Surrounded by cornfields as far as the eye can see, Iowa City might not top the list of places you'd think to call the "Athens of the Midwest." But this progressive midwestern berg is home to the University of Iowa, an educational institution of the highest caliber that offers world-class degree programs in just about every academic discipline imaginable.

AT A GLANCE

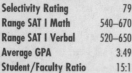

Selectivity Rating	79
Range SAT I Math	540–670
Range SAT I Verbal	520–650
Average GPA	3.49
Student/Faculty Ratio	15:1

CAMPUS TOURS

Appointment	Preferred
Dates	Year-round
Times	Mon–Fri, 10:30AM & 3:30PM; selected Sats, 10:30AM
Average Length	1 hour

ON-CAMPUS APPOINTMENTS

Admissions

Start Date–Juniors	Anytime, but preferably at the end of junior year
Appointment	Required
Advance Notice	Yes, 2 weeks
Saturdays	No
Average Length	45 min.
Info Sessions	Yes

Faculty and Coaches

Dates/Times	Year-round
Arrangements	Contact Admissions Office 2 weeks prior

CLASS VISITS

Dates	Academic year
Arrangements	Contact Admissions Office

TRANSPORTATION

The Cedar Rapids Airport is 25 miles (a 25-minute drive on I-380) away from campus. Van service to campus is supplied by Airport Express (319-626-5466 or 800-383-2219) and Airport Shuttle Service (319-337-2340 or 800-725-8460); call at least one day ahead to arrange for this service. Intercity bus service to Iowa City is provided by Greyhound and Burlington Transit buses; call the Union Bus Depot (319-337-2127) for information and schedules. Iowa City Transit (319-356-5151) and the University's Cambus (319-335-8633) provide local transportation throughout the Iowa City area.

FIND YOUR WAY

From I-80 (which connects Iowa City with Chicago, Illinois and Omaha, Nebraska), turn south on the Dubuque St. exit, which leads to the downtown/campus area. The Admissions Visitors' Center is one block west of Dubuque St. on the corner of Bloomington and N. Clinton Streets.

STAY THE NIGHT

Nearby: You can't beat the **Iowa House** (319-335-3513), also known as the Student Union. The proximity to students, three restaurants, university bookstore, theater, recreation center, pool tables, video games, and the on-campus field house, which has badminton and basketball courts, a weight room, and an indoor track, make it hard to beat. Within walking distance is the **Sheraton Hotel** (210 S. Dubuque St.; 319-337-4058), moderately-priced in downtown Iowa City. The **Golden Haug** (319-338-6452) is a bed-and-breakfast downtown near the university. Two motels are a convenient 10 minutes from the campus grounds. The **Quality Inn and Suites** and **Highlander Conference Center** (I-80 and Hwy. 1; 319-354-2000) has an indoor pool and pub, and its well-liked restaurant, the Highlander Prime Grill, specializes in prime rib and seafood. Rates are moderate. Less expensive accommodations can be found at the **Hampton Inn** (1st Ave. N., Coralville; 319-351-6600). For additional suggestions peruse the Cornell College entry.

HIGHLIGHTS

ON CAMPUS
- The University of Iowa Museum of Art
- The University of Iowa Museum of Natural History
- Old Capitol Museum
- Hawkeye Hall of Fame
- Hancher Auditorium

OFF CAMPUS
- Arts Iowa City Center & Gallery
- Plum Grove Historic Home
- Amana Colonies
- Coral Ridge Mall Attractions
- Coralville Reservoir

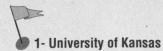

1- University of Kansas

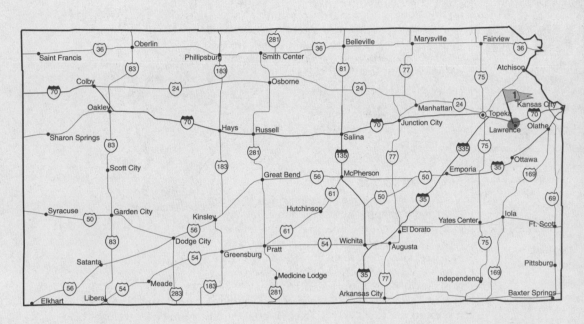

Kansas	Univ. Kansas	Kansas City	Wichita
Univ. Kansas	—	37	162
Kansas City	37	—	190
Wichita	162	190	—

UNIVERSITY OF KANSAS

Office of Admissions and Scholarships, 1502 Iowa St.,
Lawrence, KS 66045 • Telephone: 785-864-3911 • www.admissions.ku.edu •
Email: adm@ku.edu

Hours: Monday–Friday, 8:00AM–5:00PM; Saturday, 9:00AM–noon

The University of Kansas boasts first-rate pre-professional schools in architecture and engineering, and is also strong in pharmacy, nursing, journalism, and education. KU's library draws raves, and students rate the computer facilities very highly. Actor Don Johnson and basketball god Wilt Chamberlain are KU alums.

AT A GLANCE

Selectivity Rating	80
Average ACT Composite	24
Average GPA	3.4
Student/Faculty Ratio	15:1

CAMPUS TOURS

Appointment	Preferred
Dates	Year-round
Times	Summer: Mon, Wed, & Fri, 10:30AM
Average Length	1 hour

ON-CAMPUS APPOINTMENTS

Admissions

Appointment	Not required
Saturdays	No

Faculty and Coaches

Dates/ Arrangements	Contact Admissions Office 3 weeks prior

CLASS VISITS

Arrangements	Contact Admissions Office

TRANSPORTATION

Kansas City International Airport is 40 miles away from campus. Amtrak trains and Greyhound buses provide service to Kansas City, MO. The KCI Express shuttle bus operates from the airport to the Greyhound terminal and many hotels in the greater Kansas City area.

FIND YOUR WAY

Take I-70 to Lawrence; take U.S. 59 South to the main campus. The KU Visitor Center is located at 15th and Iowa.

STAY THE NIGHT

Nearby: There are a few choices within a mile or so of the campus. Across the street from the girls freshman dorm, and four or five blocks away from campus, is **Halcyon House Bed-and-Breakfast** (1000 Ohio St.; 785-841-0314), a restored Victorian with eight cozy guest rooms. Downtown there is **SpringHill Suites** (6th and New Hampshire; 785-841-2700). There are several motels within a mile or so, including the **Days Inn** (2309 Iowa, 785-843-9100), **Hampton Inn** (2300 W. 6th, 785-841-4994), **Holiday Inn** (200 McDonald Drive; 785-841-7077), **Ramada Inn** (2222 W. 6th; 785-842-7030) **Super 8 Motel** (515 McDonald Drive; 785-842-5721) and **Holiday Inn Express Hotel** (3411 Iowa; 785-749-7555).

A Little Farther: Both Topeka (to the west) and Kansas City (to the east) have a wide seclection of hotels and motels available.

HIGHLIGHTS

ON CAMPUS
- Spencer Museum of Art
- Kansas Union and bookstore
- Natural History Museum
- Visitor Center

OFF CAMPUS
- Downtown Lawrence shopping
- Country Club Plaza, Kansas City, MO
- Worlds of Fun (amusement park) KC, MO
- Cabela's, Kansas City, KS
- State capital, Topeka, KS

1- Centre College
2- University of Kentucky
3- Bellarmine U.

Walton

Maysville

3 Louisville

71

75

68

Grayson

64

Frankfort

64

Lexington

402

23

60

65

PKY

1

Richmond

Danville

31E

27

Mt. Vernon

80

Pikeville

60

Owensboro

Elizabethtown

Morgan-field

60

41

PKY

Madisonville

Bowling Green

PKY

Somerset

Barbourville

Paducah
Wickliffe

24

Glasgow

PKY

75

25E

Cadiz

Hopkinsville

68

65

31E

Middlesboro

PKY

51

Mayfield

80

Russellville

Kentucky	Bellarmine	Centre Coll.	Univ. Kentucky	*Louisville*
Bellarmine	—	85	77	0
Centre Coll.	85	—	36	92
Univ. Kentucky	77	36	—	74
Louisville	0	92	74	—

BELLARMINE UNIVERSITY

Office of Admission, 2001 Newburg Road, Louisville, KY 40205 • Telephone: 800-274-4723 • www.bellarmine.edu/admissions • Email: admissions@bellarmine.edu

Hours: Monday–Friday, 8:00AM-5:00PM

Bellarmine College is a small, career-oriented Roman Catholic school in the surprisingly happening metropolis of Louisville, Kentucky. The friendly and fun-loving upper-middle class conservatives who go here rave about their excellent professors who really care about how you are doing academically and emotionally. A ton of study abroad programs are another plus.

AT A GLANCE

Selectivity Rating	74
Range SAT I Math	490–620
Average SAT I Math	576
Range SAT I Verbal	500–600
Average SAT I Verbal	576
Average ACT Composite	24
Average GPA	3.48
Student/Faculty Ratio	13:1

CAMPUS TOURS

Appointment	Preferred
Dates	Year-round
Times	Varies
Average Length	1 hour

ON-CAMPUS APPOINTMENTS

Admissions

Start Date–Juniors	During junior year
Appointment	Preferred
Advance Notice	Yes, 1 week
Saturdays	No
Average Length	45 min.
Info Sessions	No

Faculty and Coaches

Dates/Times	Academic year
Arrangements	Contact Admissions Office 2 weeks prior

CLASS VISITS

Dates	Academic year
Arrangements	Contact Admissions Office

TRANSPORTATION

Louisville International Airport is less than five miles away. Taxis and rental cars are available.

FIND YOUR WAY

From I-71 (southbound): Follow I-71 South to I-264 West (Watterson Expressway). Stay on I-264 to the Newburg Road North exit 15A. Follow Newburg Road one-and-a-half miles to Bellarmine. **From I-64 (westbound):** Follow I-64 West to I-264 West (Watterson Expressway). Stay on I-264 to the Newburg Road North exit 15A. Follow Newburg Road one-and-a-half miles to Bellarmine. **From I-64 (eastbound):** Follow I-64 East to I-264 (Watterson Expressway), one of the first exits after the Ohio River Bridge. Stay on I-264 to the Newburg Road exit 15. Turn left and follow Newburg Road one-and-a-half miles to Bellarmine. **From I-65 (southbound):** Follow I-65 South across the Kennedy Bridge to I-264 East (Watterson Expressway). Stay on I-264 to the Newburg Road exit 15. Turn left and follow Newburg Road 1.5 miles to Bellarmine. **From I-65 (northbound):** Follow I-65 North to I-264 East (Watterson Expressway). Stay on I-264 to the Newburg Road exit 15. Turn left and follow Newburg Road one-and-a-half miles to Bellarmine.

STAY THE NIGHT

Nearby: Your choices include the **Holiday Inn-Airport East** (4004 Gardiner Point Drive), **Best Western-Ashton Suites** (653 Phillips Lane), **Courtyard by Marriott** (819 Phillips Lane), **Hampton Inn** (800 Phillips Lane), **Executive West** (830 Phillips Lane), and **Candlewood Suites** (1367 Gardiner Lane).

HIGHLIGHTS

ON CAMPUS

- New Norton Health Science Center
- Our Lady of the Woods Chapel
- Campus Center
- W. L. Lyons Brown Library
- The Thomas Merton Center
- The 28,500-square-foot Norton Health Science Center

OFF CAMPUS

- Churchill Downs/Kentucky Derby Museum
- Louisville Bats Baseball/Louisville Slugger Museum
- The Kentucky Center for the Arts
- Waterfront Park/The Belle of Louisville
- Six Flags Kentucky Kingdom Amusement Park

CENTRE COLLEGE

Admissions Office, 600 West Walnut, Danville, KY 40422 • Telephone: 800-423-6236 • www.centre.edu • Email: admissions@centre.edu

Hours: Monday–Friday, 8:30AM–4:30PM; Saturday, 9:00AM–1:00PM

Greek life dominates at this small, extremely challenging liberal arts enclave in the heart of Kentucky Bluegrass country. However, while students call Centre the Harvard of the South, the surrounding town of Danville is certainly no Cambridge, as Wal-Mart is the cultural highlight. It's no slouch, either, as the university brings in lots of cultural events.

HIGHLIGHTS

ON CAMPUS
- Norton Center for the Arts
- The new College Centre athletic and library building
- Combs Center (student center)
- 21 campus buildings on National Register of History
- House of Brews (Starbucks Cafe)

OFF CAMPUS
- Historic Shaker Village
- Civil War Battle Field
- Keeneland Racetrack (30 miles away in Lexington, Kentucky)
- Danville Shopping District
- Historic Downtown Danville

TRANSPORTATION
Bluegrass Airport near Lexington is 40 miles away from campus. The college provides transportation from the airport. Call the Admissions Office a week in advance to make arrangements.

FIND YOUR WAY
From the southwest, take I-65 N. to the Cumberland Pkwy. (Exit 43); take the Pkwy. east to U.S. 127 N., which takes you to Danville. **From the north,** take I-75 S. exit to Kentucky Rte. 922 and follow signs to the Bluegrass Pkwy. W. Take the Pkwy. west to U.S. 127 S. Follow U.S. 127 S. to Danville. **From the southeast,** take I-75 N. to Exit 59. Take U.S. 150 N.W. (initially it is U.S. 25) to U.S. 127 N., which takes you into Danville.

STAY THE NIGHT
Nearby: There are several charming bed-and-breakfasts operating in the historic homes that line Danville's older streets. The best way to inquire about rooms in these homes is to call the Campus Visit Coordinator through the Admissions Office. We recommend a beautifully restored pre–Civil War home, the **Twin Hollies** (406 Maple Ave.; 859-236-8954), a short one-and-a-half blocks away from campus, and the **Elmwood Inn** (205 E. 4th St., Perryville; 859-332-2400) on the banks of the Chaplin River, 10 minutes away. **The Elmwood,** an 1842 Greek Revival house listed on the National Register of Historic Places, has two rooms, and the moderate price includes a full breakfast with homemade muffins. Less expensive accommodations can be found within five miles of the school at the **Days Inn** (U.S. Rte. 127; 859-236-8600), or the **Super 8 Motel** (U.S. Rte. 150; 859-236-8881). **The Bright Leaf Resort and Motel** (U.S. Rte. 127 S., 1742 Danville Rd., Harrodsburg; 859-734-5481), about five miles away from campus, is an inexpensive resort-type facility with a health club, outdoor pool, fishing lakes, and golf course. Special golf packages are available.

A Little Farther: About 15 miles away from the college (two miles away from Shakertown), is the **Canaan Land Farm Bed and Breakfast** (4355 Lexington Rd., Harrodsburg; 859-734-3984), an eighteenth-century brick building listed on the National Register of Historic Places as the Benjamin Daniel house. The house is filled with antiques; sheep and goats are raised on the farm, and there's a pool. Rates are inexpensive and include a full country breakfast. About 10 miles away from the college is the **Beaumont Inn** (638 Beaumont Dr., Harrodsburg; 859-734-3381). This full-service hotel has tennis courts and a swimming pool and offers golf privileges. See the University of Kentucky entry for other suggestions.

AT A GLANCE

Selectivity Rating	76
Range SAT I Math	560–650
Average SAT I Math	603
Range SAT I Verbal	550–650
Average SAT I Verbal	612
Average ACT Composite	27
Average GPA	3.9
Student/Faculty Ratio	11:1

CAMPUS TOURS

Appointment	Required
Dates	Year-round
Times	Sept–May: Mon–Fri 10AM, 1PM, & 3PM; Sat, 10AM
Average Length	1 hour

ON-CAMPUS APPOINTMENTS

Admissions

Start Date–Juniors	No earlier than spring of junior year
Appointment	Required
Advance Notice	Yes, 1 week
Saturdays	Sometimes
Average Length	1 hour
Info Sessions	Yes

Faculty and Coaches

Dates/Times	Year-round
Arrangements	Contact Admissions Office 1 week prior

CLASS VISITS

Dates	Academic year
Arrangements	Contact Admissions Office

UNIVERSITY OF KENTUCKY

Office of Undergraduate Admission, 100 W.D. Funkhouser Building, Lexington, KY 40506 • Telephone: 800-432-0967 • www.uky.edu/Admissions/ • Email: admission@uky.edu

Hours: Monday–Friday, 8:00AM–4:30PM

Basketball is almost a religion at the University of Kentucky, but students say the top-notch academics here are the biggest strength of the school. Accessible and helpful professors are highly praised, and such pre-professional departments as business and management, communications, health sciences, education, and engineering are extremely popular.

AT A GLANCE

Selectivity Rating	79
Range SAT I Math	510–630
Range SAT I Verbal	500–620
Average ACT Composite	25
Average GPA	3.5
Student/Faculty Ratio	16:1

CAMPUS TOURS

Appointment	Required
Dates	Year-round
Times	Mon–Fri 10AM & 2PM; select Sat, 11AM
Average Length	120 min.

ON-CAMPUS APPOINTMENTS

Admissions

Appointment	Required, 2 weeks
Saturdays	No
Info Sessions	Yes

Faculty and Coaches

Dates/Times	Academic year
Arrangements	Contact Visitor Center 2 weeks prior

CLASS VISITS

Dates	Varies
Arrangements	Contact Visiting Center

TRANSPORTATION

Bluegrass Airport, located just outside Lexington, is five miles (a 20-minute drive) away from campus. Rental cars are available at the airport; the university has no shuttle service.

FIND YOUR WAY

From I-75/64 (which comes into Lexington from the north, south, east and west and merges briefly around the city), take Exit 113 (marked Paris/Lexington). Turn right off the exit ramp onto North Broadway (U.S. 68). Follow through downtown for three-and-a-half miles. One block past the Hyatt Regency Lexington, turn left onto West Maxwell Street. At the fourth light, turn right onto Martin Luther King Blvd. At the first light, turn left onto Avenue of Champions/Euclid Ave. Turn right into the Student Center parking lot. The Visitor Center is located on the first floor of the Student Center, across from the university bookstore. Please note that the Visitor Center is not located in the same building as the Office of Undergraduate Admissions.

STAY THE NIGHT

Nearby: The following are a list of hotels located near the University of Kentucky: **Best Western Regency** (2241 Elkhorn Road; 859-299-2613), **Hampton Inn** (Elkhorn Road; 859-299-2613), **Courtyard by Marriott** (775 Newtown Court; 859-253-4646), **Embassy Suites** (1801 Newtown Pike; 859-455-5000), **Marriott's Griffin Gate Resort and Golf Club** (1800 Newtown Pike; 859-231-5100), **Hyatt Regency Downtown** (401 West High Street; 859-253-1234), **Fairfield Inn** (3050 Lakecrest Circle; 859-224-3338), The **Springs Inn** (2020 Harrodsburg; 859-277-5751), and the **Shaker Village of Pleasant Hill** (3501 Lexington Road, Harrodsburg; 859-734-5411).

HIGHLIGHTS

ON CAMPUS

- W. T. Young Library
- Johnson Fitness Center
- Memorial Coliseum
- Arboretum
- Memorial Hall

OFF CAMPUS

- Rupp Arena
- Kentucky Horse Park
- Henry Clay Estate
- Keeneland Racetrack
- Applebee's Park

1- **Louisiana State University**
2- **Loyola University**
   Tulane University
   Univ. of New Orleans

Louisiana

	LSU	Loyola Univ.	Tulane Univ.	Univ. New Orleans	*New Orleans*	*Shreveport*
LSU	—	90	90	84	90	239
Loyola Univ.	90	—	0	0	0	329
Tulane Univ.	90	0	—	0	0	329
Univ. New Orleans	84	0	0	—	0	345
New Orleans	90	0	0	0	—	329
Shreveport	239	329	329	345	329	—

LOUISIANA STATE UNIVERSITY—BATON ROUGE

161 Pleasant Hall,
Baton Rouge, LA 70803 • Telephone: 225-578-1175 • www.lsu.edu •
Email: admissions@lsu.edu

Hours: Monday–Friday, 8:00AM–5:00PM

On the gorgeous campus of Louisiana State University, Fighting Bengal Tiger Football is an institution. A wide array of liberal arts and vocational educational options are available. LSU is one of the nation's few land- and sea-grant universities and is actively seeking space-grant status.

AT A GLANCE

Average ACT Composite	24
Average GPA	3.39
Student/Faculty Ratio	21:1

CAMPUS TOURS

Appointment	Preferred
Dates	Year-round
Times	Mon–Fri, 10AM
Average Length	120 min.

ON-CAMPUS APPOINTMENTS

Admissions

Info Sessions	Yes

Faculty and Coaches

Dates/Times	Year-round
Arrangements	Contact Athletic Department 1 week prior

CLASS VISITS

Dates	Varies
Arrangements	Recruitment and Tours Office

TRANSPORTATION

LSU contracts with Capitol Transportation Corporation to provide bus service for students, faculty, staff, and visitors both on and off campus. Taxis are available from the airport to campus. Baton Rouge Metro Airport is the closest airport (225-357-4165).

FIND YOUR WAY

Route 1: **From I-10 East,** exit at Nicholson Dr./Highland Rd (Exit 155A). Take Highland Road to Dalrymple Dr. (about 1.4 miles). Route 2: Exit at Dalrymple Dr. (Exit 156B). Both eastbound and westbound traffic will take a right onto Dalrymple Dr. from the off-ramp. Take Dalrymple Dr. from the off-ramp. Take Dalrymple Dr. to Highland Road (about half a mile). Route 3: Exit at Acadian Thruway (Exit 157 B). If exiting from the eastbound off-ramp you will take a right onto Acadian Thruway; if exiting from the westbound off-ramp you will take a left onto Acadian Thruway. Take Acadian Thruway (which turns into Stanford Avenue and then into LSU Avenue) to Highland Road. Take a right onto Highland Rd. to Dalrymple Drive (about 1.8 miles) All routes get you to the Visitors' Center on the corner of Dalrymple Dr. and Highland Rd.

STAY THE NIGHT

Nearby: You have a couple of choices, which include the **Lod Cook Conference Center** on campus (1-866-610-COOK) and the **Marriott Baton Rouge** (1-800-621-5116).

A Little Farther: Choices that are farther away include the **Comfort Suites** at the airport (225-356-6500) and the **Residence Inn** in Siegen (225-293-8700).

HIGHLIGHTS

ON CAMPUS

- LSU Student Union
- Mike V Tiger Cage
- Indian Mounds
- Tiger Stadium
- Alex Box Stadium

OFF CAMPUS

- Old State Capitol
- Mall of Louisiana
- Mall at Cortana
- The Old Governor's Mansion
- Louisiana State Capitol

LOYOLA UNIVERSITY NEW ORLEANS

Office of Admissions, 6363 St. Charles Avenue, Box 18, New Orleans, LA 70118 • Telephone: 800-456-9652 • www.loyno.edu/admissions • Email: admit@loyno.edu

Hours: Monday–Friday, 8:30AM–4:45PM

"The great thing about Loyola is that it accepts students who may not have shown their true academic capabilities in high school and gives them a second chance," says one student at Loyola University New Orleans. Course work in religion and philosophy is mandatory at this Catholic school, as is a 16-course Common Curriculum, but students may begin taking courses in their major during their first semester. Outside of class, life in New Orleans is a ball.

HIGHLIGHTS

ON CAMPUS
- Bookstore
- Monroe Library
- Recreational/sports complex
- Peace Quad

OFF CAMPUS
- French quarter
- Restaurants
- Audubon Zoo/Aquarium
- New Orleans Museum of Art
- D-Day Museum

TRANSPORTATION

New Orleans is accessible by car, train (Amtrak, 1-800-872-7245), or plane. New Orleans International Airport is served by major carriers including American, Continental, Delta, Northwest, Southwest, America West, United, and U.S. Airways. For more information about the New Orleans International Airport call 504-464-0831. Airport shuttles are available for $20 round-trips. The streetcar line passes directly in front of Loyola University along St. Charles Avenue and offers public transportation to visitors for only $1.25. Most taxi services are around $28.

FIND YOUR WAY

From 1-10, west traveling east, follow the signs toward the Central Business District. Take the Carrollton Avenue exit, Exit 232. Follow South Carrollton until it ends in a sharp left-hand curve and becomes St. Charles Avenue. Loyola's main campus is located on the left at 6363 St. Charles Avenue across from Audubon Park. The Broadway campus is located at 7214 St. Charles Avenue at the corner of Broadway. **From 1-10, east traveling west,** as you enter the downtown area, follow the signs to Hwy. 90 Business/West Bank. Exit at St. Charles Avenue/Carondelet Street (do not cross the bridge). At the second traffic light, make a right onto St. Charles Avenue. Follow St. Charles Avenue for four miles; Loyola's main campus is on the right at 6363 St. Charles Avenue. The Broadway Campus is located on the left at 7214 St. Charles Avenue.

STAY THE NIGHT

Nearby: The following are hotels located in New Orleans: **The Fairmont Hotel** (123 Baronne St.; 1-800-527-4727), **Grand Boutique Hotel** (2001 St. Charles Ave.; 1-800-976-1755), **Hampton Inn** (3626 St. Charles Ave.; 1-800-426-7866), **LePavillion Hotel** (Poydras St. at Baronne; 1-800-535-9095), **Maison St. Charles** (1319 St. Charles Ave.; 1-800-831-1783), **Mandevilla B & B** (7716 St. Charles Ave.; 1-800-288-0484), **The Pontchartrain Hotel** (2031 St. Charles Ave.; 1-800-777-6193), **St. Charles Inn** (3636 St. Charles Ave.; 504-899-8888), **W Hotel** (333 Poydras St.; 1-888-625-5144), **Hotel Intercontinental** (444 St. Charles Ave.; 1-800-327-0200), **Hotel Le Cirque** (2 Lee Circle; 504-962-0900), **Hotel Monaco** (333 St. Charles Ave.; 504-561-0010), **Hotel Monteleone** (124 Rue Royale; 1-800-535-9595), and **Homewood Suite** (901 Poydras; 1-800-225-5466).

AT A GLANCE

Selectivity Rating	76
Range SAT I Math	520–620
Average SAT I Math	605
Range SAT I Verbal	540–650
Average SAT I Verbal	629
Average ACT Composite	27
Average GPA	3.76
Student/Faculty Ratio	13:1

CAMPUS TOURS

Appointment	Preferred
Dates	Year-round
Times	Mon–Fri, 11:30AM & 3:30PM
Average Length	1 hour

ON-CAMPUS APPOINTMENTS

Admissions

Start Date–Juniors	At their preference
Appointment	Preferred
Advance Notice	Yes, 2 weeks
Saturdays	No
Average Length	30 min.
Info Sessions	Yes

Faculty and Coaches

Dates/Times	Academic year
Arrangements	Contact Admissions Office 2 weeks prior

CLASS VISITS

Dates	Academic year
Arrangements	Contact Admissions Office

TULANE UNIVERSITY

Office of Undergraduate Admission, 210 Gibson Hall, 6823 St. Charles Ave., New Orleans, LA 70118 • Telephone: 800-873-9283 • www.tulane.edu • Email: undergrad.admission@tulane.edu

Hours: Monday–Friday, 8:00AM–5:00PM; Saturday (select), 9:00AM–noon

Everything old is new again at Tulane, where new buildings, facilities, and programs keep popping up with delirious swiftness. Tulane's largely traditional undergraduate student body of about 7,800 benefits from an easygoing atmosphere and tremendous research programs. A visit to Tulane can be especially entertaining when coordinated with New Orleans' annual Mardi Gras celebration.

AT A GLANCE

Selectivity Rating	83
Range SAT I Math	610–700
Average SAT I Math	659
Range SAT I Verbal	610–700
Average SAT I Verbal	668
Average ACT Composite	30
Student/Faculty Ratio	10:1

CAMPUS TOURS

Appointment	Preferred
Dates	Year-round
Times	Mon–Fri, 2 tours daily; Sat 1 tour (fall only)
Average Length	120 min.

ON-CAMPUS APPOINTMENTS

Admissions

Start Date–Juniors	N/A

Faculty and Coaches

Dates/Arrangements	Contact Athletic Department 2 weeks prior

CLASS VISITS

Dates	Academic year
Arrangements	Contact Admissions Office

TRANSPORTATION

New Orleans International Airport is 15 miles away from campus. Airport Shuttle Service, taxis, and rental cars are available for the trip from airport to campus. Amtrak trains and Greyhound/Trailways buses serve New Orleans. Taxis are available for the ride from the terminal to campus.

FIND YOUR WAY

If you are heading east on I-10, follow the signs to the Central Business District as you approach downtown New Orleans. When I-10 divides, do not bear left toward I-610 to Slidell. Just after this split, take the Carrollton Ave. exit. Remain on Carrollton to the end and at St. Charles Ave., turn left, following the streetcar tracks. Continue on St. Charles to the Admissions Office. **If you are heading west on I-10,** follow the signs to Hwy. 90 Business. Exit at St. Charles Ave./Carondelet St. (do not cross the bridge). At the second traffic light, make a right onto St. Charles Ave. Follow St. Charles for four miles; Tulane and Gibson Hall will be on your right.

STAY THE NIGHT

Nearby: The **Tulane Travel Connection** (504-865-5673), which is on campus but not run by the university, can get special rates at several of the hotels and motels nearby. During certain times of the year, they offer even cheaper rates as part of special packages with some airlines. A number of hotels and motels are located on the St. Charles Ave. streetcar line that leads directly to the university. Of these, the least expensive is **Prytania Park** (1525 Prytania St.; 504-524-0427 or 800-862-1984), which is in the Garden District. About two miles away in the Garden District is the **Ramada Hotel** (2203 St. Charles Ave.; 504-566-1200). Ask for its special double-occupancy rate for Tulane visitors. The **1927 Pontchartrain** (2031 St. Charles Ave.; 504-524-0581), with a rooftop pool, is your choice for elegance and character. Make reservations through Tulane Travel Connection and you can get the special visitors' rate. The Pontchartrain also offers complimentary limousine service to the university. **Glimmer Inn Bed and Breakfast** (1631 7th St.; 504-897-1895) is a pleasant, inexpensive bed-and-breakfast that offers a delicious continental breakfast.

A Little Farther: There are hundreds of places to stay in the downtown and French Quarter areas. A couple of places that offer discounts to Tulane visitors are **Le Pavillon Hotel** (833 Poydras St.; 800-535-9095) and the **Meridien Hotel** (614 Canal St.; 504-525-6500 or 800-543-4300). The Meridien boasts Henri's, a fine French restaurant.

HIGHLIGHTS

ON CAMPUS

- Amistad Research Center
- Newcomb Art Gallery
- Reily Recreation Center
- Howard Tilton Memorial Library

OFF CAMPUS

- Audobon Zoo
- City Park and The New Orleans Museum of Art
- St. Charles Avenue Street Car
- Aquarium of Americaa
- National D-Day Museum
- French Quarter Mississippi River

UNIVERSITY OF NEW ORLEANS

Office of Admissions, AD 103, Lakefront,
New Orleans, LA 70148 • Telephone: 800-256-5866 • www.uno.edu/~admi/ •
Email: admissions@uno.edu

Hours: Monday–Friday, 8:30AM–5:00PM; open until 6:30PM on Tuesdays

UNO is a great commuter school with a growing national reputation. This public university offers a good education at an affordable price and what with the heart of the French Quarter a mere two miles away, who needs campus life, anyway?

HIGHLIGHTS

ON CAMPUS
- Recreation & Fitness Center
- The University Center
- Cove (Dining & recreation area)
- The Homer L. Hitt Alumni & Visitors Center
- UNO Lakefront Area

OFF CAMPUS
- National D-Day Museum & The Eisenhow Center for American Studies
- Ogden Museum of Southern Art
- Audubon Zoo
- Historic Garden District
- Historic French Quarter

TRANSPORTATION
The closest airport to the University of New Orleans is the Louis Armstrong International Airport. There are several types of transportation available to campus including RTA buses and taxi services.

FIND YOUR WAY
From West: Interstate 10 East to Interstate 610 East to Elysian Fields Avenue exit. Continue North for three miles; the campus is on the left. **From East:** Interstate 10 West to Inerstate 610 West. Exit at Elysian Fields Avenue. Continue about three miles; the campus is on the left.

STAY THE NIGHT
Nearby: Your choices include **Hampton Inn-Downtown French Quarter** (504-529-9990), **Holiday Inn French Quarter** (504-529-7211), **Motel 6 New Orleans** (504-240-2862), and **Studio 6 New Orleans** (504-240-9778).

AT A GLANCE

Selectivity Rating	73
Range SAT I Math	450–590
Average SAT I Math	535
Range SAT I Verbal	480–610
Average SAT I Verbal	553
Average ACT Composite	21
Student/Faculty Ratio	25:1

CAMPUS TOURS

Appointment	Preferred
Dates	Year-round
Times	Mon–Fri, 10AM & 3PM
Average Length	1 hour

ON-CAMPUS APPOINTMENTS

Admissions
Start Date–Juniors	Anytime
Appointment	Preferred
Advance Notice	Yes, 2 weeks
Saturdays	Sometimes
Average Length	1 hour
Info Sessions	Yes

Faculty and Coaches
Dates/Times	Year-round
Arrangements	Contact Admissions Office 2 weeks prior

CLASS VISITS

Dates	Varies
Arrangements	Contact Admissions Office

MAINE

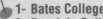

1- Bates College
2- Bowdoin College
3- Colby College
4- University of Maine—Orono
5- University of New England
6- University of Southern Maine

Ft .Kent
Van Buren
1
Presque-isle
11
Houlton
95
Sherman
Millinocket
Jackman
1
West Forks
Calais
Stratton
201
4
16
3
9
1
Skowhegan
Bangor
2
Rumford
95
Belfast
Bethel
3
Ellsworth
1
Augusta
1
Rockland
Lewiston
2
6
1
5
495
Bath
Portland
Kenne-bunk
95

Maine	Bates College	Bowdoin College	Colby College	Univ. Maine-Orono	Univ. New England	Univ. So. Maine	Augusta	Bangor	Portland
Bates College	—	22	51	109	53	42	28	105	40
Bowdoin College	22	—	56	110	48	28	31	108	26
Colby College	51	56	—	66	90	76	17	58	74
Univ. Maine-Orono	109	110	66	—	164	149	86	11	141
Univ. New England	53	48	90	164	—	18	74	154	15
Univ. So. Maine	42	28	76	149	18	—	58	136	0
Augusta	28	31	17	86	74	58	—	78	56
Bangor	105	108	58	11	154	136	78	—	134
Portland	40	26	74	141	15	0	56	134	—

BATES COLLEGE

Admissions Office, Lindholm House, Lewiston, ME 04240-9917 • Telephone: 207-786-6000 • www.bates.edu/admission.xml • Email: admissions@bates.edu

Hours: Monday–Friday, 8:00AM–5:00PM; Saturday (September–November), 8:00AM–noon

Bates College is a small and intimate liberal arts college in Maine that follows a 4-4-1 calendar. There is a fall and a winter semester, then a short term in May that provides students with opportunities to study less tradition-al topics or to study or intern off campus. An intense academic workload keeps the library packed throughout the week.

HIGHLIGHTS

ON CAMPUS

- Pettengill Hall
- Bates College Museum of Art
- Memorial Commons Dining Hall
- The George and Helen Ladd Library

OFF CAMPUS

- Bates-Morse Mountain Conservation Area
- Freeport Outlet Shopping

TRANSPORTATION

The Portland International Jetport is a 40-minute drive away from campus. Shuttle van service is available at the airport for the ride to campus. Arrangements must be made in advance through the campus travel agency. Greyhound provides service to Lewiston.

FIND YOUR WAY

The college is located approximately three miles away from Maine Tpke. Exit 13 (Lewiston Exit). Northbound travelers should take Exit 13 and turn left onto Alfred A. Plourde Pkwy. at the stop sign at the end of the off ramp. Southbound travelers should take Exit 13 and bear right onto Plourde Pkwy. Continue on Plourde straight to the stoplight on the intersection of Plourde and Pleasant; continue on Plourde 0.6 miles to the stoplight on Webster Street. Turn left onto Webster and travel one mile to the stoplight on Farwell Street. Turn right onto Farwell and follow 0.6 miles to stoplight. Continue straight across intersection onto Russell Street and follow for 0.9 miles to the third stoplight. Turn left onto College Street, and go to the second blinking stoplight; turn left onto Campus Avenue. Take your first right onto Wood Street, and turn right into the parking lot. The Admissions Office (Lindholm House) is at 23 Campus Avenue.

STAY THE NIGHT

Nearby: The new **Hilton Garden Inn** (207-784-4433) is located just seven minutes away from campus and the **Ware Street Bed & Breakfast** is adjacent to campus (207-783-8171). If you're on a budget, there's the **Super 8 Motel** (1440 Lisbon St.; 207-784-8882) and **Motel 6** (207-782-6558), both about five away minutes from campus. The **Ramada Inn** (490 Pleasant St.; 207-784-2331) has an indoor pool, an exercise room, and a live band with country rock every night in the lounge.

A Little Farther: See the University of Southern Maine entry for suggestions in Portland, Bowdoin College for suggestions in Brunswick and Freeport, and the University of New England for suggestions in the resort area of Kennebunkport.

AT A GLANCE

Selectivity Rating	97
Range SAT I Math	630–720
Average SAT I Math	677
Range SAT I Verbal	630–710
Average SAT I Verbal	671
Student/Faculty Ratio	10:1

CAMPUS TOURS

Appointment	Not required
Dates	Year-round
Times	Varies throughout year
Average Length	1 hour

ON-CAMPUS APPOINTMENTS

Admissions

Start Date—Juniors	May 1
Appointment	Required
Advance Notice	Yes, 1 week
Saturdays	Sometimes
Average Length	45 min.
Info Sessions	Yes

Faculty and Coaches

Dates/Times	Year-round
Arrangements	Contact coach directly 1 week prior

CLASS VISITS

Dates	Academic year
Arrangements	Other

BOWDOIN COLLEGE

Office of Admissions, 5000 College Station, Brunswick, ME 04011-8441 •
Telephone: 207-725-3100 • www.bowdoin.edu/admissions/ •
Email: admissions@bowdoin.edu

Hours: Monday–Friday, 8:30AM–5:00PM; open most Saturday mornings during the fall and summer

The alma mater of Nathaniel Hawthorne, Henry Wadsworth Longfellow, and Franklin Pierce has undergone significant changes in recent years. Bowdoin boasts two new state-of-the-art science facilities and new residential halls, and it has bid a fond adieu to the traditional Greek system. Sports are huge here, and the great outdoors of Maine provide ample outdoor opportunities.

AT A GLANCE

Selectivity Rating	95
Range SAT I Math	640–720
Average SAT I Math	680
Range SAT I Verbal	640–730
Average SAT I Verbal	680
Student/Faculty Ratio	10:1

CAMPUS TOURS

Appointment	Not required
Dates	Year-round
Times	Mon–Fri, 9:30AM, 11:30AM, & 3:30PM; Sat, 11:30AM
Average Length	1 hour

ON-CAMPUS APPOINTMENTS

Admissions

Start Date—Juniors	Mid-May
Appointment	Required
Advance Notice	Yes, 3 weeks
Saturdays	Sometimes
Average Length	45 min.
Info Sessions	Yes

Faculty and Coaches

Dates/Times	Year-round
Arrangements	Contact faculty directly 2 weeks prior

CLASS VISITS

Dates	Varies
Arrangements	Contact faculty directly

TRANSPORTATION

Portland International Jetport is about a 40-minute drive from campus. Mid Coast Limo (800-937-2424) is available for the trip from the airport to campus. Hertz (207-774-4544), Budget (800-527-0700), and other major rental car companies serve the airport. Arrange for limousine service or a rental car as early as possible.

FIND YOUR WAY

From the south, take the Maine Tpke. N. At Exit 6A (I-295, Portland), take I-295 N. Beyond Portland, I-295 rejoins I-95 N. Exit I-95 at Exit 22 (Bath-Brunswick/Coastal Rte. 1) and follow Rte. 1 into Brunswick, following signs for Maine St. At the intersection with Maine St., turn right; proceed straight (Bowdoin will be on the left), then turn left on College St., which takes you into the campus. **From the north,** take I-95 S. to the Topsham-Brunswick exit. Turn right onto Rte. 196; proceed to Maine St. in Brunswick and the college.

STAY THE NIGHT

Nearby: Down the main drag from the college is the **Captain Daniel Stone Inn** (10 Water St.; 207-725-9898). Rooms have color television, video cassette players (get movies from the desk), and phones. (Note: Rooms facing the highway are noisy.) **Brunswick B&B** (165 Park Row; 207-729-4914) is an appealing small bed-and-breakfast only a short walk from the college. Rates are moderate and include breakfast. For an indoor pool, exercise room, golf privileges, and game room, the best choice is **Atrium Inn and Convention Center** (U.S. 1; 207-729-5149; one mile north from campus). There is the **Comfort Inn** (800-221-2222), which isn't very far from the campus, either. Bowdoin suggests the **Tower Hill Bed and Breakfast** (207-833-2311) located on the lovely Orr's Island. For information on other accomidations call the Chamber of Commerce of the Bath-Brunswick Region at 207-725-8797.

A Little Farther: Many interesting, moderately-priced bed-and-breakfasts are 10 to 20 minutes away from campus. The **Captain York House** (207-833-6224) has the virtue of being on Bailey Island and has spectacular ocean views. If closets are a must, this is not the place for you. **Harpswell Inn,** also on the water (141 Lookout Point Rd; 207-833-5509), is a rambling federal period house 12 minutes away from campus, with charm, character, and a range of accommodations plus a full breakfast. Your host is a Bowdoin graduate.

HIGHLIGHTS

ON CAMPUS
- Bowdoin College Museum of Art
- Peary-MacMillan Arctic Museum
- Hawthorne-Longfellow Library
- Wish/Picard Theater
- Smith Student Union

OFF CAMPUS
- Maine Maritime Museum
- Beautiful coastline and islands
- Plenty of seafood/lobster restaurants

COLBY COLLEGE

Office of Admissions and Financial Aid, 4800 Mayflower Hill Drive, Waterville, ME 04901-8848 • Telephone: 800-723-3032 • www.colby.edu/admissions/ • Email: admissions@colby.edu

Hours: Monday–Friday, 8:00AM–5:00PM; Saturday (September–January and April), 8:00AM–12:30PM

This small, selective college located in the woods of Maine, but not too far from civilization, offers a great liberal arts education. The wealthy students at Colby College work intensely, party with determination, work out religiously, and rarely leave campus when school is in session. A unique Jan Plan allows students to study nontraditional subjects or intern during the month of January.

HIGHLIGHTS

ON CAMPUS

- Colby College Museum of Art
- Perkins Arboretum and Bird Sanctuary
- Johnson Pond
- Gravity Monument
- Colby bookstore

OFF CAMPUS

- Railroad Square Cinema (Maine International Film Festival)
- Belgrade Lakes Region
- Marden's Surplus and Salvage
- Jorgensen's Cafe
- Waterville Opera House

TRANSPORTATION

The Augusta State Airport is 20 miles away from campus. Taxis are available for the ride from the airport to campus. Most people fly to the Portland International Jetport, an hour and fifteen-minute drive from Colby. Vermont Transit/Greyhound buses (800-231-2222) or Star Livery Shuttle (207-353-5244) can take you to Waterville from Portland.

FIND YOUR WAY

Take I-95 to Exit 33. Follow the signs off the exit ramp to get to Colby.

STAY THE NIGHT

Nearby: You have a number of motel choices in the area, including the **Best Western** (356 Main St.; 207-873-3335), the **Holiday Inn** (375 Main St.; 207-873-0111), and the **Hampton Inn** (425 Kennedy Memorial Drive; 207-873-0400). For a nearby bed-and-breakfast, The Pressey House B&B (207-465-3500) is on Snow Pond in Oakland.

A Little Farther: In Augusta, a 20-minute drive from Waterville, try **Best Western Senator Inn** (284 Western Ave.; 207-622-5804). Also, at Exit 31 from I-95 you can find the **Comfort Inn** (Civic Center Dr.; 207-623-1000) and the **Holiday Inn** (Civic Center Dr.; 207-622-4751). Rates are moderate. See the Bates College entry for suggestions in and around Lewiston and the University of Southern Maine entry for suggestions in Portland.

AT A GLANCE

Selectivity Rating	95
Range SAT I Math	640–710
Average SAT I Math	670
Range SAT I Verbal	620–700
Average SAT I Verbal	660
Average ACT Composite	28
Student/Faculty Ratio	11:1

CAMPUS TOURS

Appointment	Not required
Dates	Year-round
Times	Varies
Average Length	1 hour

ON-CAMPUS APPOINTMENTS

Admissions

Start Date–Juniors	May 1
Appointment	Required
Advance Notice	Yes, 2 weeks
Saturdays	Sometimes
Average Length	45 min.
Info Sessions	Yes

Faculty and Coaches

Dates/Times	Year-round
Arrangements	Contact coach directly

CLASS VISITS

Dates	Academic year
Arrangements	Contact Admissions Office

UNIVERSITY OF MAINE

Visitors' Center, Chadbourne Hall,
Orono, ME 04469-5713 • Telephone: 877-486-2364 • www.go.umaine.edu/ •
Email: um-admit@maine.edu

Hours: Monday–Friday, 8:00AM–4:30PM; Saturday, 10:00AM–3:00PM

Engineering and forestry are both nationally esteemed at the University of Maine, but students say there are a wealth of excellent programs here. Social life at UMaine is pretty laid back; students enjoy outdoor activities, men's hockey, women's basketball, cheap movies on the big screen, and snowball fights during the longest winter in the world. Scary novelist extraordinaire Stephen King is an alum.

AT A GLANCE

Selectivity Rating	75
Range SAT I Math	490–610
Average SAT I Math	547
Range SAT I Verbal	480–590
Average SAT I Verbal	539
Average ACT Composite	23
Average GPA	3.21
Student/Faculty Ratio	15:1

CAMPUS TOURS

Appointment	Preferred
Dates	Year-round
Times	Mon–Fri, 9:15AM, 11:15AM, & 1:15PM; Sat 11:15AM & 1:15PM
Average Length	1 hour

ON-CAMPUS APPOINTMENTS

Admissions

Start Date–Juniors	Anytime
Appointment	Preferred
Advance Notice	Yes, 1 week
Saturdays	No
Average Length	30 min.
Info Sessions	Yes

Faculty and Coaches

Dates/Times	Year-round
Arrangements	Contact coach directly

CLASS VISITS

Dates	Varies
Arrangements	Contact faculty directly

TRANSPORTATION

Bangor International Airport is 10 miles away from campus. Taxis and rental cars are available at the airport. Concord Trailways Bus also stops on campus once a day during the academic year.

FIND YOUR WAY

The university is located off Exit 51 from I-95. Follow the signs.

STAY THE NIGHT

Nearby: About a mile away from campus is the **University Inn Academic Suites** (5 College Ave.; 800-321-4921), which has an outdoor pool and restaurant. While downtown, visit Margarita's for a taste of the border. If Mexican doesn't sound just right, try the Bear Brew Pub or Pat's Pizza for some of the students' favorite foods. The **Best Western Black Bear Inn** (4 Godfrey Ave.; 800-523-1234) only two-and-a-half miles away from campus. It includes an exercise room and continental breakfast.

A Little Farther: Check out the **Ramada Inn** (357 Odlin Road; 207-947-6961) by the Bangor Airport, which has an indoor pool and is about 20 minutes away from campus. The **Days Inn** (250 Odlin Road; 207-942-8272) also has an indoor pool. For a choice at the airport try the **Budget Traveler Motor Lodge** (327 Odlin Road; 207-945-0110). For eating in Bangor, the Whig and Courier makes a great sandwich, and the Bugaboo Creek Steak House provides a taste of the usual.

HIGHLIGHTS

ON CAMPUS

- Maine Center for the Arts
- Alfond Ice Arena
- Market Place (Memorial Union)
- Planetarium
- Page Farm and Home Museum

OFF CAMPUS

- Acadia National Park
- Hermon Ski Mt.
- Leonard Mills
- Cole Transportation Museum
- Fort Knox

UNIVERSITY OF NEW ENGLAND

Admissions Office, 11 Hills Beach Rd.,
Biddeford, ME 04005 • Telephone: 800-477-4863 • www.une.edu/admissions/ •
Email: jshea@mailbox.une.edu

Hours: Monday–Friday, 9:00AM–4:00PM; Saturday (October–November), 9:00AM–1:00PM

Five-year programs in physical therapy and occupational therapy highlight the various health-related offerings at the University of New England, a small independent college on the shores of the Atlantic Ocean in Biddeford, Maine. Practical experience is available at the university-run clinics of community health, physical therapy, and sports medicine.

HIGHLIGHTS

ON CAMPUS
- The Jack S. Ketchum Library
- The Campus Center
- The Point

OFF CAMPUS
- Maine Aquarium
- Dyer Library
- York Institute Museum

TRANSPORTATION

The Portland International Jetport is 17 miles away from campus. Taxis and rental cars are available at the airport. Special transportation from the airport can be arranged for students by calling 207-283-0171, ext. 297, one week in advance. New England Transit and Maine Lines buses serve Biddeford.

FIND YOUR WAY

From I-95 (the Maine Tpke.), take Exit 4 (Biddeford), and turn left at the end of the toll gates onto Rte. 111. Follow Rte. 111 (Alfred St.) through the intersection with U.S. Rte. 1, and at the next light turn right onto Rte. 9/208 (Pool St.). Follow Pool St. approximately four miles to the university on the left.

STAY THE NIGHT

Nearby: You have two budget choices near the campus. **Sleepy Hollow** (297 Elm St. on U.S. Rte. 1; 207-282-0031) is an inexpensive motel in Biddeford, four miles away from campus. **Beachwood Motel** (Rte. 9, Kennebunkport; 207-967-2483) is seven miles away in nearby Kennebunkport (home of former president George Herbert Walker Bush) and is a little less expensive than Sleepy Hollow. **Captain Jefferds Inn** (Pearl and Pleasant Sts., Kennebunkport; 207-967-2311) is an early nineteenth-century former sea captain's home, now a delightful 15-room inn a half mile from the beach. Rates range from moderate to expensive and include a full breakfast in the dining room. **The Welby Inn** (92 Ocean Ave., Kennebunkport; 207-967-4655) is a comfortable bed-and-breakfast with seven guest rooms (some with private baths). Rates are moderate and include a full breakfast. The **Captain Lord Mansion** (just off Ocean Ave., Kennebunkport; 207-967-3141) is listed on the National Register of Historic Places. The inn has 16 rooms and is a short walk to town. Midweek rates in May, June, November, and December are significantly lower than the normal, expensive rate. Ask about special packages. **Shawmut Inn** (Turbots Creek Rd., in Kennebunkport; 207-967-3931) is a 105-room motor hotel right on the ocean with pool, tennis courts, and golf privileges. There are supervised children's activities and live entertainment in the summer. Rates are expensive.

A Little Farther: See the University of Southern Maine entry for suggestions in Portland. See the Bowdoin College entry for suggestions in Brunswick and Freeport.

AT A GLANCE

Range SAT I Math	460–540
Average SAT I Math	509
Range SAT I Verbal	460–530
Average SAT I Verbal	511
Average GPA	3.2
Student/Faculty Ratio	11:1

CAMPUS TOURS

Appointment	Required
Dates	Year-round
Times	Mon–Fri, 10AM–1PM
Average Length	1 hour

ON-CAMPUS APPOINTMENTS

Admissions

Start Date–Juniors	Preferably after application is made
Appointment	Required, 1 week
Saturdays	No
Info Sessions	Sept–March

Faculty and Coaches

Dates/Times	Year-round
Arrangements	Contact Admissions Office 1 week prior

CLASS VISITS

Dates	Year-round
Arrangements	Contact Admissions Office

UNIVERSITY OF SOUTHERN MAINE

Office of Admission, 37 College Ave.,
Gorham, ME 04038 • Telephone: 800-800-4876 • www.usm.maine.edu/admissions/ •
Email: usmadm@usm.maine.edu

Hours: Monday–Friday, 8:00AM–4:30PM; selected Saturdays, 10:00AM–noon

The three cities of Lewiston, Portland, and Gorham host different branches of the University of Southern Maine. All the campuses build their degree offerings around a three-pronged, fancy-sounding core curriculum: basic competence, methods of inquiry/ways of knowing, and interdisciplinary. Nearly 50 percent of the students attend the school part-time.

AT A GLANCE

Selectivity Rating	67
Range SAT I Math	460–560
Average SAT I Math	512
Range SAT I Verbal	470–560
Average SAT I Verbal	516
Average GPA	2.99
Student/Faculty Ratio	13:1

CAMPUS TOURS

Appointment	Required
Dates	Year-round
Times	Mon–Fri
	& selected Sats
Average Length	1 hour

ON-CAMPUS APPOINTMENTS

Admissions

Start Date–Juniors	N/A
Appointment	Required
Advance Notice	Yes, 1 week
Saturdays	Yes
Average Length	45 min.
Info Sessions	Yes

Faculty and Coaches

Dates/Times	Academic year
Arrangements	Contact Admissions
	Office 3 weeks prior

CLASS VISITS

Dates	Academic year
Arrangements	Contact Admissions
	Office

TRANSPORTATION

Portland International Jetport is approximately five miles away from campus. Taxis or rental cars are available at the airport; call 207-774-3941 to make arrangements. New England Transit buses serve Portland. Amtrak offers round-trips to Boston.

FIND YOUR WAY

From the north, take the Maine Turnpike to Exit 7B (Rand Road/Westbrook). Follow Route 25 west for six-and-a-half miles to Gorham. At Gorham center, the intersection of Routes 25 and 114, turn right onto Route 114. Take the first left onto College Avenue. The entrance to campus will be on your right. Follow the white signs to the Office of Admission. **From the south,** take the Maine Turnpike to Exit 6 (Scarborough). Turn left after exiting the Turnpike onto Payne Road. At the second traffic light turn left onto Route 114 north. Follow Route 114 for 6.5 miles to Gorham center, the intersection of Routes 25 and 114. Go straight through the intersection and take the first left onto College Avenue. The entrance to campus will be on your right. Follow the white signs to the Office of Admission. **From Portland/I-295,** take I-295 south to Exit 1 (Maine Mall Road). Turn right at the exit sign to Route 114/Maine Mall Road. Immediately bear left at the fork in the road. At the traffic light turn left onto Payne Road. At the fifth traffic light take a right onto Route 114 north. Follow Route 114 north for 6.5 miles to Gorham center, the intersection of Routes 25 and 114. Go straight through the intersection and take the first left onto College Avenue. The entrance to campus will be on your right. Follow the white signs to the Office of Admission.

STAY THE NIGHT

Nearby: In the town of Gorham, there is **Pine Crest Bed and Breakfast** (207-839-5843), located on Route 114. This is a quaint old home within half a mile of the Gorham campus. The **Portland Regency in the Old Port** (20 Milk St.; 207-774-4200 or 800-727-3436) is a small hotel in the heart of the lively Old Port District. A 10-minute drive from the Portland campus, the Regency provides valet parking and has a well-equipped health club. Also located in the city of Portland, the **Eastland Hotel** (157 High St.; 207-775-5411 or 800-333-3333) is at Congress Square, near the Arts District. Also nearby is the **Holiday Inn by the Bay** (88 Spring St.; 775-2311 or 800-HOLIDAY). Located beyond the downtown area are the **Double Tree Hotel** (1230 Congress St.; 207-774-5611 or 800-222-TREE) and the **Holiday Inn-Portland West** (81 Riverside St.; 207-774-5601 or 800-HOLIDAY).

A Little Farther: See the University of New England for suggestions in the Kennebunk area or Bowdoin College for suggestions in the Brunswick/Freeport area.

HIGHLIGHTS

ON CAMPUS

- Art Gallery
- Costello Sports Complex
- Russell Theater and Concert Hall
- Southworth Planetarium
- TV/radio station

OFF CAMPUS

- Portland's Old Port District
- Casco Bay Cruise Lines
- Portland Head Light/Ft. William's State Park
- LL Bean, Freeport, ME
- Portland Museum of Art
- Sebago Lake
- Sunday River Ski Resort

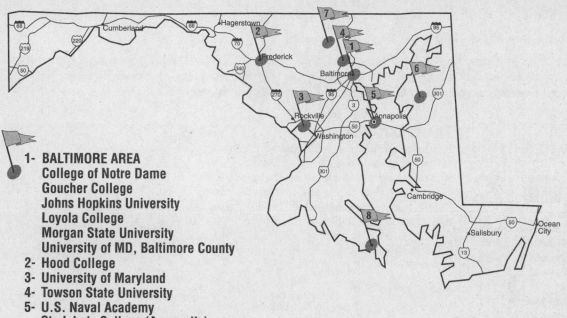

1- BALTIMORE AREA
College of Notre Dame
Goucher College
Johns Hopkins University
Loyola College
Morgan State University
University of MD, Baltimore County
2- Hood College
3- University of Maryland
4- Towson State University
5- U.S. Naval Academy
St. John's College (Annapolis)
6- Washington College
7- Western Maryland College
8- St. Mary's College of MD

Maryland	Coll. Notre Dame	Goucher College	Hood College	Johns Hopkins	Loyola College	Morgan State	St. John's Coll.	St. Mary's Coll.	Towson State	U.S. Naval Acad.	U. MD, Balt. Cty.	Univ. Maryland-C.P.	Washington Coll.	Western Maryland	Baltimore
Coll. Notre Dame	—	3	52	6	3	4	37	115	3	25	15	37	70	27	0
Goucher College	3	—	51	6	3	4	44	114	1	25	19	39	71	26	0
Hood College	52	51	—	51	50	51	73	124	53	69	46	48	114	31	46
Johns Hopkins	6	6	51	—	1	3	34	104	4	25	12	37	70	30	0
Loyola College	3	3	50	1	—	1	37	114	3	25	15	38	69	30	0
Morgan State	4	4	51	3	1	—	37	107	4	25	19	39	68	31	0
St. John's Coll.	37	44	73	34	37	37	—	85	45	0	29	31	47	60	30
St. Mary's Coll.	115	114	124	104	114	107	85	—	115	85	103	82	129	135	108
Towson State	3	1	53	4	3	4	45	115	—	34	20	40	67	28	2
U.S. Naval Academy	25	25	69	25	25	25	0	85	34	—	30	30	49	54	25
Univ. Maryland, Balt.	15	19	46	12	15	19	29	103	20	30	—	27	68	32	0
Univ. Maryland-C.P.	37	39	48	37	38	39	31	82	40	30	27	—	92	61	28
Washington Coll.	70	71	114	70	69	68	47	129	67	49	68	92	—	97	67
Western Maryland	27	26	31	30	30	31	60	135	28	54	32	61	97	—	29
Baltimore	0	0	46	0	0	0	30	108	2	25	0	28	67	29	—

COLLEGE OF NOTRE DAME OF MARYLAND

Office of Admissions, 4701 N. Charles St.,
Baltimore, MD 21210 • Telephone: 800-435-0300 • www.ndm.edu •
Email: admiss@ndm.edu

Hours: Monday–Friday, 8:30AM–4:30PM

The College of Notre Dame of Maryland is a primarily all-women's Catholic college with a park-like, waterfront campus in the middle of Baltimore. CND intercollegiate sports include volleyball, lacrosse, and field hockey. A coeducational weekend program is available for busy nontraditional students.

AT A GLANCE

Selectivity Rating	75
Range SAT I Math	460–560
Average SAT I Math	520
Range SAT I Verbal	490–570
Average SAT I Verbal	535
Average GPA	3.3
Student/Faculty Ratio	13:1

CAMPUS TOURS

Appointment	Preferred
Dates	Year-round
Times	Tours given at 2PM daily or by appointment
Average Length	1 hour

ON-CAMPUS APPOINTMENTS

Admissions

Start Date–Juniors	Anytime
Appointment	Required, 1 week
Saturdays	Sometimes
Average Length	30 min.
Info Sessions	Yes

Faculty and Coaches

Dates/Times	Year-round
Arrangements	Contact Admissions Office 1 week prior

CLASS VISITS

Dates	Academic year
Arrangements	Contact Admissions Office

TRANSPORTATION

Baltimore-Washington International Airport is 18 miles away from campus. Taxis can be hailed outside the airport or limousine service can be used to get to selected hotels in the area. Rental cars are also available. Amtrak trains and Greyhound/Trailways buses also serve Baltimore. MARC train service is available from Washington, D.C. and surrounding communities.

FIND YOUR WAY

From I-95 S., exit to I-695 toward Towson, then take Exit 25 (Charles St.). Travel south on Charles St. for approximately five miles, then turn left onto campus. **From I-83,** exit onto Cold Spring Lane east and continue to the intersection with Charles St. Turn left on Charles St., then turn right onto campus.

STAY THE NIGHT

Nearby: The **Double Inn at the Colonnade** (4 W. University Pkwy.; 410-235-5400) is a small hotel located only minutes away from campus. Also consider the Sheraton Baltimore (903 Dulaney Valley Rd., Towson; 410-321-7400). It has a pool, exercise room, sauna, Jacuzzi, and two restaurants. Ask for the special college visitor rate.

A Little Farther: There are a broad range of hotels available at Baltimore's Inner Harbor area, within 15 minutes of the college.

HIGHLIGHTS

ON CAMPUS
- Gator Alley (pub-like eatery)
- MBK Sports and Activities center (fitness center)
- Loyola/Notre Dame library
- Doyle Hall (residence hall, student activity area)

OFF CAMPUS
- National Aquarium
- Inner Harbor
- Baltimore Museum of Art
- Oriole Park at Camden Yards
- Maryland Science Center

GOUCHER COLLEGE

Admissions Office, 1021 Dulaney Valley Rd.,
Baltimore, MD 21204-2794 • Telephone: 800-468-2437 • www.goucher.edu •
Email: admission@goucher.edu

Hours: Monday–Friday, 9:00AM–5:00PM; select Saturdays (hours vary)

Once an all-women's institution, this tiny liberal arts college with a strong emphasis on liberal arts and writing proficiency and a fantastic pre-medical program took the great coeducational leap about a decade ago. Social life is laid-back and the well-liked administration sponsors a number or events, including the Blind Date Ball and Goucherfest—an all-campus celebration.

HIGHLIGHTS

ON CAMPUS

- The Julia Rogers Library
- The Rosenberg Art Gallery
- Sports and Recreation Center
- Pearlstone Cafe
- Gopher Hole

OFF CAMPUS

- National Aquarium
- Inner Harbor
- Baltimore Museum of Art
- Oriole Park at Camden Yards
- Maryland Science Center

TRANSPORTATION

Baltimore-Washington International Airport (BWI) is 25 miles away from campus. A hotel shuttle to the Baltimore North Sheraton (which is adjacent to campus, located in Towson) is relatively cheap; reservations are not required. The hotel shuttle desk is located on the lower level at BWI near baggage carousel #4. Taxis are also available for the ride from the airport to campus; they are much more expensive than the hotel shuttle. Amtrak trains and Greyhound/Trailways buses serve Baltimore. Taxis are available from the stations to campus.

FIND YOUR WAY

From I-695 (Baltimore Beltway), take Exit 27A (Dulaney Valley Rd. S.). The entrance to the college is immediately on the left.

STAY THE NIGHT

Nearby: The **Sheraton Baltimore North** (903 Dulaney Valley Rd., Towson; 410-321-7400) is within walking distance of Goucher. It has a pool, exercise room, sauna, Jacuzzi, and two restaurants. Ask for the special college visitor rate. A moderately-priced **Holiday Inn** (1100 Cromwell Bridge Rd., Towson; 410-823-4410) with similar amenities is about 10 minutes away from campus. For Maryland bed-and-breakfasts, call The **Traveler in Maryland** (410-269-6232).

A Little Farther: Goucher is actually in the suburb of Towson, eight miles north of the center of Baltimore. If you prefer to stay in the center of town, there are many hotels from which to select. It might be fun to explore historic Annapolis, which is 45 minutes away from campus. See the U.S. Naval Academy entry for suggestions there.

AT A GLANCE

Selectivity Rating	79
Range SAT I Math	520–640
Average SAT I Math	575
Range SAT I Verbal	540–650
Average SAT I Verbal	605
Average ACT Composite	26
Average GPA	3.16
Student/Faculty Ratio	10:1

CAMPUS TOURS

Appointment	Preferred
Dates	Year-round
Times	Varies throughout the year
Average Length	1 hour

ON-CAMPUS APPOINTMENTS

Admissions

Start Date–Juniors	April 1
Appointment	Required
Advance Notice	Yes, 1 week
Saturdays	No
Info Sessions	Yes

Faculty and Coaches

Dates/Times	Academic year
Arrangements	Contact Admissions Office 1 week prior

CLASS VISITS

Dates	Academic year
Arrangements	Contact Admissions Office

HOOD COLLEGE

Office of Admissions, 401 Rosemont Avenue,
Frederick, MD 21701 • Telephone: 800-922-1599 • www.hood.edu/admissions/ •
Email: admissions@hood.edu

Hours: Monday–Friday, 8:30AM–5:00PM; select Saturdays, 9:00AM–noon

About 900 students take advantage of the dynamic liberal arts education at Hood College, a residential college for women (Hood also offers commuter and evening programs for male students). Located in historic Frederick, Maryland, the school's proximity to Washington, D.C. makes for phenomenal internship options at the White House, the American Red Cross, and CNN, to name a few.

AT A GLANCE

Selectivity Rating	75
Range SAT I Math	473–590
Average SAT I Math	531
Range SAT I Verbal	493–620
Average SAT I Verbal	552
Average ACT Composite	21
Average GPA	3.23
Student/Faculty Ratio	9:1

CAMPUS TOURS

Appointment	Preferred
Dates	Year-round
Times	Mon–Fri, 10AM & 2PM
Average Length	1 hour

ON-CAMPUS APPOINTMENTS

Admissions

Start Date–Juniors	Beginning of junior year
Appointment	Preferred
Advance Notice	Yes, 1 week
Saturdays	Sometimes
Average Length	45 min.
Info Sessions	No

Faculty and Coaches

Dates/Times	Year-round
Arrangements	Contact Admissions Office 1 week prior

CLASS VISITS

Dates	Academic year
Arrangements	Contact Admissions Office

TRANSPORTATION

Baltimore-Washington International (BWI), Washington-Reagan National (DCA), Washington-Dulles International (IAD) airports all are within an hour's drive of Hood. The college provides transportation to and from the BWI Airport during vacation and busy travel times. Amtrak provides service to and from the BWI Airport Train Station, the Pennsylvania Station in Baltimore, and the Union Station in Washington. From there, buses, taxis, and a commuter train provide service to Frederick. Greyhound buses provide daily transportation to Frederick from Baltimore, Washington, New York, and other major cities. Trailways buses also offer limited service to Frederick.

FIND YOUR WAY

From points north, follow U.S. 15 south from Gettysburg and points north to Frederick. Take the Rosemont Avenue exit. Turn right onto Rosemont Avenue. Travel approximately half a mile and turn left at the entrance to Hood. **From points west,** follow I-70 east from Hagerstown and points west. Take the first Frederick exit onto U.S. 40. Follow U.S. 40 east to U.S. 15 north to Rosemont Avenue. Turn left onto Rosemont Ave. Travel approximately half a mile and turn left at the entrance to Hood. **From Washington,** follow I-270 northwest from Washington, D.C., toward Frederick and Gettysburg. Avoid turning to I-70. I-270 ends and the highway becomes U.S. 15 North. Follow U.S. 15 north to Rosemont Avenue. Turn left onto Rosemont Ave. Travel approximately half a mile and turn left at the entrance to Hood. **From Baltimore,** follow I-70 west from Baltimore to junction with U.S. 15 North (Exit 53). Follow U.S. 15 north to Rosemont Avenue exit. Turn left onto Rosemont Avenue. Travel approximately half a mile and turn left at the entrance to Hood.

STAY THE NIGHT

Nearby: Close to the college (about 10 minutes away) is the **Courtyard by Marriott** (5225 Westview Drive; 301-631-9030), which features an indoor pool fully equipped with a whirlpool, an exercise room, and provides dinner six nights per week. The **Fairfield Inn by Marriott** (5220 Westview Drive; 301-631-2000) features an indoor pool, exercise room, and complimentary breakfast seven days per week. Also located within 10 minutes driving distance from campus is the **Holiday Inn Express** (5579 Spectrum Drive; 301-695-2881) located on Spectrum Drive, which is adjacent to the Francis Scott Key shopping mall. This motel offers complimentary breakfast seven days per week, allows family pets, and also gives a discount on rates just for mentioning Hood College. The **Tyler-Spite Inn** (112 West Church Street; 301-831-4455) is located in the heart of Frederick's historic district and is walking distance to campus.

HIGHLIGHTS

ON CAMPUS

- Whitaker Campus Center
- The residence halls
- Coblentz Dining Hall
- Gambrill Gymnasium
- Hodson Science and Technology Building

OFF CAMPUS

- Downtown historic Frederick, Maryland
- The Inner Harbor in Baltimore, Maryland
- Museums & attractions at the Smithsonian in Washington, D.C.
- Harper's Ferry National Park
- Gettysburg
- Francis Scott Key Mall

JOHNS HOPKINS UNIVERSITY

Office of Undergraduate Admissions, 3400 N. Charles St./140 Garland Hall, Baltimore, MD 21218 • Telephone: 410-516-8171 • apply.jhu.edu • Email: gotojhu@jhu.edu

Hours: Monday–Friday, 8:30AM–5:00PM; Saturday, 11:00AM–noon

If you choose highly regarded and highly competitive Johns Hopkins University, be prepared for a tremendous workload and advanced course work. First-year students at this Baltimore school take their first semester pass/fail, which offers them a little more time to find their niches while academically staying afloat. Students say self-motivation is a requirement.

HIGHLIGHTS

ON CAMPUS
- Ralph S. O'Connor Recreation Center
- Mattin Student Arts Center
- Homewood House Museum
- Lacrosse Hall of Fame & Museum
- M.S.E. Library

OFF CAMPUS
- Baltimore Museum of Art (adjacent to the campus)
- Maryland Science Center
- National Aquarium in Baltimore
- Oriole Park at Camden Yards
- Pavilions at the Inner Harbor

TRANSPORTATION

Baltimore-Washington International Airport is a 30-minute drive from campus. We recommend that you take a taxi to the campus from the airport; be sure to ask to be driven to Garland Hall on the Homewood Campus of Johns Hopkins. The Amtrak station is a 10-minute drive south of campus; the Greyhound bus terminal is in downtown Baltimore.

FIND YOUR WAY

By car from the north on I-95 (Wilmington, Philadelphia, New Jersey, New York), take the Baltimore Beltway (I-695) toward Towson to Exit 25 (Charles Street). Take Charles Street south for about seven miles (when Charles Street splits a block after Cold Spring Lane, stay right). As you cross University Parkway, continue southbound in the right-hand access lane. After you pass the university on the right, turn right onto Art Museum Drive. Just after the Baltimore Museum of Art, bear right at the traffic island onto Wyman Park Drive. Take an almost immediate right through the university gates. Garland Hall is the first building on the left. **By car from the North on I-81 or I-83 (Pennsylvania, etc.),** go south on I-81 or I-83 to I-695 East (Towson) and continue on the exit to Charles Street (the next right). Continue on Charles Street south for about seven miles (when Charles Street splits a block after Cold Spring Lane, stay right). As you cross University Parkway, continue southbound in the right-hand access lane. Follow the preceeding directions. **By car from the south on I-95 (BWI Airport, Washington, D.C., Richmond etc.),** take I-95 N to exit 53 (I-395). Stay in the right lane. As I-395 ends you will see Oriole Park at Camden Yards in front of you on your left. Make a right turn onto Pratt Street; go 10 blocks (stay in the left lane). Turn left onto President Street and follow the signs for I-83 N. Take exit 9A East (Cold Spring Lane). Take the third right from Cold Spring Lane onto Roland Avenue (stay to the left); it turns into University Parkway after it splits. Follow University Parkway to Charles Street and turn right into the right-hand access lane. Follow the preceeding directions. **By car from the east on Route 50 or I-97 (Annapolis, Eastern Shore, Southern Delaware),** take Route 50 East to Exit 21 (I-97) toward Baltimore. Continue on I-97 to exit 17A (I-695) Baltimore/Towson. Continue on I-695 to exit 11A (I-95) North Baltimore. Follow the directions above from the South on I-95. **By car from the West on I-70 (Pittsburgh, Chicago, etc.),** go toward Baltimore; take the exit for I-695/Glen Burnie (exit 91 A). Continue to I-95 North. Take I-95 N to exit 53 (I-395). Follow the directions above from the South on I-95. The visitor parking lot will be on your left as you enter the campus gates. Please bring your ticket to the Admissions Office receptionist to have it validated on weekdays. The visitor lot is free on Saturdays.

STAY THE NIGHT

Nearby: Across the street is the **Inn at the Colonnade** (4 W. University Pkwy.; 410-235-5400) which has a special university visitor rate. Also nearby are the **Quality Inn** (410-889-4500) and the **Raddison Cross Keys,** (410-532-6900).

AT A GLANCE

Selectivity Rating	97
Range SAT I Math	660–760
Average SAT I Math	703
Range SAT I Verbal	620–730
Average SAT I Verbal	671
Average ACT Composite	29
Average GPA	3.73
Student/Faculty Ratio	8:1

CAMPUS TOURS

Appointment	Not required
Dates	Year-round
Times	Mon–Fri, 10AM & 1PM; Jul-Nov: Sat, 11AM
Average Length	1 hour

ON-CAMPUS APPOINTMENTS

Admissions

Start Date–Juniors	May
Appointment	Required
Advance Notice	Yes, 3 weeks
Saturdays	No
Average Length	1 hour
Info Sessions	Yes

Faculty and Coaches

Dates/Times	Year-round
Arrangements	Contact faculty or coach directly 2 weeks prior

CLASS VISITS

Dates	Academic year
Arrangements	Contact Admissions Office

LOYOLA COLLEGE IN MARYLAND

Admissions Office, 4501 N. Charles St., Baltimore, MD 21210 • Telephone: 800-221-9107 • www.loyola.edu/admission/index.html •

Hours: Monday–Friday, 9:00AM–5:00PM; Saturdays open only for special programs

The course load is heavy at Loyola College in Baltimore, and the core curriculum allows few options the first two years, but classes are small, professors are concerned with helping students succeed, and the students tell us they are challenged but satisfied. Novelist Tom Clancy is an alum.

AT A GLANCE

Selectivity Rating	81
Range SAT I Math	570–650
Range SAT I Verbal	560–640
Average GPA	3
Student/Faculty Ratio	12:1

CAMPUS TOURS

Appointment	Required
Dates	Year-round
Times	Mon–Fri, following info sessions at 10AM & 2PM
Average Length	1 hour

ON-CAMPUS APPOINTMENTS

Admissions

Start Date–Juniors	Late April
Appointment	Required
Advance Notice	Yes, 1 week
Saturdays	No
Info Sessions	Yes

Faculty and Coaches

| Dates/Times | Year-round |
| Arrangements | Contact faculty directly 2 weeks prior |

CLASS VISITS

| Dates | Academic year |
| Arrangements | Contact Admissions Office |

TRANSPORTATION

The Baltimore-Washington International Airport is 23 miles away from campus. Taxis and rental cars are available at the airport, and limousine service is provided to area hotels. Amtrak trains and Greyhound buses also serve Baltimore.

FIND YOUR WAY

From I-695 (Baltimore Beltway), take Exit 25 (Charles St.). Proceed south on Charles St. approximately seven miles. The college's main entrance is on North Charles St., just north of the Cold Spring Lane intersection.

STAY THE NIGHT

Nearby: Your choices include the **Inn at the Colonade** (410-235-5400) and the **Radisson Hotel at Cross Keys** (410-532-6900). For Maryland bed-and-breakfasts, call the **Traveler in Maryland** (410-269-6232).

HIGHLIGHTS

ON CAMPUS

- Loyola/Notre Dame Library
- The Loyola College Art Gallery
- Fitness and Aquatic Center
- Boulder Garden Cafe
- Primo's: The New Marketplace

OFF CAMPUS

- Baltimore's Inner Harbor
- National Aquarium
- Babe Ruth Museum
- Walters Art Gallery
- Oriole Park at Camden Yards

McDaniel College

2 College Hill (The office is in Carroll Hall),
Westminster, MD 21157 • Telephone: 800-638-5005 • www.mcdaniel.edu •
Email: admissio@mcdaniel.edu

Hours: Monday–Friday, 8:30AM–4:30PM; Saturday, 9:00AM–noon (by arrangement only)

Situated between Chesapeake Bay and the Blue Ridge Mountains, in the central Maryland community of Westminster, Western Maryland College is a private, liberal arts college with an enrollment of 1,500. Students rave about the exceptional scholarship offerings, as well as the breathtaking views available from most dorm windows.

HIGHLIGHTS

ON CAMPUS

- The Hoover Library
- Peterson Hall
- Golf course
- Bair stadium
- Decker College Center

OFF CAMPUS

- Pour House coffee shop
- Town Mall of Westminster
- Harry's Main Street Grille
- Carroll County Arts Center
- Classico Pizzeria

TRANSPORTATION

BWI airport is 45 minutes away from campus. A free college shuttle is available during major college breaks to the airport and train station. On most Saturdays there's a free college van to take students around Westminster and to the Baltimore Metro station. There is also 24-hour Carroll County Taxi service.

FIND YOUR WAY

From I-95, exit to I-695 W. (Baltimore Beltway). From I-695, take Exit 19 to I-795 (the Northwest Expy.). Follow I-795 to its end, then follow signs to Westminster via Rte. 140 W. Proceed around Westminster and turn left onto Rte. 31. Continue for half a mile (with the McDaniel College golf course on the left); at the first traffic light, turn left onto Main Street. Proceed for a third of a mile and turn right into the college parking lot. From I-495 (Washington Beltway), exit onto I-270 toward Frederick, then onto Rte 27N/Damascus. At the intersection of Rtes. 27 and 32 (Main Street), turn left and drive half a mile. Bear right at the fork; then make the first left into the college parking lot.

STAY THE NIGHT

Nearby: A **Best Western** (451 WMC Dr.; 410-876-0010) is across the street from campus. Ask for the college visitor rate, and you get tennis, golf, and health club privileges through the college. For something a little different, consider the **Winchester Country Inn** (430 Bishop St.; 410-876-7373), a five-minute drive from campus. This eighteenth-century inn, with five guest rooms (some with private baths), is very close to the Carroll County Farm Museum and the Farmers' Market. The moderate price includes a full breakfast and afternoon tea or sherry. The **Westminster Inn** (5 S. Center St.; 410-857-4445), half a mile away, is elegantly fitted with a Jacuzzi and private bath in each room. Prices, which include a full breakfast, are fairly expensive. A good budget choice is the **Boston Inn** (533 Baltimore Blvd.; 410-848-9095), two miles away from campus. A **Days Inn** (Cranberry Rd.; 410-857-0500) is also two miles away from campus.

A Little Farther: Westminster is 30 minutes away from Gettysburg. See the Gettysburg College entry for suggestions in this historic area. Westminster is 30 minutes away from Owings Mills. There's an **AmeriSuites** (4730 Painters Mill.; 800-246-8357) and a **Hilton Garden Inn** (Owings Mills Blvd.; 410-654-0300).

AT A GLANCE

Range SAT I Math	510–610
Average SAT I Math	556
Range SAT I Verbal	500–590
Average SAT I Verbal	554
Average GPA	3.43
Student/Faculty Ratio	12:1

CAMPUS TOURS

Appointment	Required
Dates	Varies
Times	Summer: Mon, Wed, & Fri, 10AM & 2PM; Academic: Mon–Fri, 10:15AM–2PM
Average Length	1 hour

ON-CAMPUS APPOINTMENTS

Admissions

Start Date–Juniors	Spring of junior year
Appointment	Required
Advance Notice	Yes, 1 week
Saturdays	No
Average Length	90 min.
Info Sessions	Yes

Faculty and Coaches

Dates/Times	Academic year
Arrangements	Contact coach directly 1 week prior

CLASS VISITS

Dates	Academic year
Arrangements	Contact Admissions Office

MORGAN STATE UNIVERSITY

1700 East Cold Spring Lane and Hillen Rd.,
Baltimore, MD 21251 • Telephone: 800-332-6674 • www.morgan.edu •
Email: tjenness@moac.morgan.edu

Hours: Monday–Friday, 8:00AM–5:00PM

Morgan State, Maryland's Public Urban University, is a primarily African American school that has gained national recognition in the past 10 years. Morgan boasts more than 30 specialized, nontraditional programs of study, including several for pre-college students.

AT A GLANCE

CAMPUS TOURS

Appointment	Preferred
Dates	Academic year
Average Length	120 min.

ON-CAMPUS APPOINTMENTS

Admissions

Appointment	Not required
Advance Notice	3 weeks
Saturdays	No
Info Sessions	Yes

Faculty and Coaches

Dates/Times	Academic year
Arrangements	Contact coach directly

CLASS VISITS

Dates	Academic year
Arrangements	Contact Admissions Office

FIND YOUR WAY

Take I-695 (the Baltimore Beltway) to Exit 30 S. (Perring Pkwy.). Take Perring Pkwy. for five miles to the campus at Cold Spring Lane. Take I-95 north through the Fort McHenry Tunnel. Get off I-95 at the Moravia Road Exit. (The distance to campus is about three-and-a-half miles.) You will go through major intersections at Belair Road and then at Harford Road. Moravia Road will become Cold Spring Lane at Harford Road. Cold Spring Lane goes through the middle of campus. Take I-95 South past the interchange for the beltway, I-695. Shortly thereafter, I-95 will split in I-895 (left two lanes) and I-95 (right two lanes). Go to the left onto I-895. Get off at Moravia Road Exit. Bear to the right off the exit ramp onto Moravia Road. (The distance to campus is about three-and-a-half miles). You will go through major intersections at Belair Road and then at Harford Road. Moravia Road will become Cold Spring Lane ay Harford Road. Cold Spring Lane goes through the middle of campus.

HIGHLIGHTS

ON CAMPUS
• Fine Arts Center
• Hughes Stadium
• Mitchell Building
• Research Facility
• University Museum

OFF CAMPUS
• Blacks in Wax Museum
• Baltimore Harbor
• Ravens/Orioles Athletic Stadiums
• Baltimore Museum of Art
• Aquarium

ST. JOHN'S COLLEGE (MD)

PO Box 2800,
Annapolis, MD 21404 • Telephone: 800-727-9238 • www.sjca.edu/admissions/ •
Email: admissions@sjca.edu

Hours: Monday–Friday, 8:00AM–5:00PM

The incredibly articulate, abstract, and wacky students at St. John's College in Annapolis share a thirst for knowledge and a stimulating curriculum. It's not a multiple-choice kind of place, though. The unique Great Books program requires Johnnies to study a strict four-year curriculum of ancient Greek, French, classical mathematics, science, music, literature, and philosophy—all from the original texts.

HIGHLIGHTS

ON CAMPUS

- Mitchell Art Gallery
- Greenfield Library
- McDowell Hall
- Caroll Barrister House
- French Monument
- The entire campus is a registered national landmark

OFF CAMPUS

- State House
- Paca House
- Naval Academy
- Banneker Douglass Museum
- City Dock and Market

TRANSPORTATION

Baltimore-Washington International Airport is a 45-minute drive away from the college. Ground transportation to Annapolis is available from lower level by a super shuttle van. Washington National and Dulles International airports are more expensive to use and ground transportation is piecemeal. Trains come into both Baltimore and Washington; however, it is necessary to take a cab from the train station to the bus station to get to Annapolis. Bus transportation is more convenient from Baltimore. There is hourly bus service between Baltimore and Annapolis; the bus driver will let you off near campus. Buses from Washington are less frequent and unload passengers about four blocks away from campus.

FIND YOUR WAY

Take Route 50 from Washington. From Baltimore take Route 2 or I-97. Annapolis is approximately a one hour drive away from each city. After arriving in Annapolis, follow the signs for the Naval Academy. The campus is located across the street from the academy; parking is available on campus.

STAY THE NIGHT

Nearby: The **Annapolis Marriott Waterfront Hotel** at 80 Compromise St. is 10 minutes away from the campus by car and is priced in the $200-plus range per night (410-268-7555). The **Loews Annapolis Hotel** at 126 West St., is also 10 minutes away from the campus by car and also is priced in the $200-plus range per night (410-263-7777). **Historic Inns of Annapolis** located at 58 State Circle are three restored inns that operate as one. All are a 15-minute walk from the campus and are priced in the $200-plus range per night. (410-263-2641).

A Little Farther: **Radisson** at 210 Holiday Court/Riva Road is approximately three miles away from the campus and is priced in $100 to $150 range (410-224-3150). The **Hampton Inn** at 124 Womack Drive is approximately three miles away from the campus and is priced at the $90 to $120 range (410-571-0200). The **Days Inn of Annapolis,** at 2451 Riva Rd. is two-and-a-half miles away from the campus and is priced at $70 to $110 range (410-224-4317).

AT A GLANCE

Selectivity Rating	83
Range SAT I Math	590–690
Range SAT I Verbal	660–750
Student/Faculty Ratio	8:1

CAMPUS TOURS

Appointment	Required
Dates	Year-round
Times	Mon–Fri, 9AM & 2PM
Average Length	1 hour

ON-CAMPUS APPOINTMENTS

Admissions

Appointment	Required
Advance Notice	Yes, 2 weeks
Saturdays	No
Average Length	45 min.

Faculty and Coaches

Dates/Times	N/A

CLASS VISITS

Dates	Varies

ST. MARY'S COLLEGE OF MARYLAND

Admissions Office, 18952 East Fisher Road, St. Mary's City, MD 20686-3001 •
Telephone: 800-492-7181 • www.smcm.edu/admissions/ •
Email: admissions@smcm.edu

Hours: Monday–Friday, 8:00AM–5:00PM

A small, private liberal arts school experience at state school prices regularly puts St. Mary's College in Maryland at or near the top of everyone's "Best Buys in Education" lists. The campus is gorgeous and secluded—St. Mary's City, Maryland's first capital, is twenty minutes away by car—so students work and play hard.

AT A GLANCE

Selectivity Rating	89
Range SAT I Math	560–650
Average SAT I Math	608
Range SAT I Verbal	570–670
Average SAT I Verbal	624
Average GPA	3.49
Student/Faculty Ratio	12:1

CAMPUS TOURS

Appointment	Preferred
Dates	Year-round
Times	Varies
Average Length	120 min.

ON-CAMPUS APPOINTMENTS

Admissions

Appointment	Required
Advance Notice	Yes, 1 week
Saturdays	No
Average Length	45 min.
Info Sessions	Yes

Faculty and Coaches

Dates/Times	Academic year
Arrangements	Contact Admissions Office 1 week prior

CLASS VISITS

Dates	Academic year
Arrangements	Contact Admissions Office

TRANSPORTATION

St. Mary's is within two hours by car from three major airports. From Baltimore-Washington International Airport (BWI), follow airport signs to I-97 South and the driving directions from the north (Baltimore) below. From Reagan National (DCA) and Dulles International (IAD) airports, follow the driving directions from Washington, D.C.

FIND YOUR WAY

From the North (Baltimore, Annapolis), take I-97 South to MD Route 3 in Bowie, Maryland. Follow Rte. 3 to MD Route 4 in Upper Marlboro. Take Rte. 4 South through Prince Frederick and cross the Thomas Johnson Bridge at Solomons. About three miles away from the bridge, turn left at the first traffic light onto MD Route 235 South. Travel four-and-a-half miles through Lexington Park, turning right onto Shangri La Drive (Donut Connection on corner). Proceed through the next traffic light. Bear left at the fork in the road on Willows Road and drive three miles to the stop sign at MD Route 5 South. Turn left and continue four miles to the college. **From Washington, D.C.,** take the Capital Beltway (I-495/95) to Exit 11A for MD Route 4 South. Follow Rte. 4 through Prince Frederick and cross the Thomas Johnson Bridge at Solomons. Follow detailed directions from the north above. **From the South (Richmond),** take U.S. Route 301 North over the Potomac River Bridge. Turn right at the second set of blinking lights onto MD Route 234. Follow Rte. 234 approximately 23 miles to where it ends at MD Route 5. Turn right (south) on Rte. 5, traveling through Leonardtown and continue 15 miles to St. Mary's College. The campus is located on Rte. 5. Once you see the beautiful St. Mary's River on your right, you will know you have arrived!

STAY THE NIGHT

Nearby: For a complete list of accommodations please see our website: www.smcm.edu/accomodations.cfm. The **Hampton Inn** (22211 Three Notch Rd., Rte. 235, Lexington Park, MD 20653; 301-863-3200) is 10 minutes away from campus. The **Comfort Inn at the Beacon Marina** (Solomons Island; 410-326-6303) is 30 minutes away from campus. The **Holiday Inn** (Solomons Island; 800-356-2009) is also 30 minutes away from campus. For extended stay, consider **America Lexington Park** (240-725-0100).

HIGHLIGHTS

ON CAMPUS

- Boathouse
- Student Center
- Somerset Athletics Building
- Townhouse Greens
- Garden of Remembrance

OFF CAMPUS

- Historic St. Mary's City
- Solomons Island
- Point Lookout State Park
- Evans Seafood
- Elms Beach State Park

TOWSON UNIVERSITY

Office of Admission, 8000 York Road, Towson, MD 21252-0001 • Telephone: 888-486-9766 • www.towson.edu/discover/ • Email: admissions@towson.edu

Hours: Monday–Friday, 8:30AM–5:00PM; Saturday, 10:00AM–2:00PM

Located near Baltimore, Towson University is a comprehensive public institution with almost 15,000 students of both the traditional and nontraditional varieties. Towson boasts a perennially strong women's gymnastics team and entertainment options abound in Baltimore—from the National Aquarium to Oriole Park at Camden Yards.

HIGHLIGHTS

ON CAMPUS
- Johnny Unitas Stadium
- University Union
- Burdick Hall
- The Den

OFF CAMPUS
- Towson Town Center (shopping)
- Baltimore Inner Harbor
- Movie Theater (The Commons)
- Washington, D.C.

TRANSPORTATION

BWI Airport is 20 miles away from campus (www.bwiairport.com). You can take Amtrak trains at Baltimore's Penn Station, which is eight miles away from campus (www.amtrak.com). For Greyhound bus service, go to Baltimore's West Fayette Station, which is 10 miles away from campus (www.greyhound.com). For local transit and rail, call 410-539-5000 or see our website at www.mtamaryland.com. For local taxi, call Jimmy's Cab at 410-296-7200.

FIND YOUR WAY

Directions to Towson University Admissions Office from I-95 (northbound and southbound): take the Baltimore Beltway I-695 west (toward Towson). Take exit 25, Charles Street, south. Proceed approximately 1.7 miles. Turn left on Towson Boulevard, and proceed to the first stoplight. Turn right on Osler Drive and make the first right to the Enrollment Services Center parking lot. **From I-83 (northbound and southbound):** take the Baltimore Beltway I-695 east (toward Towson). Take exit 25, Charles Street, south. Proceed approximately 1.7 miles. Turn left on Towsontown Boulevard and proceed to the fist stop light. Turn right on Osler Drive, and make the first right to the Enrollment Services Center parking lot. **From I-70 (eastbound):** take the Baltimore Beltway I-695 north (toward Towson). Take Exit 25, Charles Street south. Proceed approximately 1.7 miles. Turn left on Townsontown Boulevard, and proceed to the first stoplight. Turn right on Osler Drive, and make the first right to the Enrollment Services Center parking lot.

STAY THE NIGHT

Nearby: The following are accommodations in the Towson area: the **Burkshire Guest Suites** (10 West Burke Ave.; 800-435-5986), is across the street from campus; **Sheraton** (903 Dulaney Valley Rd.; 410-321-7400); the **Holiday Inn** (1100 Cromwell Bridge Rd.; 410-823-4410); **Ramada Inn** (8712 Loch Raven Blvd.; 410-823-0900); and **Days Inn** (8801 Loch Raven Blvd.; 410-882-0900).

AT A GLANCE

Selectivity Rating	66
Range SAT I Math	510–600
Average SAT I Math	555
Range SAT I Verbal	500–580
Average SAT I Verbal	540
Average ACT Composite	23
Average GPA	3.45
Student/Faculty Ratio	17:1

CAMPUS TOURS

Appointment	Required
Dates	Varies
Times	Varies
Average Length	1 hour

ON-CAMPUS APPOINTMENTS

Admissions

Start Date–Juniors	Spring semester
Appointment	Required
Advance Notice	Yes, 2 weeks
Saturdays	No
Average Length	30 min.
Info Sessions	Yes

Faculty and Coaches

Dates/Times	Academic year
Arrangements	Contact coach directly 1 week prior

CLASS VISITS

Dates	Academic year
Arrangements	Varies

UNITED STATES NAVAL ACADEMY

117 Decatur Road, United States Naval Academy, Annapolis, MD 21402 • Telephone: 410-293-4361 • www.usna.edu/Admissions/ • Email: webmail@gwmail.usna.com

Hours: Monday–Friday, 9:00AM–5:00PM; Saturday, 9:00AM–noon

The United States Naval Academy in Annapolis provides a stellar and rigorous education in the arts and sciences and, of course, training in military and naval service. The Midshipmen eagerly anticipate the annual Army-Navy football game, perhaps the most historic of college gridiron contests.

AT A GLANCE

Selectivity Rating	99
Range SAT I Math	560–670
Average SAT I Math	663
Range SAT I Verbal	530–640
Average SAT I Verbal	637
Student/Faculty Ratio	7:1

CAMPUS TOURS

Appointment	Not required
Dates	Year-round
Times	Jun–Sept: Mon–Sat, 9:30AM-3:30PM; Sun 12:30PM–3:30PM
Average Length	1 hour

ON-CAMPUS APPOINTMENTS

Admissions

Appointment	Preferred
Advance Notice	Yes
Saturdays	Sometimes
Average Length	1 hour
Info Sessions	Yes

Faculty and Coaches

Dates/Times	Year-round
Arrangements	Contact Athletic Department

CLASS VISITS

Dates	Academic year
Arrangements	Contact Admissions Office

TRANSPORTATION

Baltimore-Washington International Airport is 25 miles away from the academy. Shuttle service is available from the airport.

FIND YOUR WAY

From I-95, take the Beltway to the east around Washington, D.C. (toward New Carrollton). Exit to U.S. Rte. 50/301 E. toward Annapolis. **From U.S. 50/301,** take Exit 24 Rowe Blvd. into Annapolis, then turn left onto College Ave. Proceed on College Avenue, and at the stoplight turn right onto King George Street. The academy's entrance is at King George and Randall streets.

STAY THE NIGHT

Nearby: The academy is at one end of the historic town of Annapolis. **Gibson's Lodgings** (110 Prince George St.; 410-268-5555) is adjacent to the academy and offers 20 rooms, some with private baths, in three houses. The moderate rate includes continental breakfast and parking. Rooms with shared baths are cheaper. Another moderately-priced bed-and-breakfast near the academy is the **Victorian Prince George Inn** (232 Prince George St.; 410-263-6418), with four guest rooms sharing two baths. Rooms are air-conditioned, and the price includes a large continental breakfast. There are four historic inns restored and run by Historic Inns of Annapolis, all close to the academy. The **Maryland Inn,** the farthest away but the liveliest (44 rooms and a restaurant), is only a 10-minute walk from the academy. All of these inns are booked through Historic Inns of Annapolis (410-263-2641 or 800-847-8882 outside of MD). Mail requests to 16 Church Circle, Annapolis, MD 21401. For an indoor pool, exercise room, restaurant, and weekend dancing, head for the **Sheraton Barcelo** (173 Jennifer Rd.; 410-266-3131), five miles away from the academy.

A Little Farther: There are a variety of hotels in both Washington, D.C. and Baltimore, Maryland.

HIGHLIGHTS

ON CAMPUS

- Bancroft Hall
- U.S. Naval Academy Museum
- Armel-Leftwich Visitor Center
- U.S. Naval Academy Chapel
- Lejeune Hall

OFF CAMPUS

- The downtown and waterfront areas of Annapolis are showcases filled with beautifully preserved eighteenth-century buildings.
- Walking tours and boat cruises are offered at many different sites in town and at the docks.
- Maryland State House
- Maryland State War Memorial
- Eastern Shore

UNIVERSITY OF MARYLAND, BALTIMORE COUNTY

Office of Undergraduate Admissions, 1000 Hilltop Circle, Baltimore, MD 21250 • Telephone: 800-862-2482 • www.umbc.edu/Admissions/ • Email: admissions@umbc.edu

Hours: Monday–Friday, 8:30AM–4:30PM

University of Maryland, Baltimore County is a public school strategically located in suburbia between Baltimore, Maryland and Washington, D.C. Students have the big-time resources of a state university and the friendly atmosphere of a small college. UMBC has an impressive track record of placing students in leading graduate programs and promising careers.

HIGHLIGHTS

ON CAMPUS
- Albin O. Kuhn Library & Gallery
- The Commons (Community Center)
- Center for Art and Visual Culture
- Howard Hughes Medical Institute
- Retriever Activities Center

OFF CAMPUS
- Baltimore Inner Harbor
- Washington, D.C.
- Potapsaco State Park
- Historic Ellicott City
- Annapolis

TRANSPORTATION

The campus is located four miles away from BWI airport. UMBC offers daily shuttle services for students from campus to the BWI Rail Station, downtown Baltimore, and the nearby towns of Catonsville and Arbutus. The university also schedules van trips to Washington, D.C.

FIND YOUR WAY

From the north, take Interstate 95 to Route 166 (Exit 47B, Catonsville) or take Interstate 83 to the Baltimore Beltway (I-695, west) and then take Exit 12C (Wilkens Avenue, west); follow the signs to UMBC. **From the south,** take Interstate 95 to Route 166 (Exit 47B, Catonsville); follow the signs to UMBC.

STAY THE NIGHT

Nearby: You can stay at a variety of places, including the **Days Inn** (Baltimore–Inner Harbor; 410-576-1000), the **Embassy Suites** (BWI Airport; 410-850-0747), the **Hampton Inn** (BWI Airport; 410-850-0600), the **Wingate Inn** (BWI Airport; 410-859-0003), the **Holiday Inn** (Inner Harbor; 410-685-3500), the **Hyatt Regency** (Baltimore–Inner Harbor; 410-528-1234), and the **Marriott** (BWI Airport; 410-859-8300).

AT A GLANCE

Selectivity Rating	79
Range SAT I Math	570–670
Average SAT I Math	621
Range SAT I Verbal	540–640
Average SAT I Verbal	592
Average ACT Composite	25
Average GPA	3.5
Student/Faculty Ratio	17:1

CAMPUS TOURS

Appointment	Preferred
Dates	Year-round
Times	Varies
Average Length	1 hour

ON-CAMPUS APPOINTMENTS

Admissions

Appointment	Preferred
Saturdays	No
Average Length	1 hour
Info Sessions	Yes

Faculty and Coaches

Dates/Times	Year-round
Arrangements	Contact Athletic Department 1 week prior

CLASS VISITS

Dates	Academic year
Arrangements	Contact Admissions Office

UNIVERSITY OF MARYLAND—COLLEGE PARK

Mitchell Building, College Park, MD 20742-5235 •
Telephone: 800-422-5867 • www.umd.edu/admissions/ •
Email: um-admit@uga.umd.edu

Hours: Monday–Friday, 8:00AM–4:30PM; Saturday by appointment

The very affordable University of Maryland is a major research university that offers a professional atmosphere and an exemplary honors program. Maryland's core curriculum requires students to fulfill a wide range of distribution requirements; during senior year, students take two seminars designed to help integrate these disparate courses into their majors. Newscaster Connie Chung and muppet creator Jim Henson are alums.

AT A GLANCE

Selectivity Rating	80
Range SAT I Math	600–700
Range SAT I Verbal	570–670
Average GPA	3.86
Student/Faculty Ratio	13:1

CAMPUS TOURS

Dates	Academic year
Times	Call in advance for current schedule
Average Length	2 hours

ON-CAMPUS APPOINTMENTS

Admissions

Start Date—Juniors	N/A
Info Sessions	Call in advance for current schedule

Faculty and Coaches

Dates/Times	Year-round
Arrangements	Contact faculty directly 4 weeks prior

CLASS VISITS

Dates	Year-round
Arrangements	Contact Visiting Center

TRANSPORTATION

Baltimore-Washington International Airport is 25 miles away from campus. MARC trains (800-325-7245) and airport shuttles are available for the trip from the airport to campus. Washington National Airport is 15 miles away from campus. Metrorail trains (202-637-7000) are available for the trip from the airport to campus. Amtrak and Greyhound are available to Washington, D.C. Switch to Metrorail at Union Station and take it to College Park. University shuttle buses (301-314-2255) provide transportation from the College Park MARC and Metrorail stations to campus.

FIND YOUR WAY

From Baltimore and the north, take I-95 S. to the Capital Beltway (I-495 around Washington, D.C.); follow the signs to College Park. At Exit 25, take U.S. 1 S. for approximately two miles, then turn right into campus at the Visitors' Center. **From the west,** follow the preceding directions from the Capital Beltway (I-495). **From the east,** take U.S. 50 W. to the Capital Beltway (I-495); head north on I-495 to College Park. At Exit 25, take U.S. 1 S. for two miles and turn right into campus. **From Washington, D.C.,** take New Hampshire Ave. (U.S. 29) or Riggs Road (N. Capitol St. in D.C., Maryland Rte. 212) north to the East-West Highway (Maryland Rte. 410); turn right onto Rte. 410 and proceed to U.S. 1 and turn left on it. Continue on U.S. 1 to the campus, turning left at the Visitors' Center.

STAY THE NIGHT

Nearby: **The Center of Adult Education** (301-985-7300), a conference center on campus, has moderately-priced rooms. The **Quality Inn** (7200 Baltimore Ave.; 301-864-5829) is half a mile away. Slightly less expensive is **Econo Lodge** (9113 Baltimore Blvd.; 301-345-4900), which is one mile away. Your rock-bottom budget choice is **Comfort Inn** (9020 Baltimore Blvd.; 301-441-8110), which is a mile-and-a-half away. For a more upscale chain motel, try the **Holiday Inn** (10000 Baltimore Blvd.; 301-345-6700), or **Courtyard by Marriott** (8330 Corporate Dr., Landover; 301-577-3373). There is an even fancier Marriott, the **Marriott Greenbelt** (6400 Ivy Lane, Greenbelt; 301-441-3700), which is 15 minutes away. Two bed-and-breakfast referral agencies with listings in the area are the **Traveller in Maryland** (410-269-6232), and **Amanda's B&B Reservation Service** (410-225-0001).

A Little Farther: A little farther from the school is College Park, which is 20 minutes away from downtown Washington, D.C. See entries for any of the Washington, D.C. schools for suggestions.

HIGHLIGHTS

ON CAMPUS

• Campus Recreation Center
• Adele H. Stamp Student Union
• Cole Student Activities Building
• Byrd Stadium
• Memorial Chapel

OFF CAMPUS

• Washington, D.C. attractions
• Baltimore's Inner Harbor

WASHINGTON COLLEGE

300 Washington Ave.,
Chestertown, MD 21620 • Telephone: 800-422-1782 • www.washcoll.edu •
Email: adm.off@washcoll.edu

Hours: Monday–Friday, 8:30AM–4:30PM

About 1,000 students study at this, the nation's tenth oldest university, located in historic Chestertown, Maryland. In addition to offering a fine liberal arts education, the school boasts a creative writing program with exceptional resources at the O'Neill Literary House: a social haven, publishing house, and writers' think tank rolled into one.

HIGHLIGHTS

ON CAMPUS

- Miller Library
- Johnson Lifetime Fitness Center
- Gibson Center & Tawes Theater
- O'Neill Literary House
- Casey Academic Center

OFF CAMPUS

- Chesapeake Bay
- Chesapeake Bay Maritime Museum
- Eastern Neck Island National Wildlife Refuge
- Chestertown Historic District
- Rock Hall

TRANSPORTATION

Baltimore-Washington and Philadelphia International airports are 75 miles away from campus. Public transportation is not available.

FIND YOUR WAY

From the north, take I-95 S. to Rte. 896 S. in Newark, Delaware. Follow to Rte. 301 S. and exit at Galena. Proceed to Rte. 213. Take Rte. 213 S. to Chestertown. **From the south,** take I-95 N. to U.S. 50 and 301 (Exit 19). Take U.S. 50 and 301 E.; stay on U.S. 301 N. when it splits from U.S. 50. Continue on U.S. 301 to the intersection with Maryland Rte. 213; then take Rte. 213 N. into Chestertown.

STAY THE NIGHT

Nearby: **Comfort Suites** (160 Scheeler Rd.; 410-810-0555), a moderately-priced motel, is just five blocks away from campus. If you venture a little farther into historic Chestertown, you have a terrific choice of bed-and-breakfasts and inns. **Widow's Walk Bed and Breakfast** (402 High St.; 410-778-6864) is six blocks away from campus and moderately-priced. About eight blocks away from campus is the **White Swan Tavern** (231 High St.; 410-778-2300), a beautifully restored inn dating back to the 1700s with six rooms, private baths, and complimentary wine on arrival; bicycles are available for guests. Rates range from moderate to expensive. (Note: The inn does not take credit cards.) The **Imperial Hotel** (208 High St.; 410-778-5000) has 13 air-conditioned guest rooms with televisions and private baths. Rates are expensive. If you prefer a rural setting, consider **Brampton Bed and Breakfast** (Rte. 20; 410-778-1860), a wonderful brick house sitting on 35 lush acres and only one mile away from campus (and from historic Chestertown).

A Little Farther: **Mears Great Oak Landing** (22170 Great Oak Landing Rd.; 410-778-2100) is a 70-acre yachting resort on a tributary of the Chesapeake Bay with a nine-hole golf course, tennis courts, pool, and private beach. The resort is nine miles away from campus and rates are moderate.

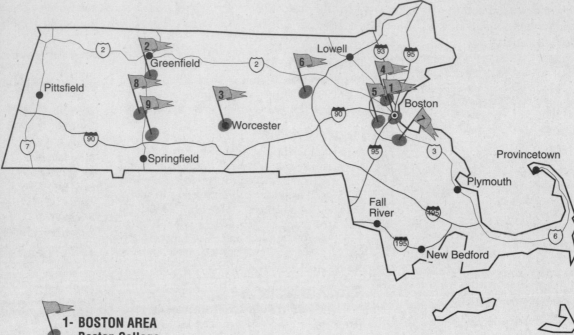

1- **BOSTON AREA**
   Boston College
   Boston University
   Emerson College
   Northeastern University
   Simmons College
2- **AMHERST AREA**
   Amherst College
   Hampshire College
   University of Massachusetts—Amherst
3- **WORCESTER AREA**
   Clark University
   College of the Holy Cross
   Worcester Polytechnic Institute
4- **CAMBRIDGE AREA**
   Harvard-Radcliffe Colleges
   Massachusetts Institute Technical
   Tufts University
5- **WELLESLEY AREA**
   Babson College
   Wellesley College
6- **WALTHAM AREA**
   Bentley College
   Brandeis University
7- **Curry College**
8- **Smith College**
9- **Mount Holyoke**

Mass.

	Amherst College	Babson College	Bentley College	Boston College	Brandeis Univ.	Curry College	Hampshire College	Harvard-Radcliffe	M. I. T.	Merrimack Coll.	Mt. Holyoke Coll.	Smith College	Tufts University	U. Mass-Amherst	Wellesley College	Wheaton College	Williams College	Boston*	Springfield	Worcester**
Amherst College	—	88	98	99	96	111	7	102	104	96	12	8	108	2	84	106	57	103	25	47
Babson College	88	—	8	7	6	15	86	11	12	34	87	92	14	90	2	33	130	15	79	31
Bentley College	98	8	—	7	2	17	96	6	7	26	98	104	8	100	9	41	140	9	86	40
Boston College	99	7	7	—	9	9	97	6	5	25	99	105	7	101	9	41	141	6	87	38
Brandeis Univ.	96	6	2	9	—	16	94	8	11	28	97	102	10	98	7	39	138	6	84	38
Curry College	111	15	17	9	16	—	108	11	9	32	110	114	16	113	17	28	142	7	101	59
Hampshire College	7	86	96	97	94	108	—	100	101	100	5	7	105	9	82	104	56	101	18	45
Harvard-Radcliffe	102	11	6	6	8	11	100	—	2	21	102	108	2	104	13	41	144	1	89	44
M. I. T.	104	12	7	5	11	9	101	2	—	22	104	109	4	106	14	40	146	1	93	44
Merrimack Coll.	96	34	26	25	28	32	100	21	22	—	108	103	18	94	36	70	130	25	112	55
Mt. Holyoke Coll.	12	87	98	99	97	110	5	102	104	108	—	5	108	14	85	107	60	104	11	47
Smith College	8	92	104	105	102	114	7	108	109	103	5	—	112	10	90	112	54	109	20	53
Tufts University	108	14	8	7	10	16	105	2	4	18	108	112	—	106	15	43	146	4	91	46
U. Mass-Amherst	2	90	100	101	98	113	9	104	106	94	14	10	106	—	86	108	55	105	27	49
Wellesley College	84	2	9	9	7	17	82	13	14	36	85	90	15	86	—	34	131	12	77	29
Wheaton College	106	33	41	41	39	28	104	41	40	70	107	112	43	108	34	—	148	31	89	52
Williams College	57	130	140	141	138	142	56	144	146	130	60	54	146	55	131	148	—	143	70	100
Boston*	103	15	9	6	6	7	101	1	1	25	104	109	4	105	12	31	143	—	90	42
Springfield	25	79	86	87	84	101	18	89	93	112	11	20	91	27	77	89	70	90	—	53
Worcester**	47	31	40	38	38	59	45	44	44	55	47	53	46	49	29	52	100	42	53	—

*Use Boston mileage for Boston University, Emerson College, Northeastern University, and Simmons College.

**Use Worcester mileage for Clark University, College of the Holy Cross, and Worcester Polytechnic Institute.

AMHERST COLLEGE

Admissions Office, Box 2231, Amherst, MA 01002 •
Telephone: 413-542-2328 • www.amherst.edu/admission/ •
Email: admission@amherst.edu

Hours: Monday–Friday, 8:30AM–4:30PM; Saturday (only during the fall), 9:00AM–noon

Concerned and friendly professors highlight the occasionally stressful experience at this truly outstanding, small liberal arts college. The campus is often somewhat dead, but there are numerous ways to get involved; when students become claustrophobic, nearby UMass, Smith, Hampshire, and Mount Holyoke offer a nice change of pace.

AT A GLANCE

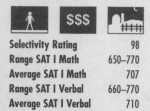

Selectivity Rating	98
Range SAT I Math	650–770
Average SAT I Math	707
Range SAT I Verbal	660–770
Average SAT I Verbal	710
Average ACT Composite	30
Student/Faculty Ratio	9:1

CAMPUS TOURS

Appointment	Not required
Dates	Varies
Times	Varies throughout the year
Average Length	1 hour

ON-CAMPUS APPOINTMENTS

Admissions

Faculty and Coaches

Dates/Times	Academic year
Arrangements	contact the faculty member or coach directly 2 weeks prior

CLASS VISITS

Dates	Academic year
Arrangements	Contact Admissions Office

TRANSPORTATION

Bradley International Airport near Hartford, Connecticut is 45 miles away from campus. Peter Pan bus line (800-237-8747), Valley Transporter limousines (800-237-8747 or 413-253-1350), rental cars, and taxis are available for the trip from the airport to campus. Amtrak trains provide regular service from New York City to Springfield, Massachusetts. Greyhound buses serve Springfield hourly from Boston and New York. Buses also run hourly from Springfield to Amherst. Taxis (and, during the academic year, the free Five College Bus Service) are available for the trip from town to campus.

FIND YOUR WAY

From the south, take I-91 N. to Exit 19. Take Rte. 9 E. for seven miles. In the town of Amherst, turn right onto Rte. 116 S. Proceed a quarter mile to the Admissions Office on the left. **From the east,** take I-90 W. (Massachusetts Tpke.) to Exit 8 (Palmer-Amherst). Take Rte. 181 N. to Rte. 9 W. From Rte. 9, turn left onto Rte. 116 S. for a quarter mile to the Admissions Office. **From the west,** take I-90 E. to the W. Springfield exit. Head north on I-91 to Exit 19; then head east on Rte. 9 for seven miles to the town of Amherst. Turn right onto Rte. 116 S. for a quarter mile to the Admissions Office. **From the north,** take I-91 S. to Exit 25 (Amherst). Take Rte. 116 S. to the Admissions Office.

STAY THE NIGHT

Nearby: Visit www.amherst.edu/about_amh/visit/lodging.html. **Lord Jeffery Inn** (413-253-2576), on the Common in Amherst, is a popular place with Amherst visitors. It has character and is conveniently located within walking distance of the campus. Rates are moderate. There is also the **Howard Johnson Motor Lodge in Hadley** (413-586-0114). **Amherst Motel** (408 Northampton Rd.; 413-256-8122) is cheap and it has a pool; there is a Friendly's across the street. **Aqua Vitae Motel** (Bay Rd., Hadley; 413-586-0300) is even cheaper and is only five miles away. No breakfast is served, but there is a cafe nearby. A third choice is **Econo Lodge** (Rte. 9, Hadley; 413-584-9816), 10 minutes away. Just like the Aqua Vitae, no breakfast is served, but a cafe is nearby. Smith College, in Northampton, is only 15 minutes away. Check that entry. A couple of other motels convenient to Amherst are listed under the University of Massachusetts, which is only two miles to the north.

HIGHLIGHTS

ON CAMPUS
- Mead Art Museum
- Pratt Museum of Natural History
- Russian Cultural Center
- Japanese Peace Garden

OFF CAMPUS
- Emily Dickinson Homestead
- Yankee Candle
- Basketball Hall of Fame
- Eric Carle Museum
- Yiddish Center

BABSON COLLEGE

Mustard Hall,
Babson Park, MA 02457 • Telephone: 800-488-3696 • www3.babson.edu •
Email: ugradadmission@babson.edu

Hours: Monday–Friday, 8:30AM–4:30PM; Saturdays (during January and fall only)

This small, rigorous, career-oriented, and well-rounded school in Massachusetts is touted by its very conservative and wealthy students as the number one business school in the country. A highly praised and compulsory entrepreneurship curriculum requires teams of students to start and operate their own actual businesses.

HIGHLIGHTS

ON CAMPUS

- Sorenson Arts Center
- Blank Center for Entrepreneurship
- Glavin Family Chapel
- Reynolds Student Center
- Webster Athletic Center

OFF CAMPUS

- Fenway Park
- The Museum of Fine Arts Boston
- Wellesley Center (shopping and restaurants)
- Newbury Street (shopping)
- Harvard Square

TRANSPORTATION

Logan International Airport is approximately 12 miles away from campus. Taxis are available for the ride to campus, but they are quite expensive. Public transportation by commuter rail line is the way to go. Take the MBTA train from the Airport (Blue Line) inbound into Boston. Transfer at Government Center to the Green Line, and take the Riverside train to Riverside Station. From there, you can take a taxi for the three-mile ride to campus. Amtrak trains and Greyhound buses run to Boston.

FIND YOUR WAY

From I-90 (Massachusetts Tpke.), exit to I-95/Route 128 S. Follow I-95 to Exit 20B (Route 9W). Continue on Rte. 9 W for 1.9 miles and take the Rte. 16 exit. At the end of the exit ramp, turn left onto Rte. 16 W. (Washington St.). Follow Rte. 16 W. for half a mile and turn left at the traffic lights onto Forest St. Follow Forest St. for one mile to the stop sign. Proceed straight through the intersection for 0.2 miles. The main entrance to the Babson campus will be on your right.

STAY THE NIGHT

Nearby: Stay right on campus at the **Babson Center for Executive Education** (781-239-4000) for afforadable, luxurious accomodations, which include a great breakfast. Also available are the **Courtyard Marriott** (342 Speen Street, Natick; 800-321-2211 or 508-655-6100), the **Crowne Plaza** (1360 Worcester Road, Rte. 9 East, Natick; 508-653-8800), and **Travelodge Natick** (1350 Worcester Road, Natick; 508-655-2222).

A Little Farther: You have many choices, including the **DoubleTree Guest Suites** (550 Winter Street, Waltham; 781-890-6767), the **Four Seasons Hotel** (200 Boylston Street, Boston; 617-338-4400 or 800-332-3442), the **Hilton at Dedham** (25 Allied Drive, Dedham; 800-445-8667 or 781-329-7900), the **Holiday Inn Newton** (399 Grove Street, Newton; 617-969-5300 or 800-325-2525), the **Marriott Newton** (2345 Commonwealth Avenue, Newton; 617-969-1000 or 800-228-9290), the **Hampton Inn** (319 Speen Street, Natick; 508-653-5000), the **Ritz Carlton** (15 Arlington Street, Boston; 800-241-3333), the **Sheraton Newton** Hotel (320 Washington St, Newton; 800-325-3535 or 617-969-3010), the **Sheraton Needham Hotel** (100 Cabot St, Needham; 781-444-1110 or 800-325-3535), the **Sheraton Framingham Hotel** (1657 Worcester Rd., Framingham; 800-325-3535), and the **Westin Hotel** (70 Third Avenue, Waltham; 800-228-3000 or 781-290-5600).

AT A GLANCE

Selectivity Rating	88
Range SAT I Math	600–690
Average SAT I Math	640
Range SAT I Verbal	550–630
Average SAT I Verbal	600
Student/Faculty Ratio	13:1

CAMPUS TOURS

Appointment	Not required
Dates	Varies
Times	Mon–Fri, 10AM & 2PM
Average Length	1 hour

ON-CAMPUS APPOINTMENTS

Admissions

Start Date–Juniors	April 1
Appointment	Required
Advance Notice	Yes, 2 weeks
Saturdays	No
Average Length	30 min.
Info Sessions	Yes

Faculty and Coaches

Dates/Times	Academic year
Arrangements	Contact Admissions Office 2 weeks prior

CLASS VISITS

Arrangements	Other

BENTLEY COLLEGE

Undergraduate Admissions Office, 175 Forest Street, Waltham, MA 02452-4705 • Telephone: 800-523-2354 • www.bentley.edu/admission/ • Email: ugadmission@bentley.edu

Hours: Monday–Friday, 8:30AM–4:30PM; Saturday (select), 9:00AM–1:00PM

Modern, technological, information-based, and business-oriented Bentley College is really big on that whole business core thing and requires all students to take accounting, business law, computer information systems, finance, and marketing. Bentley is built on a mountain only 15 minutes away from Waltham, a Boston suburb only 15 minutes away from Harvard Square.

AT A GLANCE

Selectivity Rating	80
Range SAT I Math	560–650
Average SAT I Math	603
Range SAT I Verbal	520–600
Average SAT I Verbal	559
Student/Faculty Ratio	14:1

CAMPUS TOURS

Appointment	Required
Dates	Year-round
Times	Varies throughout the year
Average Length	1 hour

ON-CAMPUS APPOINTMENTS

Admissions

Start Date–Juniors	Anytime
Appointment	Required, 2 weeks
Saturdays	Yes
Info Sessions	N/A

Faculty and Coaches

Dates/Times	Year-round
Arrangements	Contact Admissions Office 3 weeks prior

CLASS VISITS

Dates	Academic year
Arrangements	Contact Admissions Office

TRANSPORTATION

Logan International Airport in Boston is 12 miles away from Bentley College, with transportation to campus available by taxi, MBTA trains and buses, and rental car. Amtrak offers frequent passenger service to South Station in Boston from all points along the Northeast Corridor. Public transportation is available from South Station to campus.

FIND YOUR WAY

From the south, take Route 95/128 North to Exit 28A (Trapelo Road). Turn right at the end of exit ramp and follow 2.6 miles toward Belmont. Turn right onto Forest Street. Approximately one mile on the left is the main entrance to the Bentley campus. **From the west,** take the Massachusetts Tpke. to Exit 14 and follow signs to Rte. 95/128 N; follow the directions listed for people coming from the south.

STAY THE NIGHT

Nearby: There are several hotels located near the Bentley campus. They include the **Doubletree Guest Suites** (550 Winter St.; 781-890-6767), the **Westin Hotel** (70 Third Avenue; 781-290-5600), and **Wyndham Garden Hotel** (420 Totten Pond Road; 781-890-0100).

HIGHLIGHTS

ON CAMPUS

- Financial Trading Room
- Smith Academic Technology Center
- Coffeehouse
- Center for Marketing Technology
- Dana Athletic Center

OFF CAMPUS

- Harvard Square
- Downtown Boston shopping
- Boston's Club scene
- Major league sports (Red Sox, Patriots, Bruins, Celtics)
- Boston North End

BOSTON COLLEGE

Office of Undergraduate Admissions, Devlin Hall, Room 120, Chestnut Hill, MA 02467-3809 • Telephone: 800-360-2522 • www.bc.edu/admission • Email: ugadmis@bc.edu

Hours: Monday–Friday, 9:00AM–4:45PM; select Saturdays (fall only) 9:00AM–3:00PM

Boston College is neither a college (it's a university) nor in Boston (it's in Chestnut Hill). It is, however, a large Jesuit school with a rich Catholic tradition and nationally recognized schools of business, nursing, and education. Downtown Boston, with its vital, college-oriented nightlife, is only 20 minutes away by car or public transportation.

HIGHLIGHTS

ON CAMPUS
- McMullen Museum of Art
- Alumni Stadium
- Robsham Theater
- Higgins Biology and Physics Center

OFF CAMPUS
- Fenway Park
- Boston Commons
- Museum of Fine Arts
- Freedom Trail
- Waldom Pond

TRANSPORTATION

Logan International Airport in Boston is seven miles away from campus. Public transportation, rental cars, and taxis are available from the airport to campus. Amtrak trains and Greyhound buses provide service to Boston. Local public transportation to the college is provided by the Boston College branch of the Massachusetts Bay Transit authority's Green Line. The Green Line ends at the Boston/Newton boundary on Commonwealth Ave. The walk up the hill brings you to the entrance of the Chestnut Hill campus.

FIND YOUR WAY

From I-95 (also known as Rte. 128), take Exit 24 (Rte. 30). Proceed east on Rte. 30 (Commonwealth Ave.) for approximately five miles to the campus. **From the west,** take the Massachusetts Tpke. to Exit 17. At the first set of lights after the exit ramp, turn right onto Center St. and follow it to the fourth set of lights. Turn left onto Commonwealth Ave. and proceed on it for a mile-and-a-half to the campus.

STAY THE NIGHT

Nearby: A conveniently-located hotel is **Marriot-Newton** (2345 Commonwealth Avenue; 1-800-228-9290), which offers accomodations for moderate to expensive prices. Ten minutes away is a **Holiday Inn** (399 Grove Street; 1-800-HOLIDAY), which has a special BC rate. The **Best Western Terrace** (1650 Commonwealth Avenue; Brighton, 1-800-528-1234) is one-and-a-half miles away from campus and has rates ranging from inexpensive to moderate.

AT A GLANCE

Selectivity Rating	95
Range SAT I Math	620–710
Range SAT I Verbal	600–690
Student/Faculty Ratio	13:1

CAMPUS TOURS

Dates	Year-round
Times	Varies throughout the year
Average Length	1 hour

ON-CAMPUS APPOINTMENTS

Admissions

Start Date–Juniors	N/A
Info Sessions	Call for campus tour and info sessions schedule

Faculty and Coaches

Dates/Times	Year-round
Arrangements	Contact faculty directly 2 weeks prior

CLASS VISITS

Dates	Academic year
Arrangements	Contact Admissions Office

BOSTON UNIVERSITY

Admissions Office, 121 Bay State Rd.,
Boston, MA 02215 • Telephone: 617-353-2300 • www.bu.edu/admissions/ •
Email: admissions@bu.edu

Hours: Monday–Friday, 9:00AM–5:00PM; select Saturdays during fall and spring, 9:00AM–1:00PM

Large, private Boston University has a diverse student population, superior faculty, and great atmosphere. There's a lot of red tape, but the academic experience is marvelous and the tremendous social life is second to none. Talk about prominent alumni: Jason Alexander ("George" on Seinfeld) and National Public Radio's Nina Totenberg were students here, and Martin Luther King, Jr. received his doctorate here.

AT A GLANCE

Selectivity Rating		90
Range SAT I Math		610–690
Average SAT I Math		647
Range SAT I Verbal		590–680
Average SAT I Verbal		634
Average ACT Composite		28
Average GPA		3.5
Student/Faculty Ratio		14:1

CAMPUS TOURS

Appointment	Not required
Dates	Year-round
Times	Varies
Average Length	1 hour

ON-CAMPUS APPOINTMENTS

Admissions

Appointment	Required
Advance Notice	3 weeks
Saturdays	No
Average Length	30 min.
Info Sessions	Yes

Faculty and Coaches

Dates/Times	Year-round
Arrangements	Contact Athletic Department 2 weeks prior

CLASS VISITS

Dates	Academic year
Arrangements	Contact Visiting Center

TRANSPORTATION

By the MBTA (the T line): Take the Green Line train (Boston College, B line, Cleveland Circle C line, or Riverside D line) to Kenmore Square Station. Exit to the street level (Commonwealth Avenue) and walk west one block (past the Barnes and Noble bookstore) to Deerfield Street, and turn right. Walk one block to Bay State Road, and turn left. The Admissions Reception Center is located on the right side, at 121 Bay State Road. **From the airport:** Taxis to Boston University from Boston's Logan International Airport may take approximately 30 minutes (approximate $25 fare). From the airport, the T may take an hour and requires a transfer from the Blue Line to the Green Line at Government Center Station (for directions to Boston University by MBTA, see above). **By bus or train:** Amtrak service and major bus companies arrive at Boston's South Station. Taxis to Boston University take approximately 20 minutes (approximate $20 fare). The T may take 40 minutes and requires a transfer from the Red Line to the Green Line at Park Street Station (for direction to Boston University by MBTA, see above).

FIND YOUR WAY

From west of Boston: Take Interstate 90 (Massachusetts Turnpike) to Exit 18 (Brighton/Cambridge). Pay the toll, then follow the signs for Cambridge down the ramp to the second set of lights. Turn right at the lights (do not cross over the bridge/Charles River) and travel on Soldiers Field Road/Storrow Drive to the second Boston University exit. Follow the local directions below. **From north of Boston:** Take Route 93 South to the Storrow Drive exit (Exit 26). Continue on Storrow Drive to the Kenmore Square exit (left exit). Follow the signs for Kenmore Square. Follow the local directions below. **From south of Boston:** Take Interstate 93 North/Route 3 North to Storrow Drive exit (exit 26). Go west on Storrow Drive to Kenmore Square exit (left exit). Follow the signs for Kenmore Square. Follow the local directions below. **Local Directions:** Turn right off the exit ramp at the traffic light (Beacon Street). Stay to the right to enter Bay State Road. The Admissions Reception Center will be on the right, 121 Bay State Road. **Parking:** Metered parking is available in front of the Reception Center on Bay State Road. Meters accept quarters only. A campus parking lot, which offers parking for a flat fee, is located off Commonwealth Avenue just west of Kenmore Square.

STAY THE NIGHT

Nearby: Boston University is located in the Back Bay/Fenway area of Boston. The university does not endorse any particular hotel establishment. A list of local hotels can be found at www.bu.edu/admissions/explore/coming.html.

HIGHLIGHTS

ON CAMPUS

- Marsh Chapel Plaza
- Mugar Memorial Library (special collections)
- DeWolfe Boathouse
- George Sherman Student Union
- The Photonics Center

OFF CAMPUS

- Museum of Fine Arts
- Boston Red Sox at Fenway Park
- Charles River Esplanade
- Newbury Street shopping district
- Symphony Hall

BRANDEIS UNIVERSITY

Shapiro Admissions Center, Box 9110, Waltham, MA 02454 •
Telephone: 800-622-0622 • www.brandeis.edu/admissions/ •
Email: sendinfo@brandeis.edu

Hours: Monday–Friday, 9:00AM–5:00PM

The academic opportunities are awesome at relatively young Brandeis University (founded in 1948), a liberal arts school in suburban Boston with world-class research programs, amazing professors, and a slew of great undergraduate programs. About one in six Brandeis graduates goes on to law school, and one in eleven go to medical school.

HIGHLIGHTS

ON CAMPUS
- Volan Center for Complex Systems
- Usen Castle
- Rose Art Museum
- Shapiro Campus Center

OFF CAMPUS
- Harvard Square
- Faneuil Hall/Quincy Market
- Freedom Trail
- Museum of Fine Arts
- Boston Common and Public Garden

TRANSPORTATION

Logan International Airport in Boston is 15 miles away from campus. To get to campus, you can take the U.S. Shuttle service to Brandeis (617-489-4701; about $20) or take a Share-a-Cab, regular taxi, or airport shuttle and subway to campus from the airport. The Admissions Office will supply information on these transportation possibilities. Greyhound buses (and some other lines) serve the Riverside Terminal in Newton; from there you can take a taxi to campus. Amtrak trains and Greyhound and other bus lines serve Boston. Commuter trains from Boston bring you within walking distance of campus.

FIND YOUR WAY

From I-90 (Massachusetts Tpke.) eastbound, take exit 14 for I-95/Rte. 128 and Rte. 30 exit in Weston. Follow the signs to Rte. 30 (exit 24); at the top of the ramp, turn left onto Rte. 30. Take the first right and continue to campus, which is two miles ahead on the left. **From I-90 westbound,** take exit 15 for I-95/Rte. 128 and Rte. 30. After the tollgate, go straight. At the top of the ramp, turn right; at the traffic light, turn right, and at the next traffic light, turn left. Campus is two miles ahead on the left. **From Rte. 128/I-95 northbound,** take Exit 24. At the top of the ramp, turn left onto Rte. 30; take the first right; campus is two miles ahead on the left. **From Rte. 128/I-95 southbound,** take Exit 24. At the traffic light, go straight; campus is two miles ahead—you guessed it—on the left.

STAY THE NIGHT

Nearby: A slightly expensive **Best Western TLC** (477 Toten Pond Rd.; 781-890-7800 or 800-424-2900) has an indoor pool and exercise room. For a bit more money, there is the newly renovated **Wyndham Garden Hotel** (420 Toten Pond Rd.; 781-890-0100 or 800-996-3426). The **Double Tree Guest Suites** (550 Winter St.; 617-890-6767), 10 minutes away from campus, is cool but pricey. The **Westin Hotel** (70 3rd Ave.; 781-290-5600 or 800-332-3773) has an indoor pool and a health club and a special moderate rate for university visitors.

A Little Farther: For a dose of history, stay at the eighteenth-century **Longfellow's Wayside Inn** (508-443-8846), 15 miles west of campus. This charming spot was called Howe's Tavern when Longfellow wrote of it in *Tales of a Wayside Inn*. Rates are moderate. See the Harvard-Radcliffe entry for places to stay in Cambridge. See the Wellesley College entry for other suggestions in the western suburbs of Boston. Also see the Tufts, Boston University, and Massachusetts Institute of Technology entries for other suggestions in the Boston area.

AT A GLANCE

Selectivity Rating	90
Range SAT I Math	630–710
Average SAT I Math	670
Range SAT I Verbal	627–710
Average SAT I Verbal	660
Average GPA	3.82
Student/Faculty Ratio	8:1

CAMPUS TOURS

Appointment	Not required
Dates	Year-round
Times	Mon–Fri, 10AM, 11AM, 1PM & 3PM
Average Length	1 hour

ON-CAMPUS APPOINTMENTS

Admissions

Start Date–Juniors	May 15 of junior year or before Feb 15 of senior year
Appointment	Required
Advance Notice	Yes, 3 weeks
Saturdays	No
Average Length	1 hour
Info Sessions	Yes

Faculty and Coaches

Dates/Arrangements	Contact Admissions Office 3 weeks prior

CLASS VISITS

Arrangements	Contact Admissions Office

CLARK UNIVERSITY

950 Main St.,
Worcester, MA 01610 • Telephone: 800-462-5275 • www.clarku.edu •
Email: admissions@clarku.edu

Hours: Monday–Friday, 8:30AM–5:00PM; select Saturdays (during academic term), 9:00AM–3:00PM

The social sciences and the natural sciences offer the strongest programs at this small research university in Massachusetts where students say individualism is the rule. Clark is a member of the Worcester Consortium, which allows undergraduates to take courses at any of nine other schools in the area.

AT A GLANCE

Selectivity Rating	81
Range SAT I Math	540–640
Average SAT I Math	586
Range SAT I Verbal	540–650
Average SAT I Verbal	589
Average ACT Composite	25
Average GPA	3.35
Student/Faculty Ratio	10:1

CAMPUS TOURS

Appointment	Not required
Dates	Year-round
Times	Call for times
Average Length	1 hour

ON-CAMPUS APPOINTMENTS

Admissions

Start Date–Juniors	Mid-March
Appointment	Required
Advance Notice	Yes, 2 weeks
Saturdays	Sometimes
Average Length	30 min.
Info Sessions	Yes

Faculty and Coaches

Dates/Times	Academic year
Arrangements	Contact Admissions Office 2 weeks prior

CLASS VISITS

Dates	Academic year
Arrangements	Contact Admissions Office

TRANSPORTATION

Amtrak trains serve Worcester; the station is approximately three miles away from campus. Greyhound/Trailways and Peter Pan Bus lines also stop in Worcester. Contact the following for taxis from the train or bus station: Arrow Cab at 508-756-5184, Yellow Cab at 508-754-3211, or Red Cab at 508-756-5000. You can fly into Boston's Logan International Airport or TF Green Airport in Providence, Rhode Island; shuttle-van and limousine service are available from there to campus. Worcester Airport Limousine provides service from Logan and TF Green to the Worcester area; call 800-660-0992 if you are in Massachusetts or 508-835-6436 if you are outside Massachusetts.

FIND YOUR WAY

First, some advice. If you get lost, it's pronounced Wuh-stuh. **From the Mass Pike:** Take the Mass Pike (I-90) to Route I-290 (exit 10), then follow the directions below. **From I-290:** Take Exit 11 (College Square exit) off of I-290. Coming off the exit ramp, get into the middle lane so that you can proceed straight through the first traffic light. (If you are exiting from I-290 West bear left off the exit ramp and then get into the middle lane.) At the second traffic light, take a left onto Cambridge Street (Church on the corner, Wendy's and Culpepper's Bakery on the right). Follow Cambridge Street to the third traffic light and take a sharp right onto Main Street. Follow Main Street to the first traffic light and take a left onto Maywood Street. Take the first left into the Admissions House parking lot. The Admissions House is located on the corner of Main Street and Maywood Street, and the entrance is located at the back of the building. For additional directions, please visit our website.

STAY THE NIGHT

Nearby: Clark University is southwest of the downtown area. Only 10 minutes away is the **Hampton Inn** (110 Summer St.; 508-757-0400 or 800-426-7866), which is located downtown. **Beechwood Inn** (363 Plantation St.; 508-754-5789) is four miles away from Clark. Rooms are rather expensive, but you get passes to a local health club. Right off the Massachusetts Tpke. (Exit 10), and at Exit 8 off I-290 (a 15-minute drive from school), is the **Ramada Yankee Drummer Motor Inn and Conference Center** (508-832-3221 or 800-528-5012). Rates are moderate, and there is an indoor pool. The **Baymont Inn** (444 Southbridge St.; 800-428-3438) is only 15 minutes away from campus. If you are heading east toward Boston, or coming from that direction, try the **Courtyard Marriott** (3 Technology Dr., Westborough; 508-836-4800).

HIGHLIGHTS

ON CAMPUS

- Larger than life statue of Freud
- Rare book room, Goddard Library
- Traina Center for the Arts
- Dolan Field House and updated fields
- The Green

OFF CAMPUS

- Higgin's Armory
- Worcester Art Museum
- Old Sturbridge Village
- Ecotarium
- Tower Hill Botanical Gardens

COLLEGE OF THE HOLY CROSS

Admissions Office, 1 College St.,
Worcester, MA 01610-2395 • Telephone: 800-442-2421 • www.holycross.edu •
Email: admissions@holycross.edu

Hours: Monday–Friday, 8:30AM–5:00PM; select Saturdays 8:30AM–noon

It goes without saying that you will always give 110 percent at Holy Cross, an excellent Catholic liberal arts college where grading is difficult and where enthusiastic, dedicated, and involved professors are the norm. Students describe themselves as conservative, driven, and competitive. Supreme Court Justice Clarence Thomas is an alum.

HIGHLIGHTS

ON CAMPUS
- Library
- Smith Hall
- St. Joseph Chapel
- Hart Recreation Center
- Hogan Campus Center

OFF CAMPUS
- Shrewsbury Street Restaurants
- Worcester Art Museum
- Boston
- Providence

TRANSPORTATION

Worcester Airport is a 15-minute drive from campus; taxis are available for the ride to campus. Logan International Airport in Boston is a one-hour drive from campus. Worcester Airport Limousine provides service from Logan to the Worcester area; call 800-322-0298 (in Massachusetts), 800-343-1369 (outside Massachusetts), or 508-756-4834. (You can make advance reservations or call on arrival). Greyhound/Trailways and Peter Pan buses serve Worcester.

FIND YOUR WAY

Note: See Clark University Driving instructions for important pronunciation tips. **From I-90 (Massachusetts Tpke.),** take Exit 10 (Auburn/Worcester) to I-290 E. **From I-290,** take Exit 11 (College Square). To reach campus, make the first right turn after Howard Johnson's.

STAY THE NIGHT

Nearby: Choices in Auburn include the **Baymont Inn & Suites, Days Inn,** and **Ramada Inn.** Choices in Worcester include the **Beechwood Hotel, Courtyard by Marriot,** and **Crowne Plaza.** All of these places offer special rates to Holy Cross visitors.

A Little Farther: There are numerous hotels in Sturbridge and Framingham.

AT A GLANCE

Selectivity Rating	90
Range SAT I Math	590–670
Average SAT I Math	630
Range SAT I Verbal	570–650
Average SAT I Verbal	627
Student/Faculty Ratio	11:1

CAMPUS TOURS

Appointment	Not required
Dates	Varies
Times	Sept–Dec: Mon–Fri, 9AM–4PM; Jan–Aug: Mon–Fri, 9AM, noon, & 3PM
Average Length	1 hour

ON-CAMPUS APPOINTMENTS

Admissions

Start Date–Juniors	June (April for students who travel long distance)
Appointment	Required
Advance Notice	Yes, 2 weeks
Saturdays	Sometimes
Average Length	45 min.
Info Sessions	Yes

Faculty and Coaches

Dates/Times	Academic year
Arrangements	Contact Admissions Office 1 week prior

CLASS VISITS

Dates	Academic year
Arrangements	Contact Admissions Office

CURRY COLLEGE

Admissions Office, 1071 Blue Hill Ave., Milton, MA 02186 • Telephone: 800-669-0686 • www.curry.edu/admission/ • Email: curryadm@curry.edu

Hours: Monday–Friday, 8:30AM–4:30PM; select Saturday, 8:30AM–3:00PM

Curry College is perhaps best known for its Program for Advancement of Learning, the first college level program in the nation to help learning disabled students to achieve in college. Beyond PAL, this suburban liberal arts college of about 1,600 students located just seven miles away from downtown Boston has satellite campuses in, among other places, Plymouth, Cambridge, Medford, and Peabody.

AT A GLANCE

Average SAT I Math	420
Average SAT I Verbal	440
Average GPA	2.3

CAMPUS TOURS

Appointment	Required
Dates	Academic year
Times	Mon–Fri; 9AM–3PM hourly; Selected Sats, 10AM–2PM
Average Length	1 hour

ON-CAMPUS APPOINTMENTS

Admissions

Start Date–Juniors	Spring of junior year
Appointment	Required, 2 weeks
Saturdays	Sometimes
Info Sessions	N/A

Faculty and Coaches

Dates/Times	Year-round
Arrangements	Contact Admissions Office 1 week prior

CLASS VISITS

Dates	Year-round
Arrangements	Contact Admissions Office

TRANSPORTATION

Logan International Airport in Boston is approximately 10 miles away from campus. From the airport, you can take the MBTA (public transportation) and then the Curry College Shuttle to campus, or you can take the Collegiate Limousine Service (617-477-0441) for the whole trip. Amtrak trains, Greyhound buses, and Vermont Transit (New England, New York, and Montreal) serve Boston. The MBTA (public transportation) combined with the Curry College Shuttle can bring you to campus from downtown.

FIND YOUR WAY

From I-90 (Massachusetts Tpke.), exit to Rte. 128 S. Proceed to Exit 2B and take Rte. 138 N. for two-and-a-half miles; the college will be on the left. **From Providence,** Rhode Island, take I-95 N. to Rte. 128 S. Proceed to Exit 2B and take Rte. 138 N. for two-and-a-half miles; the college will be on the left. **From Boston,** take I-93 S. to Rte. 128 N. Proceed to Exit 2B and take Rte. 138 N. for two-and-a-half miles; the college will be, yes, on the left.

STAY THE NIGHT

Nearby: Curry College is south of Boston in the suburb of Milton. In the immediate area, choices include a number of chain motels and hotels. **Motel 6** (125 Union Street, Braintree; 781-848-7890) offers basic accommodations and is 15 minutes away from campus. Rates are reasonable. Three motels offer moderate rates: **Holiday Inn** (1374 North Main St., Randolph; 781-961-1000), and **Holiday Inn** (55 Ariadne Rd., Dedham; 781-329-1000), and **Comfort Inn** (235 Elm St., Dedham; 781-326-6700). All three are 15 minutes away from the campus. A more expensive option is the **Sheraton Tara** (South Shore Plaza, Braintree; 781-848-0600), which has an indoor pool, a health club, and two restaurants. There is also the **Hilton at Dedham Place** (95 Dedham Place, Dedham; 781-329-7900).

A Little Farther: See entries for other Boston-area colleges; Emerson College has listings in the center of Boston. Boston University has guest house listings in the Back Bay and Brookline areas. If you're coming from the south, you might consider breaking up your trip in Attleboro. See the Wheaton College entry for **Colonel Blackinton Inn,** which is about a 40-minute drive from Curry.

HIGHLIGHTS

ON CAMPUS
- Drapkin Student Center
- Levin Library
- WMLN campus radio station
- The Suites (new residence hall)
- Hafer Academic Center

OFF CAMPUS
- Quincy Market/Faneuil Hall (Boston)
- New England Aquarium
- Museum of Fine Arts
- Newbury Street—Boston
- Blue Hills Nature Reservation

EMERSON COLLEGE

Admissions Office, 120 Boylston St., Boston, MA 02116-4624 • Telephone: 617-824-8600 • www.emerson.edu/admission • Email: admission@emerson.edu

Hours: Monday–Friday, 9:00AM–5:00PM; Saturday (during academic term), 10:00AM–noon

"You can say you are from Emerson and get a high-paying job in the entertainment industry," according to the very artsy, open, brooding, chain-smoking crowd of artists and communicators at this world-class school for communications and performing arts in Boston. Alums with the aforementioned high-paying jobs include Jay Leno.

HIGHLIGHTS

ON CAMPUS
- WERS—88.9 FM (New England's oldest noncommercial radio station
- Emerson Majestic Theatre (Boston's second oldest theater)
- The Apple Store
- The College Library

OFF CAMPUS
- Massachusetts State House
- Freedom Trail
- Public Garden, Swanboat rides
- Boston Red Sox at Fenway Park
- Newbury Street shopping district

TRANSPORTATION

Emerson is conveniently located on Boston's subway/street trolley system—the T (Green Line). Transferring to the Green Line from the Red, Orange, or Blue Lines can be made at several downtown T stations (Park Street, Haymarket, or Government Center, respectively). While most Emerson students use Boylston Station, visitors to the Admissions Office should exit at Arlington Station and walk one block west to 420 Boylston Street (The Berkeley Building). Logan International Airport is five miles away from Emerson campus. Taxis take about 30 minutes and cost approximately $20. Amtrak, the Commuter Rail, and major bus companies arrive at Boston's South Station, a 15-minute taxi ride from the campus.

FIND YOUR WAY

From the Massachusetts Turnpike (I-90), take exit 18 Allston/Cambridge. After the toll booth, follow the signs for Cambridge, bearing right down the exit ramp. Keep to the right and make a right turn at the second set of lights onto Storrow Drive East. Proceed approximately two miles to the Downtown exit. Follow the directions from Storrow Drive. **From Interstate I-93, Route 3, or U.S. Route 1,** take Exit 26 for Storrow Drive West and proceed one mile to the Back Bay exit. Follow directions from Storrow Drive below. **From Storrow Drive,** keep left and turn left onto Beacon Street. Make an immediate right onto Arlington Street and proceed alongside the Public Gardens. At the third traffic light onto Berkeley Street and right again at the next light onto Boylston Street. The Office of Undergraduate Admissions is located on the corner of Berkeley and Boylston Streets. **Parking:** Emerson does not have private parking facilities and we urge visitors to use parking garages or public transportation. To reach the Boston Common Garage, continue on Boylston Street past the Admissions Office and turn left at the third light onto Charles.

STAY THE NIGHT

Nearby: Emerson is located in the heart of Boston's theater district. Close to the campus are the **Park Plaza Hotel** (64 Arlington Street; 800-225-2008), **Wyndham Tremont House Hotel** (275 Tremont Street; 800-331-9998), and the **Radisson Hotel-Boston** (200 Stuart Street; 617-482-1800). See Northeastern University and Boston University entries for more hotel options.

A Little Farther: The **Lenox Hotel** (710 Boylston Street; 800-471-1422), **Westin** (10 Huntington Avenue; 617-262-9600), and **Marriott Copley** (110 Huntington Avenue; 617-236-5800) are located in the historic Copley Square neighborhood (four blocks from campus). Less expensive hotels may be found in Boston's suburbs. The grande dame of Boston is the **Ritz Carlton** (15 Arlington St.; 617-536-5700 or 800-241-3333).

AT A GLANCE

Selectivity Rating	81
Range SAT I Math	540–630
Average SAT I Math	584
Range SAT I Verbal	570–660
Average SAT I Verbal	619
Average ACT Composite	27
Average GPA	3.48
Student/Faculty Ratio	15:1

CAMPUS TOURS

Appointment	Required
Dates	Academic year
Times	Mon–Fri, some Sats
Average Length	2 hours

ON-CAMPUS APPOINTMENTS

Admissions

Start Date–Juniors	Anytime
Appointment	Required, 2 weeks
Saturdays	Sometimes
Info Sessions	During class sessions

Faculty and Coaches

Dates/Times	Year-round
Arrangements	Contact Admissions Office 2 weeks prior

CLASS VISITS

Dates	Academic year
Arrangements	Contact Admissions Office

HAMPSHIRE COLLEGE

Admissions Office, 893 West Street, Amherst, MA 01002 • Telephone: 877-937-4267 • www.hampshire.edu • Email: admissions@hampshire.edu

Hours: Monday–Friday, 8:30AM–4:30PM; Saturday (late-September to January) 8:30AM–2:00PM

Academic freedom is the name of the game at Hampshire College, a progressive, alternative institution with committed and intellectually mature students and dedicated and caring professors. Hampshire is part of the Five College Consortium (including Amherst, Mount Holyoke, Smith, and UMass—Amherst), which gives students abounding academic and social opportunities off campus.

AT A GLANCE

Selectivity Rating	82
Range SAT I Math	540–660
Average SAT I Math	597
Range SAT I Verbal	600–700
Average SAT I Verbal	648
Average GPA	3.38
Student/Faculty Ratio	11:1

CAMPUS TOURS

Appointment	Not required
Dates	Year-round
Times	Varies
Average Length	1 hour

ON-CAMPUS APPOINTMENTS

Admissions

Start Date—Juniors	April of junior year
Appointment	Required
Advance Notice	Yes, 1 week
Saturdays	Sometimes
Average Length	45 min.
Info Sessions	Yes

Faculty and Coaches

Dates/Times	N/A
Arrangements	Contact Admissions Office

CLASS VISITS

Dates	Academic year
Arrangements	Contact Admissions Office

TRANSPORTATION

Bradley International Airport near Hartford, Connecticut is 45 miles away from campus. Peter Pan buses (413-253-1350), Valley Transporter limousines (800-872-8752), rental cars, and taxis are available for the trip from the airport to campus. Amtrak trains provide regular service from New York City to Springfield, Massachusetts. Greyhound buses serve Springfield hourly from Boston and New York. Buses also run hourly from Springfield to Amherst. The free Five College Bus Service is available for the trip from Amherst to Hampshire's campus, or call City Transportation (413-247-9000) for a taxi.

FIND YOUR WAY

From the south, take I-91 to Exit 19 (Northampton). Take Rte. 9 E. for seven miles. In the town of Amherst, turn right onto Rte. 116 S. and proceed three miles to the campus. **From the east or west,** take I-90 (Massachusetts Tpke.) to Exit 4. Take I-91 N. to Exit 19 (Northampton). Take Rte. 9 E. for seven miles to Amherst; then turn right onto Rte. 116 S. for three miles to campus. **From the north,** take I-91 S. to Exit 25 (Amherst). Take Rte. 116 S. to campus.

STAY THE NIGHT

Nearby: **Amherst Motel** (408 Northampton Rd, Rte. 9, Amherst, MA 01002; 413-256-8122), four-and-a-half miles away from Hampshire, is from $49 to $110 per night. **Autumn Inn** (259 Elm St. Northampton, MA 01060; 413-584-7660), eight-and-a-half miles away from Hampshire and within walking distance to downtown Northampton, is $99 per night or $89 per night with AAA discount. **Best Western** (117 Conz St. Northampton, MA 01060; 800-941-3066 or 413-586-1500), nine miles away from Hampshire and one mile from Smith College, is from $69 to $139 per night. **Campus Center Hotel University** of Massachusetts—Amherst, MA 01002; 413-549-6000), five miles away from Hampshire, is from $65 to $95 per night. **Clarion Hotel** (1 Attwood Dr. Northampton, MA 01060; 413-586-1211), nine-and-a-quarter miles away from Hampshire, is from $99 to $189 per night. **Granby Motel** (5 West State St., Rte. 202, Granby, MA 01033; 413-467-9256), six-and-a-half miles away from Hampshire, is from $68 to $70 per night. **Holiday Inn Express** (400 Russell St., Rte. 9, Hadley, MA 01035; 413-582-0002), four miles away from Hampshire, is from $99 to $259 per night. **Hotel Northampton** (36 King St. Northampton, MA 01060; 413-584-3100), seven-and-a-half miles away from Hampshire and located in downtown Northampton, is $160 per night. **Howard Johnson's** (401 Russell St., Rte. 9, Hadley, MA 01035; 800-446-4656 or 413-586-0114), four miles away from Hampshire, is from $69 to $149 per night. **Lord Jeffery Inn** (30 Boltwood Ave. Amherst, MA 01002; 800 742-0358), three-and-a-half miles away from Hampshire, is from $89 to $129. **Norwottuck Inn** (208 Russell St., Rte. 9, Hadley, MA 01035; 877-667-9688 or 413-587-9866) four-and-a-half miles away from Hampshire, is from $55 to $129.

HIGHLIGHTS

ON CAMPUS
- National Yiddish Book Center
- 650-acre working farm
- Eric Carle Museum

OFF CAMPUS
- Old Deerfield historic village, Deerfield, MA
- Skinner State Park (hiking, biking)
- Emily Dickenson Homestead

HARVARD COLLEGE

Harvard College, 8 Garden St., Cambridge, MA 02318 •
Telephone: 617-495-1551 • www.admission.college.harvard.edu/ •
Email: college@fas.harvard.edu

Hours: Monday–Friday, 9:00AM–5:00PM

Home to a distinguished faculty and phenomenal world-class research facilities, Harvard is perhaps the most prestigious hub of intellectual activity in America. "The really challenging professors are the college faculty equivalent of rock stars, but the single greatest strength Harvard has to offer is its students—the most incredibly talented group of people I've ever met," says one student.

HIGHLIGHTS

ON CAMPUS

- Widener Library
- Harvard Yard
- Fogg Museum
- Annenburg/Memorial Hall
- Science Center

OFF CAMPUS

- Harvard Square
- Faneuil Hall/Quincey Market
- Museum of Fine Arts
- Freedom Trail
- Boston Commons and Public Garden

TRANSPORTATION

Logan International Airport is five miles away from campus. The least expensive way to get to campus from the airport is the subway MBTA (the T). Taxis and rental cars are also available. Amtrak trains and Greyhound and Mass Transit buses serve Boston. From the train and Mass Transit bus stations, go to MBTA's South Station and take the Red Line subway toward Alewife. Go six stops to Harvard. The campus is a three-minute walk from Harvard Square. From the Greyhound station, go to the Arlington MBTA station and take the Green Line subway inbound to Park St. (two stops). Transfer to the Red Line outbound toward Alewife. Go four stops to Harvard. The campus is a three-minute walk from Harvard Square.

FIND YOUR WAY

From I-90 (Massachusetts Tpke.), take the Cambridge exit and turn left immediately onto Storrow Dr. West. At the second light, cross the bridge (Anderson), and drive straight into Harvard Square. For Byerly Hall, turn left at the third traffic light onto Brattle St. and get into the right lane, bearing right immediately at the traffic island. The Radcliffe Yard is two blocks north on the right side of the street.

STAY THE NIGHT

Nearby: The **Harvard Square Hotel** (110 Mount Auburn St.; 617-864-5200) is a moderately-priced, 72-room hotel within walking distance of the college. The price includes an informal continental breakfast. An old favorite with Harvard visitors is the **Sheraton Commander** (16 Garden St.; 617-547-4800), right on the Cambridge Common and a short walk from the university. Prices range from expensive during the week to moderate on weekends. The posh **Charles Hotel** (Harvard Sq.; 617-864-1200) is a short stroll from campus. There is also the **Inn at Harvard** in Harvard Square (1201 Massachusetts Ave.; 800-458-5886).

A Little Farther: Harvard is about two miles north of MIT, which is also in Cambridge. See suggestions in the MIT entry, especially the **Hyatt Regency,** which has hourly van service to Harvard Square. See the Boston University entry for guest houses and hotel suggestions in Back Bay and Brookline, across the river. See the Emerson College entry for suggestions in Boston center.

AT A GLANCE

Selectivity Rating	99
Range SAT I Math	700–790
Range SAT I Verbal	700–800
Student/Faculty Ratio	8:1

CAMPUS TOURS

Appointment	Not required
Dates	Varies
Times	Varies throughout the year
Average Length	1 hour

ON-CAMPUS APPOINTMENTS

Admissions

Start Date–Juniors	June of junior year
Appointment	Required, 2 weeks
Saturdays	No
Average Length	45 min.
Info Sessions	Yes

Faculty and Coaches

Dates/Times	Academic year
Arrangements	Contact faculty directly

CLASS VISITS

Dates	Academic year
Arrangements	Contact Admissions Office

MASSACHUSETTS INSTITUTE OF TECHNOLOGY

Admissions Office, Rm. 3-108, 77 Massachusetts Ave., Room 3-108, Cambridge, MA 02139 • Telephone: 617-253-4791 • web.mit.edu •

Hours: Monday–Friday, 9:00AM–5:00PM

Students at MIT say the workload is heavy, but it's worth it to study directly under Nobel Prize-winning professors and to work in some of the best research facilities in the universe. Freshmen are graded on a pass/no credit basis, which takes a great deal of the pressure off.

AT A GLANCE

Selectivity Rating	99
Range SAT I Math	740–800
Average SAT I Math	757
Range SAT I Verbal	680–760
Average SAT I Verbal	712
Average ACT Composite	31
Student/Faculty Ratio	6:1

CAMPUS TOURS

Appointment	Not required
Dates	Year-round
Times	Mon–Fri, 10:45AM & 2:45PM
Average Length	120 min.

ON-CAMPUS APPOINTMENTS

Admissions

Start Date–Juniors	N/A
Info Sessions	Yes

Faculty and Coaches

Dates/Times	Year-round
Arrangements	Contact coach directly 1 week prior

CLASS VISITS

Dates	Academic year
Arrangements	Contact Admissions Office

TRANSPORTATION

Logan International Airport in Boston is less than six miles away from campus. The subway (MBTA) and taxis are available for the trip from the airport to campus. Taxi fare from the airport is about $20 to $25. The taxi ride will take about 15 minutes during nonrush hour and could take 30 minutes during rush hour. Amtrak trains and Greyhound and Mass Transit buses serve Boston. From the stations, take a taxi or take the MBTA subway (Red Line) to the Kendall Square stop, which will bring you to the east end of campus. The Route 1 Harvard-Dudley bus stops at MIT on Massachusetts Ave.

FIND YOUR WAY

From I-90 (Massachusetts Turnpike), take the Cambridge/Brighton exit (exit 18) and follow the Cambridge signs over the River Street Bridge. Continue straight about one mile to Central Square, and bear right onto Massachusetts Ave. Proceed for half a mile mile to the main entrance, which will be on the left. If you cross the river again, you have gone too far. **From Route I-93,** take exit 26, and follow the signs to Back Bay along Storrow Drive West, approximately one-and-a-half miles to the exit for Route 2A. The exit will be on the left, just before the Harvard Bridge (more appropriately called the Massachusetts Avenue Bridge). The Charles River will be on your right. As you cross the bridge, you will be looking at MIT. The main entrance is at the second light on your right.

STAY THE NIGHT

Nearby: Accommodations closest to campus are the **Boston Marriott Cambridge** (800-228-9290), **The Kendall Hotel** (617-577-1300), **Marriott Residence Inn Boston Cambridge Center** (800-331-3131), and **University Park Hotel** (800-222-8733). A more extensive list of accommodations, including places farther away from the MIT campus, can be found at:

http://web.mit.edu/admissions/www/undergrad/visiting/hotels.html

HIGHLIGHTS

ON CAMPUS
- Killian Court
- Z Center
- Thirsty Ear Pub (run by MIT students)
- Room 26-100 (show new and old movies)
- The Zesiger Sports and Fitness Center (Z Center)

OFF CAMPUS
- Museum of Science
- Museum of Fine Arts
- Freedom Trail
- Faneuil Hall
- New England Aquarium

MERRIMACK COLLEGE

Office of Admission,
North Andover, MA 01845 • Telephone: 978-837-5100 • www.merrimack.edu • Email: admission@merrimack.edu

Hours: Monday–Friday, 8:30AM–4:30PM; some Saturdays during fall

Merrimack College is a small Roman Catholic institution about 25 miles away from Boston in North Andover that offers programs in the liberal arts and sciences, business, education, and pre-professional and vocational programs. Red Sox legend Carl Yastrzemski is a Merrimack alum.

HIGHLIGHTS

ON CAMPUS
- Sakowich Student Center
- Rogers Center for the Arts
- New Residence Hall for juniors
- McQuade Library
- Volpe Athletic Complex

OFF CAMPUS
- Boston, MA (North End, museums, schools, sporting events)
- Museum of Fine Arts
- Rockingham Mall (Salem, NH)
- Bertuccis Restaurant
- New Hampshire (skiing)

TRANSPORTATION

Four student-operated shuttle vans are available to take you to surrounding stores and public transportation. Metro train takes you the one mile from campus to Boston. The closest airports are Boston Logan Airport in Massachusetts and Manchesters New Hampshire National Airport.

FIND YOUR WAY

From Boston and Logan Airport: Route 93 North to exit 41, Route 125 to Andover/North Andover. Campus is on the left at the intersection of Routes 125 and 114. **From points north:** Route 95 south to 495 South (traveling from Maine) or Route 93 South or 3 South to 495 North (traveling from New Hampshire) exit 42A. Follow Route 114 toward Middleton one mile to campus. **From points south and west:** Massachussetts Turnpike (Route 90) to Auburn exit. Route 290 East to 495 North to exit 42A. Follow Route 114 East toward Middleton, one mile to campus.

STAY THE NIGHT

Nearby: Local accommodations include the **Andover Inn** (Chapel Avenue, Andover, 800-242-5903), the **Hampton Inn** (Junction of Routes 495 and 114 North, Andover/Lawrence, 800-HAMPTON), the **Wyndham Hotel** (123 Old River Road, Andover), the **Holiday Inn** (Four High Wood Drive, Tewksbury, 978-640-9000), and the **Ramada Rolling Green Inn & Conference Center** (311 Lowell Street, Andover, 978-475-5400).

AT A GLANCE

Selectivity Rating	76
Range SAT I Math	520–620
Average SAT I Math	530
Range SAT I Verbal	510–610
Average SAT I Verbal	522
Average ACT Composite	23
Average GPA	3.1
Student/Faculty Ratio	13:1

CAMPUS TOURS

Appointment	Required
Dates	Year-round
Times	Varies
Average Length	1 hour

ON-CAMPUS APPOINTMENTS

Admissions

Start Date—Juniors	March of junior year
Appointment	Required
Advance Notice	Yes, 2 weeks
Saturdays	Sometimes
Average Length	30 min.
Info Sessions	Yes

Faculty and Coaches

Dates/Times	Year-round
Arrangements	Contact Athletic Department 2 weeks prior

CLASS VISITS

Dates	Academic year
Arrangements	Contact Admissions Office

MOUNT HOLYOKE COLLEGE

Office of Admission, Newhall Center,
South Hadley, MA 01075 • Telephone: 413-538-2023 • www.mtholyoke.edu/adm/ •
Email: admission@mtholyoke.edu

Hours: Monday–Friday, 9:00AM–5:00PM; select Saturdays, 9:00AM–noon

Mount Holyoke College was the nation's first all-women's college, and it is still one of the most academically challenging and rewarding schools in the country. Students enjoy great and very approachable professors, a nurturing and supportive atmosphere, and a picturesque New England campus.

AT A GLANCE

Selectivity Rating	86
Range SAT I Math	580–670
Average SAT I Math	627
Range SAT I Verbal	608–700
Average SAT I Verbal	651
Average ACT Composite	28
Average GPA	3.66
Student/Faculty Ratio	10:1

CAMPUS TOURS

Appointment	Not required
Dates	Year-round
Times	Mon–Fri, 9AM–3PM;
	Sat, 10AM & 11AM
Average Length	Varies

ON-CAMPUS APPOINTMENTS

Admissions

Start Date—Juniors	May of
	junior year
Appointment	Required
Advance Notice	Yes, 2 weeks
Saturdays	Yes
Average Length	45 min.
Info Sessions	Yes

Faculty and Coaches

Dates/Times	Academic year
Arrangements	For faculty visits,
	contact Admissions
	Office 2 weeks prior

CLASS VISITS

Dates	Academic year
Arrangements	List available in
	Admissions Office

TRANSPORTATION

Bradley International Airport near Hartford, Connecticut is 34 miles south of campus by way of I-91. Bus service between the airport and campus (with a transfer in Springfield, Massachusetts) is offered by Peter Pan Express Service (413-781-3320). Limousine service to campus is easier and faster than bus service but more expensive. The two limousine companies that service the college are Valley Transporter (800-872-8752) and Allard's College Limousine Service (413-539-9339). Amtrak trains serve Springfield; from there, take a bus, limousine, or taxi to campus.

FIND YOUR WAY

From the south, take I-91 N. to Exit 16 (Holyoke-S. Hadley/Rte. 202). Proceed north on Rte. 202 through the city of Holyoke and over the Connecticut River across the Muller Bridge. Take the exit marked South Hadley Center—Amherst to Rte. 116 N. The college is approximately two miles away from the exit, on the right side of the road. The Admissions Office is in a white building marked "The Newhall Center," across the street from the college just before the Village Commons. **From the north,** take I-91 S. to Exit 16 (Holyoke-South Hadley/Rte. 202). Proceed north on Rte. 202 through the city of Holyoke and follow the preceding directions from that point. **From east or west on I-90 (Massachusetts Tpke.),** take Exit 5 (Holyoke-Chicopee) and bear right. At the end of the exit ramp, turn left on Rte. 33 for five miles to Rte. 116. Turn right on Rte. 116 and proceed approximately two miles north to the college.

STAY THE NIGHT

Nearby: **Willets-Hallowell Center** (413-538-2217), located on campus, offers moderately-priced rooms for visitors with full breakfast included. Dinner is served to parties of six or more. The **Yankee Pedlar Inn** (1866 Northampton St., Holyoke; 413-532-9494) is an eighteenth-century country inn with private baths, televisions, and phones. Rates are moderate and include continental breakfast. And it's conveniently located 20 minutes away from the college. For referrals to bed-and-breakfasts in the area, call Pineapple Hospitality at 508-990-1696.

A Little Farther: See the Smith College entry; the **Northampton Hilton** is 25 minutes away from Mount Holyoke. Also see the Amherst College and University of Massachusetts entries. Suggestions there are approximately 30 minutes away from Mount Holyoke. **Howard Johnson's Motor Lodge** in Hadley, detailed under the University of Massachusetts, is 20 minutes away from campus.

HIGHLIGHTS

ON CAMPUS

- Unified Science Center
- The Mount Holyoke College Art Museum
- The Equestrian Center
- Blanchard Campus Center
- Williston Memorial Library

OFF CAMPUS

- Village Commons, South Hadley, MA (shopping & theater)
- Downtown Amherst, MA (dining & shopping)
- Downtown Northampton, MA (dining & shopping)
- Mount Skinner State Park, Hadley, MA
- Downtown Springfield, MA (museums, dining, & night life)

NORTHEASTERN UNIVERSITY

Undergraduate Admissions, 360 Huntington Ave.,
Boston, MA 02115 • Telephone: 617-373-2200 • www.admissions.neu.edu •
Email: admissions@neu.edu

Hours: Monday–Friday, 8:30AM–5:00PM; Saturday, 8:30AM–1:00PM

Northeastern University's vaunted five-year co-op program—a tremendous hit with these business-oriented students—requires students to spend half of each year (after their first year) at work for one of thousands of employers. Jobs are predominantly in the New England area, although students do go across the country and even overseas.

HIGHLIGHTS

ON CAMPUS
- Marino Recreation Center
- The Snell Library
- The Curry Student Center
- Behrakis Health Science Center
- Cyber Cafe

OFF CAMPUS
- Museum of Fine Arts
- Symphony Hall
- Boston Red Sox at Fenway Park
- Cultural District
- The Charles River

TRANSPORTATION

Logan International Airport in Boston is 10 miles away from campus. The MBTA subway (public transportation) and taxis are available for the trip from campus to the airport. Amtrak trains, private buses, and mass transit buses serve Boston. The MBTA subway can bring you to campus from the stations.

FIND YOUR WAY

From the west (via Route 90, Masschusetts Turnpike), take Exit 22 (Copley Square), and bear right. Proceed to the first traffic light, and turn right onto Dartmouth Street. Take a right onto Tremont Street. Continue on Tremont Street and take a right onto Ruggles Street. Turn right onto Leon Street, and park in the West Village garage that is located on the left. The Admissions Visitor Center resides directly beside the garage (110 Behrakis Center).

STAY THE NIGHT

Nearby: The moderately-priced **Midtown Hotel** (220 Huntington Avenue; 617-262-1000, 800-343-1177) is within walking distance of the campus. A few others include **Boston Back Bay Hilton** (40 Dalton Street; 617-236-1100, 800-445-8667), the **Boston Marriott Copley Place** (110 Huntington Avenue; 617-236-5800), **The Colonnade** (120 Huntington Avenue; 617-424-7000, 800-962-3030), and **Sheraton Boston Hotel and Towers** (39 Dalton Street; 617-236-2000, 800-325-3535).

AT A GLANCE

Selectivity Rating	76
Range SAT I Math	540–640
Average SAT I Math	588
Range SAT I Verbal	520–620
Average SAT I Verbal	565
Average ACT Composite	24
Average GPA	3.18
Student/Faculty Ratio	16:1

CAMPUS TOURS

Appointment	Not required
Dates	Year-round
Times	Mon–Fri, 9AM–3PM;
	Sat, 9AM, 10AM, & 11AM
Average Length	1 hour

ON-CAMPUS APPOINTMENTS

Admissions
Appointment	Not required
Saturdays	No
Info Sessions	Yes

Faculty and Coaches
Dates/Times	N/A
Arrangements	Contact coach directly 3 weeks prior

CLASS VISITS

Arrangements	Contact Admissions Office

SIMMONS COLLEGE

Admissions Office, 300 The Fenway, Boston, MA 02115 •
Telephone: 800-345-8468 • www.simmons.edu/admission/ •
Email: ugadm@simmons.edu

Hours: Monday–Friday, 8:30AM–4:30PM; Saturday, 8:30AM–noon

Students at Simmons College in the excellent college town of Boston consider their all-women's school a great place where women become leaders. Small classes, a low student/teacher ratio, a strong career-oriented emphasis, and a mind-boggling set of requirements help with the transition.

AT A GLANCE

Selectivity Rating	76
Range SAT I Math	490–590
Average SAT I Math	542
Range SAT I Verbal	500–600
Average SAT I Verbal	554
Average ACT Composite	23
Average GPA	3.13
Student/Faculty Ratio	12:1

CAMPUS TOURS

Dates	Year-round
Times	Mon–Fri, 10AM, 11:30AM, 1PM & 2:30PM
Average Length	1 hour

ON-CAMPUS APPOINTMENTS

Admissions

Start Date–Juniors	Anytime after sophomore year
Appointment	Required, 2 weeks
Saturdays	Sometimes
Info Sessions	No available

Faculty and Coaches

Dates/Times	Year-round
Arrangements	Contact Admissions Office 2 weeks prior

CLASS VISITS

Dates	Academic year
Arrangements	Contact Admissions Office

TRANSPORTATION

Logan International Airport is approximately a 25-minute drive from campus, but the time varies with the amount of traffic. Taxis, local trains (see directions below), and rental cars are available for the trip to campus from the airport. Amtrak trains and Greyhound and Mass Transit buses serve Boston. From the Greyhound station, walk to the Arlington MBTA station. Take any Green Line E Huntington Ave. car outbound to the Museum/Ruggles stop. Walk to the right down Louis Prang St. to the Fenway. The college is on the Fenway just after the Gardner Museum. From the train or Mass Transit bus, walk to MBTA's South Station and take the Red Line inbound to the Park St. station. Transfer to the Green Line E Huntington Ave. outbound and follow the preceding directions.

FIND YOUR WAY

From the south (Rte. 3) and from the north (Rtes. 1, I-93, or I-95), take Storrow Dr. W. to the Fenway, Rte. 1 S., overpass. Exit to the right onto Boylston St. outbound. Turn left at the next light onto Park Dr.; follow Park Dr., staying to the left. The first major intersection is Brookline Ave./Boylston St.; cross Brookline and bear left at the first opportunity, following the green sign pointing to the Fenway. (You will have made a U-turn.) Continue straight, again crossing Brookline, onto the Fenway. Immediately after Emmanuel College, take the first right onto Ave. Louis Pasteur. The college parking lot then is the first drive on the left. **From the west and Rte. 2,** take Storrow Dr. E. and follow the preceding directions.

STAY THE NIGHT

Nearby: There are a few places within walking distance of Simmons. The **Best Western Longwood** (342 Longwood Ave.; 617-731-4700) has a health club. Rates are impressively high. For a reasonable alternative consider tried-and-true **Howard Johnson's** (575 Commonwealth Ave.; 617-267-3100). The **Copley Square Hotel** and the **Eliot Hotel** also are within walking distance; see the Northeastern University entry for details. See the Boston University entry for inn and hotel accommodations in nearby Brookline and Back Bay.

A Little Farther: See the Emerson College entry for more accommodations in Boston, and the MIT, Harvard, and Tufts entries for accommodations in Cambridge.

HIGHLIGHTS

ON CAMPUS

- Trustman Art Gallery
- Beatley Library
- Park Science Center

OFF CAMPUS

- Museum of Fine Arts
- Isabella Stewart Gardner Museum
- Boston Red Sox at Fenway Park

SMITH COLLEGE

Office of Admissions, 7 College Lane, Northampton, MA 01063 • Telephone: 413-585-2500 • www.smith.edu/admission/ • Email: admission@smith.edu

Hours: Monday–Friday, 8:30AM–4:30PM; Saturday, 9:00AM–1:00PM,

All-women's Smith College is an intense and competitive school with an incredibly demanding workload, but students would have it no other way. Time permitting, there is a wide range of things to do; it's easy to get involved in clubs and activities even if you just want to experiment—you can go from pianist to fencer to actor to astronomer. Also, the lesbian social scene on campus is buzzing.

HIGHLIGHTS

ON CAMPUS
- Lyman Plant House
- The Botanical Gardens
- Campus Center
- Mendenhall Center for Performing Arts
- Smith Art Museum

OFF CAMPUS
- The Summit House, Skinner State Park
- Old Deerfield
- Look Park
- Historic Northampton
- Yankee Candle

TRANSPORTATION

Bradley International Airport near Hartford, Connecticut, is approximately 30 miles away from campus. Shuttle-bus service is available from the airport to campus; call Valley Transporter at 800-872-8752 or 413-253-1350 as early as possible to arrange for this service. Amtrak train service is available to Springfield, Massachusetts. Valley Transporter also provides shuttle service from the train station to campus; call as early as possible.

FIND YOUR WAY

Take I-91 to Exit 18; then take U.S. 5 N. into the center of Northampton. Turn left on Massachusetts Rte. 9. Go straight through four traffic lights. Turn left on College Lane shortly after the fourth set. The Office of Admission is on your right, overlooking Paradise Pond.

STAY THE NIGHT

Nearby: A favorite with Smith visitors is **Hotel Northampton** (36 King St. N.; 413-584-3100), a restored 1926 building in the heart of Northampton within walking distance of the college. Also within walking distance is the **Autumn Inn** (259 Elm St.; 413-584-7660), a colonial-style, moderately-priced hostelry located on Rte. 9, adjacent to Smith. It has a swimming pool and provides parking.

A Little Farther: Sixteen miles north of Smith is historic Deerfield, a village of 12 museum houses. The **Deerfield Inn** (81 Old Main St., Deerfield, MA; 413-774-5581) is a great place. The **Yankee Pedlar Inn** in Holyoke is about 25 minutes south of Smith. On the main drag in Stockbridge (an hour's drive away) is the **Red Lion Inn** (413-298-5545), a bustling old inn with moderate to expensive rates. Lenox is only a few miles away and has great shops and restaurants. The **Village Inn** (Church St.; 413-637-0020) is a charming and elegant place to stay the night. Rates are moderate; some rooms with shared baths are inexpensive.

AT A GLANCE

Selectivity Rating	95
Range SAT I Math	580–670
Average SAT I Math	630
Range SAT I Verbal	590–700
Average SAT I Verbal	660
Average ACT Composite	27
Average GPA	3.8
Student/Faculty Ratio	9:1

CAMPUS TOURS

Appointment	Not required
Dates	Year-round
Times	Varies throughout the year
Average Length	1 hour

ON-CAMPUS APPOINTMENTS

Admissions

Start Date–Juniors	Mid-March
Appointment	Required
Advance Notice	Yes
Saturdays	Sometimes
Average Length	30 min.
Info Sessions	Yes

Faculty and Coaches

Dates/Times	Year-round
Arrangements	Contact Athletic Department

CLASS VISITS

Dates	Academic year
Arrangements	Contact faculty directly

TUFTS UNIVERSITY

Office of Undergraduate Admissions,
Medford, MA 02155 • Telephone: 617-627-3170 • www.tufts.edu •
Email: admissions.inquiry@ase.tufts.edu

Hours: Monday–Friday, 9:00AM–5:00PM; Saturday (select during fall and spring), 9:30AM–10:30AM

Many a student stuck on Ivy League wait lists has opted for Tufts, an academically rigorous liberal arts college in Boston where about 5,000 hard-working, career-driven students turn into well-educated, well-rounded individuals, professionals, and scholars. Few people have been disappointed with their choice. A diverse group of alums includes singer Tracy Chapman, actor William Hurt, and Senator Patrick Moynihan.

AT A GLANCE

Selectivity Rating	96
Range SAT I Math	640–720
Range SAT I Verbal	610–710
Student/Faculty Ratio	9:1

CAMPUS TOURS

Appointment	Preferred
Dates	Varies
Times	Varies
Average Length	1 hour

ON-CAMPUS APPOINTMENTS

Admissions

Start Date–Juniors	N/A
Info Sessions	Yes

Faculty and Coaches

Dates/Arrangements	Contact faculty directly 1 week prior

CLASS VISITS

Arrangements	Contact Admissions Office

TRANSPORTATION

Logan International Airport in Boston is a 15-minute drive from campus. You can take a subway, bus, or taxi to campus from the airport. Amtrak trains and Greyhound buses serve Boston; public transportation and taxis can take you to Tufts from the bus and train stations.

FIND YOUR WAY

Take I-90 (Massachusetts Tpke.) to the Rte. 128 exit (exit is also I-95, which coincides with Rte. 128 here). Take Rte. 128 (I-95) N. to Exit 29A (Massachusetts Rte. 2 E.). Take Rte. 2 E. (toward Cambridge) to Massachusetts Rte. 16 (this is at the end of Rte. 2). Turn left on Rte. 16 (marked 16 E.) and go through two full traffic lights (not counting blinking lights); after the second traffic light, take the next right turn, a sharp turn uphill, onto Powderhouse Blvd. Proceed to Packard Ave., which is the third left; turn onto Packard, which takes you to campus. Signs will then lead you to visitors' parking and the Admissions Office.

STAY THE NIGHT

Nearby: The **Cambridge House** (2218 Massachusetts Ave., Cambridge; 617-491-6300 or 800-232-9989) is an elegant turn-of-the-century colonial. Most, though not all, of the rooms share baths. Rates are moderate to very expensive and higher during the summer than during the rest of the year. The price includes a full breakfast and refreshments in the afternoon. Cambridge House also has a referral service to bed-and-breakfasts in the area. **Susse Chalet** (211 Concord Tpke., Cambridge; 617-661-7800) is inexpensive and a scant two miles away from campus. **Days Inn** (19 Commerce Way, Woburn; 617-935-0039) is also close to campus and has an indoor swimming pool and a restaurant. See the Harvard-Radcliffe entry for suggestions around Harvard Square about two miles south and the MIT entry for some posh hotel suggestions in southern Cambridge, about four miles south.

A Little Farther: You might want to go across the river into the Back Bay area of Boston. See the Boston University entry, which has some guest house and hotel suggestions. The Lenox Hotel, mentioned there, is about 20 minutes from Tufts. Brandeis University is 10 miles to the west, Boston College is 7 miles to the southwest, and Wellesley College is 15 miles to the southwest. See these entries if you wish to stay in the suburbs.

HIGHLIGHTS

ON CAMPUS

- The Aidekman Arts Center
- Tisch Library & Edwin Ginn Library
- Cousens Gymnasium
- Ellis Oval

OFF CAMPUS

- Museum of Fine Arts
- Isabella Stewart Gardner Museum
- Boston Red Sox at Fenway Park

UNIVERSITY OF MASSACHUSETTS—AMHERST

Undergraduate Admissions Office, University Admissions Center, University Box 30120, Amherst, MA 01003-9291 • Telephone: 413-545-0222 • www.umass.edu • Email: mail@admissions.umass.edu

Hours: Monday–Friday, 9:00AM–4:00PM; Saturday–Sunday, 10:30AM–3:30PM

UMass—Amherst has much to offer, including sports management, communications disorders, biochemistry, political science, and landscape architecture. There are many groups available for students to join, including the hand gliding club, dance team, animal rights coalition, and bridge club.

HIGHLIGHTS

ON CAMPUS
- The Mullins Center
- The Campus Center/Student Union
- The Fine Arts Center
- The Visitors' Center
- Isenberg School of Management

OFF CAMPUS
- Downtown Amherst
- Downtown Northampton
- Yankee Candle (Deerfield)
- Basketball Hall of Fame (Springfield)

TRANSPORTATION

Bradley International Airport near Hartford, Connecticut, is 45 miles south of the University. Logan International Airport in Boston is 90 miles to the east. Peter Pan Bus Lines (800-343-9999) links the campus to Bradley and Logan airports as well as to points throughout the region. Amtrak trains (800-872-7245) serve Springfield; the station is two blocks away from the Springfield bus station, where you can get a Peter Pan bus to campus. Amtrak also serves Amherst, with a station stop two miles away from campus. Once on campus, the Pioneer Valley Transportation Authority serves the Five College Area. For more information on transportation, log on to The Point, a UMass guidebook: www.umass.edu/thepoint/basics/parking/parking2.html.

FIND YOUR WAY

For driving instructions to campus, please visit the UMass Visitors' Center website: www.umass.edu/visitorsctr/directions.html.

STAY THE NIGHT

Nearby: **Campus Center Hotel** (413-549-6000) is on campus and its rates are moderate. The small **University Motor Lodge** (345 N. Pleasant St.; 413-256-8111) is within walking distance (half a mile walk). Rates range from inexpensive to moderate. The **Lord Jeffery Inn** is located approximately one mile away in downtown Amherst. Log on to their website www.lordjefferyinn.com or call 413-253-2576 for more information. There are numerous other lodging options slightly farther from campus. Visit the Hampshire Hospitality Group's website (www.hampshirehospitality.com) for information on the local **Holiday Inn Express** and **Howard Johnson's,** as well as several other nearby accomodations. The most comprehensive listing of information for visitors to the area—including numerous bed-and-breakfasts—is found on the Chamber of Commerce's website: www.amherstarea.com/index.cfm.

A Little Farther: For comprehensive information on lodging, food, and attractions in Western Massachusetts, please visit MassLive: www.masslive.com/visitorsguide.

AT A GLANCE

Selectivity Rating	74
Range SAT I Math	510–630
Average SAT I Math	571
Range SAT I Verbal	500–620
Average SAT I Verbal	554
Average GPA	3.42
Student/Faculty Ratio	19:1

CAMPUS TOURS

Appointment	Not required
Dates	Varies
Times	Mon–Fri, 11AM & 1:30PM
Average Length	1 hour

ON-CAMPUS APPOINTMENTS

Admissions

Appointment	Required, 2 weeks
Saturdays	No
Info Sessions	Yes

Faculty and Coaches

Dates/Times	Year-round
Arrangements	Contact coach directly

CLASS VISITS

Dates	Varies
Arrangements	Contact Visiting Center

WELLESLEY COLLEGE

Board of Admission, 106 Central St., Wellesley, MA 02481-8203 •
Telephone: 781-283-2270 • www.wellesley.edu/admission/ •
Email: admission@wellesley.edu

Hours: Monday–Friday, 8:30AM–4:30PM; Saturday (during academic year), 8:30AM–12:30PM

Personalization is the big thing and academics are absolutely fantastic at the stressful all-women's Wellesley College in Massachusetts, which is home to 2,300 or so very motivated, career-oriented, ambitious, and intelligent future leaders. Cross registration at MIT and cooperative education programs at Babson and Brandeis are available. Madeline Albright and Hillary Rodham Clinton are two of Wellesley's many prominent alums.

AT A GLANCE

Selectivity Rating	97
Range SAT I Math	630–720
Average SAT I Math	671
Range SAT I Verbal	620–720
Average SAT I Verbal	671
Average ACT Composite	29
Student/Faculty Ratio	9:1

CAMPUS TOURS

Appointment	Not required
Dates	Year-round
Times	Mon–Fri, 10AM–3PM, hourly; Sat, 9AM, 10AM, & 11AM
Average Length	1 hour

ON-CAMPUS APPOINTMENTS

Admissions

Start Date—Juniors	April 1
Appointment	Required
Advance Notice	Yes, 2 weeks
Saturdays	Sometimes
Average Length	45 min.
Info Sessions	Yes

Faculty and Coaches

Dates/Times	Academic year
Arrangements	Contact Admissions Office

CLASS VISITS

Dates	Academic year
Arrangements	Contact Admissions Office

TRANSPORTATION

Logan International Airport in Boston is approximately 15 miles away from campus; travel time to campus from the airport varies widely depending on traffic. Public transportation, taxis, and rental cars are available for the ride to campus. For public transportation, take the Logan Express bus to Framingham (call 800-23-LOGAN for schedules) and a taxi from Framingham to campus. If necessary, call Veteran's Taxi at 781-235-1600. It is also possible to take the subway: First take the free shuttle bus to the Airport MBTA stop; then take the inbound Blue Line four stops to Government Center. Go upstairs and change to the Green Line marked Riverside-D. Get off at Woodland, the next-to-last stop. From Woodland take a taxi to campus. If necessary, call Veteran's Taxi at 781-235-1600. By public transportation, the trip from airport to campus takes approximately two hours. Have plenty of change because exact fares are required. Amtrak trains serve South Station in Boston. From there, take the Red Line (MBTA subway) two stops to Park St. Change to the Green Line marked Riverside-D. Get off at Woodland, the next to last stop, and take a taxi to campus. If you travel by bus, take the Greyhound or Peter Pan bus to the Riverside Terminal at Route 128. From there, take a taxi to campus.

FIND YOUR WAY

From the west, take I-90 (Massachusetts Tpke.) to Exit 14 (Weston). Head south on I-95 (also called Rte. 128) for a half mile to the Rte. 16 exit. Follow Rte. 16 W. through the town of Wellesley for four miles to the college entrance, opposite the golf course. **From the east,** take the Massachusetts Tpke. to Exit 16 (West Newton). Take Rte. 16 W. and follow the preceding directions from that point. **From the north,** take I-95 (also called Rte. 128) S. to Exit 21B/22 (Rte. 16 W.). Take Rte. 16 W. and follow the preceding directions from that point. **From the south,** take I-95 (also called Rte. 128) N. to Exit 21B (Rte. 16 W.). Take Rte. 16 W. and follow the preceding directions from that point.

STAY THE NIGHT

Nearby: **The College Club** (781-283-2700) is on campus. The **Crowne Plaza** (508-653-8800) is on nearby Rte. 9 in Natick. A couple of other choices include the **Wellesley Inn** (Washington Street; 781-235-0180) and the **Holiday Inn** in Newton (Route 128 Exit 22, 617-969-5300).

A Little Farther: Waltham is readily accessible. For suggestions in that area, see the Brandeis University entry. See the Emerson College entry for accommodations in Boston.

HIGHLIGHTS

ON CAMPUS

- Davis Museum and Cultural Center
- Whitin Observatory
- Science Center
- Betsy Wood Knapp Media and Technology Center
- Margaret C. Ferguson Greenhouses

OFF CAMPUS

- Harvard Square
- Faneuil Hall Marketplace
- Boston Public Garden/Boston Commons
- Museum of Fine Arts
- Symphony Hall

WHEATON COLLEGE (MA)

Admissions Office, Norton, MA 02766 •
Telephone: 800-394-6003 • www.wheatoncollege.edu/Admission/ •
Email: admission@wheatoncollege.edu

Hours: Monday–Friday, 8:30AM–4:30PM; Saturdays (September–January only), 8:30AM–1:00PM

Wheaton College is a fun, enthusiastic, competitive college that offers a rigorous liberal arts education and a challenging core curriculum. Wheaton's beautiful and rural campus is located in Norton, a boring town equidistant from Boston, Providence, and Rhode Island.

HIGHLIGHTS

ON CAMPUS

- Mars Arts & Humanities (a 20 million dollar arts facility)
- Haas Athletic Center
- Beard Hall (new 100-bed residence hall)
- Mary Lyon Hall (college's oldest building)
- Cole Library

OFF CAMPUS

- Boston
- Providence
- Cape Cod and the islands
- Wrentham Outlet Malls
- Newport

TRANSPORTATION

Logan International Airport in Boston and Green State Airport in Providence, Rhode Island, are 45 minutes away from campus. To get to campus from Logan, take a Bonanza bus to Foxfield Plaza in Foxboro and a taxi from the plaza to Wheaton. The Bonanza bus leaves hourly on the half hour from most terminals; call Bonanza at 800-556-3815 for bus information. Bonanza buses also run from downtown Providence to Foxboro. Taxis and rental cars are available at both airports. Amtrak provides rail service to Boston and Providence. From Boston's South Station, an MBTA commuter rail serves Mansfield and Attleboro, which are towns near campus; take a taxi from either town to Wheaton.

FIND YOUR WAY

From the west, take I-90 (Massachusetts Tpke.) E. to Exit 11A; then take I-495 S. Follow I-495 to Exit 11. **From Boston and northern New England,** take I-93 S. (the Southeast Expy.) to I-93 S./128 N. Continue to the junction with I-95 S. and take I-95 S. to I-495 S. At Exit 11 from I-495, turn onto Massachusetts Rte. 123 W., and follow that for a mile-and-a-half to the college. **From Providence and southern New England,** take I-95 N. to Exit 6A; then take I-495 S. to Exit 11 and Massachusetts Rte. 123 W. Follow Rte. 123 for a mile-and-a-half to the college.

STAY THE NIGHT

Nearby: Our first choice for charm is the **Colonel Blackinton Inn** (203 N. Main St. Rte. 152, Attleboro; 508-222-6022), six miles away from campus. This nineteenth-century inn is listed on the National Register of Historic Places and has an informal country atmosphere. Continental breakfast and afternoon tea are included in the moderate price. The **Holiday Inn** (700 Miles Standish Blvd., Taunton; 508-823-0430) is only 10 minutes away and has a health club, a restaurant, and a comedy club on the weekends. Rates vary between the inexpensive and moderate ranges. **Red Roof Inn** (60 Forbes Blvd., Mansfield; 508-339-2323) has inexpensive to moderate rates and is a 15-minute drive away. For an indoor pool and a health club, try the **Holiday Inn** (31 Hampshire St., Mansfield; 508-339-2200). Rates begin at the top end of the moderate range and go into the expensive range.

A Little Farther: Providence, Rhode Island, is less than 30 minutes to the south. See the Brown University entry for suggestions there.

AT A GLANCE

Selectivity Rating	71
Range SAT I Math	550–650
Average SAT I Math	610
Range SAT I Verbal	590–670
Average SAT I Verbal	630
Average ACT Composite	27
Average GPA	3.4
Student/Faculty Ratio	11:1

CAMPUS TOURS

Appointment	Preferred
Dates	Year-round
Times	Mon–Fri, 9:30AM–3:30PM, hourly; Sat, 10AM–noon, hourly
Average Length	1 hour

ON-CAMPUS APPOINTMENTS

Admissions

Start Date–Juniors	April
Appointment	Required
Advance Notice	Yes, 2 weeks
Saturdays	Sometimes
Average Length	30 min.
Info Sessions	Yes

Faculty and Coaches

Dates/Times	Academic year
Arrangements	Contact Admissions Office 2 weeks prior

CLASS VISITS

Dates	Academic year
Arrangements	Contact Admissions Office

WILLIAMS COLLEGE

Admissions Office, 33 Stetson Court,
Williamstown, MA 01267 • Telephone: 413-597-2211 • www.williams.edu •
Email: admission@williams.edu

Hours: Monday–Friday, 8:30AM–4:30PM; Saturdays (July–October), 9:00AM–noon

For some reason or another some professors at Williams College have European accents even though they are from Ohio, but the knowledgeable, hilarious, world-class, and always accessible professors truly make this tough school worthwhile. Life and academics are perfect at Williams, says one student, "With each passing day, I feel more sorrow for the students applying early at the Ivy League schools because they don't know what they are missing."

AT A GLANCE

Selectivity Rating	98
Range SAT I Math	660–750
Average SAT I Math	694
Range SAT I Verbal	660–760
Average SAT I Verbal	701
Average ACT Composite	30
Student/Faculty Ratio	8:1

CAMPUS TOURS

Appointment	Not required
Dates	Year-round
Times	Varies throughout the year
Average Length	1 hour

ON-CAMPUS APPOINTMENTS

Admissions

Start Date—Juniors	Summer before senior year (June)
Appointment	Required
Advance Notice	Yes, 1 week
Saturdays	No
Average Length	30 min.
Info Sessions	Yes

Faculty and Coaches

Dates/Times	Year-round
Arrangements	Contact Athletic Department 1 week prior

CLASS VISITS

Dates	Academic year
Arrangements	Contact faculty directly

TRANSPORTATION
The Albany, New York, airport is 50 miles away from campus. Taxis and rental cars are available for the drive from the airport to campus.

FIND YOUR WAY
From the south, take the Taconic State Pkwy. (in New York) north to E. Chatham (the last exit before the toll). Take Rte. 295 E. to Rte. 22 N.; then take Rte. 22 N. and make a sharp right turn onto Rte. 43 E. Proceed on Rte. 43 to U.S. Rte. 7 N., which takes you to Williamstown, where you turn right onto Rte. 2 E. The Admissions Office is on Stetson Court (just off Rte. 2). **From the east and west,** take Rte. 2 to campus. **From the north,** take I-91 S. to Rte. 2; then take Rte. 2 W. to Williamstown.

STAY THE NIGHT
Nearby: The **Williams Inn** (West Main St. on the green; 413-458-9371) is a big colonial-style inn within walking distance of campus. An indoor pool makes it very popular with college visitors. Rates are expensive. Two inexpensive motels are also within walking distance. **Northside Inn and Motel** (45 North St.; 413-458-8107) and **Maple Terrace Motel** (555 Main St.; 413-458-8101), both with outdoor pools, are worth checking out. There are many appealing bed-and-breakfast choices nearby. (You can get a long list from the Admissions Office.) Here are a few: **Field Farm Guest House B&B** (413-458-3135) is a bit farther out in a quiet rural setting on 247 acres and has a tennis court, hiking trails, a pond, and cross-country skiing available on the property. Its five bedrooms have private baths; rates are moderate. **River Bend Farm B&B** (413-458-5504) is an eighteenth-century colonial home. All five rooms share baths, and the inexpensive-to-moderate rates include a deluxe continental breakfast. **Steep Acres Farm B&B** (413-458-3774) also has inexpensive to moderate rates. It is on a working farm of 54 acres and its four rooms share two baths. Continental breakfast with homemade bread is included in the price. The **Orchards** (222 Adams Rd.; 413-458-9611) is a European-style country inn one mile away from campus. Don't be put off by the location, which is on a busy commercial street across from a supermarket. Inside, it's gorgeous. Rates are expensive, and tennis and golf privileges are provided.

HIGHLIGHTS

ON CAMPUS
- Williams College Museum of Art
- Chapin Library of Rare Books
- Hopkins Forest
- Adams Memorial Theater
- Williamstown Theater Festival

OFF CAMPUS
- Clark Art Institute
- Tanglewood (summers only)
- Norman Rockwell Museum
- Images Theater
- Taconic Golf Course

WORCESTER POLYTECHNIC INSTITUTE

Admissions Office, 100 Institute Rd., Worcester, MA 01609 •
Telephone: 508-831-5286 • www.wpi.edu/admissions.html •
Email: admissions@wpi.edu

Hours: Monday–Friday, 8:30AM–5:00PM; Saturdays (fall and April), 9:00AM–noon

The undergraduate experience at Worcester Polytechnic Institute centers around the WPI Plan—a series of required independent projects designed to build research ability and teamwork skills. Engineering and sciences are the name of the game, and students gain a lot of good lab experience under the guidance of professors so dedicated some have nonoffice hours: They pass out the schedule of when they won't be in their offices.

HIGHLIGHTS

ON CAMPUS
- Robotics Lab
- Laser Labs
- Wind Tunnels
- Fire Protection Engineering Lab

OFF CAMPUS
- Worcester Art Museum
- Higgins Armory Museum

TRANSPORTATION

Logan International Airport in Boston is a one-hour drive from campus. Buses, limousines, and rental cars are available at the airport for the trip to campus. For limousine service, call Worcester Airport Limousine at 800-660-0992 (Massachusetts), 800-343-1369 (outside Massachusetts), or 508-756-4834; reservations are recommended. Worcester Airport, a 10-minute ride from the Institute, is served by USAir and Delta; taxis are available for the ride to campus. Amtrak trains (800-872-7245), Greyhound buses (508-754-3247), and Peter Pan buses (508-754-4600) provide regular service to Worcester. Train and bus stations are five-minute taxi rides from campus. TF Green airport in Providence, Rhode Island, is also an hour drive. Bradley International in Hartford, Connecticut, is an hour-and-a-half drive away from campus.

FIND YOUR WAY

Remember if you get lost, it's pronounced Wuh-stuh. **From the south and west,** take I-90 (the Massachusetts Tpke.) to Exit 10 (Auburn). Proceed east on I-290 into Worcester. Take Exit 17 (Lincoln Square, Rte. 9), and follow Rte. 9 W. straight through Lincoln Square onto Highland St. Turn right at the traffic light onto West St. and proceed two blocks to campus. **From the east,** take I-90 to Exit 11A (Rte. I-495). Take I-495 N. to I-290, and take I-290 W. into Worcester. Take Exit 18 and turn right at the first traffic light; then make an immediate right before the next traffic light. At the third light, proceed straight through, then bear right onto Salisbury Street. Follow Salisbury to Boynton St. and turn left. Turn right at stop sign onto Institute Rd. Turn right at stop sign onto West St. entrance to visitor parking.

STAY THE NIGHT

Nearby: The **Holiday Inn Worcester** (500 Lincoln St.; 508-852-4000) is only 10 minutes away and has an indoor pool, sauna, and fitness room. Rates are on the high end of the moderate range. The **Auburn Motel** (1 Buckley Drive, Auburn; 508-832-7003) is five miles away from campus. **Crowne Plaza Motel** (10 Lincoln St.; 508-791-1600) is half a mile from campus and has recreational facilities, swimming pool, a baggage handling fee, and handicap access. See the Clark University entry for other suggestions in Worcester.

AT A GLANCE

Selectivity Rating	83
Range SAT I Math	630–730
Average SAT I Math	660
Range SAT I Verbal	540–660
Average SAT I Verbal	620
Average ACT Composite	29
Average GPA	3.4
Student/Faculty Ratio	12:1

CAMPUS TOURS

Appointment	Not required
Dates	Year-round
Times	Varies throughout the year
Average Length	1 hour

ON-CAMPUS APPOINTMENTS

Admissions

Start Date–Juniors	April 15
Appointment	Required
Advance Notice	Yes
Saturdays	No
Average Length	30 min.
Info Sessions	Yes

Faculty and Coaches

Dates/Times	Academic year
Arrangements	Contact Admissions Office

CLASS VISITS

Dates	Varies
Arrangements	Contact Admissions Office

1- Kalamazoo College
2- University of Michigan
3- Michigan State U.

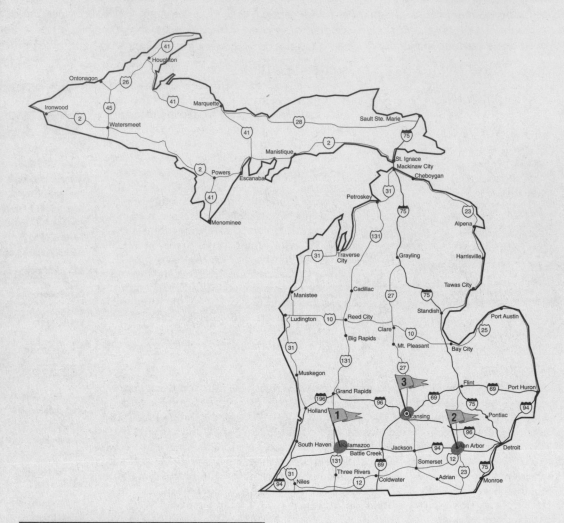

Michigan	Kalamazoo Coll.	Michigan State U.	Univ. Michigan	Detroit	Grand Rapids
Kalamazoo Coll.	—	80	90	140	52
Michigan State	80	—	62	88	72
Univ. Michigan	97	62	—	38	55
Detroit	140	88	38	—	156
Grand Rapids	52	72	55	156	—

KALAMAZOO COLLEGE

Admissions Office, 1200 Academy St.,
Kalamazoo, MI 49006 • Telephone: 800-253-3602 • www.kzoo.edu/admiss/ •
Email: admission@kzoo.edu

Hours: Monday–Friday, 8:00AM–5:00PM; Saturdays (only when classes are in session), 8:30AM–1:00PM

Kalamazoo College's greatest asset is a unique program called the K Plan, which integrates a traditional liberal arts education with an abundant amount of internship programs, a required graduate-quality senior project, and awesome study abroad opportunities. Nearly 85 percent of all students go abroad at least once during their four years at Kalamazoo.

HIGHLIGHTS

ON CAMPUS
- The Bells of Stetson Chapel
- Western Tennis Hall of Fame
- Upjohn Library
- Hicks Center

OFF CAMPUS
- Kalamazoo Institute of Arts
- Kalamazoo Air Zoo
- Kalamazoo Valley Museum
- Kal-Haven Trail
- Kellogg Biological Station

TRANSPORTATION

The Kalamazoo-Battle Creek International Airport is three-and-a-half miles away from campus. The Admissions Office will arrange a pick-up service if you call five working days in advance. Taxis are also available at the airport. Amtrak trains traveling between Detroit and Chicago stop in Kalamazoo four times daily. Major bus lines also serve the city. Taxis are available for the short trip to campus from the bus and train terminal.

FIND YOUR WAY

When traveling east-west on I-94, take exit 75 Oakland Drive and proceed north toward Kalamazoo through nine traffic lights (about three miles). As you come down the hill through the Old Campus of Western Michigan University, Oakland Drive merges with Stadium Drive at the ninth light. Stay to the left as you proceed onto Stadium Drive. You will see a green Kalamazoo College sign and will need to make a sharp left-hand turn onto Academy Street at the end of the median. As soon as you cross the railroad tracks, you are on campus. **When traveling north-south on US 131,** take exit 38A West Main Street (M-43) and proceed east towrd Kalamazoo. After three-and-a-half miles you will begin descending a steep hill. There will be a cemetery on your left. Look for the Dow Science Center on your right at the corner of West Main and Thompson Streets. Turn right onto Thompson Street or onto Catherine Street, the second street further on. You are on campus. Visitors may park on the street or in campus lots where space is available. Permits are required and available from the Admissions Office.

STAY THE NIGHT

Nearby: **Stuart Avenue Inn Bed and Breakfast** (229 Stewart Ave.; 800-461-0621), across the street from the college, is an inn that consists of several lovingly restored Victorian mansions, each of which has a parlor and a concierge. One of the mansions, the Bartlett Upjohn House, is featured in the 1987 book, *Daughters of Painted Ladies: America's Resplendent Victorians.* Rates run the gamut and include a continental breakfast with home-baked goods. Two lower priced motels are the **Baymore Inn** (2203 S. Eleventh St.; 800-301-0200) and **Red Roof Inn West** (5425 W. Michigan Ave.; 800-843-7663); both are about three miles away from the campus. Upscale **Radisson Plaza Hotel** (100 W. Michigan Ave.; 800-333-3333) is six blocks away from campus in downtown Kalamazoo. It has a health club, indoor pool, whirlpool, sauna, shops, and three restaurants.

AT A GLANCE

Selectivity Rating	81
Range SAT I Math	580–690
Average SAT I Math	630
Range SAT I Verbal	590–680
Average SAT I Verbal	631
Average ACT Composite	28
Average GPA	3.64
Student/Faculty Ratio	12:1

CAMPUS TOURS

Appointment	Preferred
Dates	Year-round
Times	Call for times
Average Length	1 hour

ON-CAMPUS APPOINTMENTS

Admissions

Start Date–Juniors	Weekdays
Appointment	Preferred
Advance Notice	Yes, 2 weeks
Saturdays	Sometimes
Average Length	1 hour
Info Sessions	Yes

Faculty and Coaches

Dates/Times	Academic year
Arrangements	Contact Admissions Office 2 weeks prior

CLASS VISITS

Dates	Academic year
Arrangements	Contact Admissions Office

MICHIGAN STATE UNIVERSITY

Office of Admissions, 250 Administration Building, East Lansing, MI 48824-1046 •
Telephone: 517-355-8332 • www.msu.edu/admissions/index.html •
Email: admis@msu.edu

Hours: Monday–Friday, 8:00AM–5:00PM; Saturday, 8:00AM–noon

Students at Michigan State University have a wide range of majors to choose from—over 150—and if you somehow manage to avoid finding a major you like, you can design your own. Professors are great in upper-level classes, but teaching assistants run the show at the introductory level.

AT A GLANCE

Selectivity Rating	73
Range SAT I Math	520–640
Average SAT I Math	579
Range SAT I Verbal	490–610
Average SAT I Verbal	552
Average ACT Composite	24
Average GPA	3.55
Student/Faculty Ratio	18:1

CAMPUS TOURS

Appointment	Preferred
Dates	Year-round
Times	Mon–Fri, 11:30AM, Sat, 11:30 AM
Average Length	1 hour

ON-CAMPUS APPOINTMENTS

Admissions

Appointment	Required
Advance Notice	No, 2 weeks
Saturdays	Sometimes
Average Length	30 min.
Info Sessions	Yes

Faculty and Coaches

Dates/Times	Academic year
Arrangements	Contact Athletic Department 2 weeks prior

CLASS VISITS

Dates	Year-round
Arrangements	Tour consortium: call 517-432-9508

TRANSPORTATION

Capitol City Airport serves the Greater Lansing Area and is a 20-minute taxi ride to the MSU campus. Amtrak trains and Greyhound buses go to East Lansing and are a short walk or taxi ride to campus.

FIND YOUR WAY

Traverse City or points north via I-75: Proceed south on I-75 to US 27 near Grayling. Proceed south on US 27 past St. Johns; then follow US 127 towards Lansing. Proceed south on US 127 to the Saginaw Street (M-43)/Grand River Avenue/Michigan Avenue exit; continue straight through the intersection at Saginaw Street; continue straight through the intersection at Michigan Avenue; continue straight to the Kalamazoo Street intersection and turn left; continue traveling east on Kalamazoo Street, and go through the stoplight at the Harrison Road intersection onto the MSU Campus. Follow the curve to the left; at the statue of Sparty, turn right (east) onto Red Cedar Road; Lot 62W, the visitors' parking lot, will be on your right. Take a lot ticket and park. Bring your lot ticket with you to have it validated. **Detroit or points east via I-96:** Proceed west on I-96 to northbound US-127; proceed north on US-127, exit on Flint/Clare (exit #8), then take the Kalamazoo Street/Michigan Avenue exit. At the stoplight, turn right onto Kalamazoo Street and go through the stoplight at the Harrison Road intersection onto the MSU Campus. Follow the preceding directions. **Grand Rapids or points west via I-96:** Proceed east on I-96 to eastbound I-69; proceed east on I-69 to southbound US-127; proceed south on US-127 to the Saginaw Street (M-43)/Grand River Avenue/Michigan Avenue exit; continue straight through the intersections at Saginaw Street, Michigan Avenue, and Kalamazoo Street, and turn left onto Kalamazoo street; follow the preceding directions. **Flint or points east via I-69:** Proceed southwest on I-69 to southbound US-127; proceed south on US-127 to the Saginaw Street (M-43)/Grand River Avenue/Michigan Avenue exit; follow the preceding directions. **Jackson or points south via US-127:** Proceed north on US-127 to the Flint/Clare exit (exit #8); take this exit, then take the Kalamazoo Street/Michigan Avenue exit. At the stoplight, turn right onto Kalamazoo Street; follow the preceding directions.

STAY THE NIGHT

Nearby: Hotels in the East Lansing include the **Kellogg Center** (S. Harrison Road; 1-800-875-5090), **East Lansing Marriott** (300 M.A.C. Ave.; 1-800-646-4MSU), **Residence Inn** (1600 E. Grand River; 1-517-332-7711), **Towneplace Suites by Marriott** (Hannah Boulevard; 1-800-257-3000), the **Ramada Inn** (1100 Trowbridge Road; 517-351-5500), and the **Hampton Inn Hotel** (2500 Coolidge Road; 517-324-2072).

HIGHLIGHTS

ON CAMPUS

- MSU Student Union
- Jack Breslin Student Events Center
- MSU Main Library & Cyber Cafe
- The International Center
- Wharton Center for the Performing Arts

OFF CAMPUS

- The State of Michigan Capitol Building
- The State of Michigan Library & Historical Center
- The Meridian Mall
- Downtown East Lansing shops & restaurant
- Oldsmobile Park, home of the Lansing Lugnuts baseball team

UNIVERSITY OF MICHIGAN—ANN ARBOR

Office of Undergraduate Admissions, 1220 SAB, Ann Arbor, MI 48109-1316 •
Telephone: 734-764-7433 • www.umich.edu/prospective.html •
Email: ugadmiss@umich.edu

Hours: Monday–Friday, 8:00AM–5:00PM; Saturdays (during fall), 9:00AM–noon

With several outstanding academic departments scattered among its 12 undergraduate schools, particularly the highly regarded engineering and business colleges, the University of Michigan offers the resources and opportunities only dreamed of at other universities. Students say, and we agree, that U of M is one of the very best public schools in all the land.

HIGHLIGHTS

ON CAMPUS
- Bentley Historic Library
- Gerald R. Ford Library
- Matthaes Botanical Gardens
- Museum of Art
- Margaret Dow Towsley Sports Museum

OFF CAMPUS
- Cobblestone Farm
- Hands-on Museum
- Leslie Science Center
- Kempf House
- Kerrytown

TRANSPORTATION

Detroit Metropolitan Airport is 28 miles east of campus. Hourly limousine service is available between the airport and the Michigan Union on campus (a short walk to Admissions in the Student Activities Building). The service leaves the airport on the hour; allow an hour to travel to campus. Tickets can be purchased at the airport. Taxis at the airport will take passengers to campus; rental cars are also available. Amtrak trains (those that run between Chicago and Detroit) and Greyhound buses serve Ann Arbor.

FIND YOUR WAY

From I-80/I-90 (Ohio Tpke.), exit to U.S. 23 N. (near Toledo, OH). Take U.S. 23 N. to I-94 W to State Street N. **From the Detroit Airport,** take I-94 W. to State Street N onto Campus.

STAY THE NIGHT

Nearby: The **Michigan League** (911 N. University Ave.; 734-764-3177) and the **Oxford Conference Center** (627 Oxford St.; 734-764-5297) are University-owned facilities located on central campus. The **Campus Inn** (615 E. Huron St.; 800-666-8693) and the **Bell Tower Hotel** (300 S. Thayer St.; 800-562-3559) are hotels within walking distance of campus. Numerous hotel chains have locations near State St. (a short drive from Central Campus) and near Plymouth Rd. (a short drive from North Campus). For a complete list, call the Huetwell Visitors Center at 734-647-5692 or see the Visiting Campus section of the Admissions website at www.admissions.umich.edu.

AT A GLANCE

Selectivity Rating	90
Range SAT I Math	610–720
Average SAT I Math	661
Range SAT I Verbal	570–670
Average SAT I Verbal	622
Average ACT Composite	28
Average GPA	3.8
Student/Faculty Ratio	15:1

CAMPUS TOURS

Appointment	Required
Dates	Year-round
Times	Varies throughout the year
Average Length	1 hour

ON-CAMPUS APPOINTMENTS

Admissions

Start Date—Juniors	N/A
Info Sessions	Year-round

Faculty and Coaches

Dates/Times	Year-round
Arrangements	Contact faculty directly 1 week prior

CLASS VISITS

Dates	Year-round
Arrangements	Contact Admissions Office

1- **Carleton College**
   St. Olaf College
2- **Macalester College**
3- **University of Minnesota—Twin Cities**
4- **Gustavus Adolphus**

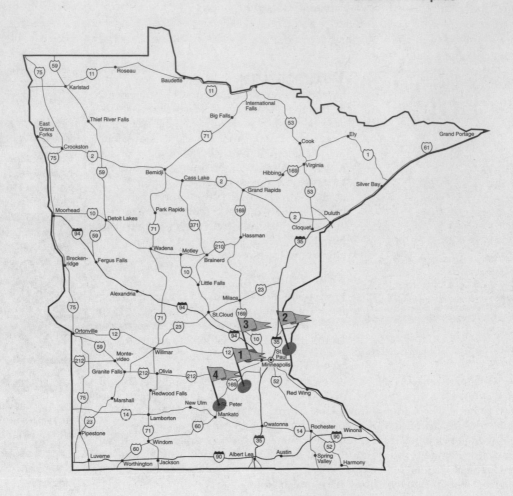

Minnesota	Carleton College	Gustavus Adolphus	Macalester College	St. Olaf College	Univ. Minnesota-TC	*Minneapolis*
Carleton College	—	60	35	0	44	32
Gustavus Adolphus	60	—	73	58	71	71
Macalester College	35	73	—	41	42	33
St. Olaf College	0	58	41	—	42	33
Univ. Minnesota-TC	44	71	4	42	—	0
Minneapolis	32	71	0	33	0	—

CARLETON COLLEGE

Admissions Office, 100 S. College St., Johnson House, Northfield, MN 55057 • Telephone: 800-995-2275 • www.carleton.edu/admissions/ • Email: admissions@acs.carleton.edu

Hours: Monday–Friday, 8:00AM–5:00PM; Saturday (during academic year), 8:30AM–noon

The 1,900 or so students at Carleton College tell us their little liberal arts school in a small, snowy, mostly uneventful Minnesota town has very few negative characteristics. They say Carleton has the integrity, drive, and pride of any great eastern school mixed with the charming, casual, friendly atmosphere of a small Midwestern town.

HIGHLIGHTS

ON CAMPUS

- Cowling Arboretum
- Art Gallery
- Historic Goodsell Observatory
- Japanese Garden
- Recreation Center

OFF CAMPUS

- Mall of America
- Guthrie Theatre
- Walker Outdoor Sculpture Garden
- Science Museum of Minnesota

TRANSPORTATION

The Minneapolis-St. Paul International Airport is 35 miles away from campus. Carleton offers a very limited schedule of rides between the airport and campus; call the Admissions Office to make arrangements. Taxi service runs from the airport to the college. Rental cars are also available at the airport. Amtrak trains serve Minneapolis/St. Paul. These trains generally arrive late at night; therefore, you should plan to stay overnight near the station, and take a bus or taxi to Northfield the following day.

FIND YOUR WAY

From I-35, take Exit 69 to Minnesota Hwy. 19 and head east for seven miles to Northfield. At the first stoplight (where Hwy. 19 merges with Hwy. 3), turn left. Proceed to the next stoplight (2nd St./Hwy. 19) and turn right onto 2nd St. You will come to a stop sign at Division St.; continue straight ahead up the hill on 2nd St. Turn left at College St., which takes you to campus and the Admissions Office.

STAY THE NIGHT

Nearby: The **Archer House** (212 Division St.; 507-645-5661) is a restored turn-of-the-century inn just a couple of blocks from campus. Highlights are its convenient downtown location and gorgeous views of the Cannon River. Rates range from inexpensive to expensive; special rates may be available during the week. The price includes continental breakfast. The **College City Motel** (Hwy. 3 N.; 507-645-4426) and **Country Inn** (300 Hwy. 3 S.; 800-456-4000) are both one mile away from campus. **AmericInn** (1320 Bollenbacher Dr.; 507-645-7761) is within three miles of campus. There are numerous hotels in the southern metro area of Minneapolis/St. Paul that will be within 45 miles of campus.

GUSTAVUS ADOLPHUS COLLEGE

800 West College Avenue,
Saint Peter, MN 56082 • Telephone: 800-487-8288 • www.gustavus.edu/admission/ •
Email: admission@gustavus.edu

Hours: Monday–Friday, 8:00AM–4:45PM; Saturdays (during academic year), 9:00AM–noon

Gusties must choose one of two required core curriculums. Curriculum I is the standard set of arts and sciences distribution requirements. Curriculum II, open to only 60 first-year students each year, presents material in a sequence designed to help students develop a comprehensive understanding of global society. Either way, the fairly conservative and religious students at Gustavus Adolphus receive a tremendous liberal arts education.

AT A GLANCE

Selectivity Rating	83
Range SAT I Math	540–670
Average SAT I Math	620
Range SAT I Verbal	550–660
Average SAT I Verbal	610
Average ACT Composite	26
Average GPA	3.64
Student/Faculty Ratio	13:1

CAMPUS TOURS

Appointment	Preferred
Dates	Year-round
Average Length	120 min.

ON-CAMPUS APPOINTMENTS

Admissions

Appointment	Preferred
Advance Notice	Yes, 1 week
Saturdays	Yes
Average Length	30 min.
Info Sessions	Yes

Faculty and Coaches

Dates/Times	Academic year
Arrangements	Contact Admissions Office 1 week prior

CLASS VISITS

Dates	Academic year
Arrangements	Contact Admissions Office

TRANSPORTATION

Airport shuttle buses to and from Minneapolis/St. Paul Lindbergh International Airport are available.

FIND YOUR WAY

The college is located four blocks west of Hwy. 169.

STAY THE NIGHT

Nearby: A variety of hotels are available in St. Peter and nearby Mankato.

HIGHLIGHTS

ON CAMPUS

- Campus Center
- Courtyard Cafe
- Lund Athletic Center
- Christ Chapel
- Hillstrom Art Museum

OFF CAMPUS

- Local coffee shops
- Area antique stores

MACALESTER COLLEGE

Office of Admissions, 1600 Grand Ave., St. Paul, MN 55105 •
Telephone: 800-231-7974 • www.macalester.edu/admissions/ •
Email: admissions@macalester.edu

Hours: Monday–Friday, 8:00AM–5:00PM; Saturdays (during fall and April), 9:00AM–noon

The facilities are exceptional, and the academics at this rigorous liberal arts college in the Twin Cities are second to none. The cold and dreary winters are a downer for some, but financial aid is good at Mac, and the professors are brilliant.

HIGHLIGHTS

ON CAMPUS
- Second Floor Campus Center
- Bateman Plaza (our front patio)
- The Quad (our front yard)
- Shaw Field

OFF CAMPUS
- Coffee News and Dunn Brothers
- Mississippi River
- Grand Ave/Crocus Hill
- Uptown in Minneapolis
- Mall of America

TRANSPORTATION

The Minneapolis-St. Paul International Airport is seven miles away from campus. Amtrak trains and Greyhound buses serve St. Paul. If you are arriving in town by plane, bus, or train, we recommend that you come to campus by taxi. The campus is approximately 15 minutes away from all terminals, and the fare should be from $10 to $15.

FIND YOUR WAY

From I-95, take the Snelling Ave. exit and go south on Snelling to Grand Ave. Turn right (west) on Grand Ave. and go one block. Turn left (south) on Macalester St. **From the north on I-35,** take I-35E into St. Paul. Exit to I-94 westbound, and follow the directions above. **From the south on I-35,** take I-35E into St. Paul. Exit at Randolph Ave. and proceed west on Randolph about one mile. Turn right (north) on Snelling and proceed to Grand Ave. and go one block. Turn left (south) on Macalester St. The Admissions Office is located at 62 Macalester St. Parking for visitors is available in a lot across the street.

STAY THE NIGHT

Nearby: Four rooms are available at the on-campus **Hugh S. Alexander Alumni House.** A double room is inexpensive, and the rate includes breakfast. A five-minute drive gets you to **Chatsworth Bed and Breakfast** (984 Ashland Ave.; 651-227-4288), a peaceful, 1902 Victorian home near good restaurants and shops. The elegant **St. Paul Hotel** (350 Market St.; 651-292-9292), Minnesota's only four-star hotel, is a 10-minute drive from the school. Here's a quick list of lower-priced places accessible to Macalester: **Holiday Inn** (1010 W. Bandana Blvd.; 651-647-1637) is five miles away, and the **Sheraton Four Points** (400 Hamline Ave. N.; 651-642-1234 or 800-535-2339). The Sheraton has a pool, whirlpool, sauna, exercise room, restaurant, and bar.

A Little Farther: Stillwater is 30 minutes from Macalester. Try **River Town Inn** (306 W. Olive St., Stillwater; 651-430-2955). Its nine guest rooms range in price from inexpensive to expensive, with full breakfast included. **Lowell Inn** (102 N. 2nd St.; 651-439-1100) offers nice rooms and high rates with no breakfast during the week. The **Holiday Inn International** (3 Appletree Square, Bloomington; 651-854-9000) is near the airport and Mall of America (20 minutes away by car).

AT A GLANCE

Selectivity Rating	95
Range SAT I Math	620–710
Average SAT I Math	670
Range SAT I Verbal	630–730
Average SAT I Verbal	690
Average ACT Composite	29
Student/Faculty Ratio	10:1

CAMPUS TOURS

Appointment	Required
Dates	Year-round
Times	Mon–Sat
Average Length	1 hour

ON-CAMPUS APPOINTMENTS

Admissions

Start Date—Juniors	January prior to senior year
Appointment	Required
Advance Notice	Yes, 2 weeks
Saturdays	Sometimes
Average Length	45 min.
Info Sessions	Yes

Faculty and Coaches

Dates/Times	Year-round
Arrangements	Contact coach directly 2 weeks prior

CLASS VISITS

Dates	Academic year
Arrangements	Contact Admissions Office

SAINT OLAF COLLEGE

Office of Admissions, 1520 St. Olaf Ave., Northfield, MN 55057-1098 •
Telephone: 800-800-3025 • www.stolaf.edu/admissions/ •
Email: admissions@stolaf.edu

Hours: Monday–Friday, 8:00AM–5:00PM; Saturday, 8:30AM–noon

St. Olaf, a small Lutheran college in Minnesota, has an excellent liberal arts program with strong departments in music, economics, and the sciences, a demanding core curriculum, and a 4-1-4 academic calendar, which allows students a winter term to travel or pursue individual projects.

AT A GLANCE

Selectivity Rating	85
Range SAT I Math	580–690
Average SAT I Math	635
Range SAT I Verbal	590–690
Average SAT I Verbal	639
Average ACT Composite	27
Average GPA	3.63
Student/Faculty Ratio	13:1

CAMPUS TOURS

Appointment	Preferred
Dates	Year-round
Times	Varies
Average Length	1 hour

ON-CAMPUS APPOINTMENTS

Admissions

Start Date—Juniors	Anytime
Appointment	Preferred
Advance Notice	No, 1 week
Saturdays	Sometimes
Average Length	45 min.
Info Sessions	Yes

Faculty and Coaches

Dates/Times	Academic year
Arrangements	Contact Admissions Office 1 week prior

CLASS VISITS

Dates	Academic year
Arrangements	Contact Admissions Office

TRANSPORTATION

The Minneapolis-St. Paul Airport is 40 miles away from campus. Please contact the Admissions Office for information regarding transportation options from the airport to campus.

FIND YOUR WAY

From I-35 W., take Rte. 19 E. for seven miles to the entrance to the college. **From I-90 near Rochester,** take U.S. 52 N. to Cannon Falls; then take Rte. 19 W. to the college.

STAY THE NIGHT

Nearby: Please contact the Admissions Office for a listing of accommodations or visit our website.

HIGHLIGHTS

ON CAMPUS

- Buntrock Commons
- Tostrud Recreation Center
- The Lion's Pause
- Beautiful 350-acre campus

OFF CAMPUS

- Mall of America
- Many Arts Activities in Twin Cities
- Museum in Twin Cities
- Historic downtown Northfield

UNIVERSITY OF MINNESOTA, TWIN CITIES

Admissions Office, 240 Williamson Hall, 231 Pillsbury Dr. S.E., Minneapolis, MN 55455-0213 • Telephone: 800-752-1000 • www.umn.edu • Email: admissions@tc.umn.edu

Hours: Monday, 8:00AM–6:00PM; Tuesday–Friday, 8:00AM–4:30PM; selected Saturdays from September to May

The University of Minnesota—located in the heart of the Twin Cities—boasts excellent programs to choose from across the board, including pre-professional majors like business and management, journalism, psychology, and engineering. This school is a big place that demands self-reliance, but students say it offers cultural opportunities at every turn.

HIGHLIGHTS

ON CAMPUS

- Weisman Art Museum
- McNamara Alumni Center
- Goldstein Gallery
- Northrup Memorial Auditorium
- University Theater, Rang Center

OFF CAMPUS

- Science Museum
- Mall of America
- Walker Art Center
- Valleyfair Amusement Park
- Target Center Metrodome

TRANSPORTATION

The Minneapolis-St. Paul International Airport is approximately 12 miles away from campus. Two hotels on campus provide daytime limousine service from the airport. For details, call Radisson University Hotel (800-333-3333 or 612-379-8888) or Holiday Inn Metrodome (800-HOLIDAY or 612-333-4646). Amtrak trains and Greyhound buses serve the Minneapolis-St. Paul area. Taxis are available for the drive from the terminals to campus. Public transportation to campus is available: Metro Transit provides bus service to and from the Minneapolis-St. Paul airport. For more information, call 612-344-7000.

FIND YOUR WAY

From I-94 (east or west), take the Huron Blvd. exit (235B). **From I-35 (east or west),** take the University Ave. SE exit (18).

STAY THE NIGHT

Nearby: Dormitory housing is available on campus from mid-June through August. Call 612-624-2994 to book a spot. You can also purchase meal tickets and eat on campus. The **Radisson University Hotel** (615 Washington Ave. S.E.; 612-379-8888) has moderate rates and a good location on the East Bank Campus. The **Econo Lodge** (2500 University Ave. S.E.; 612-331-6000) is just five blocks away. It has an outdoor pool and the price includes a continental breakfast. The **Holiday Inn Metrodome** (1500 Washington Ave. S.; 612-333-4646), only four blocks away, has a special moderate double-occupancy rate, an indoor pool, sauna, whirlpool, exercise room, game room, and restaurant.

A Little Farther: A solid suggestion is **Hyatt Regency Minneapolis** (1300 Nicollet Mall; 612-370-1234 or 800-233-1234), which provides you with the usual Hyatt amenities and activities. Rates are very expensive during the week, but drop on weekends. Ask for a special rate for University of Minnesota visitors.

AT A GLANCE

Selectivity Rating	80
Range SAT I Math	550–670
Average SAT I Math	612
Range SAT I Verbal	540–660
Average SAT I Verbal	593
Average ACT Composite	25
Student/Faculty Ratio	15:1

CAMPUS TOURS

Times	10:30AM and 2:15PM

ON-CAMPUS APPOINTMENTS

Admissions

Start Date–Juniors	Fall
Appointment	Required, 3 weeks
Saturdays	Sometimes

Faculty and Coaches

Dates/Arrangements	Contact faculty directly 3 weeks prior

CLASS VISITS

Arrangements	Contact Visiting Center

1- University of Mississippi
2- Millsaps College

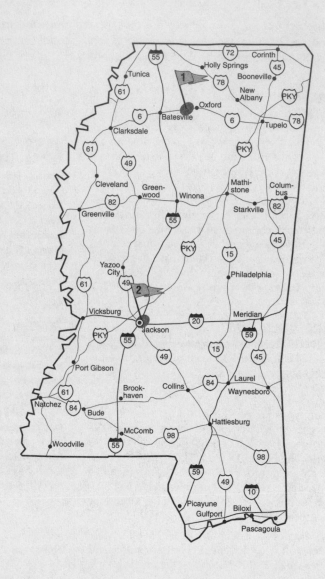

Mississippi	Millsaps Coll.	Univ. Mississippi	Jackson
Millsaps Coll.	—	167	0
Univ. Mississippi	167	—	157
Jackson	0	157	—

MILLSAPS COLLEGE

Office of Admissions, 1701 North State Street, Jackson, MS 39210 •
Telephone: 800-352-1050 • www.millsaps.edu/future_students/ •
Email: admissions@millsaps.edu

Hours: Monday–Friday, 8:00AM–4:30PM

Millsaps College boasts some of the finest pre-professional and liberal arts programs in the South—and the nation—in the pre-medical sciences, political science, and music, as well as an interdisciplinary Heritage Program (a year-long western civilization survey). Professors communicate enthusiasm, and all students must complete intense written and oral comprehensive exams before graduation.

HIGHLIGHTS

ON CAMPUS
- Hall Activities Center
- Kava House (coffee-shop/chat room)
- The Bowl (natural outdoor green space at the heart of campus)
- The Millsaps Bell Tower
- Faternity Row

OFF CAMPUS
- Downtown Jackson (shopping, nightlife, internship opportunities)
- Mississippi Museum of Art (and Davis Planetarium)
- Ross Barnett Reservoir
- Highland Village
- NorthPark/County Line District

TRANSPORTATION
We are located in Mississippi's capital city. You can get to Jackson via all major airlines, Amtrak, or bus. Taxi and local bus services are available.

FIND YOUR WAY
From I-55: Woodrow Wilson Exit #98A to the second light. Turn left on North State Street. Go past first light to the circular drive; turn right to enter campus. The Office of Admissions is in Sanders Hall on the first floor.

STAY THE NIGHT
Nearby: The **Cabot Lodge Millsaps** (800-874-4737) is located adjacent to the Millsaps campus. Other places near the campus include the **Holiday Inn Express** (High Street; 800-465-4329), the **Red Roof Inn** (High Street; 601-969-5006), the **Edison Walthall Hotel** (800-932-6161), and the **Hampton Inn** (Greymont; 800-426-7866).

AT A GLANCE	
Selectivity Rating	80
Range SAT I Math	530–650
Average SAT I Math	590
Range SAT I Verbal	550–640
Average SAT I Verbal	590
Average ACT Composite	25
Average GPA	3.5
Student/Faculty Ratio	13:1

CAMPUS TOURS	
Appointment	Preferred
Dates	Year-round
Times	Varies
Average Length	1 hour

ON-CAMPUS APPOINTMENTS	
Admissions	
Start Date–Juniors	Anytime
Appointment	Preferred
Advance Notice	Yes, 1 week
Saturdays	Sometimes
Average Length	30 min.
Info Sessions	Yes
Faculty and Coaches	
Dates/Times	Academic year
Arrangements	Contact Admissions Office 1 week prior

CLASS VISITS	
Dates	Academic year
Arrangements	Contact Admissions Office

UNIVERSITY OF MISSISSIPPI

Admissions Office, P O Box 1848, University, MS 38677 •
Telephone: 800-653-6477 • www.olemiss.edu/admissions •
Email: admissions@olemiss.edu

Hours: Monday–Friday, 8:00AM–5:00PM

The University of Mississippi—or Ole Miss as it is often called—offers over 100 academic programs everything from engineering to telecommunications to politics to pharmacy. The surrounding town of Oxford is also a great college town.

AT A GLANCE

Selectivity Rating	76
Average ACT Composite	23
Average GPA	3.37
Student/Faculty Ratio	21:1

CAMPUS TOURS

Appointment	Required
Times	Mon–Fri, 9AM–3PM;
	Sat, 9AM–noon

ON-CAMPUS APPOINTMENTS

Admissions

Start Date–Juniors	Anytime
Appointment	Required, 2 weeks
Saturdays	Yes
Info Sessions	Yes

Faculty and Coaches

Dates/Arrangements	Contact coach directly 2 weeks prior

CLASS VISITS

Dates	Academic year
Arrangements	Contact Admissions Office

TRANSPORTATION

Memphis International Airport is 70 miles away from campus. Memphis (the largest nearby city) is also served by Amtrak and Greyhound.

FIND YOUR WAY

Take I-55 or U.S. 45 to Mississippi Highway 6 and turn onto it heading toward Oxford. From the Hwy. 6 bypass, take the University of Mississippi exit marked Old Taylor Road. Go north on Old Taylor Road (you will pass the baseball stadium on the right after about a quarter mile), continuing until it ends at University Ave. Turn left (west) on University Ave. and you will soon be in the heart of campus. The Lyceum is at the top of the loop formed by University Ave.

STAY THE NIGHT

Nearby: If you want to stay close to campus, you can choose from the **Alumni House** (662-915-2331), the **Oliver Britt House Inn** (662-234-8043), the **Comfort Inn** (662-234-6000), the **Days Inn** (662-234-9500), the **Downtown Inn** (800-606-1497), the **Hampton Inn** (662-236-2500), the **Holiday Inn Express** (662-236-2500), or the **Ramada Inn** (662-234-7013).

A Little Farther: The **Peabody** in Memphis, Tennessee is another option a little farther away from campus; call 800-PEABODY for more information.

HIGHLIGHTS

ON CAMPUS

- Lyceum
- Gertrude C. Ford Center for the Performing Arts
- Paris-Yates Chapel
- Antebellum Buildings (Barnard Observatory, Croft)
- Blues Library (B.B. King's personal collection)

OFF CAMPUS

- Rowan Oak (home of William Faulker)
- Courthouse Square (dining and shopping)
- Square Books (unique bookstore)
- Double Decker bus tours
- Casinos in nearby Tunica, Mississippi

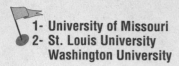

1- University of Missouri
2- St. Louis University
   Washington University

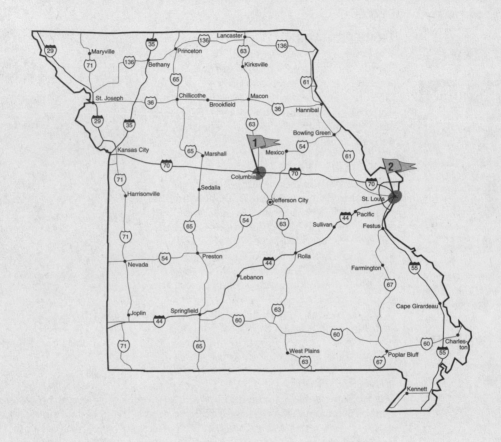

Missouri	St. Louis Univ.	Univ. Missouri	Washington Univ.	St. Louis	Springfield
St. Louis Univ.	—	132	5	0	215
Univ. Missouri	132	—	127	130	168
Washington Univ.	5	127	—	0	210
St. Louis	0	130	0	—	215
Springfield	215	168	210	215	—

SAINT LOUIS UNIVERSITY

Office of Undergraduate Admission, 221 N. Grand Blvd.,
St. Louis, MO 63103 • Telephone: 800-758-3678 • www.imagine.slu.edu •
Email: admitme@slu.edu

Hours: Monday–Friday, 8:30AM–5:00PM; Saturday, 9:00AM–2:00PM

Prestigious Saint Louis University is a small, private university with a strong Jesuit tradition that offers an excellent academic environment at a very affordable price. Career-oriented students say SLU is on the upswing, and they are thrilled to be here watching it grow. Socially, students definitely party, but spirituality and a sense of family are reportedly very noticeable.

AT A GLANCE

Selectivity Rating	76
Range SAT I Math	530–655
Average SAT I Math	595
Range SAT I Verbal	530–640
Average SAT I Verbal	585
Average ACT Composite	26
Average GPA	3.45
Student/Faculty Ratio	12:1

CAMPUS TOURS

Appointment	Preferred
Dates	Year-round
Times	Mon–Fri, 11AM, 1PM, & 3PM;
	Sat, 10AM & noon
Average Length	1 hour

ON-CAMPUS APPOINTMENTS

Admissions

Start Date–Juniors	Anytime
Appointment	Required
Advance Notice	Yes, 2 weeks
Saturdays	No
Average Length	1 hour
Info Sessions	Yes

Faculty and Coaches

Dates/Times	Year-round
Arrangements	Contact Admissions
	Office 2 weeks prior

CLASS VISITS

Dates	Academic year
Arrangements	Contact Admissions
	Office

TRANSPORTATION

The Lambert-St. Louis International Airport is 13 miles away from campus. Airport limousines, taxis, and rental cars are available for the ride from the airport to campus. Amtrak trains and Greyhound buses serve St. Louis. Taxis are available for the ride from the stations to campus.

FIND YOUR WAY

From the northeast, take I-55/70 S. across the Poplar St. Bridge to I-64 W. Follow to the Grand Blvd. exit. Make a right on Grand Blvd. and proceed one block to campus. **From the northwest,** take I-70 E. to I-170 S. Proceed to I-64 E. and continue to the Grand Blvd. exit. Make a right on Grand and continue on it for one block until you reach campus. **From the south,** take I-55 N. to I-44 W. Follow to the Grand Blvd. exit. Make a left at the stop sign and then a right on Grand Blvd. Stay on it for two miles to campus. **From the southwest,** take I-44 E. to the Grand Blvd. exit. Make a left on Grand and stay on it for two miles to campus.

STAY THE NIGHT

Nearby: Saint Louis University is proud to present our newest on-campus facility, the **Water Tower Inn.** Complete with 62 guest rooms, five meeting rooms, food service, and a fitness center, the Water Tower Inn is perfect for both short-term and extended stay guests. Saint Louis University's Water Tower Inn Sales Center is on 3545 Lafayette Ave. St. Louis, MO 63104; the phone number is 314-977-7500.

HIGHLIGHTS

ON CAMPUS
- St. Francis Xavier Church
- Busch Student Center
- Museum of Contemporary Art
- Simon Recreation Center
- Robert R. Hermann Soccer Stadium

OFF CAMPUS
- The Fabulous Fox Theatre
- Powell Symphony Hall
- Forest Park
- St. Louis Arch
- St. Louis Union Station

UNIVERSITY OF MISSOURI—COLUMBIA

Admissions Office, 230 Jess Hall, Columbia, MO 65211 •
Telephone: 573-882-7786 • www.missouri.edu/admissions.htm •
Email: admissions@missouri.edu

Hours: Monday–Friday, 8:00AM–5:00PM

The University of Missouri at Columbia (or Mizzou, as it is affectionately called by students) offers as its crown jewel a nationally renowned journalism program. Greek life is big, and the men's basketball and football teams enjoy a great deal of popularity. Sam Walton, founder of Wal-Mart, is an alum.

HIGHLIGHTS

ON CAMPUS
- Francis Quadrangle, The Columns
- Jesse Hall
- Memorial Union
- Memorial Stadium/Faurot Field
- Brady Commons

OFF CAMPUS
- Columbia Downtown District
- Rock Bridge State Park
- MKT Fitness/Biking Trail
- Shelter Gardens
- The Blue Note

TRANSPORTATION

Columbia Regional Airport is 15 minutes away from campus. Tiger Taxi is available for the ride from the airport to campus. Shuttles are also available to many of the hotels in town; check with the individual hotels/motels for such services.

FIND YOUR WAY

From the east or west, take I-70 to Stadium Blvd.; then take Stadium Blvd. south to campus (approximately four miles). The campus is at the corner of Stadium and Providence Rd. **From the north or south,** take U.S. Rte. 63 to Stadium Boulevard (State Rte. 740). Take Stadium Blvd. west to the campus, which is at the corner of Stadium and Providence Rd.

STAY THE NIGHT

Nearby: **Drury Inn** (1000 Knipp Street; 573-445-1800) has 123 rooms, offers suites and an indoor pool; it's next to the Columbia Mall and many nearby restaurants. Another choice is the **Hampton Inn** (3410 Clark Lane; 573-449-2491). The **Holiday Inn Select** (2200 I-70 Drive SW; 573-449-4422) has 311 rooms, indoor and outdoor pools, and two restaurants. The **Ramada Inn** (1100 Vandiver Drive; 573-449-0051) has 190 rooms, an outdoor pool, and a restaurant.

AT A GLANCE

Average ACT Composite	25

CAMPUS TOURS

Appointment	Required
Dates	Year-round
Times	Mon–Fri, almost hourly
Average Length	2 hours

ON-CAMPUS APPOINTMENTS

Admissions

Start Date–Juniors	N/A
Appointment	Required, 2 weeks
Info Sessions	Year-round

Faculty and Coaches

Dates/Times	Year-round
Arrangements	Contact Admissions Office

CLASS VISITS

Dates	Year-round
Arrangements	Contact Admissions Office

WASHINGTON UNIVERSITY IN ST. LOUIS

Office of Undergraduate Admissions, Campus Box 1089, One Brookings Drive, 1 Brookings Dr., St. Louis, MO 63130-4899 • Telephone: 800-638-0700 • www.wustl.edu/admissions.htm/ • Email: admissions@wustl.edu

Hours: Monday–Friday, 8:30AM–5:00PM; Saturdays (during fall and summer), 9:00AM–2:00PM

Although it has a great faculty, top-caliber students, and all the resources of the Ivies, Washington University in St. Louis is very underrated. It's a great school, as its students attest. A slew of students pursue graduate study, particularly in medicine (15 percent of all Washington University graduates head straight to medical school).

AT A GLANCE

Selectivity Rating	96
Range SAT I Math	670–750
Range SAT I Verbal	640–730
Student/Faculty Ratio	7:1

CAMPUS TOURS

Appointment	Preferred
Dates	Year-round
Times	Varies throughout the year
Average Length	1 hour

ON-CAMPUS APPOINTMENTS

Admissions

Start Date–Juniors	N/A
Appointment	Required
Saturdays	No
Average Length	30 min.
Info Sessions	Yes

Faculty and Coaches

Dates/Times	Academic year
Arrangements	Contact Admissions Office 1 week prior

CLASS VISITS

Dates	Academic year
Arrangements	Contact Admissions Office

TRANSPORTATION

Lambert-St. Louis International Airport is approximately 10 miles away from campus. Limousines and taxis are available for the ride from the airport to campus. County Cab (314-991-5300) should need only a few minutes notice.

FIND YOUR WAY

From I-55/70 south or west, exit to I-64 west (U.S. 40/61). Exit I-64 at the Clayton Road exit. Turn right (north) on Skinker Blvd. for one mile to campus. **From I-55 north or I-44 east,** take I-270 north to I-64 east (U.S. 40/61). Exit at the McCausland Ave. exit. Turn left (north) on McCausland for 1.2 miles to campus. **From the airport (heading east on I-70),** take I-70 east to I-170 south. Exit at Delmar Blvd., turn left on Delmar to Big Bend Blvd. Turn right on Big Bend to Forsyth Blvd. Turn left (east) on Forsyth Blvd. to Hoyt Drive.

STAY THE NIGHT

Nearby: The most conveniently located (two to three miles away from campus) are the following six hotels: **Clayton on the Park** (8025 Bonhomme Avenue; 314-721-6543) offers an off-site indoor/outdoor pool and on-site exercise facilities; car service from the airport is available. The **Daniele Hotel** (216 North Meramec Avenue; 314-721-0101 or 800-325-8302) offers an outdoor pool; limousine service is available. **Radisson Clayton** (7750 Carondelet Avenue; 314-726-5400 or 800-333-3333) offers an indoor/outdoor pool; airport shuttle is available. **Ritz Carlton** (100 Carondelet Plaza; 314-863-6300 or 800-241-3333) offers an indoor pool; limousine service is available. **Seven Gables Inn** (26 North Meramec Avenue; 314-863-8400 or 800-433-6590) has no pool, but offers free access to off-site exercise facilities; no shuttle service is available. **Sheraton Clayton** (7730 Bonhomme Avenue; 314-863-0400 or 888-337-1395) offers an indoor pool/whirlpool and exercise facilities; airport shuttle is available. The following two hotels are three to seven miles away from campus: **Residence Inn by Marriott** at St. Louis Galleria (1100 McMarrow; 314-862-1900 or 800-331-3131) offers an outdoor pool and free access to off-site exercise facilities; no shuttle service is available and **Courtyard by Marriott** (2340 Market Street; 314-241-9111 or 800-321-2211) offers an indoor pool and exercise facilities; no shuttle is available.

HIGHLIGHTS

ON CAMPUS

- Gallery of Art
- Edison Theatre
- Olin Library
- Francis Gymnasium & Francis Field
- Residence Halls

OFF CAMPUS

- The Fabulous Fox Theatre
- Powell Symphony Hall
- Forest Park
- Gateway Arch
- Zoo and Science Center

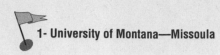

1- University of Montana—Missoula

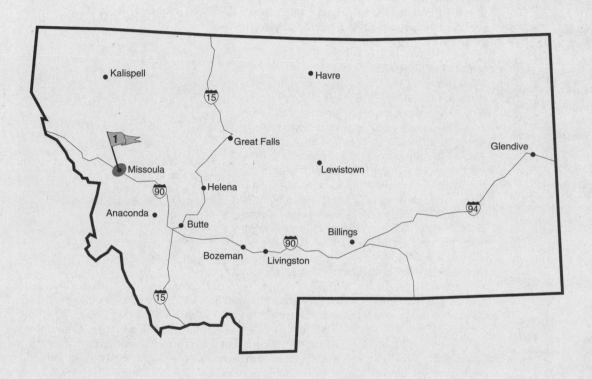

Kalispell

Havre

15

Great Falls

1
Missoula

Glendive

Lewistown

90

Helena

94

Anaconda

Butte

Billings

90

15

Bozeman   Livingston

Montana	U. Montana	Helena
U. Montana	—	113
Helena	113	—

UNIVERSITY OF MONTANA—MISSOULA

Enrollment Services—Admissions, 103 Lommasson Center,
Missoula, MT 59812 • Telephone: 800-462-8636 • www.umt.edu •
Email: admiss@selway.umt.edu

Hours: Monday–Friday, 8:00AM–5:00PM; Saturdays by appointment

The University of Montana ranks fourth in the nation among public universities in producing Rhodes scholars, and students say you'll find a great academic experience. The school also boasts good facilities, including nearby Lubrecht Forest, a huge 29,000-acre teaching and research forest located 35 miles northeast of Missoula, and not one but two working ranches.

AT A GLANCE

Selectivity Rating	76
Range SAT I Math	470–590
Average SAT I Math	540
Range SAT I Verbal	450–600
Average SAT I Verbal	550
Average ACT Composite	22
Average GPA	3.18
Student/Faculty Ratio	22:1

CAMPUS TOURS

Appointment	Preferred
Dates	Year-round
Times	Mon–Fri, 11AM & 2 PM
Average Length	1 hour

ON-CAMPUS APPOINTMENTS

Admissions

Appointment	Preferred
Advance Notice	Yes, 1 week
Saturdays	Sometimes
Average Length	1 hour
Info Sessions	Yes

Faculty and Coaches

Dates/Times	Year-round
Arrangements	Contact Admissions Office 2 weeks prior

CLASS VISITS

Dates	Varies
Arrangements	Contact Admissions Office

TRANSPORTATION

Missoula Interntational Airport is located about 15 minutes from campus. Shuttle service and taxis are available from the airport to campus.

FIND YOUR WAY

West Bound I-90: Take Missoula's first exit onto Van Buren Street, turn left at the stop sign and merge into the right lane. At the stop light, turn right onto Broadway street. Move into the furthest left lane, and turn left onto Madison at the stoplight. When driving over the bridge, stay in the left lane, and veer left at the fork; keep to the left and turn at the stop light. After making a left, get into the right lane. You will be heading due east and directly in front of you will be the Adams Center. You are now on campus. **East Bound I-90:** Take Missoula's last Exit onto Van Buren street, Exit 105. Turn right at the stop sign and merge into the right lane. At the stop light, turn right onto Broadway street. Move into the furthest left lane, and turn left onto Madison at the stoplight. Follow the preceding directions. **From the Missoula County Airport:** Leaving the airport, turn right onto Broadway Street. Take the first left leading you to the entrance of East Bound I-90. Follow I-90 and take Missoula's last exit onto Van Buren Street, turning right at the stop sign. At the stop light, turn right onto Broadway street. Move into the furthest left lane, and turn left onto Madison at the stoplight. Follow the preceding directions. **From Highway 12 & 93 North:** Highway 12 & 93 become Brooks Street through Missoula. To Higgins Avenue. Brooks Merges with Higgins at Hellgate Highschool. Be sure you are in the right lane, and turn right onto Sixth Street. Follow Sixth Street for six blocks until you reach the campus entrance.

STAY THE NIGHT

Nearby: Close to the university (just across the river) is the **Doubletree Hotel** (100 Madison St.; 406-728-3100). The prices are moderate and discounts are given to prospective students. There is a restaurant/lounge, pool, and fitness center in the hotel. Close to downtown and campus is the **Holiday Inn Parkside** (200 S Patte; 406-721-8550), which also offers a discount to prospective students. Also across the river from campus is the **Campus Inn** (744 E. Broadway; 406-549-5134). Rooms are moderately-priced and a discount is offered.

HIGHLIGHTS

ON CAMPUS

- Adams Events Center
- Washington Grizly Stadium
- Campus Recreation Center
- University Center
- Main Hall

OFF CAMPUS

- Missoula Smoke Jumpers Center
- Bison Range
- Missoula Carousel & Caras Park
- Glacier & Yellowstone National Parks

1- University of Nebraska—Lincoln
2- University of Nebraska—Omaha

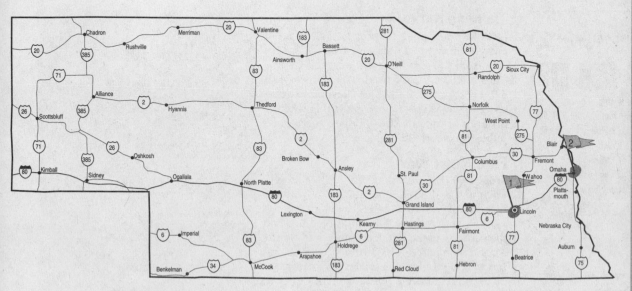

Nebraska	U. Nebraska-Lin.	U. Nebraska-Oma.	Omaha
U. Nebraska-Lin.	—	58	58
U. Nebraska-Oma.	58	—	0
Omaha	58	0	—

UNIVERSITY OF NEBRASKA—LINCOLN

Office of Admissions, 313 N.13th Street, PO Box 880417, Lincoln, NE 68588-0417 •
Telephone: 800-742-8800 • www.unl.edu/unlpub/admissions.shtml •
Email: nuhusker@unl.edu

Hours: Monday–Friday, 8:00AM–5:00PM; Saturdays by appointment

The University of Nebraska provides the kinds of academic resources you would expect from a mammoth, world-class state university along with a quality of life that can only be found in the Midwest. And, as if it needed any verification, Sports Illustrated listed UN among the Top Ten "Best Sports Colleges" in the country.

AT A GLANCE

Selectivity Rating		90
Range SAT I Math		520–660
Average SAT I Math		589
Range SAT I Verbal		500–640
Average SAT I Verbal		570
Average ACT Composite		24
Student/Faculty Ratio		19:1

CAMPUS TOURS

Appointment	Preferred
Dates	Year-round
Times	Varies
Average Length	Varies

ON-CAMPUS APPOINTMENTS

Admissions

Start Date—Juniors	Anytime
Appointment	Preferred
Advance Notice	Yes, 2 weeks
Saturdays	Sometimes
Average Length	1 hour
Info Sessions	Yes

Faculty and Coaches

Dates/Times	Year-round
Arrangements	Contact Athletic Department 2 weeks prior

CLASS VISITS

Dates	Varies
Arrangements	Contact Admissions Office

TRANSPORTATION

Lincoln Municipal Airport is seven miles away from campus. Taxis are available for the ride from the airport to campus; call Capitol Cabs at 402-477-6074 or Husker Cabs at 402-477-4111. Amtrak trains and Greyhound buses serve Lincoln. The stations are within walking distance of campus. The city also has a good public transportation system.

FIND YOUR WAY

From I-80 (E. and W.), take the 9th St. downtown exit and head south toward downtown Lincoln. After three miles, you go over a viaduct and will see Memorial Stadium and the campus to the left. Continue south to the second stoplight (P St.). Turn left on P St. and proceed eight blocks east to 17th St. Turn left on 17th St. and drive north one block to Q St. Turn left and travel west two blocks to the Admissions Office. From U.S. Rte. 77 S., turn right onto Cornhusker Highway (the first major intersection when you get to Lincoln). Proceed west to 27th St. and turn left. Proceed south three miles to Q St. Turn right onto Q St. and continue west to 14th St. and the Admissions Office. If you enter Lincoln from U.S. Rte. 77 N. turn right on capital Parkway, proceed east into downtown Lincoln. Turn left onto 17th St. and travel north one block to Q St. Turn left on Q St. and travel west two blocks to the Admissions Office.

STAY THE NIGHT

Nearby: You have a few choices within walking distance. The larger **Holiday Inn** (141 N. 9th St.; 402-475-4011) has some special rates (depending on occupancy) in the inexpensive range. (Ask for the inexpensive student/faculty rate.) The hotel offers free parking and has an indoor pool and Jacuzzi, a restaurant, and a coffee shop. Also consider the **Cornhusker Hotel** (333 S. 13th St.; 402-474-7474), which tends to run a bit higher. Lower rates are sometimes available on weekends. The hotel has an indoor pool and an exercise room. It also has two restaurants, one of which is reputed to be the only four-star restaurant in the state. There is a small fee for parking.

HIGHLIGHTS

ON CAMPUS

- Student Union
- Student Recreation
- Library
- Memorial Stadium and Hewitt Center
- Residence Halls

OFF CAMPUS

- The Mill
- Nebraska Historical Museum
- Nebraska State Capital
- Hay Market Area
- Hay Market Ball Park

UNIVERSITY OF NEBRASKA—OMAHA

Office of Recruitment Services, 6001 Dodge St.,
Omaha, NE 68182 • Telephone: 800-858-8648 • www.unomaha.edu •
Email: unoadm@unomaha.edu

Hours: Monday–Friday, 8:00AM–5:00PM

The urban campus of the University of Nebraska at Omaha has a large percentage of part-timers among its 12,000 students, many of whom take advantage of weekend, evening, and summer programs. The school offers a wide range of majors as well as study abroad opportunities in Japan and Mexico. However, there is no on-campus housing.

HIGHLIGHTS

ON CAMPUS
- University Library
- Strauss Performing Arts Center
- Caniglia Field Football Stadium

OFF CAMPUS
- Joslyn Art Museum
- Omaha's Children Museum
- USS Hazard and USS Marlin
- Henry Doorly Zoo

TRANSPORTATION

Eppley Airfield in Omaha is eight miles away from campus. Airport taxis are available for the ride to campus.

FIND YOUR WAY

From I-680, take Dodge St. eastbound for four miles to the campus at 60th St. **From I-80,** take the 72nd N. St. exit to Dodge St. East.

STAY THE NIGHT

Nearby: You can stay five minutes away from campus at **The Offutt House** (140 N. 39th St.; 402-553-0951), an 1894 mansion with fireplaces and antique-filled rooms. This renovated seven-room bed-and-breakfast is near museums and the old market. Rates vary from inexpensive to moderate, and include breakfast. **Hampton Inn** (9720 W. Dodge Rd.; 402-391-5300) is two miles west of campus, near a shopping area in town. Rates are inexpensive (and lower on weekends) and include continental breakfast. The **Embassy Suites Hotel** (555 S. 10th St.; 402-346-9000) in the Old Market area is another good place to stay. If an indoor pool is important, the **Holiday Inn** (3321 72nd St.; 402-393-3950), five miles away from school, fills the bill. Moderate rates, a game room, exercise room, sauna, and whirlpool round out the experience. **Ramada Inn** (7007 Grover Street, 402-397-7030 or 800-228-5299) five miles away from campus, it is at the 72nd Street exit of I-80.

AT A GLANCE

Selectivity Rating	65
Average ACT Composite	22
Student/Faculty Ratio	18:1

CAMPUS TOURS

Appointment	Required
Dates	Year-round
Times	Varies throughout the year
Average Length	120 min.

ON-CAMPUS APPOINTMENTS

Admissions
Start Date–Juniors	Anytime
Appointment	Required, 1 week
Saturdays	No

Faculty and Coaches
Dates/Times	Year-round
Arrangements	Contact Admissions Office 1 week prior

CLASS VISITS

Dates	Academic year
Arrangements	Varies

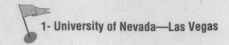

1- University of Nevada—Las Vegas

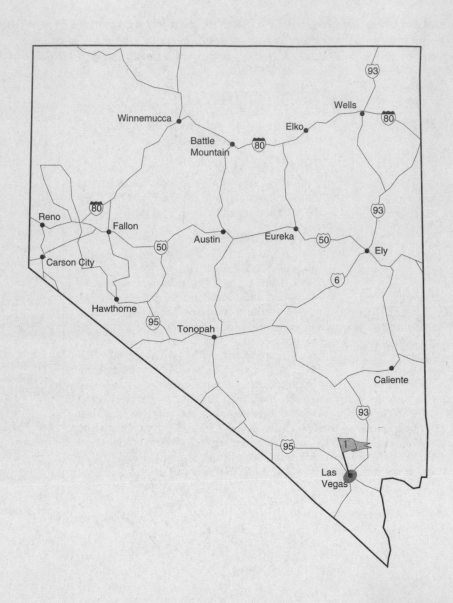

Nevada	U. Montana	Carson City
U. Nevada	—	442
Carson City	442	—

UNIVERSITY OF NEVADA—LAS VEGAS

Office of Undergraduate Recruitment, 4505 Maryland Parkway, Box 451021, Las Vegas, NV 89154 • Telephone: 702-895-3443 • www.unlv.edu • Email: Undergraduate.Recruitment@ccmail.nevada.edu

Hours: Monday–Friday, 8:00AM–5:00PM; open until 6:00PM on Mondays

The University of Nevada at Las Vegas bills itself as a teaching and research university that provides students an excellent education at a reasonable cost. On campus, check out the huge variety of trees, shrubs, and desert plants (take the self-guided tour, even) or gawk at the full-scale replica of the H-1 Racer—a record-setting plane flown by Howard Hughes—that is suspended from the ceiling of the Great Hall of Engineering.

HIGHLIGHTS

ON CAMPUS
- Lied Library
- Artemus W. Ham Concert Hall
- Moyer Student Union
- Judy Bailey Theatre
- Student Services Complex

OFF CAMPUS
- Las Vegas Boulevard
- Lake Mead
- Mount Charleston
- Hoover Dam
- Guggenheim-Hermitage Museum at The Venetian

TRANSPORTATION

McCarran Airport is only a 10 minute drive from campus. Other forms of available transportation include bus and taxi services. Monorail service will be available in 2004.

FIND YOUR WAY

The University of Nevada at Las Vegas is only a short drive from the Las Vegas Strip. **From I-15,** exit east on Tropicana. Turn north on Maryland Parkway to Harmon Avenue. The college entrance will be on the left.

STAY THE NIGHT

Nearby: For the most up-to-date information in hotel accomodations please refer to www.lasvegas.com.

AT A GLANCE	
Selectivity Rating	72
Range SAT I Math	450–570
Average SAT I Math	514
Range SAT I Verbal	430–560
Average SAT I Verbal	501
Average ACT Composite	21
Average GPA	3.2
Student/Faculty Ratio	19:1

CAMPUS TOURS	
Appointment	Preferred
Dates	Year-round
Times	Varies
Average Length	1 hour

ON-CAMPUS APPOINTMENTS	
Admissions	
Start Date–Juniors	Fall
Appointment	Required
Advance Notice	Yes
Saturdays	No
Average Length	30 min.
Info Sessions	Yes
Faculty and Coaches	
Dates/Times	Year-round
Arrangements	Contact Athletic Department 2 weeks prior

CLASS VISITS	
Dates	Year-round
Arrangements	Contact department faculty

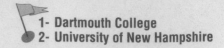

1- Dartmouth College
2- University of New Hampshire

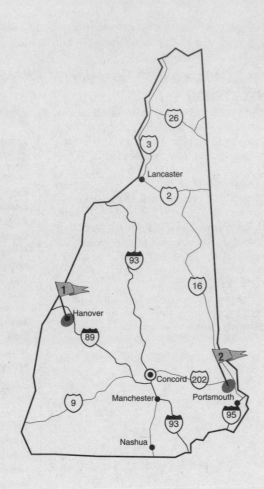

New Hampshire	Dartmouth College	U. New Hampshire	*Manchester*
Dartmouth College	—	114	86
U. New Hampshire	114	—	33
Manchester	86	33	—

DARTMOUTH COLLEGE

Office of Admissions, 6016 McNutt Hall,
Hanover, NH 03755 • Telephone: 603-646-2875 • www.dartmouth.edu •
Email: admissions.office@dartmouth.edu

Hours: Monday–Friday, 8:00AM–4:30PM (until 4:00PM in summer); Saturdays (September–mid-November), 9:00AM–noon

Few schools offer the winning combination of caring, world-class professors and gorgeous setting that Dartmouth College does. Academically, the D-Plan allows students to design an absolutely unique curriculum for themselves. Socially, frats and sororities aren't as popular as they once were in Hanover, though beer certainly still is. Daniel Webster and Theodore Geisel (a.k.a. Dr. Seuss) are just two of Dartmouth's many talented alumni.

HIGHLIGHTS

ON CAMPUS
- Hopkins Center for Creative and Performing Arts
- Hood Museum of Art
- Murals by Jose Clemente Orozco
- Ten library system (all open to tourists)
- Ledyard Canoe Club (oldest in the country)

OFF CAMPUS
- Montshire Museum of Science (Norwich, Vermont)
- Simon Pierce Glass Blowing
- Appalachian Trail
- Dartmouth Skiway (Lyme, New Hampshire)
- Quechee Gorge (Quechee, Vermont)

TRANSPORTATION

A commuter airport in Lebanon, a 15-minute ride from campus, is serviced by US Airways. Manchester Airport (75 minutes from campus) is serviced by several major airlines, and visitors can drive or take a Vermont Transit bus. Logan Airport in Boston, Massachusetts (two-and-a-half hours to campus) is serviced by most major airlines. The Dartmouth Mini-Coach (603-448-2800) operates shuttles from Logan directly to Hanover several times a day. Burlington, Vermont airport (90 minutes from campus) is serviced by several major airlines, and visitors can drive or take a Vermont Transit bus.

FIND YOUR WAY

From Boston (a two-and-a-half hour trip): Take I-93 N. to I-89 N. Take Exit 18 (Rte. 120, Lebanon-Hanover). Turn right onto Rte. 120, then left onto Rte. 10 to campus. **From New York City (a five-hour trip), southern New England, and points south:** take I-95 to New Haven or I-684 and I-84 to Hartford. Pick up I-91 N. to Vermont. Take Exit 13 (Hanover-Norwich). Turn right off the ramp, cross the bridge, and drive straight to the campus (less than one mile from the I-91 exit).

STAY THE NIGHT

Nearby: On campus next door to the Hood Museum is the **Hanover Inn** (Main and E. Wheelock Streets; 800-443-7024), and nightly entertainment. Sports facilities, including tennis and golf, are available at the college. Rates are expensive, but check for special deals. Also in Hanover (about two miles north of campus) is the **Chieftain Motel** (New Hampshire Rte. 10; 603-643-2550), featuring an outdoor pool and a view of the Connecticut River. Local hotels within a ten minute drive of campus include the **Holiday Inn Express** (603-448-5070) and the **Residence Inn** (603-643-4511) in Lebanon, New Hampshire; the **Airport Economy Inn** (603-298-8888), **Fireside Inn and Suites** (603-298-5906), and the **Sunset Motel** (603-298-8721) in West Lebanon, New Hampshire; and the **Best Western** (802-295-3000), **Comfort Inn** (802-295-3051), **Hampton Inn** (802-296-2800), and **Ramada Inn** (802-295-3000) in White River Junction, Vermont. Local inns and bed-and-breakfasts within a ten-minute drive of campus include the **Alden Inn** (603-795-2222) and **Dowd's Country Inn** (603-795-4712) in Lyme, New Hampshire; the **Norwich Inn** (802-649-1143) in Norwich, Vermont; and **Stonecrest Farm** (800-730-2425) in Wilder, Vermont. Additional accommodations exist in Quechee and Woodstock, Vermont (including the renowned **Woodstock Inn Resort**), which are about a 20- to 30-minute car ride from campus.

UNIVERSITY OF NEW HAMPSHIRE

Office of Admissions, Grant House, 4 Garrison Ave.,
Durham, NH 03824 • Telephone: 603-862-1360 • www.unh.edu •
Email: admissions@unh.edu

Hours: Monday–Friday, 8:00AM–5:00PM

The affordable University of New Hampshire provides a variety of pre-professional and liberal arts majors—some of the more popular ones are occupational therapy, communications, nursing, and the pre-medical sciences. Life in Durham is generally easygoing, and the Greek system dominates weekends at UNH.

AT A GLANCE

Selectivity Rating	77
Range SAT I Math	510–610
Average SAT I Math	558
Range SAT I Verbal	500–590
Average SAT I Verbal	546
Student/Faculty Ratio	14:1

CAMPUS TOURS

Appointment	Not required
Dates	Varies
Times	Varies throughout the year
Average Length	1 hour

ON-CAMPUS APPOINTMENTS

Admissions

Appointment	Not required
Saturdays	No

Faculty and Coaches

Dates/Times	Year-round
Arrangements	Contact Athletic Department 3 weeks prior

CLASS VISITS

Dates	Academic year
Arrangements	Contact Admissions Office

TRANSPORTATION

Boston's Logan International Airport is approximately 60 miles away from Durham. Manchester Airport is approximately 40 miles away from Durham. C & J Trailways bus lines has routes to the Seacoast area and the UNH campus from Logan Airport and South Station in Boston. For information and costs, call 742-5111 (from inside New Hampshire) or 800-258-7111 (from outside New Hampshire).

FIND YOUR WAY

From Boston, take I-95 N. to Exit 4 (New Hampshire Lakes and Mountains, Spaulding Tpke.). Continue to Exit 6 W. and take Rte. 4 W. past the UNH/Durham Rte. 108 exit. Exit at Rte. 155A and turn east toward Durham. Follow 155A through a short stretch of fields to the UNH campus. After passing through a blinking light and a traffic light, take the second left onto Garrison Ave. The Office of Admissions, Grant House, will be directly ahead on the right with parking behind. **From Portland,** take I-95 S. to Exit 5. Continue on the Spaulding Tpke. to Exit 6 W and follow Rte 4 W. Follow the preceding directions from Boston. **From Concord,** take Rte. 4 E. to the Rte. 155A exit. Follow the above directions from Boston. **From Manchester,** take Rte. 101 to Epping and exit onto Rte. 125 N. Continue to the Lee Traffic Circle and take Rte. 4 E. to the Rte. 155A exit. Follow the above directions from Boston.

STAY THE NIGHT

Nearby: On campus is the **New England Center Hotel** (15 Strafford Ave., 800-590-4334). The rooms are in an unusual hexagonal tower (one side for each of the six New England states), and priced in the moderate range. It has a nice restaurant and a workout room, and you can use the pool, racquetball courts, tennis courts, and indoor track on campus. Accommodations in Durham include: **Hickory Pond Inn** (603-659-2227), **Holly House** (603-868-7345), **The Pines Guest House** (603-868-3361), and **Three Chimney's Inn** (603-868-7800). In Portsmouth, accommodations include: **Holiday Inn** (603-431-8000), **Howard Johnson's** (603-436-7600), **Marriott Courtyard** (603-436-2121), **Sheraton Portsmouth** (603-431-2300), **Susse Chalet** (603-436-6363), and **Hampton Inn** (800-926-7866). In Dover, accommodations include the **Days Inn** (603-742-0400).

A Little Farther: Many charming bed-and-breakfasts and seaside hotels are available everywhere from Newburyport, Massachusetts to Kennebunkport, Maine and beyond. Similar tourist accomodations are available inland.

HIGHLIGHTS

ON CAMPUS

- Dimond Library
- Whittemore Center
- Hamel Recreation Center
- Student Union/Holloway Commons
- College Woods

OFF CAMPUS

- Durham eateries
- Strawberry Banke/Prescott Park (Portsmouth)
- Atlantic Ocean
- White Mountains
- Portsmouth sights and shopping

1- Drew University
2- Princeton University
3- Rutgers University

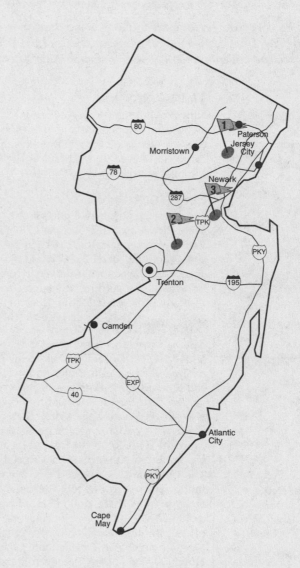

New Jersey	Drew University	Princeton Univ.	Rutgers Univ.	*Trenton*
Drew University	—	42	20	47
Princeton Univ.	42	—	18	11
Rutgers Univ.	20	18	—	26
Trenton	47	11	26	—

DREW UNIVERSITY

College Admissions, 36 Madison Ave.,
Madison, NJ 07940-1493 • Telephone: 973-408-3739 • www.drew.edu •
Email: cadm@drew.edu

Hours: Monday–Friday, 9:00AM–5:00PM; Saturdays (October–January), 9:00AM–2:00PM

Located amid the corporate headquarters and housing developments of Northern New Jersey, just baby steps from New York City, Drew University offers stellar financial aid to topflight students who are willing to forgo the Ivies and an excellent education to all. Every first-year student gets a laptop.

AT A GLANCE

Selectivity Rating	87
Range SAT I Math	540–640
Average SAT I Math	590
Range SAT I Verbal	560–670
Average SAT I Verbal	620
Student/Faculty Ratio	12:1

CAMPUS TOURS

Appointment	Not required
Dates	Varies
Times	Varies
Average Length	1 hour

ON-CAMPUS APPOINTMENTS

Admissions

Start Date—Juniors	April 15
Appointment	Required
Advance Notice	Yes, 2 weeks
Saturdays	Sometimes
Average Length	45 min.
Info Sessions	Yes

Faculty and Coaches

Dates/Times	Academic year
Arrangements	Contact Admissions Office 2 weeks prior

CLASS VISITS

Arrangements	Contact Admissions Office

TRANSPORTATION

Newark International Airport is 20 miles away from campus. Private limousine services are available for the trip from the airport to campus; one of these services is Airport Limousine Express (800-624-4410).

FIND YOUR WAY

From the New Jersey Tpke. or the Garden State Pkwy., exit to I-78. Take I-78 W. to N.J. Rte. 24 W., then take Rte. 124 W. to the university. **From I-80,** take I-287 S. to N.J. Rte. 124 E. Take Rte. 124 E. to the university. For more information regarding directions to Drew, visit: www.drew.edu/about/directions.html.

STAY THE NIGHT

Nearby: There are many hotels close to Drew University. Here is a list of some possible choices. Please call for rates and availability; some hotels may have special rates for Drew visitors. The **Best Western Morristown Inn** (270 South Street Morristown, N.J., 07960; 973-540-1700 or 800-688-4646) offers complimentary continental breakfast, an exercise room with sauna, and efficiency rooms; check www.boylehotels.com. The **Hanover Marriott** (1401 Route 10 East Whippany, N.J. 07981; 973-538-8811 or 800-242-8681) has indoor and outdoor pools, health club, and two restaurants; check www.marriott.com. The **Courtyard by Marriott** (157 Route 10 Whippany, N.J. 07981; 973-877-8700) has an indoor pool with hot tub, exercise room, and a cafe; check www.marriott.com. The **Headquarters Plaza Hotel** (3 Headquarters Plaza Morristown, N.J. 07960; 973-898-9100 or 800-225-1941 if you are in New Jersey and 800-225-1942 if you are outside New Jersey) offers complimentary continental breakfast in the lobby, a health club, and complimentary late-night snack in the lobby; check www.hqplazahotel.com. The **Embassy Suites Hotel** (909 Parsippany Boulevard Parsippany, N.J. 07981; 973-334-1440 or 800-Embassy) offers complimentary breakfast and a recreational facility; check www.embassysuites.com. The **Hilton at Short Hills** (41 J.F.K. Parkway Short Hills, N.J. 07078; 973-379-0100) offers indoor and outdoor pool, spa, and two restaurants; check www.hiltonshorthills.com. The **Grand Summit Hotel** (570 Springfield Avenue Summit N.J. 07901; 908-273-3000 or 800-346-0773) offers complimentary full American breakfast, newspapers, mini-gym, outdoor pool, shuttle service to airport, and a restaurant; check www.grandsummit.com. The **Howard Johnson** (625 Route 46 East Parsippany, N.J. 07054; 973-882-8600) offers complimentary continental breakfast; check www.hojo.com.

HIGHLIGHTS

ON CAMPUS
- Dorothy Young Center for the Arts
- Simon Forum
- Rose Memorial Library
- University Center

OFF CAMPUS
- New Jersey Shakespeare Festival
- Museum of Early Trades and Crafts
- New York City is only 30 miles away

PRINCETON UNIVERSITY

Admissions Office, PO Box 430, Princeton, NJ 08544-0430 • Telephone: 609-258-3060 • www.princeton.edu • Email: sreynold@princeton.edu

Hours: Monday–Friday, 9:00AM–5:00PM; Saturdays (in fall), 9:30AM–1:00PM

Truly gorgeous Princeton University offers the best undergraduate education in the country. Other prestigious institutions feature famous medical, law, and/or business schools, but Princeton has none of these. Here, the focus is on the college student. Princeton's famous eating clubs (which are a lot like fraternities: they provide meals, host parties, and place students in a subcommunity) are the backbone of the social scene.

HIGHLIGHTS

ON CAMPUS
- Nassau Hall
- Firestone Library
- McCarter Theater
- Princeton University Art Museum
- University Chapel
- Frist Campus Center

OFF CAMPUS
- Washington's Crossing (Delaware River)
- Institute for Advanced Study
- Jersey Shore
- Access to cities: New York and Philadelphia
- Waterfront Park

TRANSPORTATION

Newark and Philadelphia International Airports are an hour away from campus. Princeton Airporter courtesy phones are located at the airport terminal's limousine counters. The vans take passengers to the Nassau Inn, one block from the university. From the Philadelphia Airport, take either a limousine or the airport shuttle train to Philadelphia's 30th St. Station; from there, take an Amtrak train to Princeton Junction. Rental cars are available at both airports. Amtrak train service to Princeton Junction is available through New York City and through Philadelphia. From Princeton Junction the Princeton Shuttle, a one-car train (the Dinky), makes the five-minute trip to Princeton. (Note: The Dinky does not meet every train; contact New Jersey Transit for a current schedule before making plans.) Bus service to Princeton is provided by New Jersey's Suburban Transit Corporation; every half hour throughout the day, buses leave New York City's Port Authority terminal for Princeton. The same schedule is followed for buses from Princeton to New York City.

FIND YOUR WAY

For a recording of travel instructions to campus, call 609-258-2222. **From north and south,** take the New Jersey Tpke. to Exit 8 (Hightstown) and follow signs for Hightstown, then for Princeton. (Note that the N.J. Tpke. is coincident with I-95 from central to northern New Jersey.) **From the Philadelphia area,** you also can take I-95 N. to U.S. 1 N. Follow U.S. 1 to the Hightstown/Princeton circle, and follow signs to Princeton. **From the west,** the Pennsylvania Tpke. (I-76, then I-276 E.) connects to the N.J. Tpke.; take the N.J. Tpke. north to Exit 8 (Hightstown) and follow signs for Hightstown, then for Princeton.

STAY THE NIGHT

Nearby: The **Peacock Inn** (20 Bayard Lane, at the junction of Rte. 206 and Nassau St.; 609-924-1707) is a historic country inn with simple accommodations for overnight visitors. Rates for its 17 rooms range from moderate to expensive. **Nassau Inn** (10 Palmer Square; 609-921-7500) is within walking distance of the university, but it's expensive. The closest and cheapest motel is the **MacIntosh Inn** (3270 Brunswick Pike, Lawrenceville; 609-896-3700), five miles away from campus. About the same distance away is **Red Roof Inn** (3203 Brunswick Pike, Lawrenceville; 609-896-3388).

A Little Farther: New Hope, Pennsylvania is close to where George Washington crossed the Delaware River. If that's not reason enough to stay in New Hope, there are also lots of quaint shops and restaurants, as well as a theater.

AT A GLANCE

Selectivity Rating	99
Student/Faculty Ratio	6:1

CAMPUS TOURS

Appointment	Not required
Dates	Year-round
Times	Varies throughout the year
Average Length	1 hour

ON-CAMPUS APPOINTMENTS

Admissions

Start Date–Juniors	May 1
Appointment	Not required
Advance Notice	Yes, 3 weeks
Saturdays	No
Average Length	1 hour
Info Sessions	Yes

Faculty and Coaches

Dates/Arrangements	Contact Athletic Department

CLASS VISITS

Dates	Varies
Arrangements	Contact Admissions Office

RUTGERS, THE STATE UNIVERSITY OF NEW JERSEY

Office of University Undergraduate Admissions, Administrative Services Building, PO Box 2101, New Brunswick, NJ 08854-8097 • Telephone: 732-932-4636 • www.rutgers.edu •

Hours: Monday–Friday, 8:30AM–4:30PM

The University College of New Brunswick offers working and adult students a chance to complete one of many degrees through day and/or evening courses. The school enrolls nearly 3,000 students and offers courses designed to improve students' marketability in the professional world.

AT A GLANCE

Range SAT I Math	560–670
Range SAT I Verbal	530–630
Student/Faculty Ratio	14:1

CAMPUS TOURS

Appointment	Required
Dates	Varies
Times	Mon–Sat, mornings, following info sessions
Average Length	1 hour

ON-CAMPUS APPOINTMENTS

Admissions

Start Date—Juniors	N/A
Info Sessions	Oct–Dec, Feb–April, excluding breaks; June–Aug

Faculty and Coaches

Dates/Times	Year-round
Arrangements	Contact faculty directly

CLASS VISITS

Dates	Year-round
Arrangements	Contact Admissions Office

TRANSPORTATION

The Newark International Airport is approximately 20 miles away from campus. Taxis and rental cars are available at the airport. The Amtrak train and public bus station is two blocks from the Undergraduate Admissions Office.

FIND YOUR WAY

From the New Jersey Tpke., take Exit 9 and follow signs for Rte. 18 N./New Brunswick. To get to the College Ave. campus, proceed two-and-a-half miles along Route 18 N., past Rte. 27, to the second George St. exit, marked George St.-Rutgers University. For visitors' parking, bear left on exit ramp, then turn left at the light onto George St. and proceed three blocks to Somerset St. Turn right through the entrance gate.

STAY THE NIGHT

Nearby: A very expensive **Hyatt Regency** (2 Albany St.; 732-873-1234) is about three blocks from campus. It has a health center, a pool, a sauna, tennis courts, basketball, a jazz quartet on the weekends, and a pianist during the week. For a more reasonably priced option, try the **Quality Inn** (1850 Easton Ave., Somerset; 732-469-5050). It has a special inexpensive rate for university visitors. The inn, three miles away from campus, has a full health club and Olympic-size pool. It is close to shopping and near bus service to Rutgers.

HIGHLIGHTS

ON CAMPUS

- Geology Museum
- Jane Voorhees Zimmereli Art Museum
- Rutgers Display Gardens and Heylar Woods
- Hutchenson Memorial Forest

OFF CAMPUS

- New York City is only 45 minutes away

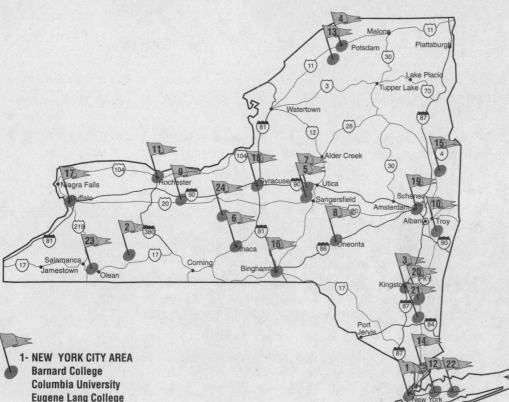

1- **NEW YORK CITY AREA**
   Barnard College
   Columbia University
   Eugene Lang College
   Fordham University
   Julliard School
   New York University
2- **Alfred University**
3- **Bard College**
4- **Clarkson University**
5- **Colgate University**
6- **Cornell University**
   Ithaca College
7- **Hamilton College**
8- **Hartwick College**
9- **Hobart College**
   William Smith College
10- **Rensselaer Polytechnic Institute**
11- **University of Rochester**
   Rochester Institute of Technology
12- **St. John's University**
13- **St. Lawrence University**
14- **Sarah Lawrence College**
15- **Skidmore College**
16- **SUNY Binghamton**
17- **SUNY Buffalo**
18- **Syracuse University**
19- **Union College**
20- **U.S. Military Academy**
21- **Vassar College**
   Marist College (Poughkeepsie)
22- **Hofstra U.**
23- **St. Bonaventure U.**
24- **Wells College**

New York

	Alfred Univ.	Bard College	Clarkson Univ.	Colgate Univ.	Cornell Univ.	Hamilton Coll.	Hartwick Coll.	Hobart & Wm. Smith	Hofstra	Ithaca Coll.	Marist Coll.	RPI	St. Bonaventure U.	St. Lawrence Univ.	Sarah Lawrence	Skidmore Coll.	SUNY Binghamton	SUNY Buffalo	Union Coll.	U.S. Military Acad.	Vassar Coll.	Wells Coll.	New York City*	Rochester**	Syracuse***
Alfred Univ.	—	287	270	187	99	180	194	81	334	97	265	293	47	260	309	299	127	109	279	287	277	119	311	80	133
Bard College	287	—	299	51	221	158	101	295	130	219	22	78	309	301	67	108	169	385	9851	27	90	240	328	235	0
Clarkson Univ.	270	299	—	197	199	172	223	192	389	201	297	203	327	10	355	173	223	282	197	311	287	180	357	225	140
Colgate Univ.	187	51	197	—	80	24	49	96	267	82	204	119	238	199	238	115	69	192	97	212	188	78	240	129	35
Cornell Univ.	99	221	199	80	—	92	118	48	253	2	184	206	141	189	235	204	49	149	184	218	202	21	237	90	54
Hamilton Coll.	180	158	172	24	92	—	66	95	278	94	186	104	237	174	238	109	96	185	89	205	181	98	242	128	39
Hartwick Coll.	194	101	223	49	118	66	—	187	249	116	157	90	229	225	181	107	64	250	73	141	117	108	179	195	97
Hobart & Wm. Smith	81	295	192	96	48	95	187	—	332	46	270	195	120	182	281	200	138	102	179	265	241	42	283	43	50
Hofstra	334	130	389	367	253	278	249	332	—	253	103	181	391	395	31	209	207	421	187	71	99	291	31	363	277
Ithaca Coll.	97	219	201	82	2	94	116	46	253	—	184	208	140	191	233	206	47	147	186	218	200	24	235	88	56
Marist Coll.	265	22	297	204	184	186	157	270	103	184	—	89	308	303	68	117	137	360	95	35	4	266	98	301	221
RPI	293	78	203	119	206	104	90	195	181	208	89	—	313	205	150	29	145	285	15	109	85	199	152	216	147
St. Bonaventure U.	47	309	327	238	141	237	229	120	391	140	308	313	—	318	357	330	171	81	317	332	307	169	345	124	194
St. Lawrence Univ.	260	301	10	199	189	174	225	182	395	191	303	205	318	—	357	175	213	272	199	313	289	179	359	215	130
Sarah Lawrence	309	67	355	238	235	238	181	281	31	233	68	150	357	357	—	178	186	399	162	40	64	267	3	342	252
Skidmore Coll.	299	108	173	115	204	109	107	200	209	206	117	29	330	175	178	—	158	289	24	139	115	191	182	232	146
SUNY Binghamton	127	169	223	69	49	96	64	138	207	47	137	145	171	213	186	158	—	226	135	162	146	72	185	175	79
SUNY Buffalo	109	385	282	192	149	185	250	102	421	147	360	285	81	272	399	289	226	—	269	385	361	133	406	65	142
Union Coll.	279	98	197	97	184	89	73	179	187	186	95	15	317	199	162	24	135	269	—	128	104	178	156	212	130
U.S. Military Acad.	287	51	311	212	218	205	141	265	71	218	35	109	332	313	40	139	162	385	128	—	24	242	41	326	248
Vassar Coll.	277	27	287	188	202	181	117	241	99	200	4	85	307	289	64	115	146	361	104	24	—	217	75	302	224
Wells Coll.	119	240	180	78	21	98	108	42	291	24	266	199	169	267	267	191	72	133	178	242	217	—	254	74	55
New York City*	311	90	357	240	237	242	179	283	31	235	98	152	345	359	3	182	185	406	156	41	75	254	—	365	265
Rochester**	80	328	225	129	90	128	195	43	363	88	301	216	124	215	342	232	175	65	212	326	302	74	365	—	83
Syracuse***	133	235	140	35	54	39	97	50	277	56	221	147	194	130	252	146	79	142	130	248	224	55	265	83	—

*   Use New York City mileage for Barnard College, Columbia University, Eugene Lang College, Fordham University, The Juilliard School, NewYork University, and St, John's University.
**   Use Rochester mileage for Rochester Institute of Technology and University of Rochester.
***   Use Syracuse mileage for Syracuse University.

ALFRED UNIVERSITY

Office of Admissions, Alumni Hall Saxon Drive, Alfred, NY 14802-1205 • Telephone: 800-541-9229 • www.alfred.edu • Email: admwww@alfred.edu

Hours: Monday–Friday, 8:30AM–4:30PM; Saturday (fall and some spring), 9:00AM–1:00PM

You can unearth one of the best ceramics programs on the planet at this small college named for Alfred the Great. Alfred U. is located in the Finger Lakes region of upstate New York, about two hours away from Buffalo. Traying, which involves sledding down a snow-covered hill on a cafeteria tray, is a favorite activity among the very creative students during the long winters.

HIGHLIGHTS

ON CAMPUS
- Powell Campus Center
- Binns Merrill Hall
- Schein-Joseph International Museum of Ceramic Art
- John L. Stull Observatory
- Robert Turner Student Gallery

OFF CAMPUS
- Corning Glass Museum; 40 min. away
- Rockwell Museum; 40 min. away
- Letchworth State Park; 30 min. away
- Stony Brook State Park; 25 min. away
- Glen H. Curtis Museum; 30 min. away

TRANSPORTATION

Greater Rochester International Airport is 70 miles away from campus. Corning-Elmira Regional Airport is 55 miles away from campus. A smaller airport in Wellsville is only 15 minutes from campus. Bus lines serve Alfred and surrounding communities. New York Trailways Short Line buses provide service between Alfred and New York City with transfers to all major cities.

FIND YOUR WAY

From Rte. 17 E. (I-86) or W. (the Southern Tier Expy.), take Exit 33 at Almond and follow signs for the university to Rte. 21 S. and to Rte. 244 into Alfred. **From Rochester,** take I-390 S. to Exit 4, the second Dansville exit. Turn right onto Rte. 36 S. and continue through Arkport. Turn onto Rte. 17 W (I-86) and follow the preceding directions from that point. **From the northeast,** take I-90 to Exit 42 at Geneva. Take Rte. 14 S.; near Dresden, turn right onto Rte. 54 and follow it through Penn Yan to Bath and Rte. 17 W (I-86) Follow the preceding directions from that point.

STAY THE NIGHT

Nearby: Luxurious accommodations are available on campus at **The Saxon Inn** (1 Park St., 607-871-2600), located across from the Office of Admissions. Continental breakfast is included and suites sleeping five people are available. Four options in Hornell (15 minutes away from campus) are the **Comfort Inn** (1 Canisteo Square; 607-324-4300), **Econo Lodge** (Rte. 36 North; 607-324-0800), **Sunshine Motel** (607-324-4565), and **Days Inn** (607-324-6222). Fifteen minutes southwest of campus in Wellsville are inexpensive motels: **Wellsville Motel** (Rte. 417; 585-593-2494), **Cook's Motel** (Rte. 417; 585-593-1747), and **Microtel Inn and Suites** (585-593-3449).

A Little Farther: Corning is about 45 minutes to the east of Alfred. Choices include **Lodge on the Green** (607-962-2456), **Holiday Inn** (607-962-5021), **Radisson Corning Hotel** (125 Denison Pkwy. E.; 607-962-5000), and **Hampton Inn** (607-936-3344). Bath is about 35 minutes and choices there include the **Days Inn** (607-776-7644) and **Bath Super 8 Motel** (607-776-2187).

AT A GLANCE

Selectivity Rating	77
Range SAT I Math	490–640
Range SAT I Verbal	490–640
Student/Faculty Ratio	12:1

CAMPUS TOURS

Appointment	Required
Times	Mon–Fri, 9AM–4PM, 9AM–noon
Average Length	1 hour

ON-CAMPUS APPOINTMENTS

Admissions

Start Date–Juniors	Anytime
Appointment	Required
Advance Notice	Yes, 2 weeks
Saturdays	No
Info Sessions	Yes

Faculty and Coaches

Dates/Times	Academic year
Arrangements	Contact Admissions Office 2 weeks prior

CLASS VISITS

Dates	Academic year
Arrangements	Contact Admissions Office

BARD COLLEGE

Admissions Office,
Annandale-on-Hudson, NY 12504 • Telephone: 845-758-7472 • www.bard.edu •
Email: admission@bard.edu

Hours: Monday–Friday, 9:00AM–5:00PM; Saturday (April, October, & November), 9:00AM–1:00PM

The very exceptional and even more creative students at Bard College come from diverse ethnic backgrounds and lifestyles. The school motto is "a place to think." Bard offers a rich academic environment and requires each of its highly self-motivated students to complete a senior project. The progressive Excellence and Equal Cost Program makes Bard available to top students at a state-school price.

AT A GLANCE

Selectivity Rating	93
Range SAT I Math	590–690
Average SAT I Math	630
Range SAT I Verbal	650–750
Average SAT I Verbal	670
Average GPA	3.5
Student/Faculty Ratio	9:1

CAMPUS TOURS

Appointment	Required
Dates	Year-round
Times	Mon–Fri, 9:30AM, 11:30AM, 1:30PM, & 3:30PM
Average Length	1 hour

ON-CAMPUS APPOINTMENTS

Admissions

Start Date–Juniors	For applicants only
Appointment	Required
Advance Notice	Yes, 2 weeks
Saturdays	No
Average Length	45 min.
Info Sessions	Yes

Faculty and Coaches

Dates/Times	Academic year
Arrangements	Contact Admissions Office 1 week prior

CLASS VISITS

Dates	Academic year
Arrangements	Accepted students only

TRANSPORTATION

The closest airports are Albany and Stewart/Newburgh—both of which are about 60 miles away from campus. In Albany, visitors can get a taxi or ground transportation to the Albany/Rennsalaer train station and take the Amtrak train south to Rhinecliff. Otherwise a rental car is necessary from both airports. All three New York City airports have ground transportation directly to Penn. Station in Manhattan and the Amtrak train goes regularly to Rhinecliff station; from there it is a short taxi ride to campus or you can take the shuttle bus. Check the Bard shuttle schedules on the Bard website at: www.bard.edu.

FIND YOUR WAY

From New England or New York City, take the Taconic State Pkwy to the Red Hook exit. Take Rte. 199 through Red Hook to Rte. 9G. Make a right (north) onto 9G and proceed two miles to campus. **From the mid-atlantic region,** take the New York State Thruway (I-87) to Exit 19 (Kingston). Follow the signs to and cross the Kingston-Rhinecliff Bridge to Rte. 96. Turn left onto Rte. 9G and proceed north four miles to the campus, which is on the left.

STAY THE NIGHT

Nearby: **The Gaslight** is quaint and comfortable (Rte. 9, north of Red Hook; 917-758-1571) and is about three miles east of campus. Bard is just north of Rhinebeck where you can find one of the oldest inns in America, the **Beekman Arms** (Rte. 9; 914-876-7077), 10 minutes from campus. Just south of Rhinebeck, about 15 minutes from the campus, lies the **Village Inn Motel** (Rte. 9; 914-876-7000) or try the **Ramada Inn** (914-339-3900) also 15 minutes from campus, in Kingston (Exit 19 off the thruway). There is also a **Holiday Inn** (914-338-0400).

A Little Farther: See our website for further suggestions.

HIGHLIGHTS

ON CAMPUS

- Richard B. Fisher Center for the Performing Arts
- Stevenson Library
- Bertelsmann Campus Center
- Center for Curatorial Studies
- Levy Economics Institute (Blithewood Mansion)

OFF CAMPUS

- Tivoli, Rhinebeck, Red Hook, Kingston
- Montgomery Place, Mills Mansion
- Dia—Beacon
- Roosevelt Home, Val Kill
- Olana

BARNARD COLLEGE

Office of Admissions, 3009 Broadway,
New York, NY 10027 • Telephone: 212-854-2014 • www.barnard.edu •
Email: admissions@barnard.edu

Hours: Monday–Friday, 9:00AM–5:00PM; Saturday (during fall), 10:00AM–3:00PM

Barnard is an all women's college located on the Upper West Side of Manhattan right across the street from the Ivy League's own Columbia University. Barnard's extremely ambitious, independent, and very New York students enjoy the luxury of their own small and intimate classes, and they can also take any course offered at Columbia. The one and only Martha Stewart is an alum.

HIGHLIGHTS

ON CAMPUS
- Milbank Hall-Minor Latham Playhouse
- Arthur Ross Greenhouse
- Held Auditorium
- Smart Media Classrooms
- Java City Cafe at McIntosh Student Center

OFF CAMPUS
- Metropolitan Museum of Art
- Central Park
- Riverside Church
- The Cloisters
- The Guggenheim Museum

TRANSPORTATION

Local airports include LaGuardia, Kennedy, and Newark. Taxi, bus, and subway service is available to get you to campus. The college recommends that you take a taxi from Kennedy and La Guardia; while expensive, it is efficient. Tell the driver that the most direct route to Barnard is the Triborough Bridge, not the Queens-Midtown Tunnel. Amtrak, Metro-North, New Jersey Transit, and Long Island Railroad trains serve New York City, as does Greyhound and several local bus lines. Public transportation is available from Grand Central Station, Penn Station, and New York Port Authority. Four public bus lines (M4, M11, M5, and M104) and two subways (the Broadway IRT local, numbers 1 and 9) stop at 116th St./Columbia University.

FIND YOUR WAY

From the Henry Hudson Pkwy. (West Side Hwy.) in New York City, take the 95th/96th St. exit. Use the 95th St. off-ramp and drive two blocks east to Broadway. Turn left (uptown) to Barnard's main gate at 117th St. To reach the Henry Hudson Pkwy. **From the north,** take the NY State Thruway (I-87) or the New England Thruway (I-95) to the Cross-Bronx Expy., toward the George Washington Bridge. Bear right as you approach the bridge and take the exit for the Henry Hudson Pkwy. S. **From the east,** take the Grand Central Pkwy. or Long Island Expy. west to the Cross-Island Pkwy. north. Cross over the Throgs Neck Bridge to the Cross-Bronx Expy., toward the George Washington Bridge. Exit onto the Henry Hudson Pkwy. S. **From the south and west,** take I-95 N. or I-80 E. to the George Washington Bridge. Exit the bridge onto the Henry Hudson Pkwy. S.

STAY THE NIGHT

Nearby: Barnard College, an affiliate of Columbia University, is on the Upper West Side of Manhattan at 116th Street and Broadway. We suggest that you arrange your accommodations as early as possible. When making reservations, ask if any special packages are offered, and be aware that rates change according to availability. **The Union Theological Seminary** (3041 Broadway; 212-280-1313) has reasonable prices. Visitors can ask for the Columbia University rate at the moderately-priced **Empire Hotel** (44 W. 63rd Street; 888-822-3555), **Excelsior** (45 W. 81st Street; 212-362-9200), and On the Avenue (2178 Broadway; 800-509-7598). **Double Tree Guest Suites** (800-222-8733) is a bit more expensive and located on W. 47th and Broadway; ask for the Columbia University rate.

A Little Farther: The moderately priced **Milburn Hotel** (242 W. 76th St.; 212-362-1006) offers modest accommodations that are clean and quiet. On the east side of Central Park, the **Hotel Wales** (1295 Madison Ave.; 212-876-6000) is within walking distance of museums and surrounded by shops and restaurants.

AT A GLANCE

Selectivity Rating	95
Range SAT I Math	620–700
Average SAT I Math	670
Range SAT I Verbal	630–710
Average SAT I Verbal	660
Average ACT Composite	29
Average GPA	3.9
Student/Faculty Ratio	10:1

CAMPUS TOURS

Appointment	Not required
Dates	Year-round
Times	Mon-Fri, 10:30AM & 2:30PM; Sat (fall), 10:30AM & 2:30PM
Average Length	1 hour

ON-CAMPUS APPOINTMENTS

Admissions

Start Date–Juniors	June 1
Appointment	Required
Advance Notice	Yes, 2 weeks
Saturdays	Sometimes
Average Length	30 min.
Info Sessions	Yes

Faculty and Coaches

Dates/Times	Academic year
Arrangements	Contact Admissions Office

CLASS VISITS

Dates	Academic year
Arrangements	Contact Admissions Office

CLARKSON UNIVERSITY

Office of Undergraduate Admission, Holcroft House, Box 5605, Potsdam, NY 13699 • Telephone: 800-527-6577 • www.clarkson.edu • Email: admission@clarkson.edu

Hours: Monday–Friday, 8:00AM–4:00PM; Saturdays, 9:00AM–3:00PM

The faculty at Clarkson University is unusually helpful and approachable, especially for an engineering-intensive school. Students also laud the small classes and great laboratories. On campus, the Greek system is popular, as is the perennially powerful hockey team. Clarkson also boasts a student-run television station (WCKN-TV 31), which students unabashedly call one of the best in the country.

AT A GLANCE

Selectivity Rating	81
Range SAT I Math	580–670
Average SAT I Math	621
Range SAT I Verbal	520–620
Average SAT I Verbal	570
Average GPA	3.51
Student/Faculty Ratio	17:1

CAMPUS TOURS

Appointment	Preferred
Dates	Year-round
Times	Mon–Sat, 10AM, 11AM, 12PM, 2PM, & 3PM
Average Length	1 hour

ON-CAMPUS APPOINTMENTS

Admissions

Start Date–Juniors	Anytime
Appointment	Preferred
Advance Notice	Yes, 1 week
Saturdays	Yes
Average Length	1 hour
Info Sessions	No

Faculty and Coaches

Dates/Times	Year-round
Arrangements	Contact Admissions Office 1 week prior

CLASS VISITS

Dates	Academic year
Arrangements	Contact Admissions Office

TRANSPORTATION

The Massena airport is 21 miles away from campus; the Ogdensburg airport is 35 miles away from campus. Major airports include Syracuse (two-and-a-half hours away), Montreal's Dorval Airport (two hours away), and Montreal's Marabel International Airport (two-and-a-half hours away). You can fly to Syracuse and rent a car or take a Greyhound bus from Syracuse to Potsdam; or you can fly from Syracuse to Massena on a commuter airline, and rent a car. Trailways bus lines (315-764-1331) and Greyhound buses (315-265-2270) serve Potsdam.

FIND YOUR WAY

From Syracuse, take I-81 N. to Exit 48 N. of Watertown. Proceed to U.S. Rte. 11, turning left (north) onto it. Continue for approximately 67 miles. Take the Sandstone entrance to campus on the right beyond the tennis courts as you enter the village of Potsdam. **From Albany**, take I-87 (the Northway) to Exit 23 (Warrensburg). From there, follow Rte. 28 to Indian Lake, where Rtes. 28 and 30 merge. Follow the combined routes to Blue Mountain Lake; from there, take Rte. 30 N. to Tupper Lake; then head west on Rte. 3 for approximately 18 miles to Rte. 56. Proceed north on Rte. 56 to Potsdam. Turn left at the second traffic light in the village (onto U.S. Rte. 11 S.), and continue for three-quarters-of-a-mile to the university. Driving time from Albany to Potsdam is approximately four hours.

HIGHLIGHTS

ON CAMPUS

- New Academic Building (Bertrand H. Snell Hall)
- The new outdoor Lodge
- Cheel Campus Center
- CAMP Building
- Center for Health Sciences

OFF CAMPUS

- St. Lawrence River (Seaway)
- Lake Placid, NY
- Thousand Island region
- Fredrick Remmington Museum
- Adirondack Mountains

COLGATE UNIVERSITY

Office of Admissions, 13 Oak Dr.,
Hamilton, NY 13346 • Telephone: 315-228-7401 • offices.colgate.edu •
Email: admission@mail.colgate.edu

Hours: Monday–Friday, 8:00AM–5:00PM; select Saturdays, 8:00AM–noon

Colgate University has snow-covered trees, big limestone buildings, a vibrant party scene, high quality academics, and professors that make students gush with joy. Great liberal arts programs are plentiful, and all students must complete a core curriculum regardless of major. Students are also very involved in athletics and supportive of Colgate's teams.

HIGHLIGHTS

ON CAMPUS

- Picker Art Gallery
- Longyear Museum of Anthropology
- ALANA Culture Center
- Observatory
- Everett Needham Case Library

OFF CAMPUS

- Downtown Hamilton
- Cooperstown
- Bouckville Antique Center
- Munson Williams Proctor Museum, Utica
- Museum of Science and Technology

TRANSPORTATION

The Syracuse-Hancock International Airport is approximately 40 miles away from campus. Rental cars are available at the airport. A local taxi service is also available if you make arrangements in advance. Hamilton Taxi can be reached at 315-824-TAXI (8294).

FIND YOUR WAY

From New York City: Take the Tappan Zee Bridge, Rte. 87; NYS Thruway N. to Exit 16 (Harriman); Rte. 17 W. to Exit 84 (Deposit). At Deposit, take Rte. 8 N. to New Berlin, then Rte. 80 W. to Sherburne and Rte. 12 N. In Sherburne, bear left on Rte. 12B N. to Hamilton. **From north of Westchester:** Take the NYS Thruway to Exit 25A to I-88 W., and exit on Rte. 20 W. Follow Rte. 20 to Madison; make a left on Rte. 12B S. into Hamilton. **From north/central New Jersey:** Follow I-80 W. into Pennsylvania. Exit on I-380 northwest toward Scranton to I-81 N. to Binghamton. Take Exit 6 to Rte. 12 N. to Sherburne; bear left on Rte. 12B N. to Hamilton. **From Syracuse and points west:** Take I-81 S., exit on I-690 E. to I-481 S. to Exit 3E off I-481 for Rte. 92 E. Follow Rte. 92 to Cazenovia and take Rte. 20 E. Follow Rte. 20 E. to Rte. 46 S and then bear right. Take Rte. 46 S. to Rte. 12B S. to the Village of Hamilton. Stay on Rte. 12B S. through town. Colgate University will be on your left. Turn left at the traffic light onto Oak Drive. From Boston and the east: Take Mass Pike to NYS Thruway W. to Exit 25A for I-88 (Duanesburg), then I-88 W. to Exit 24 for Rte. 20 W.; beyond Madison turn left onto Rte. 12B S. to Hamilton. In bad weather, or for more highway driving, stay on NYS Thruway W. to Exit 31 (Utica); follow the sign for Rte. 12 S. through Utica; then take Rte. 12B S. to Hamilton. **From Philadelphia:** Take the northeast extension of the PA Turnpike to I-81 at Scranton; go north on I-81 to Binghamton. Take Exit 6 for Rte. 12 N. to Sherburne; bear left on Rte. 12B N. to Hamilton.

STAY THE NIGHT

Nearby: The **Colgate Inn** (315-824-2300) is on Payne Street within walking distance of the university, and it offers moderate rates. The rates at **Hamilton Inn** (East Lake Rd.; 315-824-1245) range from moderate to expensive and include a continental breakfast. **Landmark Inn** (Rte. 20, Bouckville; 315-893-1810) is about three-and-a-half miles away from campus. Its rooms are reasonably priced and comfortable.

A Little Farther: Cazenovia is an old resort town just 30 minutes away from Colgate; the **Brewster Inn** (Rte. 20; 315-655-9232) has a view of Cazenovia Lake. The **Brae Loch Inn** (5 Albany St. Rte. 20; 315-655-3431) is a family-run Scottish inn with great charm across from the lake. Rooms range from moderate to expensive, and there is a fine restaurant on the premises.

AT A GLANCE

Selectivity Rating	93
Range SAT I Math	630–710
Average SAT I Math	665
Range SAT I Verbal	610–700
Average SAT I Verbal	652
Average ACT Composite	29
Average GPA	3.55
Student/Faculty Ratio	10:1

CAMPUS TOURS

Appointment	Not required
Dates	Varies
Times	Mon–Fri, 10:15AM, 12PM, 2PM, & 3:30PM
Average Length	1 hour

ON-CAMPUS APPOINTMENTS

Admissions

Start Date–Juniors	May 1
Appointment	Required
Advance Notice	Yes, 2 weeks
Saturdays	No
Average Length	45 min.
Info Sessions	Yes

Faculty and Coaches

Dates/Arrangements	Contact Athletic Department 2 weeks prior

CLASS VISITS

Dates	Academic year
Arrangements	Contact Admissions Office

COLUMBIA UNIVERSITY

Visitors Center, 212 Low Library,
New York, NY 10027 • Telephone: 212-854-2521 • www.columbia.edu •

Hours: Monday–Saturday, 9:00am–5:00pm

Without the extensive, western civilization-focused core curriculum at this vaunted Ivy League bastion on Manhattan's Upper West Side, graduating would be a breeze. Accomplished scholars with mind-boggling brainpower are everywhere, but there's no hand-holding and only the self-motivated thrive. Socially, New York City offers, well, everything.

AT A GLANCE

Selectivity Rating	98
Range SAT I Math	660–750
Average SAT I Math	693
Range SAT I Verbal	660–760
Average SAT I Verbal	701
Average GPA	3.79

CAMPUS TOURS

Appointment	Not required
Dates	Year-round
Times	Campus tours year-round, Mon–Fri, 11AM & 3PM
Average Length	120 min.

ON-CAMPUS APPOINTMENTS

Admissions
Start Date–Juniors	N/A
Info Sessions	Yes

Faculty and Coaches
Dates/Times	Academic year
Arrangements	Contact Visiting Center 2 weeks prior

CLASS VISITS

Dates	Academic year
Arrangements	Contact Visiting Center

TRANSPORTATION

La Guardia is the closest airport, and taxis are available for the ride to campus. Kennedy and Newark airports also serve the New York City area; bus service is available from all of these airports to the Port Authority Bus Terminal in the city. Public transportation is available from the bus terminal to the campus; five local bus lines (M4, M11, M5, M60, and M104) and two subway lines (Broadway IRT locals 1 and 9) serve the Columbia/Morningside Heights area. Amtrak and commuter trains serve the city at Pennsylvania and Grand Central Stations. Long distance buses arrive at the Port Authority Bus Terminal.

FIND YOUR WAY

Columbia is best reached by taking the 95th/96th St. exit from the Henry Hudson Pkwy. (West Side Highway). Use the 95th St. off-ramp and turn left onto Riverside Dr. Proceed north to 116th St. A right turn at 116th St. leads you to the campus gate. Parking available on street or in local garage (120th between Claremont and Riverside).

STAY THE NIGHT

Nearby: Columbia University is on the Upper West Side of Manhattan at 116th St. and Broadway. Located about 35 blocks to the south, between Central Park W. and Columbus Ave., on the West Side, is the Excelsior Hotel (45 W. 81st St.; 212-362-9200 or 800-368-4575). This is a very simple and clean hotel with moderate prices. A little farther south is the Empire Hotel (63rd St. and Broadway; 212-265-7400 or 888-822-3555). The hotel offers special rates for university visitors, but it is still fairly expensive. Other Upper West Side hotels that may have special rates for Columbia visitors are the Lucerne (79th Street and Amsterdam Avenue; 212-875-1000 or 800-492-8122), On the Ave (77th Street and Broadway; 212-362-1100 or 800-509-7598), and the Beacon (75th Street and Broadway; 212-787-1100 or 800-572-4969).

A Little Farther: Additional information available at:

www.studentaffairs.columbia.edu/admissions/visit/accommodations.php.

HIGHLIGHTS

ON CAMPUS
- Low Plaza
- Dodge Physical Fitness Center
- Alfred Lerner Hall
- St. Paul's Chapel
- Butler Library

OFF CAMPUS
- Central Park
- Statue of Liberty
- Metropolitan Museum of Art
- American Museum of Natural History
- Rockefeller Center
- Greenwich Village

CORNELL UNIVERSITY

Admissions Office, 410 Thurston Ave., Ithaca, NY 14850 • Telephone: 607-255-5241 • www.info.cornell.edu • Email: admissions@cornell.edu

Hours: Monday–Friday, 8:00AM–4:30PM

Not surprisingly, the academic experience is very rewarding at Cornell University, an Ivy League beast that offers over 4,000 undergraduate courses. Socially, the Greek System is big at Cornell, and the surrounding area, though often too cold, provides abundant opportunities for fishing, hiking, cross-country and downhill skiing, sailing, and other such activities.

HIGHLIGHTS

ON CAMPUS
- Johnson Art Museum
- Gorges and waterfalls bordering campus
- Center for Theater Arts
- Cornell Plantations, including Beebe Lake
- Willard Straight Hall

OFF CAMPUS
- Four state parks, including Taughannock Falls
- Cornell's Ornithology Lab in Sapsucker Woods
- Collegetown next to campus
- Stewart Park/Cayuga Lake
- Ithaca Commons (shopping)

TRANSPORTATION

The Ithaca-Tompkins County Airport is five miles (a 10-minute drive) from campus. Taxis and limousine service are available for the ride from the airport to campus. Greyhound Bus and shortline serve Ithaca; from the bus station you can take a taxi (607-277-8294) or a Tompkins Consolidated Area Transit (TCAT) Bus Routes to campus.

FIND YOUR WAY

For directions, check out www.info.cornell.edu/CUHomePage/directions/directions.

STAY THE NIGHT

Nearby: If you're willing to shell out some cash, we recommend the **Statler Hotel** (800-541-2501), a fine campus hotel run by students of Cornell's hotel management school. **Peregrine House Inn** (140 College Ave.; 607-272-0919) is an eight-room bed-and-breakfast within walking distance of campus. This old, three-story brick house with Victorian furnishings offers moderate rates. For a convenient budget choice, try **Hillside Inn** (518 Stewart Ave.; 607-273-6864), just three blocks from campus. About one mile away from the university is **Best Western University Inn** (East Hill Plaza; 607-272-6100), which offers reasonable rates, a pool, a health club, and nearby golf privileges. A no-frills **Super 8** (400 S. Meadow St., Rte. 13; 607-273-8088) is also just two miles away from campus.

A Little Farther: A **Super 8** (400 S. Meadow St., Rte. 13; 607-273-8088) is just two miles away from campus. Other hotels and motels include the **Holiday Inn** (607-272-1000, in downtown Ithaca), **Ramada Inn** (607-257-3100, one mile away near Pyramid Mall), **Ithaca Courtyard Marriott** (607-330-1000, near the airport), and **Clarion University Hotel** (607-257-2000, one mile from Cornell). Tompkins county offers numerous beautiful bed-and-breakfasts For more information, visit www.visitithaca.com/places_to_stay.htm.

AT A GLANCE

Selectivity Rating	97
Range SAT I Math	660–750
Average SAT I Math	700
Range SAT I Verbal	620–720
Average SAT I Verbal	667
Average ACT Composite	27
Student/Faculty Ratio	9:1

CAMPUS TOURS

Appointment	Not required
Dates	Year-round
Times	See our website
Average Length	1 hour

ON-CAMPUS APPOINTMENTS

Admissions

Start Date–Juniors	Contact Admissions Office
Appointment	Required
Advance Notice	Yes, 3 weeks
Saturdays	No
Average Length	1 hour
Info Sessions	Yes

Faculty and Coaches

Dates/Times	Academic year
Arrangements	Contact Admissions Office 3 weeks prior

CLASS VISITS

Dates	Academic year
Arrangements	See our website

[handwritten notes:]

Tour   9, 11, 1, 3   (1:15)

Info - 11

EUGENE LANG COLLEGE

Admissions Office, Eugene Lang College- New School University, 65 W. 11th St., New York, NY 10011 • Telephone: 877-528-3321 • www.lang.edu • Email: Lang@newschool.edu

Hours: Monday–Friday, 9:00AM–5:00PM

Eugene Lang, the undergraduate division of the New School for Social Research, is an ideal choice if you are a left-leaning, self-reliant student with an interest in the humanities and social sciences and a pretty clear idea of what you want to do. Life ain't cheap in New York City, but the cultural mecca of the world is right outside the door.

AT A GLANCE

Selectivity Rating	76
Range SAT I Math	510–610
Average SAT I Math	570
Range SAT I Verbal	580–690
Average SAT I Verbal	610
Average ACT Composite	27
Average GPA	3.22
Student/Faculty Ratio	11:1

CAMPUS TOURS

Appointment	Not required
Dates	Academic year
Times	Mon–Fri, 11AM & 2PM
Average Length	1 hour

ON-CAMPUS APPOINTMENTS

Admissions

Start Date–Juniors	Winter of junior year
Appointment	Not required
Advance Notice	Yes, 1 week
Saturdays	Sometimes
Average Length	30 min.
Info Sessions	Yes

Faculty and Coaches

Dates/Times	Academic year
Arrangements	Contact Admissions Office 1 week prior

CLASS VISITS

Dates	Academic year
Arrangements	Contact Admissions Office

TRANSPORTATION

Kennedy International, La Guardia, and Newark airports all serve New York City. At Kennedy and La Guardia, Carey bus service provides group rides into the city at regular intervals; check with your airline for details. Taxis are also available, though expensive. From Newark, Carey Bus brings passengers into the Port Authority Bus Terminal, which is a subway ride away from the college. Amtrak, Metro-North, New Jersey Transit, and Long Island Railroad trains all serve New York City. Greyhound and several local bus lines also come into the city. Public transportation is available from the terminals to the college. New Jersey's PATH train stops at 14th St. and 6th Ave., only two blocks from campus. The BMT, IND, and IRT subway lines all have stops within walking distance of the school.

FIND YOUR WAY

From north of New York City, take the Saw Mill River Pkwy. to the Henry Hudson Pkwy. S. (Rte. 9A) and continue to the West Side Highway (which becomes 12th Ave./West St.). Exit at 14th St. and continue east on 14th. Turn right onto 7th Ave., then left onto 12th St. The college is one-and-a-quarter blocks ahead. **From west of New York City,** take the George Washington Bridge to the Henry Hudson Pkwy. S. and proceed according to the previous directions. From the Lincoln Tunnel, follow signs to 39th or 40th Street and head east (one block) to 9th Ave. Proceed south on 9th Ave. to 14th St. Turn left onto 14th St. and continue east to 7th Ave. Turn right onto 7th Ave., then left onto West 12th St. The college is one-and-a-quarter blocks ahead. **From east of New York City,** take the Long Island Expressway (I-495) west to the Midtown Tunnel. Follow signs to 34th St. and the F.D.R. Dr. Take the F.D.R. south to the 15th St. exit and continue south to 14th St. Proceed west on 14th, then turn left onto 7th Ave. Turn left again on 12th St. and proceed to the college.

STAY THE NIGHT

Nearby: Eugene Lang College is in Greenwich Village, just north of New York University, so see the New York University entry for suggestions. Note that the **Hotel Chelsea** (with the coolest lobby you are ever going to see, though the rooms are a bit shabby) and the **Gramercy Park Hotel** are both within walking distance of Eugene Lang. Another possibility, about a 40-block bus ride from Eugene Lang, is the **Hotel Elysee** (60 E. 54th St.; 212-753-1066). Rates are expensive but quite reasonable for New York City.

A Little Farther: Check the Columbia and Juilliard entries for suggestions uptown and near Lincoln Center.

HIGHLIGHTS

ON CAMPUS
- Harry Scherman Library
- Raymond Fogelman Library
- Adam & Sophie Gimbel Design Library
- Student Center

OFF CAMPUS
- The Empire State Building
- American Museum of Natural History
- Union Square
- Fifth Avenue (shopping)
- The Museum of Modern Art

FORDHAM UNIVERSITY

Office of Undergraduate Admissions, Dealy Hall 115, Bronx, NY 10458 • Telephone: 800-367-3426 • www.fordham.edu • Email: enroll@fordham.edu

Hours: Monday–Friday, 9:00AM–5:00PM

Fordham University has traditional green lawn and a Gothic architecture campus in the Bronx, and it has a concrete campus near Lincoln Center in Manhattan. The Bronx campus remains a traditional liberal arts and sciences school while Lincoln Center offers a wide range of courses but focuses on media studies, visual arts, and theater. At both campuses, students must complete a solid liberal arts core curriculum. Denzel Washington is a proud Fordham alum.

HIGHLIGHTS

ON CAMPUS
- Millennium Hall (Rose Hill Campus)
- Willian D. Walsh Family Library
- Keating Hall/Edwards Parade
- McMahon Hall (Lincoln Center)
- Pope Auditorium (Lincoln Center)

OFF CAMPUS
- Arthur Avenue (Little Italy)
- Bronx Zoo
- Botanical Gardens
- Lincoln Center/ Broadway (Lincoln Center Campus)
- Central Park

TRANSPORTATION

La Guardia, Kennedy International, Newark, and Westchester County airports all serve New York City. The closest to Fordham's Rose Hill Campus (on E. Fordham Rd. at 190th St. in the Bronx), is La Guardia, which is a 20-minute drive from campus. Taxis and limousine service (call Riverdale Jitney, 718-884-9400) are available for the ride from the airport to campus. The other area airports are also served by shuttle and taxi service. Amtrak, Long Island Railroad, and New Jersey Transit trains all serve New York City. Greyhound buses come into the Port Authority Terminal. Several local train and subway lines offer access to campus: the Metro-North commuter railroad (Fordham station), the Woodlawn-Jerome IRT subway (#4 to the Fordham Rd. station), and the IND subway (Concourse D line). A number of local bus lines pass the campus along Fordham Rd.

FIND YOUR WAY

New York City can be approached on many highways. After you are in the city area, any of the following roads and exits will get you close to Fordham: Bronx River Pkwy. (Pelham Parkway westbound exit), Saw Mill River Pkwy. (Mosholu Pkwy. exit), and the Cross-Bronx Expy. (Bronx River Pkwy. W. exit). Ample parking facilities are available on campus. The Lincoln Center campus (113 W. 60th Street and Columbus Ave) is easily reached by the George Washington Bridge and Lincoln and Holland Tunnels. Follow the West Side Highway to the 79th St. exit.

STAY THE NIGHT

Nearby: Fordham University's Rose Hill campus is in the Bronx, north of Manhattan. The closest place to stay is in Yonkers at the **Holiday Inn** (125 Tuckahoe Rd.; 914-476-3800) only 15 minutes away. Rates are moderate. **Days Inn** (Tarrytown Rd., Elmsford; 914-592-5680), 25 minutes away, is always a reliable, inexpensive choice. It also has an outdoor pool and health club privileges. For an indoor pool, pick the **Ramada Inn** (540 Saw Mill River Rd., Elmsford; 914-592-3300). Rates range from moderate to expensive. Options in upper Manhattan include the **Empire Hotel** (1889 Broadway), the **Comfort Inn Central Park West** (31 W. 71st St), and the **Excelsior Hotel** (45 W. 81st St.) See our website for more details.

A Little Farther: For those who do not wish to stay in New York City, Fort Lee in New Jersey is readily accessible from the George Washington Bridge and within easy driving distances to both campuses. Hoboken, New Jersey may also be an attractive option for it's proximity to New York City transportation (PATH trains and buses to Port Authority).

AT A GLANCE

Selectivity Rating	82
Range SAT I Math	530–630
Average SAT I Math	606
Range SAT I Verbal	530–630
Average SAT I Verbal	606
Average ACT Composite	26
Average GPA	3.63
Student/Faculty Ratio	11:1

CAMPUS TOURS

Appointment	Preferred
Dates	Varies
Times	Varies between campuses
Average Length	1 hour

ON-CAMPUS APPOINTMENTS

Admissions

Start Date—Juniors	May 19th
Appointment	Required
Advance Notice	Yes, 2 weeks
Saturdays	No
Average Length	30 min.
Info Sessions	Yes

Faculty and Coaches

Dates/Times	Year-round
Arrangements	Contact coach directly

CLASS VISITS

Dates	Varies
Arrangements	Contact faculty directly

HAMILTON COLLEGE

Admissions Office, 198 College Hill Rd.,
Clinton, NY 13323 • Telephone: 800-843-2655 • www.hamilton.edu •
Email: admission@hamilton.edu

Hours: Monday–Friday, 8:30AM–4:30PM; Saturday (during fall), 8:30AM–1:00PM

*"I have several friends at Ivy League schools and feel I'm getting as good or even better an education as they are,"
gushes a student at Hamilton College, an intimate liberal arts college with energetic professors in upstate New York.
Students are very preppy, and though Hamilton has the feeling of being off in the wilderness with its tremendous
beauty, a 24-hour supermarket, a commercial airport, and a minor league hockey team are all just 15 minutes away.*

AT A GLANCE

Selectivity Rating	91
Range SAT I Math	610–700
Range SAT I Verbal	600–700
Student/Faculty Ratio	10:1

CAMPUS TOURS

Appointment	Not required
Dates	Year-round
Times	Times subject to change. Contact Admissions Office
Average Length	Varies

ON-CAMPUS APPOINTMENTS

Admissions

Start Date–Juniors	April 1
Appointment	Required, 2 weeks
Saturdays	Sometimes

CLASS VISITS

Arrangements	Contact Admissions Office

TRANSPORTATION

Oneida County Airport (served by USAir) is eight miles away from campus. Taxis and limousine service are available at the airport for the ride to campus. (Note that taxis are approximately twice as expensive as the limousines.) Syracuse Airport is 45 miles away from campus. Limousine service to campus is available but must be arranged in advance by calling 315-736-9601 or 315-736-5221. Amtrak trains are available to Union Station in Utica, a 20-minute drive to campus. Taxis are available for the drive to campus.

FIND YOUR WAY

From the NY State Thruway (I-90), take Exit 32 (Westmoreland). After the exit, bear right, then turn left onto Rte. 233 S. Proceed for approximately five miles into Clinton (crossing Rte. 5). At the blinking light at the foot of a steep hill (look for the Hamilton College sign on the right), turn right up the hill onto College Hill Rd. The Admissions Office is a yellow house on the left of College Hill Rd. **From the south,** take I-81 N. through Binghamton to Exit 6 (sign says Rte. 12, Norwich). Follow Rte. 12 N. for approximately 50 miles; in the village of Sherburne, bear left onto Rte. 12B. Follow 12B N. for approximately 35 miles. Turn left onto Rte. 233. approximately three miles north of the village of Deansboro. Follow Rte. 233 to the flashing red light. Turn left and the follow the signs to campus.

STAY THE NIGHT

Nearby: On campus, the newly renovated fourth floor of the **Bristol Campus Center** (315-859-4194) has moderately-priced rooms available. During the academic year, a snack bar is open for breakfast. Bed-and-breakfasts in the area are **The Hedges** (180 Sanford Avenue; 800-883-5883/315-859-5909) and **The Artful Lodger** (7 East Park Row; 315-853-3672), both about one mile from campus. The recently remodeled **Alexander Hamilton Inn** (21 West Park Row; 315-853-2061) offers guest rooms and fine dining in a centuries old building on the Village Green.

A Little Farther: The moderately-priced **Comfort Suites** (800-221-2222) in Vernon, New York, is 15 minutes away from campus. The **Utica Radisson** (315-797-8010) has an indoor swimming pool, game room, Jacuzzi, weight room, a restaurant, and a nightly band (except Sunday). A special dining experience can be found at **La Petite Maison** (Waterville, 315-841-8030), 20 minutes south of campus. See the Colgate entry for more suggestions in the area (a 25-minute drive away).

HIGHLIGHTS

ON CAMPUS

- Emerson Gallery
- Root Glen
- Hamilton College Jazz Archive

OFF CAMPUS

- Adirondack Park
- Stanley Performing Arts Center
- Munson-Williams Proctor Art Institute
- National Baseball Hall of Fame
- Glimmerglass Opera

HARTWICK COLLEGE

Admissions Office, 1, Hartwick Dr., Bresee Hall, Oneonta, NY 13820-4020 • Telephone: 888-427-8925 • www.hartwick.edu • Email: admissions@hartwick.edu

Hours: Monday–Friday, 9:00AM–5:00PM; select Saturdays, 10:00AM–2:00PM

Hartwick College offers a traditional liberal arts school in the upstate village of Oneonta, New York with about 1,400 students. The upstate campus is near a variety of attractions, including the Boxing Hall of Fame. Dilbert creator Scott Adams is an alum.

HIGHLIGHTS

ON CAMPUS

- Yagen Museum
- Stevens-German Library
- Miller Hall of Science
- Binder Athletic Facility
- Shineman Chapel

OFF CAMPUS

- Baseball Hall of Fame/Farmers Museum
- National Soccer Hall of Fame
- Catskills Park
- Glimmerglass Opera & State Park
- Gilbert Lake

TRANSPORTATION

Oneonta has a small airport that can handle private planes. Albany and Binghamton have larger airports, which are 75 miles (an hour to an hour-and-a-half drive) from Oneonta. Greyhound buses are available from these airports to Oneonta. Greyhound also provides service into Oneonta. Taxis to campus are available at the station.

FIND YOUR WAY

From the New York City area, take the NY State Thruway N. (I-87) to Exit 19 (Kingston), then take Rte. 28 W. to Shandaken. Turn right onto Rte. 42 to Lexington. Turn left at Lexington to Rte. 23A, which becomes Rte. 23 W. Follow this into Oneonta. **From the south,** get onto I-81 N. through Scranton, PA, into Binghamton, NY. Take I-88 E. to Oneonta. Use Oneonta Exit 15, marked Colleges, Airport.

STAY THE NIGHT

Nearby: Three motels are within 10 minutes of the college. From least expensive to most expensive, they are the **Christopher's Country Lodge,** (Rte. 28; 607-432-2444), **Cathedral Farms Country Inn** (Rte. 205; 607-432-7483), **Clarion Hotel** (Main Street; 607-432-7500), and **Holiday Inn** (NY Rte. 23; 607-443-2250).

A Little Farther: From May to October, you can stay in **Cooperstown** (home of the Baseball Hall of Fame) at the **Otesaga Hotel** (60 Lake St.; 607-547-9931), situated on beautiful Lake Otesaga. There's a groovy porch and a formal dining room with music and all-American cuisine. There is also an annex to the Otesaga: Cooper Inn, a wonderful old building a block or so closer to the Baseball Hall of Fame. You can use all the facilities of the Otesaga, which include a golf course and a heated swimming pool. Lunch is served buffet-style by the pool. Rates at the Otesaga are very expensive but include breakfast and dinner. Rates at the Cooper Inn are at the low end of the expensive range, but meals are not included.

AT A GLANCE

Selectivity Rating	67
Range SAT I Math	510–620
Average SAT I Math	567
Range SAT I Verbal	520–610
Average SAT I Verbal	565
Average ACT Composite	2
Student/Faculty Ratio	11:1

CAMPUS TOURS

Appointment	Preferred
Dates	Varies
Times	Mon–Fri, 9:45AM–3:30PM, hourly; Sat 11:30AM, 12PM, & 1PM
Average Length	1 hour

ON-CAMPUS APPOINTMENTS

Admissions

Start Date–Juniors	None during March
Appointment	Preferred
Advance Notice	Yes, 1 week
Saturdays	Yes
Average Length	45 min.
Info Sessions	Yes

Faculty and Coaches

Dates/Times	Year-round
Arrangements	Contact Admissions Office 1 week prior

CLASS VISITS

Dates	Academic year
Arrangements	Contact Admissions Office

HOBART AND WILLIAM SMITH COLLEGES

Admissions Office, Pulteney St.,
Geneva, NY 14456 • Telephone: 800-245-0100 • www.hws.edu •
Email: admissions@hws.edu

Hours: Monday–Friday, 8:30AM–5:00PM; Saturday (during academic term), 9:00AM–2:00PM

Hobart and William Smith Colleges are separate, single-sex institutions sharing the same beautiful and histori-cal campus in the gorgeous Finger Lakes region of upstate New York. In an effort to combine the best aspects of single-sex and coeducational instruction, the schools share classes and even a common faculty, yet maintain separate traditions and curricular priorities.

AT A GLANCE

Selectivity Rating	85
Range SAT I Math	540–630
Average SAT I Math	600
Range SAT I Verbal	540–630
Average SAT I Verbal	550
Average GPA	3.34
Student/Faculty Ratio	11:1

CAMPUS TOURS

Appointment	Preferred
Dates	Year-round
Times	Mon–Fri, 9AM–11AM, 1PM–3PM; Sat, 9AM–1PM
Average Length	1 hour

ON-CAMPUS APPOINTMENTS

Admissions

Start Date–Juniors	April
Appointment	Required
Advance Notice	Yes, 1 week
Saturdays	Sometimes
Average Length	45 min.
Info Sessions	Yes

Faculty and Coaches

Dates/Times	Year-round
Arrangements	Contact Admissions Office 1 week prior

CLASS VISITS

Dates	Academic year
Arrangements	Contact Admissions Office

TRANSPORTATION

From I-90, take Exit 42. Take Rte. 14 S. to the first light (approximately five-and-a-half miles). Turn right on North St.; pass Geneva General Hospital and take the next left turn onto Main St. The Admissions Office is on S. Main St. in Durfee House. From downstate, take I-81 N. to Binghamton; then take Rte. 17 W. to Rte. 96, and follow 96 through Ithaca to Rte. 96A at Ovid. Follow 96A to Rtes. 5 and 20 W., and take them into Geneva. Enter campus by turning left at Pulteney St. Proceed to St. Clair St. and turn left to S. Main St. Turn left again onto S. Main to Durfee House and the Admissions Office.

FIND YOUR WAY

From I-90, take Exit 42. Take Rte. 14 S. to the first light (approximately five-and-a-half miles). Turn right on North St.; pass Geneva General Hospital and take the next left turn onto Main St. The Admissions Offices are located in 629 and 639 S. Main St. **From downstate,** take I-81 N. to Binghamton; then take Rte. 17 W. to Rte. 96, and follow 96 through Ithaca to Rte. 96A at Ovid. Follow 96A to Rtes. 5 and 20 W., and take them into Geneva. Enter campus by turning left at Pulteney St. Proceed to St. Clair St. and turn left to S. Main St. Turn left again onto S. Main to the Admissions Offices.

STAY THE NIGHT

Nearby: Seneca Lake is home to a few great accomodations. The **Inn at Bellhurst Castle** (Rte. 14 S.; 315-781-0201) is a grand, heavily paneled Victorian mansion with grounds that run down to the lake. Rates are moderate to expensive. **Geneva on the Lake** (10001 Lochland Rd.; 315-789-7190) is a handsome, all-suite resort with a pool, boating, and access to many sporting activities. Rates are expensive. More moderately-priced is the **Ramada Geneva Lake Front** (315-789-0400), with 148 rooms on the shore of Seneca Lake. A budget option within half a mile of campus is the **Motel 6** (485 Hamilton St.; 315-789-4050). There are numerous bed-and-breakfasts throughout the area (see our website).

A Little Farther: A **Holiday Inn** is nine miles away from campus (Rtes. 414, 5, and 20 E. in Waterloo; 315-539-5011). Rates are moderate, and there is a restaurant and weekend entertainment. See also the University of Rochester and Rochester Institute of Technology entries (Rochester is 35 miles to the northwest), the Syracuse University entry (Syracuse is 50 miles to the northeast), and the Cornell University entry (Ithaca is 45 miles to the southeast).

HIGHLIGHTS

ON CAMPUS
- Scandling Center
- Rosenberg Hall
- Stern Hall
- Houghton House
- Bristol Field House

OFF CAMPUS
- Seneca Lake
- Women's Hall of Fame
- Women's Rights National Historic Park
- Finger Lakes Wineries
- Smith Opera House

HOFSTRA UNIVERSITY

Admissions Center, Bernon Hall,
Hempstead, NY 11549 • Telephone: 800-HOFSTRA • www.hofstra.edu •
Email: admitme@hofstra.edu

Hours: Monday–Friday, 9:00AM–5:00PM; Saturday, open until 2:00PM

Hofstra University offers its largely pre-professional undergraduates superb facilities, competent instruction, and easy access to New York City at an affordable price. The high-profile drama department hosts an annual Shakespeare Festival and New College at Hofstra focuses on creativity, discussion, and writing a la the Oxford model. Film icon Francis Ford Coppola is an alum.

HIGHLIGHTS

ON CAMPUS

- CV Starr Hall (high-tech business computer facility)
- Dempster Hall (Home of the School of Communication's WRHU radio station, the largest noncommercial TV studio on the East Coast.)
- Axinn Library
- Eight theaters on campus (including J.C.A Playhouse)
- Hofstra Student Center

OFF CAMPUS

- New York City
- Jones Beach
- Nassau Coliseum
- Eisenhower Park
- Roosevelt Field Mall

TRANSPORTATION

The closest airports to campus are JFK, La Guardia, and McArthur; taxi and limo services are available from all of them. Long Island Railroad is available from New York City; take it to the final stop, Hempstead, where a bus is available to take you to Hofstra.

FIND YOUR WAY

From Southern New Jersey, Southeast Pennsylvania, Maryland, Washington, DC, and Virginia: Take the N.J. Turnpike to Exit 13. Follow Rte. 278 to the Verrazano-Narrows Bridge. Exit left off the bridge onto the Belt Parkway east and take Exit 25A (Southern State Pkwy. east/Belt Pkwy. Splits; stay left), then take Exit 22N (Meadowbrook Pkwy. North). Take the Meadowbrook Pkwy. to exit M4 (signs says Hempstead, Coliseum). From exit M4 you will be on Rte. 24 W. (also known as Hempstead Turnpike.) Stay on 24 W for about one mile. Pass the Nassau Veterans Memorial Coliseum on the right. Hofstra University is on both sides of the Hempstead Turnpike. You will see two overhead walkways. Make a left at the light just after the second walkway. The Admissions Center, Bernon Hall, is the first building on your left. **From northwestern New Jersey, nothern Pennsylvania, and the Middle States:** Take either Interstate 78, Interstate 80, US Rte. 22, New Jersey Rte. 4, or New Jersey Rte. 17 to the George Washington Bridge. Proceed over the bridge to the Cross Bronx Expressway onto the Throgs Neck Bridge. Take the Cross Island Pkwy. to the Grand Central Pkwy. East. The Grand Central Pkwy. will turn into the Northern State Pkwy. Take this to exit 31A, the Meadowbrook Pkwy. South. Take the Meadowbrook Pkwy. to exit M4 (Sign says Hempstead, Coliseum). Follow the preceding directions. **From Upstate New York:** Take the New York Thruway over the Tappan Zee Bridge to the cross Westchester Expressway (Itnerstate 287). Stay on the Expressway to the New England Thruway. Proceed south on the Thruway to the Throgs Neck Bridge. Follow the directions from northwestern New Jersey, etc. **From New England:** Proceed South to the New England Thruway (Interstate 95) and take this to the Throgs Neck Bridge. Follow the directions from northwestern New Jersey, etc. **From Manhattan:** Take the Midtown Tunnel to the Long Island Expressway (Interstate 495) cast to exit 38, which is the Northern State Parkway East. Take this to exit 31A, the Meadowbrook Pkwy. South, and follow the directions from northwestern New Jersey, etc.

STAY THE NIGHT

Nearby: Your choices include the **Long Island Marriott** (101 James Doolittle Blvd., Uniondale, NY; 516-794-3800), the **Howard Johnson's** (120 Jericho Tpk., Westbury, NY; 516-333-9700), the **Comfort Inn/Econo Lodge** (333 South Service Road, Plainview, NY; 516-694-6500), the **Wingate Inn** (821 Stewart Avenue, Garden City, NY; 516-705-9000), the **Red Roof Inn** (699 Dibblee Drive, Westbury, NY; 516-794-2555), and the **Garden City Hotel** (Garden City, NY; 516-747-3000).

AT A GLANCE

Selectivity Rating	74
Range SAT I Math	520–610
Average SAT I Math	570
Range SAT I Verbal	510–600
Average SAT I Verbal	559
Average ACT Composite	25
Average GPA	2.92
Student/Faculty Ratio	15:1

CAMPUS TOURS

Appointment	Preferred
Dates	Year-round
Times	Mon–Fri, 10:15AM–2PM; Sat, 9AM–11AM
Average Length	120 min.

ON-CAMPUS APPOINTMENTS

Admissions

Start Date—Juniors	End of September of junior year
Appointment	Preferred
Advance Notice	Yes
Saturdays	Yes
Average Length	30 min.
Info Sessions	Yes

Faculty and Coaches

Dates/Times	Academic year
Arrangements	Contact Athletic Department 2 weeks prior

CLASS VISITS

Dates	Academic year
Arrangements	Contact Admissions Office

ITHACA COLLEGE

Admissions Office, 100 Job Hall, Ithaca, NY 14850-7020 • Telephone: 800-429-4274 • www.ithaca.edu • Email: admission@ithaca.edu

Hours: Monday–Friday, 8:30AM–5:00PM; most Saturdays (please call to confirm), 8:30AM–12:30PM

The other college in Ithaca is Ithaca College, a wonderful institution that originated as a Conservatory of Music and has grown into a nationally renowned pre-professional college with a highly diverse curriculum and one of the best physical therapy programs on the East Coast. Communications is big as well, and the absolutely gorgeous campus is only five minutes from Cornell, state parks, and the countryside.

AT A GLANCE

Selectivity Rating	81
Range SAT I Math	550–640
Average SAT I Math	595
Range SAT I Verbal	540–630
Average SAT I Verbal	587
Student/Faculty Ratio	12:1

CAMPUS TOURS

Appointment	Preferred
Dates	Year-round
Times	Mon–Fri, 9AM–3PM, hourly; Select Sats; 9AM–11AM, hourly
Average Length	1 hour

ON-CAMPUS APPOINTMENTS

Admissions

Start Date–Juniors	Anytime
Appointment	Required
Advance Notice	Yes, 2 weeks
Saturdays	Sometimes
Average Length	30 min.
Info Sessions	No

Faculty and Coaches

Dates/Times	Academic year
Arrangements	Contact Admissions Office 2 weeks prior

CLASS VISITS

Dates	Academic year
Arrangements	Contact Admissions Office

TRANSPORTATION

Ithaca is served by US Airways at the Tompkins County Airport and by Greyhound, Shortline, and other bus companies. Limousine service is available from the airport, and taxis and city buses serve the campus from the bus terminal. Hancock International Airport in Syracuse is approximately 60 miles north of Ithaca.

FIND YOUR WAY

From the New York City Area, follow Route 17 west to Binghamton and take I-81 north to Whitney Point (exit 8). Pick up Route 79 west to Ithaca. At T-intersection in Ithaca turn left onto Route 96B (Aurora St.). An alternate route of about the same distance is through Owego: Stay on Route 17 west through Binghamton to Route 96/96B in Owego. Follow 96/96B for about 25 miles. The campus will be on your right. **From Albany and New England,** follow the New York State Thruway (I-90) west to I-88 (exit 25A). Take I-88 west to Bainbridge (exit 8) and then Route 206 to Whitney Point. Pick up Route 79 west to Ithaca. At T-intersection in Ithaca turn left onto Route 96B (Aurora St.). **From Rochester and Buffalo,** follow the New York State Thruway (I-90) east to Waterloo (exit 41) and take Route 414 south to Route 318 east to Route 89 south to Ithaca. In Ithaca turn right onto Route 13 south. After passing Green St., move into the far left lane and go straight onto Route 96 B (Clinton St.). Turn right onto Aurora St. (still 96B).

STAY THE NIGHT

Nearby: **Holiday Inn** (222 S. Cayuga St.; 607-272-1000) is only one mile away from Ithaca College and is moderately-priced. It has an indoor swimming pool. For other choices see www.visitithaca.com.

Tour   9:30, 11, 1:30. 3

HIGHLIGHTS

ON CAMPUS

- New academic facilities
- Art gallery
- Music and theater performances
- The Tower Club restaurant
- Division III intercollegiate sports

OFF CAMPUS

- Ithaca Commons
- Numerous gorges and parks
- Wineries
- Ithaca Farmers' Market

THE JUILLIARD SCHOOL

Admissions Office, 60 Lincoln Center Plaza, New York, NY 10023-6588 • Telephone: 212-799-5000 • www.juilliard.edu • Email: mgray@juilliard.edu

Hours: Monday–Friday, 9:00AM–5:00PM

The prestigious Juilliard School in New York City's Lincoln Center is perhaps the world's finest school for the performing arts. Juilliard enrolls about 750 highly diverse students and offers a variety of programs, including dance, theater, and music. Juilliard boasts a host of famous alumni, including actor Robin Williams and musician Wynton Marsalis.

HIGHLIGHTS

ON CAMPUS
• Lila Acheson Wallace Library

OFF CAMPUS
• Central Park
• The Statue of Liberty
• American Museum of Natural History
• The Guggenheim Museum
• Times Square

TRANSPORTATION

La Guardia, Newark International, and Kennedy International serve the New York City area. Limousine, taxi, bus, and subway service can get you to Lincoln Center and Juilliard. Taxi service is the most expensive means of travel. Carey bus service operates from La Guardia and Newark airports. Airport shuttles operate from Kennedy. Your airline should be able to help you plan how to get into the city. Amtrak trains and Greyhound and several other bus lines serve New York City. The closest subway to the school is the #1 subway; the closest bus is the M104 at West 66th St.

FIND YOUR WAY

Take your favorite route into New York City (check the Barnard and Columbia entries), then head for Lincoln Center and the school near 65th and Broadway, west of Central Park.

STAY THE NIGHT

Nearby: Within walking distance is the **Alcott** (27 W. 72nd St.; 212-877-4200), which has moderate rates. In the other direction is the **Salisbury** (123 W. 57th St.; 212-246-1300). Rates are rather expensive, but remember to ask for its musician's discount. See the Columbia University entry for other suggestions, especially the **Empire Hotel** and the **Excelsior,** which are both within walking distance of Juilliard. (Ask the Empire for their musician's discount as well.)

A Little Farther: See the New York University and Eugene Lang College entries for midtown and downtown choices.

AT A GLANCE		
Selectivity Rating		99
Student to Faculty Ratio		4:1

CAMPUS TOURS	
Times	Mon–Fri, 2:30PM

ON-CAMPUS APPOINTMENTS

Admissions	
Start Date–Juniors	N/A

Faculty and Coaches	
Arrangements	Contact Admissions Office

CLASS VISITS

Arrangements	Contact faculty directly

MARIST COLLEGE

Office of Admissions, 3399 North Road,
Poughkeepsie, NY 12601-1387 • Telephone: 800-436-5483 • www.marist.edu •
Email: admissions@marist.edu

Hours: Monday–Friday, 9:00AM–5:00PM; Saturday, during academic year by appointment

Private and nondenominational Marist College offers its 4,000 or so full-time undergraduates a solid liberal arts education with a career-oriented focus. The campus in Poughkeepsie, New York (which is midway between New York City and Albany) offers a picturesque view of the Hudson River. Looking to transfer? Marist has one of the more flexible transfer policies around.

AT A GLANCE

Selectivity Rating	84
Range SAT I Math	510–610
Average SAT I Math	565
Range SAT I Verbal	500–600
Average SAT I Verbal	506
Average ACT Composite	24
Average GPA	3.2
Student/Faculty Ratio	14:1

CAMPUS TOURS

Appointment	Required
Dates	Varies
Times	Varies
Average Length	120 min.

ON-CAMPUS APPOINTMENTS

Admissions

Info Sessions	Yes

Faculty and Coaches

Dates/Times	Academic year
Arrangements	Contact coach directly 2 weeks prior

CLASS VISITS

Dates	Academic year
Arrangements	Contact faculty directly

TRANSPORTATION

Poughkeepsie Train station is one mile away from campus. The station is served by Metro-North trains and Amtrak. Stewart Airport is 30 minutes away in Newburgh, New York.

FIND YOUR WAY

Marist can be reached from Interstate 84 and 87. **From I-87,** take exit 17, follow signs to 84 east, take 84 east to exit 13. Follow Rte. 9 North to campus. **From 84 or the west,** take exit 13 to Rte. 9 North.

STAY THE NIGHT

Nearby: Places to stay include the **Holiday Inn Express,** with rates that go from $90 to $130; and the **Courtyard by Marriott,** with rates that go from $100 to $150.

HIGHLIGHTS

ON CAMPUS

- James A. Cannavino Library
- James J. McCann Recreation Center
- Student Center
- Newly renovated freshman residence halls

OFF CAMPUS

- Mohonk Mountain Preserve
- Lake Minewaska
- FDR Home & Library
- Vanderbilt Mansion
- Locust Grove, Samuel Morse Estate

NEW YORK UNIVERSITY

Office of Undergraduate Admissions, 22 Washington Square North, New York, NY 10011 • Telephone: 212-998-4500 • www.nyu.edu • Email: admissions@nyu.edu

Hours: Monday–Friday, 9:00AM–5:00PM

New York University offers a bevy of highly regarded and nationally competitive programs, especially the prestigious Tisch School of the Arts and the Stern School of Business. The hefty price tag for attending NYU still frustrates some students, but for most, Greenwich Village—the heart of the social universe of young New York—helps to make it all worthwhile. Joseph Heller, Martin Scorsese, and Oliver Stone are alums.

HIGHLIGHTS

ON CAMPUS
- Kimmel Center for Student Life
- Silver Center for Arts & Science
- Coles Athletic Center

OFF CAMPUS
- Central Park
- Statue of Liberty
- Museum of Modern Art
- Empire State Building
- Times Square

TRANSPORTATION

La Guardia Airport is 20 miles away from campus, ordinarily a one-hour drive, but longer at rush hours. Kennedy and Newark airports also serve New York City. To get to campus from any of the airports, you can take a taxi or a bus to Grand Central Station and then take a taxi or the Lexington Ave. subway downtown to Astor Place. Long Island Railroad and Amtrak trains bring you to Penn Station; from there take the 8th Ave. subway (IND) downtown (A express or C or E local) to the West 4th St. stop. Metro-North trains bring you into Grand Central Station; from there take the Lexington Ave. subway (IRT) downtown (#6 local) to the Astor Place stop. Interstate buses come into the city's Port Authority Bus Terminal. Take either a taxi or the 8th Ave. downtown subway to West 4th St. to get to campus.

FIND YOUR WAY

From the north, take I-87 (NY State Thruway), which becomes the Major Deegan Expy. in the Bronx. From there take the F.D.R. Drive south to Houston St.; head west to La Guardia Pl. (two blocks west of Broadway). Turn north three blocks to Washington Square and the university. **From the west and south,** take an interstate highway or the New Jersey Tpke. through the Holland Tunnel, then go north on Ave. of the Americas (6th Ave.) to W. 4th St. Take W. 4th St. east to Washington Square.

STAY THE NIGHT

Nearby: New York University is in Greenwich Village, at the foot of Fifth Avenue, and south of midtown. If you consult a general New York City guide, look for accommodations south of 38th St., which will put you within a one- to two-mile range of the school. Taxis and public transportation are readily available. For convenience, you cannot do better than the **Washington Square Hotel** (103 Waverly Pl.; 212-777-9515), just down the block from the Admissions Office. Accommodations are very modest, with rates to match. A 15-minute walk past shops, galleries, and restaurants will bring you to the dazzlingly sophisticated, new **Soho Grand Hotel** (310 W. Broadway; 212-965-3000) in the exciting art center of Soho, where, for a moderate (for New York!) rate, you can have a New York experience. This is a favorite of artists and photographers. The rooms have great views, and there is valet parking. Bed-and-breakfasts are located all around town in the $80 to $100 range. Two reservation agencies to call are **Abode Bed and Breakfast** (212-472-2000) and **Bed and Breakfast and Books** (212-865-8740). NYU has arranged for guests of the university to receive special rates (moderately expensive) at **Club Quarters** (52 William St.; 212-443-4700) in the heart of the Wall Street District.

AT A GLANCE

Selectivity Rating	89
Range SAT I Math	630–720
Average SAT I Math	666
Range SAT I Verbal	620–710
Average SAT I Verbal	672
Average ACT Composite	29
Average GPA	3.7
Student to Faculty Ratio	12:1

CAMPUS TOURS

Appointment	Required
Dates	Year-round
Times	Contact Admissions Office.
Average Length	1 hour

ON-CAMPUS APPOINTMENTS

Admissions

Start Date–Juniors	
Appointment	Required
Advance Notice	Yes, 2 weeks
Saturdays	Sometimes
Average Length	1 hour
Info Sessions	Yes

Faculty and Coaches

Dates/Times	Year-round
Arrangements	Contact Athletic Department 2 weeks prior

CLASS VISITS

Dates	Academic year
Arrangements	Contact Admissions Office

RENSSELAER POLYTECHNIC INSTITUTE

Office of Admissions, 110 8th Street,
Troy, NY 12180-3590 • Telephone: 518-276-6216 • admissions.rpi.edu •
Email: admissions@rpi.edu

Hours: Monday–Friday, 8:30–5:00PM; Saturday (select), 9:30AM–3:00PM

Rensselaer Polytechnic Institute is a top-flight engineering school (with strong computer science and business and management departments) where mostly male, bookish students hit the books furiously and occasionally go on road trips, frat parties, or watch the perennially-competitive hockey team. George Ferris, inventor of the ferris wheel, and Washington Roebling, architect of the Brooklyn Bridge, are alums.

AT A GLANCE

Selectivity Rating	82
Range SAT I Math	640–720
Average SAT I Math	684
Range SAT I Verbal	580–680
Average SAT I Verbal	626
Average ACT Composite	26
Student to Faculty Ratio	16:1

CAMPUS TOURS

Appointment	Not required
Dates	Year-round
Times	Mon–Fri, 11AM & 2PM;
	Sat, during academic year
Average Length	1 hour

ON-CAMPUS APPOINTMENTS

Admissions

Start Date–Juniors	Not required
Advance Notice	Yes, 3 weeks
Saturdays	No
Info Sessions	Yes

Faculty and Coaches

Dates/Times	Year-round
Arrangements	Contact Admissions
	Office 3 weeks prior

CLASS VISITS

Dates	Year-round
Arrangements	Contact Admissions
	Office

TRANSPORTATION

The Albany International Airport is 10 miles away from campus. Taxis and rental cars are available for the ride from the airport to campus. Amtrak provides service to the Albany-Rensselaer train station; from there, take a taxi to campus. Bus service is available to Albany and Troy; take a taxi from these terminals to campus.

FIND YOUR WAY

From north, east, south, or west, Rensselaer is centrally located near the major highways in New York State. **From the North:** Take I-87, the Adirondack Northway, south to Exit 7 east. Get on Route 7 headed eastbound. Follow the directions to campus below. **From the South:** Take I-87, the New York State Thruway, north to exit 23. At exit 23, get on I-787 north to Route 7 East, Exit 9E. Disregard the sign for Rensselaer and Russell Sage College at the previous exit. Exit 9E, Route 7 east, provides an easier approach to campus. Follow the directions to campus below. **From the East:** Take I-90 (Massachusetts Turnpike, Berkshire Spur of the New York Thruway), to exit B1. Continue west (13.5 miles) to I-787 north to Route 7 east, exit 9E. Disregard the sign for Rensselaer and Russell Sage College at the previous exit. Exit 9E, Route 7 east, provides an easier approach to campus. Follow the directions to campus below. **From the West:** Take I-90, the New York State Thruway, to exit 24. From exit 24, take I-87 north, exit 1N, to exit 7 east. Follow the directions to campus below. **Directions to Campus:** Cross the Collar City Bridge and follow signs for Route 7, Hoosick Street. At the fourth traffic light, turn right onto 15th Street. You will see the large Rensselaer sign in granite at the intersection of 15th Street and Sage Avenue. Make a left at the third traffic light onto Sage Avenue. The Admissions Building will be directly in front of you. Bear to the left of the building onto Eaton Road. The parking lot will be on your right, directly behind the Admissions Building.

STAY THE NIGHT

Nearby: We look forward to your visit to Rensselaer. Our recommended lodging accommodations include: **The Albany Marriott** (189 Wolf Road; 518-458-8444), **Best Western—Albany Airport** (200 Wolf Road; 518-458-1016), **Clarion Suites** (611 Troy-Schenectady Road; 518-758-5891), **Days Inn** (16 Wolf Road; 518-459-3600), **The Desmond** (660 Albany-Shaker Road; 518-869-8100), **Franklin Plaza Inn & Suites** (1 Fourth Street, Troy; 518-274-8800), **Hampton Inn-Latham** (981 New London Road; 518-785-1285), **Hampton Inn-Wolf Road** (10 Ulenski Drive; 518-438-2822), **Holiday Inn Express** (946 New London Road; 518-783-6161), **The Inn at the Century** (997 New London Road; 518-785-0931), and **Microtel-Colonie** (7 Rensselaer Avenue; 800-782-9121).

HIGHLIGHTS

ON CAMPUS

- The Approach
- The Playhouse
- The Mueller Fitness Center
- The Houston Field House
- Mother's Wine Emporium

OFF CAMPUS

- The Troy Music Hall
- The Junior Museum
- Palace Theatre
- Saratoga Performing Arts Center (SPAC)
- Pepsi Arena

ROCHESTER INSTITUTE OF TECHNOLOGY

60 Lomb Memorial Dr.,
Rochester, NY 14623-5604 • Telephone: 716-475-6631 • www.rit.edu •
Email: admissions@rit.edu

Hours: Monday–Friday, 8:30AM–4:30PM; Saturday, 10:00AM–noon

Rochester Institute of Technology offers a demanding arts and technology school that has valuable relationships with major industries, state-of-the-art facilities, and an intense (but not cutthroat) student body. Located as it is in the hometown of Xerox, Kodak, and Bausch & Lomb, RIT provides its career-minded students with plenty of opportunities for internships. If you can stand cold weather, this is the place for you.

HIGHLIGHTS

ON CAMPUS
- Center for Manufacturing Studies
- Student Life Center/Field House/Ice Arena
- ESPN Zone at the RIT Student Union
- The Sentinel (largest metal sculpture)
- Microelectronic Engineering Facilities

OFF CAMPUS
- International Museum of Photography
- Frontier Field (AAA Baseball)
- Lake Ontario
- Eastman Theatre
- High Falls Entertainment

TRANSPORTATION
The Greater Rochester International Airport is approximately five miles away from campus. Taxis and rental cars are available for the ride from the airport to campus.

FIND YOUR WAY
From I-90, take Exit 46 and proceed north on I-390 to Exit 13 (Hylan Dr.). Turn left on Hylan and continue north to Jefferson Rd., then turn left. Proceed west on Jefferson a short distance to the main campus.

STAY THE NIGHT
Nearby: Most campus visitors stay at the **RIT Inn & Conference Center** (5257 W. Henrietta Rd; 585-359-1800; www.ritinn.com) located three miles away from campus and offering free shuttle service and special rates for campus visitors. The **Radisson Inn** (175 Jefferson Rd.; 585-475-1910) is within walking distance of campus. Rates are at the top end of the moderate range. A full range of hotel or motel options and prices are available within a five mile radius of campus.

A Little Farther: Visitors could combine a campus visit with visits to nearby attractions in the Finger Lakes area or Buffalo-Niagara Falls (about one hour away).

AT A GLANCE

Selectivity Rating	84
Range SAT I Math	570–670
Range SAT I Verbal	540–640
Average GPA	3.7
Student to Faculty Ratio	13:1

CAMPUS TOURS

Appointment	Preferred
Dates	Year-round
Times	Mon–Fri, 10AM, noon, & 2PM; Sat, 10AM
Average Length	1 hour

ON-CAMPUS APPOINTMENTS

Admissions

Start Date–Juniors	September of junior year
Appointment	Required
Advance Notice	Yes, 1 week
Saturdays	Sometimes
Average Length	1 hour
Info Sessions	Yes

Faculty and Coaches

Dates/Times	Academic year
Arrangements	Contact coach directly 2 weeks prior

CLASS VISITS

Dates	Academic year
Arrangements	Contact Admissions Office

ST. BONAVENTURE UNIVERSITY

PO Box D, Saint Bonaventure, NY 14778 •
Telephone: 800-462-5050 • www.sbu.edu •
Email: admissions@sbu.edu

Hours: Monday–Friday, 8:30AM–5:00PM; select Saturdays by appointment

Excellent professors who are very receptive to students' needs characterize St. Bonaventure University, an intimate Catholic liberal arts college about an hour from Buffalo. Sports are very huge, especially basketball, and intervisitation rules are strictly enforced in the single-sex dormitories.

AT A GLANCE

Selectivity Rating	76
Range SAT I Math	480–580
Average SAT I Math	531
Range SAT I Verbal	480–570
Average SAT I Verbal	523
Average ACT Composite	22
Average GPA	3.1
Student to Faculty Ratio	15:1

CAMPUS TOURS

Appointment	Preferred
Dates	Year-round
Times	Mon–Fri, 8:30AM–3:30PM
Average Length	1 hour

ON-CAMPUS APPOINTMENTS

Admissions

Start Date—Juniors	Anytime
Appointment	Preferred
Advance Notice	No, 1 week
Saturdays	Sometimes
Average Length	1 hour
Info Sessions	Yes

Faculty and Coaches

Dates/Times	Year-round
Arrangements	Contact Admissions Office 2 weeks prior

CLASS VISITS

Dates	Academic year
Arrangements	Contact Admissions Office

TRANSPORTATION

The closest airports to campus are the Buffalo/Niagara International Airport and the Bradford Regional Airport. Available bus service is available through Coach USA.

FIND YOUR WAY

For directions, please see our website at www.sbu.edu.

STAY THE NIGHT

Nearby: Your choices include the **Country Inn and Suites** (716-372-7500), the **Hampton Inn** (716-375-1000), and the **Motel DeSoto** (716-373-1400).

A Little Farther: If you don't mind staying a little farther away, the **Holiday Valley Resort** (716-699-2345) is a good choice.

HIGHLIGHTS

ON CAMPUS

- Reilly Center
- Richter Center
- Quick Arts Center
- Allegany River Trail
- The Rathskeller

OFF CAMPUS

- Ellicottville, NY (skiing, shopping)
- Old Library Restaurant
- Rock City
- Allegany State Park
- O'Deas Snow Tubing and Golf Paradise

ST. JOHN'S UNIVERSITY

Office of Admission, 8000 Utopia Pkwy., Jamaica, NY 11439 •
Telephone: 888-978-5646 • www.stjohns.edu •
Email: admhelp@stjohns.edu

Hours: Monday, 8:30AM–7:00PM; Tuesday–Thursday, 8:30AM–4:30PM; Friday, 8:30AM–3:00PM; Saturday by appointment

St. John's University is a solid, very large liberal arts institution (about 18,000 students) in Queens, New York that has a strong Catholic heritage. Besides the main campus, St. John's has additional campuses on Staten Island and in Rome, Italy. Former New York Governor Mario Cuomo is an alum.

HIGHLIGHTS

ON CAMPUS
- 100-acre Queens campus
- Magnificent new residence halls
- Famous Alumni Hall Athletics
- A handsome Staten Island campus with harbor views

OFF CAMPUS
- Major beaches and parklands
- Safe residential neighborhoods
- Manahattan is just minutes away

TRANSPORTATION

Kennedy and La Guardia Airports are 7 to 10 miles away from campus. Taxi service is available from both airports. Amtrak trains and Greyhound buses serve New York City. Public transportation is available to campus. On the subway, take the E or F train to Kew Gardens; take the Q-44A bus to Utopia Pkwy. and Union Tpke. Or take the #7 train to Main St., Flushing; then take the Q-17 bus to Utopia Pkwy. And the Long Island Expy. Transfer to the Q-30 or 31 bus to 82nd Ave. and Utopia Pkwy. From Long Island, take the Long Island Railroad to Jamaica Station; then take the Q-30 or 31 bus to 82nd Ave. and Utopia Pkwy.

FIND YOUR WAY

Take I-95 or I-80 to the George Washington Bridge. Cross the bridge and take the Cross Bronx Expressway to I-295 to the Throgs Neck Bridge. Take the Throgs Neck Bridge to the Clearview Expressway, exit at Union Tpke. and make a right, follow to Utopia Pkwy. and make a left, then a right onto campus. For directions to the Staten Island campus, please call 718-990-2000.

STAY THE NIGHT

Nearby: The nearest accommodations are at La Guardia Airport, about 15 minutes away by car. We suggest the **Holiday Inn Crowne Plaza** (104-04 Ditmars Blvd., 94th St. exit from Grand Central Pkwy.; 718-457-6300). It has an indoor pool, health club, and sauna. Rates are expensive during the week and moderate on the weekends. Consider the **Marriott La Guardia** (102-05 Ditmars Blvd., at the 94th St. exit from Grand Central Pkwy.; 718-565-8900). If you reserve and pay for your room (nonrefundable) 21 days in advance, they offer moderate room rates. In Garden City, Long Island, about 20 minutes in the other direction from St. John's, is the fancy **Garden City Hotel** (45 7th Street, Garden City; 516-747-3000 or 800-547-0400 from out of state). It is located five miles south of Northern State Pkwy. (the extension of Grand Central Pkwy.) at Exit 26. This full-service hotel is quite expensive, and on weekends breakfast is included.

A Little Farther: A 30- to 45-minute drive will take you into Manhattan. Check the Columbia entry for suggestions in uptown Manhattan (take the Triborough Bridge from the Grand Central Pkwy.). If you would prefer to be in midtown Manhattan, check the suggestions in the NYU entry.

AT A GLANCE

Selectivity Rating	68
Range SAT I Math	480–580
Average SAT I Math	535
Range SAT I Verbal	460–560
Average SAT I Verbal	516
Average GPA	3
Student to Faculty Ratio	19:1

CAMPUS TOURS

Appointment	Preferred
Dates	Year-round
Times	Please call office for times
Average Length	1 hour

ON-CAMPUS APPOINTMENTS

Admissions

Start Date–Juniors	Anytime
Appointment	Preferred
Advance Notice	Yes, 2 weeks
Saturdays	Sometimes
Average Length	1 hour
Info Sessions	Yes

Faculty and Coaches

Dates/Times	Year-round
Arrangements	Contact Admissions Office 2 weeks prior

CLASS VISITS

Dates	Academic year
Arrangements	Contact Admissions Office

ST. LAWRENCE UNIVERSITY

Payson Hall, St. Lawrence University,
Canton, NY 13617 • Telephone: 800-285-1856 • www.stlawu.edu •
Email: admissions@stlawu.edu

Hours: Monday–Friday, 8:00AM–5:00PM; Saturday, 9:00AM–4:00PM

Students at this traditional liberal arts enclave in remote, frigid, rural upstate New York get a good liberal arts education and have a darned good time. Good research resources and a strong placement rate throughout the Northeast corridor are a hit with students. The Greek system is immense and SLU's competitive Division I hockey team is also very popular.

AT A GLANCE

Selectivity Rating	85
Range SAT I Math	520–620
Average SAT I Math	570
Range SAT I Verbal	520–620
Average SAT I Verbal	570
Average ACT Composite	24
Average GPA	3.33
Student to Faculty Ratio	12:1

CAMPUS TOURS

Appointment	Preferred
Dates	Year-round
Times	Varies
Average Length	1 hour

ON-CAMPUS APPOINTMENTS

Admissions

Start Date–Juniors	Summer before senior year
Appointment	Required
Advance Notice	Yes
Saturdays	Yes
Average Length	1 hour
Info Sessions	No

Faculty and Coaches

Dates/Times	Year-round
Arrangements	Contact Admissions Office

CLASS VISITS

Dates	Academic year
Arrangements	Contact Admissions Office

TRANSPORTATION

Greyhound and Trailways buses provide service to Canton, New York. The nearest regional airport is Ogdensburg, New York, which has commuter service. The nearest large airport is Ottawa, Ontario, which is 90 minutes away. Taxi service is available in Canton.

FIND YOUR WAY

From Albany, New York Metropolitan area, western Connecticut, and Massachusetts: I-87 (the Adirondack Northway) north to exit 23, Warrensburg; Rte. 9 N. to Rte. 28 to Blue Mountain Lake; Rte. 30 N. to Tupper Lake; Rte. 3 W. to Rte. 56 N.; Rte. 56 N. to Colton; Rte. 68 to Rte. 11 on the outskirts of Canton; make a left on Rte. 11/Main Street to the traffic light at Park Street (Village Park and post office are at this intersection); make a left on Park Street and go 6/10 mile to the parking lot on the right. Payson Hall (Admissions and Financial Aid offices) are across the street. **From Syracuse, N.Y.:** I-81 N. to exit 48 north of Watertown; Rte. 342 to Rte. 11; Rte. 11 N. to Canton; follow Main Street into center of town to traffic light at Park Street and follow the above directions. **From Burlington, VT., Boston area, Rhode Island, eastern Connecticut, Massachusetts, northern New England:** I-89 N. to Exit 17, Rte. 2; and follow the signs to Grand Isle Ferry (daily, year-round); upon exiting ferry, take Rte. 314 to I-87 S. to Exit 38; Rte. 374 W. to Chateaugay; Rte. 11 S. to Malone; Rte. 11B to Potsdam; Rte. 11 to Canton, to traffic light at Park Street and follow the above directions. **From Detroit/Windsor:** Highway 401 to Prescott, Ont.; bridge to USA; Rte. 37 west one mile to Rte. 68 south to Canton; follow Main Street to the traffic light at Park Street and follow the preceding directions. **Montreal:** Highway 20/40 west to Highway 401 to Cornwall; bridge to USA, Rte. 37 W. to Massena; Rte. 56 S. to Raymondville; Rte. 310 south to Rte. 11; right on Rte. 11 into Canton, to traffic light at Park Street; follow the above directions. **Ottawa:** Highway 16/416 south to Prescott; bridge to USA; Rte. 37 W. one mile to Rte. 68 S. to Canton, to traffic light at Park Street; follow the above directions. **Toronto:** Highway 401 to Prescott, Ont.; bridge to USA; Rte. 37 W. one mile to Rte. 68 S. to Canton, to traffic light at Park Street; follow the above directions.

STAY THE NIGHT

Nearby: Your choices include the **Best Western University Inn, Comfort Suites,** and numerous bed-and-breakfast establishments. Contact Admissions for a list or check online for visitor information: www.stlawu.edu.

HIGHLIGHTS

ON CAMPUS

- Newell Field House
- Brewer Bookstore
- Brush Art Gallery
- Owen D. Young Library
- As of January 2004, we will open a new Student Center

OFF CAMPUS

- Adirondack Mountains
- Lake Placid
- Ottawa, Ontario
- Montreal, Quebec
- Thousand Islands

SARAH LAWRENCE COLLEGE

Office of Admissions, 1 Mead Way, Bronxville, NY 10708-5999 • Telephone: 800-888-2858 • www.sarahlawrence.edu • Email: slcadmit@slc.edu

Hours: Monday–Friday, 9:00AM–5:00PM; Saturday (during fall), 9:00AM–5:00PM

Sarah Lawrence College is a small, atypical, and intense school that is highly conducive to independent thought. There are no general education courses and no tests; the self-described creative, curious, open-minded, bizarre, egocentric, and melodramatic students usually take only three intensive courses per semester. Barbara Walters and Brian De Palma are notable alumni.

HIGHLIGHTS

ON CAMPUS
- Cambell Sports Center
- Communitea House
- Siegel Center
- Library
- Bates Hall

OFF CAMPUS
- The Metropolitan Museum of Art
- The Museum of Modern Art
- Broadway
- The Village
- New York Public Library

TRANSPORTATION

LaGuardia Airport is 18 miles (a 25-minute drive) from campus. Taxis are available for the trip from the airport to campus. National Mountain Line Limousine Service provides moderately priced service directly to the college from LaGuardia Airport. You must call 718-884-9400 ahead for a reservation. Cost is $21 per person, not including tip. From the airport, you can also take a bus to Grand Central Terminal in New York City. At the Ground Transportation desk by the baggage claim, purchase tickets for Gray Line Bus Service. Tickets are $13 per person, and buses depart every 20 minutes. The bus makes several stops in Manhattan, including Grand Central Terminal from which you can take a train to Bronxville. Amtrak trains and Greyhound buses serve New York City. Public transportation or taxis can take you from the Amtrak station or the Port Authority Bus Terminal to Grand Central Station. From Grand Central take the Harlem Line of the Metro North Railway to the Bronxville station. The trip takes approximately 30 minutes and trains generally leave every half-hour (check specific times at Grand Central or call 212-532-4900). Taxi service is available from the Bronxville station to the college for approximately $3 per person.

FIND YOUR WAY

Take any of the following to New York's Cross-County Pkwy.: I-87 (NY State Thruway), Henry Hudson/Saw Mill River Pkwy., Hutchinson River Pkwy., or Sprain Brook Pkwy. **From the Thruway and the Henry Hudson/Saw Mill River Pkwy.,** head east on the Cross-County Pkwy. and exit at Kimball Ave. Turn left on Kimball to the second traffic light, then turn right on Glen Washington Rd. **From the Hutchinson River and Sprain Brook Parkways,** head west on the Cross-County Pkwy. to Exit 5. Make a short right on Midland Ave. to Kimball Ave.; turn left on Kimball to the first traffic light, then turn right on Glen Washington Rd.

STAY THE NIGHT

Nearby: There are a number of choices within 30 minutes of the campus. The **Westchester Marriott** (670 White Plains Rd., Tarrytown; 914-631-2200) has nicely appointed rooms. There's also an indoor pool, a health club, and a disco on weekends. The **Holiday Inn Crown Plaza** (66 Hale Ave., White Plains; 914-682-0050) has an indoor pool, exercise room, and running track. The **Rye Town Hilton Inn** (699 Westchester Ave., Port Chester; 914-939-6300) is set on 40 wooded acres and has indoor exercise facilities, tennis courts, and two restaurants. The **Royal Regency** (165 Tuckahoe Rd., Yonkers; 914-476-6200) has a fitness room, restaurant, lounge, live entertainment, and includes a continental breakfast.

AT A GLANCE

Selectivity Rating	89
Range SAT I Math	530–650
Average SAT I Math	590
Range SAT I Verbal	610–710
Average SAT I Verbal	660
Average ACT Composite	27
Average GPA	3.6
Student to Faculty Ratio	6:1

CAMPUS TOURS

Appointment	Required
Dates	Year-round
Times	Mon–Fri, 9AM–4PM; Sat, 9AM–4PM
Average Length	1 hour

ON-CAMPUS APPOINTMENTS

Admissions

Start Date–Juniors	Spring of junior year
Appointment	Required
Advance Notice	Yes, 2 weeks
Saturdays	Sometimes
Average Length	1 hour
Info Sessions	Yes

Faculty and Coaches

Dates/Times	
Arrangements	Contact Admissions Office 2 weeks prior

CLASS VISITS

Dates	Academic year
Arrangements	One per family

SKIDMORE COLLEGE

Office of Admissions, 815 N. Broadway,
Saratoga Springs, NY 12866-1632 • Telephone: 800-867-6007 • www.skidmore.edu •
Email: admissions@skidmore.edu

Hours: Monday–Friday, 8:30AM–4:30PM; Saturday, 8:30AM–noon

With a beautiful library, great computer resources, and over 60 degree programs, Skidmore College is a competitive liberal arts college that has come a long way and continues to improve. Most students at Skidmore live on campus, which is a good thing because Skidmore's dorms are some of the most livable in the country.

AT A GLANCE

Selectivity Rating	82
Range SAT I Math	580–660
Average SAT I Math	620
Range SAT I Verbal	580–670
Average SAT I Verbal	630
Average ACT Composite	27
Average GPA	3.43
Student to Faculty Ratio	11:1

CAMPUS TOURS

Appointment	Preferred
Dates	Year-round
Times	Varies
Average Length	1 hour

ON-CAMPUS APPOINTMENTS

Admissions

Start Date–Juniors	May 1
Appointment	Required
Advance Notice	Yes, 2 weeks
Saturdays	Sometimes
Average Length	45 min.
Info Sessions	Yes

Faculty and Coaches

Dates/Times	Academic year
Arrangements	Contact Admissions Office 2 weeks prior

CLASS VISITS

Dates	Academic year
Arrangements	Contact Admissions Office

TRANSPORTATION

The Albany airport is 25 miles away from campus. Taxis, bus service, and rental cars are available for the trip from airport to campus.

FIND YOUR WAY

From I-87, take Exit 15 and turn left on New York Rte. 50 S. toward Saratoga Springs. At the third set of traffic lights, turn right on East Ave.; turn right again on North Broadway and continue about a quarter-of-a-mile to the main entrance to campus. The Admissions Office is located just beyond the main entrance and across the street.

STAY THE NIGHT

Nearby: You have some very interesting choices in Saratoga Springs, but beware. The rates skyrocket in August because of the racing season. You'll probably enjoy staying on the main drag, Broadway, where you can rub shoulders with the college students and get a good feel for the social life in Saratoga Springs. Just five minutes from the college is the **Inn at Saratoga** (231 Broadway; 518-583-1890), a historic Victorian structure with 34 rooms. Rates range from moderate to expensive and include continental breakfast. The **Adelphi Hotel** (365 Broadway; 518-587-4688), open from May through October (weekends only in May), has prices that range from moderate to very expensive. **Prime Hotel** (534 Broadway; 518-584-4000) is a good modern pick with an indoor pool, sauna, weight room, and tennis and golf privileges. Rates range from moderate to expensive. The **Holiday Inn** (232 Broadway; 518-584-5000) is another safe bet. One of the majestic old resort hotels, the **Gideon Putnam Hotel** (Saratoga Spa State Park; 518-584-3000) stands amidst 1,500 acres, with loads of activities including golf, swimming, tennis, cross-country skiing, and ice-skating. They even have mineral baths. Rates vary with the season, from moderate to expensive. There are a ton of bed-and-breakfasts. **Westchester House** (102 Lincoln Ave.; 518-587-7613) has seven guest rooms. **Eddy House** (Nelson and Crescent Aves.; 518-587-2340) has five rooms, with prices in the moderate to expensive range. **Six Sisters Bed and Breakfast** (149 Union Ave.; 518-583-1173) is 10 minutes from campus (as are the others), and the prices vary from moderate to expensive. Inexpensive accommodations can be found at the **Grand Union** (92 S. Broadway; 518-584-9000), about a mile from Skidmore.

HIGHLIGHTS

ON CAMPUS
- Tang Teaching Museum
- Lucy Scribner Library
- Case Student Center

OFF CAMPUS
- SPAC (Saratoga Performing Arts Center)
- National Museum of Dance
- NYRA (New York Racing Association) Race Course
- Saratoga National Battlefield
- National Museum of Racing and Hall of Fame

SUNY AT BINGHAMTON

Office of Undergraduate Admissions, PO Box 6001, P.O. Box 6001, Binghamton, NY 13902-6001 • Telephone: 607-777-2171 • www.binghamton.edu • Email: admit@binghamton.edu

Hours: Monday–Friday, 8:30AM–5:00PM

Binghamton University offers a top-notch education at a state school price. Pre-professional programs, most notably in psychology, accounting, and nursing, are particularly strong, and students say on-campus activities are varied and plentiful.

HIGHLIGHTS

ON CAMPUS
- Anderson Center for the Arts
- University Union
- Fitspace (East Gym)
- Nature Preserve
- Events Center
- Rosefsky Art Gallery, Summer Music Festival

OFF CAMPUS
- Cider Mill Playhouse
- Binghamton Mets Stadium
- Tri Cities Opera/Binghamton Philharmonic
- Roberson Science Center
- Ross Park Zoo
- Spiedie Fest and Balloon Rally

TRANSPORTATION

Binghamton Regional Airport (607-763-4471) is seven miles away from campus. Taxi and airport limousine service is available to campus. Contact Broome Transit (607-778-1692) for information about the county bus. Greyhound, Chenango Valley, and Short Line buses serve the area. Buses, taxis, and limousines provide service from the bus terminals to campus. Off Campus College Transport provides free bus service throughout the area.

FIND YOUR WAY

From north and south, take I-81 to NY Rte. 17 W. Pass the Binghamton exit. Take Rte. 17 W. to Exit 70 S. (Rte. 201). Follow Rte. 201 and the SUNY signs to Rte. 434 E., which runs in front of the campus. The main entrance to campus is the first right turn. **From the I-87 (NY State Thruway),** take Exit 16 (Harriman exit), which will put you on NY Rte. 17 W. Follow the preceding directions from that point.

STAY THE NIGHT

Nearby: Accommodations closest to Binghamton University include the **Holiday Inn SUNY** (4105 Vestal Pkwy. E., Vestal; 607-729-6371 or 800-465-4329), the **Howard Johnson Express Inn** (3601 Vestal Pkwy. E., Vestal; 607-729-6181 or 800-446-4656), **Courtyard Marriott** (3801 Vestal Parkway East; 607-644-1000), the **Hampton Inn** (3708 Vestal Pkwy.; 607-797-5000), and **Residence Inn by Marriott** (4610 Vestal Pkwy. E., Vestal; 607-770-8500). About 10 to 20 minutes from campus you will find the **Best Western Binghamton Regency Hotel** (1 Sarbro Sq.; 607-722-7575 or 800-528-1234), **Best Western of Johnson City** (569 Harry L Drive, Johnson City; 607-729-9194 or 800-528-1234), **Comfort Inn** (1156 Front Street; 607-722-5353, 800-228-5150), and **Days Inn Motel** (1000 Front Street; 607-724-3297, 800-329-7466).

A Little Farther: Check the Alfred University entry for suggestions in Corning, to the west of Binghamton. Check the Cornell University entry for suggestions in and around Ithaca, which is to the northwest of Binghamton.

AT A GLANCE

Selectivity Rating	89
Range SAT I Math	590–690
Average SAT I Math	637
Range SAT I Verbal	550–640
Average SAT I Verbal	599
Average ACT Composite	26
Average GPA	3.6
Student to Faculty Ratio	21:1

CAMPUS TOURS

Appointment	Preferred
Dates	Year-round
Times	Mon–Sat, noon;
	Summer: Mon–Fri, noon
Average Length	120 min.

ON-CAMPUS APPOINTMENTS

Admissions

Start Date–Juniors	N/A
Info Sessions	Yes

Faculty and Coaches

Arrangements	Contact coach directly

SUNY AT BUFFALO

Office of Admissions, 17 Capen Hall, Box 601660,
Buffalo, NY 14260 • Telephone: 888-822-3648 • www.buffalo.edu •
Email: ub-admissions@buffalo.edu

Hours: Monday–Friday, 8:30AM–5:00PM; Saturday, 1:00PM, but call first.

University at Buffalo, as this SUNY school is calling itself these days, offers an excellent education in just about anything. Engineering, business, and pre-med are the major draws, but other disciplines (especially communications and the liberal arts and sciences) also offer competitive programs, and the library, research, and recreational facilities are all very impressive.

AT A GLANCE

Selectivity Rating	81
Range SAT I Math	520–630
Average SAT I Math	589
Range SAT I Verbal	500–600
Average SAT I Verbal	566
Average ACT Composite	29
Average GPA	3.1
Student to Faculty Ratio	14:1

CAMPUS TOURS

Appointment	Required
Dates	Varies
Times	Mon–Fri, 1PM; selected Sats

ON-CAMPUS APPOINTMENTS

Admissions

Start Date—Juniors	Anytime
Appointment	Required
Advance Notice	Yes, 2 weeks
Saturdays	No

Faculty and Coaches

Arrangements	Contact Admissions Office

CLASS VISITS

Dates	Varies
Arrangements	Contact faculty directly

TRANSPORTATION

Greater Buffalo International Airport is 20 minutes from campus. Taxis and buses are available for the trip from the airport to campus. The taxis can be picked up at the airport; for bus departure times and routes call 800-231-2222. Amtrak trains and Greyhound buses provide service to Buffalo.

FIND YOUR WAY

To reach the North Campus from the New York State Thruway (I-90), take Exit 50 to I-290 (Youngmann Memorial Hwy.). Take I-290 west to Exit 4 (I-990 North) and follow signs for State University (exit 1). Exit 1 will bring you to the Audubon Pkwy. Make the first U-turn (just before the traffic light), then get into the right lane. Turn right at the first exit (White Rd.). The Fronczak Lot (long-term parking, accessed through the Governors A Lot) and Hamilton Loop (short-term parking) will be on your right. The South Campus is located at the corner of State Routes 5 (Main St.) and 62 (Bailey Ave.). **From the New York State Thruway (I-90),** take Exit 50 to I-290, then Rte. 5 west, to Rte. 62. Directions are available online at Web: www.buffalo.edu.

STAY THE NIGHT

Nearby: University at Buffalo has two campuses: north and south. The Admissions Office and the majority of undergraduate academic departments are on the north campus. The south campus houses the School of Architecture and Planning, the School of Health Related Professions, and the School of Medicine and Biomedical Sciences. Because Buffalo is the second-largest city in the state, there are many nationally affiliated hotels and motels in the metropolitan area, including more than 20 close to the university. Those nearest include the **Marriott, Hampton Inn, Motel 6, Red Roof Inn, Residence Inn, Super 8 Motel, University Inn and Conference Center, Extended Stay America, Holiday Inn, Microtel, Sleep Inn,** and **Courtyard.** Airport area hotels include the **Comfort Suites, Days Inn, Fairfield Inn, Holiday Inn, Quality Inn, Radisson Hotel,** and **Sheraton Inn.** Popular downtown hotels are **Adam's Mark, Hyatt Regency,** and **Radisson.** To obtain a special UB discount on selected hotels, call NFT Travel at 1-800-633-6782; mention the code UB LOOK. Area maps and a list of accommodations and restaurants are available on our website at www.buffalo.edu.

HIGHLIGHTS

ON CAMPUS
- Center for the Arts
- Alumni Arena and Athletic Stadium
- Center for Computational Research
- Apartment-style student housing (new)
- The Commons (on-campus shopping)

OFF CAMPUS
- Major league sports
- Shea's Theater
- Niagra Falls
- Albright-Knox Art Gallery
- Buffalo Philharmonic Orchestra

SYRACUSE UNIVERSITY

Office of Admissions, 201 Tolley Administration Building, Syracuse, NY 13244 • Telephone: 315-443-3611 • www.syracuse.edu • Email: orange@syr.edu

Hours: Monday–Friday, 8:30AM–5:00PM; Summer, 8:00AM–4:30PM; select Saturdays

Syracuse University in upstate New York is probably best known for its outstanding school of communications, which includes one of the nation's top broadcast journalism programs (Ted Koppel is an alum). Those programs are excellent, but this large, private, and very challenging institution also offers a wide variety of academic and social opportunities.

HIGHLIGHTS

ON CAMPUS
- Schine Student Center
- Lowe Art Gallery
- Archbold Ahtletic Complex
- Carrier Dome
- Bird Library

OFF CAMPUS
- Marshall Street shopping area
- Armory Square
- Everson Museum of Art
- Carousel Center Mall & Theaters
- Finger Lakes recreational region

TRANSPORTATION

Syracuse-Hancock International Airport is six miles away from campus. Taxis, limousines, and rental cars are available at the airport for the trip to campus. Arrangements can be made on arrival at the airport. Syracuse is served by Amtrak trains and Greyhound buses; taxis are available for the ride from the stations to campus.

FIND YOUR WAY

Northbound and Southbound travelers on I-81 should exit at Adams Street (Exit 18). Proceed one block up the Adams Street hill to Irving Avenue. Turn right onto Irving Avenue and continue through the two traffic lights. At the end of Irving Avenue, by the Carrier Dome, turn right onto E. Raynor Ave. Proceed one block then turn right onto Stadium Place. Turn right into Irving Garage (the first parking garage entrance). Look for the Admissions Office Visitor parking sign. Please park on the fourth or fifth level of Irving Garage to be closer to the Pedestrian Bridge (located on the fifth floor of the Irving Garage) to cross over Irving Avenue. Follow the walkway to the left (the College of Law will be on your right.) Take the stairs to the College of Law plaza and continue on the left sidewalk (Eggers Hall will be on your left) toward Hendricks Chapel. Turn the corner and proceed to the rear entrance of the Tolley Administration Building. Proceed to the Office of Admissions, which is in room 201.

STAY THE NIGHT

Nearby: **Sheraton University Hotel** (800-395-2105) is right on campus. Three other possibilities near campus include the **Genesee Inn Golden Tulip & Executive Quarters** (1060 E. Genesee St.; 800-365-4663), about five blocks away; the **Hawthorn Suites Hotel** at Armory Square (416 S. Clinton Street, Syracuse; 800-527-1133); 3); and the **Marx Hotel & Conference Center** (701 East Genesee St., Syracuse; 877-843-6279). Twenty minutes northeast of campus (Thruway exit 35, Carrier Circle) you can find several hotels and motels, including **Candlewood Suites** (800-946-6200), **Courtyard by Marriott** (800-205-6520), **Crest Hill Suites** (888-723-1655), **Embassy Suites** (800-362-2779), **Fairfield Inn by Marriott** (800-228-2800), the **Hampton Inn** (800-426-7866), **Holiday Inn Carrier Circle** (800-465-4329), and the **Wyndham Hotel** (800-782-9847).

AT A GLANCE

Selectivity Rating	87
Range SAT I Math	570–660
Range SAT I Verbal	550–640
Average GPA	3.5
Student to Faculty Ratio	12:1

CAMPUS TOURS

Appointment	Required
Dates	Year-round
Times	Mon–Fri, varies; selected Saturdays
Average Length	1 hour

ON-CAMPUS APPOINTMENTS

Admissions

Start Date–Juniors	Juniors are not interviewed.
Appointment	Preferred
Advance Notice	Yes, 1 week
Saturdays	No
Average Length	30 min.
Info Sessions	Yes

Faculty and Coaches

Dates/Times	Year-round
Arrangements	Contact Admissions Office 1 week

CLASS VISITS

Dates	Academic year
Arrangements	Contact Admissions Office

UNION COLLEGE

Admissions Office, Grant Hall,
Schenectady, NY 12308 • Telephone: 888-843-6688 • www.union.edu •
Email: admissions@union.edu

Hours: Monday–Friday, 8:00AM–5:00PM; Summer, 8:00AM–4:30PM; Saturday (during academic year), 10:00AM–1:00PM

Union College provides rigorous liberal arts, science, and engineering programs that cater to the individual paths of over 2,000 students. The campus, which is located about three hours away from New York City in Schenectady, is the nation's first to be architecturally designed. Entertainment ranges from the Adventurers gaming club, to an annual beach volleyball tournament.

AT A GLANCE

Selectivity Rating	90
Range SAT I Math	590–680
Average SAT I Math	630
Range SAT I Verbal	550–650
Average SAT I Verbal	610
Average GPA	3.49
Student to Faculty Ratio	11:1

CAMPUS TOURS

Appointment	Not required
Dates	Year-round
Times	Mon–Fri, 10AM–3PM, on the hour
Average Length	1 hour

ON-CAMPUS APPOINTMENTS

Admissions

Start Date—Juniors	May 1
Appointment	Required
Advance Notice	Yes, 2 weeks
Saturdays	Sometimes
Average Length	1 hour
Info Sessions	Yes

Faculty and Coaches

Dates/Times	Year-round
Arrangements	Contact Admissions Office 2 weeks prior

CLASS VISITS

Dates	Year-round
Arrangements	Contact Admissions Office

TRANSPORTATION

The Albany Airport is 10 miles away from campus. Taxis are available at the airport for the ride to campus. The Schenectady Amtrak rail and Trailways bus stations are each a mile from campus. Taxi service is available.

FIND YOUR WAY

Coming from any direction, take Exit 24 of the New York State Thruway to Rte. 87 (The Northway). Take Rte. 87 to Exit 6 (Rte. 7 W.) and drive west toward Schenectady for approximately six miles. Make a right at Union St. and proceed for approximately two miles through eight traffic lights. The college will appear on the right. Turn and follow the signs to the Admissions Office, which will be the third building on the right.

STAY THE NIGHT

Nearby: There are two chain motels within walking distance of campus. One with special inexpensive rates for Union visitors is the **Days Inn** (167 Nott Terrace; 518-370-3297 or 800-325-2525). The **Holiday Inn** (100 Nott Terrace; 518-393-4141 or 800-HOLIDAY), with rates in the moderate range, has an indoor pool and is three blocks away from campus. For nearby bed-and-breakfast accommodations, call the American Country Collection at 518-370-4948 from 10:00 AM to noon and from 1:00 PM to 5:00 PM, Mondays through Fridays, or write to them at 1353 Union St., Schenectady, NY 12309. The **Glen Sanders Mansion** (518-374-7262) offers elegant accommodations right on the Mohawk River, three miles away from campus.

A Little Farther: **Microtel** (7 Rensselaer Avenue; 518-782-9161 or 1-800-782-9121, within 12 miles of campus), **Hampton Inn** (981 New Loudon Road; 518-785-0000, within 14 miles of campus) and **Marriott Residence Inn** (One Residence Inn Dr.; 518-783-0600, within seven miles of campus) are in Latham, NY. The **Holiday Inn Turf** (205 Wolf Road; 518-458-7250 within 12 miles of campus), **Best Western Albany** (200 Wolf Road; 518-458-1000, within one mile of campus), **Albany Marriott Hotel** (189 Wolf Road; 518-458-8444, within 12 miles of campus), and the **Desmond** (660 Albany-Shaker Road; 518-869-8100, within 12 miles of campus) are near Albany Airport. For a more extensive list of accomodations, see the Union website, www.union.edu/Visitor_Center/lodging.php.

HIGHLIGHTS

ON CAMPUS

- The Nott Memorial, a national historic monument
- Schaffer Library
- Reamer Campus Center
- Jackson's Garden
- Memorial Chapel

OFF CAMPUS

- Proctor's Theatre
- Jay Street area
- Pepsi Arena
- Crossgates Mall
- Plotterkill Nature Preserve

10, 11, 12, 1, 2, 3

UNITED STATES MILITARY ACADEMY

606 Thayer Rd.,
West Point, NY 10996-1797 • Telephone: 845-938-4041 • www.usma.edu •
Email: 8dad@exmail.usma.army.mil

Hours: Monday–Friday, 7:30AM–4:00PM; Saturday, 8:00AM–noon

Better known as West Point, the United States Military Academy provides an excellent education in the arts and sciences. Students get to use live ammunition. Training ranges from the liberal arts to engineering to mountain warfare in Vermont to winter warfare in Alaska.

HIGHLIGHTS

ON CAMPUS
• Cadet Chapel
• West Point Museum

OFF CAMPUS
• Bear Mountain State Park
• Hudson River
• Hyde Park

TRANSPORTATION

Stewart Airport in Newburgh is 20 miles away from the academy. Rental cars and taxis are available at the airport for the trip to West Point.

FIND YOUR WAY

The main highways leading to the academy are U.S. Rte. 9W and the Palisades Interstate Pkwy.; a more scenic route is NY State Rte. 218. From these roads, follow the signs to West Point and the academy.

STAY THE NIGHT

Nearby: **Hotel Thayer** is on campus (914-446-4731) overlooking the majestic Hudson River, and has moderate rates. Within a couple of miles of West Point are the **U.S. Academy Motel** (Rte. 218, Highland Falls; 914-446-2021) and the **Best Western Palisades Motel** (Rtes. 218 and 94, Highland Falls; 914-446-9400), which are inexpensive. By far the most interesting choice is **Bear Mountain Inn** (Bear Mountain State Park, Bear Mountain; 914-786-2731), a 1920 lodge with a lovely view of the Hudson, an outdoor pool, a gift shop, a restaurant, and hiking trails. Rates are moderate on the weekend and at the top of the inexpensive range during the week.

A Little Farther: Cold Spring is 20 miles away from West Point. **Pig Hill Bed and Breakfast** (73 Main St.; 914-265-9247) has eight rooms in its 1850s brick building. Some have fireplaces and four-poster and canopy beds. Rates vary from moderate to expensive and include a full breakfast. See the Vassar College entry for another suggestion in Cold Spring and for suggestions in Poughkeepsie (about 30 miles away from West Point).

AT A GLANCE	

Selectivity Rating	99
Range SAT I Math	600–690
Average SAT I Math	641
Range SAT I Verbal	570–660
Average SAT I Verbal	627
Average ACT Composite	28
Average GPA	3.67
Student to Faculty Ratio	7:1

CAMPUS TOURS	
Appointment	Required
Dates	Varies
Times	Mon–Fri, beginning at 9AM
Average Length	Varies

ON-CAMPUS APPOINTMENTS	
Admissions	
Start Date–Juniors	Spring of junior year
Appointment	Required
Advance Notice	Yes, 3 weeks
Saturdays	Yes
Info Sessions	Available as part of tour
Faculty and Coaches	
Dates/Times	Year-round
Arrangements	Contact Admissions Office

CLASS VISITS	
Dates	Year-round
Arrangements	Contact Admissions Office

UNIVERSITY OF ROCHESTER

Admissions Office,
Rochester, NY 14627-0251 • Telephone: 888-822-2256 • www.rochester.edu •
Email: admit@admissions.rochester.edu

Hours: Monday–Friday, 8:30AM–5:00PM; select Saturdays

The tough but extremely rewarding University of Rochester has traditionally been best known for math and science, but the home of the Bausch & Lomb scholars and Xerox has enough diversity in its academic offerings to dispel the myth that the school is solely an engineering/pre-med breeding ground. Take Five is a program for students who find themselves unable to fit enough courses of interest into a four-year schedule.

AT A GLANCE

Selectivity Rating	88
Range SAT I Math	620–710
Average SAT I Math	687
Range SAT I Verbal	600–700
Average SAT I Verbal	665
Average ACT Composite	30
Student to Faculty Ratio	8:1

CAMPUS TOURS

Appointment	Required
Dates	Year-round
Times	Mon–Fri, call Admissions for times
Average Length	1 hour

ON-CAMPUS APPOINTMENTS

Admissions

Start Date—Juniors	N/A
Info Sessions	N/A

Faculty and Coaches

Dates/Times	Year-round
Arrangements	Contact Admissions Office 2 weeks prior

CLASS VISITS

Dates	Acadmic Year
Arrangements	Contact Admissions Office

TRANSPORTATION

Greater Rochester International Airport is two miles away from campus. Taxis are available at the airport for the drive to campus. Amtrak trains and Greyhound buses serve Rochester; their stations are close to municipal bus lines that serve the university's River Campus.

FIND YOUR WAY

From the east, take I-90 to Exit 46; then take I-390 N. to Exit 17. Turn left onto Scottsville Rd., bear right onto Elmwood Ave. and cross the Genesee River bridge. Turn left onto Wilson Blvd. and proceed to the information booth for parking instructions and directions. **From the south,** take I-390 N. to Exit 17 and proceed as above. **From the west,** take the I-90 to Exit 47, then take I-490 E. to I-390 S. Leave I-390 at Exit 17 and proceed as above.

STAY THE NIGHT

Nearby: One mile away from campus you will find a cheerful, turn-of-the-century bed-and-breakfast that's popular with university visitors called the **428 Mount Vernon** (716-271-0792). It's on the edge of Highland Park, and if you're in good shape, it's a beautiful hike to the Admissions Office. Other lodgings include the **Hampton Inn** (717 E. Henrietta Rd.; 716-272-7800 or 800-HAMPTON), **Days Inn** (4853 W. Henrietta Rd.; 716-334-9300 or 800-329-7466), **Courtyard by Marriott** (33 Corporate Woods; 716-292-1000); **Hyatt Regency Rochester** (125 E. Main St.; 716-546-1234), and the **Marriott Thruway** (5257 W. Henrietta Rd.; 716-359-1800). All are within 15 minutes of campus.

HIGHLIGHTS

ON CAMPUS

- Eastman Theater
- Memorial Art Gallery
- Rush Rhees Library
- Interfaith Chapel
- Robert B. Goergen Athletic Center

OFF CAMPUS

- Niagra Falls
- Museum of Photography and Film
- Rochester Museum and Science Center
- Susan B. Anthony House
- Park Avenue neighborhood

VASSAR COLLEGE

Admissions Office, 124 Raymond Ave.,
Poughkeepsie, NY 12604 • Telephone: 800-827-7270 • www.vassar.edu •
Email: admissions@vassar.edu

Hours: Monday–Friday, 8:30AM–5:00PM; Saturday (some fall and spring)

There are no core requirements at Vassar College, a small liberal arts school not terribly far from New York City. A first-year student's courseload can include anything from ancient Chinese philosophy to a techno-lit English class using the Internet. Over four years, Vassar students design their own majors and pursue interdisciplinary studies. Actress Meryl Streep is an alum.

HIGHLIGHTS

ON CAMPUS

- Library
- Shakespeare Garden
- Observatory
- Frances Lehman Loeb Art Center
- Center for Drama and Film

OFF CAMPUS

- Franklin Roosevelt House and Museum
- Eleanor Roosevelt House
- Vanderbilt Mansion
- Rhinebeck
- Mills Mansion

TRANSPORTATION

Stewart Airport in Newburgh is 20 miles away from campus. Taxis are available for the trip from the airport to campus.

FIND YOUR WAY

From the New York State Thruway, use Exit 17 (Newburgh) and take I-84 eastbound across the Newburgh-Beacon Bridge to Route 9 north. Follow the directions below. **From Route 9 northbound,** drive 9.5 miles north of the intersection of I-84 and Route 9, and exit on Spackenhill Road (Route 113). The IBM main facility is on the left. Proceed about half a mile on Spackenhill Road. Turn left at the second traffic light onto Wilbur Boulevard. Turn right when Wilbur ends at Hooker Avenue. Turn left at the first traffic light onto Raymond Avenue. Enter the college through the stone archway on the right. **From Route 9 southbound,** exit at Spackenhill Road (Route 113) and follow the directions above.

STAY THE NIGHT

Nearby: **Inn at the Falls** (50 Red Oaks Mill Rd.; 845-462-5770), a luxurious country place beautifully situated on the river, is about 10 minutes away from campus. A simple motel, **Best Inn** (62 Haight Ave.; 845-454-1010), is two blocks away from the college; rates are inexpensive. There is a **Sheraton Hotel** (40 Civic Center Plaza; 845-485-5300) less than a 15 minutes away, with a special rate in the moderate range for college visitors. The hotel has a well-equipped exercise room and steam room, as well as comedy club entertainment.

A Little Farther: Why not visit the quaint, historic town of Cold Spring? **Hudson House** (845-265-9355), the second oldest inn in New York State, is right on the river, which you can see from some of the rooms. Rates, which include a continental breakfast, vary from moderate to expensive. See the United States Military Academy entry for another Cold Spring suggestion.

AT A GLANCE

Selectivity Rating	94
Range SAT I Math	630–700
Average SAT I Math	664
Range SAT I Verbal	640–730
Average SAT I Verbal	686
Student to Faculty Ratio	9:1

CAMPUS TOURS

Appointment	Not required
Dates	Year-round
Times	Mon–Fri, 11:30AM & 2PM; Fall and Summer: Mon–Fri, 9AM, 11:30AM, & 2PM
Average Length	1 hour

ON-CAMPUS APPOINTMENTS

Admissions

Start Date–Juniors	N/A

Faculty and Coaches

Dates/Times	Academic year
Arrangements	Contact coach directly

CLASS VISITS

Dates	Academic year
Arrangements	Contact faculty directly

WELLS COLLEGE

Office of Admissions, 170 Main Street,
Aurora, NY 13026 • Telephone: 800-952-9355 • www.wells.edu •
Email: admissions@wells.edu

Hours: Monday–Friday, 8:30AM–4:30PM

It's like one big, happy family at tiny, isolated, all-women's Wells College in the far reaches of upstate New York, where students revel in discussion-oriented classes, traditional liberal arts education, sisterhood, and dozens of traditions, including campus serenades.

TRANSPORTATION

There are airports in Ithaca (Tompkins-Cortland Regional), Syracuse (Hancock Field), and Rochester (Rochester International). Flights on US Air arrive in Ithaca from major cities of the northeast. Both Syracuse and Rocheser, each approximately one hour from campus, are served by the nation's major airlines and have direct flights and connections everwhere in the United States and abroad. Through the Admissions Office, visitors to Wells can arrange for transportation to campus from any of these airports (there is a fee for this service). Visitors traveling by train will arrive in Syracuse. Visitors traveling by bus will arrive in Ithaca. The college van can be scheduled to pick up and bring visitors to campus (there is a fee for this service).

FIND YOUR WAY

Aurora is located on the eastern shore of Cayuga Lake in Cetral New York. The New York State Thruway (Interstate Rte. 90) is 25 to the north. Rte. 17 (the Southern Tier Expressway and the future I-86) is approximately 50 miles to the south. **From New York City and Long Island:** Follow I-87 N. to Rte. 17 at exit 16 in Harriman. Take 17 W. to I-81 N. in Binghamton. Take I-81 to Homer exit (#12); make a right at the end of the exit ramp onto Rte. 281 N., and soon after that, make a left onto Rte. 90 and take it local to Aurora (approximately 40 miles). **From the New York State Thruway and traveling west:** Exit at weedsprot (#40); make a right onto Rte. 34 S. to Auburn; make a right onto Rtes. 5 & 20 W. and a left onto Rte. 326 to the village of Union Springs; turn left on local Rte. 90 to Aurora. **From New Jersey:** Follow I-80 W. to I-380 W. to Scranton, PA. Follow I-380 W. to I-81 N. to Binghamton. Take I-81 to the Homer exit (#12), and follow the directions from New York City and Long Island. **From Massachussetts and points in New England:** Follow the Massachussetts Turnpike (I-90) west into New York State. Continue on I-90 (which turns into the New York State Thruway) in New York to exit 40 (Weedsport). Make a right onto Rte. 34 S to Auburn; make a righ onto Rte.s 5 & 20 west and a left onto Rte. 326 to the village of Union Springs; turn left on local Rte. 90 to Aurora. **From Maryland/DC and southern states:** Follow I-95 N. to I-695 around Baltimore. Take I-83 N. to Harrisburg, PA. In Harrisburg, exit from I-83 to I-81 N. Take I-81 north to the Homer exit (#12) and follow the directions from New York City and Long Island.

STAY THE NIGHT

Nearby: Choices include the **Aurora Inn** (315-364-8888) and **Wells College Guest Housing** (315-364-3399). Just a few miles away from campus are the **Holiday Inn** (315-253-4531), **Microtel Inn & Suites** (315-253-5000), and **Springside Inn** (315-252-7247).

A Little Farther: Approximately 25 miles away from campus you will find the **Best Western** (607-272-6100), the **Holiday Inn** (607-272-6100), the **Ramada Inn** (607-257-3100), and **LaTourelle Country** (607-273-2734).

HIGHLIGHTS

ON CAMPUS

- Sommer Center
- Boat House
- Schwartz Student Union
- Macmillan Hall
- Main Building

OFF CAMPUS

- Mackenzie-Childs
- Ithaca Commons
- Pyramid Mall
- Cayuga Lake
- Cornell University

1- Davidson College
2- Duke University
   UNC—Chapel Hill
3- Guilford College
4- Wake Forest University
5- UNC-Asheville

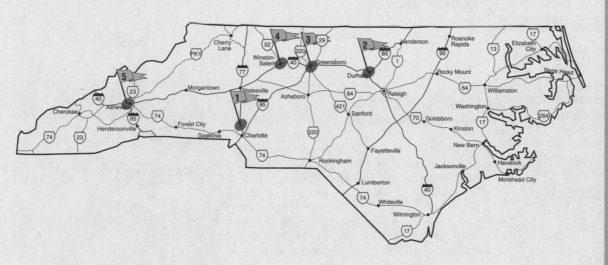

North Carolina	Davidson Coll.	Duke Univ.	Guilford Coll.	UNC-Asheville	UNC-Chapel Hill	Wake Forest Univ.	*Charlotte*	*Raleigh*
Davidson Coll.	—	135	80	129	129	62	18	144
Duke Univ.	135	—	58	13	13	84	144	20
Guilford Coll.	80	58	—	54	54	25	99	74
UNC-Asheville	129	227	168	—	228	146	132	252
UNC-Chapel Hill	129	13	54	228	—	78	142	28
Wake Forest Univ.	62	84	25	146	78	—	80	104
Charlotte	18	144	99	132	142	80	—	169
Raleigh	144	20	74	252	28	104	169	—

DAVIDSON COLLEGE

Admissions Office, P.O. Box 7156,
Davidson, NC 28035-1719 • Telephone: 800-768-0380 • www.davidson.edu •
Email: admission@davidson.edu

Hours: Monday–Friday, 8:30AM–5:00PM; select Saturdays during fall and spring, 10:00AM–2:00PM

According to students on Davidson's beautiful wooded campus, almost every conversation either begins or ends with a description of all the work students have to do and how no one will ever be able to get it done. Professors at this excellent liberal arts school push students pretty hard, but they are incredible teachers with a great deal of enthusiasm for their subjects. Self-scheduled exams diminish the academic stress to some extent.

AT A GLANCE

Selectivity Rating	97
Range SAT I Math	640–720
Average SAT I Math	656
Range SAT I Verbal	640–720
Average SAT I Verbal	659
Average ACT Composite	28
Student to Faculty Ratio	11:1

CAMPUS TOURS

Appointment	Preferred
Dates	Year-round
Times	Varies
Average Length	1 hour

ON-CAMPUS APPOINTMENTS

Admissions

Appointment	Preferred
Advance Notice	Yes, 2 weeks
Saturdays	Sometimes
Info Sessions	Yes

Faculty and Coaches

Arrangements	Contact Admissions Office 2 weeks prior

CLASS VISITS

Dates	Academic year
Arrangements	Contact Admissions Office

TRANSPORTATION

Douglas International Airport in Charlotte is 25 miles away from campus. Amtrak trains and Greyhound/Trailways buses serve Charlotte. Taxis are available for the ride from the airport and stations.

FIND YOUR WAY

From I-77, take Exit 30 and proceed east a quarter mile to the traffic light. The campus is immediately ahead, and parking is to the left. **From I-85,** take Exit 55 to Rte. 73 W. Proceed west for eight miles into Mecklenburg County. At the sign to Davidson, turn right onto Davidson-Concord Rd. Proceed three miles to a stop sign and turn left into town. At the stoplight, turn right. Proceed to the next light and look for the designated parking area.

STAY THE NIGHT

Nearby: Your best bet is **Davidson College Guesthouse** (704-892-2127), an on-campus establishment that offers eight rooms and continental breakfast for an inexpensive rate. You can use the college's sports facilities and dine on campus at the Vail Commons and Union Cafe. In Davidson, **The Village Inn** (704-892-8044) is a small inn that serves breakfast and afternoon tea. In Cornelius, the Best Western (704-896-0660) has continental breakfast, an outdoor pool, and a fitness room. Four basic choices within a five-minute drive are the **Comfort Inn** (20740 Torrance Chapel Rd.; 704-892-3500) where the inexpensive rate (special for college visitors) includes breakfast. Some rooms even have jacuzzis, and there's a fully equipped Nautilus club across the street. **Hampton Inn** (19501 Statesville Rd.; 704-892-9900) offers a complimentary continental breakfast. **Holiday Inn** (19901 Holiday Lane, Cornelius; 704-892-9120) has an outdoor pool, Jacuzzis in some of the rooms, and a Nautilus center nearby.

A Little Farther: There's a charming bed-and-breakfast in Charlotte called the **Home Place** (5901 Sardis Rd.; 704-365-1936); it's a restored Victorian with a big porch and three guest rooms.

HIGHLIGHTS

ON CAMPUS

• Belk Visual Arts Center

OFF CAMPUS

• Lake Norman
• Botanical Garden
• Mint Museum
• Afro-American Cultural Center
• Museum of the New South

DUKE UNIVERSITY

Office of Undergraduate Admissions, 2138 Campus Dr., Box 90588, Durham, NC 27708 • Telephone: 919-684-3214 • www.duke.edu • Email: undergrad-admissions@duke.edu

Hours: Monday–Friday, 8:30AM–5:00PM; Saturday, 9:00AM–1:00PM

The intellectual, yet cool, fun, and relaxed students at prestigious and extremely competitive Duke University don't much like the way the administration is trying to turn this place into Harvard because according to them, Duke is a better place to go to college. Duke students continue to find release in the incredible academics and their first love, Blue Devils basketball.

HIGHLIGHTS

ON CAMPUS
- Duke Chapel
- Primate Center
- Sarah P. Duke Gardens
- Duke Forest
- Levine Science Research Center

OFF CAMPUS
- Duke Homestead
- N.C. Museum of Life and Science
- Durham Bulls Athletic Park
- Ninth Street
- Southpointe Mall

TRANSPORTATION

The Raleigh-Durham International Airport is 18 miles away from campus. Limousines, taxis, and rental cars are available at the airport. Amtrak trains serve Raleigh and Durham. You must make your own arrangements for transportation from there to campus. Greyhound bus service is available to Durham, approximately three miles away from campus. Taxis are available at the station.

FIND YOUR WAY

From I-40 (from Raleigh and the airport), bear right onto Durham Freeway north (NC Rte. 147); continue into Durham and exit at Swift Ave./Duke University-East Campus. Turn left at the top of the ramp; turn right at the flashing light (Campus Dr.). Proceed for one mile to the Admissions Office; the driveway is to the right as you approach the traffic circle. **From I-85 S.,** take the exit for 15-501 S. Bypass-Duke University/Chapel Hill; proceed for two miles and exit at the sign for NC 751/Duke University. Turn left on Rte. 751 and go one mile to the fourth stoplight; turn left onto Duke University Rd. and continue for one mile. Turn left onto Chapel Dr. at the stone pillars. At the circle, turn right onto Campus Dr.; the Admissions Office is the first building on the left. **From I-85 N.,** exit onto Rte. 70 E. at the sign to NC 751/Duke University. Proceed on Rte. 70 for two miles to the intersection with Rte. 751; turn right onto Rte. 751 for approximately four-and-a-half miles. Turn left at the fifth stoplight (Duke University Rd.), and proceed for one mile; turn left onto Chapel Dr. at the stone pillars. At the circle, turn right onto Campus Dr.; the Admissions Office is the first building on the left.

STAY THE NIGHT

Nearby: The **Millennium Hotel-Durham** (2800 Campus Walk Ave.; 800-633-5379) and the **Durham Hilton** (3800 Hillsborough Rd.; 919-383-8033 or 800-445-8667) are a short drive from campus. The inexpensive **Brookwood Inn** (2306 Elba St.; 919-286-3111 or 800-716-6401) is across the street from the university hospital and has a shuttle to campus. The **Washington Duke Inn and Golf Club** (3001 Cameron Blvd.; 919-490-0999 or 800-443-3853) is conveniently located near campus. The inn has a golf course, tennis and swimming facilities nearby. A complimentary shuttle service is available within the city of Durham.

A Little Farther: Several bed-and-breakfast inns are also in Durham, not too far from campus, including **Arrowhead Inn Bed and Breakfast** (106 Mason Rd., Durham; 919-477-8430), **Morehead Manor** (914 Vickers Ave.; 919-687-4366 or 888-437-6333), and **Old North Durham Inn** (922 North Mangum St.; 919-683-1885).

AT A GLANCE

Selectivity Rating	98
Range SAT I Math	670–770
Range SAT I Verbal	650–740
Average ACT Composite	30
Average GPA	3.85
Student to Faculty Ratio	11:1

CAMPUS TOURS

Appointment	Not required
Dates	Year-round
Times	Varies throughout the year (see website)
Average Length	1 hour

ON-CAMPUS APPOINTMENTS

Admissions

Start Date–Juniors	June 1, between junior and senior years
Appointment	Required
Advance Notice	Yes
Saturdays	No
Average Length	30 min.
Info Sessions	Yes

Faculty and Coaches

Arrangements	Contact coach directly

CLASS VISITS

Dates	Year-round
Arrangements	Contact Admissions Office

GUILFORD COLLEGE

Admissions Office, 5800 W. Friendly Avenue,
Greensboro, NC 27410 • Telephone: 800-992-7759 • www.guilford.edu •
Email: admission@guilford.edu

Hours: Monday–Friday, 8:30AM–5:00PM; Saturday, call for appointment

Guilford College is an intimate, Quaker-affiliated liberal arts college where students have a real say and responsibility in the running of the school. Professors and the administration receive high marks.

AT A GLANCE

Selectivity Rating	73
Range SAT I Math	490–620
Average SAT I Math	550
Range SAT I Verbal	500–640
Average SAT I Verbal	570
Average ACT Composite	25
Average GPA	2.95
Student to Faculty Ratio	15:1

CAMPUS TOURS

Appointment	Preferred
Dates	Year-round
Times	Mon–Fri, 10AM & 2PM; Sat, 11AM
Average Length	1 hour

ON-CAMPUS APPOINTMENTS

Admissions

Start Date–Juniors	August 1 of junior year
Appointment	Preferred
Advance Notice	Yes, 1 week
Saturdays	Yes
Average Length	1 hour
Info Sessions	Yes

Faculty and Coaches

Dates/Times	Academic year
Arrangements	Contact Admissions Office 1 week prior

CLASS VISITS

Dates	Academic year
Arrangements	Contact Admissions Office

TRANSPORTATION

The Triad Piedmont International Airport in Greensboro is five miles away from campus. A shuttle is available at the airport. Amtrak is also located near downtown Greensboro.

FIND YOUR WAY

From I-40 or I-85, exit to Holden Road N. Follow Holden Rd. to Friendly Ave., and turn left (west) to the college.

STAY THE NIGHT

Nearby: For an inexpensive stay about five minutes away, try the **Innkeeper** (336-854-0090), and for a moderately priced place about two miles away, try the **Greensboro Courtyard by Marriott** (4400 W. Wendover Ave.; 336-294-3800). If you want to treat yourselves, however, you won't want to miss the newly opened **O. Henry Hotel,** about 10 minutes east of Guilford, near the Friendly Shopping Center. The rooms are luxurious and the service is impeccable. Be sure to ask for their Guilford College rate, which includes a wonderful breakfast buffet.

HIGHLIGHTS

ON CAMPUS
• The Art Gallery
• Hege Library
• Frank Family Science Center
• Founders Student Center

OFF CAMPUS
• Greensboro Historical Museum
• Guilford Battleground Park
• Old Salem

UNIVERSITY OF NORTH CAROLINA—ASHEVILLE

CPO #2210, 117 Lipinsky Hall,
Asheville, NC 28804-8510 • Telephone: 800-531-9842 • www.unca.edu •
Email: admissions@unca.edu

Hours: 8:30AM–5:00PM; some Saturdays, 11:00AM–1:00PM

Students at the University of North Carolina at Asheville say their school that's tucked away in the mountains is not just the next best thing compared to a small private school. It's better. Attending UNCA means small classes with a lot of hard work, and accessible, friendly, and knowledgeable faculty and staff—without the big price tag of a private school.

HIGHLIGHTS

ON CAMPUS

- Health and Fitness Center
- Governor's Hall
- Student Center
- Asheville Botanical Gardens

OFF CAMPUS

- Over 1 million acres of National Forest
- Over 100 great restaurants
- Music venues that attract world-class musicians
- Semi-pro baseball and hockey teams
- Variety of shopping opportunities
- Surrounding areas provide numerous opportunities for hiking, kayaking, cycling, etc.

TRANSPORTATION

Asheville Regional Airport is located 17 miles south of Asheville. A Greyhound passenger bus terminal is located three miles south of campus. Amtrak passenger train service is available in Greenville, SC, 60 miles south of Asheville. UNC Asheville is serviced by public buses (Asheville Transit) and private taxi services.

FIND YOUR WAY

The Office of Admissions is located in 117 Lipinsky Hall. Turn onto University Heights at the round-about on Weaver Boulevard (see the directions below). At the top of the hill, stay to the left at the Y in the road. You may park in the Admissions parking spaces near Robinson Hall or in the Visitors Parking located in the lot just past the first stop sign. See the campus map kiosks for directions to Lipinsky once you are on campus. Lipinsky is just to the left of the Ramsey Library. Driving directions: **approaching from the north on US 19-23:** Take the NC 251/UNC Asheville exit. Turn left at traffic light at bottom of ramp. Proceed approximately half a mile to second traffic light; turn left onto W.T. Weaver Blvd. Proceed approximately a third of a mile to second left-hand turn for the main entrance road away from UNCA campus. **Approaching from the east on I-40:** Take exit 53B for I-240. Follow I-240 for approximately four-and-a-half miles. Take exit 5A for Merrimon Avenue. Turn right at the light at the bottom of the ramp. Proceed approximately one mile to third light; turn left onto W.T. Weaver Blvd. Proceed approximately a quarter of a mile on Weaver Blvd. to right-hand turn for main entrance road away from UNCA campus. **Approaching from the south or west on I-26 or I-40:** Take I-240 for Asheville. As you cross the river, move into the left-hand lane. Take US 19-23 north. Proceed approximately one mile away from UNCA exit. Turn right at bottom of exit ramp. Proceed approximately a third of a mile mile to second traffic light; turn left onto W.T. Weaver Blvd. Proceed approximately a third of a mile mile to second left-hand turn for the main entrance road away from UNCA campus.

STAY THE NIGHT

Nearby: Please mention UNC Asheville when making your reservations. Rates are applicable for the 2002 to 2003 academic year and are subject to availability. The **American Court Motel** (85 Merrimon Avenue, 28801; 800-233-3582), one-and-a-half miles away from UNCA, offers a 15 percent discount. There are many more possible choices.

AT A GLANCE

Selectivity Rating	81
Range SAT I Math	520–630
Average SAT I Math	574
Range SAT I Verbal	530–640
Average SAT I Verbal	586
Average ACT Composite	24
Average GPA	3.72
Student to Faculty Ratio	14:1

CAMPUS TOURS

Appointment	Required
Dates	Year-round
Times	Varies
Average Length	1 hour

ON-CAMPUS APPOINTMENTS

Admissions

Start Date–Juniors	April of junior year
Appointment	Required
Advance Notice	Yes, 1 week
Saturdays	Sometimes
Average Length	30 min.
Info Sessions	Yes

Faculty and Coaches

Dates/Times	Academic year
Arrangements	Contact Admissions Office 2 weeks prior

CLASS VISITS

Dates	Academic year
Arrangements	Contact Admissions Office

UNIVERSITY OF NORTH CAROLINA—CHAPEL HILL

Undergraduate Admissions, Jackson Hall,
Chapel Hill, NC 27599 • Telephone: 919-966-3621 • www.unc.edu •
Email: uadm@email.unc.edu

Hours: Monday–Friday, 8:00AM–5:00PM

With first-rate academic offerings that include great programs in business and journalism, the University of North Carolina is one of the nation's top state universities. Students at UNC say their school represents the true college experience—from theater to tennis, from baseball to basketball, and from academics to amusement.

AT A GLANCE

Selectivity Rating	90
Range SAT I Math	600–690
Average SAT I Math	642
Range SAT I Verbal	580–680
Average SAT I Verbal	625
Average ACT Composite	27
Average GPA	4.14
Student to Faculty Ratio	14:1

CAMPUS TOURS

Appointment	Preferred
Dates	Year-round
Times	Mon–Fri, 10AM & 2:30PM; no tours on Oct. 23 & 24
Average Length	1 hour

ON-CAMPUS APPOINTMENTS

Admissions

Start Date–Juniors	N/A
Appointment	Preferred
Advance Notice	Yes, 2 weeks
Saturdays	No
Average Length	30 min.
Info Sessions	Yes

Faculty and Coaches

Dates/Times	N/A
Arrangements	Contact faculty directly 1 week prior

CLASS VISITS

Dates	Academic year
Arrangements	Send email request to: classvisit@unc.edu; also see: www.admissions.unc.edu/visit/visit.html

TRANSPORTATION

The Raleigh-Durham International Airport is approximately 20 miles away from campus. Taxis and limousines are available for the drive from the airport to campus.

FIND YOUR WAY

From the east, take I-40 W. to Chapel Hill; then follow the signs to the campus. **From the north,** take the Hwy. 15/501 S. bypass to Chapel Hill; then follow the signs to campus. **From the west,** take I-85 N., then I-40 E. to Chapel Hill, then follow the signs to campus. **From the south,** take Hwy. 15/501 N. to Chapel Hill, then follow the signs to campus.

STAY THE NIGHT

Nearby: The university has a colonial-style inn right on campus called the **Carolina Inn** (211 Pittsboro St.; 919-933-2001 or 800-962-8519). Less than a mile away is the **Best Western University Inn** (Raleigh Rd./NC Hwy. 54 East; 919-932-3000). No surprises here, nor are there any at the **Hampton Inn** (1740 U.S. Hwy. 15; 919-968-3000), which is three miles away. Its inexpensive rate includes continental breakfast. The **Sheraton** (Europa Dr.; 919-968-4900) is a moderately priced, full-service hotel with an outdoor pool, tennis court, and nightclub; it's about four miles away from the university.

A Little Farther: **Fearrington House** (919-542-2121), technically in Pittsboro, eight miles south of Chapel Hill, has a charming courtyard, gardens, and a wonderful restaurant. Double rooms are expensive. Ten miles away from the university is the **Inn at Bingham School** (NC Hwy. 54 at Mebane Oaks Rd.; 919-563-5583), a restored headmaster's home listed on the National Register of Historic Places. This six-bedroom inn offers rooms with a delicious southern breakfast for a moderate rate. Also check the suggestions in the entry for Duke University, which is not too far to the northeast.

HIGHLIGHTS

ON CAMPUS

- Morehead Planetarium
- Coker Arboretum
- Morehead-Patterson Bell Tower
- Ackland Art Museum
- Dean Smith Center
- Forest Theatre

OFF CAMPUS

- Franklin Street
- North Carolina Botanical Gardens
- Chapel Hill Museum
- Fearrington Village
- University Lake
- Jordan Lake State Recreation Area

WAKE FOREST UNIVERSITY

Admissions Office, P.O. Box 7305,
Winston-Salem, NC 27109 • Telephone: 336-758-5201 • www.wfu.edu •
Email: admissions@wfu.edu

Hours: Monday–Friday, 8:30AM–5:00PM

Classes at Wake Forest University are challenging and usually interesting, and a solid, broad-based core curriculum obligates all students to pursue a well-rounded academic program. Work Forest, as students often call it, has a very tough grading system and savage workload, but social life is reportedly excellent and walking onto the gorgeous campus is like walking into heaven.

HIGHLIGHTS

ON CAMPUS
- Charlotte and Philip Hanes Art Gallery
- Museum of Anthropology
- The Z. Smith Reynolds Library
- Wait Chapel
- Benson University Center

OFF CAMPUS
- Reynolda House, Museum of American Art
- Tanglewood Park (golf)
- Old Salem
- Southeastern Center for Contemporary Art
- Hanes Mall

TRANSPORTATION

Piedmont Triad International Airport in Greensboro is 26 miles away from campus. Call Airport Express Limousine (336-668-0164) for service to campus. The limousine leaves the baggage claim area every hour on the hour until midnight. Blue Bird Cab (336-722-7121) also provides transportation to campus. Right in Winston-Salem, five minutes from campus, is the Smith Reynolds Airport, a small commuter airport.

FIND YOUR WAY

From I-40 E., take the Wake Forest University/Silas Creek Pkwy. exit; proceed north on the Pkwy., which will bring you to the Reynolda Rd. entrance to the university. **From I-40 W.,** take the Cherry St. exit, which will bring you to University Pkwy. Take the Pkwy. to the university entrance. **From U.S. Rte. 52 S.,** exit to University Pkwy. and follow the Pkwy. to the university entrance. **From U.S. Rte. 52 N.,** exit to I-40 W. and follow preceding directions from there.

STAY THE NIGHT

Nearby: A very popular place to stay is the university-owned **Graylyn International Conference Center** (1900 Reynolda Rd.; 336-758-2600), within a mile of Wake Forest. Ask for the special university visitors rate and advise them in advance if you would like to have meals provided. Two inexpensive choices are close to campus. The **Courtyard by Marriott** (3111 University Pkwy.; 336-727-1277) is two miles away. The other, priced slightly higher, is the **Ramada Plaza** (3050 University Pkwy.; 336-723-2911), about six blocks away. They both offer a fitness room and pool. **Brookstown Inn** (200 Brookstown Ave.; 336-725-1120), 10 minutes from campus, is a restoration of an 1837 cotton mill listed on the National Register of Historic Places. The moderate price includes continental breakfast and wine and cheese in the afternoon. For a little more glitz try the **Adam's Mark Winston Plaza** (425 N. Cherry St.; 336-725-3500), a fairly expensive hotel with an indoor pool and full fitness center. For a change of pace, the **Colonel Ludlow Bed and Breakfast Inn,** located close to Old Salem (a restored 1700s Moravian village), offers rates that include breakfast and range from moderate to expensive. The Inn is located at Summit and W. 5th Streets; 336-777-1887.

AT A GLANCE

Selectivity Rating	94
Range SAT I Math	620–710
Range SAT I Verbal	600–680
Student to Faculty Ratio	10:1

CAMPUS TOURS

Appointment	Required
Dates	Academic year
Times	Mon–Fri, 10AM & 3PM
Average Length	1 hour

ON-CAMPUS APPOINTMENTS

Admissions

Start Date–Juniors	Available during the summer before senior year
Appointment	Required
Advance Notice	Yes, 1 week
Saturdays	No
Average Length	30 min.
Info Sessions	Yes

Faculty and Coaches

Dates/Times	Academic year
Arrangements	Contact department directly 2 weeks prior

CLASS VISITS

Dates	Academic year
Arrangements	Contact department directly

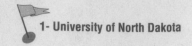

1- University of North Dakota

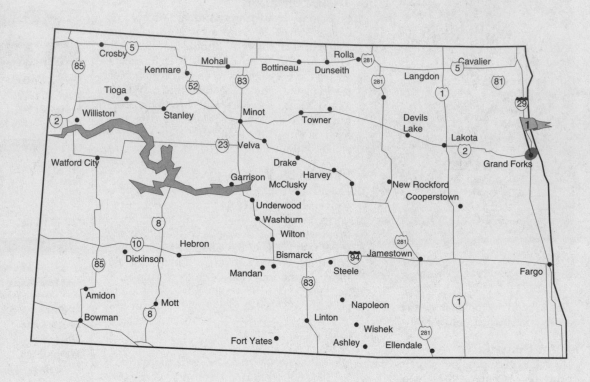

North Dakota	Univ. of North Dak	*Bismarck*
Univ. of North Dak	—	270
Bismarck	270	—

UNIVERSITY OF NORTH DAKOTA

Enrollment Services, Box 8135, Grand Forks, ND 58202 • Telephone: 800-CALL-UND • www.und.edu • Email: enrollment_services@mail.und.nodak.edu

Hours: Monday–Friday, 8:00AM–4:30PM; one Saturday per month, 10:00AM–2:00PM

The University of North Dakota offers choices comparable to a large university, but it has the atmosphere of a small close-knit school, according to its students. The strongest and most popular department at UND is aviation, and the nationally renowned Center for Aerospace Science attracts many out-of-state students.

HIGHLIGHTS

ON CAMPUS

- Engelstad Arena
- Hyslop Sports Center
- Tabula Coffee Shop
- International Centre
- North Dakota Museum of Art

OFF CAMPUS

- Alerus Center
- Empire Arts Theatre
- Columbia Mall
- Red Pepper (Subs)
- Cabela's

TRANSPORTATION

Free shuttle buses around campus and $1 taxi are available for full-time students. There is bus service at the Greyhound Bus station and train service at the Amtrak train station. The closest airport is the Grand Fork International Airport.

FIND YOUR WAY

UND is located between Winnipeg and Fargo on Interstate 29. UND is approximately five hours northwest of Minneapolis traveling from I-94 to I-29 North.

STAY THE NIGHT

Nearby: **Best Western Town House** (710 1st Ave. N), 800-867-9797), located downtown just off of Demers Ave., offers you access to a restaurant, lounge, and casino. Prices range from inexpensive to expensive. On the South Side of town, located near our shopping centers, the **Road King Inn** (3300 30th Ave. S., 800-707-1391) also ranges from inexpensive to expensive. Both have special rates for college visitors.

AT A GLANCE

Selectivity Rating	76
Average ACT Composite	23
Average GPA	3.38
Student to Faculty Ratio	18:1

CAMPUS TOURS

Appointment	Preferred
Dates	Year-round
Times	Mon–Fri, 8AM–4:30PM
Average Length	1 hour

ON-CAMPUS APPOINTMENTS

Admissions

Start Date–Juniors	Anytime
Appointment	Preferred
Advance Notice	No
Saturdays	Sometimes
Average Length	30 min.
Info Sessions	Yes

Faculty and Coaches

Dates/Times	Academic year
Arrangements	Enrollment Services

CLASS VISITS

Dates	Academic year
Arrangements	Enrollment Services

OHIO

1- Antioch College
2- Case Western Reserve University
3- Denison University
4- Hiram College
5- Kenyon College
6- Miami University (Ohio)
7- Oberlin College
8- Ohio University
9- Ohio State University
10- Ohio Wesleyan University
11- Wittenburg University
12- College of Wooster
13- University of Dayton

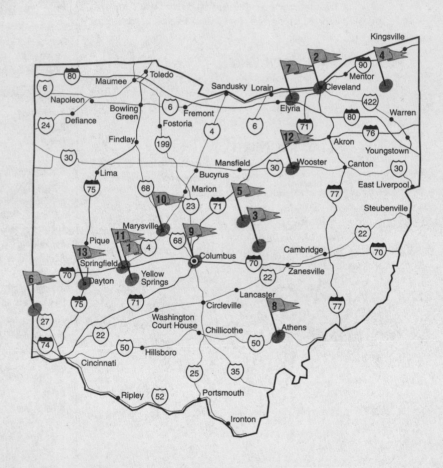

Ohio

	Antioch Coll.	Case Western	Coll. of Wooster	Denison Univ.	Hiram Coll.	Kenyon Coll.	Miami Univ.	Oberlin Coll.	Ohio State Univ.	Ohio Univ.	Ohio Wesleyan	Univ. of Dayton	Wittenberg Univ.	Cincinnati	Cleveland	Columbus	Dayton
Antioch Coll.	—	190	151	78	216	103	65	162	50	125	75	21	9	70	190	50	20
Case Western	190	—	52	117	42	97	262	25	144	202	115	221	183	249	0	144	209
Coll. of Wooster	151	52	—	71	63	45	219	50	101	138	85	171	135	212	52	101	173
Denison Univ.	78	117	71	—	131	25	150	97	32	70	34	112	80	143	117	27	104
Hiram Coll.	216	42	63	131	—	112	275	58	156	195	138	233	196	265	35	156	228
Kenyon Coll.	103	97	45	25	112	—	171	85	52	110	35	132	95	163	97	52	124
Miami Univ.	65	262	219	150	275	171	—	232	118	190	138	45	75	33	262	118	47
Oberlin Coll.	162	25	50	97	58	85	232	—	114	216	97	189	145	225	26	114	186
Ohio State Univ.	50	144	101	32	156	52	118	114	—	75	20	80	40	111	144	0	72
Ohio Univ.	125	202	138	70	195	110	190	216	75	—	95	136	115	160	202	75	143
Ohio Wesleyan	75	115	85	34	138	35	138	97	20	95	—	99	55	131	115	20	92
Univ. of Dayton	21	221	171	112	233	132	45	189	80	136	99	—	33	48	218	77	0
Wittenberg Univ.	9	183	135	80	196	95	75	145	40	115	55	33	—	73	183	40	25
Cincinnati	70	249	212	143	265	163	33	225	111	160	131	48	73	—	255	110	56
Cleveland	190	0	52	117	35	97	262	26	144	202	115	218	183	255	—	147	209
Columbus	50	144	101	27	156	52	118	114	0	75	20	77	40	110	147	—	72
Dayton	20	209	173	104	228	124	47	186	72	143	92	0	25	56	209	72	—

ANTIOCH COLLEGE

Office of Admissions and Financial Aid, 795 Livermore Street, Yellow Springs, OH 45387 • Telephone: 800-543-9436 • www.antioch-college.edu • Email: admissions@antioch-college.edu

Hours: Monday–Friday, 8:30AM–5:00PM

The Antioch College Environmental Field Program is a major attraction of this ultra-liberal and progressive liberal arts school in Southern Ohio. A somewhat notorious Sexual Offense Prevention Policy requires students to obtain verbal consent for each specific act of any sexual encounter they have with each other.

AT A GLANCE

Average GPA	3.0
Student to Faculty Ratio	10:1

CAMPUS TOURS

Appointment	Required
Dates	Academic year
Times	Mon–Fri, 10:30AM; afternoons are possible
Average Length	1 hour

ON-CAMPUS APPOINTMENTS

Admissions

Start Date–Juniors	Anytime
Appointment	Required
Advance Notice	Yes, 1 week
Saturdays	Sometimes
Average Length	30 min.
Info Sessions	Yes

Faculty and Coaches

Dates/Times	N/A
Arrangements	Contact Admissions Office 1 week prior

CLASS VISITS

Dates	Academic year
Arrangements	Contact Admissions Office

TRANSPORTATION

The nearest airport to campus is in Dayton, 30 miles away, followed by airports in Columbus (72 miles) and Cincinnati (84 miles). The Dayton bus station is 25 miles away. The Admissions Office will arrange for student shuttles (cost varies by distance) between the airport or bus station and campus. Rental cars and taxis are also available at all the airports.

FIND YOUR WAY

From I-70, take Exit 52 to U.S. Rte. 68 S. and follow it approximately six miles through Yellow Springs. Turn left at the second stop light on E. Limestone Street. Turn right on President Street and park at the dead end. **From 675 bypass,** take Dayton-Yellow Springs Road (Exit 20) and turn right (east). Go about six miles. Turn right at traffic light on S. Walnut Street, then turn left on Limestone Street. After crossing Xenia Ave turn right on President St. and park at the dead end. The Office of Admissions and Financial Aid is located in Weston Hall next to the Student Union.

STAY THE NIGHT

Nearby: **Morgan House** (120 W. Limestone St.; 937-767-7509), a bed-and-breakfast in Yellow Springs, is a comfortable home within walking distance of campus and the downtown area. It has a limited number of rooms, shared bathrooms, a pay phone, and lots of local charm. Fairborn, about 12 miles west, has a number of hotels and motels off the 675 bypass across from Wright State University. They include the **Holiday Inn** (800-HOLIDAY), **Homewood Suites** (937-429-0600), **Red Roof Inn** (800-843-7663), and **Hampton Inn** (800-HAMPTON). The **Springfield Inn** (800-234-3611) is located approximately 12 miles northeast in Springfield, Ohio.

HIGHLIGHTS

ON CAMPUS

- Herndon Gallery
- Glen Hellen Nature Preserve
- Japanese Tea Garden
- Community Bike Shop
- Alternative Library

OFF CAMPUS

- Little Art Movie Theater
- Clifton Gorge
- National Afro-American Museum and Cultural Center
- Little Miami Scenic Trail Bike Path

CASE WESTERN RESERVE UNIVERSITY

Office of Undergraduate Admission, 10900 Euclid Ave., Cleveland, OH 44106-7055 • Telephone: 216-368-4450 • admission.case.edu • Email: admission@po.cwru.edu

Hours: Monday–Friday, 8:30AM–5:00PM; select Saturdays (January–April)

Small classes, world-class facilities, and brilliant professors are what you'll find at this sleeper school in Cleveland. While Case Western is widely known for churning out topflight engineers, the very studious, serious, diverse, and conservative students report that the liberal arts programs are excellent as well.

HIGHLIGHTS

ON CAMPUS

- Kelvin Smith Library
- Peter B. Lewis Building
- Veale Convocation Athletic Center
- Turning Point sculpture
- Elephant steps

OFF CAMPUS

- Severance Hall, home of the Cleveland Orchestra
- Cleveland Museum of Art
- Cleveland Botanical Gardens
- Cleveland Museum of Natural History
- Crawford Auto and Aviation museum and Historical Society

TRANSPORTATION

Cleveland Hopkins Airport is the closest to the university. To get to the campus, take the Regional Transit Authority (RTA) Rapid Transit from the airport terminal to University Circle; the ride takes approximately 40 minutes and is very cheap. Amtrak's Lake Shore Limited provides service to Cleveland via Toledo, Erie, and Buffalo, connecting from those cities to many other locations throughout the country. Greyhound buses also provide service to Cleveland. The Greater Cleveland Regional Transit Authority (RTA) offers extensive and economical bus and rail service throughout the metropolitan area.

FIND YOUR WAY

From I-71 and I-77, exit to I-90 in Cleveland. Take I-90 N. to U.S. 20 E. (Euclid Ave.). Proceed on Euclid Ave. to the Admissions Office.

STAY THE NIGHT

Nearby: A particular favorite is **Glidden House** (1901 Ford Dr.; 216-231-8900), a large, Gothic-style bed-and-breakfast within walking distance of campus. Prices are moderate, and a special rate is available for Case Western Reserve visitors. Also in the neighborhood is the posh **Baricelli Inn** (2203 Cornell Rd.; 216-791-6500). Somewhat smaller than Glidden House, this converted mansion is within walking distance of the school. Visitors to the university frequently stay at the **Intercontinental Suite Hotel** (8800 Euclid Ave.; 216-707-4300), a nice hotel (don't be turned off by the antiseptic name) near the campus. Special rates for Case Western Reserve visitors are at the high end of the moderate range. To get to campus, you can walk or take the convenient loop bus across the street from the hotel. There is a parking charge.

A Little Farther: If you want to stay downtown, try the **Stouffer Renaissance Hotel.** This is a convenient, though pricey, place to stay. It has all the amenities of a large metropolitan hotel and the added attraction of public transportation from inside the building directly to the campus.

THE COLLEGE OF WOOSTER

Admissions Office, 847 College Ave,
Wooster, OH 44691 • Telephone: 800-877-9905 • www.wooster.edu •
Email: admissions@wooster.edu

Hours: Monday–Friday, 9:00AM–5:00PM; Saturdays (not during summer or winter break), 9:00AM–noon

This small Presbyterian liberal arts college south of Cleveland has small classes and fabulous professors. A first year seminar in critical inquiry is required of all students, but judging from the wealth of interesting course titles, that's far from a bad thing. Recent course offerings have included Go Directly to Jail: Locking Up Minorities in America and The Truth About Lies.

AT A GLANCE

Selectivity Rating	78
Range SAT I Math	550–650
Average SAT I Math	598
Range SAT I Verbal	550–650
Average SAT I Verbal	595
Average ACT Composite	26
Average GPA	3.54
Student to Faculty Ratio	13:1

CAMPUS TOURS

Appointment	Required
Dates	Year-round
Times	On the hour
Average Length	1 hour

ON-CAMPUS APPOINTMENTS

Admissions

Start Date—Juniors	Anytime, usually in the spring or summer
Appointment	Required
Advance Notice	Yes, 1 week
Saturdays	Sometimes
Average Length	45 min.
Info Sessions	No

Faculty and Coaches

Dates/Times	Year-round
Arrangements	Contact Admissions Office 1 week prior

CLASS VISITS

Dates	Academic year
Arrangements	Contact Admissions Office

TRANSPORTATION

Cleveland-Hopkins Airport is 55 miles away from campus. A college shuttle is available if arranged in advance through the Admissions Office.

FIND YOUR WAY

The college is near the intersection of U.S. Rte. 30 and Ohio Rte. 83. **From the south,** take I-71 N.; exit to U.S. 30 E. (east of Mansfield) and continue to Ohio Rte. 83 in Wooster. Or, take I-77 N. to U.S. 250 N.W. to Wooster. **From the north,** take I-71 S. to Ohio Rte. 83 S. Or, take I-77 S. to Ohio Rte. 21 S. Then take Ohio Rte. 585 S.W. to Wooster. **From the east or west,** take I-76 to Ohio Rte. 3 S. to Wooster. Or, take I-76 to Ohio Rte. 21 S.; then take Rte. 585 S.W. to Wooster.

STAY THE NIGHT

Nearby: If you fly into Cleveland, a 45-minute drive from the College of Wooster, you may be tempted to stay the night in Cleveland and push off in the morning for the campus. Don't do it! You'll miss the chance to stay at some very nice places in and around Wooster. The perfect choice for visiting the college is the **Wooster Inn** (801 E. Wayne Ave.; 330-264-2341), which is owned by the college. It's just two blocks away from campus, and the college's athletic facilities, including a golf course, are available to guests. Rates are moderate and include a full breakfast. For a pleasant and inexpensive bed-and-breakfast within walking distance (five blocks) of the college, try the **Gasche House** (340 North Bever Street; 330-264-8231). This is a beautifully restored 141-year-old Victorian, with four-poster beds and period furniture. The price includes a continental breakfast. If you are not the bed-and-breakfast type but want an inexpensive place to stay in Wooster, try the **Econo Lodge** (2137 Lincoln Way East; 330-264-8883).

A Little Farther: Just 22 miles away is the **Inn at Honey Run** (Millersburg; 800-468-6639 in Ohio or 330-674-0011). Honey Run offers a variety of rates ranging from moderate to expensive (continental breakfast included). The inn's earth-shelter rooms (described in the Kenyon entry) may be of interest to you. Take something other than jeans to wear in the evening; more formal attire is in order.

HIGHLIGHTS

ON CAMPUS

- Severance Hall Chemistry Building
- Timken Science Library
- Armington Physical Education Center/Swigart Fitness Center
- Ebert Art Center
- Rubbermaid Student Development Center

OFF CAMPUS

- Rock-and-Roll Hall of Fame
- Inventure Place (National Inventor's Hall of Fame)
- Professional Football Hall of Fame, Canton

DENISON UNIVERSITY

Admissions Office, Box H,
Granville, OH 43023 • Telephone: 800-336-4766 • www.denison.edu •
Email: admissions@denison.edu

Hours: Monday–Friday, 8:30AM–4:30PM; Saturdays (select during fall and spring), 8:30AM–12:30PM

Denison is a high-quality liberal arts school not far from Columbus, Ohio. Over the past several years, Denison has been making a concerted effort to create a more studious image for itself; students appreciate the attentiveness and dedication of the DU faculty.

HIGHLIGHTS

ON CAMPUS
- F. W. Olin Science Hall
- Mitchell Recreation and Athletics Center
- Swasey Chapel
- Biological Reserve and Polly Anderson Field Station
- Burke Hall Art Gallery

OFF CAMPUS
- Granville Historical Society Museum
- Dawes Arboretum
- Easton Town Center

TRANSPORTATION

Port Columbus International Airport is 22 miles (a 35-minute drive) from campus. During the academic year (from September to May), the Denison University Student Taxi Service provides shuttle service between the campus and the airport; call the Admissions Office one week before your visit to arrange for this shuttle. During the summer, visitors can rent a car at the airport or take a taxi to and from the campus.

FIND YOUR WAY

From I-70, exit to Ohio Rte. 37 N.; the university is near the intersection of Rte. 37 with Rtes. 16 and 661. **From the north,** take I-71 S.; exit to Ohio Rte. 13 (south of Mansfield). Take Rte. 13 S. through Mount Vernon; then make a right turn onto Rte. 661. Take Rte. 661 S. into Granville; you will pass the Denison athletic fields. The university is on Rte. 37 just west of Rte. 661.

STAY THE NIGHT

Nearby: If you have a morning visit scheduled at Denison, it's worth making the effort to spend the preceding night in Granville. The first of two delightful inns in this picture-postcard town (a five-minute drive from the Admissions Office) is the **Buxton Inn** (313 E. Broadway; 740-587-0001). Founded in 1812, it is still operating in its original building in the middle of the village. Another gem is the **Granville Inn** (314 E. Broadway; 740-587-3333). It's also moderately priced and offers a continental breakfast. This is an English Tudor manor house with carved oak paneling and lots of character. It includes a pleasant restaurant. Another outstanding overnight and dining location just outside of Granville is the **Cherry Valley Lodge** (2299 Cherry Valley Road; 740-788-1200).

A Little Farther: Check the places in the Kenyon College entry, especially **Russell-Cooper House** (in Mount Vernon, 23 miles away from Denison).

AT A GLANCE

Selectivity Rating	81
Range SAT I Math	560–670
Average SAT I Math	615
Range SAT I Verbal	550–650
Average SAT I Verbal	602
Average ACT Composite	26
Average GPA	3.5
Student to Faculty Ratio	11:1

CAMPUS TOURS

Appointment	Preferred
Dates	Year-round
Times	Varies throughout the year
Average Length	1 hour

ON-CAMPUS APPOINTMENTS

Admissions

Start Date—Juniors	Spring Recommended
Appointment	Preferred
Advance Notice	Yes, 1 week
Saturdays	Sometimes
Average Length	1 hour
Info Sessions	No

Faculty and Coaches

Dates/Times	Year-round
Arrangements	Contact Admissions Office 1 week prior

CLASS VISITS

Dates	Academic year
Arrangements	Contact Admissions Office

HIRAM COLLEGE

Admissions Office, Box 96,
Hiram, OH 44234 • Telephone: 800-362-5280 • www.hiram.edu •
Email: admission@hiram.edu

Hours: Monday–Friday, 9:00AM–4:00PM; Saturdays (during academic year), 9:00AM–noon

The innovative Hiram Plan at Hiram College divides each semester into two sessions that last three and twelve weeks respectively. The three-week sessions take the form of hands-on learning experiences like study abroad, research, internships, and field trips. Also, over the past decade or so, Hiram's medical school acceptance rate has been among the highest in the nation.

AT A GLANCE

Selectivity Rating	79
Range SAT I Math	480–620
Average SAT I Math	566
Range SAT I Verbal	510–630
Average SAT I Verbal	573
Average ACT Composite	24
Average GPA	3.39
Student to Faculty Ratio	11:1

CAMPUS TOURS

Appointment	Preferred
Dates	Year-round
Times	See Admissions Office for times
Average Length	1 hour

ON-CAMPUS APPOINTMENTS

Admissions

Start Date–Juniors	Anytime
Appointment	Preferred
Advance Notice	Yes, 2 weeks
Saturdays	Sometimes
Average Length	1 hour
Info Sessions	No

Faculty and Coaches

Dates/Times	Academic year
Arrangements	Contact Admissions Office 2 weeks prior

CLASS VISITS

Dates	Academic year
Arrangements	Contact Admissions Office

TRANSPORTATION

Cleveland-Hopkins and Akron-Canton airports are an hour's drive from the campus. The Admission Office supplies free transportation to the campus; contact the receptionist to arrange for this service. Rental cars are also available at both airports.

FIND YOUR WAY

From the east, take I-80 to Exit 209; then take Ohio Rte. 5 E. (toward Warren). At the intersection with Rte. 82, turn left (north and west, away from Warren) and continue on Rte. 82, which merges with Rte. 700 just south of the college. The college is at the intersection of Routes 82/700 and 305. **From the west,** take I-80 to Exit 193 (S.R. 44). Take Rte 44 north 6 miles to Rte. 82. Take Rte. 82 E. to Hiram.

STAY THE NIGHT

Nearby: Located right on campus, the **Hiram Inn** (888-447-2646) offers all the modern amenities in a nineteenth-century setting. The 12 guest rooms, though decorated in the style of the early 1800s, come equipped with air conditioning, cable television, and access to a computer hookup. Some rooms offer a whirlpool spa or fireplace. Ask for college visitor rates. Aurora, which is 15 to 20 minutes to the west, offers several quite respectable possibilities. Ask for college visitor rates at each. **Aurora Inn** (Ohio Rtes. 82 and 306; 330-562-6121) offers moderate prices, indoor and outdoor pools, tennis courts, and Jacuzzis. The **Inn at Six Flags** (800 N. Aurora Rd.; 330-562-9151) is moderately priced, and has an indoor pool with a glass dome that opens in warm weather. For the fitness-minded, there is **Mario's International Aurora House Spa and Hotel** (35 E. Garfield Rd.; 330-562-9171). Each room has a whirlpool. Mario's is normally very expensive and would probably make sense only if you wanted to use the spa facilities, but the hotel does have a moderate visitor rate that might make this an appealing choice.

A Little Farther: To the east of Hiram, about a 40-minute drive away, is **Avalon Inn** (Warren-Sharon Rd., off Market St.; 330-856-1900). This is a moderately priced, modern, resort motel with indoor/outdoor lighted tennis courts, an indoor pool, and two golf courses. Just 26 miles to the east of Hiram is the town of Streetsboro, which offers many lodging options including the **Hampton Inn** (330.422.0500), the **Comfort Inn** (330-626-5511), the **Holiday Inn Express** (330-422-1888), and the **Wingate Inn** (330-422-9900). Streetsboro is located at Exit 187 of the Ohio Turnpike (I-80).

HIGHLIGHTS

ON CAMPUS

- James H. Barrow Field Station
- The Hiram College Library
- Kennedy Center
- Hiram Church
- Stevens Memorial Observatory

OFF CAMPUS

- Cleveland
- The Flats
- The Science Discovery Center
- Rock and Roll Hall of Fame
- Agora Theater

KENYON COLLEGE

Admissions Office,
Gambier, OH 43022-9623 • Telephone: 800-848-2468 • www.kenyon.edu •
Email: admissions@kenyon.edu

Hours: Monday–Friday, 8:30AM–4:30PM; Saturdays (during academic year), 9:00AM–noon

Kenyon is an environment where professors really care whether students are learning. The liberal arts-filled academic environment is competitive and rigorous, but in a lighthearted, self-motivating kind of way; the hardworking, fun-loving, insomniac students seem to really enjoy themselves.

HIGHLIGHTS

ON CAMPUS
- Kenyon College Bookstore
- Horn Gallery
- Mather Science Quadrangle
- Brown Family Environmental Center
- Olin Library & Chalmers Library; Olin Art Gallery
- Construction has begun on our new $60 million fitness, recreation, and athletic facility, which is scheduled to be completed in Spring 2005.

OFF CAMPUS
- Gap Trail (walking; biking; rollerblading)
- Mt. Vernon movie theater
- Hunan Garden (Chinese restaurant)

TRANSPORTATION

Port Columbus International Airport is approximately 50 miles away from campus. Call the Admissions Office receptionist to arrange for the college's shuttle service from the airport. (Note that this service is not free.) Rental cars are available at the airport if you prefer to drive.

FIND YOUR WAY

From Port Columbus International Airport, take I-270 North to OH-161 East. Follow OH-161 to the exit for New Albany/Johnstown (OH-62), exit and turn left onto OH-62. After about 20 miles, turn left onto OH-661 North toward Mount Vernon. Rte. 661 merges with Rte. 13 S. of Mount Vernon. In Mount Vernon, look for the small, green Kenyon College signs. At the intersection of Rtes. 13 and 229, turn right (east) on Rte. 229 (East Gambier St.) and stay on it for about five miles. Kenyon will be on your left.

STAY THE NIGHT

Nearby: You can roll out of bed and onto campus if you stay at the **Kenyon Inn** (740-427-2202), a pleasant colonial with rates at the low end of the moderate range. Gambier is tiny (the campus, inn, and post office make up the whole town), so you might prefer to stay in the big city of Mount Vernon, which is 10 minutes away. The first choice in Mount Vernon is the **Russell-Cooper House** (115 E. Gambier St.; 740-397-8638), a restored Victorian mansion with rooms that are moderately priced (rates include breakfast). If this doesn't appeal to you, try **The Curtis** (12 Public Sq.; 800-828-7847 outside Ohio or 800-634-6835 in Ohio), a nice, simple, inexpensive motel. Also located in Mt. Vernon are **The Holiday Inn Express** (11555 Upper Gilchrist Rd., 740-392-1900) and the **Dan Emmett House** (150 Howard St., 740-392-6886) where local professors play the blues.

A Little Farther: A very special place about one mile away is the **White Oak Inn** (29683 Walhonding Rd., Danville; 614-599-6107). For recreation, you can go canoeing, fishing, and hiking; and horseshoes, badminton, and croquet are available on the grounds, and golf courses are nearby. If you prefer serenity to glamour, this is the place for you. The **Inn at Honey Run** (6920 County Rd. 203, Millersburg; 330-674-0011 or 800-468-6639 in Ohio) is a great place to stay and well worth the 40-mile drive northeast from Kenyon. Located in Amish country, this unusual contemporary inn blends well with the wooded surroundings. You might consider staying in their Honeycombs, an earth-sheltered annex (a cave that's not a cave). The rates range from moderate to expensive, depending on your room. Roscoe Village Inn (200 N. White Woman St.; 614-622-2222). The inn, which has a nice restaurant and a tavern, offers 50 rooms. It is moderately priced; check for AAA discounts.

AT A GLANCE

Selectivity Rating	90
Range SAT I Math	610–690
Average SAT I Math	661
Range SAT I Verbal	620–720
Average SAT I Verbal	681
Average ACT Composite	30
Average GPA	3.73
Student to Faculty Ratio	9:1

CAMPUS TOURS

Appointment	Not required
Dates	Varies
Times	Mon–Fri, 10AM–4PM; Sat 10AM–1PM (every hour)
Average Length	1 hour

ON-CAMPUS APPOINTMENTS

Admissions

Start Date–Juniors	Later part of junior year
Appointment	Required
Advance Notice	Yes, 2 weeks
Saturdays	Sometimes
Average Length	1 hour
Info Sessions	No

Faculty and Coaches

Dates/Times	Year-round
Arrangements	Contact coach directly 2 weeks prior

CLASS VISITS

Dates	Academic year
Arrangements	Contact Admissions Office

MIAMI UNIVERSITY

Admissions Office, 301 S. Campus Ave.,
Oxford, OH 45056 • Telephone: 513-529-2531 • www.miami.muohio.edu •
Email: admission@muohio.edu

Hours: Monday–Friday, 8:00AM–5:00PM; Summer, 7:30AM–4:30PM; Saturdays (September–April, but not December), 8:00AM–noon

The Harvard of Ohio is widely known for offering top-rate programs in combination with state school afford-ability, and students beam that Miami University prides itself on its strong academic tradition and prepares its students well for their futures. The surrounding town of Oxford is a bit sedate, but it is beautiful and student-friendly. Humorist P. J. O'Rourke is an alum.

AT A GLANCE

Selectivity Rating	82
Range SAT I Math	580–660
Average SAT I Math	610
Range SAT I Verbal	550–640
Average SAT I Verbal	590
Average ACT Composite	26
Average GPA	3.7
Student to Faculty Ratio	17:1

CAMPUS TOURS

Appointment	Preferred
Dates	Year-round
Times	Mon–Fri, 10AM & 2PM;
	Sat 10AM, during academic year
Average Length	120 min.

ON-CAMPUS APPOINTMENTS

Admissions

Start Date—Juniors	N/A

Faculty and Coaches

Dates/Times	Academic year
Arrangements	Contact Admissions
	Office 2 weeks prior

CLASS VISITS

Dates	Academic year
Arrangements	Contact Admissions
	Office

TRANSPORTATION

Greater Cincinnati International Airport is 55 miles south of Oxford in northern Kentucky. Dayton International Airport is 55 miles northeast of Oxford in Vandalia. Miami University Airport is quite near campus, but is suitable only for small private planes; call 513-529-2735 for information. Door-to-Door Transportation Services (513-641-0088) offers service between Oxford and the Cincinnati airport approximately every hour-and-a-half for less than $50; make reservations in advance. Similar fees for airport-to-campus transportation (Cincinnati or Dayton) are charged by Joan's Cab Service (513-523-2211); reservations are suggested. Rental cars are available at both major airports. Amtrak trains provide no direct service to Oxford, but make tri-weekly stops in Cincinnati (a one-hour drive from Oxford) and Hamilton (a 30-minute drive from Oxford).

FIND YOUR WAY

From the east, take I-70 W. to I-75 S. (north of Dayton). Take I-75 S. to Ohio Rte 63 W. Take Rte. 63 W. to Ohio Rte. 4 N. From Rte. 4 N., turn west onto Ohio Rte 73. Rte. 73 joins U.S. Rte. 27 and takes you into Oxford. **From the north,** take I-75 S. and follow the preceding directions from there. **From the west,** take I-70 E. to U.S. Rte. 27 (near Richmond, IN). Take Rte. 27 S. into Oxford. **From the south,** take I-75 N. to U.S. Rte. 27 (in Cincinnati); take U.S. Rte 27 N. into Oxford.

STAY THE NIGHT

Nearby: For a moderate price (including continental breakfast), two people can stay at the **Marcum Conference Center** (513-529-6911). The university advises that reservations be made 60 days ahead, but walk-ins will be accommodated, if possible. You may use the university athletic facilities. The **Marcum Conference Center and Inn** (100 N. Patterson Ave.; 513-529-2404) is a great college-town hotel. It is somewhat more expensive but still within the moderate range and very convenient. Another moderately priced choice in Oxford is the **Alexander House Country Inn** (22 N. College Ave.; 513-523-1200), six blocks from campus. Inexpensive choices include the **College View Motel** (513-523-6311), a mile-and-a-half south on Rte. 27 S.; **Cottage Inn** (513-523-6306), two miles northwest of Oxford on Rte. 27 N.; and **Oxford Motel** (5399 College Corner Pike; 513-523-1880). Check the Oxford Visitors and Convention Bureau at www.oxfordchamber.org

A Little Farther: For a more vacation-like ambiance, try **Hueston Woods Lodge** (800-282-7275 or 513-523-6381), five miles north on Ohio Rte. 732. The rooms are moderately priced (ask for a cottage with kitchenette).

HIGHLIGHTS

ON CAMPUS

- McGuffey Museum
- Center for the Performing Arts
- Amos Music Library
- Recreational Sports Center
- Peabody Hall (National Historical Landmark)

OFF CAMPUS

- The Pioneer Farm and House Museum
- Hueston Woods State Park

OBERLIN COLLEGE

Admissions Office, Carnegie Building, 101 N. Professor St.,
Oberlin, OH 44074 • Telephone: 800-622-6243 • www.oberlin.edu •
Email: college.admissions@oberlin.edu

Hours: Monday–Friday, 8:30AM–5:00PM; Saturdays, 9:00AM–noon

Academically intense, (yet noncompetitive) Oberlin College is an outstanding liberal arts school connected to a world-renowned conservatory of music that has something to offer to pretty much everyone. Oberlin's left-leaning undergraduates say they are free thinkers who prefer political debates, concerts, and plays to drinking or playing sports.

HIGHLIGHTS

ON CAMPUS

- Allen Art Museum
- Oberlin College Science Center
- Adam Joseph Lewis Center for Environmental Studies
- Mudd Library
- Jesse Philips Recreational Center

OFF CAMPUS

- Rock and Roll Hall of Fame
- Cleveland Art Museum
- Cleveland Natural History Museum
- Severance Hall (concert hall)
- Tower City

TRANSPORTATION

Cleveland-Hopkins International Airport is 25 minutes from the college. Public transportation is available from the airport to campus; see bus route 33 at www.loraincountytransit.com. Relatively inexpensive limousine service is also available for the ride from the airport to campus; call 216-267-8282 to make arrangements for this.

FIND YOUR WAY

From the east, take I-80 (the Ohio Tpke.) to Exit 9; then take Ohio Rte. 10 W. to Rte. 20 W. Take Rte. 20 to the SR 511 exit, and take Rte. 511 W. into Oberlin. **From the west,** take I-80/90 to Exit 8 (Elyria-Lorain). Do not use Exit 8A. Take Ohio Rte. 57 S. to Ohio Rte. 113; then take Rte. 113 W. to Ohio Rte. 58. Proceed south on Rte. 58 to Oberlin. **From the north,** take Rte 58 S. to Oberlin. **From the south,** take I-71 N. to the Ashland exit; take U.S. Rte. 250 E. to Ohio Rte. 89. Head north on Rte. 89 to Ohio Rte. 58, then follow Rte. 58 N. to Oberlin.

STAY THE NIGHT

Nearby: The **Oberlin College Inn** (Main and College Sts. across from Tappan Square; 440-775-1111) is conveniently located in downtown Oberlin, just one block from the Admissions Office. Downtown you will find a variety of restaurants, coffee shops, bookstores, and a movie theater. The Ohio Tpke. (I-80 & I-90) passes approximately 10 minutes north of Oberlin, heading west from Cleveland to Toledo. You will find familiar chains of hotels located near these major highways.

A Little Farther: Oberlin is close to several cities including Elyria, North Olmsted, and Cleveland, so check out www.oberlin.edu/outside for hotels, great restaurants, museums, and shopping.

AT A GLANCE

Selectivity Rating	90
Range SAT I Math	610–710
Average SAT I Math	659
Range SAT I Verbal	630–740
Average SAT I Verbal	691
Average ACT Composite	30
Average GPA	3.52
Student to Faculty Ratio	10:1

CAMPUS TOURS

Appointment	Not required
Dates	Year-round
Times	Mon–Fri, 10AM, noon, 2:30PM, & 4:30PM; Sat 10AM & noon
Average Length	1 hour

ON-CAMPUS APPOINTMENTS

Admissions

Start Date—Juniors	January 2
Appointment	Required
Advance Notice	Yes, 2 weeks
Saturdays	Yes
Average Length	30 min.
Info Sessions	Yes

Faculty and Coaches

Dates/Times	Academic year
Arrangements	Contact Admissions Office

CLASS VISITS

Dates	Academic year
Arrangements	Contact Admissions Office

OHIO STATE UNIVERSITY—COLUMBUS

Student Visitor Center, 131 Enarson Hall, 154 West 12th, Columbus, OH 43210 • Telephone: 614-292-3980 • www.osu.edu • Email: telecounseling@fa.adm.ohio-state.edu

Hours: Monday–Friday, 9:00AM–5:00PM; open until 6:00PM on Wednesdays

With over 30,000 full-time undergraduates (and another 5,000 part-timers), Ohio State University is like a small city that has anything and everything both academically and socially. As an added perk, OSU is extremely affordable. Students caution, however, that you must get involved to have an enjoyable experience.

AT A GLANCE

Selectivity Rating		72
Range SAT I Math		540–660
Average SAT I Math		594
Range SAT I Verbal		520–630
Average SAT I Verbal		575
Average ACT Composite		25
Average GPA		4.0
Student to Faculty Ratio		13:1

CAMPUS TOURS

Appointment	Required
Dates	Varies
Times	Mon–Fri, 10AM & 2PM
Average Length	2 hours

ON-CAMPUS APPOINTMENTS

Admissions

Start Date—Juniors	Anytime
Saturdays	No
Info Sessions	See Admissions Office for times

Faculty and Coaches

Dates/Times	Year-round
Arrangements	Contact faculty directly 2 weeks prior

CLASS VISITS

Dates	Year-round
Arrangements	Contact Admissions Office

TRANSPORTATION

Port Columbus International Airport is a 25-minute drive from campus, depending on traffic. Taxis are available at the airport for the trip; some hotels run regular shuttles from the airport into town. Greyhound buses serve downtown Columbus; no passenger train service is available.

FIND YOUR WAY

Routes I-70, I-670, and I-71 intersect or join State Rte. 315. Exit 315 at Lane Ave. Travel east (left if you are traveling south on 315 or right if you are traveling north on 315) on Lane Ave. to Fyffe Road. Turn south (right) on Fyffe Road. to Woody Hayes Dr. Turn east (left) on Woody Hayes Dr. to College Rd. Turn south (right) on College Rd. to 12th Ave. Turn west (right) on 12th Ave. The Student Visitor Center can be followed from Lane Ave. When you check in, you will be given a parking pass.

STAY THE NIGHT

Nearby: Just across the street from the university (its northern edge) is the moderately priced **Holiday Inn** on the Lane (328 W. Lane Ave.; 800-465-4329 or 614-294-4848). A free shuttle service will bring you to a hotel from the airport. The **University Plaza Hotel** (3110 Olentangy River Rd.; 877-677-5292 or 614-267-7461) is convenient and moderately priced too. An inexpensive motel one-and-a-half miles away is **Cross Country Inn-OSU North** (3246 Olentangy River Rd.; 800-621-1429 or 614-267-4646). Because Ohio State is located in Columbus, one of Ohio's major cities, there are a variety of places to stay. They range from the inexpensive **Red Roof Inn** (441 Ackerman Rd.; 800-843-7663 or 614-267-9941), to the **Hyatt Regency of Columbus** (350 N. High St.; 800-233-1234 or 614-463-1234), which is an expensive hotel with the usual amenities.

HIGHLIGHTS

ON CAMPUS

- Hale Cultural Center
- Chadwick Arboretum
- Jack Nicklaus Golf Museum
- Schottenstein Center and Value City Arena

OFF CAMPUS

- Columbus Zoo
- Columbus Crew
- Wyandotte Lake
- Easton (shopping)
- MSL Columbus Crew

OHIO UNIVERSITY—ATHENS

Undergraduate Admissions, 120 Chubb Hall,
Athens, OH 45701 • Telephone: 740-593-4100 • www.ohiou.edu •
Email: admissions.freshmen@ohiou.edu

Hours: Monday–Friday; 8:00AM–5:00PM; Saturday, 10:30AM–noon

Beautiful and safe Ohio University prides itself on offering a private school–like education at a bargain, public school–like price. The excellent honors tutorial program allows select students to work more closely with professors than is usually possible at a large university.

HIGHLIGHTS

ON CAMPUS
- Charles J. Ping Recreation Center
- Kennedy Museum of Art
- Templeton-Blackburn Memorial Auditorium
- Convocation Center
- Alden Library

OFF CAMPUS
- Stuart's Opera House-Nelsonville
- Dairy Barn (Cultural Arts Center)
- Hocking Valley Science Railway
- Athens County Historical Society and Museum
- Hocking Hill Recreation Area

TRANSPORTATION

Port Columbus International Airport in Columbus is 75 miles (a two-hour drive) from campus. Rental cars are available at the airport. The Ohio University Airport, which is 12 miles away from campus, has a 4,200-foot lighted runway and is open to the public. Ground transportation from the airport to Athens should be arranged in advance. Bus service to and from Athens is available by calling Lakefront Trailways at 1-800-638-6338 ext. 162 or All Points Transportation at 740-927-9778.

FIND YOUR WAY

From U.S. Rte. 50 or U.S. Rte. 33 (which merge near Athens), take the Athens exit for Rte. 682 N. At the traffic light, turn right onto Richland Ave. Stop at the Ohio University Visitors' Center (the log structure on your left at the corner of Richland Ave. and South Shafer St.) for directions to parking locations and other specific places on campus.

STAY THE NIGHT

Nearby: For convenience, you cannot beat the **Ohio University Inn and Conference Center** (331 Richland Ave.; 740-593-6661), adjacent to the campus (about a 15-minute walk to the Admissions Office). The prices are in the moderate range.

A Little Farther: If you can't get into the **Ohio University Inn,** call the Athens County Convention and Visitors' Bureau at 800-878-9767 for a list of other are hotels. **Lake Hope State Park** (740-596-5253), 30 minutes from campus, has inexpensive cabins available year-round (rent by the week during summer) and various types of campsites. **Burr Oak State Park** (800-282-7275), also 30 minutes away, has a lodge and two-bedroom cabins equipped with kitchenettes. The views are beautiful and costs range from inexpensive to moderate. Rates vary seasonally and by the day of the week. Check for special packages.

AT A GLANCE

Selectivity Rating		78
Range SAT I Math		500–610
Average SAT I Math		550
Range SAT I Verbal		500–600
Average SAT I Verbal		540
Average ACT Composite		23
Average GPA		3.3
Student to Faculty Ratio		20:1

CAMPUS TOURS

Appointment	Required
Dates	Year-round
Times	Mon–Fri, 10AM, 12PM, & 2PM; Sat, NOON
Average Length	1 hour

ON-CAMPUS APPOINTMENTS

Admissions

Start Date–Juniors	N/A
Appointment	Not required
Advance Notice	No
Saturdays	No
Average Length	45 min.
Info Sessions	Yes

Faculty and Coaches

Dates/Times	Academic year
Arrangements	Contact coach directly 2 weeks prior

CLASS VISITS

Dates	Academic year
Arrangements	Contact faculty directly

OHIO WESLEYAN UNIVERSITY

Office of Admissions, 61 S. Sandusky St., Delaware, OH 43015 • Telephone: 800-922-8953 • www.owu.edu • Email: owuadmit@owu.edu

Hours: Monday–Friday, 8:30AM–5:00PM; Saturday (during academic term), 9:00AM–2:00PM

The Admissions Office is picky at Ohio Wesleyan University, a midwestern liberal arts college with small classes and a reportedly excellent administration. Students say OWU's extremely accessible professors provide additional study sessions before exams and a lot of personal attention to help students with academic and personal problems.

AT A GLANCE

Selectivity Rating	79
Range SAT I Math	540–650
Average SAT I Math	608
Range SAT I Verbal	540–650
Average SAT I Verbal	602
Average ACT Composite	27
Average GPA	3.3
Student to Faculty Ratio	13:1

CAMPUS TOURS

Appointment	Required
Dates	Year-round
Times	10AM, noon, 2PM, & 4PM; Sat 10AM, 11AM, noon, & 1PM
Average Length	1 hour

ON-CAMPUS APPOINTMENTS

Admissions

Start Date–Juniors	At the student's convenience
Appointment	Required
Advance Notice	Yes, 1 week
Saturdays	Yes
Average Length	45 min.
Info Sessions	Yes

Faculty and Coaches

Dates/Times	Academic year
Arrangements	Contact Admissions Office 1 week prior

CLASS VISITS

Dates	Academic year
Arrangements	Contact Admissions Office

TRANSPORTATION

The Port Columbus International Airport in Columbus is a 45-minute drive from campus. Call the Admissions Office to arrange for transportation from the airport.

FIND YOUR WAY

The campus is located near the junction of U.S. Rtes. 23 and 36. From Rte. 36 (William St. in Delaware), head south on Sandusky St. The Admissions Office is near the third traffic light on Sandusky. Use the parking lot off Sandusky St. and follow the signs to Admissions.

STAY THE NIGHT

Nearby: Numerous hotels and motels are available throughout the Delaware and the northwest Columbus area. Delaware, located in the approximate center of Ohio, is 20 miles due north of downtown Columbus and 120 miles southwest of Cleveland. Worthington is a nearby north suburb of Columbus and is 15 minutes directly south of Delaware. Accommodations in the area include **Amerihost** (1720 Columbus Pike, Rte. 23; 740-363-3510) **Best Western Delaware Hotel** (351 S. Sandusky St.; 740-363-1262), **Hampton Inn** (171-Route 36/37; 740-363-4700), **Long View Farm B & B** (3780 Bowtown Road; 740-362-0387), **Super 8** (Route 23; 740-363-8869), **Travelodge** (U.S. Route 23 North; 740-369-4421), **Welcome Home Inn B & B** (6640 Home Road; 740-881-6588).

A Little Farther: Other options include **The Courtyard** (7411 Vantage Dr.; 800-321-2211), **Holiday Inn at Crosswoods** (175 Hutchinson; 614-885-3334), Homewood Suites (115 Hutchinson; 614-785-0001), **Microtel** (7500 Vantage Dr.; 800-433-3690), **Red Roof Inn** (7474 N. High St.; 800-THE-ROOF), **Sheraton Suites** (201 Hutchinson; 614-436-0004), **Travelodge** (7480 N. High St.; 614-836-2525), **Worthington Inn** (1881 Carriage House, High St. & New England; 614-885-2600), and **AmeriSuites** (Columbus/Worthington; 800-833-1516). Also, **The Frederick Fitting House** (72 Fitting Ave.; 419-886-2863) is a charming, quiet, country village bed-and-breakfast. Prices vary from inexpensive to moderate (including full breakfast). Nearby you will find a golf course, tennis courts, jogging trails, canoeing, shops, and skiing.

HIGHLIGHTS

ON CAMPUS

- R. W. Corns Building
- Hamilton Williams Campus Center
- Selby Stadium
- Beeghiy Library
- Sanborn Hall (music)

OFF CAMPUS

- The Arts Castle
- Highbanks Nature Preserve
- Delaware State Park
- Columbus Zoo
- Delaware County Fairgrounds

UNIVERSITY OF DAYTON

Office of Admissions, 300 College Park Drive, Dayton, OH 45469-1300 • Telephone: 800-837-7433 • admission.udayton.edu • Email: admission@udayton.edu

Hours: Monday–Friday, 8:30AM–4:30PM; Saturday (second semester only), 8:30AM–noon

The University of Dayton is a Catholic school with a broad set of general requirements that is just big enough to provide self-motivated students with a wealth of opportunities. Campus facilities are on the upswing, and UD sponsors both a University Scholars Program, which offers enrollees special classes, seminars, and symposia, and an even more rigorous honors program.

HIGHLIGHTS

ON CAMPUS
- John F. Kennedy Memorial Union
- Ryan C. Harris Learning-Teaching Center
- University of Dayton Arena
- University of Dayton Science Center
- Kettering Laboratories; UDRI

OFF CAMPUS
- Schuster Performing Arts Center
- United States Air Force Museum
- The Dayton Art Institute
- RiverScape
- Fifth Third Field

TRANSPORTATION

The University of Dayton campus is located 20 minutes south of Dayton International Airport. Cincinnati and Columbus airports are also located within a 75-minute drive. Greyhound bus service is available to downtown Dayton. Transportation from the bus terminal to campus is available by Yellow, Cliff, and Checker cab companies, as well as the Regional Transit Authority (RTA) public bus service. The RTA bus stop is located two blocks west of the Greyhound Terminal, at the corner of Fourth and Ludlow streets. The RTA bus to UD is #16. In addition, the university provides a ride board for students, which allows students with cars to post that they can give rides and students without cars to post that they need rides.

FIND YOUR WAY

From I-75, southbound (from Toledo): Exit #51 at Edwin C. Moses Boulevard. Turn left and follow Edwin C. Moses Boulevard east to Stewart Street. Turn right and continue on Stewart Street to the University of Dayton entrance at College Park. **From I-75, northbound** (from Cincinnati): Exit #51 at Edwin C. Moses Boulevard. Turn right and follow Edwin C. Moses Boulevard east to Stewart Street. Follow the preceding directions. **From I-70, westbound (from Columbus):** Exit I-70 at I-675. Proceed southbound to state route 35. Go west toward Dayton to I-75. Take I-75 south one exit to #51 Edwin C. Moses Boulevard. Turn left and follow Edwin C. Moses Boulevard east to Stewart Street. Follow the preceding directions. **From I-70, eastbound (from Indianapolis and Dayton Airport):** Exit I-70 at I-75 south. Proceed southbound through Dayton and exit at Edwin C. Moses Boulevard. Turn left and follow Edwin C. Moses Boulevard east to Stewart Street. Follow the preceding directions.

STAY THE NIGHT

Nearby: Please visit the Office of Admissions' website (http://admission.udayton.edu/visitud/hotels.asp) for a full list.

AT A GLANCE

Selectivity Rating	77
Range SAT I Math	510–630
Average SAT I Math	575
Range SAT I Verbal	500–610
Average SAT I Verbal	557
Average ACT Composite	24
Student to Faculty Ratio	15:1

CAMPUS TOURS

Appointment	Preferred
Dates	Year-round
Times	Contact the Office of Admissions for further information.
Average Length	Varies

ON-CAMPUS APPOINTMENTS

Admissions

Appointment	Preferred
Advance Notice	Yes, 2 weeks
Saturdays	Sometimes
Average Length	30 min.
Info Sessions	Yes

Faculty and Coaches

Dates/Times	Year-round
Arrangements	Contact Admissions Office 2 weeks prior

CLASS VISITS

Dates	Year-round
Arrangements	Contact Admissions Office

WITTENBERG UNIVERSITY

Admissions Office, Ward St. & North Wittenberg Ave., P.O. Box 720, Springfield, OH 45501 • Telephone: 800-677-7558 • www.wittenberg.edu • Email: admission@wittenberg.edu

Hours: Monday–Friday, 9:00AM–5:00PM; Saturday (during term), 9:00AM–noon

"What they sell in the brochure is what you get and more," exclaims one satisfied student at Wittenberg University. This school is a great place to learn and grow as a person, according to its students. A unique trimester system keeps academic life interesting, and the Financial Aid Office receives especially high praise.

AT A GLANCE

Selectivity Rating	79
Range SAT I Math	484–684
Average SAT I Math	582
Range SAT I Verbal	490–680
Average SAT I Verbal	576
Average ACT Composite	26
Average GPA	3.4
Student to Faculty Ratio	14:1

CAMPUS TOURS

Appointment	Required
Dates	Academic year
Times	Every hour on the hour
Average Length	1 hour

ON-CAMPUS APPOINTMENTS

Admissions

Start Date–Juniors	Anytime
Appointment	Required
Advance Notice	Yes, 2 weeks
Saturdays	Sometimes
Info Sessions	N/A

Faculty and Coaches

Dates/Times	Subject to faculty/ coach availability
Arrangements	Contact Admissions Office 1 week prior

CLASS VISITS

Dates	Year-round
Arrangements	Contact Admissions Office

TRANSPORTATION

Dayton International Airport is 27 miles away from the campus. Car rentals are available from the airport. During the academic year, student drivers provide free shuttle service between the airport and the campus; call the Admissions Office at least one week in advance to arrange for this service.

FIND YOUR WAY

From I-70, take U.S. Rte. 68 N. to Ohio Rte. 41. Proceed west for two miles on Rte. 41 following signs to the university.

STAY THE NIGHT

Nearby: Located conveniently on campus, Wittenberg runs its very own guest house. Not only convenient, Benjamin Prince Guest House is a historic landmark filled with antiques. Check with the Admissions Office about availability. If you are staying in Springfield, the best choice for the money is the **Springfield Inn** (100 S. Fountain Ave.; 937-322-3600). This full-service modern hotel is one mile from campus across from Market Place. Mention you are a guest of the Wittenberg Admissions Office to obtain a special rate. For a change of pace, try the **Buck Creek State Park Cottages** (1901 Buck Creek Ln.; 937-322-5284). The cottages are pretty, modern, and in a lovely setting about four miles away from campus, and there are boating and fishing places nearby. This is a very inexpensive choice for a family; the two-bedroom cottages are inexpensive.

A Little Farther: Tipp City, about 30 minutes west of Springfield and somewhat north of Dayton, has some charming little inns and bed-and-breakfasts. A small (four-room) bed-and-breakfast with particular charm and elegance is **Willow Tree Inn** (1900 W. State Rte. 571; 937-667-2957). Rates range from inexpensive to moderate (less on weekdays than on weekends), and you will enjoy a glass of wine in the evening in addition to the continental breakfast.

HIGHLIGHTS

ON CAMPUS

- Thomas Library
- Weaver Observatory
- Chakeres Theatre
- Alumni & Visitors Center

OFF CAMPUS

- Springfield Art Center
- Kings Island
- United States Air Force Museum

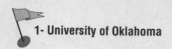

1- University of Oklahoma

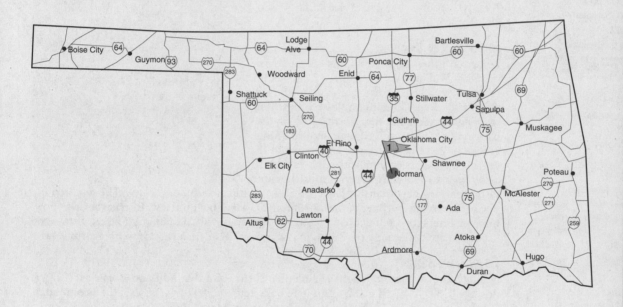

Boise City · 64
Guymon 93
270
283
Shattuck ·
60
Woodward ·
Seiling
64
Lodge
Alve
60
270
183
El Reno
40
Clinton
Elk City ·
281
44
283
Altus
62
Lawton
70
44
Enid
64
35
Ponca City
77
Stillwater ·
Guthrie ·
Oklahoma City
Norman
Anadarko
177
Ada ·
Bartlesville
60
60
Tulsa ·
69
Sapulpa ·
75
Muskagee
44
Shawnee
75
McAlester
Atoka ·
69
Ardmore ·
Duran
Hugo
Poteau ·
270
271
259

Oklahoma	Univ. of Oklahoma	Oklahoma City
Univ. of Oklahoma	—	21
Oklahoma City	21	—

UNIVERSITY OF OKLAHOMA

Prospective Student Services, 550 Parrington Oval, L-1,
Norman, OK 73019-4076 • Telephone: 800-234-6868 • www.goz.ou.edu •
Email: admrec@ou.edu

Hours: Monday–Friday, 8:00AM–5:00PM

Full scholarships for National Merit scholars and an honors program open to students who score above 1100 on the SAT create an ambitious intellectual atmosphere at the University of Oklahoma. Business programs are reputedly very good, as are engineering programs (studies in petroleum are especially strong, due to the proximity of the oil industry). A phenomenally pretty campus and maniacal school spirit are pluses.

AT A GLANCE

Selectivity Rating	76
Average SAT I Math	591
Average SAT I Verbal	582
Average ACT Composite	25
Average GPA	3.56
Student to Faculty Ratio	21:1

CAMPUS TOURS

Appointment	Preferred
Dates	Year-round
Times	Mon–Fri, 9AM & 2PM; Sat, 9:30AM
Average Length	120 min.

ON-CAMPUS APPOINTMENTS

Admissions

Start Date–Juniors	Six-semester high school transcript required for administrative process
Appointment	Preferred
Advance Notice	Yes, 2 weeks
Saturdays	Sometimes
Average Length	30 min.
Info Sessions	Yes

Faculty and Coaches

Dates/Times	Academic year
Arrangements	Contact Prospective Student Services 2 weeks prior

CLASS VISITS

Dates	Academic year
Arrangements	Prospective Student Services

TRANSPORTATION

Will Rogers World Airport is 20 miles away from Norman and serves as the closest commercial airport. There are shuttles, buses, and taxis that transport visitors to and from Will Rogers World Airport in Oklahoma City. Metro Transit Cart buses have routes that cover Norman every half hour to hour. Metro Transit also offers daily service to and from Oklahoma City.

FIND YOUR WAY

I-35 from OKC: Take Main Street Downtown exit, east. Follow Main Street for 2.2 miles to University Blvd. Turn right (south) on University Blvd. Go through Boyd Street (first stop light) and into the North Oval of the University. There are eight visitor parking spaces as you enter the Oval, and there are 15 spaces available as you leave the Oval. In order to park on campus, you must obtain a visitor parking permit inside Jacobson Hall. Your license tag number will be required for you to receive the parking permit. **I-35 from Dallas,** Take Lindsey Street east exit. Follow Lindsey Street for 1.6 miles to Elm Street, turn left (north). Go to Boyd Street, turn right (east). Go approximately one block to University Blvd. Turn right into the North Oval.

STAY THE NIGHT

Nearby: Local accommodations include the **Cutting Garden Bed and Breakfast** (927 W. Boyd; 405-329-4522), the **Days Inn** (609 Interstate Dr.; 800-DAYSINN), the **Econolodge** (100 26th Dr.; 800-55ECONO), the **Fairfield Inn by Marriott** (301 Norman Center Court; 405-447-1661), the **Guest Inn** (2543 West Main Street; 800-460-4619), the **Hampton Inn** (309 Norman Court Center; 73072, 800-HAMPTON), the **Holiday Inn** (1000 Interstate Drive; 1-800-HOLIDAY), the **Holmberg House Bed and Breakfast** (766 De Barr Ave.; 405-321-6221), **La Quinta Inns and Suites** (930 Ed Noble Parkway I-35 and Lindsey; 1-800-NU-ROOMS), the **Montford Inn Bed and Breakfast and Cottage** (322 Tonhawa St.; 800-321-8969), the **OU Motel** (2420 S. Classen Blvd; 405-321-4670), the **Ramada Inn** (1200 24th Avenue Southwest; I-35 and Lindsey, 800-500-9869), the **Residence Inn** (2681 Jefferson; 800-331-3131), the **Super 8 Motel** (2600 W. Main; 405-329-1624), and the **Travelodge** (225 N. Interstate Drive; 405-329-194).

HIGHLIGHTS

ON CAMPUS
- Jacobson Hall/OU Visitor Center
- Sam Noble Museum of Natural History
- Oklahoma Memorial Stadium
- Oklahoma Memorial Union
- The Fred Jones Jr. Museum of Art

OFF CAMPUS
- The Firehouse Art Center
- The Santa Fe Depot
- The Sooner Theatre
- The Cleveland Country Historical House
- The Little River Zoo

1- **Lewis & Clark College**
   Reed College
2- **Willamette University**

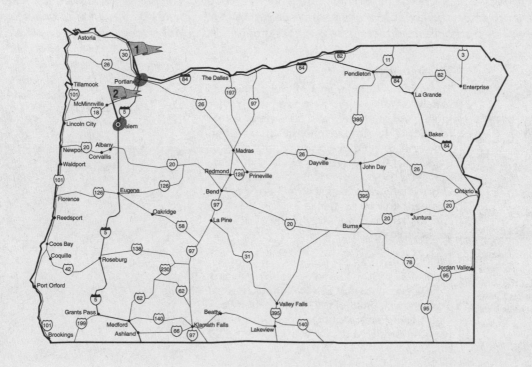

Oregon	Lewis & Clark	Reed Coll.	Willamette Univ.	Eugene	Portland
Lewis & Clark Coll.	—	5	44	114	0
Reed Coll.	5	—	49	119	0
Willamette Univ.	44	49	—	63	45
Eugene	114	119	63	—	115
Portland	0	0	45	115	—

LEWIS & CLARK COLLEGE

Office of Admissions, 0615 S.W. Palatine Hill Rd.,
Portland, OR 97219-7899 • Telephone: 800-444-4111 • www.lclark.edu •
Email: admissions@lclark.edu

Hours: Monday–Friday, 8:30AM–5:00PM; Saturday (by appointment during academic year), 9:00AM–noon

Lewis & Clark College is a small college in Portland, Oregon with a beautiful campus, small classes, and excellent, approachable professors. Lewis & Clark offers strong programs in foreign languages, English, and international affairs, as well as a school-subsidized overseas studies program that sends students virtually anywhere in the world.

AT A GLANCE

Selectivity Rating	83
Range SAT I Math	580–670
Range SAT I Verbal	600–690
Average GPA	3.6
Student to Faculty Ratio	12:1

CAMPUS TOURS

Appointment	Preferred
Dates	Year-round
Times	Mon, Wed, & Fri, 9AM & 3PM; Tues & Thurs, 9:30AM & 3PM
Average Length	1 hour

ON-CAMPUS APPOINTMENTS

Admissions

Start Date–Juniors	Anytime
Appointment	Required
Advance Notice	Yes, 1 week
Saturdays	Sometimes
Average Length	30 min.
Info Sessions	Yes

Faculty and Coaches

Dates/Times	Academic year
Arrangements	Contact Admissions Office 1 week prior

CLASS VISITS

Dates	Academic year
Arrangements	Contact Admissions Office

TRANSPORTATION

The Portland International Airport is approximately 20 miles away from campus. Tri-Met (public transportation) and taxis are available for the ride to campus from the airport; these run regularly so they do not require reservations. Lake Oswego Airporter also can transport you to campus. Call the Admissions Office if you want current schedules or phone numbers for these transportation services. Amtrak trains and Greyhound/Trailways buses serve Portland.

FIND YOUR WAY

From I-5, exit to Terwilliger Blvd. Follow Terwilliger south and east to campus (toward Tryon Creek State Park). The Admissions Office is in Frank Manor, a large brick building just inside Main Gate off Palatine Hill Road.

STAY THE NIGHT

Nearby: Lewis & Clark is six miles south of Portland center, in the southwest quadrant of the city. The popular choice is the **Lakeshore Motor Hotel** (210 N. State St., Lake Oswego; 503-636-9679), a mile-and-a-half away. The hotel, known as the parents' dorm, has decks overlooking the lake that surrounds the hotel on three sides. All the rooms have kitchenettes. There is no dining room, but there are restaurants nearby. Rates range from inexpensive to moderate. An appealing bed-and-breakfast is **MacMaster House** (1041 S.W. Vista St.; 503-223-7362), about 15 minutes away from campus. This is in the Washington Park area, famous for its rose gardens. Rates are in the moderate range and include breakfast served in a formal dining room. The large, three-story colonial house is furnished with antiques, and the owners are very hospitable. Downtown options include the **Days Inn City Center** (800-899-0248), the **Hotel Vintage Plaza** (800-243-0555), and the **Portland Hilton** (800-445-8667). See the Reed College entry for other suggestions in Portland, but be aware that Reed is a 20-minute drive from Lewis & Clark. The **Holiday Inn Crowne Plaza** (14811 Kinse Oaks Blvd, Lake Oswego; 800-277-6983) offers moderate pricing and free shuttle from the hotel to Lewis & Clark.

HIGHLIGHTS

ON CAMPUS

- Gallery of Contemporary Art
- New residence halls/Maggie's Cafe
- Library
- Templeton Student Center
- Pamplin Sports Center

OFF CAMPUS

- Downtown Portland
- Columbia River Gorge
- Mt. Hood
- Oregon Coast
- Powell's Bookstore

REED COLLEGE

Admissions Office, 3203 S.E. Woodstock Blvd., Portland, OR 97202-8199 • Telephone: 800-547-4750 • web.reed.edu • Email: admission@reed.edu

Hours: Monday–Friday, 8:30AM–5:00PM

Reed College is so tough. About half of all freshmen at Reed make it through all four years. This is despite the fact that grades, while recorded, are neither reported nor discussed. For those intelligent and work-obsessed students who can cut the mustard, this little liberal arts school is a virtual utopia. If you want to work really hard and hang out with brilliant, strange, intelligent, and interesting people, Reed is the place for you.

HIGHLIGHTS

ON CAMPUS

- Thesis Tower
- Research Nuclear Reactor
- Crystal Springs Canyon
- Cerf Amphitheatre
- The Paradox Café

OFF CAMPUS

- Powell's Bookstore
- Mt. Hood
- Washington Park
- The Waterfront
- Bagdad Theatre

TRANSPORTATION

The Portland Metro Airport is 20 miles away from campus. Taxis, Airporter buses, public buses, and rental cars are available for the ride to campus from the airport. For taxis, call Broadway Cab at 503-227-1234 or Rose City Cab at 503-282-7707. The Blue Star Airporter bus will take you from the airport's taxi/limousine area to the campus. For an even cheaper ride, take the Tri-Met.

FIND YOUR WAY

From the south, take I-5 N. to the Ross Island Bridge exit; then continue east on Powell Blvd. (which connects to the Ross Island Bridge). Turn right (south) on 39th Ave. and proceed a mile-and-a-half, then turn right on Woodstock Blvd. After half a block, turn right again into the Reed parking lot. **From the north,** take I-5 S. to the Oregon City/99E exit. Stay to the far left, then after the split in the exit, stay to the right and take the Oregon City/99E off-ramp. This will put you on McLaughlin Blvd.; continue south on McLaughlin to the Holgate exit (a right-hand exit); from Holgate, turn right onto 28th Ave. and continue to the college, which will be on the left, two miles down.

STAY THE NIGHT

Nearby: An inexpensive bed-and-breakfast is the **Portland Guest House** (1720 N.E. 15th Ave.; 503-282-1402), 15 minutes away from campus and within walking distance of the Lloyd Center Mall. Also about 15 minutes away from Reed, with rooms starting at the low end of the moderate range (ask for the special Reed visitors rate), is **Portland's White House** (1914 N.E. 22nd Ave.; 503-287-7131). None of these bed-and-breakfasts allow smoking. For other bed-and-breakfasts, call Northwest Bed-and-Breakfast Travel Unlimited (503-243-7616). About equidistant between Reed and Lewis & Clark is the **Riverplace Hotel** (1510 S.W. Harbor Way; 503-228-3233 or 800-227-1333). This four-star hotel has all amenities, and the price includes a complimentary continental breakfast. You can dine overlooking the river and enjoy a jazz trio at the bar (well, your parents can). Also check out the downtown Portland accommodations in the Lewis & Clark entry.

AT A GLANCE

Selectivity Rating	88
Range SAT I Math	620–710
Average SAT I Math	704
Range SAT I Verbal	660–760
Average SAT I Verbal	667
Average ACT Composite	30
Average GPA	3.8
Student to Faculty Ratio	10:1

CAMPUS TOURS

Appointment	Preferred
Dates	Year-round
Times	Mon–Fri, in the morning and afternoon
Average Length	1 hour

ON-CAMPUS APPOINTMENTS

Admissions

Start Date–Juniors	Anytime
Appointment	Required
Advance Notice	Yes, 1 week
Saturdays	No
Average Length	30 min.
Info Sessions	Yes

Faculty and Coaches

Dates/Times	N/A
Arrangements	Contact Admissions Office

CLASS VISITS

Dates	Academic year
Arrangements	Contact Admissions Office

WILLAMETTE UNIVERSITY

Office of Admissions, 900 State St.,
Salem, OR 97301 • Telephone: 877-542-2787 • www.willamette.edu •
Email: undergrad-admission@willamette.edu

Hours: Monday–Friday, 8:00AM–5:00PM; Saturday, 9:00AM–2:00PM

Students call Methodist-affiliated Willamette University the best small liberal arts school in the Northwest. They say the education is great, the professors are wonderful, and the classes are small enough to allow for a lot of individual attention. On campus you'll find cute squirrels and meandering ducks; and, if that gets old, Portland is only 45 minutes away.

AT A GLANCE

Selectivity Rating	84
Range SAT I Math	560–660
Average SAT I Math	610
Range SAT I Verbal	560–680
Average SAT I Verbal	620
Average ACT Composite	27
Average GPA	3.6
Student to Faculty Ratio	10:1

CAMPUS TOURS

Appointment	Preferred
Dates	Year-round
Average Length	1 hour

ON-CAMPUS APPOINTMENTS

Admissions

Start Date–Juniors	Anytime
Appointment	Preferred
Advance Notice	Yes, 1 week
Saturdays	Sometimes
Average Length	1 hour
Info Sessions	Yes

Faculty and Coaches

Dates/Times	Academic year
Arrangements	Contact Admissions Office 1 week prior

CLASS VISITS

Dates	Academic year
Arrangements	Contact Admissions Office

TRANSPORTATION

Portland International Airport is 60 miles away from campus. HUT Limousine Service offers regular transportation from the Portland airport to the Willamette Campus. Amtrak offers daily north/south train service to Salem; the station is across the street from the southeast corner of the campus. Greyhound buses serve Salem from throughout the U.S.; the bus depot is five blocks away from campus.

FIND YOUR WAY

From I-5 (N. or S.), take the Hwy. 22/Mission St. exit and travel approximately two miles west to the City Center/Willamette University exit. The off-ramp takes you to the southeast corner of campus. Keep to the left and proceed through the traffic signal half a block, turning right onto campus and into the university's main parking lot.

STAY THE NIGHT

Nearby: Salem has a variety of accommodations all within close proximity to campus. Rates range from moderate to inexpensive for university visitors depending on the time of year and number of guests. **The Best Western-Mill Creek Inn** (3125 Ryan Dr. S.E.; 503-585-3332) is five miles away from campus and within easy Interstate 5 access. Price includes a free breakfast at Denny's, health club privileges, pool, and sauna. If a walk is what you like, the **Ramada Inn** (200 Commercial St. S.E.; 503-363-4123) is convenient. Located just a short walk away from campus, the Ramada Inn is located in the heart of town and just minutes away from shopping areas. Additional hotels include the **Phoenix Inn** (4310 Commercial St. SE; 503-588-9220), **Salem Inn** (1775 Freeway Ct. N.E.; 503-588-0515), and **Comfort Suites** (630 Hawthorne Ave. S.E.; 503-585-9705). Salem also boasts a number of charming bed-and-breakfast establishments. For additional information on those, please contact the Office of Admissions (503-370-6303).

A Little Farther: Salem is less than 50 miles away from Portland via Interstate 5. A wide variety of lodging accommodations are available in Portland and along Interstate 5 between Portland and Salem.

HIGHLIGHTS

ON CAMPUS
- Hallic Ford Museum of Art
- Roger's Music Center
- Sparks Sports and Recreation Center
- Willamette Bistro
- The Star Trees

OFF CAMPUS
- State capitol (across from campus)
- Riverfront Park
- Silver Falls State Park
- Beautiful Pacific Ocean
- Bush's Pasture Park

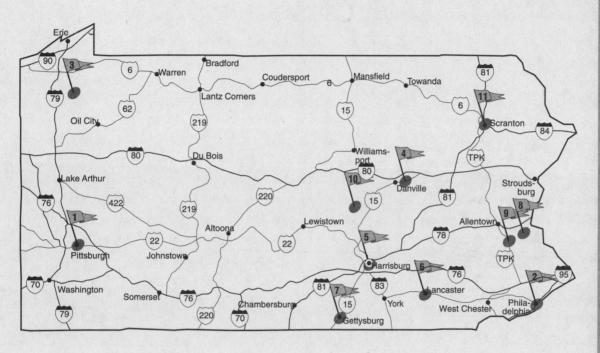

1- PITTSBURGH AREA
　Carnegie Mellon University
　Chatham College
　Duquesne U. of Pittsburgh
2- PHILADELPHIA AREA
　Bryn Mawr College
　Drexel University
　Haverford College
　University of Pennsylvania
　Swarthmore College
　Villanova College
　Temple University
3- Allegheny College
4- Bucknell University
5- Dickinson College
6- Franklin & Marshall College
7- Gettysburg College
8- Lafayette College
9- Lehigh College
10- Pennsylvania State University
11- University of Scranton

Penn.

	Allegheny Coll.	Bryn Mawr Coll.	Bucknell Univ.	Carnegie Mellon	Chatham Coll.	Dickinson Coll.	Drexel Univ.	Duquesne Univ.	Franklin & Marshall	Gettysburg Coll.	Haverford Coll.	Lafayette Coll.	Lehigh Univ.	Penn State Univ.	Swarthmore Coll.	Temple Univ.	Univ. Pennsylvania	Univ. Pittsburgh	Univ. Scranton	Villanova Univ.	Philadelphia	Pittsburgh
Allegheny Coll.	—	341	212	92	88	273	349	90	325	293	344	337	345	166	339	383	349	93	307	336	346	88
Bryn Mawr Coll.	341	—	156	295	293	112	11	293	58	113	2	73	50	188	11	11	11	291	116	2	4	293
Bucknell Univ.	212	156	—	259	253	79	169	220	104	103	157	139	126	71	162	168	169	220	92	155	165	253
Carnegie Mellon	92	295	259	—	0	182	304	0	237	198	297	306	281	136	305	303	304	0	295	293	300	0
Chatham Coll.	88	293	253	0	—	179	306	0	238	196	295	303	279	133	303	303	306	0	293	291	308	0
Dickinson Coll.	273	112	79	182	179	—	120	190	59	27	113	114	103	82	120	124	120	188	141	110	117	179
Drexel Univ.	349	11	169	304	306	120	—	304	61	124	9	62	52	196	10	4	0	303	124	13	0	306
Duquesne Univ.	90	293	220	0	0	190	304	—	238	186	294	301	290	137	305	305	304	3	296	294	294	0
Franklin & Marshall	325	58	104	237	238	59	61	238	—	55	60	86	72	123	62	79	61	237	137	56	58	238
Gettysburg Coll.	293	113	103	198	196	27	124	186	55	—	115	135	125	131	121	140	124	184	160	110	121	196
Haverford Coll.	344	2	157	297	295	113	9	294	60	115	—	74	51	189	9	9	10	293	117	4	10	295
Lafayette Coll.	337	73	139	306	303	114	62	301	86	135	74	—	16	186	73	78	63	297	66	71	58	303
Lehigh Univ.	345	50	126	281	279	103	52	290	72	125	51	16	—	173	59	58	52	289	82	48	60	279
Penn State Univ.	166	188	71	136	133	82	196	137	123	131	189	186	173	—	186	193	196	135	149	186	192	133
Swarthmore Coll.	339	11	162	305	303	120	10	305	62	121	9	73	59	186	—	22	10	303	124	12	11	303
Temple Univ.	383	11	168	303	303	124	4	305	79	140	9	78	58	193	22	—	5	301	126	18	0	305
Univ. Pennsylvania	349	11	169	304	306	120	0	304	61	124	10	63	52	196	10	5	—	303	125	13	0	306
Univ. Pittsburgh	93	291	220	0	0	188	303	3	237	184	293	297	289	135	303	301	303	—	296	290	303	0
Univ. Scranton	307	116	92	295	293	141	124	296	137	160	117	66	82	149	124	126	125	296	—	114	125	296
Villanova Univ.	336	2	155	293	291	110	13	294	56	110	4	71	48	186	12	18	13	290	114	—	0	291
Philadelphia	346	4	165	300	308	117	0	291	58	121	10	58	60	192	11	0	0	303	125	6	—	311
Pittsburgh	88	293	253	0	0	179	306	0	238	196	295	303	279	133	303	305	306	0	296	291	311	—

ALLEGHENY COLLEGE

Admissions Office,
Meadville, PA 16335 • Telephone: 800-521-5293 • www.allegheny.edu •
Email: admiss@allegheny.edu

Hours: Monday–Friday, 8:00AM–5:00PM; Saturday, select by appointment

Ninety miles away from Cleveland and Pittsburgh, this old-school college (founded in 1815) is located in Meadville, Pennsylvania (population 14,000), in the foothills of the Allegheny Mountains. Allegheny requires each student to complete an original senior project to prove effective writing, speaking, analysis, and the ability to work independently.

HIGHLIGHTS

ON CAMPUS

- Rustic Bridge
- $14.5 million science complex dedicated to biology, chemistry, and environmental science
- $13 million Wise Sport and Fitness Center
- Campus Center
- Robertson Athletic Field

OFF CAMPUS

- Market House
- Academy Theatre
- French Creek
- Diamond Park
- Ernst Bike Trail

TRANSPORTATION

Erie International Airport is 40 miles away from campus. The college will provide pickup service for students traveling alone if given advance notice; call the Admissions Office to make arrangements.

FIND YOUR WAY

To get into the city of Meadville, take I-79 to Exit 36A. You will then be traveling on Route 322 East; take the Park Ave. exit. Follow Park Avenue straight through town (six traffic lights) to Chestnut St. and turn right. Follow the sign for Allegheny at the next light, making a left turn around Diamond Park onto North Main St. After two traffic lights on North Main, bear right up the hill to Allegheny. After you pass the brick gates in the center of campus (on the left), take the second left turn onto Allegheny St. At the first stop sign, turn left onto Park Ave. After passing three large buildings, take the first left, which leads to the Admissions parking area. The Admissions Office is in Schultz Hall, which is the first building down the hill from the parking area.

STAY THE NIGHT

Nearby: The **Days Inn** (240 Conneaut Lake Rd.; 814-337-4264), two miles away from campus, has a special inexpensive rate. **Super 8 Motel** (845 Conneaut Lake Rd.; 814-333-8883) is half a mile west of I-79. **Holiday Inn Express** (250 Conneaut Lake Rd.; 814-724-6012) is half a mile east of I-79. **Motel 6** (Conneaut Lake Rd.; 814-724-6366) is one-eighth of a mile west of I-79. The motels listed above offer discounted rates for families visiting Allegheny College. Mention that you are a prospective Allegheny student when you make your reservation.

A Little Farther: The college is in Meadville, which is 88 miles north of Pittsburgh and 92 miles east of Cleveland, Ohio. See the Carnegie Mellon and Chatham entries for suggestions in Pittsburgh and the Case Western Reserve entry for suggestions in Cleveland.

AT A GLANCE

Selectivity Rating	74
Range SAT I Math	550–650
Average SAT I Math	600
Range SAT I Verbal	550–650
Average SAT I Verbal	598
Average ACT Composite	25
Average GPA	3.7
Student to Faculty Ratio	14:1

CAMPUS TOURS

Times	Mon–Fri, 8AM–5PM; Sat 8:30AM–NOON

ON-CAMPUS APPOINTMENTS

Admissions

Start Date–Juniors	Anytime
Appointment	Required
Advance Notice	Yes, 2 weeks
Saturdays	Sometimes

Faculty and Coaches

Arrangements	Contact Admissions Office

CLASS VISITS

Arrangements	Contact Admissions Office

BRYN MAWR COLLEGE

Office of Admissions, 101 North Merion Avenue, 101 N. Merion Ave.,
Bryn Mawr, PA 19010-2899 • Telephone: 800-262-1885 • www.brynmawr.edu •
Email: admissions@brynmawr.edu

Hours: Monday–Friday, 9:00AM–5:00PM; Saturday (during fall), 9:00AM–1:00PM

The women's community at Bryn Mawr offers passionate professors, a strict core curriculum, and individualized attention. But beware: Social life always comes after academics for Mawrters.

AT A GLANCE

Selectivity Rating	92
Range SAT I Math	600–690
Average SAT I Math	638
Range SAT I Verbal	630–730
Average SAT I Verbal	672
Average ACT Composite	28
Student to Faculty Ratio	8:1

CAMPUS TOURS

Appointment	Preferred
Dates	Year-round
Times	Contact Office of Admissions for times
Average Length	1 hour

ON-CAMPUS APPOINTMENTS

Admissions

Start Date–Juniors	Mid-March
Appointment	Required
Advance Notice	Yes, 1 week
Saturdays	Sometimes
Average Length	30 min.
Info Sessions	Yes

Faculty and Coaches

Dates/Times	Academic year
Arrangements	Contact coach directly 1 week prior

CLASS VISITS

Dates	Academic year
Arrangements	Contact Admissions Office

TRANSPORTATION

Philadelphia International Airport is 20 miles away from campus. Taxis, limousines, and trains are available. No advance arrangements are needed for a taxi. For limousine service, call Main Line Airport Service at 610-525-0513 (or 800-427-3464 in Pennsylvania) for information and reservations, or use the courtesy phone at the airport (push Main Line). If you want to use the trains, take the airport shuttle from the airport (it leaves every 20 minutes) to 30th St. Station in Philadelphia. From 30th St., take the SEPTA R-5 train to Bryn Mawr (leaves approximately every 30 minutes). Amtrak trains and Greyhound buses serve Philadelphia from all over the country. Take the Amtrak train to 30th St. Station in Philadelphia. From 30th St., take SEPTA commuter train R-5 (Paoli Local or Bryn Mawr Local, which goes from Lansdale and Doylestown to Downingtown and Paoli) to Bryn Mawr; the R-5 takes approximately 18 minutes to reach Bryn Mawr. The campus is a 5-minute walk from the station; walk straight ahead (on Morris Avenue) as you get off the train. After two blocks, turn left on Yarrow St.; the college stretches to your right and straight ahead. Call Bennett Taxi Service on a direct phone line from the Bryn Mawr train station if you don't want to walk. If you want to call Bennett in advance, the number is 610-525-1770. From the Greyhound Bus terminal, walk to the Market East train station and take the SEPTA R-5 train to Bryn Mawr (see preceding directions).

FIND YOUR WAY

From the Pennsylvania Tpke., take Exit 24 (Valley Forge) and follow the signs to Rte. 76 E. (Expressway to Philadelphia). After three miles, take Exit 27 (Gulph Mills and Rte. 320). Stay to the right and take Rte. 320 S. At the Spring Mill Rd. intersection, a sign indicates that 320 S. continues to the right; do not turn right there. Continue straight across the intersection; this puts you on Montgomery Ave. Continue on Montgomery for approximately two miles to Morris Ave (a four-way intersection with traffic light). Turn left onto Morris and pass the first left (Yarrow St.). The entrance to the college parking lot is just beyond Yarrow on the left. The distance from the turnpike to the college is eight miles.

STAY THE NIGHT

Nearby: On campus is the **Wyndham Alumnae House** (610-526-5236). Rates are moderate and include a continental breakfast. **Radnor Hotel** (591 E. Lancaster Ave., St. David's; 610-688-5800) is a privately owned hotel about 10 minutes from the college with an outdoor pool and a dining room. Rates are moderate. If a bed-and-breakfast accommodation appeals to you (even a room in a private home) contact Bed and Breakfast Connections (900-448-3619 or 610-687-3565). There is a $5 reservation fee.

HIGHLIGHTS

ON CAMPUS
- Thomas Hall (on National Historic Landmark registry)
- Erdman Hall (designed by famed architect Louis Kahn)
- The Cloister and Great Hall
- The Labyrinth and Taft Garden
- Rhys Carpenter Library

OFF CAMPUS
- Barnes Foundation Museum
- Philadelphia
- Longwood Gardens
- Suburban Square and King of Prussia (shopping)
- Valley Forge National Park

BUCKNELL UNIVERSITY

Admissions Office, Freas Hall,
Lewisburg, PA 17837 • Telephone: 570-577-1101 • www.bucknell.edu •
Email: admissions@bucknell.edu

Hours: Monday–Friday, 8:30AM–4:30PM; Saturday, 8:30AM–noon

With the exception of being isolated from any form of civilization, Bucknell University offers the ultimate college experience, according to students. Here in the hidden valley, you can have the multiplicity of majors and research opportunities offered by a huge, impersonal state school or the close-knit community and individualized education offered by a small liberal arts college.

HIGHLIGHTS

ON CAMPUS
- Weis Center for the Performing Arts
- Primate Facilities
- Uptown Night Club
- Stradler Poetry Center
- Library with Technology and Media Commons

OFF CAMPUS
- Variety of restaurants in historic Lewisburg
- R. B. Winter State Park
- Historic Movie Theater (downtown)
- Two malls located just a 30-minute drive away from campus.
- Skiing in the Poconos

TRANSPORTATION

Williamsport Airport is 25 miles away from campus and Harrisburg Airport is 65 miles away. The Admissions Office will provide transportation to campus if you make arrangements with them at least two weeks in advance. Rental cars and taxis are available at the airport. Susquehanna Trailways bus lines serve the Lewisburg area.

FIND YOUR WAY

Take I-80 to its intersection with Rte. 15. Exit to Rte. 15 S. and proceed for approximately seven miles to the university.

STAY THE NIGHT

Nearby: A few blocks from Bucknell in the restored downtown area is an antique-filled bed-and-breakfast, the **Pineapple Inn** (439 Market St.; 570-524-6200). Built in the 1850s, its prices range from inexpensive to moderate and include a full breakfast and tea in the afternoon. You can play tennis nearby. Many inexpensive and moderate motels and hotels are located in and around Lewisburg, particularly along U.S. Rte. 15. These include the **Days Inn** (570-523-1171), only one mile away from campus; the **Best Western Country Cupboard Inn** (570-524-5500), about two miles away from the university; the **Comfort Inn** (570-568-8000), and **Holiday Inn Express** (570- 568-1100), eight miles away in New Columbia at the junction of Rtes. 15 and 80; and **Hampton Inn** (570-743-2223), 10 miles south of campus on Rte. 15 in Shamokin Darn.

A Little Farther: If you're traveling east of the university on I-80, stop at the **Inn at Turkey Hill** (991 Central Rd., Bloomsburg; 717-387-1500) in a historic town on the Susquehanna River, 45 minutes from Bucknell (use Exit 35 from I-80). This inn is part old farmhouse and part modern wing. If you're visiting Bucknell during the summer or early fall, consider making a little detour to the northeast (about a 75-minute drive) to the charming Victorian village of Eagles Mere, a popular resort town in the 1920s. Here you will find **Eagles Mere Inn,** a delightful country place with rates in the expensive range (but they include breakfast and dinner). From November to March, the inn is open only on weekends; from March 15 to April 15 it is closed. Consider also a bed-and-breakfast in Williamsport: **Reighard House** (1323 E. 3rd St.; 570-326-3593), two blocks east of the Faxon Rd. exit from I-80. This Victorian home has six guest rooms with private baths and other modern amenities. Rates range from inexpensive to moderate.

AT A GLANCE

Selectivity Rating	89
Range SAT I Math	620–700
Average SAT I Math	659
Range SAT I Verbal	590–670
Average SAT I Verbal	631
Student to Faculty Ratio	12:1

CAMPUS TOURS

Appointment	Not required
Dates	Year-round
Times	Mon–Fri, 9:30AM–3:30PM; Sat, 10:30AM–12PM
Average Length	1 hour

ON-CAMPUS APPOINTMENTS

Admissions

Start Date—Juniors	April 15
Appointment	Required
Advance Notice	Yes, 3 weeks
Saturdays	Yes
Average Length	45 min.
Info Sessions	Yes

Faculty and Coaches

Dates/Times	Year-round
Arrangements	Contact Admissions Office 2 weeks prior

CLASS VISITS

Dates	Academic year
Arrangements	Contact Admissions Office

CARNEGIE MELLON UNIVERSITY

Admissions Office, 5000 Forbes Ave.,
Pittsburgh, PA 15213 • Telephone: 412-268-2082 • www.cmu.edu •
Email: undergraduate-admissions@andrew.cmu.edu

Hours: Monday–Friday, 8:30AM–5:00PM; select Saturdays during fall

School, friends, food, or sleep; choose three. That's Carnegie Mellon, according to the incredibly intelligent engineer types and flamboyant drama majors at this rigorous school. Excellent programs include engineering, computer science, business, architecture, and a well-respected School of Drama with several famous alums, including Ted Danson.

AT A GLANCE

Selectivity Rating	91
Range SAT I Math	680–770
Average SAT I Math	716
Range SAT I Verbal	590–700
Average SAT I Verbal	646
Average ACT Composite	29
Average GPA	3.6
Student to Faculty Ratio	11:1

CAMPUS TOURS

Appointment	Not required
Times	Mon–Fri, 9:30AM, 11:30AM, 1:30PM, & 3:30PM
Average Length	1 hour

ON-CAMPUS APPOINTMENTS

Admissions

Start Date–Juniors	May–November, during first week of the month
Appointment	Required
Advance Notice	Yes, 2 weeks
Saturdays	No
Average Length	45 min.
Info Sessions	Yes

Faculty and Coaches

Dates/Times	Year-round
Arrangements	Contact Admissions Office 2 weeks prior

CLASS VISITS

Dates	Year-round
Arrangements	Contact Admissions Office

TRANSPORTATION

Greater Pittsburgh International Airport is 25 miles away from campus. Airport Limousine Service provides transportation from the airport to campus; no advance reservation is necessary. Amtrak trains and Greyhound buses serve Pittsburgh. Taxis are available from the stations to campus.

FIND YOUR WAY

From the east on the Pennsylvania Tpke., take Exit 6 (Pittsburgh/Monroeville); then take I-376 W. to Exit 9 (Edgewood/Swissvale). At the end of the ramp, turn right onto Braddock Ave. and continue to the Forbes Ave. intersection (Frick Park will be on the left). Turn left onto Forbes Ave. and follow it approximately three miles to campus, which will be on the left. **From the west on the Pennsylvania Tpke.,** take Exit 3 (Perry Hwy.); then take I-79 S. to Exit 21 (I-279 S.). Follow I-279 S. toward Pittsburgh. As the interstate nears the city, follow signs for I-279 S. and the Fort Pitt Tunnel Bridge (left lanes). Follow signs for I-279 S./376 E. onto the bridge (right lanes). Watch carefully for signs on and after the bridge for I-376 E. (toward Monroeville). Take I-376 E. to Exit 5 (Forbes Ave. Oakland). Follow Forbes Ave. approximately a quarter of a mile to campus, which will be on the right.

STAY THE NIGHT

Nearby: Your choices include the **Hampton Inn,** the **Holiday Inn,** the **Shadyside Inn,** the **Wyndham Garden Hotel,** the **Marriott Residence Inn,** the **Marriott Courtyard Inn,** the **University Club,** and the **Appletree Bed & Breakfast.**

A Little Farther: You have some great choices 15 minutes away in downtown Pittsburgh. Across the Ninth St. Bridge over the Allegheny river is **The Priory** (614 Pressley St.; 412-231-3338). This restored nineteenth-century residence of Benedictine priests now houses an elegant inn. Rates, which include a continental breakfast, are in the moderate range and are less expensive on weekends than during the week. Well located near shops and restaurants, the **Sheraton at Station Square** (7 Station Sq. Dr.; 412-261-2000), is about 10 minutes away from campus. It offers rooms on weekends for a moderate rate, and on weekdays for an expensive rate. The Sheraton has an indoor pool and exercise equipment. Also about 10 minutes away is the **Double Tree Hotel** (1000 Penn Ave.; 412-281-3700). Lots of glitz here: an executive fitness club, a lap pool, a sauna, a whirlpool, an exercise room with fitness instructors, dancing, and a shopping arcade. Rates are moderate on the weekend and expensive during the week. See the Chatham College entry for other suggestions in the Pittsburgh area.

HIGHLIGHTS

ON CAMPUS
- Hunt Library
- Newell-Simon Building with Robotics
- College of Fine Arts
- Purnell Center for Performing Arts (new theater)
- University Center Building (Student Center)

OFF CAMPUS
- Carnegie Museum of Art
- Carnegie Museum of Natural History
- Carnegie Science Center
- Andy Warhol Museum
- Pittsburgh Zoo

CHATHAM COLLEGE

Office of Admissions, Woodland Rd.,
Pittsburgh, PA 15232 • Telephone: 800-837-1290 • www.chatham.edu •
Email: admissions@chatham.edu

Hours: Monday–Friday, 9:00AM–5:00PM; Saturday (by apppointment only)

This tiny women's college is located in the Shadyside area of Pittsburgh, one of the safest and most livable cities in the United States. Chatham offers unique programs including Chatham Abroad—a series interdisciplinary courses taught in exotic locales during the short January term—and all seniors must complete a year-long research project.

HIGHLIGHTS

ON CAMPUS
- Campus is National Arboretum
- State of the Art Science Complex
- Restored Tiffany window
- Historic Buildings

OFF CAMPUS
- Aviary
- Pittsburgh Zoo and Aquarium
- Pirates, Steelers, Penguins, and Riverhounds
- Festivals
- Theater, museums, and concerts

TRANSPORTATION

Greater Pittsburgh International Airport is 20 miles away from campus. Buses and limousines are available for the trip from the airport to campus. Amtrak trains and Greyhound buses serve Pittsburgh. The Port Authority Transit (PAT) operates the city's public transit system (buses, subway, and rail line).

FIND YOUR WAY

From the Pennsylvania Tpke., take Exit 6 (Pittsburgh) to I-376 W. Follow I-376 (the Pkwy.) W. toward the city. Continue on the Pkwy. through the Squirrel Hill Tunnel; stay in the right lane and exit immediately after the tunnel at Squirrel Hill (Exit 8). Follow the exit ramp and make the first left onto Forward Ave. At the first traffic light, bear left on Murray Ave.; stay on Murray to the dead end. Turn right on Wilkins Ave., and within half a block turn left on Woodland Rd., which leads directly into the college. The entrance is marked on each side by a red brick wall. The distance from the Tpke.'s Exit 6 to the campus is 12 miles.

STAY THE NIGHT

Nearby: **Shady Side Bed-and-Breakfast** (5516 Fifth Ave.; 412-683-6501) is a stone manor house built by a steel magnate at the turn of the century. It comes complete with billiard room, lots of antiques, and wood paneling; it is within walking distance of the school. The **Shady Side Inn** (5405 Fifth Ave.; 412-441-4444), about a mile away, is a complex of several all-suite buildings designed for short-term apartment stays. Rates for a one-bedroom apartment, with kitchen, are moderate. See the Carnegie Mellon University entry, which is very close to Chatham, for other suggestions.

AT A GLANCE

Selectivity Rating	66
Range SAT I Math	470–570
Average SAT I Math	516
Range SAT I Verbal	500–630
Average SAT I Verbal	565
Average ACT Composite	22
Average GPA	3.28
Student to Faculty Ratio	12:1

CAMPUS TOURS

Dates	Year-round
Times	Mon–Fri, & scheduled Sat., 10AM–2PM
Average Length	1 hour

ON-CAMPUS APPOINTMENTS

Admissions

Start Date–Juniors	Anytime; summer of junior year is encouraged
Appointment	Required
Advance Notice	Yes, 1 week
Saturdays	Yes
Info Sessions	Interview functions as information session

Faculty and Coaches

Dates/Times	Year-round
Arrangements	Contact Admissions Office

CLASS VISITS

Dates	Year-round
Arrangements	Contact Admissions Office

DICKINSON COLLEGE

Office of Admissions, Waidner Admissions House—PO Box 1773, Carlisle, PA 17013-2896 • Telephone: 800-644-1773 • www.dickinson.edu • Email: admit@dickinson.edu

Hours: Monday–Friday, 8:30AM–4:30PM; select Saturdays (August–mid-December and April–early May), 10:00AM–noon

This small liberal arts enclave is a great college known for its picturesque location, an extremely strong overseas education program, and the loving attention it lavishes on its undergraduates. The administration works for the students, not vice versa, and a capable, accessible faculty motivates students to achieve their best, with the result that over half of all graduates pursue advanced academic degrees.

AT A GLANCE

Selectivity Rating	81
Range SAT I Math	570–650
Average SAT I Math	612
Range SAT I Verbal	580–670
Average SAT I Verbal	623
Average ACT Composite	27
Student to Faculty Ratio	12:1

CAMPUS TOURS

Appointment	Not required
Dates	Year-round
Times	Mon–Fri, 9AM, 11AM, 1PM, & 3PM
Average Length	1 hour

ON-CAMPUS APPOINTMENTS

Admissions

Start Date–Juniors	April 1
Appointment	Required
Advance Notice	Yes, 2 weeks
Saturdays	No
Average Length	45 min.
Info Sessions	Yes

Faculty and Coaches

Dates/Times	Academic year
Arrangements	Contact Admissions Office 2 weeks prior

CLASS VISITS

Dates	Academic year
Arrangements	Contact Admissions Office

TRANSPORTATION

Harrisburg International Airport is 32 miles away from campus. Taxis and airport limousines are available for the trip from the airport to campus. For airport limousine service, call 717-258-4720 to make advance arrangements. Nearby Harrisburg is served by Amtrak trains and Greyhound/Trailways buses.

FIND YOUR WAY

From the Pennsylvania Tpke., take Exit 16 (Carlisle). Take the right ramp to Rte. 11 S. Follow Rte. 11 S. into downtown Carlisle (approximately three miles). Turn right at the intersection of Hanover and High Streets. The Waidner Admission House is at the corner of West High (Rte. 11) and South College Streets, and has available parking on the east side of the building. **From I-81 North,** use exit 47 (Hanover Street). Turn left at traffic light; then turn left at the downtown intersection of Hanover and High Streets. **From I-81 South,** use exit 49 (High Street). Turn right at the yield sign (Rte. 641). As you come into downtown Carlisle, you will be on High Street.

STAY THE NIGHT

Nearby: The following are hotels in the Dickinson area: **Clarion Inn and Convention Center** (1700 Carlisle Pike, Rte.11; 717-243-1717), **Comfort Suites** (10 S. Hanover Street; 717-960-1000 or 1-800-704-1188), **Days Inn** (101 Alexander Spring Road; 717-258-4147 or 800-325-2525), **Econo Lodge** (1460 Carlisle Pike; 717-249-7775), **Hampton Inn** (Carlisle Pike; 717-240-0200), **Holiday Inn-Carlisle** (1450 Carlisle Pike; 717-245-2400), **Sleep Inn** (5 East Garland Drive; 717-249-8863), **Allenberry Resort Inn** (717-258-3211), **Harrisburg Hilton and Towers** (1 North Second Street; 717-233-6000), **Harrisburg Marriott** (4650 Lindle Road; 717-564-5511), and the **Sheraton Inn** (Union Deposit Road & I-83; 717-561-2800).

HIGHLIGHTS

ON CAMPUS

- Old West, est. 1805
- New Math/Science Building
- Trout Art Gallery
- Kline Center

OFF CAMPUS

- Appalachian Trail
- Yellow Breeches (for fly fishing)
- Whitaker Center for Arts with IMAX
- Hershey Park Entertainment Center
- National Civil War Museum

DREXEL UNIVERSITY

Office of Enrollment and Career Management, 32nd and Chestnut Sts.,
Philadelphia, PA 19104 • Telephone: 800-237-3935 • www.drexel.edu •
Email: enroll@drexel.edu

Hours: Monday–Thursday, 8:00AM–5:30PM; Friday, 8:00AM–5:00PM; Saturday, 9:00AM–noon

With its strong research orientation, Drexel University in Philadelphia has a solid record of priming undergraduates for professions such as hotel management, graphic design, and, in particular, engineering. Drexel's co-op program is a major strength. It extends the undergraduate experience for an extra year, but it provides DU students with hands-on work experience for six months out of the year and practically guarantees a job after graduation.

HIGHLIGHTS

ON CAMPUS
- W. W. Hagerty Library
- University bookstore
- Creese Cafe
- Crossroads at the Handschumacher Dining Hall

OFF CAMPUS
- Liberty Bell
- Independence Hall
- Congress Hall
- Franklin Court
- Philadelphia Museum of Art

TRANSPORTATION

The drive from Philadelphia International Airport to campus is 20 minutes (but it could be much longer if traffic is heavy, which isn't unusual). SEPTA (the public transportation system) shuttle trains run hourly from the airport to 30th St. Station, leaving you only two blocks from campus. Taxis are also available. Amtrak trains from all parts of the country and SEPTA commuter trains stop at 30th St. Station, two blocks from campus. Greyhound bus lines serve Philadelphia from the depot in center city; from there, you can take a SEPTA bus or commuter train (from the Market East station to 30th St. Station) to campus.

FIND YOUR WAY

From Princeton, Trenton, and points north: Take 95 south to 676/Central Philadelphia exit. Then take 676 west to 76 east exit. Follow 76 east exit under railroad bridge and proceed into right lane as soon as it is safe to do so. Follow the sign for exit 39 (do not continue following 76 east). Go around the 30th St. train station. **From New York and northern New Jersey:** Take New Jersey Tpke. south to exit 4 (Camden/Philadelphia). Follow Rte. 73 north to Rte. 38 west. Travel 4.7 miles past Flower World and merge right onto Route 30 west. Follow 2.6 miles to the Ben Franklin Bridge. Cross bridge and stay in left lanes. Follow signs for 676 west. Follow 676 for one mile and take 76 east exit. Go under the bridge and get into the right lane as soon as it is safe to do so and follow signs for Exit 39 (do not continue following 76 east). Go up ramp and around 30th Street Station to the first light and make a right.

STAY THE NIGHT

Nearby: Drexel is in the same area as the University of Pennsylvania (known as Penn), so check the Penn entry. Even though the **International House** is on the Penn campus, it is open to Drexel visitors and is within walking distance of Drexel. There's a special moderate rate at the **Sheraton University City Hotel** for Drexel visitors.

AT A GLANCE

Selectivity Rating	77
Range SAT I Math	550–660
Average SAT I Math	600
Range SAT I Verbal	520–620
Average SAT I Verbal	570
Average GPA	3.26
Student to Faculty Ratio	14:1

CAMPUS TOURS

Appointment	Required
Dates	Year-round
Times	Mon–Fri, NOON & 12:30PM; Sat, 11AM
Average Length	1 hour

ON-CAMPUS APPOINTMENTS

Admissions

Start Date–Juniors	Anytime
Appointment	Required
Advance Notice	Yes, 2 weeks
Saturdays	No
Info Sessions	Year-round

Faculty and Coaches

Dates/Times	Year-round
Arrangements	Contact Admissions Office 2 weeks prior

CLASS VISITS

Dates	Year-round
Arrangements	Contact Admissions Office

DUQUESNE UNIVERSITY

Office of Admissionss, 600 Forbes Avenue,
Pittsburgh, PA 15282 • Telephone: 412-396-5000 • www.admissions.duq.edu •
Email: admissions@duq.edu

Hours: Monday–Friday, 8:30AM–4:30PM

Catholic Duquesne University—located atop a hill in central Pittsburgh—works hard to serve a determinedly career-minded (and largely commuting) student population. The health sciences are downright hard, and pre-professional programs in business, pharmacy, physical therapy, and speech pathology are a major draw. Duquesne professors are accessible and demanding.

AT A GLANCE

Selectivity Rating	76
Range SAT I Math	490–600
Average SAT I Math	545
Range SAT I Verbal	490–590
Average SAT I Verbal	545
Average ACT Composite	24
Average GPA	3.4
Student to Faculty Ratio	15:1

CAMPUS TOURS

Appointment	Preferred
Dates	Year-round
Times	Mon–Fri, 10AM, noon, & 2PM, Sat, varies
Average Length	1 hour

ON-CAMPUS APPOINTMENTS

Admissions

Start Date–Juniors	Anytime
Appointment	Preferred
Advance Notice	Yes, 2 weeks
Saturdays	No
Average Length	45 min.
Info Sessions	Yes

Faculty and Coaches

Dates/Times	Year-round
Arrangements	Contact Admissions Office 2 weeks prior

CLASS VISITS

Dates	Academic year
Arrangements	Contact Admissions Office

TRANSPORTATION

Pittsburgh International Airport, ranked as one of the nation's busiest and best, is 30 to 45 minutes from downtown. All major car rental agencies are represented. Cab service from the airport into Pittsburgh is approximately $30. Airlines Transportation Company buses depart from the airport's lower level every 30 minutes and drop off visitors at all downtown hotels. Bus fare is $10. Duquesne is a 10- to 15-minute walk or a $3 cab ride from major downtown hotels. Airlines Transportation also provides return service to the airport from downtown hotels at half-hour intervals. Both Amtrak and Greyhound terminals are located downtown, a 15- to 20-minute walk or approximately a $5 cab ride to Duquesne.

FIND YOUR WAY

From I-80: Follow I-80 to I-79 S. Exit 19A. From I-79, proceed to Exit 72, Pittsburgh/I-279 S. (see below). From I-76 Pennsylvania Tpke. (eastbound): Use Exit 28 Cranberry, I-79. Follow I-79 S. to Exit 72, Pittsburgh/I-279 S. (see below). **From I-279 S./I-579 S.:** Follow I-279 S. approximately 15 miles to Exit 8A, I-579 S./Veteran's Bridge. Follow all signs indicating Mellon Arena. Proceed to the traffic light and turn right onto Washington Place. Proceed through the next two intersections and turn left at the second intersection onto Forbes Ave. Proceed on Forbes to Duquesne University parking garage; turn right at main garage entrance. **From I-76 Pennsylvania Tpke. (westbound)/I-376:** Follow I-76 W. to Exit 57, Pittsburgh/Monroeville I-376. Proceed on I-376 W. approximately 12 miles to Exit 2B, Blvd. of the Allies. Continue on Blvd. of the Allies approximately one mile and stay in the right lane. Blvd. of the Allies divides into a Y as you pass Mercy Hospital. Follow the far right lane to the stop sign. Proceed straight ahead to Bluff Street and the Duquesne University campus. At the intersection of Bluff Street and McAnulty Drive, turn right down the hill. Proceed through the stop sign; turn right onto Forbes Avenue at the traffic light. Proceed on Forbes to Duquesne University parking garage; turn right at main garage entrance. **From I-70:** Go to I-79 N. and take Exit 59A, Pittsburgh/I-279 N.; follow the directions below. **From I-79 N.:** Use Exit 59A, Pittsburgh/I-279 N., and follow the directions below. **From I-279 N./I-376:** Go on I-279 N. approximately seven miles through the Fort Pitt Tunnel, staying in the right lane as you approach the tunnel. Use the right exit for Monroeville/I-376 East at the end of the Fort Pitt Bridge. Proceed approximately two-tenths of a mile and exit left at Grant Street/Exit 1C. Proceed on Grant to the fifth traffic light at Forbes Avenue. Turn right onto Forbes Avenue and proceed approximately one-half mile to Duquesne University parking garage; turn right at main garage entrance.

STAY THE NIGHT

Nearby: You will find the usual chain hotels close to campus. When you make reservations, ask whether there is a special rate for Duquesne visitors.

HIGHLIGHTS

ON CAMPUS

- Academic Walk (Main walkway on campus, nick-named A-walk)
- A. J. Palumbo Center for the Duquesne Dukes, Athletic facility for student and faculty use.
- The Nite Spot (Located on the first floor of the Student Union, offers students late night activities right on campus.)
- The Off Ramp (Located in the Student Union, weekly shows featuring bands, comedians, etc.)

OFF CAMPUS

- The South Side
- Oakland (The Carnegie Museum and music venues)

FRANKLIN & MARSHALL COLLEGE

Admissions Office, P.O. Box 3003,
Lancaster, PA 17604-3003 • Telephone: 717-291-3953 • www.fandm.edu •
Email: admission@fandm.edu

Hours: Monday–Friday, 8:30AM–4:30PM; select Saturdays by appointment, 10:00AM–noon

Professors are very knowledgeable, and the deans and administration are awesome at Franklin & Marshall College, an outstanding liberal arts college about an hour away from Philadelphia. Be prepared if you attend, though; the demanding workload is, in the words of one exhausted student, "Rigorous, man, rigorous." Greek life consumes the social scene.

HIGHLIGHTS

ON CAMPUS
- Alumni Sport and Fitness Center
- Barshinger Center in Hensel Hall
- Steinman College Center
- Roschel Performing Arts Center
- Shadek-Fackenthal Library

OFF CAMPUS
- Central Market
- The Fulton Opera House
- Tanger and Rockvale Square Outlet Malls
- Hershey Park (20 minutes away from campus)
- Pennsylvania Dutch Country

TRANSPORTATION

Harrisburg International Airport is a 40-minute drive from campus. Rental cars are available at the airports. Amtrak trains provide regular east/west daily service to Lancaster. Continental Trailways buses also provide regular daily bus service to Lancaster.

FIND YOUR WAY

From Rte. 30 in Lancaster, take the Harrisburg Pike Exit. Follow Harrisburg Pike East (toward downtown Lancaster) approximately two miles. F&M will be on your right. For more detailed information please refer to: www.fandm.edu/departments/admission/see/visiting.html

STAY THE NIGHT

Nearby: Your choices include the **Comfort Inn** (50 Centerville Rd.; 717-898-2431), the **Eden Resort Inn** (222 Eden Rd.; 717-569-6444), the **Hampton Inn** (545 Greenfield Rd.; 717-299-1200), the **Hilton Garden Inn** (101 Granite Run Dr.; 717-560-0880), the **Holiday Inn East** (521 Greenfield Rd.; 717-299-2551), the **Apple Bin Inn** (2835 Willow Street Pike; 717-464-5881), the **Ramada Inn** (2250 Lincoln Hwy. East; 717-393-5499), the **Sleep Inn** (U.S. Route 30 Mountville Exit; 717-285-0444), the **King's Cottage** (1049 E. King Street; 717-397-1017), and the **Mainstay Suites** (U.S. Route 30 Mountville Exit; 717-285-1779).

A little farther: In Ephrata, about 30 minutes away from campus, is the eighteenth-century **Smithton Inn** (900 W. Main St.; 717-733-6094). Double rooms are priced in the moderate range during the week and expensive on the weekends. The price includes a country breakfast. All rooms have private baths and fireplaces and are furnished to maintain the pre-revolutionary character of the building. Also about 30 minutes away is the **Churchtown Inn Bed and Breakfast** (Rte. 23; 215-445-7794), deep in Pennsylvania Dutch country. On Saturday evening, you can go to an Amish or Mennonite home for dinner.

AT A GLANCE

Selectivity Rating	86
Range SAT I Math	590–680
Average SAT I Math	633
Range SAT I Verbal	570–660
Average SAT I Verbal	615
Student to Faculty Ratio	11:1

CAMPUS TOURS

Appointment	Not required
Dates	Year-round
Times	Mon–Fri, 10AM, 11AM, 2PM, & 3PM
Average Length	1 hour

ON-CAMPUS APPOINTMENTS

Admissions

Start Date–Juniors	March 1
Appointment	Required
Advance Notice	Yes, 2 weeks
Saturdays	Sometimes
Average Length	45 min.
Info Sessions	Yes

Faculty and Coaches

Dates/Times	Academic year
Arrangements	Contact Admissions or Athletics 2 weeks prior

CLASS VISITS

Dates	Academic year
Arrangements	Contact Admissions Office

GETTYSBURG COLLEGE

Admissions Office, Campus Box 416,
Gettysburg, PA 17325-1484 • Telephone: 800-431-0803 • www.gettysburg.edu •
Email: admiss@gettysburg.edu

Hours: Monday–Friday, 9:00AM–5:00PM; Summer, 9:00AM–4:30PM; Saturday, 9:00AM–noon

An attentive administration, affable professors, and a broad set of distribution requirements covering the humanities, natural and social sciences, mathematics, foreign language, writing skills, and nonwestern civilization make small Gettysburg College a good find.

AT A GLANCE

Selectivity Rating	85
Range SAT I Math	590–660
Range SAT I Verbal	580–650
Average ACT Composite	28
Student to Faculty Ratio	11:1

CAMPUS TOURS

Appointment	Preferred
Dates	Year-round
Times	Available on the hour
Average Length	1 hour

ON-CAMPUS APPOINTMENTS

Admissions

Start Date–Juniors	April 1
Appointment	Required
Advance Notice	Yes, 2 weeks
Saturdays	Sometimes
Average Length	45 min.
Info Sessions	Yes

Faculty and Coaches

Arrangements	Contact Admissions Office 2 weeks prior

CLASS VISITS

Dates	Academic year
Arrangements	Contact Admissions Office

TRANSPORTATION

A number of airports are within easy driving distance of Gettysburg, including Harrisburg International Airport (40 miles) and Baltimore/Washington International Airport (55 miles). Gettysburg sponsors a low cost transportation service to and from area airports and the Harrisburg train station (Amtrak). Call Admissions (800-431-0803 or 717-337-6100) for more details.

FIND YOUR WAY

Please see our website for detailed driving directions to campus:
www.gettysburg.edu/admissions/visiting-campus/directions.html.

STAY THE NIGHT

Nearby: The **Gettysburg Hotel** (1 Lincoln Square; 717-337-2000) is an elegant choice located half a mile away from campus.

HIGHLIGHTS

ON CAMPUS

- Beautiful 200-acre campus
- Musselman Library
- Christ Chapel
- Glatfelter Hall
- Science Center

OFF CAMPUS

- Gettysburg National Park
- Appalachian Trail
- Easy Acess to Washington DC
- Easy Acess to Baltimore's Inner Harbor

HAVERFORD COLLEGE

Admissions Office, 370 Lancaster Avenue, Haverford, PA 19041 • Telephone: 610-896-1350 • www.haverford.edu • Email: admitme@haverford.edu

Hours: Monday–Friday, 9:00AM–5:00PM; Summer, 8:30AM–4:30PM; Saturday (during fall), 10:00AM–1:00PM

With its tradition of excellence in the liberal arts, Haverford College demands intense study from its 1,100 students. Under Haverford's honor code, all examinations are self-scheduled and unproctored, and Ford students sit on most academic committees and have a vote in every aspect of Haverford life. And—we are not making this up—Dave Barry is an alum.

HIGHLIGHTS

ON CAMPUS
- Integrated Natural Sciences Center
- John Whitehead Campus Center
- Cantor Fitzgerald Gallery
- Arboreteum
- The Coop (coffee shop)

OFF CAMPUS
- Philadelphia
- Philadelphia Museum of Art
- Franklin Institute of Natural Science Museum
- Historical Valley Forge Park
- Penn's Landing, South Street

TRANSPORTATION

Philadelphia International Airport is 20 miles away from campus. Main Line Airport Limousine Service will take you directly to Stokes Hall on the Haverford campus; to call for this service, use the airport courtesy phones (push Main Line). If you want to call in advance, Main Line's number is 610-525-0513 (or 800-427-3464 in Pennsylvania). Limousines leave approximately every 45 minutes. Public transportation is also available from the airport to campus. Take a SEPTA Airport Express from the airport to 30th St. Station in Philadelphia; trains run every 30 minutes and take 20 minutes to reach 30th St. **From 30th St. Station,** take either the R-5 Paoli Local or the Bryn Mawr Local to Haverford (not all trains stop at Haverford; check timetables available at the station). Walk down Haverford Station Road. Turn left onto Lancaster Avenue; then turn right onto campus at College Lane. If you don't want to walk, the Bennett Taxi Service can drive you from the station to campus; call 525-1770 (a local call). Amtrak trains and Greyhound buses serve Philadelphia. Amtrak takes you to 30th St. Station; to get to campus from there, use the SEPTA commuter trains as described above. From the Greyhound station, walk to the Market East SEPTA train station and take the R-5 Paoli Local or the Bryn Mawr Local as described above; the ride from Market East to Haverford takes approximately 25 minutes.

FIND YOUR WAY

From the Pennsylvania Tpke., take Exit 24 (Valley Forge Interchange) and follow the signs to I-76 E. (Expy. to Philadelphia). Take I-76 to Exit 28A for I-476 (South/Chester). Proceed south on I-476 to Exit 5, U.S. 30 St. Davids-Villanova exit. Turn east on U.S. 30 (Lancaster Ave.) and proceed for approximately three-and-a-half miles through Villanova, Rosemont, and Bryn Mawr to Haverford. After you see the Haverford Post Office on the left, turn right onto the main entrance of the Haverford campus at College Lane. Follow the signs to the visitor parking lot. For additional details check our website at www.haverford.edu.

STAY THE NIGHT

Nearby: Your choices for accommodations near campus include the **Adams Mark Hotel** (Bala Cynwyd, City Ave. and Monument Road, Philadelphia, PA 19131; 215-581-5000), the **Holiday Inn** (4100 Presidential Blvd, Philadelphia, PA 19131; 215-477-0200), the **Courtyard by Marriott** (762 West Lancaster Ave., Wayne, PA 19087; 610-687-6633), the **Radnor Hotel** (591 East Lancaster Ave., St. Davids, PA 19087; 610-688-5800), the **Philadelphia Marriott** (111 Crawford Ave West, Conshohocken, PA 19428; 610-941-5600), the **Desmond Hotel and Conference Center** (One Liberty Blvd., Malvern, PA 19355; 610-296-9800), and the **Wayne Hotel** (139 East Lancaster Ave., Wayne, PA 19087; 610-687-5000).

AT A GLANCE

Selectivity Rating	97
Range SAT I Math	640–720
Range SAT I Verbal	640–740
Student to Faculty Ratio	8:1

CAMPUS TOURS

Appointment	Not required
Dates	Varies
Times	Mon–Fri, 9:45AM–3:45PM; Sat, 10:45AM–1PM
Average Length	1 hour

ON-CAMPUS APPOINTMENTS

Admissions

Start Date–Juniors	April 1
Appointment	Required
Advance Notice	Yes, 2 weeks
Saturdays	Sometimes
Average Length	45 min.
Info Sessions	No

Faculty and Coaches

Dates/Times	Year-round
Arrangements	Contact coach directly 2 weeks prior

CLASS VISITS

Dates	Academic year
Arrangements	Contact Admissions Office

LAFAYETTE COLLEGE

Admissions Office, 118 Markle Hall,
Easton, PA 18042 • Telephone: 610-330-5100 • www.lafayette.edu •
Email: admissions@lafayette.edu

Hours: Monday–Friday, 9:00AM–5:00PM; Saturday (open only for information sessions), 9:00AM–noon

Challenging, yet rewarding, Lafayette College is a small liberal arts school in Pennsylvania with a nationally-renowned engineering program and some of the best opportunities for research in the nation. Campus life revolves around the Greek system.

AT A GLANCE

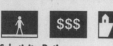

Selectivity Rating	82
Range SAT I Math	610–700
Average SAT I Math	665
Range SAT I Verbal	560–650
Average SAT I Verbal	620
Average ACT Composite	28
Average GPA	3.8
Student to Faculty Ratio	11:1

CAMPUS TOURS

Dates	Year-round
Times	Mon–Fri, 10AM, 11AM, 1PM, 2PM, & 3:15PM
Average Length	1 hour

ON-CAMPUS APPOINTMENTS

Admissions

Start Date—Juniors	May 1
Appointment	Required
Advance Notice	Yes, 3 weeks
Saturdays	Sometimes
Info Sessions	Saturdays: Group information sessions only

Faculty and Coaches

| Dates/Times | Year-round |
| Arrangements | Contact faculty directly as soon as possible |

CLASS VISITS

| Dates | Academic year |
| Arrangements | Contact Admissions Office |

TRANSPORTATION

The Lehigh Valley International Airport is a 20-minute drive from campus. Taxis are available for the trip from the airport to campus.

FIND YOUR WAY

From the Northeast Extension of the Pennsylvania Tpke., take Exit 33 (Lehigh Valley) to Rte. 22 E. From Rte. 22, take the 4th St. exit (the last exit in Pennsylvania before you cross the Delaware River to go to New Jersey). At the stoplight at the end of the exit ramp, make a left turn. At the next traffic light, make a left turn onto 3rd St. Go up College Hill and make the first left onto McCartney St. At the next stop sign, make another left onto High St. The Admissions Office is in Markle Hall, which is on the right. Parking is available on the street or on the parking deck behind Markle Hall. **From the New York area,** take the George Washington Bridge to Rte. 80 W.; then take Rte. 287 S. to I-78 W. Take I-78 to Exit 3 (Rte. 22). Proceed on Rte. 22 to the toll bridge that connects Phillipsburg, NJ, to Easton, PA. Take the first exit labeled Easton (a right-hand exit). At the end of the exit ramp, make a right turn at the traffic light. Follow the preceding directions from College Hill.

STAY THE NIGHT

Nearby: The **Lafayette Inn** (525 Monroe St.; 610-253-4500) is within walking distance of campus. There is no pool or restaurant. There also is a **Holiday Inn** (Route 22 in Phillipsburg, NJ; 908-459-9135).

A little farther: Lafayette is about 15 minutes away from Bethlehem and about a 30 minutes away from Allentown. Check the Lehigh University entry for suggestions in these towns.

HIGHLIGHTS

ON CAMPUS

- Skillman & Kirby Libraries
- Farinon College Center
- Williams Center for the Arts

OFF CAMPUS

- Hugh Moore Park
- Lehigh Canal
- Canal Museum
- Crayola Factory
- Two Rivers Landing

LEHIGH UNIVERSITY

Office of Admissions, 27 Memorial Dr.West,
Bethlehem, PA 18015 • Telephone: 610-758-3100 • www.lehigh.edu •
Email: admissions@lehigh.edu

Hours: Monday–Friday, 8:15AM–4:45PM; select Saturdays (only during fall), by appointment

The quality of academic programs and the facilities at Lehigh University are the best money can buy. Traditionally, Lehigh has been noted for its distinguished engineering school and strong College of Business and Economics but a push in recent years to improve the quality of the liberal arts programs—highlighted by a brand-spanking new performing arts facility—has paid off quite handsomely. Lee Iacocca is an alum.

HIGHLIGHTS

ON CAMPUS
- Athletics (Division 1)
- Performing Arts Center
- Greek Life
- On Campus Café

OFF CAMPUS
- Downtown/Historic Bethlehem
- Lehigh Valley Mall
- Pocono Mountain
- Dorney Park
- Music Fest

TRANSPORTATION

The renamed Lehigh Valley International Airport (formerly the Allentown-Bethlehem-Easton Airport) is a 15-minute drive from campus. Taxis are available for the ride from the airport to campus. A bus station is within walking distance of campus.

FIND YOUR WAY

From I-78, take the Hellertown exit; at the exit, turn left onto Rte. 412 and drive through Hellertown about one mile to the traffic light at Water St. (becomes Friedensville Rd.). Turn right and go half a mile to a traffic island; bear right onto Mountain Dr. South at the entrance to the Goodman Campus. Follow Mountain Dr. to the top of South Mountain (to the first stop sign), then descend on Mountain Dr. North. Keep to the right after the first stop sign. Take the second left after the next stop sign. Follow the road to the first fork and bear right. Bear right around the next curve, then at the bottom of the incline (the green-painted Taylor College is in front of you), bear left. At the stop sign at the gate, turn left; bear right at the first intersection and follow the curve around to the stop sign. Make a left; at the next stop sign turn left again. The Alumni Memorial Building is at the left. The parking lot is behind the building.

STAY THE NIGHT

Nearby: The **Comfort Suites** (3rd St. and Brodhead Ave.; 610-882-9700) is within walking distance of campus and has moderate rates. A chain of Marriott's has recently opened (Rte. 22 and Catasauqua Rd.) 10 minutes away from campus: **Marriott-Courtyard** (800-321-2211), **Marriott-Fairfield Inn** (800-228-2800), and **Marriott-Residence Inn** (800-331-3131). Prices vary. Another choice is **Holiday Inn-East** (Rtes 22 and 512; 610-866-5800), 15 minutes away, which includes a nightclub, a restaurant, and offers moderate rates. The **Sheraton Jetport** (3400 Airport Rd.; 610-266-1000) is located 15 minutes away in Allentown and has moderate rates. For the physically active, the **Allentown Hilton** (Hamilton Mall; 610-433-2221) is about 20 minutes away and offers an exercise room and an indoor pool. Several bed-and-breakfasts are located in the area. Five miles away from campus, in Bethlehem on Old Philadelphia Pike, is the **Wydnor Hall Inn** (800-839-0020). It's a comfortable 1820s stone Georgian house with four guest rooms. The **Sayre Mansion Inn** (250 Wyandotte St.; 610-882-2100) is a bit more expensive, yet more convenient because it's only five minutes away from campus. The downtown area offers the **Radison Hotel Bethlehem** (437 Main St.; 610-867-2200).

AT A GLANCE

Selectivity Rating	88
Range SAT I Math	630–710
Average SAT I Math	665
Range SAT I Verbal	580–670
Average SAT I Verbal	617
Average GPA	3.6
Student to Faculty Ratio	10:1

CAMPUS TOURS

Dates	Year-round
Times	Mon–Fri, 10:15AM, 11:15AM, 1PM, 2PM, & 3PM
Average Length	1 hour

ON-CAMPUS APPOINTMENTS

Admissions
Start Date—Juniors	April 1
Appointment	Required
Advance Notice	Yes, 2 weeks
Saturdays	Sometimes
Info Sessions	Daily

Faculty and Coaches
Dates/Times	Year-round
Arrangements	Contact Admissions Office 2 weeks prior

CLASS VISITS

Dates	Year-round
Arrangements	Contact Admissions Office

PENN STATE UNIVERSITY PARK

Undergraduate Admissions Office, 201 Shields Building, Box 3000, University Park, PA 16802-3000 • Telephone: 814-865-5471 • www.psu.edu • Email: admissions@psu.edu

Hours: Monday–Friday, 8:00AM–5:00PM

Penn State University is the quintessential state-sponsored university. It provides a reasonably priced education to the masses, offers studies in a mind-boggling range of areas, and maintains top departments, particularly in those fields geared toward career training. And Penn State offers students a million and one things to do, including football games, women's field hockey, parties, Bible study groups, the Unimart, the library, the Nittany mall, and concerts.

AT A GLANCE

Selectivity Rating	85
Range SAT I Math	560–670
Average SAT I Math	617
Range SAT I Verbal	530–630
Average SAT I Verbal	593
Average GPA	3.53
Student to Faculty Ratio	17:1

CAMPUS TOURS

Appointment	Required
Dates	Year-round
Times	Mon–Fri, 12:30PM (bus tour) & 3PM (walking tour)
Average Length	2 hours

ON-CAMPUS APPOINTMENTS

Admissions

Start Date–Juniors	N/A
Info Sessions	Year-round

Faculty and Coaches

Dates/Times	Year-round
Arrangements Contact faculty directly	

CLASS VISITS

Dates	Year-round
Arrangements Contact faculty directly	

TRANSPORTATION

University Park (State College-Bellefonte) Airport is five miles away from campus. The airport is served by Air Atlantic and Allegheny Commuter airlines. Limousine or taxi service (on call) is available. Airline connections to University Park are available from the Philadelphia, Pittsburgh, and Harrisburg airports. Greyhound/Trailways buses serve State College.

FIND YOUR WAY

From I-80, exit to Pennsylvania Rte. 26 S. To reach the Admissions Office, exit from Rte. 26 to University Dr. west toward campus; turn left on Curtin Road to the office, which is in Shields Building. To get to the information booth and visitors' parking, take Rte. 26 S. (College Avenue) to Atherton St. Turn right on Atherton to Pollock Rd.; the information booth is to the right on Pollock.

STAY THE NIGHT

Nearby: On campus is the **Nittany Lion Inn** (N. Atherton St. at Park Ave.; 814-231-7500), which has reasonable rates and a restaurant. One block away is a moderately priced **Days Inn** (240 Pugh St.; 814-238-8454), which has an indoor pool, sauna, exercise room, restaurant, and a live band in the lounge on weekends. For inexpensive accommodations, try **Autoport** (1405 S. Atherton St.; 814-237-7666), about a mile away from campus. A nice, clean motel with an outdoor pool, it has been run by the same family for over 50 years. There is also an inexpensive **Holiday Inn Penn State** (1450 S. Atherton St.; 814-238-3001), which has lighted tennis courts, an outdoor pool, a disc jockey (on weekends), and privileges at an athletic club. For bed-and-breakfasts in the area, which are generally less expensive, call **Rest and Repast** (814-238-1484). You can also stay at a Mediterranean-style resort and conference center called **Toftrees** (1 Country Club Ln.; 814-234-8000), about 10 minutes away. It has tennis courts, putting greens, a driving range, a golf course, an exercise room, an outdoor heated pool, and music every evening. The resort is nicely situated among rolling hills and has moderate rates.

HIGHLIGHTS

ON CAMPUS
- Mineral Museum
- Palmer Museum of Art
- Frost Entomological Museum

OFF CAMPUS
- Football Hall of Fame

SWARTHMORE COLLEGE

Admissions Office, 500 College Ave.,
Swarthmore, PA 19081 • Telephone: 800-667-3110 • www.swarthmore.edu •
Email: admissions@swarthmore.edu

Hours: Monday–Friday, 8:30AM–4:30PM; Saturday (fall, March, and April), 9:00AM–noon

Students study like crazy at Swarthmore College, which is arguably the best and almost definitely the most extraordinarily rigorous small liberal arts school in the country. Students say the dedication of the professors is simply amazing, and they give the administration a thumbs up for running a tight ship and staying out of the way.

HIGHLIGHTS

ON CAMPUS

- McCabe Library
- Lang Performing Arts Center
- Benjamin West House
- Clothier Memorial

TRANSPORTATION

Philadelphia International Airport is approximately a 20-minute drive from campus. Taxis, rental cars, or SEPTA commuter trains are available. If you are using the trains, take the airport shuttle train to 30th St. Station (in Philadelphia); then transfer to the Media Local (train number R-3) to Swarthmore. From the Swarthmore station, follow the wide walkway up the hill directly to Parrish Hall. The train trip takes an hour or more. Amtrak trains from New York and Washington arrive hourly at Philadelphia's 30th St. Station. From there, take the SEPTA Media Local (train number R-3) to Swarthmore. From the Swarthmore station, follow the wide walkway up the hill directly to Parrish Hall. Greyhound buses serve Philadelphia from many cities. From the bus station, walk to the Market East train station and take the SEPTA Media Local (train number R-3) to Swarthmore as described above.

FIND YOUR WAY

If heading east on the Pennsylvania Tpke., take Exit 326 (Valley Forge); then, take I-76 E. (Schuylkill Expressway) 2.5 miles to I-476 S. Proceed on I-476 for 13 miles to Exit 3 (Media/Swarthmore). At the bottom of the exit ramp, follow the sign for Swarthmore by turning left onto Baltimore Pike. Stay in the right lane, and in less than a quarter mile, turn right onto Rte. 320 S. Follow Rte. 320 carefully, watching out for turns. Proceed to the second traffic light (College Ave.) and turn right. Follow the road to visitor parking. The entrance to the Admissions Office is through the archway at the back of Parrish Hall. **If heading west on the Pennsylvania Tpke.,** take Exit 333 (Norristown) and follow the signs for I-476 S. Stay on I-476 for 17 miles to Exit 3 (Media/Swarthmore). Follow above directions from that point. **From the New Jersey Tpke.,** take Exit 3 and follow the signs to the Walt Whitman Bridge. After crossing the bridge, stay to the right and follow the signs for I-95 S. Take I-95 S., pass the Philadelphia International Airport, and continue to Exit 7 (I-476 N./Plymouth Meeting). Take I-476 N. to Exit 3 (Media/Swarthmore). At the bottom of the exit ramp, follow the sign for Swarthmore by turning right onto Baltimore Pike. Follow above directions from that point. **If heading north on I-95,** pass the Chester exits and continue to Exit 7 (I-476 N./Plymouth Meeting). Take I-476 N. to Exit 3 (Media/Swarthmore). At the bottom of the exit ramp, follow the sign for Swarthmore by turning right onto Baltimore Pike. Follow above directions from that point.

AT A GLANCE

Selectivity Rating	97
Range SAT I Math	680–760
Average SAT I Math	715
Range SAT I Verbal	670–770
Average SAT I Verbal	718
Student to Faculty Ratio	8:1

CAMPUS TOURS

Appointment	Not required
Dates	Varies
Times	10:30AM, 12:30PM, 2:30PM, & 3:30PM
Average Length	1 hour

ON-CAMPUS APPOINTMENTS

Admissions

Start Date–Juniors	June 1
Appointment	Required
Advance Notice	Yes, 2 weeks
Saturdays	Sometimes
Average Length	30 min.
Info Sessions	Yes

Faculty and Coaches

Dates/Times	Year-round
Arrangements	Contact Admissions Office, or contact coach directly 2 weeks prior

CLASS VISITS

Dates	Academic year
Arrangements	Contact Admissions Office

TEMPLE UNIVERSITY

Office of Admissionss, 1801 North Broad Street, Philadelphia, PA 19122-6096 • Telephone: 888-340-2222 • www.temple.edu • Email: tuadm@mail.temple.edu

Hours: Monday–Friday, 8:30AM–5:00PM; select Saturdays, 10:00AM–1:00PM

About 18,000 students attend Temple University, an urban, underrated public school in the lively city of Philadelphia that offers a wide array of degree options including easily some of the best communications programs in the country. A core curriculum ensures that you get a good solid education regardless of major.

AT A GLANCE

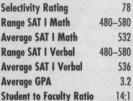

Selectivity Rating	78
Range SAT I Math	480–580
Average SAT I Math	532
Range SAT I Verbal	480–580
Average SAT I Verbal	536
Average GPA	3.2
Student to Faculty Ratio	14:1

CAMPUS TOURS

Appointment	Not required
Dates	Year-round
Average Length	1 hour

ON-CAMPUS APPOINTMENTS

Admissions

Appointment	Preferred
Advance Notice	No
Saturdays	Sometimes
Average Length	1 hour
Info Sessions	Yes

Faculty and Coaches

Dates/Times	Year-round
Arrangements	Contact Admissions Office 1 week prior

CLASS VISITS

Dates	Academic year
Arrangements	Contact Admissions Office

TRANSPORTATION

Amtrack/SEPTA rail station is available on campus; you have access to two subway stops; and Philadelphia International Airport is 10 miles away.

FIND YOUR WAY

The school is two miles north of Philadelphia City Hall on Broad Street (US 611).

STAY THE NIGHT

Nearby: See Center City hotels.

HIGHLIGHTS

ON CAMPUS

- Tuttleman Learning Center
- Student Center
- 1300 C.B. Moore Ave. (new dorm)

OFF CAMPUS

- Liberty Bell
- Independence Hall
- Philadelphia Art Museum
- Franklin Institute
- South Street

UNIVERSITY OF PENNSYLVANIA

Admissions Office, 1 College Hall, Philadelphia, PA 19104 • Telephone: 215-898-7507 • www.admissionsug.upenn.edu • Email: info@admissions.ugao.upenn.edu

Hours: Monday–Friday, 9:00AM–5:00PM

Students are quick to remind us that the University of Pennsylvania is not one school but four and that each school at the Ivy League University of Pennsylvania is pretty much impeccable. Wharton, the business school, is indisputably among the nation's best; both the School of Nursing and the School of Engineering and Applied Sciences are top-rated as well.

HIGHLIGHTS

ON CAMPUS
- University of Pennsylvania Museum
- Institute of Contemporary Art
- Walnut Street shops and restuarants
- Annenburg Center
- Franklin Field

OFF CAMPUS
- Philadelphia Museum of Art
- Independence Hall/Liberty Bell/Old City
- National Constitution Center
- Reading Terminal Market
- Flyers, Phillies, Eagles

TRANSPORTATION

Philadelphia International Airport is five miles away from campus (see driving instructions below). Airport shuttle trains leave every 30 minutes and stop at 30th St. Station, a 15-minute walk from campus. Amtrak train service is available to 30th St. Station in Philadelphia, which is a 15-minute walk or short taxi ride from campus.

FIND YOUR WAY

For directions to campus, visit www.admissionsug.upenn.edu/visiting/directions.php. The Office of Undergraduate Admissions is located in 1 College Hall (between 34th/36th Streets and Walnut/Spruce Streets). As you enter campus at 34th and Walnut Streets, you will see the main thoroughfare, Locust Walk. Proceed southwest on Locust Walk and you will spot "The Button" to your right and a statue of Ben Franklin to your left. College Hall is the building to your left behind the statue of Ben Franklin. The Office of Undergraduate Admissions is located on the ground floor of College Hall. **Walking from 30th St. Station:** Make a right (head west) onto Market Street, turn left on 34th, and go to the intersection of 34th and Walnut Streets. Follow the directions listed above. **From the north via NJ Tpke.:** Take the NJ Tpke. S. and get out on Exit 4. Bear right out of the toll and follow the signs to Philadelphia and the Ben Franklin Bridge. After crossing the bridge, take I-676 W. to I-76 E., and take that to Exit 346A (a left-lane exit marked South St.). Turn right onto South St. to enter campus. To find parking, turn right at the second light onto 33rd Street. Make the first left onto Walnut Street and there will be a lot on the right at 38th and Walnut. **From the west via PA Tpke.:** On the PA Tpke., use Exit 326, the Valley Forge Interchange. Take I-76 E. for approximately 17 miles until Exit 346A (marked South Street), and follow the directions from the north via NJ Tpke. **From the north via PA Tpke.:** Follow the signs for I-476. Take I-476 S. to the I-76/Philadelphia exit. Take I-76 E. for approximately 12 miles to Exit 346A, and follow the diretions from the north via NJ Tpke. **From the north via 95 south:** Taking I-95 S., use the 676/Central Philadelphia Exit. Follow the signs to I-676 W., and follow 676 W. until 76 E. Follow I-76 E. until Exit 346A, and follow the directions from the north via NJ Tpke. **From the south via 95 north:** Taking I-95 N., use the I-676/Central Philadelphia Exit, which is approximately seven miles north of the airport. Follow 676 W. until I-76 E. Follow I-76 E. until Exit 346A, and follow the directions from the north via NJ Tpke. **From the airport:** Take I-95 N. to the I-676/Central Philadelphia exit, which is approximately seven miles north of the airport. Follow directions from the south via 95 north.

STAY THE NIGHT

You will find the usual chain hotels including the **Sheraton-University City Hotel**.

AT A GLANCE	
Selectivity Rating	98
Range SAT I Math	680–760
Average SAT I Math	716
Range SAT I Verbal	650–740
Average SAT I Verbal	688
Average ACT Composite	30
Average GPA	3.84
Student to Faculty Ratio	6:1

CAMPUS TOURS	
Appointment	Not required
Dates	Year-round
Times	Varies
Average Length	Varies

ON-CAMPUS APPOINTMENTS

Admissions	
Start Date–Juniors	N/A
Info Sessions	Yes

Faculty and Coaches	
Dates/Times	Academic year
Arrangements	Contact Admissions Office 2 weeks prior

CLASS VISITS	
Dates	Academic year
Arrangements	Contact Admissions Office

UNIVERSITY OF PITTSBURGH

Office of Admissionss, 4227 Fifth Avenue, Alumni Hall,
Pittsburgh, PA 15260 • Telephone: 412-624-7488 • www.pitt.edu •
Email: oafa@pitt.edu

Hours: Monday–Friday, 8:30AM–5:00PM; select Saturdays by appointment

The University of Pittsburgh is a large research-oriented public university with especially strong programs in health sciences (health information management, pre-med, pre-pharmacy, physical therapy) and engineering. Students also mention that English, philosophy, and business and management have excellent programs.

AT A GLANCE

Selectivity Rating	82
Range SAT I Math	560–650
Average SAT I Math	607
Range SAT I Verbal	540–640
Average SAT I Verbal	595
Average ACT Composite	26
Student to Faculty Ratio	17:1

CAMPUS TOURS

Dates	Year-round
Times	Mon–Fri, 10AM–3PM
Average Length	Varies

ON-CAMPUS APPOINTMENTS

Admissions

Start Date–Juniors	Anytime
Advance Notice	Yes, other
Saturdays	No
Average Length	1 hour
Info Sessions	Yes

Faculty and Coaches

Dates/Times	Academic year
Arrangements	Subject to faculty/ coach availability

CLASS VISITS

Dates	Academic year
Arrangements	Contact Admissions Office

TRANSPORTATION

The Greyhound-Trailways bus station in Pittsburgh is located at 11th St. and Liberty Ave., downtown, and can be reached by local PAT buses or by taxi service (391-2300 or 261-5400). Fares for Port Authority Transit System (PAT bus) vary within a five-zone system extending in all directions from downtown to the outer suburbs. Basic fare ranges from $0.60 to $2.10, and exact change is required. Transfers can be purchased for a quarter and can be used for one connection in any direction within three hours of the time of purchase. Local buses numbered 71 (A, B, C, or D), 67 (A or F), or 61 (A, B, or C) come into Oakland and may be boarded along Fifth Ave. For bus routes and times call 231-5707. Yellow Cab (412-655-8100) and People's Cab (412-681-3131) provide service to the Oakland area. Fares from downtown are approximately $11, and fares from the airport are approximately $37. Pittsburgh International Airport is about 15 miles west of campus. Pittsburgh Airlines Transportation Co. (412-471-8900) provides buses to downtown and other areas; call for schedules and rates. Amtrak (1-800-872-7245) in Western, PA has two east-bound trains and two west-bound trains each day. Connections can be made in Chicago and New York. The terminal is located at Liberty and Grant Streets downtown.

FIND YOUR WAY

From the east via the PA Tpke. (I-76): Take Exit 57 (Old Exit 6) to I-376 W. From 376 take Exit 3B (Old Exit 7A), Oakland, onto Bates Street. Stay on Bates until it ends at Bouquet Street. Turn left onto Bouquet, then right at the first light onto Forbes Ave. **From the west via the PA Tpke. (I-76):** Take Exit 28 (Old Exit 3) and follow I-79 South to I-279 South. (You exit to the left off I-79.) Follow 279 into the city, to the I-376 Monroeville Exit. Follow 376 to the Forbes Ave./Oakland Exit. Forbes Ave. then leads right into the Pitt campus. **From the north:** Take I-79 South to I-279 South. (You exit to the left off I-79.) Follow 279 into the city, to the I-376 Monroeville Exit. Follow 376 to the Forbes Ave./Oakland Exit. Forbes Ave. then leads right into the Pitt campus. **From the South:** Follow I-79 N. to the I-279 N. Exit. Take 279 through the Fort Pitt Tunnels and across the bridge to the I-376 Monroeville Exit (first exit on the right). Follow 376 to the Forbes Ave./Oakland Exit. Forbes Ave. leads into the Pitt campus.

STAY THE NIGHT

Nearby: A few of the many hotels available in the University of Pittsburgh area include the **Hampton Inn** (800-426-7866), the **Holiday Inn** (800-864-8287), the **Residence Inn by Marriott** (1-800-331-3131), the **Wyndham Garden Hotel University Place** (877-299-1890 or 877-662-6242), and the **Shadyside Inn** (800-767-8483).

HIGHLIGHTS

ON CAMPUS

- Cathedral of Learning
- William Pitt Union
- Heinz Chapel
- Peterson Event Center
- Sennott Square

OFF CAMPUS

- Carnegie Museum and Scaife Art Gallery
- PNC Park (Home of the Pittsburgh Pirates)
- Andy Warhol Museum
- Heinz Field
- Shadyside/Walnut Street shopping district

THE UNIVERSITY OF SCRANTON

Office of Admissionss, 800 Linden Street, Scranton, PA 18510-4699 • Telephone: 888-727-2686 • www.scranton.edu • Email: admissions@scranton.edu

Hours: Monday–Friday, 8:30AM–4:30PM; Saturday, during academic year, 11:00AM

One-fifth of the students at the liberal arts and pre-professional University of Scranton (a private Roman Catholic college in northeastern Pennsylvania) come from the college's home town of Scranton, while the other members of undergraduate population come from over twenty states and ten countries. Off-campus opportunities include studying at twenty-seven additional Jesuit campuses.

HIGHLIGHTS

ON CAMPUS
- Brennan Hall
- The Harry and Jeanette Weiberg Memorial Library
- The Murray Room (workout facility)
- The Gunster Student Center

OFF CAMPUS
- Montage Mountain
- First Union Arena
- The Mall at Steamtown
- Steamtown National Historic Site
- Lake Scranton

TRANSPORTATION

The University of Scranton is easily reached by car and air. Located off of Interstate 81 in Northeastern Pennsylvania, driving time from New York City, Philadelphia, and Syracuse is just two hours; Trenton and Hartford are less than three hours away. For those traveling by air the metropolitan Scranton area is serviced by the Wilkes-Barre/Scranton International Airport with USAir, United Express, Continental, and Delta flights available. The airport is off of Exit 178A (49A) of Interstate 81 (about 10 miles south of Scranton).

FIND YOUR WAY

From New York and Northern New Jersey, take I-80 West to I-380 North. Then take I-81 South to Exit 185 (53). **From Philadelphia and Southern New Jersey,** take the Northeast Extension of the Pennsylvania Turnpike (I-476) to Exit 37, then I-81 North to Exit 185 (53). **From Connecticut and New England,** take I-84 West to I-81 South, then to Exit 185 (53). **From Baltimore and Washington, DC,** take I-83 North to I-81 North to Exit 185 (53). (Former exit numbers are listed in parentheses.) **From I-81 Exit 185 (53) (Central Scranton expressway),** follow the visitors' parking signs to campus. You will see the campus on your right. At the first traffic signal, turn right onto Madison Ave. Proceed two blocks and turn right onto Mulberry St. Proceed one block to the five-story parking and public safety pavilion and park on the second level. There are campus maps and help available at the public safety office in the parking garage. The Admissions Visitors' Center (Rupert Mayer House) is a three-minute walk from the parking garage.

STAY THE NIGHT

Nearby: For more information about hotel accommodations, please contact the Northeast Territory Visitors Bureau at 1-800-22-WELCOME or visit www.visitnepa.org.

VILLANOVA UNIVERSITY

Office of University Admissions, 800 Lancaster Ave.,
Villanova, PA 19085-1672 • Telephone: 610-519-4000 • www.admission.villanova.edu •
Email: gotovu@villanova.edu

Hours: Monday–Friday, 9:00AM–5:00PM; select Saturdays, 9:00AM–1:00PM

A very strong honors program, great colleges of engineering and business, and an all-around excellent academic experience lead students at Villanova University to proudly declare their school the best school in the Northeast. Well-attended daily masses and somewhat strict dorm policies make Villanova very Catholic as well.

AT A GLANCE

Selectivity Rating	82
Range SAT I Math	610–680
Average SAT I Math	633
Range SAT I Verbal	580–650
Average SAT I Verbal	605
Average ACT Composite	27
Average GPA	3.63
Student to Faculty Ratio	13:1

CAMPUS TOURS

Appointment	Not required
Dates	Year-round
Times	Times vary, Contact Admissions Office
Average Length	1 hour

ON-CAMPUS APPOINTMENTS

Admissions

Start Date–Juniors	N/A
Saturdays	No
Info Sessions	Yes

Faculty and Coaches

Arrangements	Contact Athletic Department 2 weeks prior

CLASS VISITS

Dates	Varies
Arrangements	Contact faculty directly

TRANSPORTATION

Philadelphia International Airport is approximately 20 miles away from campus. Bennetts Limousine Service is available for the ride from airport to campus; call it from the courtesy phone at the airport or call in advance at 610-525-0513. Public train transportation is also available. Take the SEPTA shuttle train from the airport to 30th St. Station in Philadelphia; transfer to the R-5 Paoli Local train which will take you to the Villanova station (and campus). Amtrak trains and Greyhound buses serve Philadelphia. Amtrak will bring you into 30th St. Station; from there, take the SEPTA R-5 Paoli Local train to Villanova. From the bus station, go to SEPTA's Market East station to get the R-5 Paoli Local train to Villanova.

FIND YOUR WAY

From the Pennsylvania Tpke., take Exit 326 (formerly 24A—Midcountry Exchange Rte. 476 S.). After the tollbooths, take I-476 S. to Exit 13 (Villanova, St. David's). Bear right to Rte. 30 E. (Lancaster Ave.). Take Rte. 30 E. through five traffic lights; at the fifth light, make a right onto Ithan Avenue and proceed to the Main Entrance on the left.

STAY THE NIGHT

Nearby: See Villanova's site at www.parents.villanova.edu/travel2campus/hotele.htm for a complete listing of accomodations. The closest accomodations are **Villanova Conference Center** (610-523-1776), the **Radnor Hotel** (610-688-5800), and the **Marriott West-Conshohocken** (610-941-5600).

A little farther: See the University of Pennsylvania entry for downtown Philadelphia accommodations.

HIGHLIGHTS

ON CAMPUS

- Arboretum
- Villanova Theatre (Vasey Hall)
- Art Gallery
- Five Holy Grounds Coffee Shops
- Cyber Cafe
- Augustinian Historical Museum

OFF CAMPUS

- Valley Forge National Historic Park
- King of Prussia Mall
- Franklin Institute
- Philadelphia Zoo
- Boat House Row/Philadelphia Museum of Art

1- Brown University
   Rhode Island School of Design
   Providence College
2- University of Rhode Island

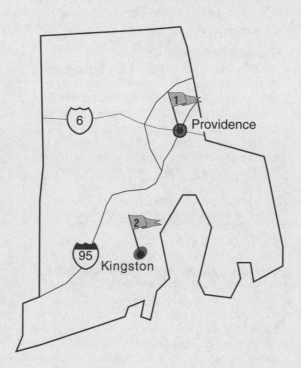

Rhode Island	Brown Univ.	Providence Coll.	RISD	Univ. Rhode Island	Providence
Brown Univ.	—	3	1	34	0
Providence Coll.	3	—	3	31	0
RISD	1	3	—	34	0
Univ. Rhode Island	34	31	34	—	34
Providence	0	0	0	34	—

BROWN UNIVERSITY

Admissions Office, 45 Prospect St.,
Providence, RI 02912 • Telephone: 401-863-2378 • www.brown.edu •
Email: admission_undergraduate@brown.edu

Hours: September–May: Monday–Friday, 8:30AM–5:00PM; Saturdays, 9:00AM–noon. June–August: Monday–Friday, 8:00AM–4:00PM

Professors really make an effort to help students learn at Brown University, and advisors are readily accessible. Courses can be taken either ABC/No Credit, wherein any grade below a C does not appear on the student's transcript, or Satisfactory/No Credit, a pleasant version of Pass/Fail that leaves out the failing part. Brown's thousands of notable alumni include entertainment mogul Ted Turner and the late John F. Kennedy, Jr.

AT A GLANCE

Selectivity Rating	98
Range SAT I Math	650–750
Average SAT I Math	700
Range SAT I Verbal	640–750
Average SAT I Verbal	690
Average ACT Composite	29
Student to Faculty Ratio	8:1

CAMPUS TOURS

Times	Mon–Fri, 10AM, 11AM, 1PM, 3PM, & 4PM; Sat, 10AM–NOON

ON-CAMPUS APPOINTMENTS

Admissions

Start Date—Juniors	June
Appointment	Required
Advance Notice	Yes, 3 weeks
Saturdays	No

Faculty and Coaches

Arrangements	Contact faculty directly

CLASS VISITS

Arrangements	Contact Admissions Office

TRANSPORTATION

T. F. Green airport in Warwick is approximately 10 miles away from the campus. A limousine service is available outside the terminal building after each flight arrival; the limousine will take you downtown within walking or taxi distance from campus. If several of the people in the limousine are headed to Brown, ask the driver to take you to campus. Amtrak trains and Greyhound buses serve Providence. Near either terminal, you an get buses to the campus or the downtown area.

FIND YOUR WAY

From I-95 N. and S., take exit 20 to I-195 E. From I-195 E., take Exit 2 (Wickenden St.), and follow the loop onto Benefit St. Continue on Benefit for approximately half a mile to College St. Turn right on College and go to the top of the steep hill where College terminates at Prospect St. Turn left onto Prospect and continue for two blocks to the Admissions Office on the right corner of Prospect and Angell streets. **From I-95 W.,** exit at South Main St. and continue for approximately half a mile to College St.; follow the preceding directions.

STAY THE NIGHT

Nearby: A few blocks from downtown is the **Old Court** (144 Benefit St.; 401-751-2002), a mid-nineteenth-century mansion on historic Benefit St. It has been completely renovated and rates are expensive. For a completely different experience, you can stay at the **Omni Biltmore** (Kennedy Plaza; 401-421-0700 or 800-THE-OMNI). Built in 1922, this grand landmark hotel has nightly jazz in the lounge and is affiliated with a health club. Rates are moderate on the weekend and expensive during the week. If an indoor pool is important, try the **Marriott Inn** (Charles and Orms streets; 401-272-2400), six blocks away. Rates are moderate on the weekend and expensive during the week. The **Holiday Inn** (21 Atwells Ave.; 401-831-3900) also has an indoor pool, a game room, weight equipment, privileges at the YMCA, a piano bar, and a restaurant. Rates are moderate. For a budget choice, drive 15 minutes to **Hi-Way Motor Inn** (1880 Hartford Ave.; 401-351-7810) at the junction of US Rte. 6 and I-295. Rates are inexpensive. Inquire about special rates at the **Days Hotel** (220 India St.; 401-272-5577), a five-minute drive from Brown.

HIGHLIGHTS

ON CAMPUS

- Bell Gallery
- John Carter Bell Library
- Lyman Hall and Dill Center for the Performing Arts

OFF CAMPUS

- College Hill
- Thayer Street

PROVIDENCE COLLEGE

Office of Admissionss, River Avenue and Eaton Street, Providence, RI 02918 • Telephone: 800-721-6444 • www.providence.edu • Email: pcadmiss@providence.edu

Hours: Monday–Friday, 8:30AM–4:30AM; select Saturdays

At enormously Catholic Providence College, where you couldn't be "just a number" if you tried, all students must complete a two-year interdisciplinary western civilization survey as well as an array of distribution requirements. Many of PC's students are business and management majors; marketing, education, and accounting are among the other popular profession-oriented paths.

HIGHLIGHTS

ON CAMPUS

- St. Dominic Chapel
- Peterson Center (Athletic Facility)
- Slavin Center (Student Center)
- Harkins Hall (Classrooms, administrative offices)
- Aquinas Hall (Residence Hall)

OFF CAMPUS

- Providence Place Mall
- Thayer Street
- Atwells Avenue
- Water Place Park
- RISD Museum

TRANSPORTATION

RIPTA-City Transportation TF Green Airport is 13 minutes away. Logan Airport, East Boston, is one hour away. Amtrak is six minutes away. Bonanza Bus Lines are seven minutes away. Taxis are available outside all four transportation places.

FIND YOUR WAY

From points east: Take I-195 W. into RI and follow to I-95 N. Look for the Providence College sign, Exit 23. Take Exit 23 (state offices). Turn right onto Orms St. After the first light, bear right onto Douglas Ave. (Rte. 7). Proceed 0.7 miles to the third light on Douglas and turn left onto Eaton St. Proceed about 0.6 miles to the second light at the intersection of Eaton St. and River Ave. The main gate of the campus will be on your right. **From points south:** Take I-95 N. into Providence, RI, and look for the sign indicating Providence College, Exit 23. Follow the preceding directions. **From points west:** In Connecticut, take I-84 to Rte. 2 E. Follow Rte. 2 E. to Norwich, Connecticut, and then take I-395 N. Proceed along I-395 N. to Rte. 6 E. Take Rte. 6 E. into Johnston, RI. Proceed along Rte. 6 E. to Rte. 10 N. in Providence. Get in the left lane. Proceed to I-95 N., stay in right-hand lane, and look immediately for the sign indicating Providence College, Exit 23. Follow the preceding directions. **From points north:** Follow I-95 S. into Providence, RI, and look for the sign indicating Providence College, Exit 23. Take Exit 23 (Charles St.). Proceed right onto Charles St. and go 0.2 miles to the first light at Admiral St. Take a left onto Admiral St. and proceed approximately 1.2 miles to the third light at River Ave. Take a left onto River Ave. to the next light (0.4 miles) at Eaton St. The main gate of the campus will be on your left. **From points northwest:** Take I-90 E. to Massachusetts Exit 10A (Worcester/Providence, Rtes. 146/20), which will lead you to Rte. 146 S. (Providence). For almost an hour, follow Rte. 146 S. into Providence, RI, and look for the Providence College, the next exit sign shortly before the Admiral St. exit. Take the Admiral St. exit and turn right onto Admiral St. Proceed approximately 1.1 miles to the second light at River Ave. Take a left onto River Ave. to the next light (0.4 miles) at Eaton St. The main gate of the campus will be on your left. Note alternate campus entrance for those coming from the north or northwest, if the main gate at River Ave. and Eaton St. is closed, take a left from River Ave. onto Eaton St. and proceed east. The campus is on your left.

STAY THE NIGHT

Nearby: A couple of choices include the **Comfort Inn-Airport** (1940 Post Road, Warwick; 800-228-5150) and the **Crowne Plaza** (801 Greenwich Ave., Warwick; 800-227-6963).

AT A GLANCE

Selectivity Rating	82
Range SAT I Math	550–640
Average SAT I Math	596
Range SAT I Verbal	540–630
Average SAT I Verbal	587
Average ACT Composite	25
Average GPA	3.41
Student to Faculty Ratio	14:1

CAMPUS TOURS

Appointment	Not required
Dates	Year-round
Times	Varies
Average Length	1 hour

ON-CAMPUS APPOINTMENTS

Admissions

Info Sessions	Yes

Faculty and Coaches

Dates/Times	Academic year
Arrangements	Contact coach directly 2 weeks prior

CLASS VISITS

Dates	Academic year
Arrangements	Contact Admissions Office

RHODE ISLAND SCHOOL OF DESIGN

Admissions Office, 2 College St.,
Providence, RI 02903 • Telephone: 800-364-7473 • www.risd.edu •
Email: admissions@risd.edu

Hours: Monday–Friday, 8:30AM–4:30PM

The Rhode Island School of Design enrolls more than 2,000 students in a wide array of visual design and arts programs. The school is located in a residential section of Providence, and it's one of the few places you'll find metalsmithing and glassblowing studios. Programs of study range from animation to furniture and fashion design.

AT A GLANCE

Average SAT I Math	600
Average SAT I Verbal	603
Average ACT Composite	25
Average GPA	3.3
Student to Faculty Ratio	11:1

CAMPUS TOURS

Appointment	Required
Dates	Year-round
Times	Varies (check website)
Average Length	120 min.

ON-CAMPUS APPOINTMENTS

Admissions

Start Date—Juniors	Interview not required for admission
Info Sessions	Yes

Faculty and Coaches

Dates/Times	N/A

CLASS VISITS

Dates	Year-round
Arrangements	Contact Admissions Office

TRANSPORTATION

T. F. Green Airport in Warwick is a 20-minute drive from Campus. Taxis are available at the airport for the ride to campus. Amtrak train and Greyhound bus service are available into Providence. Taxis are available at the stations.

FIND YOUR WAY

From I-95 take exit 20 to I-195 E. From I-195, take Exit 1 Downtown Providence. Continue on road and take a right at the second traffic light (College St.). Travel on College St. three blocks and turn left on Prospect St. The RISD Admissions Office is three blocks on the left (62 Prospect St.).

STAY THE NIGHT

Nearby: Rhode Island School of Design is very close to Brown University. Please see suggestions in the Brown entry, which are equally applicable to RISD. The Marriott is within walking distance of RISD, as is the Westin Hotel. The Holiday Inn is a mile away. The Omni Baltimore is about five minutes from RISD, the Days Hotel is a short drive from the campus.

HIGHLIGHTS

ON CAMPUS

- RISD Museum
- The Edna Lawrence Nature Lab
- Metcalf (three-dimensional fine art building)
- 161 S. Main St. (Industrial Design Building)

OFF CAMPUS

- American Diner Museum
- Roger Williams National Memorial
- Providence Athenaeum
- Newport Mansions

UNIVERSITY OF RHODE ISLAND

Undergraduate Admissions, Newman Hall, 14 Upper College Road, Suite1, Kingston, RI 02881-1391 • Telephone: 401-874-7000 • www.uri.edu • Email: uriadmit@etal.uri.edu

Hours: Monday–Friday, 8:30AM–4:30PM

Though fraternities and sororities still dominate social life, this once proud party school is a shell of its former self. This is a good thing, of course, for students looking to take advantage of URI's excellent pre-professional programs, respectable academics, and very affordable in-state tuition.

HIGHLIGHTS

ON CAMPUS

- Ryan Center (new arena & ice rink)
- Ballentine Hall (new business building)
- Memorial Student Union
- Multi-cultural Center
- Six newly renovated residence halls
- Green Hall (newly renovated historic building housing Registar, Financial Aid, and Bursar, as well as the administrative offices.)

OFF CAMPUS

- Newport
- Providence
- Narragansett Beaches
- South County Bike Path
- Block Island

TRANSPORTATION

The T. F. Green Airport in Warwick is 20 miles away from campus. The airport is serviced by the major airlines. Bus transportation and rental cars are available for the trip from the airport to campus. For information on bus transportation, contact the RI Public Transportation Authority at 401-781-9400 or www.ripta.edu. Amtrak trains along the northeast corridor stop at the station in Kingston about two miles away from campus. Local buses (RIPTA) and taxis are available to get to campus from the station. (For train schedules, call Amtrak at 800-USA-RAIL or www.amtrack.com; for bus schedules, call RIPTA at 401-781-9400.) Bus service to Providence is provided by Bonanza Bus Lines (800-556-3815 or www.bonanzabus.com); service from Providence to campus is provided by RIPTA.

FIND YOUR WAY

From the north, take I-95 S. to Exit 9, then take Rhode Island Rte. 4 S. (a left-lane exit). Follow Rte. 4 S. to Rte. 1 S., then stay on Rte. 1 to Rhode Island Rte. 138 W. (Note that this is just past the Holiday Inn; do not take the first 138 exit, which is 138 E.) Take Rte. 138 W. and stay on it for approximately four miles; the university will be on the right. **From the south,** take I-95 N. to Exit 3A and Rhode Island Rte. 138 E. Proceed for approximately seven miles on Rte. 138; the university will be on the left.

STAY THE NIGHT

Nearby: About five minutes away is the **Holiday Inn** (3009 Tower Hill Road, South Kingston; 401-789-1051). Rates are moderate. **Larchwood Inn** (521 Main St.; 401-783-5454) is a mansion with 18 guest rooms—most with private baths—situated on three-and-a-half acres. The inn is 10 minutes south of the university and has a restaurant that serves three meals a day. Rates vary with the season and are inexpensive from November through mid-May and moderate from mid-May through October. **Newport, the City by the Sea,** is only about 15 miles east of the university and offers accommodations ranging from large national hotels and motels to small bed-and-breakfasts at a variety of seasonal prices. Your best bet for a stay in Newport is to contact Newport County Visitors Bureau at 800-326-6030 or 800-976-5122 or www.gonewport.com

A little farther: Approximately 45 minutes south in Westerly is the **Shelter Harbor Inn** (10 Wagner Rd.; 401-322-8883), which has a restaurant, a rooftop deck with hot tub, flower gardens, paddle tennis courts, a shuttle to a private beach two miles away, and golf and fishing nearby. This cheerful bed-and-breakfast, with 24 rooms with private baths, has moderate prices that include a full breakfast.

AT A GLANCE

Selectivity Rating		71
Range SAT I Math		500–610
Average SAT I Math		562
Range SAT I Verbal		490–590
Average SAT I Verbal		549
Average GPA		3.4
Student to Faculty Ratio		18:1

CAMPUS TOURS

Appointment	Not required
Dates	Varies
Times	Mon–Fri, 10AM, NOON, & 2PM; Sat, 10AM & 2PM
Average Length	Varies

ON-CAMPUS APPOINTMENTS

Admissions

Start Date–Juniors	Sept–Nov only
Appointment	Required
Advance Notice	Yes, 3 weeks
Saturdays	No
Average Length	30 min.
Info Sessions	Yes

Faculty and Coaches

Dates/Times	Year-round
Arrangements	Contact coach directly 2 weeks prior

CLASS VISITS

Dates	Varies
Arrangements	Contact department directly

1- Clemson University
2- Furman University
3- University of South Carolina
4- Coll. of Charleston

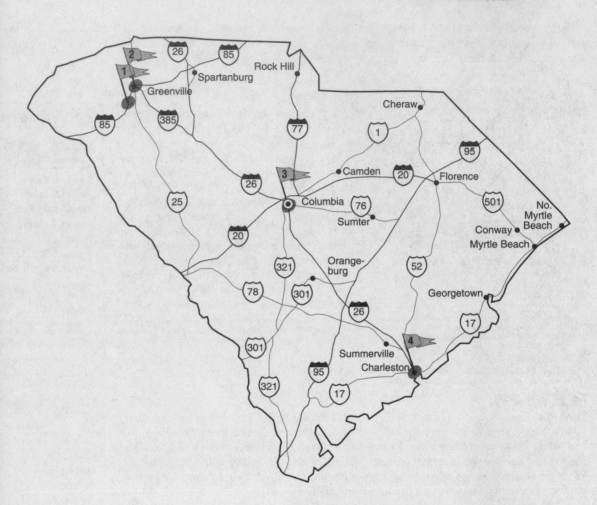

South Carolina	Clemson Univ	Coll. of Charleston	Furman Univ.	Univ. So. Carolina	Charleston
Clemson Univ.	—	248	30	118	240
Coll. of Charleston	248	—	217	113	—
Furman Univ.	30	217	—	101	210
Univ. So. Carolina	118	113	101	—	114
Charleston	240	0	210	114	—

CLEMSON UNIVERSITY

Admissions Office, 105 Sikes Hall, PO Box 345124, Clemson, SC 29634-5124 • Telephone: 864-656-2287 • www.clemson.edu • Email: cuadmissions@clemson.edu

Hours: Monday–Friday, 8:00AM–4:30PM

Clemson is a reasonably large public university in South Carolina that offers small classes (for the most part), several strong pre-professional programs, and a proud football tradition (though the team has been a bit down in recent years). Graduates of the topflight Department of Graphic Communications enjoy a 100 percent job placement rate.

HIGHLIGHTS

ON CAMPUS

- South Carolina Botanical Garden/Discovery Center/Geology Muse
- Hendrix Student Center
- Conference Center and Inn at Clemson/Walker Golf Course
- Fort Hill (Calhoun House)
- Lee Art Gallery

OFF CAMPUS

- T. Ed Garrison Livestock Arena
- Lake Hartwell
- Downtown Clemson (shopping & dining)

TRANSPORTATION

The Greenville-Spartanburg Airport in Greenville, South Carolina is a one-hour drive from campus. Arrange for a rental car or the airport shuttle for the drive from the airport to the campus.

FIND YOUR WAY

From I-85, exit to U.S. Rte. 76 (north and west). Follow U.S. 76 to South Carolina Hwy. 93 W. Follow Highway 93 to Sikes Hall (Admissions Office) and to the Visitors' Center (just off Hwy. 93 across from Sikes Hall).

STAY THE NIGHT

Nearby: Within a mile-and-a-half of Clemson there are several chain motels, including the **Days Inn, Ramada Inn, Sleep Inn, Hampton Inn, Comfort Inn,** and **Lake Hartwell Inn.** On campus, we have the **James F. Martin Inn** (864/ 656-9020), which includes golf privileges. The **Ramada Inn** (U.S. Hwy. 123 and 76; 864-654-7501) has an indoor pool, live entertainment in the lounge from Monday through Saturday, and balconies that open up into an atrium that houses the pool and a gazebo. The **Comfort Inn** (1305 Tiger Blvd.; 864-653-3600) has an outdoor pool and an exercise room. For charm the choice is the **Liberty Hall Inn** (Business Rte. 28, Pendleton; 864-646-7500), about six miles away. The Inn's inexpensive rates include breakfast and is on the National Register of Historic Places.

AT A GLANCE

Selectivity Rating	82
Range SAT I Math	570–670
Average SAT I Math	618
Range SAT I Verbal	540–640
Average SAT I Verbal	587
Average ACT Composite	26
Average GPA	3.97
Student/Faculty Ratio	15:1

CAMPUS TOURS

Appointment	Not required
Dates	Year-round
Times	Mon–Sat, 9:45AM & 1:45PM; Sun, 1:45PM
Average Length	120 min.

ON-CAMPUS APPOINTMENTS

Admissions

Start Date–Juniors	Anytime
Appointment	Not required
Advance Notice	No
Saturdays	No

Faculty and Coaches

Dates/Times	N/A
Arrangements	Contact coach directly

CLASS VISITS

Arrangements	Contact faculty directly

COLLEGE OF CHARLESTON

Office of Admissions, 66 George Street,
Charleston, SC 29424 • Telephone: 843-953-5670 • www.cofc.edu •
Email: admissions@cofc.edu

Hours: Monday–Friday, 8:30AM–5:00PM; select Saturdays

The College of Charleston, a state supported college of about 10,000 students founded in 1770, boasts one of the nation's most beautiful and historic campuses. C of C offers an abundance of degree programs in the arts, sciences (including marine biology), education, and business, and it has a perennially great NCAA Division I men's basketball team that strikes fear in the hearts of national powerhouses.

AT A GLANCE

Range SAT I Math	550–630
Average SAT I Math	590
Range SAT I Verbal	550–640
Average SAT I Verbal	595
Average ACT Composite	24
Average GPA	3.58
Student/Faculty Ratio	14:1

CAMPUS TOURS

Appointment	Required
Dates	Year-round
Times	Mon–Fri, 10AM & 2 PM, during academic year
Average Length	1 hour

ON-CAMPUS APPOINTMENTS

Admissions

Appointment	Required
Advance Notice	Yes, 2 weeks
Saturdays	No
Info Sessions	Yes

Faculty and Coaches

Dates/Times	Academic year
Arrangements	Contact Athletic Department 2 weeks prior

CLASS VISITS

Dates	Academic year
Arrangements	Contact department directly

TRANSPORTATION

The Charleston International Airport is the nearest airport to the campus and is located about twenty minutes away. This airport is serviced by Delta, Northwest, Midway, and US Air. A cab must be taken from the airport to campus. A Greyhound bus station and an Amtrak train station are also located about 20 minutes away from campus. Both the Myrtle Beach Airport and the Savannah, Georgia airport are about two hours from Charleston. There is a bus service that allows for travel around the city. The Charleston Area Regional Transit Authority (CARTA) sponsors the Downtown Area Shuttle (DASH) for travel in the Charleston peninsula. CARTA also sponsors a bus service that allows for transportation in downtown and in the surrounding areas.

FIND YOUR WAY

From I-26: Make a right at the Meeting Street Exit and go to Calhoun St., where you will make a right. Stay on Calhoun St. for two blocks and the heart of campus will be on your left between St. Phillip St. and Coming St. **From Hwy 17-S:** Take the Lockwood Dr. south (right) exit. From Lockwood Dr., turn left onto Calhoun St., and follow the preceding directions. **From Hwy. 17-N:** Follow Hwy. 17 over the Cooper River bridge. After the bridge, exit on Meeting St. Follow Meeting St. to Calhoun St. and make a right; follow the preceding directions.

STAY THE NIGHT

Nearby: Hotels in the historic district include the **Hampton Inn** (Meeting & John Streets; 800-426-7866), the **Days Inn** (Meeting Street at the Market; 800-329-7466), **King Charles Inn** (Meeting & Hassel Streets; 800-528-1234), Francis Marion Hotel (Calhoun & King Streets; 800-937-8461), **Doubletree Guest Suites** (Church Street; 800-222-8733), **Embassy Suites** (Meeting Street; 800-362-2779), **Charleston Place** (King & Market Streets; 800-611-5545), **Mills House** (Meeting & Queen Streets; 800-874-9600), the **Elliott House Inn** (Queen Street; 800-729-1855), the **Lodge Alley Inn** (East Bay Street; 800-845-1004), and the **Courtyard Marriott** (Lockwood Drive; 800-321-2211).

A Little Farther: Within one mile of the campus in West Ashley you will find the **Holiday Inn Riverview** (Savannah Highway; 800-465-4329), the **Hampton Inn Riverview II** (Ashley Point Drive; 800-426-7866), and **Spring Hill Suites** (Ripley Point Drive; 888-287-9400). Within a ten minute drive to campus in Mount Pleasant is the **Shem Creek Inn** (1409 Shrimp Boat Lane; 800-523-4951), the **Hilton Hotel** (Patriots Point; 888-856-0028), the **Hampton Inn** (Johnnie Dodds Blvd.; 800-426-7866), the **Holiday Inn** (Johnnie Dodds Blvd.; 800-465-4329), and the **Quality Inn & Suites** (Patriots Point; 877-424-6423).

HIGHLIGHTS

ON CAMPUS

- The Cistern Area
- The Promenade
- St. Phillip's Deli
- Johnson Center
- Patriot's Point

OFF CAMPUS

- Folly Beach
- Market shopping district
- King Street shops
- Battery
- Waterfront Park

FURMAN UNIVERSITY

Office of Admissions, 3300 Poinsett Hwy.,
Greenville, SC 29613 • Telephone: 864-294-2034 • www.furman.edu •
Email: admissions@furman.edu

Hours: Monday–Friday, 8:30AM–5:00PM

Furman University is a conservative liberal arts school with a caring administration, a solid core curriculum, and a well-earned reputation for rigorous academics. Furman's beautiful, well-manicured, 750-acre campus boasts tennis courts, softball fields, and an 18-hole golf course.

HIGHLIGHTS

ON CAMPUS

- Bell Tower
- Timmons Arena
- Tower Cafe
- 18-Hole Golf Course
- Lakeside Amphitheater

OFF CAMPUS

- Downtown Greenville
- Mountains
- Minor League Baseball
- Bi-Lo Center (concerts)
- Peace Center for Performing Arts

TRANSPORTATION

The Greenville-Spartanburg Airport is 20 miles away from campus. To arrange for limousine service to campus from the airport, call 864-879-2315; after business hours, call 864-235-1713. Amtrak trains serve Greenvile; public buses or taxis are available from the station to campus. Greyhound buses stop on the east side of town; taxis are available at the terminal for the ride to campus.

FIND YOUR WAY

From Asheville, North Carolina, and the northwest, take I-26 to Hendersonville, North Carolina; then take U.S. 25 S. In Traveler's Rest South Carolina, U.S. 25 S. and U.S. 276 E. join briefly; where the highways divide, take 276 East to the Furman exit. **From Charlotte, North Carolina, and the northeast,** take I-85 to Greenville, then take I-385 into downtown. Bear right onto Highway 183, which becomes Beattie Pl. Follow Beattie Pl. (which becomes College St.) and bear right onto U.S. 276 W. Continue five miles to Furman exit. **From Atlanta, Georgia, and the southwest,** take I-85 to Greenville, then take I-185 exit. Follow I-185 into Greenville, where it becomes Mills Ave., then Church St. Turn left from Church St. onto Beattie Pl. (which becomes College St.) and follow preceding directions. **From Columbia, South Carolina, and the southeast,** take I-26 to I-385. Continue on I-385 approximately 45 miles into downtown Greenville. Bear right onto Highway 183, which becomes Beattie Pl. Follow Beattie Pl. (which becomes College St.) and follow the preceding directions.

STAY THE NIGHT

Nearby: Your best deal for price and location is the **Comfort Inn-Executive Center** (540 N. Pleasantburg Dr.; 803-271-0060), a 15-minute drive from campus. A little more expensive and farther away (about 20 minutes) is **Courtyard by Marriott** (70 Orchard Park Dr.; 803-234-0300). Opened in 1991, this hotel is near downtown and shopping areas. Guests have privileges at the Greenville Health and Raquet Club. At the **Hyatt Regency-Greenville** (220 N. Main St.; 803-235-1234), about 15 minutes away, the rates are moderate and it also offers privileges at the Greenville Racquet Club. For bed-and-breakfasts in the area call Clarion Carriage House Inns in Charleston (800-CLARION).

A little farther: A 35-minute ride to the north will take you to Flat Rock, North Carolina, the home of author Carl Sandburg (his house is open to visitors), where you'll find the **Woodfield Inn** (Hwy. 25; 704-693-6016). Rates are moderate, but the inn is closed from January through March.

AT A GLANCE

Selectivity Rating	82
Range SAT I Math	590–680
Range SAT I Verbal	590–690
Average GPA	3.93
Student/Faculty Ratio	11:1

CAMPUS TOURS

Appointment	Required
Dates	Year-round
Times	Call for appointment
Average Length	1 hour

ON-CAMPUS APPOINTMENTS

Admissions

Start Date–Juniors	N/A
Appointment	Required, 2 weeks
Saturdays	Sometimes
Info Sessions	Year-round, except on holidays, breaks, & exam periods

Faculty and Coaches

Dates/Times	Year-round
Arrangements	Contact Admissions Office 1 week prior

CLASS VISITS

Dates	Academic year
Arrangements	Contact Admissions Office

UNIVERSITY OF SOUTH CAROLINA—COLUMBIA

Visitor Center,
Columbia, SC 29208 • Telephone: 800-868-5872 •
Email: admissions-ugrad@sc.edu

Hours: Monday–Friday, 8:30AM–5:00PM

The extremely affordable University of South Carolina does a great job of throwing money at academic super-stars, and students say the state's flagship university provides great overall academics and atmosphere. International studies and the business program are the crown jewels among USC's multitude of majors. For social life, Columbia's Five Points area is filled with great restaurants, shops, and bars.

AT A GLANCE

Selectivity Rating	73
Range SAT I Math	510–620
Average SAT I Math	569
Range SAT I Verbal	500–610
Average SAT I Verbal	555
Average ACT Composite	24
Average GPA	3.7
Student/Faculty Ratio	17:1

CAMPUS TOURS

Appointment	Required
Dates	Varies
Times	Mon–Fri, 10AM & 2PM;
	Summers: Mon–Fri, 10AM
Average Length	2 hours

ON-CAMPUS APPOINTMENTS

Admissions

Start Date–Juniors	Anytime
Appointment	Required, 2 weeks
Saturdays	No
Info Sessions	N/A

Faculty and Coaches

Dates/Times	Year-round
Arrangements	Contact Admissions Office 2 weeks prior

CLASS VISITS

Dates	Year-round
Arrangements	Contact Visiting Center

TRANSPORTATION

The Columbia Metropolitan Airport is a 20-minute drive from campus. Taxis, limousines, and rental cars are available at the airport for the trip to campus. City bus service is also available from the airport to points near the campus; this service is cheaper than other alternatives but takes longer. Greyhound buses serve Columbia; the terminal is six blocks away from campus.

FIND YOUR WAY

From I-20 and Florence, turn off at SC 277 (Exit 73) toward Columbia. Stay on this freeway, which becomes Bull Street. Follow Bull Street until it intersects with Pendleton Street. Turn right and proceed four blocks to Assembly Street. Turn left, and the Visitor Center will be on your immediate right. **From I-20 East and Augusta South Carolina,** turn off at Exit 58 (US 1 toward West Columbia) and stay on this highway which becomes Meeting Street and then becomes Gervais Street after you cross the Congaree River. Turn right onto Assembly Street, at the South Carolina State Capitol. The Visitor Center will be on your right at the second traffic light. **From I-26 East from Spartanburg,** follow US-126/76 toward downtown Columbia and exit at Elmwood Ave. Turn right onto Assembly Street and continue for 11 blocks until you see the Visitor Center on your right just past Pendleton Street. **From I-26 West from Charleston,** take the exit 111-B (US 1) and continue until you see the Congaree River. The street name changes from Meeting Street to Gervais Street. Proceed several blocks. Turn right on to Assembly Street, at the South Carolina State Capitol. The Visitor Center will be on your right at the second traffic light. **From US 76/378:** From Sumter, US 76/378 will change from Sumter Highway to Garners Ferry Road to Devine Street. Devine will intersect with Harden Street at Five Points. Turn left onto Harden Street and take the next right onto Blossom Street. Turn right at the sixth stoplight onto Assembly Street. The Visitor Center will be four blocks ahead on your left. **From I-77:** From Charlotte, exit onto SC 277 toward Columbia. Stay on this freeway, which becomes Bull Street. Follow Bull Street until it intersects with Pendleton Street. Turn right and proceed four blocks to Assembly Street. Turn left, and the Visitor Center will be on your immediate right.

STAY THE NIGHT

Nearby: Special University of South Carolina visitor rates apply at some hotels and inns. Be sure to inquire when you make your reservation. While there are many lodging choices throughout choices throughout Columbia, the following hotels are within a few blocks of the campus: **Holiday Inn Coliseum at USC** (800-HOLIDAY or 803-799-7800), the **Clarion Town House Hotel** (800-277-8711 or 803-771-8711), and the **Adam's Mark Hotel** (800-444-ADAM or 803-771-7000). Two bed-and-breakfast inns are within walking distance: **Rose Hall** (803-771-2288) and **Claussen's Inn** (800-622-3382 or 803-765-0440).

HIGHLIGHTS

ON CAMPUS

- McKussick Museum
- Confederate Relic Room
- Melton Observatory
- Williams Brice Stadium
- Historic Horseshoe

OFF CAMPUS

- Riverbanks Zoo
- South Carolina State Museum
- Robert Mills House
- Woodrow Wilson's boyhood home
- Columbia Museum of Art

1- Rhodes College
2- University of the South
3- Vanderbilt University
   Fisk Univ.
4- University of Tennessee—Knoxville

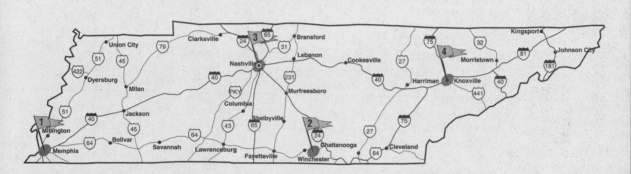

Tennessee	Fisk Univ.	Rhodes Coll.	Univ. of the South	U. Tenn. Knoxville	Vanderbilt Univ.	Knoxville	Memphis
Fisk Univ.	—	203	82	181	0	181	210
Rhodes Coll.	203	—	260	384	210	387	0
Univ. of the South	82	260	—	161	96	159	260
U. Tenn. Knoxville	181	384	161	—	180	0	391
Vanderbilt Univ.	0	210	96	180	—	178	210
Knoxville	181	387	159	0	178	—	387
Memphis	210	0	260	391	210	387	—

FISK UNIVERSITY

Office of Admission Services, 1000 Seventeenth Avenue North, Nashville, TN 37208-3051 • Telephone: 888-702-0022 • www.fisk.edu • Email: admissions@fisk.edu

Hours: Monday–Friday, 8:00AM–5:00PM

Historically African American Fisk University is a wonderful place to learn and a place where individuals are definitely allowed to excel and develop a rapport with the challenging, very open-minded and caring professors. Several affordable Southern-style restaurants and food stands are near campus, including Mary's Bar-B-Q—perhaps Nashville's best barbecue place.

AT A GLANCE

Selectivity Rating	75
Range SAT I Math	365–620
Average SAT I Math	484
Range SAT I Verbal	395–650
Average SAT I Verbal	492
Average ACT Composite	19
Average GPA	3
Student/Faculty Ratio	12:1

CAMPUS TOURS

Appointment	Required
Dates	Varies
Times	Mon, Wed, & Fri, 1PM & 3PM; Tues & Thurs, 11AM & 2PM
Average Length	1 hour

ON-CAMPUS APPOINTMENTS

Admissions

Start Date–Juniors	Spring semester of junior year
Appointment	Required
Advance Notice	Yes, 2 weeks
Saturdays	Sometimes
Average Length	1 hour
Info Sessions	Yes

Faculty and Coaches

Dates/Times	Academic year
Arrangements	Contact Admissions Office 2 weeks prior

CLASS VISITS

Dates	Academic year
Arrangements	Contact Admissions Office

TRANSPORTATION

Nashville International Airport is the closest airport. Taxi services and car rentals are available.

FIND YOUR WAY

From the north: Take I-65 South. Take the South North First Street exit (exit number 85B, toward Jefferson Street). Merge on to 1st Street. Turn right onto Spring Street. Continue on Jefferson Street. Make left on to 17th Avenue North. Park in the designated Fisk Parking Area. **From the south:** Take I-65 North. Take I-40 West. Take exit 82B (toward Memphis). Merge onto I-40 West. Take exit number 209B (Charlotte Avenue), stay right on 209B. Follow exit 209B until you reach the traffic light at Charlotte. Make left at right. Continue on Charlotte Avenue. Turn right onto DB Todd Blvd. Turn right onto Jefferson Street. Turn right onto 17th Avenue North. Park in designated Fisk parking area. **From the south/east:** Take I-24 West. Take I-40 West. Follow exit 209B until you reach the traffic light at Charlotte. Make a left at light. Continue on Charlotte Avenue. Turn right onto DB Todd Blvd. Turn right onto Jefferson Street. Turn right onto 17th Avenue North. Park in designated Fisk parking area. **From the west:** Take I-40 East. Take the I-40 East exit, exit number 12C, towards Nashville. Merge onto I-40 East. Take the Jefferson Street Exit, exit number 207. Keep right at the fork in the ramp. Merge onto Jefferson Street. Make right onto 17th Avenue North. Park in designated Fisk parking area.

STAY THE NIGHT

Nearby: Hotels within 15 minutes of campus that also have moderate rates include the **Hampton Inn Vanderbilt** (1919 West End Ave.; 615-329-1144), the **Holiday Inn Vanderbilt** (2613 West End Ave.; 615-327-4707), the **Millennium Maxwell House Hotel** (600 Metrocenter Blvd., 615-259-4343), and the **Hampton Inn-North** (2407 Brick Church Pike; 615-226-3300). Hotels with more expensive rates include the **Holiday Inn Crowne Plaza** (623 Union St., 616-259-2000), **Loews Vanderbilt Plaza** (2100 West End Ave.; 615-320-1700), and the **Sheraton Music City** (777 McGavock Pike; 615-885-2200).

HIGHLIGHTS

ON CAMPUS

- Jubilee Hall
- Fisk Memorial Chapel
- Carl Van Vechten & Aaron Douglas Art Galleries
- Cravath Hall with Douglas Murals
- Harris Music Building
- Carnegie Hall

OFF CAMPUS

- The Gaylord Entertainment Center (Nashville Arena)
- Country Music Hall of Fame
- General Jackson Dinner Cruise stop
- The Wildhorse Saloon
- Ryman Auditorium
- Parthanon/Centennial Park

RHODES COLLEGE

Office of Admissions, 2000 N. Pkwy.,
Memphis, TN 38112 • Telephone: 800-844-5969 •
Email: adminfo@rhodes.edu

Hours: Monday–Friday, 8:30AM–5:00PM; Saturday (during academic term), 9:00AM–noon

Tiny Rhodes College in Memphis offers its students the best of many worlds: a highly touted academic program, a beautiful campus, and accessibility to a major metropolis. Rhodes also boasts a highly committed faculty and a killer reputation with graduate schools; the school claims its students' acceptance rate in such programs is over 90 percent.

HIGHLIGHTS

ON CAMPUS

- Bryan Campus Life Center
- Halliburton Tower
- Briggs Student Center
- Oak Alley
- McCoy Theater

OFF CAMPUS

- Graceland
- National Civil Rights Museum
- Beale Street
- Rendezvous BBQ
- Orpheum Theater

TRANSPORTATION

Memphis International Airport is seven miles away from campus. Rhodes students provide transportation from the airport to campus between 9:00 AM and 9:00 PM every day; call the Admissions Office at least one week in advance to arrange for this service. Amtrak trains and Greyhound buses serve Memphis. Taxis are available from the stations to campus.

FIND YOUR WAY

From the north, take I-55 S. to West Memphis, AR. Exit to I-40 E. (toward Memphis). Exit at Danny Thomas Blvd. North (Exit 1B) and take the first right onto North Pkwy. Continue on North Pkwy., then turn left on University St. and continue to the Phillips Lane entrance to the campus. **From the south,** take I-55 North to Memphis and merge with I-240 North, exit Union Avenue East. Continue on Union Ave. to East Pkwy. Turn left onto East Pkwy. and continue to North Pkwy. Turn left at North Pkwy. and continue to University Street. Turn right at University to Phillips Lane Entrance. **From the east,** take I-40 W. to Memphis. Continue on Sam Cooper Blvd., which becomes Broad St. Proceed on Broad, then turn right onto East Pkwy. At the first intersection, turn left onto North Pkwy. and proceed to University St. Turn right at University to the Phillips Lane entrance. **From the west,** take I-40 E. to Memphis, then follow the directions given from the north.

STAY THE NIGHT

Nearby: The **Hampton Inn and Suites** (175 Peabody; 901-260-4000) and **Wyndam Garden Hotel** (250 N. Main St.; 901-525-1800) are located near the campus. A little bit farther is the **Hampton Inn** (1180 Union Ave.; 901-276-1175), whose inexpensive rate includes continental breakfast. For a real treat, consider the famous **Peabody Hotel** (149 Union Ave.; 901-529-4000), about 10 minutes away from the school. The special rate for college visitors puts it at the high end of the moderate range. Ducks march through the lobby in the afternoon. Need we say more?

AT A GLANCE

Selectivity Rating	80
Range SAT I Math	600–690
Average SAT I Math	640
Range SAT I Verbal	590–700
Average SAT I Verbal	644
Average ACT Composite	28
Average GPA	3.62
Student/Faculty Ratio	11:1

CAMPUS TOURS

Appointment	Required
Dates	Year-round
Times	Times vary, contact Admissions Office
Average Length	1 hour

ON-CAMPUS APPOINTMENTS

Admissions

Start Date–Juniors	Anytime
Appointment	Required, 1 week
Saturdays	Yes
Info Sessions	Yes

Faculty and Coaches

Dates/Times	Academic year
Arrangements	Contact Admissions Office 1 week prior

CLASS VISITS

Dates	Year-round
Arrangements	Contact Admissions Office

THE UNIVERSITY OF THE SOUTH

Office of Admissions, 735 University Ave.,
Sewanee, TN 37383-1000 • Telephone: 800-522-2234 • www.sewanee.edu •
Email: collegeadmission@sewanee.edu

Hours: Monday–Friday, 8:00AM–4:30PM; select Saturdays during academic term

The University of the South (a.k.a. Sewanee, to the initiated) offers a huge Greek system and one of the best liberal arts educations in the country. Students say the honor code is an integral part of the Sewanee experience; the students' commitment to abstain from lying, cheating, and stealing fosters an overwhelming trust that inspires students to feel safe leaving doors unlocked and backpacks unattended.

AT A GLANCE

Selectivity Rating	86
Range SAT I Math	550–650
Range SAT I Verbal	560–660
Average GPA	3.39
Student/Faculty Ratio	10:1

CAMPUS TOURS

Appointment	Required
Times	Mon–Fri, 10AM & 2PM;
	Sat, 11:30AM

ON-CAMPUS APPOINTMENTS

Admissions

Start Date–Juniors	Anytime
Appointment	Required
Advance Notice	Yes, 1 week
Saturdays	Sometimes
Average Length	1 hour
Info Sessions	Yes

Faculty and Coaches

Dates/Times	Academic year
Arrangements	Contact Admissions
	Office 1 week prior

CLASS VISITS

Dates	Academic year
Arrangements	Contact Admissions
	Office

TRANSPORTATION

The Nashville International Airport is 90 miles away from campus. The Chattanooga Metropolitan Airport is 50 miles away from campus. Rental cars are available at these airports, and shuttle service is available from the airports for students traveling alone. Contact the Office of Admission for details. The university has its own airport in Sewanee, a mile-and-a-half from campus. The 3,500-foot runway is available to private planes; call 913-598-1910 for more information. The university can provide a car at the Sewanee airport for visitor use. Greyhound bus lines serve Monteagle, which is four miles away from Sewanee. If you notify the Admissions Office well in advance, it will provide transportation to and from the bus station.

FIND YOUR WAY

From I-24 (between Nashville and Chattanooga), take Exit 134 (Monteagle) to Hwy. 41N. After approximately four miles, pass through the stone columns and veer right onto University Ave. The Admissions Office is approximately one mile down University Ave. on the right, across from the main quadrangle and All Saints' Chapel. If you are traveling south on Hwy. 41, Sewanee is six miles east of Cowan. At the top of the mountain, turn left onto University Ave. at the small group of shops. Proceed up the hill to the heart of campus. The Admissions Office is on the left side of the street across from the main quadrangle and All Saints Chapel.

STAY THE NIGHT

Nearby: For on-campus convenience, character, and fun, the **Sewanee Inn** (931-598-1686) has it all. Built from mountain stone with cathedral ceilings, the rooms include a continental breakfast. Alternatives include the **Best Western Smoke House** (Monteagle; 913-924-2091), a motel with cabins in the back and an outdoor pool; the **Monteagle Inn** (931-924-3869); or the **Edgeworth Inn** (931-924-2669), just seven miles away from the university. The inn's moderate price includes a full southern breakfast with biscuits. It's fun to explore the 96 acres of this Victorian village. The inn is also great for hiking and biking. The Assembly grounds are listed on the National Register of Historic Places.

A little farther: If you're ready for a change of pace, you'll find it 11 miles west of Sewanee at **Tim's Ford State Park** (Winchester; 931-967-4457). The park has campsites and two-bedroom housekeeping cabins with fireplaces that are available from April to December. The cabins are heated, air-conditioned, and located on Tim's Ford Lake. The area has an outdoor swimming pool, bike trails, a recreation building with games and sports, and a marina with a restaurant and picnic area.

HIGHLIGHTS

ON CAMPUS
- Outdoor recreation on Sewanee's 10,000-acre campus
- All Saints' Chapel
- Abbo's Alley Ravine Garden
- Memorial Cross and Univeristy View
- University Golf and Tennis Club

OFF CAMPUS
- The Tennessee Aquarium
- Nashville concerts and events
- Monteagle Assembly
- South Cumberland Recreation Area

UNIVERSITY OF TENNESSEE—KNOXVILLE

320 Student Service Building, Circle Park Drive, Knoxville, TN 37996-0230 • Telephone: 800-221-8657 • www.utk.edu • Email: admissions@tennessee.edu

Hours: Monday–Friday, 8:00AM–5:00PM

The very large University of Tennessee at Knoxville has great facilities and offers fabulous academic opportunities by the bushel, including prominent programs in the sciences, engineering, education, business, textiles, and advertising. Socially, students are not averse to partying, and they bleed orange for their beloved volunteer football and women's basketball teams.

HIGHLIGHTS

ON CAMPUS
- Ayres Hall and the Hill
- Neyland Stadium
- Hodges Library
- Rec Sports Center
- The Rock

OFF CAMPUS
- Women's Basketball Hall of Fame
- The Old City
- Knoxville Zoo
- West Town Mall
- Volunteer Landing

TRANSPORTATION
Knox Area Transit buses, taxis, McGhee Tyson Airport.

FIND YOUR WAY
From McGhee Tyson Airport: Follow U.S. 129 (Alcoa Highway) north to Knoxville. Take Neyland Drive exit. Turn left onto Neyland Dr. Continue straight through next traffic light (a left turn would take you to Ag. Campus). Turn left at the next light onto Lake Loudon Blvd. Drive to the end of Lake Loudon Blvd. Turn right onto Volunteer Blvd. The Campus Information Center is on your right. **From Atlanta:** Follow I-75/I-40 to Exit 386. Exit onto U.S. 129 (Alcoa Highway) south (toward airport and Smoky Mtns.). Follow the preceeding directions. **From Nashville:** Follow I-40 to Exit 386. Exit onto U.S. 129 (Alcoa Highway) south (toward Airport and Smoky Mtns.). Follow the preceding directions. **From Asheville:** Follow I-40 to Exit 388. Exit onto James White Parkway (left hand exit). James White Parkway turns into Neyland Drive. Turn right at second traffic light (next to arena) onto Lake Loudon Blvd. Follow the preceeding directions. **From Lexington:** Follow I-75 to I-275 to Knoxville. Exit I-275 onto Henley St. (U.S. 441). Turn right onto Cumberland Ave. immediately after you pass the World's Fair Park. Once on Cumberland Ave., turn left at the fifth traffic light, which is Volunteer Blvd. Follow Volunteer Blvd. straight through the traffic light. Volunteer Blvd. curves to the right. The Campus Information Center is on your left, past the torchbearer statue.

AT A GLANCE

Selectivity Rating		77
Range SAT I Math		500–610
Average SAT I Math		549
Range SAT I Verbal		500–600
Average SAT I Verbal		551
Average ACT Composite		24
Average GPA		3.38
Student/Faculty Ratio		18:1

CAMPUS TOURS

Appointment	Preferred
Dates	Year-round
Average Length	120 min.

ON-CAMPUS APPOINTMENTS

Admissions

Faculty and Coaches

Dates/Times	Year-round

CLASS VISITS

Dates	Year-round
Arrangements	Contact Admissions Office

VANDERBILT UNIVERSITY

Office of Undergraduate Admissions, 2305 West End Ave.,
Nashville, TN 37203 • Telephone: 800-288-0432 • www.vanderbilt.edu •
Email: admissions@vanderbilt.edu

Hours: Monday–Friday, 8:00AM–5:00PM; Saturday (mornings during the academic year by appointment), 9:00AM–1:00PM

There is a sense of academic excellence at Vanderbilt University but without the cutthroat competition found at schools of similar academic caliber. Greeks dominate campus life on this gorgeous laid-back campus, which is chock full of southern hospitality; Nashville provides plenty of social options.

AT A GLANCE

Selectivity Rating	93
Range SAT I Math	640–720
Range SAT I Verbal	610–700
Student/Faculty Ratio	9:1

CAMPUS TOURS

Appointment	Preferred
Dates	Year-round
Times	Varies; call for schedule
Average Length	1 hour

ON-CAMPUS APPOINTMENTS

Admissions

Start Date—Juniors	Interviews are not offered

Faculty and Coaches

Dates/Times	Year-round
Arrangements	Contact Athletic Department

CLASS VISITS

Dates	Varies
Arrangements	Contact Admissions Office

TRANSPORTATION

Nashville International Airport is approximately 10 miles away from campus, and taxis and rental cars are available. Capitol Limousine Service offers a van limo service from the airport to any hotel or motel in the Nashville area or to any university location. They suggest that you make a reservation prior to your arrival (615-883-6777). Greyhound buses serve Nashville, and taxis to campus are available.

FIND YOUR WAY

From the north, take I-265 to I-40 E.; from I-40 take Exit 209B. Turn right on Broadway (U.S. 70 S.). Follow Broadway and veer right to West End Ave. Continue on West End to 23 Ave. Undergraduate Admissions is located on the right. **From the east or south,** take I-40 W. to Exit 209A. Turn left on Broadway, and follow the preceding directions from there. **From the west,** take I-40 E. to Exit 209B. Turn right on Broadway, and follow the preceding directions.

STAY THE NIGHT

Nearby: Several choices are within walking distance of the university. The most expensive (the special rate for university visitors is at the high end of the moderate range) is the **Vanderbilt Plaza** (2100 West End Ave.; 615-320-1700 or 800-336-3335), which is across the street from campus. At the **Hampton Inn** (1919 West End Ave.; 615-329-1144 or 800-426-7866), you can get a cheap double room. Rates are a bit higher at the **Holiday Inn Vanderbilt** (2613 West End Ave.; 615-327-4707 or 800-663-4427), which has a pool and fitness room. We like the all-suite **Hermitage Hotel** (231 6th Ave. North; 615-244-3121 or 800-251-1908), about a five-minute drive from the university. Built in 1910, the hotel has been beautifully restored but rates are expensive. Another possibility, about 15 minutes away, is **Maxwell House** (2025 Metro Center Blvd.; 615-259-4343). Prices at this large hotel are expensive, but it has a fitness room, lighted tennis courts, a sauna, and a whirlpool, not to mention great food! Also about 15 minutes away is a **Courtyard by Marriott-Brentwood** (103 E. Park Dr.; 615-371-9200). Rates vary from inexpensive to moderate and there's a fitness room and pool.

HIGHLIGHTS

ON CAMPUS

- National Arboretum
- Freedom Forum First Amendment Center
- Free Electron Laser
- Robert Penn Warren Center for Humanities
- SEC Division I Athletics

OFF CAMPUS

- 2nd Avenue (Historic/Entertainment District)
- The Grand Ole Opry
- Percy Priest Lake
- The Parthenon

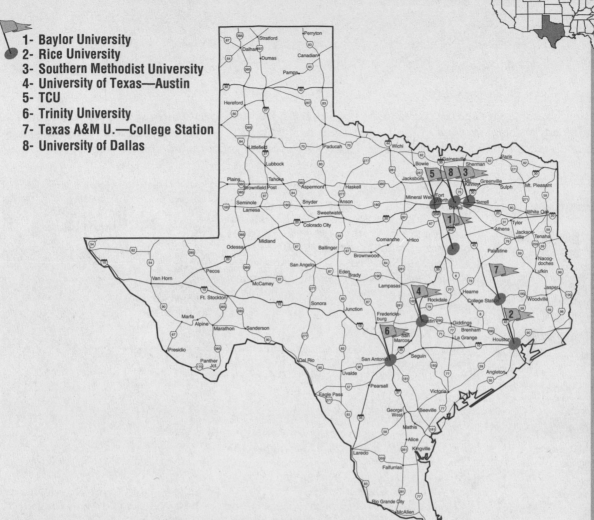

1- Baylor University
2- Rice University
3- Southern Methodist University
4- University of Texas—Austin
5- TCU
6- Trinity University
7- Texas A&M U.—College Station
8- University of Dallas

Texas

	Baylor Univ.	Rice Univ.	So. Methodist Univ.	TCU	Texas A&M U.	Trinity Univ.	Univ. of Dallas	Univ. Texas-Austin	Dallas	Houston	San Antonio
Baylor Univ.	—	245	102	91	89	186	103	100	92	236	182
Rice Univ.	245	—	253	282	99	196	253	186	243	0	189
So. Methodist Univ.	102	253	—	35	185	282	8	195	0	240	278
TCU	91	282	35	—	173	273	32	192	31	262	269
Texas A&M U.	89	99	185	173	—	167	189	104	189	98	168
Trinity Univ.	186	196	282	273	167	—	282	79	265	205	0
Univ. of Dallas	103	253	8	32	189	282	—	203	10	249	282
Univ. Texas-Austin	100	186	195	192	104	79	203	—	195	186	79
Dallas	92	243	0	31	189	265	10	195	—	243	272
Houston	236	0	240	262	98	205	249	186	243	—	197
San Antonio	182	189	278	269	168	0	282	79	272	197	—

BAYLOR UNIVERSITY

Admission Services Office, PO Box 97056,
Waco, TX 76798-7056 • Telephone: 800-229-5678 • www.baylor.edu •
Email: admissions_serv_office@baylor.edu

Hours: Monday–Friday, 8:00AM–5:00PM

This Christian school in the Lone Star State has a huge Greek system and tons of Bible studies and Christian activities. The Baylor Interdisciplinary Core Program eats up 41 credits in various subjects, emphasizes how they all relate, and replaces normal requirements for the 200 freshman the program admits each year.

AT A GLANCE

Selectivity Rating	81
Range SAT I Math	550–650
Range SAT I Verbal	530–630
Student/Faculty Ratio	17:1

CAMPUS TOURS

Appointment	Preferred
Dates	Year-round
Times	Mon–Fri, 8:30AM; 10AM; 1:30PM; & 3PM
Average Length	120 min.

ON-CAMPUS APPOINTMENTS

Admissions

Start Date–Juniors	Spring semester
Appointment	Preferred
Saturdays	No
Average Length	1 hour
Info Sessions	Yes

Faculty and Coaches

Dates/Times	Year-round
Arrangements	Contact Athletic Department 2 weeks prior

CLASS VISITS

Dates	Varies
Arrangements	Contact Visiting Center

TRANSPORTATION

Waco Regional Airport is 10 miles (a 15-minute drive) from campus. Rental cars and taxis are available at the airport for the drive to campus; call Avis at 800-331-1212 or Hertz at 800–654-3131. The Waco airport can be reached via Dallas-Fort Worth International and Houston International (George Bush) airports.

FIND YOUR WAY

From I-35, take Exit 335B on University Parks Dr. The Campus Tours Office is two blocks east of I-35 in the Wiethorn Visitors' Center.

STAY THE NIGHT

Nearby: **La Quinta Inn** (1110 S. 9th St.; 254-752-9741) has an outdoor pool and a cafe next door; rates are inexpensive. **Lexington Inn** (254-754-1266) is located at I-35 and University Parks Dr. Other options close to campus are the **Clarion Inn** (S. 4th St.; 254-757-2000), the **Marriott Courtyard** (University Parks Dr. and Washington; 254-752-8686), and the **Best Western Old Main Lodge** (I-35 and 4th St.; 254-753-0316). The **Hilton Hotel** (113 S. University Parks Dr.; 254-754-8484), one mile away from the school and near downtown, has an outdoor pool, access to a health club a tennis court, restaurant, and lounge.

A little farther: See the Southern Methodist University entry for suggestions in Dallas, approximately 95 miles to the north, and Texas Christian University for suggestions in Fort Worth, which is a little closer than Dallas.

HIGHLIGHTS

ON CAMPUS

- Strecker Museum
- Armstrong Browning Library
- Baylor Sciences Building
- Mayborn Museum Complex
- Chili's II (first on a university campus)

OFF CAMPUS

- Fort Fisher Park
- Texas Sports Hall of Fame
- Cameron Park
- Dr. Pepper Museum
- River Square Center (shopping/restuarants)

RICE UNIVERSITY

Office of Admission, 6100 Main St.,
Houston, TX 77251-1892 • Telephone: 800-527-6957 • www.rice.edu •
Email: admission@rice.edu

Hours: Monday–Friday, 8:30AM–5:00PM

Rice University, the Ivy of the South, has a varied and challenging academic program minus some of the intense competition that often accompanies other universities of such stature. Work is taken very seriously, and most of the intelligent, articulate, and approachable students study four to five hours a day.

HIGHLIGHTS

ON CAMPUS
- Rice Memorial Center
- Baker Institute for Public Policy
- Rice University Art Gallery
- Sheperd School of Music
- Rockling Park

OFF CAMPUS
- Museum of Fine Arts
- Downtown Theater District
- Rothko Chapel at the Meril Collection
- Cockrell Butterfly Centre at the Museum of Natural History
- NASA Space Center

TRANSPORTATION

Houston's Hobby Airport is a 30-minute (non-rush hour) drive from campus. Houston's Intercontinental Airport is a 45-minute (non-rush hour) drive from campus. Taxis, shuttles, and rental cars are available at both airports. The shuttle services pick up passengers at the baggage claim areas. The shuttle delivers passengers to the Harvey Suites substation (6700 S. Main St.). From the substation, take a taxi to campus. Amtrak trains and Greyhound buses serve Houston. The bus terminal on Main St. is a short distance from campus; taxis are available at the terminal for the ride to campus.

FIND YOUR WAY

Take I-10, I-45, or I-610 to U.S. Rte. 59 (the Southwest Freeway). Take U.S. 59 into the city to the Shepherd-Greenbriar/Rice University exit. At Greenbriar, head south to Rice Blvd. Turn left on Rice and continue to Main St. Turn right on Main St. and make an immediate right turn into the main campus gate. Lovett Hall (location of the Admissions Office) is at the end of the entrance driveway; visitors' parking is available in both lots in front of Lovett Hall.

STAY THE NIGHT

Nearby: The **Marriott Medical Center** (6580 Fannin St.; 713-796-0080) is within walking distance of the university. It has an indoor pool, exercise room, whirlpool, Jacuzzi, and a great seafood restaurant. It's also 15 minutes away from the Galleria, the big downtown shopping mall. For something special half a mile away from school, we suggest **La Colombe** (3410 Montrose Blvd.; 713-524-7999), a restored 1920s mansion with six suites and a wonderful French restaurant. Rates are very expensive. Two other suggestions are also close to the university: **Holiday Inn Medical Center** (6701 S. Main St.; 713-797-1110), half a mile away, with an outdoor pool and a special inexpensive rate for Rice visitors ,and the **Park Plaza Warwick** (5701 S. Main St.; 713-526-1991), an old-fashioned hotel five minutes away, near the Museum of Fine Arts and a park with a jogging trail. Another option is the **Hilton Houston Plaza** (6633 Travis Street; 713-313-4000).

AT A GLANCE

Selectivity Rating	97
Range SAT I Math	670–770
Range SAT I Verbal	650–750
Student/Faculty Ratio	5:1

CAMPUS TOURS

Appointment	Not required
Dates	Year-round
Times	Mon–Fri, 11AM & 3PM; Sat, 10:30AM, during academic year
Average Length	1 hour

ON-CAMPUS APPOINTMENTS

Admissions

Start Date–Juniors	Late May
Appointment	Required
Advance Notice	Yes, 2 weeks
Saturdays	Sometimes
Average Length	30 min.
Info Sessions	Yes

Faculty and Coaches

Arrangements	Contact department directly

CLASS VISITS

Dates	Academic year
Arrangements	Contact Admissions Office

SOUTHERN METHODIST UNIVERSITY

PO Box 750181, Dallas, TX 75275-0296 •
Telephone: 800-323-0672 • www.smu.edu •
Email: enrol_serv@mail.smu.edu

Hours: Monday–Friday, 8:30AM–5:00PM; Saturday (select during fall), 9:00AM–noon

Excellent professors and tremendous business and management programs make Southern Methodist a great choice. Students definitely love SMU thanks to a small, interacting student body, a beautiful campus, and metropolitan Dallas—a fun town if there ever was one.

AT A GLANCE

Selectivity Rating	81
Range SAT I Math	550–650
Range SAT I Verbal	540–630
Average GPA	3.48
Student/Faculty Ratio	12:1

CAMPUS TOURS

Appointment	Preferred
Dates	Year-round
Times	Mon–Fri, 11AM & 3PM; Sat, 11AM
Average Length	1 hour

ON-CAMPUS APPOINTMENTS

Admissions

Start Date—Juniors	Anytime
Appointment	Preferred
Advance Notice	Yes, 2 weeks
Saturdays	No
Average Length	1 hour
Info Sessions	Yes

Faculty and Coaches

Dates/Times	Year-round
Arrangements	Contact Admissions Office 2 weeks prior

CLASS VISITS

Dates	Year-round
Arrangements	Contact Admissions Office

TRANSPORTATION

Dallas-Fort Worth International Airport is approximately 15 miles away from campus. Airport shuttle minivans are available for the ride from the airport to campus; direct-dial free phones are located near the baggage area. The minivans and taxis leave from the lower level of the airport. Love Field (served by Southwest Airlines) is approximately four miles away from campus; airport shuttle minivans are also available at this airport. By special arrangement with SMU, American Airlines makes reduced fares available to visitors for all SMU special visitation days. For details, call the American Airlines Meeting Services Desk at 800-433-1790 and ask for Star Number S9700. Amtrak trains and Greyhound/Trailways bus lines serve Dallas.

FIND YOUR WAY

From I-30 (U.S. Routes 67/80), exit to U.S. Rte. 75 N. Exit from Rte. 75 to Mockingbird Lane West, which will take you to campus.

STAY THE NIGHT

Nearby: Within walking distance is the moderately priced (ask for the special SMU visitor rate) **Radisson** (6060 N. Central Expy.; 214-750–6060). Restaurants are just behind the hotel and theaters and shopping areas are nearby. The hotel has an indoor and outdoor pool, a Jacuzzi, and a steam room. For luxury, consider splurging on **Mansion on Turtle Creek** (2821 Turtle Creek Blvd.; 214-559-2100). For bed-and-breakfasts, contact Book a Bed Ahead (312-293-8620).

HIGHLIGHTS

ON CAMPUS
• Gerald J. Ford Stadium
• Meadows Museum
• Hughes Trigg Student Center
• Dallas Hall
• Fondren Library

OFF CAMPUS
• Morton H. Myerson Symphony Center
• Dallas Museum of Art
• West End Historical District
• Southfork Ranch
• John F. Kennedy Memorial

TCU

Office of Admission, TCU Box 297013,
Fort Worth, TX 76129 • Telephone: 800-828-3764 • www.tcu.edu •
Email: frogmail@tcu.edu

Hours: Monday–Friday, 8:00AM–5:00PM; Saturday (select during academic year), 10:00AM–noon

Located in Fort Worth, Texas, TCU offers the nation's first academically affiliated program in ballet, but students seem more attracted to the business school; nearly one in ten business majors enters an MBA program within a year of graduation. Horned Frog athletics are huge, and a strong Greek system rules social life.

HIGHLIGHTS

ON CAMPUS

- Amon Carter Stadium
- Monnig Meteorite Collection
- W. M. Lewis Collection of British Literature
- Mills Glass Collection
- Tandy Film Library

OFF CAMPUS

- Kimbell Art Museum
- Billy Bob's Honkey Tonk
- Downtown Sundance Square
- Bass Performance Hall
- Fort Worth Zoo

TRANSPORTATION

Dallas-Fort Worth International Airport is 25 miles away from campus. Taxis, rental cars, and the Super Shuttle (800-258-3826) are available for the trip from the airport to campus. About 45 miles away from campus, Dallas Love Field Airport serves as a base for Southwest Airlines; taxis and rental cars are available.

FIND YOUR WAY

From the east or west, take I-30 and exit at University Dr. (Signs on I-30 indicate the TCU exit.) Head south on University to the Admissions Office at 2800 S. University Dr. **From the north or south,** take I-35 West to I-20 West. Exit at Hulen St. (you'll see a TCU sign), then go north. Go east on Bellaire South. You will see TCU at the crest of the hill.

STAY THE NIGHT

Nearby: The **Ramada Inn-Midtown** (817-228-2828), the **Marriott Courtyard** (817-321-2221), the **Residence Inn** (871-870-1011), and **Fairfield Inn** (817-335-2000) are all approximately two miles away from the TCU campus, with rates ranging from inexpensive to moderate. All are within walking distance of a 13-mile jogging trail, great restaurants, and a spectacular shopping center. The **Worthington Hotel** (817-870-1000), the **Ramada Inn-Downtown** (817-335-7000), and the **Radisson** (817-870-2100) are in Fort Worth's thriving downtown, which is about four miles away from TCU. There you will find fantastic dining options, two movie theaters, specialty shops, coffee bars, and bookstores.

AT A GLANCE

Selectivity Rating	80
Range SAT I Math	520–630
Range SAT I Verbal	510–620
Student/Faculty Ratio	15:1

CAMPUS TOURS

Appointment	Preferred
Dates	Year-round
Times	Mon–Fri, 10AM & 2PM; Sat, 10AM
Average Length	1 hour

ON-CAMPUS APPOINTMENTS

Admissions

Start Date—Juniors	Spring of junior year
Appointment	Required
Advance Notice	Yes, 1 week
Saturdays	Sometimes
Info Sessions	Yes

Faculty and Coaches

Dates/Times	Academic year
Arrangements	Contact Admissions Office 2 weeks prior

CLASS VISITS

Dates	Varies
Arrangements	Contact Admissions Office

TEXAS A&M UNIVERSITY—COLLEGE STATION

Office of Admission, 1265 TAMU,
College Station, TX 77843-1265 • Telephone: 979-845-3741 • www.tamu.edu •
Email: admissions@tamu.edu

Hours: Monday–Friday, 8:00AM–5:00PM

Virtually every major ever invented is available on Texas A&M's huge, tradition-happy main campus in College Station. The best thing about A&M, though, is being an Aggie. The 40,000 fanatical students build towering bonfires and show their legendary school spirit in Midnight Yell Practice before big football games. Also, A&M's military training program, the Corps of Cadets is the best leadership training in the nation, according to one student.

AT A GLANCE

Selectivity Rating	83
Range SAT I Math	550–660
Average SAT I Math	602
Range SAT I Verbal	520–630
Average SAT I Verbal	576
Average ACT Composite	25
Student/Faculty Ratio	21:1

CAMPUS TOURS

Appointment	Preferred
Dates	Year-round
Times	Varies

ON-CAMPUS APPOINTMENTS

Faculty and Coaches

Arrangements	Contact coach directly 1 week prior

CLASS VISITS

Arrangements Contact faculty directly

TRANSPORTATION

Aggie Bus Operations is available, and the closest airport is Easterwood Airport.

FIND YOUR WAY

The Visitor Center is located on the first floor of Rudder Tower, across from the University Center Parking Garage. **From North Austin**, take 290 E to Hwy. 21. Go east on Hwy. 21 to Hwy. 47 (on outskirts of Bryan near Texas A&M Riverside Campus). Veer right onto Hwy. 47 (which will eventually become Hwy. 60 or University Drive). Go past the Easterwood Airport exit, veer to the right onto West By-Pass (FM 2818) and turn left on George Bush Drive. Continue on George Bush Drive to Houston Street. Turn left on Houston St. to enter the University Center Parking Garage. The Visitor Center is just across the street from the University Center Parking Garage. **From South Austin**, take Hwy. 183 South to Hwy. 71. Go east on Hwy. 71 toward Bastrop to Hwy. 21. Go past Bastrop, look for left turn to continue on State Rte 21 toward Caldwell; after left turn, travel approximately three blocks and turn right to continue on Hwy. 21. Continue northeast on Hwy. 21 to Hwy. 47 and follow the preceding directions. **From Dallas**, take I-35 S to Waco. In Waco, take Exit 339 to 340 (southeast loop around Waco). Take Hwy. 6 exit to Bryan. Exit right on University Drive (Hwy. 60). Turn left on Texas Avenue. Turn right on George Bush Drive to Houston Street. Turn right on Houston St. to enter the University Center Parking garage. The Visitor Center is just across the street from the University Center Parking Garage. **From Houston**, take Hwy. 290 (toward Austin). Stay on Hwy. 290 until you reach Hwy. 6 (just north of Hempstead). Turn right onto Hwy. 6 North towards College Station. Near College Station, continue north on Business 6 (Texas Ave.; left exit from Hwy. 6). Turn left onto George Bush Drive and follow the remaining directions from Dallas. **From San Antonio**, take I-35 north to San Marcos. Take Exit 205 (Hwy. 21 toward Bastrop/Luling), veer right, and go Past bridge; look to make a left turn to continue on Hwy. 21 toward Bastrop. Go past Bastrop, and look to make a left turn to continue on Hwy. 21 toward Caldwell; after that left turn, you will travel approximately three blocks and turn right to continue on Hwy. 21. Go east on Hwy. 21 to Hwy. 47 (on outskirts of Bryan near Texas A&M Riverside Campus) and follow the remaining directions from North Austin.

STAY THE NIGHT

Nearby: Your choices include the **Memorial Student Center Hotel** and various chains

TRINITY UNIVERSITY

Office of Admissions, One Trinity Place, San Antonio, TX 78212 • Telephone: 800-874-6489 • www.trinity.edu • Email: admissions@trinity.edu

Hours: Monday–Friday, 8:00AM–5:00PM; Saturday, 9:00AM–1:00PM (closed Saturdays during the summer)

Situated in San Antonio, Trinity University provides about 2,200 students with large school resources in a small school setting and a liberal arts and sciences education from great professors. Along with exploring San Antonio, students can enjoy a variety of campus activities, including hugely popular off-the-wall intramurals like co-ed inner-tube water polo and something called flickerball.

HIGHLIGHTS

ON CAMPUS

- Stieren Theatre
- Laurie Auditorium
- Coates Library
- Bell Atlantic Center
- Coates University Center

OFF CAMPUS

- McNay Art Museum
- San Antonio Museum of Art
- River Walk
- Alamo
- San Antonio Zoo

TRANSPORTATION

San Antonio International Airport is approximately five-and-a-half miles away from campus. SuperVan Shuttle (210-344-RIDE) and taxis are available for the ride to campus.

FIND YOUR WAY

From U.S. 281 N. or S., exit Hildebrand. Go west on Hildebrand, then south at the first light (Devine/Stadium Drive) toward the large stadium. At the bottom of the hill, turn right toward the campus, keep going south on Stadium; the Admissions Office is on the right before Mulberry Ave.

STAY THE NIGHT

Nearby: Some affordable options include **Amerisuites** (7615 Jones-Maltsberger; 210-930-2333) and **Fairfield Inn at the Airport** (88 NE Loop 410; 210-530-9899). Ask both for their Trinity visitor rate. You can also try the **Hampton Inn near the Airport** (8811 Jones-Maltsberger; 210-336-1800), the **Red Roof Inn** (333 Wolfe Rd.; 210-340-4055), and **Doubletree** (37 NE Loop 410; 210-366-2424); ask for special Trinity rates. About 10 minutes away is the **Crockett Hotel** (320 Bonham St.; 210-225-6500), a historic building across the street from the Alamo. Rates vary from moderate to expensive. Right next to the Alamo is the **Menger Hotel** (204 Alamo Plaza; 210-223-4361), a landmark dating back to 1859, which is about 15 minutes away from Trinity and has moderate rates. The new wing to the hotel opens up onto the beautiful River Walk, which you have to see to believe. The luxurious **St. Anthony** (300 E. Travis St.; 210-227-4392 or 800-338-1338) is about 20 minutes away from Trinity. The restaurant features southwestern cuisine. If you like big, lively hotels, you can't beat the **Hotel San Antonio Marriott River Center** (101 Bowie St.; 210-223-1000), about 15 minutes away from Trinity. This 38-story giant with 1,000 rooms connects to the River Center Mall, which connects to the aforementioned River Walk. Needless to say, it has every amenity, including an indoor and outdoor pool, a health club, an exercise room, and convention facilities. Rates are very expensive (higher than St. Anthony) and include a complimentary breakfast.

AT A GLANCE

Selectivity Rating	83
Range SAT I Math	610–690
Average SAT I Math	650
Range SAT I Verbal	580–690
Average SAT I Verbal	630
Average ACT Composite	29
Average GPA	3.48
Student/Faculty Ratio	11:1

CAMPUS TOURS

Appointment	Required
Dates	Year-round
Times	Mon–Fri, 11:30AM & 3:30PM; Sat, 11:30AM
Average Length	1 hour

ON-CAMPUS APPOINTMENTS

Admissions

Start Date—Juniors	Summer before senior year
Appointment	Required
Advance Notice	Yes, 2 weeks
Saturdays	Sometimes
Average Length	1 hour
Info Sessions	Yes

Faculty and Coaches

Dates/Times	Academic year
Arrangements	Contact Admissions Office 2 weeks prior

CLASS VISITS

Dates	Academic year
Arrangements	Contact Admissions Office

UNIVERSITY OF DALLAS

Office of Admissions, 1845 East Northgate Drive, Irving, TX 75062 • Telephone: 800–628-6999 • www.udallas.edu • Email: ugadmis@acad.udallas.edu

Hours: Monday–Friday, 8:00AM–5:00PM

You eat, drink, and sleep western culture at the University of Dallas—a small, Catholic liberal arts school with a rigorous and demanding core curriculum stressing classical humanities. The academically serious students rave about the intellectual push they get from their teachers; professor accessibility is high at UD.

AT A GLANCE

Selectivity Rating	80
Range SAT I Math	540–650
Average SAT I Math	600
Range SAT I Verbal	560–670
Average SAT I Verbal	620
Average ACT Composite	27
Student/Faculty Ratio	12:1

CAMPUS TOURS

Appointment	Preferred
Dates	Year-round
Times	Varies
Average Length	1 hour

ON-CAMPUS APPOINTMENTS

Admissions

Start Date–Juniors	Admissions interviews anytime
Appointment	Preferred
Advance Notice	No, 2 weeks
Saturdays	Sometimes
Average Length	90min
Info Sessions	Yes

Faculty and Coaches

Dates/Times	Year-round
Arrangements	Contact Admissions Office 2 weeks prior

CLASS VISITS

Dates	Academic year
Arrangements	Contact Admissions Office

TRANSPORTATION

DFW International Airport and Dallas Love Field are within 12 miles of campus. Super Shuttle, taxis, and rental cars are readily available.

FIND YOUR WAY

For directions call 1-800–628-6999 or refer to www.udallas.edu/about/directions.cfm.

STAY THE NIGHT

Nearby: For a list of hotels near campus, refer to www.udallas.edu/about/hotels.cfm.

HIGHLIGHTS

ON CAMPUS

- Church of the Incarnation
- Capp Bar
- The Mall
- The Rathskeller
- Plenty of Parking

OFF CAMPUS

- Dallas Restaurant Row
- Dallas Alley
- Deep Ellum
- Greenville Avenue
- The ballpark in Arlington

THE UNIVERSITY OF TEXAS AT AUSTIN

Freshman Admissions Center, John Hargis Hall, Austin, TX 78712-1111 • Telephone: 512-475-7440 • www.utexas.edu • Email: frmn@uts.cc.utexas.edu

Hours: Monday–Friday, 8:30AM–4:30PM

Tuition is so low at the University of Texas at Austin that some out-of-state students pay less than they would to go to public institutions in their own home states. Academics and research are world-class as well, and students love Austin—arguably the hippest small city in America and certainly one of the most vibrant bar and live music scenes.

HIGHLIGHTS

ON CAMPUS

- Texas Union
- Frank Erwin Center
- Performing Arts Center
- Ransom Humanities Center
- Gregory Gym/Recreational Sports

OFF CAMPUS

- Mt. Bonnell
- Town Lake/Lake Travis
- 6th Street
- State Capitol

TRANSPORTATION

Austin-Bergstrom International Airport is a seven-minute ride from campus. City buses and taxis are available for the trip from the airport to campus. Amtrak trains and Greyhound buses serve Austin. City buses and taxis are available to campus.

FIND YOUR WAY

From I-35, exit to Martin Luther King Blvd. The Admissions Center is quite close to the highway, next to the Frank Erwin Special Events Center, at the corner of Martin Luther King Blvd. and Red River.

STAY THE NIGHT

Nearby: The important thing in Austin is to be near 6th St., which is alive with restaurants, shops, bars, and entertainment. The **Marriott at the Capital** (701 E. 11th St.; 512-478-1111) is within walking distance of 6th St. and about a mile away from campus. It has an indoor pool, outdoor pool, exercise room, and game room. Another option is the **Doubletree Club Hotel** (1617 1H-35 N.; 512-479-4000) adjacent to the southeast corner of campus. Rates are expensive, but ask about special super-saver rates. The **Driskill** (604 Brazos St.; 512-474-5911 or 800-252-9367) is right in the heart of downtown near 6th St. and has a lot of character. Only 10 minutes away from campus, the hotel has moderate rates on the weekends and expensive ones during the week. If you desire tranquility, consider **Brook House** (609 W. 33rd St.; 512-459-0534) or the slightly higher priced **McCallum House** (613 W. 32nd St.; 512-451-6744). The McCallum House includes a full breakfast and has moderate rates, and the Brook House offers continental breakfast and has inexpensive rates.

AT A GLANCE

Selectivity Rating	86
Range SAT I Math	570–680
Average SAT I Math	626
Range SAT I Verbal	540–650
Average SAT I Verbal	596
Average ACT Composite	26
Student/Faculty Ratio	19:1

CAMPUS TOURS

Appointment	Not required
Dates	Year-round
Times	May–Dec: Mon–Sat, 11AM & 2PM Sat, 2PM
Average Length	1 hour

ON-CAMPUS APPOINTMENTS

Admissions

Start Date–Juniors	N/A
Appointment	Not required
Advance Notice	No
Info Sessions	Yes

Faculty and Coaches

Dates/Times	Year-round
Arrangements	Contact Athletic Department

CLASS VISITS

Dates	Year-round

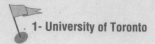
1- University of Toronto

Yukon
Territory

Northwest
Territories

Nunavut

British
Columbia

Alberta

Saskatchewan

Manitoba

Quebec

New Brunswick

Ontario

1

Toronto

Toronto	Univ. Toronto	Toronto
Univ. Toronto	—	0
Toronto	0	—

UNIVERSITY OF TORONTO

Nona Macdonald Visitors Centre, 25 King's College Circle, Toronto, ON M5S1A3 • Telephone: 416-978-2190 • www.utoronto.ca • Email: ask@adm.utoronto.ca

Hours: Monday–Friday, 9:30AM–4:30PM; Tuesday, 1:00PM–6:00PM

The vast majority of students at the University of Toronto live off campus, so the school community isn't as tight-knit as other schools; but it matters little when the totally awesome international city of Toronto is your stomping ground. Students describe the academics at this school as second to none.

HIGHLIGHTS

ON CAMPUS
- Hart House
- The Athletic Centre
- Justine Barnike Gallery
- Thomas Fisher Rare Book Library
- Convocation Hall

OFF CAMPUS
- CN Tower
- Royal Ontario Museum
- Art Gallery of Ontario
- Eaton Centre
- Harbourfront

TRANSPORTATION

The Toronto Transit Commission's buses and subways have stops near each of the school's three campuses. A bus is available into Toronto from Pearson International Airport.

FIND YOUR WAY

The University of Toronto's St. George campus is in the heart of downtown Toronto, right beside the Parliament Buildings at the top of University Avenue.

STAY THE NIGHT

Nearby: There are many nearby hotels with prices ranging from moderate to expensive, including the **Quality Inn, Howard Johnson, the Park Hyatt, the Intercontinental,** and the **Four Seasons.** Each campus has local accommodations.

A Little Farther: Toronto has many hotels and motels located near Pearson International Airport and in suburban locations.

AT A GLANCE	
Selectivity Rating	79
Average GPA	3.0
Student to Faculty Ratio	15:1

CAMPUS TOURS	
Appointment	Not required
Dates	Year-round
Times	Mon–Fri, 11AM & 2PM; Sat. & Sun, 11AM
Average Length	1 hour

ON-CAMPUS APPOINTMENTS	
Faculty and Coaches	
Dates/Times	Year-round
Arrangements	Contact Athletic Department

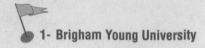

1- Brigham Young University

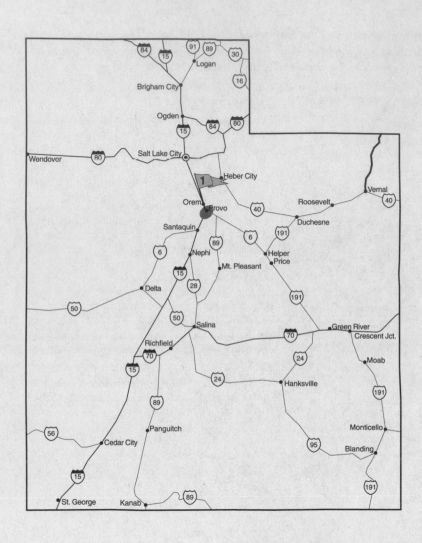

Utah	BYU	Provo	Salt Lake City
BYU	—	0	45
Provo	0	—	45
Salt Lake City	45	45	—

BRIGHAM YOUNG UNIVERSITY (UT)

Brigham Young University, A-209 ASB,
Provo, UT 84602-1110 • Telephone: 801-422-2507 • www.byu.edu •
Email: admissions@byu.edu

Hours: Monday–Friday, 8:00AM–5:00PM

You'll find a one-of-a-kind academic and religious experience at demanding Brigham Young University, a great place for physical, spiritual, and mental development where a whopping 99 percent of the tremendously homogenous and straight arrow students belong to the Mormon Church. Looking for an eternal mate and having fun without getting high or smashed are popular pastimes in the dull but nice happy Valley of Provo.

HIGHLIGHTS

ON CAMPUS

- Monte L. Bean Life Science Museum
- The Museum of Art
- Visitors' Center
- Harold B. Lee Library
- Wilkinson Student Center

OFF CAMPUS

- Sundance Ski Resort
- Mt. Timpanogus Cave
- Seven Peaks Resort Water Park
- Temple Square

TRANSPORTATION

Salt Lake City International Airport is about 45 miles north of campus. Either prior to or upon your arrival at the airport, arrangements for transportation to Provo can be made for taxis, Key Limousines, Utah Transit Authority service (bus and rail system), and rental cars. In addition, both Salt Lake and Provo have a Greyhound bus station and an Amtrak train station.

FIND YOUR WAY

From the north on I-15, take Exit 272 and continue east on University Parkway (Utah Rte. 265/12th South Street) to University Ave. (U.S. 189) in Provo. Enter campus either by continuing to the east for two more blocks and turning right at the Marriott Center or by turning right onto University Avenue for one block before turning left (east) and entering campus on 1230 North (Bulldog Avenue becomes Campus Drive once you're on the hill), at which point you'll be near the Administration Building. **From the south on I-15,** take Exit 266 and head north on University Ave. (U.S. 189) to 1230 North (Bulldog Avenue), turn right (east) and enter campus on the hill near the Administration Building.

STAY THE NIGHT

Nearby: Provo offers a number of accommodations in close proximity to BYU's campus and other local attractions, including **La Quinta Inn, Days Inn, Hampton Inn, Residence Inn, Travelodge** and **Econo Lodge.** Also located within a few miles of campus are a **Best Western Cotton Tree Inn,** the **Provo Marriott Hotel/Conference Center,** and the **Hines Mansion.**

A little farther: About 20 minutes away from campus, up Provo Canyon, Robert Redford's **Sundance** four-star resort and ski lodge rests at the base of magnificent Mt. Timpanogos. Its rates are expensive but are lower in the off-season. A wide variety of accommodations in any price range are within 30 and 40 miles of Provo in Salt Lake City and the surrouding areas.

AT A GLANCE

Selectivity Rating	87
Range SAT I Math	560–670
Range SAT I Verbal	540–650
Average ACT Composite	27
Average GPA	3.75
Student/Faculty Ratio	18:1

CAMPUS TOURS

Appointment	Preferred
Dates	Year-round
Times	Mon–Fri
Average Length	1 hour

ON-CAMPUS APPOINTMENTS

Admissions

Start Date–Juniors	N/A
Appointment	Preferred
Advance Notice	Yes
Saturdays	No

Faculty and Coaches

Dates/Times	Year-round
Arrangements	Contact Visitors' Center; arrangements will be made at the time the tour is scheduled.

CLASS VISITS

Dates	Year-round
Arrangements	Contact Visiting Center

VERMONT

1- **Bennington College**
2- **Goddard College**
3- **Marlboro College**
4- **Middlebury College**
5- **University of Vermont**

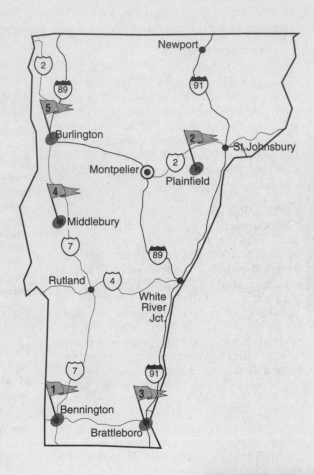

Vermont	Bennington Coll.	Goddard Coll.	Marlboro Coll.	Middlebury Coll.	Univ. Vermont	Burlington	Rutland
Bennington Coll.	—	124	28	85	119	119	57
Goddard Coll.	124	—	120	63	43	43	71
Marlboro Coll.	28	120	—	113	150	150	80
Middlebury Coll.	85	63	113	—	34	34	30
Univ. Vermont	119	43	150	34	—	0	67
Burlington	119	43	150	34	0	—	67
Rutland	57	71	80	30	67	67	—

BENNINGTON COLLEGE

Office of Admissions, One College Drive, Bennington, VT 05201 • Telephone: 802-440-4312 • www.bennington.edu • Email: admissions@bennington.edu

Hours: Monday–Friday, 9:00AM–5:00PM; Saturday (during term), 10:00AM–3:00PM

Bennington College is a small, progressive, very arts-oriented and "creative" liberal-arts college that offers students the opportunity to put together their own programs. Classes are more akin to intimate seminars, so instead of grades and tests, Benningtonians receive written evaluations of their work. Nearly weekly theme parties provide the bulk of campus entertainment.

HIGHLIGHTS

ON CAMPUS
- Edward Clark Crossett Library
- Visual & Performing Arts Center
- Hoffberger Music Library
- The Rebecca B. Stickney Observatory
- Meyer Recreation Barn

OFF CAMPUS
- Bennington Museum
- Old North Church
- Bennington Battle Monument
- Outlet stores
- Local ski and recreation areas

TRANSPORTATION

The Albany, New York airport and Albany/Rensselaer Amtrak train station are approximately 50 miles away from campus. CLS transportation provides limousine service from the airport and train station; call 802-447-1609 to make arrangements.

FIND YOUR WAY

From the New York City area, take the Taconic State Parkway north to New York Route 295; from Route 295 take New York Route 22 north for about 30 miles. At the end of Route 22 make a right onto New York Route 7 east to Vermont (New York Route 7 turns to Route 9 in Vermont). This brings you into the town of Bennington. At the intersection of Route 7 and Route 9 (Bennington's main four corners intersection) make a left onto Route 7 north. Continue on Route 7 North through two sets of lights; after the second set of lights, continue straight through on Route 7 North/Route 67A. Bear left to follow Route 67A West. Take the first exit to follow Route 67A North (North Bennington). At the end of the exit ramp at the lights, turn left onto Route 67A North. Go through one set of lights, and you will see the college entrance is a short distance ahead on the right. Turn right, go through the gates, onto College Drive. At the first stop sign, go left up the hill to the security booth (on your left). Visitor parking is located across from the security booth on your right.

STAY THE NIGHT

Nearby: The inexpensive **Best Western New Englander** (220 Northside Dr.; 802-442-6311) is only one mile away from school. This facility has an outdoor pool and lawn games in the summer. Four miles away from the school is the **Vermonter Motor Lodge** (West Rd.; 802-442-2529), which is open from May through December. A double room is inexpensive, and for a relatively modest rate you can enjoy mountain views. The lodge also has its own pond and cottages. About five miles away from the school is **South Shire Bed-and-Breakfast** (124 Elm St.; 802-447-3839). This wonderful Victorian mansion has five rooms in the main house that are moderately expensive and four (somewhat more pricey) luxurious accommodations with Jacuzzis and fireplaces in the carriage house. There is also the **Henry House Inn** located in North Bennington (802-442-7045; www.henryhouseinn.com). This charming establishment built in 1769 boasts six fireplaces and 25 acres of forest and meadows.

A little farther: **Pleasant West Mountain Inn** (Rte. 313 and River Rd.; 802-375-6516) offers good food and rooms for an expensive rate. Depending on the season, you can enjoy cross-country and downhill skiing (not far from Bromley or Stratton, important Alpine centers), trout fishing, swimming, canoeing, and tubing.

AT A GLANCE

Selectivity Rating	83
Range SAT I Math	500–630
Average SAT I Math	568
Range SAT I Verbal	580–690
Average SAT I Verbal	630
Average GPA	3.39
Student/Faculty Ratio	9:1

CAMPUS TOURS

Appointment	Preferred
Dates	Year-round
Times	During Admissions Office hours

ON-CAMPUS APPOINTMENTS

Admissions

Start Date–Juniors	Anytime
Appointment	Required
Advance Notice	Yes, 1 week
Saturdays	Yes
Info Sessions	Yes

Faculty and Coaches

Dates/Times	Academic year
Arrangements	Contact Admissions Office

CLASS VISITS

Dates	Academic year
Arrangements	Contact Admissions Office

GODDARD COLLEGE

Admissions Office, R. R. 2, Plainfield, VT 05667 • Telephone: 800-468-4888 • www.goddard.edu • Email: admissions@goddard.edu

Hours: Monday–Friday, 8:00AM–4:30PM

If you loathe the idea of a traditional school, check out Goddard College, an artsy, eccentric school located in rural Vermont where academic freedom reigns supreme. Goddard's creative, intelligent, and artistic students design an individual curriculum—a self-directed, experimental education, if you will— tailored to their own specific needs.

AT A GLANCE

Selectivity Rating	73
Range SAT I Math	480–590
Average SAT I Math	541
Range SAT I Verbal	550–680
Average SAT I Verbal	609
Average GPA	2.5
Student/Faculty Ratio	11:1

CAMPUS TOURS

| Appointment | Not required |

ON-CAMPUS APPOINTMENTS

Admissions

Start Date—Juniors	Sept
Appointment	Required, 2 weeks
Saturdays	Sometimes

Faculty and Coaches

| Arrangements | Contact Admissions Office 3 weeks prior |

CLASS VISITS

| Arrangements | Contact Admissions Office |

TRANSPORTATION

Burlington International Airport is 45 miles away from campus. Buses are available from the airport to Montpelier (10 miles away from campus), but not to Plainfield. Rental cars are available at the airport. The Barre-Montpelier Airport is a small commercial field only eight miles away from campus; it has daily flights to and from Boston. Contact the Admissions Office about transportation from this airport to campus. Arrangements to take taxis from both airports can be made in advance or on arrival; call Barre Taxi Service (802-479-1985) or Norm's Taxi (802-223-5226). Amtrak has train connections to Montpelier (10 miles away from campus) from Washington, D.C., New York City, and Montreal. Vermont Transit, a subsidiary of Greyhound Bus Lines, serves both Barre and Montpelier.

FIND YOUR WAY

Take I-91 or I-93 N. to I-89; then take I-89 N.W. to Exit 8 (Montpelier). Go northeast on U.S. Rte. 2 (for approximately 10 miles away from Montpelier); as you enter Plainfield Village, turn left at the Goddard sign. The college is approximately one-eighth of a mile up the road on the left side.

STAY THE NIGHT

Nearby: Montpelier is 10 miles to the west of Plainfield and a 20-minute drive from campus. Try **Montpelier Bed-and-Breakfast** (22 North St.; 802-229-0482), though there is no breakfast until May, since the owner is a congressman in the winter (try the Elm Street Cafe for breakfast). The moderately priced **Montpelier Inn** (147 Main St.; 802-223-2727) has some deluxe rooms and offers a game room and a comfortable living room and dining room with fireplaces, and is accessible to the shops in Montpelier. The **Capital Plaza Hotel** (802-223-5252) in downtown Montpelier is inexpensive and has an indoor swimming pool.

HIGHLIGHTS

ON CAMPUS

- Historic Gardens
- Restored Manor House

OFF CAMPUS

- Barre Granite Quarries
- Montpelier

MARLBORO COLLEGE

Admissions Office, PO Box A, South Road, Marlboro, VT 05344-0300 • Telephone: 800-343-0049 • www.marlboro.edu • Email: admissions@marlboro.edu

Hours: Monday–Friday, 8:30AM–4:30PM

Intense Marlboro College—an unusual and intimate school in the woods—is a dream for academic and social self-starters, but you have to be serious about studying to succeed. Under The Plan, juniors and seniors work one-on-one with professors to design and pursue a self-devised curriculum, culminating in a senior research paper. The process requires tons of writing homework, but students unanimously agree that it's a remarkable experience.

HIGHLIGHTS

ON CAMPUS

- The Rice Library
- Whittemore Theatre
- Mac Arthur Observatory
- Drury Gallery
- Persons Auditorium

OFF CAMPUS

- Marlboro Music Festival
- Mount Snow
- Northampton, Massachusetts
- Brattleboro, Vermont

TRANSPORTATION

Bradley International Airport near Hartford, Connecticut, is an hour-and-a-half away from campus. Buses and Amtrak stop in nearby Brattleboro.

FIND YOUR WAY

Take Exit 2 off Interstate 91 in Brattleboro, Vermont. Turn right off of the exit onto Route 9 West through West Brattleboro into Marlboro After passing the Marlboro. Elementary School on the left, watch for college signs. Make a left turn as Route 9 makes a sweeping right. Stay on the paved road through the village of Marlboro to the college (approximately three miles).

STAY THE NIGHT

Nearby: Brattleboro Vermont features many lodging options, from quaint bed-and-breakfasts to popular chain hotels. A complete listing is available on Marlboro's website.

MIDDLEBURY COLLEGE

Admissions Office, 5405 Middlebury College,
Middlebury, VT 05753-6002 • Telephone: 802-443-3000 • www.middlebury.edu •
Email: admissions@middlebury.edu

Hours: Monday–Friday, 8:00AM–5:00PM; Saturday (August–October), 9:00AM–noon

At Middlebury College, on the prettiest campus in the world, students enjoy views of the mountains. The school has its own downhill slope and lighted cross-country ski trail. In the course of completing one of the more rigorous and prestigious liberal arts curriculums in the country, students can take advantage of a wealth of amazing programs, especially in writing, the world-class Language School, and theater.

AT A GLANCE

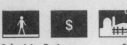

Selectivity Rating	97
Range SAT I Math	670–740
Average SAT I Math	700
Range SAT I Verbal	680–750
Average SAT I Verbal	710
Average ACT Composite	30
Student/Faculty Ratio	11:1

CAMPUS TOURS

Appointment	Not required
Dates	Year-round
Times	Mon–Fri, call for exact times
Average Length	1 hour

ON-CAMPUS APPOINTMENTS

Admissions

Start Date—Juniors	June 1
Appointment	Required
Advance Notice	Yes, 3 weeks
Saturdays	No
Average Length	30 min.
Info Sessions	Yes

Faculty and Coaches

Dates/Times	Academic year
Arrangements	Contact Athletic Department

CLASS VISITS

Dates	Academic year
Arrangements	Contact Admissions Office

TRANSPORTATION

Burlington International Airport is 35 miles away from campus. Taxi and bus service is available for the trip between the airport and campus.

FIND YOUR WAY

From New York, take I-87 N. to Exit 20 (soon after Glen Falls); take 149 E. to U.S. 4 E.; take U.S. 4 through Whitehall to the Fair Haven exit, then take Vermont Rte. 22A north to Rte. 74 E. to Rte. 30 N. to the campus. **From Boston,** take I-93 N. to I-89 (north of Manchester, NH). Take I-89 N. and west to Bethel, Vermont Rte. 107 W. Follow Rte. 107 to Rte. 100 N., then take 100 N. to Vermont Rte. 125. Take Rte. 125 W. into Middlebury.

STAY THE NIGHT

Nearby: Middlebury has some wonderful places to stay within walking distance or a very short drive from campus. Travelers have a range of options, including beautifully appointed country inns, charming bed-and-breakfasts, and convenient motels. You won't go wrong with the **Swift House Inn** (25 Stewart Lane; 802-388-9925), a 15-minute walk from the school. Rooms are beautifully decorated and the grounds are lovely. The moderate-to-expensive price includes lavish continental breakfast. Even closer to campus (a five-minute walk) is the somewhat less pricey, intimate (11 rooms), recently restored, 200-year-old **Inn on the Green** (19 S. Pleasant St.; 802-388-7512 or 888-244-7512), offering charming rooms with all amenities and continental breakfast served in your room. Around the corner, also on the green in the historic district, is the bustling, 75-room **Middlebury Inn** (14 Courthouse Sq., Rte. 7; 802-388-4961 or 800-842-4666). Rates range from moderate to expensive.

A little farther: East Middlebury offers visitors some lovely accommodations as well. For an inexpensive, small, and pleasant bed-and-breakfast about four miles away from campus, try **The October Pumpkin Inn** (Rte. 125E; 802-388-9525) in East Middlebury. Rates are inexpensive to moderate and the price includes a full breakfast. Consider also the **Waybury Inn** (Rte. 125, East Middlebury; 802-388-4015), featured as the Stratford Inn on *The Bob Newhart Show.* It's a little bit farther east (six miles away from the college). Tennis courts and a golf course are also nearby. A fitness center with an indoor pool is open to inn guests for a special rate. Room prices are on the high side and include a full country breakfast. For the traveler seeking chain motels, you can enjoy a trip north on Rte. 7 to South Burlington and Burlington. There you will find many of the national chains. Please contact the Addison County Chamber of Commerce at 802-388-7951 or 800–733-8376 for more details. Log onto www.midvermont.com/ for a complete listing of area attractions, lodging, or dining.

HIGHLIGHTS

ON CAMPUS

- Bicentennial Hall
- The Center for the Arts
- Athletic facilities
- The Commons System
- Middlebury College Snow Bowl

OFF CAMPUS

- The Green Mountains and the Adirondack Mountains
- Lake Champlain
- Sheldon Museum
- College ski area

UNIVERSITY OF VERMONT

Office of Admissions, 194 South Prospect Street, 194 S. Prospect St., Burlington, VT 05401-3596 • Telephone: 802-656-3370 • www.uvm.edu • Email: admissions@uvm.edu

Hours: Monday–Friday, 8:00AM–4:30PM; select Saturdays

The University of Vermont has a solid academic reputation, accessible professors, and a great hockey team. UVM is particularly strong in animal science and health- and environment-related areas; students report that psychology, political science, and business and management majors are also popular.

HIGHLIGHTS

ON CAMPUS

- Fleming Museum
- Billings Student Center
- Campus Green
- Athletic Complex/Fitness Center
- Spear Street Research Farm and Equine Center

OFF CAMPUS

- Lake Champlain
- Green Mountains
- Burlington (arts, cultural events)
- ECHO Lake Aquarium & Science Center
- Shelburne Museum

TRANSPORTATION

Burlington International Airport is several miles (a 15-minute drive) from campus. Taxis, local buses, and rental cars are available for the trip from the airport to campus. Taxis are at or can be called from the airport. Rental car agencies in the airport are open 24 hours a day. The CCTA bus line from the airport to campus runs Monday through Friday from 6:40 AM to 10:10 PM and Saturdays until 8:10 PM.

FIND YOUR WAY

From I-89, take Exit 14W and proceed one mile west to campus. The Admissions Office is one block left on South Prospect St. **From U.S. Rte. 7,** enter Burlington and turn up the hill at the intersection with Main St. (Rte. 2). The campus is at the top of the hill. The Admissions Office is one block right on South Prospect St. **From the east,** Rte. 2 becomes Main St. in Burlington and bisects the campus. The Admissions Office is one block left on South Prospect St.

STAY THE NIGHT

Nearby: For convenience and charm, a terrific choice is **The Willard Street Inn** (349 S. Willard St.; 802-651-8710) is a five- to ten-minute (but uphill!) walk to UVM and offers accommodations in the grand style and a fabulous breakfast. Its rates are expensive. The **Radisson Hotel** (60 Battery St.; 802-658-6500) is five minutes away from the university and within walking distance of Burlington's fabulous pedestrian mall. It is pricier, but still has rooms available for moderate rates. The hotel has the usual amenities of a big-city hotel designed to attract the business visitor. You can also try the **Sheraton Hotel and Conference Center** (intersection of I-89, Exit 14W and U.S. 2; 802-865-6600 or 800-325-3535). An inexpensive choice about one mile away is the **Anchorage Inn** (108 Dorset St. South, Burlington; 802-863-7000). It provides a continental breakfast and has an indoor pool and fitness center. For additional lodging information, please visit our website at www.uvm.edu/admissions.

A little farther: The **Inn at Shelburne Farms** (802-985-8498), about 20 minutes away from the school in Shelburne is part of a working farm. It offers beautiful views of Lake Champlain, a tennis court, boating, and lovely walks. Wonderful food is also part of the package. Its rates are very expensive. The Inn is open from Memorial Day to mid-October.

AT A GLANCE

Selectivity Rating	76
Range SAT I Math	520–620
Average SAT I Math	574
Range SAT I Verbal	520–620
Average SAT I Verbal	568
Average ACT Composite	24
Student/Faculty Ratio	13:1

CAMPUS TOURS

Appointment	Required
Dates	Year-round
Times	Mon–Fri, 10AM & 2PM
Average Length	Varies

ON-CAMPUS APPOINTMENTS

Admissions

Start Date–Juniors	Anytime
Appointment	Required
Advance Notice	Yes, 2 weeks
Saturdays	No
Average Length	30 min.
Info Sessions	Yes

Faculty and Coaches

Dates/Times	Academic year
Arrangements	Contact Admissions Office 2 weeks prior

CLASS VISITS

Dates	Academic year
Arrangements	Contact Admissions Office

1- Hollins College
2- Randolph-Macon Woman's College
3- Sweet Briar College
4- University of Virginia
5- Washington & Lee University
6- College of William & Mary
7- Hampden-Sydney College
8- James Madison University
9- Mary Washington College
10- Randolph-Macon College

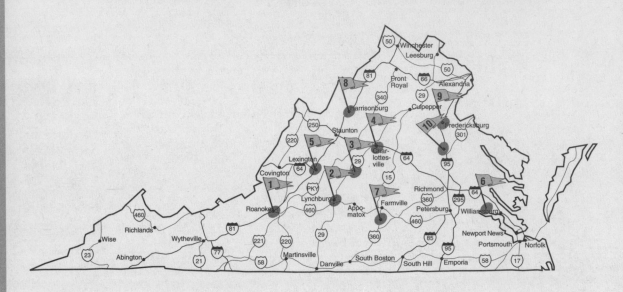

Virginia

	Coll. William & Mary	Hampden-Sydney	Hollins Coll.	James Madison	Mary Wash. Coll.	Randolph-Mac. W.C.	Ran.-Mac. Coll.	Sweet Briar Coll.	Univ. Virginia	Washington & Lee	*Richmond*	*Roanoke*
Coll. William & Mary	—	122	218	181	103	62	164	145	131	199	52	218
Hampden-Sydney	122	—	106	120	122	83	57	67	86	105	69	106
Hollins Coll.	218	106	—	102	176	182	52	65	115	53	185	0
James Madison	181	120	102	—	96	132	95	84	63	61	128	102
Mary Wash. Coll.	103	122	176	96	—	42	130	119	67	135	56	176
Randolph-Mac. W.C.	62	83	182	132	42	—	137	125	76	141	16	182
Ran.-Mac. Coll.	164	57	52	95	130	137	—	9	58	40	114	52
Sweet Briar Coll.	145	67	65	84	119	125	9	—	48	29	95	65
Univ. Virginia	131	86	115	63	67	76	58	48	—	73	69	115
Washington & Lee	199	105	53	61	135	141	40	29	73	—	117	53
Richmond	52	69	185	128	56	16	114	95	69	117	—	185
Roanoke	218	106	0	102	176	182	52	65	115	53	185	—

COLLEGE OF WILLIAM AND MARY

Office of Admissions, PO Box 8795,
Williamsburg, VA 23187-8795 • Telephone: 757-221-4223 • www.wm.edu •
Email: admiss@wm.edu

Hours: Monday–Friday, 8:00AM–5:00PM; Saturday (during term), 9:00AM–noon

The workload is obscene at William and Mary, one of the best and most competitive public schools in the nation, where the oldest honor code in the nation allows students to take unproctored exams. W&M is probably the only school to have its social scene revolve around three delis across the street from campus. A veritable catalog of distinguished alumni includes Thomas Jefferson and Glenn Close.

HIGHLIGHTS

ON CAMPUS

- The Wren Building
- Muscarelle Museum of Art
- Lake Matoaka/College Woods Recreation area
- Crim Dell Bridge
- The Sunken Garden

OFF CAMPUS

- Colonial Williamsburg
- Busch Gardens Amusement Park
- Water Country USA
- Jamestown Settlement
- Outlet shopping centers/Pottery Factory

TRANSPORTATION

Several airports serve the Williamsburg area: Newport News-Williamsburg International Airport in Newport News is a 20-minute drive from campus; Norfolk International Airport in Norfolk is a 60-minute drive from campus; Byrd International Airport in Richmond is a 60-minute drive from campus. The following companies offer airport limousine service: Williamsburg Limo (757-877-0279), Airport Transport (757-857-9477), and Groome Transport (757-222-7222); make arrangements one day in advance.

FIND YOUR WAY

From I-64, take Exit 238. At the second set of lights (Rte. 132), turn right. Turn right again at the next set of lights (Rte. 60 bypass). Follow Bypass Rd. to its end and its intersection with Richmond Rd. Turn left at the light onto Richmond Rd. At the third set of lights, you will see the Walter F. Zable Stadium on the right. The Office of Admission is in Blow Memorial Hall, just beyond the light on the right. Stop in Dawson Circle in front of the hall to obtain a parking permit from the Office of Admission.

STAY THE NIGHT

Nearby: William and Mary is on the edge of Colonial Williamsburg. The town's restoration organization runs a number of lodging facilities, all of which are within five minutes away from William and Mary. Of these, the least expensive is the **Governor's Inn Motel** (506 N. Henry St.; 757-229-1000). The **Motor House,** just opposite the visitors' center (757-229-1000 or 800-447-8679), offers rooms from the inexpensive to moderate range. Climbing up the scale, the grand **Williamsburg Inn** (Francis St.; 757-229-1000 or 800-HISTORY) is top of the line. The inn has tennis courts (with tennis pro) and a golf course. Two appealing bed-and-breakfasts are the **Applewood Colonial Bed and Breakfast** (605 Richmond Rd.; 757-229-0205), within walking distance of the college, and **Liberty Rose Bed-and-Breakfast** (1022 Jamestown Rd.; 757-253-1260), half a mile away. A romantic and charming restoration, the Liberty Rose is the more expensive of the two, with rooms priced in the moderate to expensive range. Basic lodgings are a stone's throw away. The **Quarter Path Inn Motel** (620 York St.; 757-220-0960) and the **Traveller's Inn** (800-336-0500) are decent, no-frills accommodations. There are many places to stay in the Williamsburg area. You can get a complete list from the Williamsburg Area Convention and Visitors Bureau (757-253-0192). This guide includes lists of campgrounds and very inexpensive private guest homes.

HAMPDEN—SYDNEY COLLEGE

Office of Admissions, PO Box 667,
Hampden-Sydney, VA 23943 • Telephone: 800–755-0733 • www.hsc.edu •
Email: hsapp@hsc.edu

Hours: Monday–Friday, 8:30AM–5:00PM; Saturday (during term), 9:00AM–noon

If you've been searching for a great atmosphere where you can reach your highest academic potential, a rich southern heritage, or if you just want to hang out with a bunch of guys for four years, all-male Hampden-Sydney may be the place for you. H-SC's classes are always small, and its professors are well-rounded. Also, you cannot hide if you didn't do your homework, and you are forced to be vocal and express your ideas.

AT A GLANCE

Selectivity Rating	77
Range SAT I Math	510–610
Average SAT I Math	562
Range SAT I Verbal	500–620
Average SAT I Verbal	561
Average ACT Composite	22
Average GPA	3.1
Student/Faculty Ratio	10:1

CAMPUS TOURS

Appointment	Preferred
Dates	Year-round
Times	Mon–Fri, 9AM–3:30PM; Sat, during year, 9 AM–NOON
Average Length	1 hour

ON-CAMPUS APPOINTMENTS

Admissions

Start Date—Juniors	Anytime
Appointment	Preferred
Advance Notice	Yes, 1 week
Saturdays	Yes
Average Length	45 min.
Info Sessions	No

Faculty and Coaches

Dates/Times	Year-round
Arrangements	Contact coach directly 2 weeks prior

CLASS VISITS

Dates	Academic year
Arrangements	Contact Admissions Office

TRANSPORTATION

The closest airports are in Lynchburg and Richmond; there is train service to Lynchburg & Richmond, and Greyhound Bus service to Farmville, Virginia.

FIND YOUR WAY

Campus is located three miles south of Farmville, Virginia; for driving directions see our website: www.hsc.edu/visitors.

STAY THE NIGHT

Nearby: There are a few familiar hotels and motels in Farmville, Virginia, with prices ranging from approximately $65 to $100. There are also some scattered bed-and-breakfast lodgings.

HIGHLIGHTS

ON CAMPUS

- Tiger Inn (student center)
- Kirby Fieldhouse (athletic facility)
- Residence halls
- Classrooms
- Museum on campus

OFF CAMPUS

- Area women's colleges
- Cities of Richmond, VA and Lynchburg, VA
- City of Charlottesville, VA (with historic sites)
- Civil War historical landmarks

HOLLINS UNIVERSITY

Hollins University Admissions Office, PO Box 9707, Roanoke, VA 24020-1707 • Telephone: 800-456-9595 • www.hollins.edu • Email: huadm@hollins.edu

Hours: Monday–Friday, 8:30AM–4:30PM; Saturday, 9:00AM–1:00PM

Tiny Hollins University is an all-women's liberal arts school with a great creative writing program that encourages personal growth and discovery. Hollins boasts a beautiful antebellum campus, roomy and comfortable dorms, and a wonderful community atmosphere that feels much like your second family.

HIGHLIGHTS

ON CAMPUS
- Front Quadrangle
- Wyndham Robertson Library
- Moody Student Center
- Dana Science Center
- Art Gallery and Studios

OFF CAMPUS
- Roanoke Historic Farmer's Market
- Virginia's Explore Park
- Roanoke Star/Overlook
- Blue Ridge Parkway
- Carvins Cove

TRANSPORTATION

Roanoke Airport is two miles away from campus. Limousine or taxi service from the airport to campus can be arranged on arrival. Call Roanoke Airport Limousine Service (540-345-7710), Star City Cab (540-366-6390), or Yellow Cab Company (540-345-7711).

FIND YOUR WAY

From I-81 (N. or S.), take Exit 146 onto Plantation Road. At the first traffic light, turn left onto Williamson Road and go half a mile. The entrance to Hollins is on the left.

STAY THE NIGHT

Nearby: Choices include the **Hampton Inn** (540-563-5656), the **Country Inn & Suites** (540-366-5678), the **Best Western Inn at Valley View** (540-362-2400), **AmeriSuites** (540-366-4700), the **Wyndham Roanoke Hotel** (540-563-9300), the **Clarion Hotel-Roanoke Airport** (540-362-4500), and the **Holiday Inn-Airport** (540-366-8861).

AT A GLANCE	
Selectivity Rating	78
Range SAT I Math	490–610
Average SAT I Math	550
Range SAT I Verbal	530–660
Average SAT I Verbal	595
Average ACT Composite	24
Average GPA	3.41
Student/Faculty Ratio	9:1

CAMPUS TOURS	
Appointment	Not required
Dates	Year-round
Times	Varies
Average Length	1 hour

ON-CAMPUS APPOINTMENTS

Admissions	
Start Date–Juniors	Anytime
Appointment	Preferred
Advance Notice	Yes, 1 week
Saturdays	Yes
Average Length	1 hour
Info Sessions	Yes

Faculty and Coaches	
Dates/Times	Academic year
Arrangements	Contact Admissions Office 1 week prior

CLASS VISITS	
Dates	Academic year
Arrangements	Contact Admissions Office

JAMES MADISON UNIVERSITY

Undergraduate Admissions, Sonner Hall MSC 0101,
Harrisonburg, VA 22807 • Telephone: 540-568-5681 • www.jmu.edu •
Email: gotojmu@jmu.edu

Hours: Monday–Thursday, 8:00AM–8:00PM; Friday, 8:00AM–5:00PM; Saturday, 9:30AM–5:00PM

The active, intelligent, and highly motivated students at James Madison University say their school is a true bargain for both in-state and out-of-state students. JMU provides comfortable surroundings and many strong programs including business, music, political science, and international relations.

AT A GLANCE

Selectivity Rating	83
Range SAT I Math	540–630
Average SAT I Math	587
Range SAT I Verbal	540–620
Average SAT I Verbal	578
Average GPA	3.64
Student/Faculty Ratio	17:1

CAMPUS TOURS

Appointment	Preferred
Dates	Year-round
Times	Varies
Average Length	120 min.

ON-CAMPUS APPOINTMENTS

Admissions

Start Date—Juniors	September 29, 2003
Appointment	Required
Advance Notice	Yes, 1 week
Saturdays	No
Average Length	30 min.
Info Sessions	Yes

Faculty and Coaches

Dates/Times	Year-round
Arrangements	Athletics—Contact facilities administrator; academic affairs, academic year, 1 week

CLASS VISITS

Dates	Academic year
Arrangements	Contact academic department of interest

TRANSPORTATION

Buses are available. Major airports serve Washington, D.C.; a smaller airport serves Weyers Cave (15 miles); a train serves Staunton, VA (25 miles). Public transportation serves campus. Taxis are available.

FIND YOUR WAY

Harrisonburg is located at the intersection of three major highways: Interstate 81, U.S. 33 amd U.S. 11. The campus entrance is located just off Interstate 81 and is within a two-hour drive from Richmond, Roanoke, and Washington, D.C. Directions to campus **Southbound on I-81:** Take Exit 245 Port Republic Road, make a right at the exit, and your first right onto JMU's campus. **Northbound on I-81:** Take Exit 245 Port Republic Road, make a left at the exit. After crossing the overpass, make a right onto JMU's campus. **Once on campus:** The Campus Visitation Center is located in Sonner Hall, the second building on the left. Note: Please contact the Office of Admissions before your visit. Satellite parking is required on some Saturdays. Office hours are Monday through Friday from 8:00 AM to 5:00 PM. For visitation questions, check the website: www.jmu.edu/ucenter/uinfo/directions.html.

STAY THE NIGHT

Nearby: Your choices include the **Apple Hill B&B** (430 Boyers Road; 540-432-0418 or 877-430-0418), the **Belle Meade Red Carpet Inn** (3210 South Main Street; 540-434-6704 or 800-251-1962), **By the Side of the Road B&B** (491 Garbers Church Road; 540-801-0430), the **Comfort Inn** (1440 E. Market Street; 540-433-6066 or 800-228-5150), the **Days Inn** (1131 Forest Hill Road; 540-433-9353 or 800-DAYSINN), the **Econo Lodge Harrisonburg** (1703 E. Market Street; 540-433-2576 or 800-553-2666), the **Economy Inn** (Route 11, Box N; 540-434-5301 or 800-HAMPTON), the **Four Points Hotel by Sheraton** (1400 E. Market Street; 540-433-2521 or 800-703-7037), the **Hampton Inn** (85 University Boulevard; 540-432-1111 or 800-HAMPTON), the **Holiday Inn Express** (3325 S. Main Street; 540-433-9999 or 800-HOLIDAY), the **Jameson Inn** (1891 Evelyn Byrd Avenue; 540-442-1515 or 800-822-5252), the **Joshua Wilton House** (412 S. Main Street; 540-434-4464 or 800-2WILTON), the **Journey's End** (North Valley Pike; 540-434-8250), the **Kingsway Bed & Breakfast** (3955 Singers Glen Road; 540-867-9696), the **Marriott Courtyard** (1890 Evelyn Byrd Avenue 540-432-3031 or 888-236-2427), the **Motel 6** (10 Linda Lane; 540-433-6939 or 800-4-MOTEL6), the **Ramada Inn** (1 Pleasant Valley Road; 540-434-9981 or 888-298-2054), **Rockingham Motel** (4035 South Main Street; 540-433-2538), the **GuestHouse Inn** (45 Burgess Road; 540-433-6089 or 800-21-GUEST), the **Stonewall Jackson Inn B&B** (547 East Market Street; 540-433-8233 or 800-445-5330), and **Super 8 Motel** (3330 S. Main Street; 540-433-8888 or 800-800-8000).

HIGHLIGHTS

ON CAMPUS

- University Recreation Center
- Quad
- Taylor Down Under
- College Center
- Warren Hall Loft

OFF CAMPUS

- Downtown Harrisonburg
- Skyline Drive
- George Washington National Forest
- New Market Battlefield
- Staunton

MARY WASHINGTON COLLEGE

Office of Admissions, 1301 College Avenue, Fredericksburg, VA 22401 • Telephone: 800-468-5614 • www.mwc.edu • Email: admit@mwc.edu

Hours: Monday–Friday, 8:30AM–5:00PM

Small, ultra-liberal-arts-oriented, and public Mary Washington College provides many of the amenities of the private schools—small classes and caring, eager professors—at a very affordable price. Students at MWC report an overall high level of satisfaction, particularly with their in-class experiences, and they deem the demanding core curriculum quite rewarding.

HIGHLIGHTS

ON CAMPUS
- Jepson Science Center
- Battleground Athletic facilities/Fitness Center
- Woodard Campus Center
- Combs Hall
- Palmieri Plaza Fountain

OFF CAMPUS
- Historic Fredericksburg
- Fredericksburg Battlefield
- Kenmore Plantation/Mary Washington House/Chatam Manor
- James Moroe Museum/Belmont
- Potomac Mills Mall

TRANSPORTATION

Reagan National, Dulles International, and Richmond International airports are about an hour away from campus. Fredericksburg is accessible by transportation services from all these major airports. Fredericksburg is also served by commercial buses and Amtrak.

FIND YOUR WAY

From I-95 north/south, take exit 130-A, follow Route 3 East business for one-and-a-half miles to the campus. At the traffic light at the College Ave./ William St. (Rte. 3) intersection, turn left onto College Ave. Proceed to the first light and turn right into the main gates of campus. Limited visitor parking is located just inside the gates.

STAY THE NIGHT

Nearby: You can stay just five minutes away in **Best Western Fredericksburg**—located on Rte. 3 east. **Kenmore Inn (B&B)**—located in historic Frederickburg on Princess Anne St., and **Holiday Inn Select** on Rte. 3 West at Central Park.

A little farther: Just 15 minutes away from campus is the brand new **Wingate Inn** located on Rte. 17 north, and the **Fairfield Inn** located on Rte.I South, I-95 exit 126-A.

AT A GLANCE

Selectivity Rating	84
Range SAT I Math	560–640
Average SAT I Math	595
Range SAT I Verbal	570–660
Average SAT I Verbal	613
Average ACT Composite	27
Average GPA	3.66
Student/Faculty Ratio	17:1

CAMPUS TOURS

Appointment	Preferred
Dates	Year-round
Times	Monday–Friday; 10:30AM & 2PM
Average Length	1 hour

ON-CAMPUS APPOINTMENTS

Admissions

Saturdays	No
Info Sessions	Yes

Faculty and Coaches

Dates/Times	Academic year
Arrangements	Contact Admissions Office 1 week prior

CLASS VISITS

Dates	Academic year
Arrangements	Contact Admissions Office

RANDOLPH-MACON COLLEGE

PO Box 5005,
Ashland, VA 23005 • Telephone: 800-888-1762 • www.rmc.edu •
Email: admissions@rmc.edu

Hours: Monday–Friday, 8:30AM–4:30PM; select Saturdays

Academically competitive Randolph-Macon's 4-1-4 calendar includes a January term, during which students explore nontraditional academic themes, undertake field study and internships, or travel. R-MC students may take courses at any of the other schools in the Seven Colleges Consortium of Virginia (Washington and Lee, Hampden-Sydney, Sweet Briar, Mary Baldwin, Hollins, or Randolph-Macon Woman's College).

AT A GLANCE

Selectivity Rating	76
Range SAT I Math	500–600
Average SAT I Math	552
Range SAT I Verbal	500–610
Average SAT I Verbal	560
Average GPA	3.24
Student/Faculty Ratio	11:1

CAMPUS TOURS

Appointment	Preferred
Dates	Year-round
Average Length	1 hour

ON-CAMPUS APPOINTMENTS

Admissions

Start Date—Juniors	Anytime
Appointment	Required
Advance Notice	Yes, 1 week
Saturdays	Sometimes
Average Length	30 min.
Info Sessions	Yes

Faculty and Coaches

Dates/Times	Year-round
Arrangements	Contact Admissions Office 1 week prior

CLASS VISITS

Dates	Year-round
Arrangements	Contact Admissions Office

TRANSPORTATION

The Amtrak station (on main north-south track) located at the southwest corner of campus—northbound and southbound trains each stop twice a day. Richmond International Airport is located about 25 minutes away. Taxi and limousine service to campus is available.

FIND YOUR WAY

I-95 to Exit 92 (Rte. 54 West-Ashland). Continue on Rte. 54 across Rte. 1 (third stoplight). About half a mile after Rte. 1, turn right onto Henry Street. The R-MC Welcome Center is on the corner. The Admissions Office is located three blocks down on East Patrick Street.

STAY THE NIGHT

Nearby: Lodging within Ashland, Virginia includes the **Ashland Inn, Budget Inn, Days Inn, Econo Lodge, Hampton Inn, Henry Clay Inn** (bed-and-breakfast), **Microtel Inn, Quality Inn and Suites, Super 8,** and **Travelodge.**

A little farther: Numerous hotels in Richmond, Virginia area. Richmond accommodations include the **Jefferson Hotel,** the **Berkeley Hotel,** and chain hotels such as the **Courtyard, Embassy Suites,** the **Hilton,** the **Holiday Inn,** the **Marriott,** the **Omni,** the **Radisson,** and **Sheraton Hotels.** There are also numerous bed-and-breakfast inns in the area.

HIGHLIGHTS

ON CAMPUS
- Randolph-Macon Performing Arts Center
- The Brock Sports and Recreation Center
- Frank E. Brown Campus Center
- Pace-Armistead Hall and Flippo Gallery
- Washington and Franklin Hall

OFF CAMPUS
- Paramount's Kings Dominion
- Virginia Center Commons Mall
- Downtown Richmond
- Virginia Museum of Fine Arts
- Riverwalk and Brown's Island

RANDOLPH-MACON WOMAN'S COLLEGE

Admissions Office, 2500 Rivermont Ave.,
Lynchburg, VA 24503-1526 • Telephone: 800–745-7692 • www.rmwc.edu •
Email: admissions@rmwc.edu

Hours: Monday–Friday, 8:30AM–5:00PM; Saturday, 10:00AM–noon, during the academic year

"I actually spend more time out of class talking to my professors than I do in class lectures," beams one of the
many happy students at Randolph-Macon Woman's College, a tiny all-women's bastion in Lynchburg, Virginia.
There's little to do on campus, but the elegant dining hall and resident halls make students wonder if they're living at a five-star hotel or a college.

HIGHLIGHTS

ON CAMPUS
- The Maier Museum of Art
- Botanical Gardens
- The Whiteside Amphitheater
- The Riding Center

OFF CAMPUS
- Point of Honor
- Blue Ridge Parkway
- Blackwater Creek Trail
- Poplar Forest

TRANSPORTATION
The Lynchburg Municipal Airport is a 20-
minute drive from campus. Call the
Admissions Office to make special pickup
arrangements. Taxi and limousine service is
available at the airport.

FIND YOUR WAY
The major north-south highway to Lynchburg
is U.S. Rte. 29. The major east-west highway is
U.S. Rte. 460. Both of these roads have clear
signs leading to the college. In Lynchburg,
Main St. (which is one-way) becomes
Rivermont Ave. Continue on Rivermont Ave.
about two miles until you reach the entrance
of the college, on the right.

STAY THE NIGHT
Nearby: Some hotels in Lynchburg include the
Days Inn (3320 Candlers Mountain Rd.; 800-
329-7466), the **Hampton Inn** (5604 Seminole
Ave.; 800-426-7866), the **Lynchburg Hilton** (2900 Candlers Mountain Rd.; 800-445-8667),
and the **Holiday Inn Select** (601 Main St.; 800-465-4329). Some bed-and-breakfasts are
the **Lynchburg Mansion Inn** (405 Madison St.; 804-528-5400), the **Madison House** (413
Madison St.; 877-901-1503), the **Residence** (2460 Rivermont Ave.; 888-835-0387), and the
Federal Crest Inn (1101 Federal St.; 800-818-6155).

AT A GLANCE

Selectivity Rating	79
Range SAT I Math	510–620
Average SAT I Math	564
Range SAT I Verbal	540–640
Average SAT I Verbal	592
Average ACT Composite	25
Average GPA	3.4
Student/Faculty Ratio	9:1

CAMPUS TOURS

Appointment	Preferred
Dates	Year-round
Times	Mon–Fri, 9AM–5PM;
	Sat, 9AM–12PM;
	Summer: Mon–Fri,
	8:30AM–5PM
Average Length	1 hour

ON-CAMPUS APPOINTMENTS

Admissions

Start Date–Juniors	Anytime
Appointment	Preferred
Advance Notice	Yes, 1 week
Saturdays	Sometimes
Average Length	30 min.
Info Sessions	No

Faculty and Coaches

Dates/Times	Academic year
Arrangements	Contact Admissions
	Office 1 week prior

CLASS VISITS

Dates	Academic year
Arrangements	Contact Admissions
	Office

SWEET BRIAR COLLEGE

Office of Admissions, Box B,
Sweet Briar, VA 24595 • Telephone: 800-381-6142 • www.sbc.edu •
Email: admissions@sbc.edu

Hours: Monday–Friday, 8:30AM–5:00PM; Saturday (during term by appointment)

The women of Sweet Briar College absolutely love the small, fascinating, discussion-oriented classes and accessible and enthusiastic professors. And, to top it all off, the beautiful campus of SBC—complete with wooded footpaths and bike trails—is one of the most wired colleges in the country.

AT A GLANCE

Selectivity Rating	80
Range SAT I Math	490–610
Average SAT I Math	550
Range SAT I Verbal	530–660
Average SAT I Verbal	590
Average ACT Composite	24
Average GPA	3.5
Student/Faculty Ratio	8:1

CAMPUS TOURS

Appointment	Preferred
Dates	Year-round
Times	Call for times
Average Length	1 hour

ON-CAMPUS APPOINTMENTS

Admissions

Start Date–Juniors	Anytime
Appointment	Preferred
Advance Notice	No
Saturdays	Yes
Average Length	30 min.
Info Sessions	Yes

Faculty and Coaches

Dates/Times	Year-round
Arrangements	Contact Admissions Office 1 week prior

CLASS VISITS

Dates	Academic year
Arrangements	Contact Admissions Office

TRANSPORTATION

The Lynchburg Municipal Airport is a 30-minute drive from campus. Taxi service is available for the trip from the airport to campus. The Admissions Office will arrange for transportation if you request it at least three days in advance.

FIND YOUR WAY

From Richmond, take U.S. Rte. 64 W. to U.S. Rte. 29. Head south on U.S. 29 to the college.

STAY THE NIGHT

Nearby: The **Florence Elston Inn** (www.elstoninn.com; 434-381-6207) is most convenient, as it is located on the Sweet Briar campus. A lovely bed-and-breakfast, **Dulwich Manor** (www.dulwichmanor.com; 434-946-7207), is about five minutes away from the college in Amherst. This English manor house is surrounded by woodland. **Winridge Bed & Breakfast** (Madison Heights; 434-384-7220) is about 20 minutes away from campus.

A little farther: There are more choices in Lynchburg especially on Candlers Mountain Road. Of these, the least expensive is the **Days Inn** (3320 Candlers Mountain Rd.; 434-847-8655) 16 miles south of Sweet Briar. About the same distance from the college are the **Hilton Lynchburg** (2900 Candlers Mountain Rd.; 434-237-6333), and the **Sleep Inn** (3620 Candlers Mountain Rd.; 434-846-6900).

HIGHLIGHTS

ON CAMPUS

- Bistro
- Riding Center
- Boathouse
- Book shop
- Gymnasium

OFF CAMPUS

- Lynchburg
- Charlottesville
- Lexington
- Roanoke
- Farmville

UNIVERSITY OF VIRGINIA

Admissions Office, PO Box 400160, Charlottesville, VA 22906 • Telephone: 434-982-3200 • www.virginia.edu • Email: undergradadmission@virginia.edu

Hours: Monday–Friday, 8:00AM–5:00PM

The University of Virginia is one of the best and most selective state schools in the country. The research facilities and archives are spectacular, and for the size of this university, UVA has a small and familiar feel. Students say classes for everybody except first-year students are surprisingly reasonable in size. Katie Couric is an alum.

HIGHLIGHTS

ON CAMPUS
- Historic Academical Village
- University of Virginia Museum of Art
- Football & soccer stadiums
- The Corner (shops & restaurants)
- Aquatic & fitness center
- Location of the future arts precinct new library housing original early American manuscripts (next door to Admission Office), golf course, observatory, Old Cabell Performance Hall

OFF CAMPUS
- Blue Ridge Mountains
- VA Film Festival & Festival of the Book
- Wintergreen Ski Resort
- Historic Downtown Mall
- James River

TRANSPORTATION

The Charlottesville-Abemarle Airport is 10 miles away from campus. Taxis are available for the ride from the airport to campus.

FIND YOUR WAY

From the north or south, take U.S. Rte. 29 toward Charlottesville; do not take the Rte. 29 bypass around the city, but take the business route, which becomes Emmet St. and goes through campus. **From east or west on I-64,** take Exit 22B to U.S. Rte. 29 N. Follow the preceding directions from Rte. 29.

STAY THE NIGHT

Nearby: If convenience is everything to you, you have several choices within walking distance of the university, including the **Cavalier Inn** (434-296-8111), **Hampton Inn** (brand new! 434-923-8600), and the **Red Roof Inn** (434-295-4333). Call **Guesthouses/B&B** (804-979-7264) for a selection of bed-and-breakfasts, some of which are adjacent to the university. Most are moderately priced. Inexpensive accommodations can be found at the **Knights Inn** (434-973-8133), about two miles away from the university. More expensive choices include a bed-and-breakfast called **200 South Street** (434-979-0200), a 20-room inn in the downtown historic district, and the university owned **Boar's Head Inn** (434-296-2181 or 800-476-1988).

AT A GLANCE

Selectivity Rating	94
Range SAT I Math	620–720
Average SAT I Math	668
Range SAT I Verbal	600–700
Average SAT I Verbal	647
Average ACT Composite	28
Average GPA	3.96
Student/Faculty Ratio	16:1

CAMPUS TOURS

Appointment	Not required
Dates	Year-round
Times	Varies
Average Length	1 hour

ON-CAMPUS APPOINTMENTS

Admissions

Appointment	Not required
Advance Notice	No, 3 weeks
Saturdays	No
Info Sessions	Yes

Faculty and Coaches

Dates/Times	Year-round
Arrangements	Contact Athletic Department 3 weeks prior

CLASS VISITS

Dates	Academic year
Arrangements	Contact Admissions Office

WASHINGTON AND LEE UNIVERSITY

Gilliam Admissions House, Letcher Avenue,
Lexington, VA 24450-0303 • Telephone: 540-463-8710 • admissions.wlu.edu •
Email: admissions@wlu.edu

Hours: Monday–Friday, 8:30AM–4:30PM; Saturday (May–December), 8:00AM–noon

Washington and Lee is a moderately priced traditional liberal arts school with a great reputation, a wild social scene, and a very conservative student population. The dean of the freshman program memorizes everybody's name by the first day of school, according to students, which is both impressive and eerie. The great American author Tom Wolfe is an alum.

AT A GLANCE

Selectivity Rating	97
Range SAT I Math	640–720
Range SAT I Verbal	640–720
Average GPA	3.96
Student/Faculty Ratio	11:1

CAMPUS TOURS

Appointment	Not required
Dates	Year-round
Times	Mon–Fri, 10AM–4PM;
	Sat, 9:30AM–12:30PM
Average Length	1 hour

ON-CAMPUS APPOINTMENTS

Admissions

Start Date–Juniors	May 1st
Appointment	Required
Advance Notice	Yes, 2 weeks
Saturdays	Yes
Average Length	45 min.
Info Sessions	Yes

Faculty and Coaches

Dates/Times	Year-round
Arrangements	Contact faculty/
	coach directly 2 weeks prior

CLASS VISITS

Dates	Academic year
Arrangements	Contact Admissions
	Office

TRANSPORTATION

The Roanoke Airport is 50 miles away from campus. Taxis, limousines, and rental cars are available for the ride from the airport to campus. For limousine reservations, call Shenandoah Limousine (540-464-5466) or Roanoke Airport Limousine Service (540-345-7710).

FIND YOUR WAY

From the north, take I-81 S. to the first Lexington exit and follow U.S. Rte. 11 S., which becomes Main St. in Lexington. On Rte. 11, you pass the Virginia Military Institute and then enter the Washington and Lee campus, eight miles away from I-81. **From the south,** take I-81 N. to the second Lexington exit and I-64 W.; from I-64 W. follow posted directions to U.S. Rte. 11 S. Rte. 11 S. brings you onto the Washington and Lee campus, two miles away from I-64.

STAY THE NIGHT

Nearby: A popular choice and a favorite with college kids is the warm and friendly **Llewellyn Lodge** (603 S. Main St.; 540-463-3235 or 800-882-1145), within walking distance of the university. The moderate price includes a full breakfast. Tennis courts, a public outdoor pool, and a golf course are nearby. Two interesting inns, both run by Historic Country Inns of Lexington, are only one block away from campus; they are the **Alexander-Winthrow House** (3 W. Washington St.; 540-463-2044) and the **McCampbell Inn** (11 N. Main St.; 540-463-2044). The reasonable prices include breakfast. If you are more comfortable with the usual chains, the **Days Inn Keydet General Motel** (U.S. Rte. 60 West; 540-463-2143) is inexpensive and has a lovely view of the Blue Ridge Mountains. The **Holiday Inn** (Rte. 11 N. and I-64; 540-463-7351) is somewhat more expensive and also has a mountain view. Col Alto is a restored historic home and now part of the **Hampton Inns** (401 E. Nelson St., 540-463-2223).

HIGHLIGHTS

ON CAMPUS

- Lee Chapel
- Elrod University Commons
- Lenfest Center for the Arts
- Doremus Fitness Center
- Reeves Center & Watson Pavillion

OFF CAMPUS

- Stonewall Jackson House
- George Marshall Museum at VMI
- Natural Bridge
- Lime Kiln Theater (summer)
- Virginia Horse Center

1- Evergreen State College
2- University of Puget Sound
3- University of Washington
4- Whitman College
5- Gonzaga University
6- Seattle University
7- Washington State University

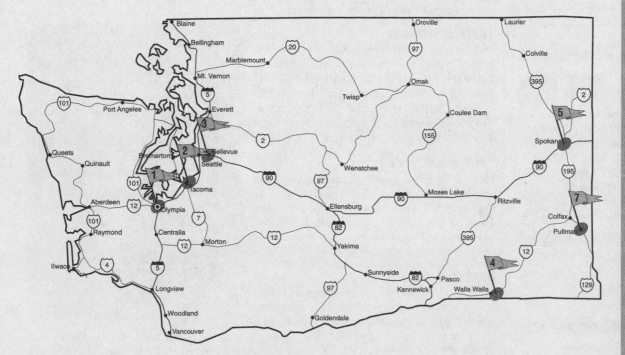

Washington	Evergreen State	Gonzaga	Seattle Univ.	Univ. Puget Sound	Univ. Washington	Wash. State U.	Whitman Coll.	Seattle	Spokane
Evergreen State	—	328	67	28	59	335	320	58	320
Gonzaga	328	—	281	298	283	78	157	283	0
Seattle Univ.	67	281	—	37	4	288	273	0	279
Univ. Puget Sound	28	298	37	—	30	305	293	30	294
Univ. Washington	59	283	4	30	—	290	274	0	280
Wash. State U.	335	78	288	305	290	—	115	288	76
Whitman Coll.	320	157	273	293	274	115	—	274	160
Seattle	58	283	0	30	0	288	274	—	280
Spokane	320	0	279	294	280	76	160	280	—

THE EVERGREEN STATE COLLEGE

Office of Admissions, 2700 Evergreen Pkwy NW,
Olympia, WA 98505 • Telephone: 360-867-6170 • www.evergreen.edu •
Email: admissions@evergreen.edu

Hours: Monday–Friday, 8:00AM–5:00PM

You want academic freedom? How much can you handle? If your answer to these questions is "How much have you got?," The Evergreen State College may be the school for you. With few tests and no letter grades (students receive narrative evaluations instead), ESC stresses education for its own sake. Students design their own majors with the guidance of professors throughout their academic careers.

AT A GLANCE

Selectivity Rating	77
Range SAT I Math	480–590
Average SAT I Math	536
Range SAT I Verbal	520–650
Average SAT I Verbal	583
Average ACT Composite	23
Average GPA	3.13
Student/Faculty Ratio	22:1

CAMPUS TOURS

Appointment	Preferred
Dates	Year-round
Times	Varies
Average Length	1 hour

ON-CAMPUS APPOINTMENTS

Admissions
Info Sessions	Yes

Faculty and Coaches
Dates/Times	Year-round
Arrangements	Contact Admissions Office 3 weeks prior

CLASS VISITS

Dates	Academic year
Arrangements	Contact Admissions Office

TRANSPORTATION

Seattle-Tacoma International Airport is approximately one hour away from Olympia. Bus and shuttle service is available for the trip from the airport to campus. For shuttle service, call Capital Aeroporter (1-800-962-3579). You may also use their website to book your transportation: www.capair.com.

FIND YOUR WAY

Take I-5 (north or south depending on where you are) to exit 104. This will put you on Highway 101. Take the third exit; it is marked The Evergreen State College exit. Travel two miles on the Evergreen Parkway to the main campus entrance which will be on your left.

STAY THE NIGHT

Nearby: The Greener Guide program offers you a hosted overnight stay in our campus housing apartments. We provide a bed and all linens; you are responsible for toiletries and some meals. There may be up to three other people sharing the bathroom. The student host will take you through the different types of housing styles we offer and even treat you to a meal in the Housing Community Center. If you would like to stay in our campus housing for a real overnight experience, please contact the Office of Admissions at 360-866-6172. Other suggestions for overnight accommodations include **Extended StayAmerica** (800-398-7829), **Holiday Inn Express** (800-465-4329), **Phoenix Inn** (877-570-0555), **Governor House** (800-272-6232), **Guest House Inn & Suites** (800-214-8378), **Red Lion Olympia** (800-325-4000), and **Motel 6** (800-466-8356).

HIGHLIGHTS

ON CAMPUS
- Longhouse Cultural and Education Center
- Organic Farm
- The College Library
- College Activities Building
- Computer Center

OFF CAMPUS
- State Capitol Campus
- Washington State Center for the Performing Arts
- Farmers' Market
- Tumwater Historical Park
- Washington State Capitol Museum

GONZAGA UNIVERSITY

Office of Admissions, 502 E. Boone Avenue, Spokane, WA 99258 • Telephone: 800-322-2584 • www.gonzaga.edu • Email: admissions@gonzaga.edu

Hours: Monday–Friday, 8:00AM–5:00PM; select Saturdays

Gonzaga University is a top-notch Jesuit university that offers a host of degree programs through five different colleges (arts and sciences, business administration, education, engineering, and professional studies). The intellectually diverse and very conservative students enjoy pretty small classes, and most students praise their dedicated professors who really try to help.

HIGHLIGHTS

ON CAMPUS

- The Wall
- Charlotte Y. Martin Athletic Center
- Jundt Art Museum
- Bing Crosby Museum in the Crosby Student Center
- The Gonzaga University Bookstore

OFF CAMPUS

- The Centennial Trail
- Riverpark Square Shopping Center
- Mt. Spokane Ski Resort and Recreational Area
- Riverfront Park
- Greenbluff Orchards

TRANSPORTATION

Transportation to Gonzaga's campus is available from Spokane International Airport as well as the train and bus depot via taxi, city bus, or hotel shuttle.

FIND YOUR WAY

From I-90 Westbound: Take Exit 281. (Newport/Colville exit.) Veer right at the bottom of the ramp. Proceed through five stop lights. Pass over the Spokane River at the Samuel C. Guess Memorial Bridge. Merge into far right lane. Turn right on Sharp Ave. Proceed four blocks east. Turn right on Addison St. **From I-90 eastbound,** take exit 281. (Division St. /Newport/Colville exit.) Veer left at the bottom of the ramp. Begin to merge right at the first stop light. Proceed to right center lane. Pass under the railroad trellis (Sprague Ave.). Merge into the far right lane. Pass over the Spokane River on the Samuel C. Guess Memorial Bridge. Turn right on Sharp Ave. Proceed four blocks east. Turn right on Addison St.

STAY THE NIGHT

Nearby: The **Davenport Hotel** (10 South Post Street, Spokane, WA 99201; www.davenporthotel.com; 509-455-8888 or 800-899-1482); the **Fairfield Inn by Marriott** (311 N. Riverpoint Blvd.; www.fairfieldinn.com; 509-747-9131), a 10-minute walk to campus, which includes complimentary continental breakfast, indoor pool, and interior corridors; the **Doubletree Hotel–Spokane City Center** (322 N. Spokane Falls Ct.; 509-455-9600 or 800-222-TREE; www.doubletree.com), a 10-minute walk to campus, which includes free airport shuttle, free local shuttle to and from Gonzaga, and free parking; the **Holiday Inn Express** (801 N. Division; www.ontherockexpress.com; 509-328-8505; a five-minute walk to campus, which includes all nonsmoking rooms, complimentary parking, continental breakfast, afternoon beverages, interior corridors, and on-site fitness and business centers; the **Hotel Lusso** (1 N. Post 509-747-9750; www.hotellusso.com), located in downtown Spokane, a 15-minute walk to campus, includes complimentary airport shuttle service, valet parking, European breakfast, afternoon beverage service, health club affiliation, business center, and Fugazzi's Restaurant located in the hotel; the **Mariana Stoltz Bed & Breakfast** (427 E. Indiana; 509-483-4316 or 800-978-6587; www.mariannastoltzhouse.com) a five-minute walk to campus and a local historic site that includes complimentary parking, home-cooked breakfast, afternoon beverage, and a home-like atmosphere.

AT A GLANCE

Selectivity Rating	79
Range SAT I Math	540–640
Average SAT I Math	593
Range SAT I Verbal	530–620
Average SAT I Verbal	578
Average ACT Composite	26
Average GPA	3.63
Student/Faculty Ratio	13:1

CAMPUS TOURS

Appointment	Required
Dates	Year-round
Average Length	Varies

ON-CAMPUS APPOINTMENTS

Admissions

Start Date–Juniors	Anytime
Appointment	Required
Advance Notice	Yes, 2 weeks
Saturdays	Sometimes
Average Length	30 min.
Info Sessions	Yes

Faculty and Coaches

Dates/Times	Academic year
Arrangements	Yes, 3 weeks

CLASS VISITS

Dates	Academic year
Arrangements	Contact Visiting Center

SEATTLE UNIVERSITY

Admissions Office, 900 Broadway, Seattle, WA 98122-4340 • Telephone: 800-426-7123 • www.seattleu.edu • Email: admissions@seattleu.edu

Hours: Monday–Tuesday, 9:00AM–6:00PM; Wednesday–Friday, 9:00AM–4:30PM; some Saturdays, 9:00AM–2:00PM

Enrolling about 3,200 students, Seattle University is a very well-respected Jesuit Catholic institution that offers strong liberal arts, a professionally oriented curriculum, and allows students to focus on personal growth. Students can choose from a wide range of extracurricular options, including marksmanship and sailing clubs.

AT A GLANCE

Selectivity Rating	80
Range SAT I Math	500–620
Average SAT I Math	561
Range SAT I Verbal	500–610
Average SAT I Verbal	562
Average ACT Composite	26
Average GPA	3.49
Student/Faculty Ratio	14:1

CAMPUS TOURS

Appointment	Preferred
Dates	Year-round
Times	Varies
Average Length	1 hour

ON-CAMPUS APPOINTMENTS

Admissions

Appointment	Required
Advance Notice	Yes, 2 weeks
Saturdays	Sometimes
Average Length	1 hour
Info Sessions	Yes

Faculty and Coaches

Dates/Times	Academic year
Arrangements	Contact Admissions Office 2 weeks prior

CLASS VISITS

Dates	Academic year
Arrangements	Contact Admissions Office

TRANSPORTATION

Airport: SeaTac International Airport. Amtrak Seattle Metro Transit Buses and taxis are available.

FIND YOUR WAY

From I-5, take the James St. exit off I-5 (coming from the north, exit 165; coming from the south, exit 164A). Turn east up the hill past Broadway until you reach 12th Avenue (0.6 miles). Turn left at the light on 12th Avenue and proceed north two blocks to East Marion Street and turn left. The visitor parking lot information booth will be directly ahead. Stop for parking information and campus directions. **From I-90,** take the Rainier Avenue North exit (3B) and merge onto Rainier Avenue South (you will be heading northbound). Follow Rainier Avenue South (0.5 miles) to the intersection of Rainier Avenue South and Boren Avenue South. Turn slightly left onto Boren Avenue South for two blocks then turn right onto 12th Avenue. Follow the preceding directions. **From Highway 520,** take 520 westbound to I-5 south. Take the James Street exit off I-5 (exit 165a). Turn left on James Street and drive up the hill past Broadway until you reach 12th Avenue. Turn left at the light on 12th Avenue and proceed north two blocks to East Marion Street and turn left. Follow the preceding directions.

STAY THE NIGHT

Nearby: Your choices include the **Best Western Executive** (200 Taylor Ave. N; 206-448-9444) with single rooms priced from $90 to $155 per night and double rooms priced from $115 to $165; the **Best Western Loyal Inn** (2301 8th Ave.; 206-682-0202) with single rooms priced from $94 to $104 per night and double rooms priced from $104 to $124 per night; the **Days Inn Towncenter** (2204 7th Ave.; 206-448-3434) with single rooms priced from $69 to $125 and double rooms from $79 to $137; **Executive Court Suites** (300 10th Ave.; 206-233-9300) with single rooms priced from $130 to $159 per night and double rooms priced from $185 to $195 per night; the **Holiday Inn Crowne Plaza** (6th & Seneca; 206-464-1980) with single rooms priced from $139 to $289; the **Spring Hill Suites** (1800 Yale Ave.; 206-254-0500) with rooms priced at $89 on weekends and $109 on weekdays; **Hotel Seattle University** (315 Seneca St.; 206-623-5110) with single rooms priced from $86 to $92 and double rooms priced at $92 per night; **Park Plaza Suites** (1011 Pike; 206-682-8282) with single rooms priced from $129 to $200 and double rooms priced from $149 to $260; and the **Quality Inn** (224 8th Ave.; 206-624-6820) with single rooms priced from $99 to $129 and double rooms priced from $109 to $139.

HIGHLIGHTS

ON CAMPUS

- Chapel of Saint Ignatius
- Brand new Student Center
- Award-winning grounds and open space
- Sullivan Hall (home of the School of Law)

OFF CAMPUS

- Space Needle/Seattle Center
- Pike Place Market
- Seattle Art Museum
- Waterfront
- Pacific Place Shopping Center

UNIVERSITY OF PUGET SOUND

Office of Admission, 1500 N. Warner St.,
Tacoma, WA 98416 • Telephone: 800-396-7191 • www.ups.edu •
Email: admission@ups.edu

Hours: Monday–Friday, 8:00AM–5:00PM; Saturday (by appointment only), 9:00AM–1:00PM

Students rave that professors with a passion for their subjects and a stimulating, rigorous learning environment make the very competitive University of Puget Sound the best school in Washington. Academics are rigorous, and people study a lot in the large and comfortable dorm rooms on the aesthetically beautiful (but rainy) campus.

HIGHLIGHTS

ON CAMPUS

- Three-story Pale Chihuly glass sculpture in Wyatt Hall
- Diversions Cafe
- Alcorn Arboretum
- Music and theater productions directed by faculty and students on campus

OFF CAMPUS

- Point Defiance Park, Zoo, and Aquarium
- Mt. Rainier National Park
- San Juan Islands
- Experience Music Project (Seattle)
- Washington State History Museum (Tacoma)
- Glass Museum (Tacoma)

TRANSPORTATION

Seattle-Tacoma International Airport is 24 miles away from campus. Capital Aeroporter provides hourly transportation from the airport to the downtown Tacoma Sheraton and, if possible, to campus. Call 800-962-3579 or 253-927-6179 (in Tacoma) or 206-838-7431 (at the airport) to arrange for this service. If the Aeroporter cannot take you directly to campus, you can take a taxi from the Sheraton. Amtrak train service is available to the station in Tacoma. From there, you can either take a taxi or a public bus (#41, #400, or #500); if you take a bus, request a transfer ticket and leave the bus at 10th and Commerce streets. Wait there for the #16A or #16B bus, and take it to N. 15th and Alder Sts., which is one block west of the Wheelock Student Center. Greyhound Bus Lines also serve Tacoma. From the bus station, take the #16A or #16B bus at 10th and Commerce streets (one block west of Pacific Ave. from the station), and follow preceding directions to campus.

FIND YOUR WAY

From the north/I-5, take Exit 133, Interstate 705 north, City Center exit. Exit at Schuster Parkway. Continue for approximately one mile; stay to the left. Exit to the left, Schuster Parkway, and follow down along the water. Stay to the right and proceed approximately one-and-a-half miles. Exit right onto North 30th. Continue through the traffic signal in Old Town and up the hill. At the top of the hill, turn left at North Alder. Continue approximately one mile to North 15th. Turn right and proceed into campus. **From I-5,** take Exit 132 for Gig Harbor/Bremerton Hwy. (Washington Rte. 16); then take the Union Ave. exit, make a right at the light, and travel north approximately two miles to the campus (on your right). Continue onto N. 18th St. and turn right. Turn right again on N. Lawrence St. (at the yield sign) and continue to the stop sign. Turn right into Jones Circle. Park in the parking circle in front of Jones Hall or in the lot just south of the Wheelock Student Center.

STAY THE NIGHT

Nearby: Just seven blocks away from campus is **Keenan House** (2610 N. Warner St.; 253-752-0702). Furnished with antiques, this Victorian home is your best bet for price and convenience. Upscale, yet reasonably priced, **Sheraton Tacoma Hotel** (1320 Broadway Plaza; 253-572-3200 or 800-845-9466) is about two-and-a-half miles away from campus. **La Quinta** (1425 E. 27th St.; 253-383-0146), located approximately four miles away from the university with a view of Mount Rainier and Commencement Bay, is more modestly priced and also has a swimming pool; request the special school rate. Approximately 15 minutes away is affordable **Shilo Inn** (7414 S. Hosmer Rd.; 253-475-4020 or 800-334-1049), near the 77th St. exit off I-5, which has a heated pool and a health club.

AT A GLANCE

Selectivity Rating	85
Range SAT I Math	580–670
Average SAT I Math	622
Range SAT I Verbal	580–685
Average SAT I Verbal	631
Average ACT Composite	27
Average GPA	3.58
Student/Faculty Ratio	11:1

CAMPUS TOURS

Appointment	Not required
Dates	Year-round
Times	Mon–Fri, 9AM–4PM (hourly)
Average Length	1 hour

ON-CAMPUS APPOINTMENTS

Admissions

Start Date–Juniors	Anytime
Appointment	Preferred
Advance Notice	Yes, 2 weeks
Saturdays	Sometimes
Average Length	1 hour
Info Sessions	Yes

Faculty and Coaches

Dates/Times	Year-round
Arrangements	Contact Admissions Office 2 weeks prior

CLASS VISITS

Dates	Academic year
Arrangements	Contact Admissions Office

UNIVERSITY OF WASHINGTON

Office of Admissions, Box 355840,
Seattle, WA 98195-5840 • Telephone: 206-543-9686 • www.washington.edu •
Email: askuwadm@u.washington.edu

Hours: Monday–Friday, 8:00AM–5:00PM

The University of Washington—the premier research institution north of Berkeley and west of Minnesota—boasts 13 colleges that offer programs for undergraduates and a picturesque and very happening Seattle location. There are a slew of outdoorsy types, and fraternities and sororities are quite popular.

AT A GLANCE

Selectivity Rating	81
Range SAT I Math	550–660
Range SAT I Verbal	510–630
Average GPA	3.66
Student/Faculty Ratio	11:1

CAMPUS TOURS

Appointment	Required
Dates	Year-round
Times	Mon–Fri, 2:30PM, except during campus holidays
Average Length	2 hours

ON-CAMPUS APPOINTMENTS

Admissions

Start Date–Juniors	N/A
Info Sessions	Year-round

Faculty and Coaches

Dates/Times	Year-round
Arrangements	Contact Admissions Office 3 weeks prior

CLASS VISITS

Dates	Year-round
Arrangements	Contact Admissions Office

TRANSPORTATION

The Seattle-Tacoma International Airport is approximately 18 miles away from campus. To get to campus from the airport, take Shuttle Express, which leaves the airport on call. For Shuttle information, call 206-622-1424; no advance reservations are required. Amtrak trains and Greyhound/Trailways buses serve Seattle.

FIND YOUR WAY

From I-5 (N. and S.), take Exit 169. Proceed east on 45th St. N.E. for approximately half a mile. Turn right on 15th Ave. N.E. and head south approximately three blocks. The Admissions Office is in Schmitz Hall, at N.E. Campus Pkwy. and 15th Ave. N.E. Visitor parking is across the street.

STAY THE NIGHT

Nearby: A nice range of choices can be found within walking distance of the university. **University Motel** (4731 12th St. N.E.; 206-522-4724), a small neighborhood place six blocks away, has great rates. All units are suites with kitchenettes. For something fancier, consider the **Meany Tower Hotel** (4507 Brooklyn Ave. N.E.; 206-634-2000), only three blocks from campus. There's a special moderate double-occupancy rate for university visitors. Astounding views of the mountains, lakes, and city, and a small workout room make it a good choice. The **Chambered Nautilus Bed-and-Breakfast** (5005 22nd St. N.E.; 206-522-2536), two blocks away, offers a tranquil retreat in the city. Prices are moderate and a gourmet breakfast is included. And who doesn't want to stay on a fully functional, exceptionally clean, restored tugboat? The **Challenger** (809 Fairview Pl. North.; 206-340-1201) has seven guest rooms (four of which have private baths), is carpeted throughout, and is furnished with nautical antiques. Rates run in the moderate range, with a full gourmet breakfast included. The tug has closed-circuit TV and videos. Five miles away is the small and lovely **Inn at the Market** (86 Pine St.; 206-443-3600), with rates that fluctuate between moderate and very expensive. Its setting is spectacular and its location is fantastic—it's near lively Pike Place Market. The **Silver Cloud Inn** (5036 25th NE; 206-526-5200,) is just east of campus and conveniently located by restaurants and shopping areas. **The Inn** (4140 Roosevelt Way NE; 206-632-5055) is just on the west side of the campus.

HIGHLIGHTS

ON CAMPUS

- Henry Art Gallery
- Burke Museum
- Meany Hall for Performing Arts
- Football games at Husky Stadium
- Waterfront Activities Center (WAC)

OFF CAMPUS

- The Experience Music Project (EMP)
- Safeco Field
- Seattle Art Museum/Asian Art Museum
- International District
- Washington Park Arboretum

WASHINGTON STATE UNIVERSITY

Office of Admissions, 342 French Administration Building, Pullman, WA 99164-1067 • Telephone: 888-468-6978 • www.wsu.edu • Email: admiss2@wsu.edu

Hours: Monday–Friday, 8:00AM–5:00PM

Underrated Washington State University is a good-size research institution that offers cutting-edge technology and a nationally recognized School of Communications (named after Edward R. Murrow, a legendary alum). There's tons of school spirit, and Wazzoo's very isolated hometown of Pullman is reportedly very student-friendly.

HIGHLIGHTS

ON CAMPUS
- CUB (Food Services, bowling alley, movies, etc.)
- Student Recreation Center
- Ferdinands (WSU's own ice cream & cheeses)
- PAC-10 Athletics
- Over 200 registered student organizations

OFF CAMPUS
- State Parks
- Lionel Hampton Jazz Festival
- Renaissance Fair
- Harvest Festival
- Lentil Festival

TRANSPORTATION
Bus and taxi transportation is available through the town and campus. The closest airport is the Pullman/Moscow Airport.

FIND YOUR WAY
From Spokane, take Interstate 90 to Colfax/Pullman exit (#279) to highway 195. Take 195 south through Colfax to Pullman. Turn left at the Pullman exit then right onto highway 270 (Davis Way). Follow 270 to N. Grand Avenue in downtown Pullman.

STAY THE NIGHT
Nearby: Choices in Pullman include the **Hawthorn Inn,** the **Holiday Inn Express,** and the **Quality Inn.**

A little farther: Choices in Moscow include the **Best Western,** the **Hampton Inn,** and **Super 8 Motel.**

AT A GLANCE	
Selectivity Rating	73
Range SAT I Math	480–590
Average SAT I Math	533
Range SAT I Verbal	470–580
Average SAT I Verbal	522
Average GPA	3.43
Student/Faculty Ratio	17:1

CAMPUS TOURS	
Appointment	Not required
Dates	Year-round
Times	Mon–Fri, 9AM or 1PM
Average Length	Varies

ON-CAMPUS APPOINTMENTS	
Admissions	
Appointment	Not required
Advance Notice	Yes
Info Sessions	Yes
Faculty and Coaches	
Dates/Times	Year-round
Arrangements	Contact coach directly 2 weeks prior

CLASS VISITS	
Dates	Year-round
Arrangements	Contact department

WHITMAN COLLEGE

Office of Admission, 345 Boyer Ave.,
Walla Walla, WA 99362-2083 • Telephone: 877-462-9448 • www.whitman.edu •
Email: admission@whitman.edu

Hours: Monday–Friday, 8:30AM–4:30PM; Saturday (during term), 10:00AM–2:00PM

Whitman is one of the best kept secrets west of the Mississippi. This highly competitive but largely undiscovered gem of the inland Northwest has almost everything going for it: a beautiful setting, a rigorous curriculum, an exceptionally willing faculty, and a helpful administration. Whitman also boasts a phenomenal success rate among its graduates (three-quarters attend professional or graduate school within a year of graduation).

AT A GLANCE

Selectivity Rating		93
Range SAT I Math		610–700
Average SAT I Math		655
Range SAT I Verbal		610–710
Average SAT I Verbal		659
Average ACT Composite		28
Average GPA		3.78
Student/Faculty Ratio		10:1

CAMPUS TOURS

Appointment	Preferred
Dates	Year-round
Times	Mon–Fri, 9AM,10AM, & 2:30PM; Sat, 11AM; Summer: Mon–Fri, 10AM & 2PM
Average Length	1 hour

ON-CAMPUS APPOINTMENTS

Admissions

Start Date–Juniors	Anytime
Appointment	Preferred
Advance Notice	Yes, 2 weeks
Saturdays	Sometimes
Average Length	1 hour
Info Sessions	Yes

Faculty and Coaches

Dates/Times	Year-round
Arrangements	Contact Admissions Office 2 weeks prior

CLASS VISITS

Dates	Year-round
Arrangements	Contact Admissions Office

TRANSPORTATION

A 10-minute drive from campus, the Walla Walla Airport is serviced by Horizon Air, which offers daily flights to Walla Walla with connections through Seattle, Washington. For city bus service from the airport to the campus or downtown, call Valley Transit (509-525-9140) to arrange for boarding (bus transportation from the airport Monday to Friday only). Rental cars in Walla Walla are available from Budget (509-525-8811), Hertz (509-522-3321), and Dollar (509-527-0812). For city taxi service, call A-1 Taxi (509-529-2525). Greyhound Bus Lines (509-525-9313 or 800-231-2222) serves Walla Walla with daily connections from Pendleton, Oregon; Pasco, Washington; Spokane, Washington; and Seattle, Washington. Delta Airlines, Alaska Airlines/Horizon Air and United Express provide additional air service with flights to Pasco (47 miles northwest of Walla Walla). Major rental car companies are on-site at the Pasco Airport.

FIND YOUR WAY

If you are traveling to Walla Walla **(from the east or west) on Highway 12,** take the Clinton Street exit and proceed six blocks south on Clinton to Boyer Avenue. Turn right on Boyer. Penrose House (the Office of Admissions) is one block ahead on the northwest corner of Boyer and Stanton. Parking is in the driveway of Penrose House. If you are traveling **from south of Walla Walla, Highway 11 from Pendleton,** Oregon becomes Highway 125 at the Washington state line, and then becomes Ninth Ave. when in enters Walla Walla. Drive north on Ninth to Main St. Turn right on Main and continue on Main until you come to a five-way intersection. Make a soft right onto Boyer Avenue. Travel on Boyer beyond the stop sign to Penrose House on the northwest corner of Boyer and Stanton.

STAY THE NIGHT

Nearby: There are several choices within walking distance of the college. The **Green Gables Inn** (922 Bonsella St.; 509-525-5501), one block north of campus, provides bed and breakfast amenities in a beautiful, 1909 Tudor-style mansion. Just across the street from the campus is the **Howard Johnson Express Inn** (325 E. Main St.; 509-529-4360 or 800-446-4656), which offers a seasonal outdoor pool, Jacuzzi, sauna, and exercise room. The reasonably priced **Travelodge** (421 E. Main St.; 509-529-4940 or 800-578-7878) has a seasonal outdoor pool and hot tub. Just a five-minute drive away is the **Hawthorne Suites** (520 N. 2nd St.; 509-525-2522 or 800-228-5150) with inexpensive rates, a free continental breakfast, indoor pool, sauna, and spa. Nearby is Walla Walla's newest motel, the **Best Western Walla Walla Suites Inn** (7 E. Oak St.; 509-525-4700), which has an indoor pool, hot tub, and fitness room. Additional guest services are available from these businesses.

HIGHLIGHTS

ON CAMPUS
- Sheehan Art Gallery, Olin Hall
- Memorial Building
- Penrose Library
- Harper Joy Theater
- Reid Campus Center

OFF CAMPUS
- Whitman Mission National Historic Site
- Columbia and Snake Rivers
- Main Street (National Historic District)
- Fort Walla Museum
- Bluewood and Spout Springs ski areas

1- West Virginia University

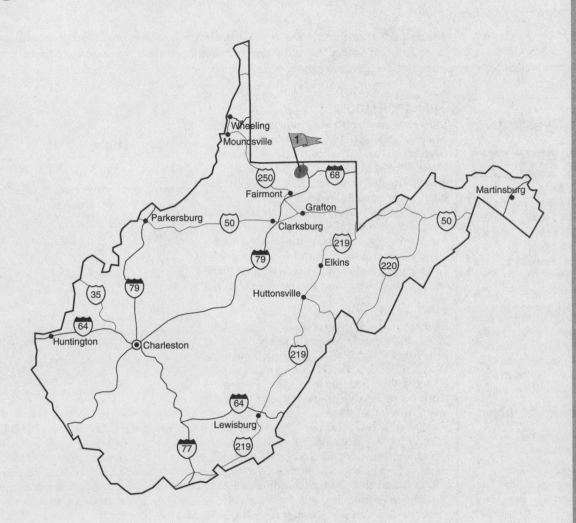

	West Virginia Univ.	Charleston
West **Virginia**		
West Virginia Univ.	—	153
Charleston	153	—

WEST VIRGINIA UNIVERSITY

WVU Visitors' Resource Center, PO Box 6693,
Morgantown, WV 26506-6009 • Telephone: 800-344-9881 • www.ia.wvu.edu •
Email: wvuadmissions@arc.wvu.edu

Hours: Monday–Friday, 8:15AM–4:45PM

A raucous Greek scene and very popular sports programs make West Virginia University in the great college hamlet of Morgantown a fun place to go to school. Excellent programs in journalism, agriculture, engineering, and business make it a very good place to get a degree.

AT A GLANCE

Selectivity Rating	75
Range SAT I Math	470–580
Average SAT I Math	528
Range SAT I Verbal	460–560
Average SAT I Verbal	514
Average ACT Composite	23
Average GPA	3.2
Student/Faculty Ratio	19:1

CAMPUS TOURS

Appointment	Required
Dates	Year-round
Times	Mon–Fri, 10:30AM & 2PM; Sat, 10AM & 12:30PM
Average Length	120 min.

ON-CAMPUS APPOINTMENTS

Admissions

| Start Date—Juniors | N/A |

Faculty and Coaches

| Dates/Times | Year-round |
| Arrangements | Contact Visitors Resource Center, 2 weeks prior |

CLASS VISITS

| Dates | Varies |
| Arrangements | Contact Visiting Center |

TRANSPORTATION

Morgantown Airport is two miles away from campus, available via county buses, taxi, or personal car. The Greater Pittsburgh International Airport is approximately 70 miles away from campus. Flights to Pittsburgh leave Morgantown Airport daily. WVU also provides transportation to and from the Pittsburgh Airport for a reasonable fee during peak holiday times. Greyhound buses also run to and from Morgantown and Pittsburgh; the station is just two blocks from campus. Rental cars are also available.

FIND YOUR WAY

By car: at the intersection of I-79 and I-68, WVU is approximately 70 miles south of Pittsburgh or 200 miles northeast of Washington, D.C. The Visitor Resource Center is accessible from Exit 1 of Interstate 68 (University Ave. exit). If you exit from I-68 West, turn left at the end of the exit ramp onto Route 119 North; go straight for three stoplights. If you exit from I-79 onto I-68 East turn left at the light on Route 119 North; go straight for three stoplights. One Waterfront Place is on the left. You will see a large blue sign labeled Visitor Resource Center. As your turn left, make a quick right into the parking garage. You will receive a parking ticket that you will need to bring inside with you to have validated for your time at the center, which is located on the ground floor. You can enter from the mezzanine floor and come down the staircase or walk around to the front door where the center is located.

STAY THE NIGHT

Nearby: There are many of the usual lodging accommodations near the school. The new **Radisson Hotel** (304-296-1700 or 1-800-333-3333; rooms priced at $100 and up) is right across from the Visitor Resource Center. Another nearby option is the **Historic Clarion** (304-292-8401; rooms priced at $100 & up) located on 127 High Street in downtown Morgantown, just blocks away from WVU's downtown campus. The **Ramada Inn** (304-296-3431 or 1-800-228-2828; rooms priced at $60 and up), located at the intersection of Rte. 119 South and I-68 is approximately one mile away from the WVU Visitor Resource Center, as is the **Comfort Inn** (304-296-9364 or 1-800-228-5150; rooms priced at $60 and up). The **Holiday Inn** (304-599-1680 or 1-800-HOLIDAY; rooms priced at $80 and up) on 1400 Saratoga Ave. is close to WVU's Coliseum and Evansdale Campus. The **Hampton Inn** (304-599-1200 or 1-800-HAMPTON; rooms priced at $80 and up) located near WVU's Medical Center, is on 1053 Van Voorhis Road. **Almost Heaven Bed and Breakfast** (304-296-4007; rooms priced at $80 and up), located at 391 Scott Avenue, is also approximately one or two miles away from the WVU Visitor Resource Center.

HIGHLIGHTS

ON CAMPUS
- New State of the Art Student Recreation Center
- Mountainlair (Student Union)
- Personal Rapid Transit (PRT)
- Mountaineer Field
- Historic Woodburn Circle
- Core Arboretum

OFF CAMPUS
- Waterfront (Wharf District)
- Cooper's Rock State Park
- Caperton Recreational Trail
- Downtown Morgantown
- Cheat Lake Area/Lakeview Scanticon Resort

1- Beloit College
2- Lawrence University
3- Marquette University
4- University of Wisconsin
5- Ripon College

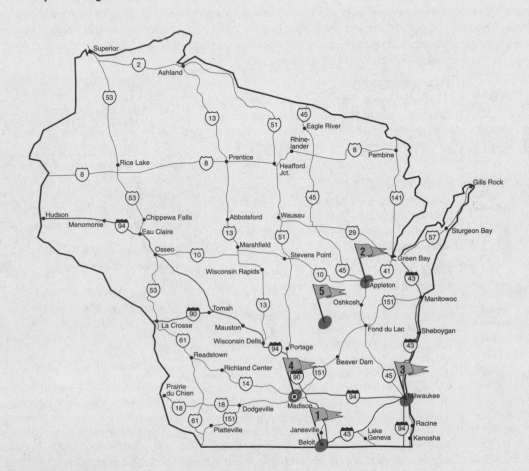

Wisconsin

	Beloit Coll.	Lawrence Univ.	Marquette Univ.	Ripon	U. Wisconsin-Mad.	Madison	Milwaukee
Beloit Coll.	—	148	76	123	56	55	70
Lawrence Univ.	148	—	102	40	103	103	102
Marquette Univ.	76	102	—	85	77	76	0
Ripon	123	40	85	—	77	77	87
Univ. Wisconsin-Mad.	56	103	77	77	—	0	78
Madison	55	103	76	77	0	—	77
Milwaukee	70	102	0	87	78	77	—

BELOIT COLLEGE

Admissions Office, 700 College St.,
Beloit, WI 53511 • Telephone: 800-9-BELOIT • www.beloit.edu •
Email: admiss@beloit.edu

Hours: Monday–Friday, 8:00AM–4:30PM; Saturday, 8:30AM–noon

Pink hair and pierced faces are not uncommon at funky and free-thinking Beloit College, where the college motto is "Invent Yourself" and jocks and freaks more or less peacefully coexist in a very demanding and intimate academic atmosphere. Student Symposium occurs each spring; for an entire day, students and faculty ditch classes to view student projects displayed all across campus.

AT A GLANCE

Selectivity Rating	79
Range SAT I Math	560–650
Average SAT I Math	610
Range SAT I Verbal	590–690
Average SAT I Verbal	640
Average ACT Composite	27
Average GPA	3.52
Student/Faculty Ratio	11:1

CAMPUS TOURS

Appointment	Required
Dates	Year-round
Times	Varies
Average Length	1 hour

ON-CAMPUS APPOINTMENTS

Admissions

Start Date–Juniors	Fall of junior year
Appointment	Required
Advance Notice	Yes, 2 weeks
Saturdays	Yes
Average Length	1 hour
Info Sessions	No

Faculty and Coaches

Dates/Times	Academic year
Arrangements	Contact Admissions Office

CLASS VISITS

Dates	Academic year
Arrangements	Contact Admissions Office

TRANSPORTATION

O'Hare International Airport in Chicago is 75 miles away from campus; the Van Galder Bus Company (608-752-5407 or www.vangalder-bus.com/) runs hourly shuttles from the airport to Beloit.

FIND YOUR WAY

I-43, I-90, U.S. Rtes. 14 and 51, and Rtes. 2, 75, 81, and 251 lead to Beloit. Signs posted on all major highways through the town will direct visitors to campus.

STAY THE NIGHT

Nearby: The college has three guest apartments on campus in a lovely historic home that has been recently renovated. All the apartments have kitchens, though you can also use dining facilities on campus. The price is incredibly inexpensive. Call the Admissions Office at 800-356-0751 or 608-363-2500 to check on availability. Within walking distance of campus is a newly constructed boutique hotel, **The Beloit Inn** (500 Pleasant St.; 608-362-5500). Opened in November 2000, hotel services and amenities include continental breakfast, newspaper, executive fitness center, limo and airport pick-up service, business center, laundry/dry cleaning pick up and delivery, on-site wine storage, personal cigar humidor in the lounge, and meeting and catering services. Also, several hotels are within two to three miles away from campus. A full-service **Holiday Inn** (200 Dearborn St.; 815-389-3481) offers special rates to college visitors, and the **Holiday Inn Express** (2790 Milwaukee Rd.; 608-365-6000) has inexpensive rates, which include a full breakfast. For other lodging options, call the Admissions Office at 800-356-0751 or visit the website at www.visitbeloit.com/.

A little farther: Lake Geneva is a year-round resort area about an hour's drive east of Beloit. Here you will find **The French Country Inn** (W. 41490 West End Rd., Lake Geneva, WI 53147; 262-245-5220), an unusual lakeside structure dating back from the 1880s. Its wonderfully furnished guestrooms overlook the lake, and all have private bathrooms. The inn has a lovely restaurant with creative menus—a real treat. Rates are moderate during the week and expensive on the weekend. A 20-minute drive from Beloit will find you in Janesville, Wisconsin, if traveling north toward Madison, or in Rockford, Illinois, if traveling south toward Chicago. Both of these cities offer several accommodation options within an easy drive of Beloit.

LAWRENCE UNIVERSITY

Admissions Office, PO Box 599,
Appleton, WI 54912-0599 • Telephone: 800-227-0982 • www.lawrence.edu •
Email: excel@lawrence.edu

Hours: Monday–Friday, 8:00AM–5:00PM; Saturday (September–May), 9:00AM–noon

Demanding Lawrence University is a little liberal arts college with a slew of excellent music programs, a strong biology department, and several other top-notch majors. Other characteristics include small classes, dedicated (but very tough) professors who are always willing to help the students, and an extremely diverse student body (given Lawrence's small Midwestern town location).

HIGHLIGHTS

ON CAMPUS
- Wriston Art Gallery
- Music Conservatory
- Main Hall
- New $18 million Science Building
- Buchanan Kiewit Recreation Center

OFF CAMPUS
- Numerous Parks and Museums
- Fox River Mall
- Barlow Planetarium
- Bjorklunden Retreat Center, Door County, WI
- Green Bay Packers, Lambeau Field

TRANSPORTATION
The Outagamie County Airport is approximately five miles away from campus. Taxis are available at the airport for the ride to campus. Greyhound Bus Lines serve Appleton; the bus station is also six blocks from campus. Taxis are available if you don't want to walk.

FIND YOUR WAY
From U.S. Hwy. 41, exit on College Ave. Proceed east four miles to the Admissions Office (Wilson House), which is on the northeast corner of College Ave. and Lawe St. Visitor parking is located behind the office.

STAY THE NIGHT
Nearby: The **Paper Valley Hotel and Conference Center** (333 W. College Ave.; 920–733-8000) is about six blocks away. You'll be able to keep busy without ever leaving the hotel. It has a nine-hole miniature golf course, ping-pong, shuffleboard, video games, an indoor swimming pool, a whirlpool, a sauna, a weight room, two restaurants, a shopping arcade, and entertainment. Rates are moderate. Another good bet is the **Best Western Midway Hotel** (3033 W. College Ave.; 920–731-4141), only three miles away from the university. It has an indoor pool, a weight room, a sauna, a whirlpool, video games all for a special moderate rate for college visitors. About four miles away, there's a **Holiday Inn** (150 Nicolet Rd.; 920–735-9955) with an indoor pool, exercise room, video games, tennis, and golf. Rates here are a bit higher than at the Best Western Midway during the week, but they offer inexpensive rates on the weekend. There are also a few fine bed-and-breakfasts within four blocks off campus; they include **Queen Anne Bed and Breakfast** (920-831-9903), **Franklin Street Inn** (920-993-1711), and the **Gathering Place** (920–731-4418). Other good options include **Comfort Suites** (920–730-3800), **Country Inn & Suites** (920-830-3240), **Fairfield Inn** (920-954-0202), the **Hampton Inn** (920-954-9211), and the **Wingate Inn** (920-933-1200).

AT A GLANCE

Selectivity Rating	85
Range SAT I Math	560–670
Average SAT I Math	625
Range SAT I Verbal	560–690
Average SAT I Verbal	620
Average ACT Composite	27
Average GPA	3.53
Student/Faculty Ratio	11:1

CAMPUS TOURS

Appointment	Required
Dates	Year-round
Times	Times vary
Average Length	1 hour

ON-CAMPUS APPOINTMENTS

Admissions

Start Date–Juniors	Anytime
Appointment	Required
Advance Notice	Yes, 1 week
Saturdays	Yes
Average Length	30 min.

Faculty and Coaches

Dates/Times	Academic year
Arrangements	Contact Admissions Office 2 weeks prior

CLASS VISITS

Dates	Academic year
Arrangements	Contact Admissions Office

MARQUETTE UNIVERSITY

Office of Undergraduate Admissions, Marquette Hall, 1217 W. Wisconsin Ave., Milwaukee, WI 53201-1881 • Telephone: 800-222-6544 • www.marquette.edu • Email: Admissions@Marquette.edu

Hours: Monday–Friday, 9:00AM–4:00PM; select Saturdays (by appointment), 10:00AM–4:30PM

The Jesuit work ethic is all the rage at Marquette University, where students say academic excellence is abundant. Distribution requirements are rigorous, including course work in mathematics, theology, science, and liberal arts. Milwaukee provides a hopping social scene.

AT A GLANCE

Selectivity Rating	77
Range SAT I Math	530–650
Average SAT I Math	590
Range SAT I Verbal	520–640
Average SAT I Verbal	560
Average ACT Composite	25
Student/Faculty Ratio	15:1

CAMPUS TOURS

Appointment	Required
Dates	Year-round
Times	Mon–Fri, 9AM–3PM, on the hour
Average Length	120 min.

ON-CAMPUS APPOINTMENTS

Admissions

Start Date–Juniors	Anytime
Appointment	Required
Advance Notice	Yes, 2 weeks
Saturdays	Sometimes
Average Length	1 hour
Info Sessions	Yes

Faculty and Coaches

Dates/Times	Academic year
Arrangements	Contact Athletic Department 2 weeks prior

CLASS VISITS

Dates	Academic year
Arrangements	Contact Admissions Office

TRANSPORTATION

General Mitchell International Airport is approximately seven miles away from campus. Taxis, limousines, rental cars, and buses run by the Milwaukee County Transit System are available for the ride from the airport to campus. Amtrak trains and Greyhound/Trailways buses serve Milwaukee. Public bus service is available from all parts of the metropolitan area.

FIND YOUR WAY

The I-94/I-43 interchange frames the south and east border of campus. Exit to W. Wisconsin Ave., which passes through the campus.

STAY THE NIGHT

Nearby: The **Pfister Hotel** (424 E. Wisconsin Ave.; 414-273-8222), one-and-a-half miles away, is a fun off-campus choice. Known as the oldest hotel in Wisconsin, this gorgeous Victorian is modern inside; it has an indoor pool, exercise equipment, and three restaurants. No surprises with the **Ramada Inn Downtown** (633 W. Michigan St.; 414-272-8410), seven blocks away, or the **Holiday Inn** (611 W. Wisconsin Ave.; 414-273-2950), six blocks away. Both provide pleasant accommodations for extremely reasonable rates.

A little farther: If you're willing to drive 20 miles or so north to Cedarburg, you can stay in a historic mill town with many activities and attractions in the area, such as the Ozaukee Pioneer Village, the Cedar Creek Settlement, the Old Woolen Mill, and the Stone Mill Winery. The **Washington House Inn** (414-375-3550), a bed-and-breakfast built in 1886, is a fun place that conjures up the frontier past. Rates run the gamut from inexpensive to expensive.

HIGHLIGHTS

ON CAMPUS
- The Memorial & Science Library
- Law Library
- Gesu Church
- Haggerty Museum of Art
- Helfaer Theatre
- Helfaer Recreation Center

OFF CAMPUS
- Santiago Calatrava addition to Milwaukee Art Museum
- Milwaukee Public Museum
- Eisner Museum of Advertising and Design
- Miller Park
- The Riverwalk

RIPON COLLEGE

Office of Admissions, 300 Seward Street, PO Box 248,
Ripon, WI 54971 • Telephone: 800-947-4766 • www.ripon.edu •
Email: adminfo@ripon.edu

Hours: Monday–Friday, 8:00AM–5:00PM; Saturday (during term), 9:00AM–noon

Ripon is a small private school with a high academic profile where professors provide old-fashioned, hands-on personal attention and individual care. The friendly, homey atmosphere engenders a community-oriented campus. Indiana Jones (well, Harrison Ford) is one of a number of prominent alums.

HIGHLIGHTS

ON CAMPUS

- Ceresco Prairie Conservancy
- Art Gallery
- Storzer Athletic Center
- Lane Library

OFF CAMPUS

- Little White Schoolhouse (start of Republicans)
- Green Lake resort town
- EAA, aviation museum (Oshkosh)
- Fox River Mall (Appleton)

TRANSPORTATION

The closest airport (40 minutes away) is Outagamie County Airport in Appleton. Milwaukee International Airport is one-and-a-half hours away. Greyhound buses are available in Oshkosh (20 minutes away).

FIND YOUR WAY

Easily accessible by state highways 23, 44, and 49, Ripon is located on the western edge of the Fox River Valley. Madison is 75 miles away, Milwaukee is 80 miles away, Chicago is 180 miles away, and Minneapolis is 250 miles away.

STAY THE NIGHT

Nearby: Your choices include the **AmericInn Motel** (920-748-7578; $65 per night on average), the **Best Western-Welcome Inn** (920-748-2821; $60 per night on average), and the **Heidel House Resort on Green Lake** (920-294-3344; $150 per night on average).

AT A GLANCE

Selectivity Rating	79
Range SAT I Math	540–670
Average SAT I Math	602
Range SAT I Verbal	570–640
Average SAT I Verbal	599
Average ACT Composite	24
Average GPA	3.34
Student/Faculty Ratio	14:1

CAMPUS TOURS

Appointment	Preferred
Dates	Varies
Average Length	1 hour

ON-CAMPUS APPOINTMENTS

Admissions

Appointment	Preferred
Advance Notice	Yes
Saturdays	Sometimes
Average Length	30 min.
Info Sessions	No

Faculty and Coaches

Dates/Times	Academic year
Arrangements	Contact Admissions Office 1 week prior

CLASS VISITS

Dates	Academic year
Arrangements	Contact Admissions Office

UNIVERSITY OF WISCONSIN—MADISON

Campus Information and Visitor Center, 716 Langdon St., Madison, WI 53706-1481 • Telephone: 608-262-3961 • www.civc.wisc.edu • Email: onwisconsin@admissions.wisc.edu

Hours: Monday–Friday, 8:00AM–4:30PM

The University of Wisconsin at Madison is a humongous institution with some of the finest academic and research facilities on the planet (including a library with a jaw-dropping five million bound volumes) and rock-bottom tuition rates. All undergraduate students must complete a broad and difficult assortment of distribution requirements throughout the liberal arts and sciences. Frank Lloyd Wright is an alum.

AT A GLANCE

Selectivity Rating	90
Range SAT I Math	610–700
Average SAT I Math	652
Range SAT I Verbal	560–670
Average SAT I Verbal	613
Average ACT Composite	27
Average GPA	3.6
Student/Faculty Ratio	13:1

CAMPUS TOURS

Appointment	Required
Dates	Year-round
Times	Mon–Fri, times vary depending on day of week
Average Length	1 hour

ON-CAMPUS APPOINTMENTS

Admissions

Start Date—Juniors	N/A

Faculty and Coaches

Dates/Times	Academic year
Arrangements	Log onto www.visit bucky.wisc.edu/learnmore.aspx 2 weeks prior

CLASS VISITS

Dates	Academic year
Arrangements	Log onto www.visit bucky.wisc.edu/learnmore.aspx

TRANSPORTATION

The Dane County Regional Airport (MSN, www.co.dane.wi.us/airport) is approximately six miles away from campus. Taxis and limousines are available for the ride from the airport to campus. Campus buses and the Madison Metro buses provide service throughout the campus and the city. The campus is also served by Greyhound, Van Galder, and Badger bus lines.

FIND YOUR WAY

From U.S. Rte. 51 and I-90, exit to U.S. Rte. 12/18 West. Take that to Park St. (Hwy. 14 North), which will take you to campus. See www.visit.wisc.edu/directions.html.

STAY THE NIGHT

Nearby: Your choices inclide the **Memorial Union** (800 Langdon Street; 608-262-1583), the **Union South** (227 N. Randall Avenue; 608-263-2600), the **Friedrick Center** (1950 Willow Drive; 608-231-1341), and the **Lowell Center** (610 Langdon Street; 608-256-2621).

A little farther: See www.wisc.edu/cac/housing/overnight.htm for more accommodation options.

HIGHLIGHTS

ON CAMPUS

- Allen Centennial Gardens
- Kohl Center
- Memorial Union Terrace
- Elvehjem Museum of Art
- Babcock Hall Dairy Plant and Store

OFF CAMPUS

- State Capitol
- Monona Terrace
- Henry Vilas Zoo
- State Street
- Arboretum
- www.visit.wisc.edu/todo.html

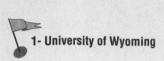

1- University of Wyoming

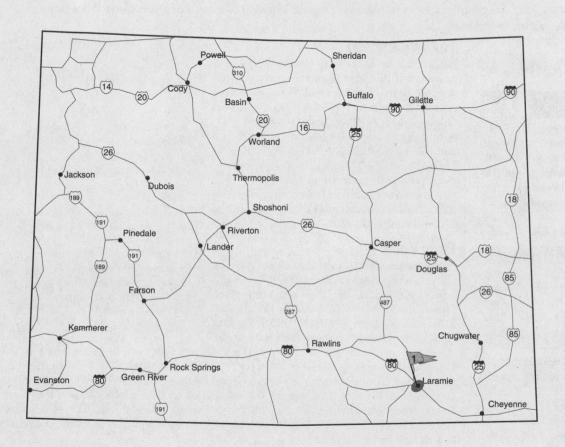

Wyoming	Univ. Wyoming	Cheyenne
Univ. Wyoming	—	49
Cheyenne	49	—

UNIVERSITY OF WYOMING

Admissions Office, PO Box 3435,
Laramie, WY 82071 • Telephone: 800-342-5996 • siswww.uwyo.edu •
Email: Why-Wyo@uwyo.edu

Hours: Monday–Friday, 8:00AM–5:00PM

The key word to describe the University of Wyoming is value, according to the students at this very cold and isolated campus. UW's other big draw is its mountain setting, the beautiful country surrounding the school in every direction, and the great outdoors in general. The sun shines 320 days each year, and there are many trails and ski resorts in the area.

AT A GLANCE

Selectivity Rating	75
Range SAT I Math	480–600
Average SAT I Math	541
Range SAT I Verbal	460–580
Average SAT I Verbal	524
Average ACT Composite	23
Average GPA	3.4
Student/Faculty Ratio	15:1

CAMPUS TOURS

Appointment	Required
Dates	Year-round
Times	Varies
Average Length	1 hour

ON-CAMPUS APPOINTMENTS

Admissions

Start Date—Juniors	After junior year
Appointment	Required
Advance Notice	Yes, 2 weeks
Saturdays	No
Average Length	30 min.

Faculty and Coaches

Dates/Times	Academic year
Arrangements	Contact Athletic Department

CLASS VISITS

Arrangements	Contact Visiting Center

TRANSPORTATION

Air service to Laramie is available by Great Lakes shuttle from Denver International Airport. Rental cars are available at Municipal Airport Laramie at 1-307-742-5296. To contact Great Lakes Airlines, call 1-800-554-5111. Alternatively, rental cars are available at Denver International Airport; the drive to Laramie, using I-25N and I-80W, takes about two-and-a-half hours. For Greyhound Bus fare and schedule information, call 1-800-231-2222. The local Greyhound Bus Terminal is on 4700 Bluebird Lane (307-742-5188).

FIND YOUR WAY

From Interstate 80: Exit 316: Head west on Grand Avenue into Laramie (HWY 30) to 15th Street, turn right and then left on Ivinson Street. The Visitors' Center will be on left. **Exit 313:** Head north on 3rd Street (HWY 287). Turn right onto Grand Avenue. Turn left on 14th street and then turn right on Ivinson. The Visitors' Center will be on the right. **Exit 311:** Head east on Snowy Range Road (HWY 130/230) into Laramie. Turn right onto 3rd street, proceed, and then make a left at Grand Avenue. Turn left on 14th street and then turn right on Ivinson. The Visitors' Center will be on the right. **Exit 310:** Head East on Curtis street into Laramie. Turn right onto 3rd street, proceed, and then make a left at Grand Avenue. Turn left on 14th street and then turn right on Ivinson. The Visitors' Center will be on the right.

STAY THE NIGHT

Nearby: Local accommodations in Laramie include the **Howard Johnson's Country Corner Hotel** (I-80 & Snowy Range Road; 307-742-8371), the **Best Western Gas Lite** (960 N. 3rd; 800-942-6610), the **Camelot** (I-80 & Snowy Range Road; 307-721-8860), the **Comfort Inn** (3420 Grand Ave.; 800-228-5150), the **Days Inn** (1368 McCue St.; 307-745-5678), the **Econo Lodge** (1370 McCue St.; 800-700-7974), the **First Inn Gold** (Junction I-80 & US 287; 800–642-4212), the **Holiday Inn** (Junction US 287 & I-80; 800-526-5245), the **Motel 6** (621 Plaza Lane; 307-742-2307), the **Motel 8** (501 Boswell; 888-745-4800), the **Sunset Inn** (1104 S. 3rd; 800-308-3744), **Super 8** (I-80 & Curtis; 800-800-8000), the **Travel Inn** (262 N. 3rd; 877-310-7381), the **Travelodge Downtown Motel** (165 N. 3rd; 800-942-6671), and the **University Inn** (1720 Grand; 307-721-8855).

HIGHLIGHTS

ON CAMPUS

- Student Union
- American Heritage Center & Art Museum
- Geology Museum
- Rocky Mountain Herbarium & Williams Conservatory
- Half-Acre Gym

OFF CAMPUS

- Historic Downtown
- Wyoming Territorial Prison & Old West Park
- Vedauwoo Recreation Area
- Snowy Range Mountains/Medicine Bow National Forest
- Laramie Plains Museum

APPENDIX ONE

Regional Mileage Matrices

New England	Amherst	Bennington Coll.	Boston	Bowdoin Coll.	Colby Coll.	Dartmouth Coll.	Marlboro Coll.	Middlebury Coll.	Providence	Providence Coll.	Trinity Coll.	Univ. Maine-Orono	Univ. New Hamp.	Univ. Vermont	Wesleyan Univ.	Worcester	Yale Univ.
Amherst	—	70	103	215	265	102	46	166	91	87	47	320	141	178	63	47	85
Bennington Coll.	70	—	143	220	271	101	28	85	152	165	110	325	148	119	126	109	136
Boston	103	143	—	137	187	129	114	216	51	51	107	242	63	224	118	42	141
Bowdoin Coll.	215	220	137	—	56	177	191	267	182	189	229	110	94	232	244	167	267
Colby Coll.	265	271	189	56	—	144	241	285	232	239	280	66	144	250	294	218	317
Dartmouth Coll.	102	101	129	177	144	—	72	100	171	179	147	272	114	95	163	129	186
Marlboro Coll.	46	28	114	191	241	72	—	113	124	148	92	296	118	150	107	72	122
Middlebury Coll.	166	85	216	267	285	100	113	—	236	242	212	326	196	34	228	194	251
Providence	91	152	51	182	232	171	124	236	—	0	74	287	108	248	78	44	110
Providence Coll.	87	165	51	189	239	179	148	242	0	—	267	302	122	267	96	38	104
Trinity Coll.	47	110	1-7	229	280	147	92	212	74	267	—	334	155	224	17	66	41
Univ. Maine-Orono	320	325	242	110	66	272	296	326	287	302	334	—	199	291	349	272	371
Univ. New Hamp.	141	148	63	94	144	114	118	196	108	122	155	199	—	199	170	93	192
Univ. Vermont	178	119	224	232	250	95	150	34	248	267	224	291	199	—	240	205	263
Wesleyan Univ.	63	126	118	244	294	163	107	228	78	96	17	349	170	240	—	77	26
Worcester	47	109	42	167	218	129	72	194	44	38	66	272	93	205	77	—	100
Yale Univ.	85	136	141	267	317	186	122	251	110	104	41	371	192	263	26	100	—

Middle Atlantic

Middle Atlantic	Wells Coll.	Vassar Coll.	Univ. Scranton	Univ. Pittsburgh	Temple Univ.	Syracuse Univ.	SUNY Buffalo	SUNY Binghamton	Skidmore Coll.	St. Lawrence Univ.	St. Bonaventure	Rutgers Univ.	Rochester	Princeton Univ.	Pittsburgh	Philadelphia	Penn State Univ.	New York City	Marist Coll.	Lehigh Univ.	Ithaca	Hofstra Univ.	Franklin & Marshall	Duquesne Univ.	Colgate Univ.	Bucknell Univ.	Allegheny Univ.	Alfred Univ.
Alfred Univ.	119	277	188	266	311	133	109	127	299	260	47	287	80	285	244	292	188	311	265	238	99	334	249	263	187	157	198	—
Allegheny Univ.	257	394	307	93	383	284	135	292	433	401	132	364	205	367	88	346	166	372	420	345	258	424	325	90	327	212	—	198
Bucknell Univ.	171	201	92	220	168	199	236	135	282	330	199	171	197	169	253	165	71	178	205	126	143	210	104	220	201	—	212	157
Colgate Univ.	78	188	121	220	245	35	192	69	115	199	238	237	129	240	357	247	240	240	204	193	80	267	248	404	—	201	327	187
Duquesne Univ.	342	408	296	0	305	361	224	357	496	483	216	348	284	336	0	294	137	370	410	290	362	401	238	—	404	220	90	263
Franklin & Marshall	281	208	137	237	79	255	328	183	301	386	278	123	289	111	238	58	123	152	223	74	230	205	—	238	248	104	325	249
Hofstra Univ.	285	202	150	400	120	277	421	207	209	395	375	62	363	75	401	121	265	31	103	114	253	—	205	401	267	210	424	334
Ithaca	24	134	82	289	229	54	149	49	209	189	140	230	90	228	298	236	181	237	184	182	—	253	230	362	80	143	258	99
Lehigh Univ.	226	134	82	289	58	199	316	128	228	330	309	70	270	68	279	44	173	81	149	—	182	114	74	290	193	126	345	238
Marist Coll.	216	4	115	409	177	221	360	137	117	303	306	120	301	127	409	178	261	98	—	149	184	103	223	410	204	205	420	265
New York City	254	65	120	369	97	265	406	185	182	359	345	36	365	51	386	104	234	—	98	81	237	31	152	370	240	178	372	311
Penn State Univ.	207	257	149	135	193	238	208	191	337	368	155	191	229	192	133	192	—	234	261	173	181	265	123	137	240	71	166	188
Philadelphia	267	165	125	303	0	253	370	182	271	384	352	55	324	43	311	—	192	104	178	44	236	121	58	294	247	165	346	292
Pittsburgh	74	396	296	0	340	354	218	325	472	484	218	355	289	346	—	311	133	386	409	279	298	401	238	0	357	253	88	244
Princeton Univ.	343	123	119	335	45	246	363	174	239	377	343	18	317	—	346	43	192	51	127	68	228	75	111	336	240	169	367	285
Rochester	160	302	217	286	340	83	65	175	232	215	124	318	—	317	289	324	229	365	301	270	90	363	289	284	129	197	205	80
Rutgers Univ.	253	111	112	347	71	248	364	176	217	379	336	—	318	18	355	55	191	36	120	70	230	62	123	348	237	171	364	287
St. Bonaventure	72	302	231	220	340	194	81	171	217	215	—	336	124	343	218	352	155	345	306	309	140	375	278	216	238	199	132	47
St. Lawrence Univ.	179	307	261	486	383	130	272	213	175	—	215	379	215	377	484	384	368	359	303	330	189	395	386	483	199	330	401	260
Skidmore Coll.	191	289	216	498	273	146	289	158	—	175	217	217	232	239	472	271	337	182	117	228	209	209	301	496	115	282	433	299
SUNY Binghamton	72	165	61	359	146	79	226	—	158	213	171	176	175	174	325	182	191	185	137	128	49	207	183	357	69	135	292	127
SUNY Buffalo	133	361	275	226	398	142	—	226	289	272	81	364	65	363	218	370	208	406	360	316	149	421	328	224	192	236	135	109
Syracuse Univ.	55	257	130	363	254	—	142	79	146	130	194	248	83	246	354	253	238	265	221	199	54	277	255	361	35	199	284	133
Temple Univ.	262	180	124	301	—	254	398	146	273	383	340	71	340	45	340	0	193	97	177	58	229	120	79	305	245	168	383	311
Univ. Pittsburgh	345	408	296	—	301	363	226	359	498	486	220	347	286	335	0	303	135	369	409	289	289	400	237	0	220	220	93	266
Univ. Scranton	137	115	—	296	124	130	275	61	216	261	231	112	217	119	296	125	149	120	115	82	82	150	137	296	121	92	307	188
Vassar Coll.	217	—	115	408	180	257	361	165	289	307	302	111	302	123	396	165	257	65	4	134	134	202	208	408	188	201	394	277
Wells Coll.	—	217	137	345	262	55	133	72	191	179	72	253	160	343	74	267	207	254	216	226	24	285	281	342	78	171	257	119

	Bradley Univ.	Chicago	Cincinnati	Grand Rapids	Indiana Univ.	Kalamazoo Coll.	Kenyon Coll.	Lawrence Univ.	Marquette Univ.	Michigan State	Oberlin Univ.	Ohio State Coll.	Ohio Univ.	Purdue Univ.	Ripon Coll.	Rose-Hulman	Springfield, IL	Univ. Dayton	Univ. Illinois	Univ. Michigan	Univ. Notre Dame	Univ. Wisconsin	Valparaiso Univ.	Wabash Coll.
Bradley Univ.	—	167	326	319	287	441	260	330	254	362	460	389	358	301	188	458	300	432	94	382	235	233	196	166
Chicago	167	—	290	170	134	352	163	189	90	221	324	320	286	236	178	432	324	336	135	126	236	48	135	148
Cincinnati	326	290	—	386	52	303	138	476	380	260	225	111	160	184	555	282	412	48	279	55	126	314	143	261
Grand Rapids	319	170	386	—	324	52	269	90	260	72	265	321	311	277	492	335	322	258	100	189	264	354	269	278
Indiana Univ.	287	134	52	324	—	272	275	418	319	80	335	230	304	105	329	289	203	336	198	264	258	424	320	189
Kalamazoo Coll.	441	352	303	52	272	—	251	224	251	72	286	320	394	211	85	277	231	361	330	419	354	200	245	229
Kenyon Coll.	260	163	138	269	275	251	—	558	323	251	56	110	40	292	413	52	85	52	264	172	132	232	209	73
Lawrence Univ.	330	189	476	380	418	224	558	—	102	312	513	547	621	310	40	547	412	360	478	500	77	145	368	350
Marquette Univ.	254	90	380	260	319	251	323	102	—	312	414	466	522	211	85	522	107	324	432	360	261	158	281	246
Michigan State	362	221	260	72	80	72	251	312	312	—	203	250	276	277	492	395	253	361	371	189	134	242	186	293
Oberlin Coll.	460	324	225	265	335	286	56	513	414	203	—	85	216	276	538	248	363	250	189	306	231	368	281	335
Ohio State Coll.	389	320	111	321	230	320	110	547	466	250	85	—	114	248	492	75	322	114	90	189	134	77	103	248
Ohio Univ.	358	286	160	311	304	394	40	621	522	276	216	114	—	276	538	216	253	216	306	134	242	145	248	246
Purdue Univ.	301	236	184	277	105	211	292	310	211	277	276	248	276	—	412	276	107	248	100	258	110	261	77	28
Ripon Coll.	188	178	555	492	329	85	413	40	85	492	538	492	538	412	—	538	412	492	479	258	412	98	269	329
Rose-Hulman	458	432	282	335	289	277	52	547	522	395	248	75	75	276	538	—	180	216	94	332	180	261	227	57
Springfield, IL	300	324	412	322	203	231	85	412	107	253	363	322	253	107	412	180	—	239	198	454	194	186	227	162
Univ. Dayton	432	336	48	252	336	361	52	360	324	361	250	172	216	248	492	332	239	—	365	200	248	269	227	168
Univ. Illinois	94	135	279	232	198	330	286	478	432	371	189	90	306	100	479	94	198	365	—	168	197	245	159	75
Univ. Michigan	382	230	55	330	264	419	184	500	360	189	306	172	134	258	258	332	454	200	365	—	233	206	206	314
Univ. Notre Dame	235	89	126	198	258	354	132	77	261	134	231	280	242	110	412	180	194	248	197	233	—	168	56	177
Univ. Wisconsin	233	144	431	278	424	200	232	145	158	242	368	103	145	261	98	261	186	269	245	206	168	—	200	326
Valparaiso Univ.	196	53	143	209	320	245	209	368	281	186	281	248	248	77	269	227	227	269	159	206	56	200	—	124
Wabash Coll.	166	148	163	261	189	229	73	350	246	293	335	350	246	28	329	57	162	168	75	314	177	326	124	—

Middle West	Bismark	Des Moines	Gustavus-Adolphus	Iowa State Univ.	Macalester Coll.	Northfield	Pierre	St. Louis	Univ. Iowa	Univ. Kansas	Univ. Missouri	U. Nebraska-Lincoln	U. Nebraska-Omaha	Wichita
Bismark	—	689	485	661	438	479	209	1034	751	811	913	675	617	839
Des Moines	689	—	228	28	245	204	514	370	112	234	234	193	135	388
Gustavus-Adolphus	485	228	—	203	73	59	384	606	287	462	542	353	300	619
Iowa State Univ.	661	28	203	—	217	176	486	398	137	262	262	221	163	416
Macalester Coll.	438	245	73	217	—	41	424	630	291	488	484	438	380	633
Northfield	479	204	59	176	41	—	392	589	250	447	443	397	339	592
Pierre	209	514	384	486	424	392	—	808	626	595	681	441	383	630
St. Louis	1034	370	606	398	630	589	808	—	283	294	132	502	444	462
Univ. Iowa	751	112	287	137	291	250	626	283	—	343	231	305	247	496
Univ. Kansas	811	234	462	262	488	447	595	294	343	—	167	215	198	162
Univ. Missouri	913	234	542	262	484	443	681	132	231	167	—	316	312	320
U. Nebraska-Lincoln	675	193	353	221	438	397	441	502	305	215	316	—	58	243
U. Nebraska-Omaha	617	135	300	163	380	339	383	444	247	198	312	58	—	301
Wichita	839	388	619	416	633	592	630	462	496	162	320	243	301	—

Southeast	Bellarmine Univ.	Birmingham	Centre Coll.	Fisk Univ.	Jackson, MS	Louisville	Millsaps Coll.	Rhodes Coll.	Tuskegee Univ.	Univ. Alabama	Univ. Kentucky	Univ. Mississippi	Univ. South	Univ. Tennessee	Vanderbilt Univ.
Bellarmine Univ.	—	365	85	175	587	0	585	376	491	420	77	460	263	245	175
Birmingham	365	—	377	192	245	360	240	249	136	49	402	175	162	257	188
Centre Coll.	85	377	—	194	603	92	604	399	514	435	36	424	241	155	189
Fisk Univ.	175	192	194	—	414	176	412	203	319	247	214	287	93	181	0
Jackson, MS	587	245	603	414	—	586	585	213	287	187	660	157	407	493	414
Louisville	0	360	92	176	586	—	208	378	492	418	74	399	264	247	175
Millsaps Coll.	585	240	604	412	585	208	—	208	286	190	623	167	414	496	411
Rhodes Coll.	376	249	399	203	213	378	208	—	386	238	424	65	260	384	210
Tuskegee Univ.	491	136	514	319	287	492	286	386	—	149	530	312	270	337	325
Univ. Alabama	420	49	435	247	187	418	190	238	149	—	462	163	220	214	246
Univ. Kentucky	77	402	36	214	660	74	623	424	530	462	—	465	277	172	214
Univ. Mississippi	460	175	424	287	157	399	167	65	312	163	465	—	274	468	249
Univ. South	263	162	241	93	407	264	414	260	270	220	277	274	—	161	96
Univ. Tennessee	245	257	155	181	493	247	496	384	337	214	172	468	161	—	180
Vanderbilt Univ.	175	188	189	0	414	175	411	210	325	246	214	249	96	180	—

South Atlantic

	Atlanta	Baltimore	Charleston, SC	Clemson Univ.	Coll. of Charleston	Coll. Wm. & Mary	Duke Univ.	Eckerd Coll.	Florida A&M	Florida State	Hampden-Sydney	James Madison	Mary Wash.	Mercer Univ.	Orlando	Randolph Macon	St. John's Coll.	St. Mary's Coll.	Univ. Delaware	Univ. Florida	Univ. Georgia	U. Maryland-B.C.	Univ. Miami	UNC-Ashville	Univ. So. Carolina	Univ. Virginia	Wake Forest Univ.	Wesleyan Coll.	West Virginia Univ.
Atlanta	—	654	291	117	321	591	374	484	272	267	457	534	588	84	426	548	673	647	796	333	66	678	688	211	215	575	350	78	654
Baltimore	654	—	568	609	582	195	296	968	922	895	227	170	100	728	892	139	30	108	58	824	615	0	1099	507	517	160	375	733	204
Charleston, SC	291	568	—	240	0	480	285	461	404	344	405	502	487	267	384	446	572	545	626	317	275	577	595	270	114	499	264	272	620
Clemson Univ.	117	609	240	—	240	478	261	561	364	351	404	428	485	210	380	445	570	543	640	253	85	576	595	271	268	540	286	271	587
Coll. of Charleston	321	582	0	240	—	464	306	261	351	405	364	501	485	282	266	445	543	543	667	268	279	580	601	204	171	565	285	204	321
Coll. Wm. & Mary	591	195	480	478	464	—	204	804	781	781	122	181	103	609	822	62	188	161	253	755	548	193	1035	497	565	131	257	615	321
Duke Univ.	374	296	285	261	306	204	—	726	646	608	102	282	210	431	649	170	295	253	351	582	375	300	862	224	275	173	84	454	391
Eckerd Coll.	484	968	461	561	261	804	726	—	204	122	805	902	801	103	181	828	945	886	980	210	405	887	278	480	717	994	206	532	381
Florida A&M	272	922	404	364	351	781	646	204	—	0	801	825	882	161	253	785	910	884	972	158	287	916	522	412	886	884	158	279	887
Florida State	267	895	344	351	405	781	608	122	0	—	803	828	828	197	254	787	913	886	953	188	285	953	518	412	913	980	158	279	886
Hampden-Sydney	457	227	405	404	364	122	102	805	801	803	—	96	120	536	721	83	215	188	285	721	254	197	913	221	83	158	215	188	285
James Madison	534	170	502	428	501	181	282	902	825	828	96	—	122	613	818	42	188	204	154	746	489	164	1033	339	285	67	206	277	223
Mary Wash.	588	100	487	485	485	103	210	801	825	828	120	122	—	621	803	88	84	154	85	786	375	94	1098	433	543	206	277	609	255
Mercer Univ.	84	728	267	210	282	609	431	103	161	197	536	613	621	—	361	591	716	689	882	159	93	722	623	292	171	543	206	98	255
Orlando	426	892	384	380	266	822	649	181	253	254	721	818	803	361	—	762	888	861	950	114	255	892	242	504	215	731	287	753	223
Randolph Macon	548	139	446	445	445	62	170	828	785	787	83	42	88	591	762	—	127	101	197	690	363	133	977	392	279	158	165	622	294
St. John's Coll.	673	30	572	570	543	188	295	945	910	913	215	188	84	716	888	127	—	85	85	816	515	29	1103	518	649	150	76	748	232
St. Mary's Coll.	647	108	545	543	543	161	253	886	884	886	188	204	154	689	861	101	85	—	154	789	166	103	1076	491	786	145	165	721	283
Univ. Delaware	796	58	626	640	667	253	351	980	972	953	285	154	85	882	950	197	85	154	—	882	673	67	1157	565	882	218	433	791	262
Univ. Florida	333	824	317	253	268	755	582	210	158	188	721	746	786	159	114	690	816	789	882	—	345	821	363	153	166	575	218	755	973
Univ. Georgia	66	615	275	85	279	548	375	405	287	285	254	489	375	93	255	363	515	166	673	345	—	633	717	166	204	515	76	98	639
U. Maryland-B.C.	678	0	577	576	580	193	300	887	916	953	197	164	94	722	892	133	29	103	67	821	633	—	633	501	623	153	165	822	973
Univ. Miami	688	1099	595	595	601	1035	862	278	522	518	913	1033	1098	623	242	977	1103	1076	1157	363	717	633	—	802	648	575	548	829	1253
UNC-Ashville	211	507	270	271	204	497	224	480	412	412	221	339	433	292	504	392	518	491	565	153	166	501	802	—	162	351	143	379	206
Univ. So. Carolina	215	517	114	268	171	565	275	717	886	913	83	285	543	171	215	279	649	786	882	166	204	623	648	162	—	367	146	285	408
Univ. Virginia	575	160	499	540	565	131	173	994	884	980	158	67	206	543	731	158	150	145	218	575	515	153	575	351	367	—	190	618	190
Wake Forest Univ.	350	375	264	286	285	257	84	206	158	158	215	206	277	206	287	165	76	165	433	218	76	165	548	143	146	190	—	392	355
Wesleyan Coll.	78	733	272	271	204	615	454	532	279	279	188	277	609	98	753	622	748	721	791	755	98	822	829	379	285	618	392	—	693
West Virginia Univ.	654	204	620	587	321	321	391	381	887	886	285	223	255	255	223	294	232	283	262	973	639	973	1253	206	408	190	355	693	—

South and Southwest

South and Southwest	Baylor Univ.	El Paso	Little Rock	LSU	New Orleans	Oklahoma City	Rice Univ.	SMU	TCU	Texas A&M	Trinity Univ.	Univ. Dallas	Univ. New Orleans	Univ. Texas-Austin
Baylor Univ.	—	679	409	460	540	274	245	102	91	89	186	103	531	100
El Paso	679	—	935	1014	1095	676	742	617	595	680	564	632	1099	575
Little Rock	409	935	—	337	417	344	434	316	344	446	583	330	534	520
LSU	460	1014	337	—	80	614	272	437	465	365	471	453	84	458
New Orleans	540	1095	417	80	—	694	352	517	545	444	547	532	0	538
Oklahoma City	274	676	344	614	694	—	461	209	190	373	477	199	727	382
Rice Univ.	245	742	434	272	352	461	—	253	282	94	196	249	364	186
SMU	102	617	316	437	517	209	253	—	35	173	282	14	527	195
TCU	91	595	344	465	545	190	282	35	—	173	273	32	559	192
Texas A&M	89	680	446	365	444	373	94	173	173	—	167	189	446	104
Trinity Univ.	186	564	583	471	547	477	196	282	273	167	—	282	546	79
Univ. Dallas	103	632	330	453	532	199	249	14	32	189	282	—	534	203
Univ. New Orleans	531	1099	534	84	0	727	364	527	559	446	546	534	—	513
Univ. Texas-Austin	100	575	520	458	538	382	186	195	192	104	79	203	513	—

Mountain

Mountain	Albertson Coll.	Albuquerque	Arizona State Univ.	BYU	Casper	Colorado Coll.	Helena	Las Vegas	Pocatello	U. of Ariz.-Tucson	U. of Colo.-Boulder	U. of Colo.-Denver
Albertson Coll.	—	981	1080	405	733	922	574	781	261	1184	846	853
Albuquerque	981	—	462	559	719	367	1213	586	703	473	463	437
Arizona State Univ.	1080	462	—	604	1017	747	1127	291	808	103	843	817
BYU	405	559	604	—	447	563	523	374	204	717	524	534
Casper	733	719	1017	447	—	351	503	821	424	1070	280	281
Colorado Coll.	922	367	747	563	351	—	854	809	634	819	96	70
Helena	574	1213	1127	523	503	854	—	895	319	1240	779	780
Las Vegas	781	586	291	374	821	809	895	—	578	404	784	758
Pocatello	261	706	808	204	424	634	319	578	—	921	563	564
U. of Ariz.-Tucson	1184	473	103	717	1070	819	1240	404	921	—	873	847
U. of Colo.-Boulder	846	463	843	524	280	96	779	784	563	873	—	26
U. of Colo.-Denver	853	437	817	534	281	70	780	758	564	847	26	—

Pacific and Northwest

	Evergreen State U.	Gonzaga Univ.	Los Angeles	Portland	St. Mary's Coll.	San Diego	San Francisco	Seattle Univ.	Spokane	U. Cal–Davis	U. Cal–Santa Cruz	Univ. Redlands	Univ. Washington	Washington State	Willamette Univ.
Evergreen State U.	—	328	1094	124	743	1218	763	67	320	711	838	1164	59	335	171
Gonzaga Univ.	328	—	1320	354	981	1438	990	281	0	927	1050	1377	283	78	402
Los Angeles	1094	1320	—	968	372	124	387	1137	1205	365	356	69	1134	1318	921
Portland	124	354	968	—	628	1086	637	173	351	584	712	1038	174	352	45
St. Mary's Coll.	743	981	372	628	—	491	21	800	980	64	80	435	804	980	582
San Diego	1218	1438	124	1086	491	—	514	1256	1297	611	484	117	1258	1437	1039
San Francisco	763	990	387	637	21	514	—	807	879	67	75	466	810	988	590
Seattle Univ.	67	281	1137	173	800	1256	807	—	279	745	868	1201	4	288	220
Spokane	320	0	1205	351	980	1297	879	279	—	827	986	1274	280	76	396
U. Cal–Davis	711	927	365	584	64	611	67	745	827	—	135	470	780	925	539
U. Cal–Santa Cruz	838	1050	356	712	80	484	75	868	986	135	—	425	920	1049	699
Univ. Redlands	1164	1377	69	1038	435	117	466	1201	1274	470	425	—	1203	1381	993
Univ. Washington	59	283	1134	174	804	1258	810	4	280	780	920	1203	—	290	219
Washington State	335	78	1318	352	980	1437	988	288	76	925	1049	1381	290	—	400
Willamette Univ.	171	402	921	45	582	1039	590	220	396	539	699	993	219	400	—

APPENDIX TWO

College Calendars

School	January	February	March	April	May	June
Alabama **Auburn University**	Winter session begins 2nd wk. No classes MLK Day.	Classes continue.	Exams 2nd–3rd wks.	Spring break 1st wk.	Exams 2nd wk. Summer session begins 3rd wk.	Classes continue.
Tuskegee University	Spring session begins 3rd wk.	Classes continue.	Spring break 2nd wk. Classes resume 3rd wk.	No classes Good Fri. through Easter Mon.	Exams 2nd wk.	Summer session begins 2nd wk.
University of Alabama— Tuscaloosa	Spring session begins 1st wk.	Classes continue.	Spring break 4th wk. Exams 3rd wk.	Classes resume 1st wk.	Exams 1st wk. Interim session begins 3rd wk.	Interim session ends 1st wk. Summer session begins 2nd wk.
Arizona **Arizona State University**	Spring session begins 3rd wk. No classes MLK Day.	Classes continue.	Spring break 3rd wk. Classes resume 4th wk.	Classes continue.	Exams 1st–2nd wks.	Summer session begins 1st wk.
University of Arizona	Spring session begins 3rd wk. No classes MLK Day.	Classes continue.	Spring break 3rd wk. Classes resume 4th wk.	Classes continue.	Exams 1st–2nd wks.	Summer session begins 1st wk.
Arkansas **University of Arkansas— Fayetteville**	Spring session begins 2nd wk. No classes MLK Day.	Classes continue.	Spring break 3rd wk.	Classes end 4th wk.	Final exams 1st wk. Sum sess. I 3rd wk. No classes Memorial Day. Summer sess. III 3rd wk.	Sum sess. I ends 3rd wk. II begins 4th wk. IV begins 1st wk. and V begins 1st wk.
California **California Institute of Technology**	Winter session begins 2nd wk.	Classes continue.	Exams 3rd wk. Spring break 4th wk.	Spring session begins 1st wk.	Classes continue.	Exams 2nd wk.
Claremont McKenna College	Spring session begins 3rd or 4th wk.	Classes continue.	Spring break 3rd wk.	Classes continue.	Final Exams 2nd wk.	No classes.
Harvey Mudd College	Spring session begins 3rd wk.	Classes continue.	Spring break 3rd wk. Classes resume 4th wk.	Classes continue.	Exams 2nd or 3rd wk.	No classes.
Mills College ✓	Spring session begins 3rd wk.	Classes continue.	Spring break 4th wk.	Classes resume 1st wk.	Exams 2nd–3rd wks.	No classes.
Occidental College	First day of classes 4th wk.	Classes continue.	Exams 2nd wk. Spring break 3rd wk. Spring session begins 4th wk.	Classes continue.	Exams 2nd wk.	Exams 1st wk. Summer session begins 3rd wk.

July	August	September	October	November	December	Additional Info
No classes July 4.	Summer session ends 1st wk. Fall session begins 3rd wk.	Labor Day holiday.	Classes continue.	Break from Wed. before Thanksgiving through following Sun.	Exams 2nd wk.	*Campus visits are not discouraged during exam periods, but visiting on a normal class day is recommended.*
No classes July 4. Summer session ends last wk.	No classes.	No classes Labor Day. Classes begin 2nd wk.	Classes continue.	Break from Wed. before Thanksgiving Day through the following Sun.	Exams 1st–2nd wks.	*Campus visits are not discouraged during exam periods.*
No classes July 4.	Summer session ends 2nd wk.	Fall session begins 2nd wk.	Classes continue.	Break from Wed. before Thanksgiving Day.	N/A	*Campus visits are not discouraged during exam periods.*
No classes July 4.	Summer session ends 1st wk. Fall sessions begins 3rd or 4th wk.	No classes Labor Day.	Classes continue.	Break from Thanksgiving Day through following Sun. Veterans' Day observed.	Exams 2nd–3rd wks.	*N/A*
No classes July 4.	Summer session ends 1st wk. Fall session begins 3rd wk.	No classes Labor Day.	Classes continue.	Break from Thanksgiving Day through the following Sun. No classes Veterans' Day.	Exams 2nd–3rd wks.	*Residence halls unavailable during exam periods.*
No classes July 4. Sum sess. ends 1st wk. VI ends first wk.	Summer II ends 1st wk. III ends 1st wk. IV ends 1st wk. V ends 1st wk. and VI ends 1st wk. Fall begins 4th wk.	Labor Day Holiday.	N/A	N/A	N/A	*N/A*
No classes.	No classes.	Fall session begins 4th wk.	Classes continue.	Break from Thanksgiving Day through following Sun.	Exams 2nd wk.	*Approximately 200 students are on campus conducting research during the summer.*
No classes.	No classes.	Fall session begins 1st wk.	Fall break 3rd wk.	Break from Thanksgiving Day through following Sun.	Exams 3rd wk.	*60 students are on campus during the summer. Interviews, group info. sessions, and student–led campus tours available.*
No classes.	Fall session begins 4th wk.	Labor Day holiday.	No classes the 3rd Mon. and Tues.	Break from Thanksgiving Day through following Sun.	Exams 3rd wk.	*Approximately 80 students are on campus during the summer.*
No classes.	Fall session begins last wk.	Labor Day holiday.	Break mid–month.	Break from Fri. before Thanksgiving Day through Sun. following Thanksgiving.	Exams 2nd wk.	*N/A*
No classes July 4.	Fall session begins 4th wk.	Labor Day holiday.	Fall break 2nd wk.	Break from Wed. before Thanksgiving Day through the following Sun.	Exams 2nd wk.	*About 100 students are on campus in the summer. Visits are not discouraged during exams, but tour/class visits are unavailable.*

School	January	February	March	April	May	June
PEPPERDINE UNIVERSITY	Winter session begins 2nd wk.	Classes continue.	No classes 2nd Fri.	Exams 2nd–3rd wks. Spring break 4th wk. Summer session starts 4th wk. or 1st wk. in May.	Summer session begins 1st wk. No classes Memorial Day.	Classes continue.
PITZER COLLEGE	Spring session begins 3rd wk.	Classes continue.	Spring break 3rd wk.	Classes continue.	Exams 2nd wk.	No classes.
POMONA COLLEGE	Spring session begins 3rd or 4th wk.	Classes continue.	Spring break 3rd or 4th wk.	Classes continue.	Exams 2nd–3rd wks.	No classes.
SAINT MARY'S COLLEGE OF CALIFORNIA	Jan. term begins 2nd wk. Open House 2nd or 3rd weekend. No classes MLK Day.	Classes continue.	Midterm exams 4th wk.	Easter recess begins Mon. before Easter. Classes resume Tues. after Easter.	Final exams 3rd wk. Limited tours finals wk. Commencement is Sat. after final exams.	No classes
SANTA CLARA UNIVERSITY ✓	Winter session begins 1st wk. No classes MLK Day.	Classes continue.	Exams 3rd wk.	Spring session begins 1st wk.	Classes continue.	Exams 2nd wk. Summer session begins 4th wk.
SCRIPPS COLLEGE	Spring session begins 4th wk.	Classes continue.	Spring break 4th wk.	Classes resume 1st wk.	Exams 2nd–3rd wks.	Science course offerings.
STANFORD UNIVERSITY ✓	Winter session begins 2nd wk. No classes MLK Day.	Classes continue.	Exams 3rd wk. Spring session begins last wk.	Classes continue.	Classes continue.	Exams 1st–2nd wks. Summer session begins 4th wk.
UNIVERSITY OF CALIFORNIA— BERKELEY ✓	Spring session begins 3rd or 4th wk. No classes MLK Day.	Classes continue.	Spring break near end of month. Classes resume after 1 wk. break.	Classes continue.	Exams 2nd–3rd wks. First summer session begins last wk.	Summer session options begin 3rd and 4th wks.
UNIVERSITY OF CALIFORNIA— DAVIS	Winter session begins 1st wk. No classes MLK Day.	Classes continue.	Exams 3rd wk. Spring break 4th wk. Spring session begins 5th wk.	Classes continue.	Classes continue.	Exams 2nd wk. Summer session begins 3rd wk.
UNIVERSITY OF CALIFORNIA— IRVINE	Winter session begins 1st wk. No classes MLK Day.	Classes continue.	Exams mid–month.	Spring session begins 1st wk.	Classes continue.	Exams 2nd wk. First summer session begins 4th wk.
UNIVERSITY OF CALIFORNIA— LOS ANGELES	Winter session begins 2nd wk. No classes MLK Day.	Classes continue.	Exams 3rd wk. Spring break 4th wk.	Spring session begins 1st wk.	Classes continue.	Exams 2nd wk. Summer session begins 4th wk.

July	August	September	October	November	December	Additional Info
No classes July 4. Summer session ends last wk. or 1st wk. in Aug.	Summer session ends 1st wk. Fall session begins last wk.	Classes continue.	Classes continue.	Break from Thanksgiving through the following Sun.	Exams 1st–2nd wks.	*Campus visits during exam periods are not discouraged.*
No classes.	No classes.	Fall session begins 1st wk.	Fall break from 3rd Sat. through the following Tues.	Break from Thanksgiving Day through the following Sun.	Exams 3rd wk.	*Approximately 25 students are on campus during the summer.*
No classes.	No classes.	Fall session begins 1st wk.	Fall break from 3rd Fri. through the following Tues.	Break from Wed. before Thanksgiving Day through the following Sun.	Exams 3rd wk.	*Very few students are on campus during the summer.*
No classes	No classes	Fall term begins wk. before Labor Day. No tours during 1st wk. of classes.	Fall Preview Day 2nd weekend. Midterm exams 3rd wk. No classes Fri. of midterm wk.	Thanksgiving recess Thurs.–Sun.	Final exams 2nd wk. Ltd. tours during finals wk. Xmas recess Sat. after finals wk. thru Sun. after New Year's Day	*N/A*
No classes July 4.	Summer session ends 1st wk.	Fall session begins 4th wk.	Classes continue.	Break from Wed. before Thanksgiving through the following Sun.	Exams 2nd wk.	*N/A*
Science course offerings.	No classes.	Fall session begins 1st wk.	Fall break from the 3rd Fri. through the following Tues.	Break from Wed. before Thanksgiving Day through the following Sun.	Exams 3rd wk.	*A very small number of students are on campus from June 1–Aug. 20.*
Classes continue.	Summer session ends 2nd wk.	Fall session begins 4th wk.	Classes continue.	Break from Thanksgiving Day through the following Sun.	Exams 2nd wk.	*N/A*
Summer session options begin 1st and last wks.	Summer session ends 3rd wk. Fall session begins last wk.	No classes Labor Day.	Classes continue.	Break from Thanksgiving Day through the following Sun. Veterans' Day holiday.	Exams 2nd–3rd wks.	*Campus visits are not discouraged during the fall exam period, but tours are limited at that time.*
No classes 4th wk.	Classes continue.	Summer session ends 2nd wk. Fall session begins 4th wk.	Classes continue.	Break from Thanksgiving Day through the following Sun.	Exams 2nd wk.	*Campus visits are not discouraged during exam periods.*
No classes July 4. First summer session ends at end of month.	Second summer session begins 1st full wk.	No classes Labor Day. Second summer ends 3rd wk.	Classes continue.	Break from Thanksgiving Day through the following Sun.	Exams 2nd wk.	*During the summer, fewer students are on campus, and most of them are students from other universities.*
No classes July 4.	Classes continue.	Summer session ends 2nd wk. Fall session begins last wk.	Classes continue.	Break from Thanksgiving Day through the following Sun.	Exams 2nd wk.	*Campus visits are not discouraged during exam periods, but tours are limited at that time.*

School	January	February	March	April	May	June
UNIVERSITY OF CALIFORNIA—RIVERSIDE	Winter session begins 1st wk. No classes MLK Day.	Classes continue.	Exams 3rd wk. Spring break 4th wk. Spring session begins at end of 4th wk.	Classes continue.	Classes continue.	Exams 2nd wk. Summer session begins 4th wk.
UNIVERSITY OF CALIFORNIA—SAN DIEGO	Winter session begins 1st wk. No classes MLK Day.	Classes continue.	Exams 3rd wk. Spring session begins last wk.	Classes continue.	No classes Memorial Day.	Exams 2nd wk. Summer session begins last wk.
UNIVERSITY OF CALIFORNIA—SANTA BARBARA	Winter session begins 2nd wk. No classes MLK Day.	Classes continue.	Exams 2nd–3rd wk.	Spring session begins 1st wk.	No classes Memorial Day.	Exams 1st–2nd wks. Commencement 2nd or 3rd weekend. Summer session begins 4th wk.
UNIVERSITY OF CALIFORNIA—SANTA CRUZ ✔	Winter session begins 2nd wk. No classes MLK Day (Jan. 17).	Classes continue.	Exams 3rd wk. Spring session begins 5th wk.	Classes continue.	No classes Memorial Day.	Exams 2nd wk. Summer session begins 4th wk.
UNIVERSITY OF REDLANDS	Spring session begins 2nd wk.	Classes continue.	Spring break 1st wk. Classes resume 2nd wk.	Exams 3rd wk.	May term begins 1st wk. and ends last wk.	No classes.
UNIVERSITY OF SAN DIEGO	Winter session: 2nd wk.–4th wk. Spring session end of month. No classes MLK holiday.	Classes continue.	Spring break sometime this month.	Classes continue.	Exams 3rd wk.	Summer session begins 1st wk.
UNIVERSITY OF SAN FRANCISCO ✔	Winter session begins 1st wk. and ends 3rd wk. Spring session begins last wk.	Classes continue.	Spring break 3rd wk.	No classes Holy Thurs., Good Fri., and Easter Mon.	Exams 3rd–4th wks. Summer session begins last wk. No classes Memorial Day.	Classes continue.
UNIVERSITY OF SOUTHERN CALIFORNIA	Spring session begins 2nd wk. No classes MLK Day.	Classes continue.	Spring break 3rd wk.	Classes resume 2nd wk. Exams last wk.–1st wk. in May.	Exams 1st wk. Summer session begins 2nd wk. No classes Memorial Day.	Classes continue.
UNIVERSITY OF THE PACIFIC	Spring session begins 3rd wk.	Classes continue.	Spring break mid–month.	No classes day after Easter.	Exams 2nd wk. Summer session begins 3rd wk. No classes Memorial Day.	Classes continue.
WHITTIER COLLEGE	Winter session begins 2nd wk. and ends at end of 4th wk.	Classes continue.	Spring break last wk.	Classes resume 1st wk.	Exams mid–month.	Limited summer term begins.
Colorado — **COLORADO COLLEGE** ✔	Spring session (5th block of academic year) begins mid–month.	Classes continue.	Spring break 1st wk. Seventh block begins 2nd wk.	Block ends 2nd wk. Eighth block begins 3rd wk.	Block ends 2nd wk.	Block A begins 2nd wk.

July	August	September	October	November	December	Additional Info
No classes July 4.	Summer session ends 1st wk.	Fall session begins 4th wk.	Classes continue.	Break from Thanksgiving Day through the following Sun.	Exams 1st or 2nd wk.	*Campus visits are not discouraged during exam periods, but tours are limited during that time.*
No classes July 4.	Classes continue.	Summer session ends 2nd wk. Fall session begins 3rd wk.	Classes continue.	Break from Thanksgiving Day through the following Sun.	Exams 2nd wk.	*Approximately 600 students are on campus during the summer.*
No classes July 4th.	Summer session ends 1st wk.	Fall session begins 3rd wk.	Classes continue.	No classes Veterans' Day. No classes Thanksgiving holiday through the following Sun.	Final exams 1st wk.	*N/A*
No classes July 4.	Summer session ends 5th wk.	Fall session begins 4th wk.	Classes continue.	Break from Thanksgiving Day through the following Sun. No classes Veterans' Day.	Exams 2nd wk. Campus closed Dec 24–Jan. 1.	*Few students are on campus during the summer.*
No classes.	No classes.	Fall session begins 2nd wk.	Fall break 2nd wk.	Break from Wed. before Thanksgiving Day through the following Sun.	Exams 3rd wk.	*During exam periods, interviews are available, but campus tours are not.*
No classes July 4.	Summer session ends 3rd wk.	Fall session begins 2nd wk.	No classes 4th Fri.	Break from Thanksgiving Day through the following Sun.	Exams 3rd wk.	*Campus visits are not discouraged during exams. Spring break varies from year to year.*
No classes July 4.	Summer session ends 1st wk.	Fall session begins 1st wk.	No classes third Fri.	Break from Thanksgiving Day through the following Sun.	Exams 3rd wk.	*For more information: www.usfca.edu*
No classes July 4.	Summer session ends 2nd wk. Fall session begins last wk.	No classes Labor Day.	Classes continue.	Break from Thanksgiving Day through the following Sun.	Exams 2nd–3rd wks.	*The summer population includes more international students and conference attendees.*
No classes July 4.	Fall semester begins last wk.	No classes Labor Day.	Classes continue.	Break from Thanksgiving Day through the following Sun.	Exams 2nd wk.	*Individual visits available throughout year. Call for appointment.*
Limited summer term.	Limited summer through Aug.	Classes begin 1st wk.	Break from 3rd Fri. through the following Sun.	Break from Thanksgiving Day through the following Sun.	Exams 2nd wk.	*Fewer than 50 students are on campus during the summer.*
Block B begins 1st wk. Block C begins 3rd wk.	Block C ends 3rd wk.	Fall session (1st block of academic year) begins 1st wk. and ends last wk.	Second block begins 1st wk. and ends 4th wk.	Third block begins 1st wk. and ends by Thanksgiving Day, then off until Sun.	Fourth block begins 1st wk. and ends 4th wk. (before Xmas).	*Year is divided into 8 3-1/2 wk. blocks with 4-1/2 day breaks in between. Exams held last 3 days of each block.*

School	January	February	March	April	May	June
COLORADO SCHOOL OF MINES ✔	Spring session begins 1st wk.	Classes continue.	Spring break 2nd wk. Classes resume 3rd wk.	Classes continue.	Exams 1st wk.	Summer session begins last wk.
UNIVERSITY OF COLORADO—BOULDER ✔	Spring session begins 2nd wk. No classes MLK Day.	Classes continue.	Spring break last full wk.	Classes continue.	Exams 1st wk. Summer session begins 2nd wk.	Classes continue.
UNIVERSITY OF COLORADO—DENVER	Spring session begins 3rd wk. No classes MLK Day.	Classes continue.	Spring break 3rd wk. Classes resume 4th wk.	Classes continue.	Exams 2nd wk. No classes Memorial Day.	Summer session begins first wk.
Connecticut						
CONNECTICUT COLLEGE ✔	Spring session begins 3rd or 4th wk.	Classes continue.	Spring break 3rd & 4th wks.	Classes resume 1st wk.	Exams 2nd–3rd wks.	No classes.
FAIRFIELD UNIVERSITY	Spring session begins 3rd wk. No classes MLK Day.	Classes continue.	Spring break 2nd wk. Break from Thurs. before Easter through Easter Mon.	Break from Thurs. before Easter through the following Mon.	Exams 1st–2nd wks. Summer session begins last wk.	Summer session continues.
TRINITY COLLEGE (CT) ✔	Spring session begins 3rd wk.	Classes continue.	Spring break 3rd wk.	Classes continue.	Exams 1st–2nd wks.	No classes.
UNIVERSITY OF BRIDGEPORT	Spring session begins 4th wk.	Classes continue.	Spring break 3rd wk. Classes resume 3rd wk.	Exams last wk.– 2nd wk. in May.	Exams 2nd wk. First summer session begins 4th wk. No classes Memorial Day.	First summer session ends last wk.
UNIVERSITY OF CONNECTICUT ✔	Spring session begins 4th wk.	Classes continue.	Spring break 3rd wk. Classes resume 4th wk.	Classes continue.	Exams 1st–2nd wks. First summer session begins 3rd wk. No classes Memorial Day.	First summer session ends last wk.
UNIVERSITY OF HARTFORD	Spring session begins 4th wk.	Classes continue.	Spring break 3rd wk.	Classes continue.	Exams 2nd wk. Summer session begins 3rd wk.	Classes continue.
WESLEYAN UNIVERSITY ✔	Spring session begins 3rd wk.	Classes continue.	Spring break 2nd and 3rd wks. Classes resume 4th wk.	Classes continue.	Exams 3rd wk.	No classes.
YALE UNIVERSITY ✔	Spring session begins 2nd or 3rd wk.	Classes continue.	Spring break from end of 1st wk. to beginning of 3rd wk.	Classes continue.	Reading period and exams 1st–2nd wks.	No classes.

July	August	September	October	November	December	Additional Info
No classes July 4.	Summer session ends 1st wk. Fall session begins 3rd wk.	Classes continue.	Classes continue.	Break from Thanksgiving Day through following Sun.	Exams 3rd wk.	*N/A*
No classes July 4.	Summer session ends 1st wk. Fall session begins last full wk.	Classes continue. Break from last Thurs. through following Sun.	Classes continue.	Break from Thanksgiving Day through the following Sun.	Exams 2nd–3rd wks.	*Campus visits are not discouraged during exams, but tour guides may be hard to find at these times.*
No classes July 4.	Summer session ends first wk. Fall session begins 4th wk.	No classes Labor Day.	Classes continue.	Break for Thanksgiving Day.	Exams 2nd wk.	*This is the only public university in capital city.*
No classes.	Fall session begins last wk.	Classes continue.	Fall break from 1st Thurs. through following Tues.	Break from Tues. before Thanksgiving Day through the following Sun.	Exams 3rd wk.	*N/A*
No classes July 4.	Summer session ends mid-month.	Fall session begins 1st wk. No classes Labor Day.	Four-day Fall Break. No classes Columbus Day.	Break from Wed. before Thanksgiving Day through the following Sun.	Exams 2nd–3rd wks.	*Campus visits are discouraged during exams.*
No classes.	Fall session begins last wk.	Classes continue.	Fall break from Sat. before Columbus Day through Sun. after Columbus Day.	Break from Thanksgiving Day through the following Sun.	Exams 3rd wk.	*Campus visits are discouraged during exam periods unless there is no alternative time.*
Second summer session begins 1st wk. No classes July 4.	Second summer session ends 1st wk.	Fall session begins 1st wk.	Fall Break Sat. before Columbus Day through Tues. after.	Break from Thanksgiving Day through the following Sun.	Exams 3rd wk.	*During exam periods, no campus tours are offered, but interviews are available.*
Second summer session begins 1st wk. No classes July 4.	Second summer session ends 1st wk. Fall session begins last wk.	Classes continue. No classes Labor Day.	Classes continue.	Break wk. of Thanksgiving.	Exams 2nd–3rd wks.	*N/A*
Classes continue.	Summer session ends 2nd wk.	Fall session begins 1st wk.	Classes continue.	Break from Tues. before Thanksgiving Day through the following Sun.	Exams 2nd–3rd wks.	*Campus visits are not discouraged during exams, but tours are limited.*
No classes.	No classes.	Fall session begins 1st wk.	Fall break 2nd Wed. to following Mon.	Break from Wed. before Thanksgiving Day through Sun.	Exams 3rd wk.	*About 200 people are on campus during the summer; they are involved in a variety of on-campus programs.*
No classes.	No classes.	Fall session begins 1st wk.	Classes continue.	Break from Sat. before Thanksgiving Day through the following Sun.	Reading period and exams 2nd–3rd wks.	*N/A*

School	January	February	March	April	May	June
Delaware						
UNIVERSITY OF DELAWARE ✓	Winter session begins 1st wk. No classes MLK Day.	Classes continue.	Spring break last wk.	Classes resume 1st wk.	No classes Memorial Day. Exams last wk.	Summer session begins 2nd wk.
Dist. of Columbia						
AMERICAN UNIVERSITY	Spring Welcome Wk. 2nd wk. Spring sessions begins 3rd wk. No classes MLK Day.	Classes continue.	Spring break 2nd wk. Classes resume 3rd wk.	Study days 4th wk. Exams from end of month–1st wk. of May.	Exams continue 1st wk. Commencement 2nd wk. No classes Memorial Day.	First summer session continues. New undergrad orientations 4th wk.
CATHOLIC UNIVERSITY OF AMERICA	Spring session begins 2nd wk. No classes MLK Day.	Classes continue.	Spring break 1st wk. Classes resume 2nd wk.	Break from Thurs. before Easter through the following Mon. Exams last wk.– 1st wk. in May.	Exams 1st wk.	No classes.
GEORGE WASHINGTON UNIVERSITY ✓	Spring session begins 3rd wk. No classes MLK Day.	No classes Presidents' Day.	Spring break 3rd wk.	Exams from end of month–1st wk. of May.	Exams 2nd wk. No classes Memorial Day.	Classes continue.
GEORGETOWN UNIVERSITY ✓	Mini term ends Jan. 9; Spring term begins Jan. 12; MLK Holiday (no classes) Jan. 19	Classes continue.	Spring break Mar. 12–22	Good Fri. (no classes) April 9; Last day of classes Apr. 28; Finals begin Apr. 30.	Finals end May 5; Graduation May 8; Mini–term May 10–21; Sum sess 1 begins May 27.	Summer session 1 continues
HOWARD UNIVERSITY	Spring session begins 2nd wk. No classes MLK Day.	No classes Presidents' Day.	Spring break 3rd wk. Classes resume 4th wk.	Reading period last wk.	Exams 1st–2nd wks. Summer session begins 3rd wk. No classes Memorial Day.	Classes continue.
Florida						
ECKERD COLLEGE ✓	Winter session begins 1st wk. and ends last wk.	Spring session begins 1st wk.	Spring break 4th wk.	Classes resume 1st wk.	Exams 3rd wk.	Summer session begins 1st wk.
FLORIDA A&M UNIVERSITY	Spring session begins 2nd wk. No classes MLK Day.	Classes continue.	Spring break 2nd wk. Classes resume 3rd wk.	Exams last wk.	Summer sessions A & C begin 2nd wk. No classes Memorial Day.	Summer session A ends 3rd wk. Summer session B begins last wk.
FLORIDA INSTITUTE OF TECHNOLOGY ✓	Spring term begins 1st full wk.	Mid term exams. Registration for summer term opens first wk.	Spring break 1st full wk. Registration for fall class opens last wk.	Final exams last wk. of the month.	Spring Commencement 1st Sat. Summer classes begin 2nd wk.	Classes continue.
FLORIDA INTERNATIONAL UNIVERSITY	Spring session begins 1st wk. No classes MLK Day.	Classes continue.	Spring break 4th wk. Classes resume 5th wk.	Exams 2nd wk. Classes end 3rd wk.	Summers A and C start 2nd wk. No classes Memorial Day.	Super Summer B starts 3rd wk. Summer A ends 3rd wk.
FLORIDA SOUTHERN COLLEGE ✓	Spring session begins 2nd or 3rd wk.	Classes continue.	Spring break 1st or 2nd wk. Classes resume 2nd or 3rd wk.	Exams 4th wk.	No classes. Optional May term offers classes all month in England.	Summer session begins 1st or 2nd wk.

July	August	September	October	November	December	Additional Info
No classes July 4.	Summer session ends 2nd wk.	Fall session begins 1st wk. No classes Labor Day.	Classes continue.	No classes Election Day. Break from Wed. before Thanksgiving through following Sun.	Exams 2nd wk.	N/A
Second summer session begins 1st wk. New undergrad orientations 1st and 2nd wks.	Second summer session ends 1st wk. Fall Welcome Wk. 3rd wk. Fall session begins 4th wk.	No classes Labor Day.	Fall break Mon. and Tues. of 2nd wk.	Thanksgiving break Wed. before holiday through Sun.	Study days 2nd wk. Exams 2nd–3rd wk.	Campus visits are generally available except on national holidays and Sundays.
No classes.	Fall session begins last wk.	No classes Labor Day.	No classes Columbus Day.	Break from Thanksgiving Day through the following Sun.	Exams 2nd wk.	N/A
No classes July 4.	Summer session ends 2nd wk. Fall session begins last wk.	No classes Labor Day.	No classes Columbus Day.	Break from Wed. before Thanksgiving Day through the following Sun.	Exams 3rd wk.	N/A
Summer session 1 ends July 1; Summer session 2 starts July 6	Summer session 2 ends Aug. 9; New Student Orientation 3rd wk.	Labor Day (no classes)	Fall break 2nd wk.	Thanksgiving break, Wed. before Thanksgiving through Sun.	Last day of classes 2nd wk.; Finals 3rd wk.; Mini term starts 5th wk.	N/A
No classes July 4.	Summer session ends 1st wk. Fall session begins last wk.	No classes Labor Day.	No classes Columbus Day.	Break from Thanksgiving Day through the following Sun.	Reading period 1st wk. Exams 2nd–3rd wks.	N/A
Summer session ends last wk.	Freshman orientation term begins 2nd wk.	Fall session begins 1st wk.	Classes continue. Fall Break is Mon. and Tues. of 3rd wk.	Break from Thanksgiving Day through the following Sun.	Exams 2nd wk.	N/A
No classes July 4.	Summer sessions B & C end first wk. Fall session begins last wk.	No classes Labor Day.	Classes continue.	No classes Veterans' Day. Break from Thanksgiving Day through following Sun.	Exams 2nd wk.	Campus tours are not scheduled during exam periods.
Last day of summer terms (lengths vary).	Fall term begins last full wk.	Classes continue.	Midterm exams. Fall break weekend mid–month.	Thanksgiving break (Wed.–Sun.)	Final exams 2nd wk. Fall Commencement Sat. after finals.	Campus visits are encouraged at most times of the year. Find more information at www.fit.edu/ugrad/visit.htm.
Classes continue. No classes July 4.	Summer sessions B and C end 2nd wk. Fall session begins last wk.	No classes Labor Day.	Classes continue. Midterms mid–month.	No classes Veterans' Day. No classes Thanksgiving holiday through the following Sun.	Exams 2nd wk. Classes end 1st wk.	The campus is very active during summer. Visits are not discouraged during exams, but regular visits are preferred.
Summer session ends last wk.	No classes.	Fall session begins 1st wk.	Fall Break Fri. to Tues. of 3rd wk.	Break from Wed. before Thanksgiving Day through following Sun.	Exams 2nd or 3rd wk.	N/A

School	January	February	March	April	May	June
Florida State University	Spring session begins 2nd wk. No classes MLK Day.	Classes continue.	Spring break 4th wk.	Classes resume 1st wk. Exams 4th wk.	Summer session begins 2nd wk. No classes Memorial Day.	Classes continue.
New College of Florida ✔	Independent Study Period begins first wk. Offices closed for MLK Day.	Spring classes begin first wk. New College Weekend Feb. 6–8.	Spring break 4th wk.	Classes resume 1st wk.	Classes end 3rd wk. Exams/Advising/Evaluation 4th wk. Commencement 4th wk.	No classes.
Rollins College ✔	Spring session begins 2nd wk. No classes MLK Day. Winter session ends last wk.	Classes continue.	Spring break 3rd wk.	Classes continue.	Exams 1st–2nd wks.	No classes.
Stetson University ✔	Spring session begins 2nd wk. No classes MLK Day.	Classes continue	Spring break 1st wk.	No classes Good Fri.	Exams 1st wk.	Summer session begins 1st wk.
University of Florida	Spring term begins Jan. 6.	Spring term continues.	Spring break begins March 6–13.	Spring term ends April 21.	Summer A and C term begins May 10.	Summer A term ends June 18. Summer B term begins June 28.
University of Miami	Spring session begins 2nd wk. No classes MLK Day.	Classes continue.	Spring break 2nd wk. Classes resume 3rd wk.	Reading period 4th wk. Exams last wk.–1st wk. in May.	Exams 1st wk. Summer session begins 3rd wk. No classes Memorial Day	Classes continue.
University of South Florida	Spring session begins 2nd wk. No classes MLK Day.	Classes continue.	Spring break 1st wk. Classes resume 2nd wk.	Exams 3rd–4th wks.	Summer session begins 1st wk. No classes Memorial Day.	Classes continue.
Georgia **Agnes Scott College**	Spring session begins 3rd wk.	Classes continue.	Spring break 3rd wk. Classes resume 4th wk.	No classes Good Fri.	Reading days and exams 1st wk.	No classes.
Clark Atlanta University	Spring session begins 2nd wk. No classes MLK Day.	Classes continue.	Spring break 2nd wk. Classes resume 3rd wk. No classes Good Fri.	No classes Good Fri.	Exams 2nd wk.	Summer session begins 1st wk.
Emory University	Spring session begins 3rd wk. No classes MLK Day.	Classes continue.	Spring break 2nd wk. Classes resume 3rd wk.	Classes continue to end of month.	Reading period and exams 1st wk. First summer session begins 3rd or 4th wk.	First summer session ends last wk.
Georgia Institute of Technology	Spring session begins 1st wk. No classes on MLK Day.	Classes continue.	Spring break 2nd wk.	Exams 4th wk.	Summer session begins 2nd wk. No classes Memorial Day.	Classes continue.

July	August	September	October	November	December	Additional Info
No classes July 4.	Summer session ends 1st wk. Fall session begins last wk.	No classes Labor Day.	Classes continue.	No classes Veterans' Day. Break from Thanksgiving Day through the following Sun.	Exams 2nd wk.	*Information sessions and tours are available during exam periods, but the campus is very quiet at those times.*
No classes.	New student orientation 3rd wk. Mini–classes (faculty course previews) end of 3rd wk.	Classes continue. Offices closed for Labor Day.	Fall break 2nd wk.	Open House 11/14. Offices closed Veterans' Day and Thanksgiving Thurs./Fri.	Classes end 1st wk. Exams/Advising/Evaluation 2nd wk. Offices closed Xmas break.	*N/A*
No classes.	Fall session begins last wk.	No classes Labor Day.	Classes continue.	Break from Thanksgiving Day through the following Sun.	Exams 2nd–3rd wks.	*Campus visiting is not discouraged during exam periods.*
No classes July 4. Summer session ends at end of month.	Fall session begins last wk.	No classes Labor Day.	Fall break 2nd Mon.–Tues.	Break from Thanksgiving Day through the following Sun.	Exams 2nd wk.	*N/A*
Summer B and C term continues.	Summer B and C term ends Aug. 6. Fall term begins Aug. 23.	Fall term continues.	Fall term continues.	Thanksgiving break begins Nov. 25–26.	Fall term ends Dec. 8.	*N/A*
No classes July 4.	Summer session ends 1st wk. Fall session begins last wk.	No classes Labor Day.	Fall break 3rd Fri.	Break from Wed. before Thanksgiving Day through the following Sun.	Reading period 2nd wk. Exams 2nd–3rd wks.	*N/A*
No classes July 4.	Summer session ends 1st wk. Fall session begins last wk.	Classes continue.	Classes continue.	Break from Thanksgiving Day through the following Sun.	Exams 2nd wk.	*About 15,000 students are on campus during the summer. Visits are not discouraged during exams.*
No classes.	Fall session begins last wk.	No classes Labor Day.	Fall break from Fri. after Columbus Day through following Sun.	Break from Wed. before Thanksgiving Day through following Sun.	Reading period 2nd wk. Exams 2nd–3rd wks.	*N/A*
No classes July 4. Summer session ends 4th wk.	Fall session begins 4th wk.	Classes continue.	Classes continue.	Break from Thanksgiving Day through the following Sun.	Exams 2nd wk.	*N/A*
Second summer session begins 1st wk.	Second summer session ends 1st wk. Fall session begins last wk.	No classes Labor Day.	Fall break from Sat. preceding Columbus Day through following Tues.	Break from Thanksgiving Day through following Sun.	Reading period and exams 2nd–3rd wks.	*N/A*
No classes Independence Day. Exams 5th wk.	Fall session begins 3rd wk.	No classes Labor Day.	Classes continue.	Break Thanksgiving Day through following Sun.	Exams 2nd wk.	*N/A*

School	January	February	March	April	May	June
MERCER UNIVERSITY—MACON	Spring session begins 2nd wk. No classes MLK Day.	Classes continue.	Spring break 2nd wk. No classes Good Fri.	No classes Good Fri. Exams last wk.–1st wk. in May.	Exams 1st wk. Summer session and Summer session 1 begins.	Summer session 1 ends. Summer session 2 begins.
MOREHOUSE COLLEGE	Spring session begins 2nd wk. No classes MLK Day.	Classes continue.	Spring break 2nd wk. Classes resume 3rd wk. No classes Good Fri.	No classes Good Fri.	Exams 1st–2nd wks.	Summer session begins 1st wk.
MORRIS BROWN COLLEGE	Spring session begins 2nd wk. No classes MLK Day.	Classes continue.	Spring break 1st wk. Classes resume 2nd wk. No classes Good Fri.	No classes Good Fri.	Reading period 1st wk. Exams 1st–2nd wks.	No classes.
OGLETHORPE UNIVERSITY	Spring session begins 3rd wk. No classes MLK Day.	Classes continue.	Spring break 3rd wk. Classes resume 4th wk.	Classes continue.	Exams 1st wk. Summer session begins 4th wk. No classes Memorial Day.	Classes continue.
SPELMAN COLLEGE	Spring session begins 2nd wk. No classes MLK Day.	Classes continue.	Spring break 2nd wk. Classes resume 3rd wk. No classes Good Fri.	No classes Good Fri.	Exams 1st or 2nd wk. Graduation 3rd Sun.	No classes.
UNIVERSITY OF GEORGIA	Spring session begins 2nd wk. No classes MLK Day.	Classes continue.	Spring break 2nd wk. Classes resume 3rd wk.	Classes continue.	Exams 2nd wk.	Classes continue.
WESLEYAN COLLEGE	Spring semester begins first Wed. in Jan. No classes MLK Day.	Classes continue	Spring break 2nd wk.	No classes Good Fri.	Exams first wk. May term begins second wk.	May term ends 1st wk. Midsummer Term begins 2nd wk.
Hawaii **UNIVERSITY OF HAWAII—MANOA**	Spring session begins 2nd wk. No classes MLK Day.	Classes continue. No classes Presidents' Day.	Spring break 3rd wk. No classes on State Holidays.	Classes continue.	Exams 2nd wk. First Summer session begins 4th wk.	Classes continue. No classes on State Holiday.
Idaho **ALBERTSON COLLEGE**	Winter Term begins 1st wk.	Wk.–long Winter Recess. Spring Term begins.	Classes continue.	Mid–Semester Recess.	Spring Term ends 4th wk.	No Classes.
IDAHO STATE UNIVERSITY	Spring session begins 2nd wk. No classes MLK Day.	No classes Presidents' Day.	Spring break 2nd wk. Classes resume 3rd wk.	Classes continue.	Exams 2nd wk. Summer session begins 3rd wk.	Classes continue.
UNIVERSITY OF IDAHO	Spring semester begins 2nd wk.; No classes MLK Day	Last day for adds/drops 2nd wk.; new frosh early–warning grades due 2nd wk.	Mid–term exams 2nd wk.; Spring break 3rd wk.	Advising for fall and registration for summer terms 1st wk.; Registration for fall 3rd wk.	Final exams 2nd wk.; Commencement 3rd Sat.; Start of Summer sessions following wk.	Additional Summer sessions begin 2nd wk.

July	August	September	October	November	December	Additional Info
No classes July 4. Summer and Summer session 2 ends.	Fall session begins 3rd wk.	No classes Labor Day.	Fall break.	Break from Wed. before Thanksgiving through following Sun.	Exams 2nd–3rd wks.	*N/A*
No classes July 4. Summer session ends last wk.	Fall session begins last wk.	No classes Labor Day.	Classes continue.	Break from Thanksgiving Day through the following Sun.	Exams 2nd wk.	*N/A*
No classes.	Fall session begins last wk.	No classes Labor Day.	Classes continue.	Break from Thanksgiving Day through the following Sun.	Reading period 1st wk. Exams 2nd wk.	*N/A*
No classes July 4.	Summer session ends 2nd wk. Fall session begins last wk.	Classes continue.	Classes continue.	Break from Wed. before Thanksgiving through the following Sun.	Exams 2nd wk.	*N/A*
No classes.	Fall session begins last wk.	Classes continue.	Classes continue.	Break Thanksgiving Day through following Sun.	Exams 2nd wk.	*N/A*
Classes continue.	Fall session begins 3rd wk.	Classes continue. No classes Labor Day.	Classes continue.	Break Thanksgiving Day through following Sun.	Exams 2nd wk.	*N/A*
No classes July 4.	Midsummer Term ends 1st wk. Fall semester begins third wk.	No classes Labor Day.	Fall break first Mon. and Tues. of month.	Break from Thanksgiving Day through following Sun.	Exams second wk.	*N/A*
First Summer session ends 1st wk. II Summer session begins 2nd wk. No classes July 4.	Second Summer session ends 2nd wk. Fall session begins 4th wk. No classes State Holiday.	Classes continue. No classes Labor Day.	Classes continue.	Break from Thanksgiving Day through the following Sun.	Exams 3rd wk.	*Campus visits Mon–Fri. Make reservations.*
No Classes.	No Classes.	Fall term begins after Labor Day.	Wk.–long Fall Recess.	Recess: Thanksgiving through Sun.	Fall term ends 2nd wk. Break until after New Year.	*Campus visits are encouraged anytime during the year.*
No classes July 4.	Summer session ends 2nd wk. Fall session begins last wk.	Classes continue. No classes Labor Day.	Classes continue.	Break from day before Thanksgiving day through following Sun.	Exams 2nd–3rd wks.	*N/A*
No classes July 4th; Additional Summer sessions begin 2nd wk.	Application deadline for fall Aug. 1; Classes for fall term start 4th wk.	No classes Labor Day; Last day to add courses 1st wk.; Last day to drop courses 3rd wk..	Classes do meet Columbus Day; Mid–term exams 3rd wk.; Advising for spring begins 3rd wk.	On–line registration for spring begins 2nd wk.; Classes do meet Veterans' Day.	Final exams 2nd wk.; Fall Commencement 3rd Sat.; Winter intersession begins 3rd wk.	*UI Undergraduate Catalog is online at www.students.uidaho.edu/registrar*

School	January	February	March	April	May	June
Illinois						
BRADLEY UNIVERSITY	N/A	N/A	N/A	N/A	N/A	N/A
ILLINOIS INSTITUTE OF TECHNOLOGY	Spring session begins 3rd wk. No classes MLK Day.	Classes continue.	Spring break 3rd wk. Classes resume 4th wk.	Classes continue.	Exams 2nd wk.	Summer session begins 1st wk.
KNOX COLLEGE	Spring session begins 3rd wk. No classes MLK Day.	Classes continue.	Spring break 3rd wk. Classes resume 4th wk.	Classes continue.	Exams 3rd wk.	Summer session begins last wk.
LAKE FOREST COLLEGE ✔	Spring session begins 3rd wk.	Classes continue.	Spring break 2nd wk. Classes resume 3rd wk.	Exams last wk.– 1st wk. in May.	Graduation 2nd wk.	Summer session begins 2nd wk.
NORTHWESTERN UNIVERSITY ✔	Winter session begins 1st or 2nd wk.	Classes continue.	Exams 3rd wk. Spring session begins last wk. (or 1st wk. in April).	Spring session begins 1st wk. (or last wk. in March).	Classes continue.	Exams 2nd wk. Summer session begins 3rd or 4th wk.
UNIVERSITY OF CHICAGO ✔	Winter session begins 2nd wk.	No classes 2nd Mon.	Reading period and exams 2nd–3rd wks.	Spring session begins 1st wk.	No classes Memorial Day.	Reading period and exams 1st–2nd wks. Summer session begins last wk.
UNIVERSITY OF ILLINOIS—URBANA–CHAMPAIGN	Spring session begins 3rd wk.	Classes continue.	Spring break mid–month.	Classes continue.	Exams 2nd full wk. Summer session begins 3rd wk.	2nd summer session begins 3rd wk.
WHEATON COLLEGE (IL) ✔	Spring session begins 2nd wk. No classes MLK Day.	No classes Presidents' Day.	Spring break 2nd wk. Classes resume 3rd wk. No classes Good Fri.	Classes continue.	Exams first wk. Summer session begins 3rd wk. No classes Memorial Day.	1st summer session ends 2nd wk. 2nd summer session begins 3rd wk.
Indiana						
DePAUW UNIVERSITY	Winter session begins 2nd wk. and ends last wk.	Spring session begins 1st wk.	Spring break last wk.	Classes resume 1st wk.	Exams 3rd wk.	No classes.
EARLHAM COLLEGE	Spring session begins 2nd wk.	Classes continue.	Spring break 3rd wk. Classes resume 4th wk.	Classes continue.	Exams 1st wk. May term begins 2nd wk.	No classes.
INDIANA UNIVERSITY—BLOOMINGTON	Spring session begins 2nd wk.	Classes continue.	Spring break 3rd wk. Classes resume 4th wk.	Classes continue.	Final exams 1st wk. IUB commencement 1st wk. Summer session begins 2nd wk.	1st summer session ends. 2nd summer session begins.

July	August	September	October	November	December	Additional Info
N/A	N/A	N/A	N/A	N/A	N/A	N/A
No classes July 4. Exams last wk.	Fall session begins last wk.	Classes continue.	Fall break 3rd wk. Classes resume 4th wk.	Break from Thanksgiving Day through the following Sun.	Exams 2nd wk.	N/A
Classes continue.	Summer session ends at end of 2nd full wk. Fall session begins last wk.	Classes continue.	Classes continue.	Break from Thanksgiving Day through the following Sun.	Exams 2nd–3rd wks.	N/A
No classes July 4. Exams last wk.	Fall session begins last wk.	Classes continue.	Fall break from 3rd Sat. through following Tues.	Break from Thanksgiving Day through the following Sun.	Exams 3rd wk.	Approximately 100 students are on campus during the summer.
No classes July 4.	Summer session ends at end of 2nd wk.	Fall session begins 3rd wk.	Classes continue.	Break from Wed. before Thanksgiving through the following Sun.	Exams 2nd wk.	Many of the students on campus during the summer session are from other colleges and universities.
No classes July 4.	Summer session ends 4th wk.	Fall session begins last wk.	Classes continue.	Break from Thanksgiving Day through the following Sun.	Reading period and exams 1st–2nd wks.	N/A
No classes July 4.	Summer session ends 1st wk. Fall session begins last wk.	Classes continue.	Classes continue.	Break from Tues. before Thanksgiving Day through the following Sun.	Exams 3rd wk.	N/A
No classes July 4. Summer session ends Fri. of 2nd wk.	Fall session begins last wk.	No classes Labor Day.	Break 3rd Sat. through the following Tues.	Break from day before Thanksgiving day through following Sun.	Exams 3rd wk.	N/A
No classes.	Fall session begins last wk.	Classes continue.	Classes continue.	Break from Fri. before Thanksgiving Day through Sun. following Thanksgiving.	Exams 3rd wk.	Fewer than 50 students are on campus during the summer. Campus visits are not discouraged during exam periods.
No classes.	Falls session begins last wk.	Classes continue.	Break Fri.–Sun. of end of 2nd wk.	Break from Wed. before Thanksgiving Day through the following Sun.	Exams 3rd wk.	N/A
Classes continue.	2nd summer session ends 2nd wk. Fall session begins Aug. 30.	Classes continue.	Classes continue.	Break from Tues. before Thanksgiving Day through the following Sun.	Exams 3rd wk. IUB commencement end of 3rd wk.	Campus visits are not discouraged during exam periods.

School	January	February	March	April	May	June
PURDUE UNIVERSITY— WEST LAFAYETTE	Spring session begins 2nd wk. No classes MLK Day.	Classes continue.	Spring break 3rd wk. Classes resume 4th wk.	Exams last wk.– 1st wk. of May	Exams 1st wk.	Summer session begins 2nd wk.
ROSE–HULMAN INSTITUTE OF TECHNOLOGY	N/A	N/A	N/A	N/A	N/A	N/A
UNIVERSITY OF NOTRE DAME ✔	Spring session begins 2nd or 3rd wk.	Classes continue.	Spring break 2nd wk. Classes resume 3rd wk.	Break from Good Fri. to Easter Mon.	Exams 1st wk.	Summer session begins 3rd wk.
✔ **VALPARAISO UNIVERSITY**	N/A	N/A	N/A	N/A	N/A	N/A
WABASH COLLEGE	Spring semester classes begin. Celebration of Student Research. National Merit Visit Day.	Fine Arts Fellowship Weekend.	Honor Scholarship Weekend	Lilly Awards Weekend.	Classes End. Commencement.	No Classes.
Iowa **CORNELL COLLEGE**	Spring session (5th course of academic year) begins 2nd wk. Course ends last wk.	Six course begins 1st wk. and ends last wk.	Seventh course begins 1st wk. and ends last wk. Spring vacation begins last wk.	Eighth course begins 1st wk. and ends last wk.	Ninth course begins 1st wk. and ends last wk.	No classes.
GRINNELL COLLEGE	Spring session begins 3rd wk.	Classes continue	Spring break, 3rd and 4th wk. Classes resume 5th wk.	Classes continue	Exams held 2nd wk.	No summer session
IOWA STATE UNIVERSITY	Spring session begins Jan. 10. Holiday Jan. 11.	Classes continue.	Spring break 2nd wk. Classes resume 3rd wk.	Classes continue.	Exams mid–month.	Summer session begins 2nd wk.
UNIVERSITY OF IOWA	Classes begin 3rd wk.	Classes continue.	Spring break 3rd wk. Classes resume 4th wk.	Classes continue.	Exams 2nd wk.	Summer session begins 2nd or 3rd wk.
Kansas **UNIVERSITY OF KANSAS**	Spring session begins 3rd wk.	Classes continue.	Spring break 3rd or 4th wk. Classes resume following wk.	Classes continue.	Exams 2nd–3rd wks.	Summer session begins 2nd wk.
Kentucky **BELLARMINE UNIVERSITY**	N/A	N/A	N/A	N/A	N/A	N/A

July	August	September	October	November	December	Additional Info
No classes July 4	Summer session ends 1st wk. Fall sessions begins 3rd wk.	No classes Labor Day	Fall break– 2nd Mon/Tue	Break from Tues before Thanksgiving Day through following Sun.	Exams 2nd wk.	*Always call ahead for tour reservations.*
N/A	N/A	N/A	N/A	N/A	N/A	N/A
Classes continue.	Summer session ends 1st wk. Fall session begins last wk.	Classes continue.	Fall break 3rd wk. Classes resume 4th wk.	Break from Thanksgiving Day through the following Sun.	Exams 3rd wk.	N/A
N/A	N/A	N/A	N/A	N/A	N/A	N/A
No Classes.	Fall semester Classes Begin	N/A	Homecoming. Fall Visit Weekends.	Monon Bell Weekend.	Classes End. Final Exams.	N/A
No classes.	No classes.	Fall session (1st course of academic year) begins 1st wk. and ends last wk.	Second course begins 1st wk. and ends last wk.	Third course begins 1st wk. and ends by Thanksgiving break.	Fourth course begins 1st wk. and ends by Xmas.	N/A
No summer session	Fall session begins 4th wk.	Classes continue	Fall break 3rd wk., classes resume 4th wk.	Classes continue, no classes Thanksgiving and day after	Exams held 2nd wk.	N/A
No classes July 4. Summer session 1 ends July 7.	Summer session ends 1st wk. Commencement Aug. 5. Fall session begins last wk.	Classes continue.	Classes continue.	Break from Sat. before Thanksgiving Day through the following Sun.	Exams 2nd wk. Holiday Dec. 25–26.	N/A
No classes July 4th. Summer session ends last wk.	Fall session begins last wk.	No classes Labor Day.	Classes continue.	No classes Thanksgiving wk.	Exams 3rd wk.	N/A
No classes July 4. Summer session ends last wk.	Fall session begins 3rd wk. First day of classes is Aug. 19.	Classes continue.	Classes continue. Fall break 2 days of 3rd wk.	Break from Wed. before Thanksgiving Day through the following Sun.	Exams 3rd wk.	N/A
N/A	N/A	N/A	N/A	N/A	N/A	N/A

School	January	February	March	April	May	June
CENTRE COLLEGE	Winter session begins 1st wk. (Jan. 6). Winter session ends 3rd wk. (Jan. 24).	Spring session begins first wk. (Feb. 2).	Spring break 4th wk. (March 19–27).	Classes continue.	Exams 2nd and 3rd wk. (May 12–14 & 16–17).	No Classes
UNIVERSITY OF KENTUCKY	Spring session begins 2nd wk. No classes MLK Day.	Classes continue.	Spring break 2nd wk. Classes resume 3rd wk.	Exams last wk.–1st wk. in May.	Exams 1st wk. Summer session begins 2nd wk. No classes Memorial Day.	Classes continue.
Louisiana **LOUISIANA STATE UNIVERSITY— BATON ROUGE**	Spring semester begins 3rd wk. No classes MLK Day.	No classes from Mon. before Ash Wed. through Ash Wed.	Mid–semester exams 2nd wk.	Spring break 2nd wk.	Final exams 2nd wk.	Summer term begins 2nd wk. Mid–term exams last wk.
LOYOLA UNIVERSITY NEW ORLEANS	Jan. 12– Classes Begin Jan. 19– MLK Day/no classes.	Feb. 23–27– Mardi Gras Holiday/no classes.	3/1– Classes Resume 3/12–14 Family Weekend 3/29– President's Open House.	April 5–12– Easter Holiday/ No Classes April 13– classes resume.	May 5– Last Day of Classes	No classes.
TULANE UNIVERSITY ✔	Spring session begins 2nd wk. No classes MLK Day.	No classes the Mon. and Tues. of Mardi Gras (before Ash Wed.).	Classes continue.	Classes resume 1st wk. Exams last wk–1st wk. in May. Easter break.	Exams 1st wk. Summer session begins 3rd wk.	Classes continue.
UNIVERSITY OF NEW ORLEANS	N/A	N/A	N/A	N/A	N/A	N/A
Maine **BATES COLLEGE** ✔	Winter session begins 2nd wk. No classes MLK Day.	Break from end of 2nd wk. to beginning of 4th wk.	Classes continue.	Reading period 1st wk. Exams 2nd wk. Short term begins 4th wk.	Short term ends last wk.	No classes.
BOWDOIN COLLEGE ✔	Spring session begins 4th wk.	Classes continue.	Spring break 3rd–4th wks.	Classes continue.	Reading period and exams 2nd–3rd wk. Commencement May 29th.	No classes.
COLBY COLLEGE ✔	Winter session begins 1st wk. and ends last wk.	Spring session begins 1st wk.	Spring break 3rd wk.	Classes continue.	Exams 2nd wk.	No classes.
UNIVERSITY OF MAINE	Spring session begins 2nd wk. No classes on MLK Day.	Spring break begins end of Feb.	Spring break ends mid–March.	Classes continue	Exams 1st wk. Summer session begins.	Classes continue.
UNIVERSITY OF NEW ENGLAND ✔	Winter session begins 3rd wk. and ends last wk.	Spring session begins 1st wk.	Spring break 4th wk.	Classes resume 1st wk.	Exams 2nd wk. Summer session begins 3rd wk. No classes Memorial Day.	Classes continue.

July	August	September	October	November	December	Additional Info
No Classes	No Classes	Fall session begin first wk. (Sept. 6)	Fall break 2nd wk. Thurs. and Fri.	Break from Wed. before Thanksgiving Day through the following Sun.	Exams 2nd wk.	N/A
No classes July 4. Summer session ends last wk.	Fall session begins last wk.	No classes Labor Day.	Oct. 6 academic holiday.	Break from Thanksgiving Day through the following Sun. Election Day holiday.	Exams 2nd wk.	Many students are on campus during the summer.
No classes July 4. Summer term ends last wk.	Fall semester begins 3rd wk.	No classes Labor Day.	Fall holiday Thurs. & Fri. 1st wk. Mid–semester exams 2nd wk.	Break from Thanksgiving Day through following Sun.	Final exams 1st wk.	N/A
No classes.	Aug. 30– classes begin.	Sept. 6– Labor Day Holiday/no classes.	Oct. 18–19– Fall Break/no classes Oct. 20– classes resume.	Nov. 24–26– Thanksgiving holidays/No Classes Nov. 29– classes resume.	Dec. 10– Last day of classes.	N/A
No classes July 4.	Summer session ends 3rd wk. Fall session begins last wk.	No classes Labor Day. No classes Yom Kippur.	Classes continue.	Break from Wed. before Thanksgiving Day through the following Sun.	Exams 3rd wk.	N/A
N/A	N/A	N/A	N/A	N/A	N/A	N/A
No classes.	No classes.	Fall session begins 2nd wk.	Fall break 3rd wk. Classes resume 4th wk.	Break from Fri. before Thanksgiving Day through Sun. following Thanksgiving.	Reading period 1st wk. Exams 2nd–3rd wks.	Campus visits are not discouraged during exam periods.
No classes.	First–Year Orientation begins Aug. 28th.	Fall session begins first wk. Common Good Day Sept. 18th.	Sarah & James Bowdoin Day Oct. 1st. Fall break 2nd wk. Homecoming Oct. 23rd.	Break from Wed. before Thanksgiving to following Sun.	Reading period and exams 2nd–3rd wk.	Sarah & James Bowdoin Day is a commemoration of the college's founders.
No classes.	No classes.	Fall session begins 2nd wk.	Fall break from Sat. before Columbus Day through following Tues.	Break from Wed. before Thanksgiving Day through the following Sun.	Exams 2nd–3rd wks.	Approximately 60 students are on campus during the summer.
Classes continue	Summer session ends 3rd wk.	Fall session begins 1st wk. No classes Labor Day.	Fall break from Fri. before Columbus Day through the following Tues.	Break from Wed. before Thanksgiving Day through the following Sun.	Exams 3rd wk.	N/A
No classes July 4. Summer session ends 4th wk.	No classes.	Fall session begins 2nd wk.	No classes Columbus Day.	Break from Wed. before Thanksgiving Day through the following Sun.	Exams 2nd–3rd wks.	Approximately 80 students are on campus from mid-June through Aug.

School	January	February	March	April	May	June
UNIVERSITY OF SOUTHERN MAINE	Spring session begins 3rd wk. No classes MLK Day.	Break from Sat. before Presidents' Day through Sun after Presidents' Day.	Spring break last wk.	Classes resume 1st wk.	Exams 1st–2nd wks. Summer session begins 2nd or 3rd wk.	Classes continue.
Maryland						
COLLEGE OF NOTRE DAME OF MARYLAND	Winter session begins 2nd wk. and ends 4th wk. Spring session begins at end of month.	Classes continue.	Spring break from wk. before Easter to wk. after Easter.	Spring break from wk. before Easter to wk. after Easter.	Exams 2nd–3rd wks. Summer session begins last wk.	Classes continue.
GOUCHER COLLEGE	Spring session begins 4th wk.	Classes continue.	Spring break 3rd wk. Classes resume 4th wk.	Classes continue.	Exams 1st wk.	No classes.
HOOD COLLEGE	Spring session begins 3rd wk. No classes MLK Day.	Classes continue.	Spring break 2nd wk. Classes resume 3rd wk.	Easter break from Fri. before Easter through the following Mon.	Exams 2nd wk.	No classes.
JOHNS HOPKINS UNIVERSITY	Winter session: 1st–3rd wks. No classes MLK Day. Spring session begins 4th wk.	No classes Presidents' Day.	Spring break 3rd wk. Classes resume 4th wk.	Classes continue.	No classes 1st wk. (reading period). Exams 2nd wk.	No classes.
LOYOLA COLLEGE ✓ IN MARYLAND	Spring session begins 3rd wk. No classes MLK Day.	No classes Presidents' Day	Spring break 1st wk. Classes resume 2nd wk.	Break from Thurs. before Easter through the following Mon.	Exams 1st Wk.	Summer session begins 1st wk.
McDANIEL COLLEGE	Winter session begins 1st wk. and ends 4th wk. Spring session begins at end of month.	Classes continue.	Spring break 3rd wk. Classes resume 4th wk.	Classes continue.	Exams 1st–2nd wks.	Summer session begins 4th wk.
MORGAN STATE UNIVERSITY	Spring session begins 3rd wk. No classes MLK Day.	Classes continue.	No classes Good Fri. Spring break last wk.	Classes resume 1st wk. No classes Good Fri.	Exams 2nd–3rd wks.	Summer session begins 2nd wk.
SAINT JOHN'S COLLEGE (MD)	N/A	N/A	N/A	N/A	N/A	N/A
SAINT MARY'S ✓ COLLEGE OF MARYLAND	Spring semester begins 3rd wk. No classes on MLK Day.	Classes continue.	Spring break 3rd wk. Classes resume 4th wk.	Classes continue.	Exams 2nd wk.	Summer session begins 1st wk.
TOWSON ✓ UNIVERSITY	Winter session begins 1st wk. and ends 4th wk. Spring session begins at end of month.	Classes continue.	Spring break 3rd wk. Classes resume 4th wk.	Classes continue.	Exams 2nd to 3rd wk.	Summer session begins 1st wk. or earlier.

July	August	September	October	November	December	Additional Info
No classes July 4.	Summer session ends 2nd wk.	Fall session begins 1st wk.	Classes continue.	Break from Tues. before Thanksgiving Day through the following Sun.	Exams 3rd wk.	*Call ahead for tour availability. Many students on campus during summer.*
No classes July 4. Summer session ends last wk.	No classes.	Fall session begins 1st wk.	No classes 3rd Fri.	Break from Wed. before Thanksgiving Day through the following Sun.	Exams 3rd wk.	*Very few College of Notre Dame students are on campus during the summer session.*
No classes.	No classes.	Fall session begins 1st wk.	No classes 3rd Mon. and Tues.	Break from Wed. before Thanksgiving Day through the following Sun.	Exams 3rd wk.	*Visits are permitted during exams, but student–led tours are not guaranteed. 25 students are on campus during summer.*
No classes July 4.	Fall session begins last wk.	Classes continue. No classes Labor Day.	Oct. break mid–month.	Break from Wed. before Thanksgiving Day through the following Sun.	Exams 3rd wk.	*Hood offers 3 summer terms with classes in 3–, 5–, and 6–wk. sessions.*
No classes.	No classes.	Fall session begins 1st wk.	No classes 2nd Mon.	Break from Thanksgiving Day through the following Sun.	No classes 2nd wk. (reading period). Exams from end of 2nd–3rd wks.	*Visits are not discouraged during exams.*
N/A	Summer session ends 4th wk.	Fall classes begin 2nd wk.	No classes 3rd Fri.	Break from Wed. before Thanksgiving Day through the following Sun.	Exams 3rd–4th wk.s	*Summer classes are held in the evening; there are daytime programs, but they are few.*
Classes continue.	Summer session ends 3rd wk.	Fall session begins 1st wk.	Break from 3rd Fri. through the following Tues.	Break from Tues. before Thanksgiving Day through the following Sun.	Exams 2nd wk.	*Campus visits are not discouraged during exam periods.*
No classes July 4. Summer session ends last wk.	Classes begin.	No classes Labor Day.	Classes continue.	Break from Thanksgiving Day through the following Sun.	Exams mid–month.	*N/A*
N/A	N/A	N/A	N/A	N/A	N/A	*N/A*
Classes end 2nd wk.	Fall semester begins last wk.	No classes on Labor Day.	Classes continue.	Break from Wed. before Thanksgiving through the following Sun.	Exams 3rd wk.	*N/A*
Classes continue.	Summer session ends 2nd wk.	Fall session begins 1st wk. (sometimes last wk. in Aug). No classes Labor Day.	Classes continue.	Break from Wed. 8/4 Thanksgiving Day through the following Sun.	Exams 2nd–3rd wks.	*N/A*

School	January	February	March	April	May	June
UNITED STATES NAVAL ACADEMY ✓	Winter session begins 2nd wk. No classes MLK Day.	No classes Presidents' Day.	Spring break 2nd wk. Classes resume 3rd wk.	Classes continue.	Exams 1st–2nd wks. Graduation last wk.	Summer session begins 1st wk.
UNIVERSITY OF MARYLAND, BALTIMORE COUNTY	Winter session begins 1st wk. and ends 3rd wk. Spring session begins at end of month.	Classes continue.	Spring break 4th wk. Classes resume last wk.	Classes continue.	Exams 2nd–3rd wks.	Summer sessions begin 1st wk.
UNIVERSITY OF MARYLAND—COLLEGE PARK	Spring session begins 4th wk. No classes MLK Day.	Classes continue.	Spring break 3rd or 4th wk.	Classes resume 1st wk.	Exams 3rd wk.	Summer session begins 1st wk.
WASHINGTON COLLEGE	Spring session begins 3rd wk.	Classes continue.	Spring break 2nd wk. Classes resume 3rd wk.	Classes continue.	Exams 2nd wk.	No classes.
Massachusetts **AMHERST COLLEGE** ✓	Winter session begins 1st wk. and ends 3rd wk. Spring session begins at end of 3rd wk.	Classes continue.	Spring break begins at end of 2nd wk. Classes resume last wk.	Classes continue.	Exams 2nd wk.	No classes; some students work on campus.
BABSON COLLEGE ✓	Winter session 2nd–4th wk. Spring session begins 4th wk. No classes MLK Day.	No classes Presidents' Day.	Spring break 3rd wk. Classes resume 4th wk.	Classes continue. No classes Patriot Day.	Exams 2nd wk. First summer session begins 4th wk. No classes Memorial Day.	Classes continue.
BENTLEY COLLEGE	Spring session begins 2nd wk. No classes MLK Day.	No classes Presidents' Day.	Spring break 2nd wk. Classes resume 3rd wk.	No classes Patriots' Day.	Exams 1st–2nd wks. First summer session begins 3rd wk.	First summer session ends last wk.
BOSTON COLLEGE	Classes begin 3rd wk. No classes MLK Day.	No classes Presidents' Day.	Spring break 1st wk. Classes resume 2nd wk. No classes Thurs.–Fri. before Easter.	No classes Thurs.–Fri. before Easter.	Exams 1st–2nd wks. Summer session begins late May. No classes Memorial Day.	Classes continue.
BOSTON UNIVERSITY ✓	Spring session begins 2nd wk. No classes MLK Day.	No classes Presidents' Day.	Spring break 2nd wk. Classes resume 3rd wk.	Classes continue. No classes Patriots' Day.	Summer session begins 1st wk. No classes Memorial Day.	First summer session ends last wk.
BRANDEIS UNIVERSITY	Spring session begins 4th wk.	Spring recess 1st wk.	Classes continue.	No classes Passover wk.	Exams 1st–2nd wks.	Limited summer classes.
CLARK UNIVERSITY ✓	Spring session begins 3rd wk.	Classes continue.	Spring break 1st wk. Classes resume 2nd wk.	Classes continue.	Exams 1st wk. First summer session begins 3rd wk. No classes Memorial Day.	First summer session ends last wk.

July	August	September	October	November	December	Additional Info
No classes July 4.	Summer session ends and Fall session begins at end of month.	No classes Labor Day.	No classes Columbus Day.	Break from Thanksgiving Day through the following Sun. No classes Veterans' Day.	Exams 2nd–3rd wks.	About 1,000 midshipmen are at the academy during summer (except June). Visits are not discouraged.
No classes July 4.	Summer session ends 3rd wk. Fall session begins last wk.	No classes Labor Day.	Classes continue.	Break from Thanksgiving Day through the following Sun.	Exams 2nd–3rd wk.s	N/A
No classes July 4.	Summer session ends 3rd wk.	Fall session begins 1st wk.	Classes continue.	Break from Thanksgiving Day through the following Sun.	Exams 2nd–3rd wks.	Campus visits encouraged any time except Spring break and Dec. 25–Jan. 1.
No classes.	Fall session begins last wk.	Classes continue.	Break from 2nd Fri. through the following Sun.	Break from Wed. before Thanksgiving Day through the following Sun.	Exams 2nd–3rd wks.	Campus visits any time except Spring break and Dec. 25–Jan.1.
No classes.	No classes.	Fall session begins Tues. after Labor Day.	Break from end of 2nd wk. through Mon. and Tues. of 3rd wk.	Break from Sat. before Thanksgiving Day through the following Sun.	Exams from end of 2nd wk. through Wed. of 3rd wk.	N/A
No classes July 4. First sum sess ends 1st wk. Second sum sess begins 2nd wk.	Second summer session ends 3rd wk.	Fall session begins 1st wk. No classes Labor Day.	No classes Columbus Day.	Break from Sat. before Thanksgiving Day through the following Sun.	Exams 3rd wk.	N/A
Second summer session begins 1st wk. No classes July 4.	Second summer session ends 2nd wk.	Fall session begins 1st wk.	No classes Columbus Day.	Sat. classes held on Veterans' Day. Break Wed. before Thanksgiving thru following Sun.	Exams 2nd–3rd wks.	Campus visits are not discouraged during exam periods.
No classes July 4.	Summer session ends early Aug.	Classes begin Wed. after Labor Day.	No classes Columbus Day.	Break from Wed. before Thanksgiving Day through the following Sun.	Exams 2nd–3rd wks.	N/A
No classes July 4. Second summer session begins July 6.	Summer session ends 2nd wk.	Fall session begins 2nd wk.	No classes Columbus Day.	Break from Wed. before Thanksgiving Day through the following Sun. No classes Veterans' Day.	Exams 3rd–4th wks.	Campus visits are not discouraged during exam periods.
Limited summer classes.	Limited summer classes. Fall session begins last wk.	No classes Labor Day, Rosh Hashanah, Yom Kippur, and Succoth.	Classes continue.	Break from Wed. before Thanksgiving Day through the following Sun.	Exams 2nd wk.	Campus visits are not discouraged during exam periods.
Second summer session begins 1st wk. No classes July 4.	Second summer session ends 1st wk. Fall session begins last wk.	No classes Labor Day.	Fall break from 3rd Fri. through the following Tues.	Break from Tues. before Thanksgiving Day through the following Sun.	Exams 2nd–3rd wks.	Approximately 200 students are on campus for summer sessions.

School	January	February	March	April	May	June
COLLEGE OF THE HOLY CROSS ✔	Spring session begins 3rd wk.	Classes continue.	Spring break 1st wk. Classes resume 2nd wk.	Break from Wed. before Easter through the following Mon.	Reading period 1st wk. Exams 2nd wks.	No classes.
CURRY COLLEGE ✔	Spring session begins 4th wk.	No classes Presidents' Day.	Spring break 2nd wk. Classes resume 3rd wk.	No classes Patriots' Day.	Exams 2nd–3rd wks.	Summer session begins 2nd wk.
EMERSON COLLEGE ✔	Spring session begins 3rd wk. No classes MLK Day.	No classes Presidents' Day.	Spring break 2nd wk. Classes resume 3rd wk.	No classes Patriots' Day.	Exams 1st wk. First summer session begins last wk.	Classes continue.
HAMPSHIRE COLLEGE ✔	Winter session begins 1st wk. and continues for 3 wks. Spring session begins last wk.	Classes continue.	No classes on Exam Day during 2nd wk. Spring break 3rd–4th wks.	No classes on Advising/Exam Day during 2nd wk.	Exams 2nd wk.	No classes.
HARVARD COLLEGE	Fall reading period 1st and 2nd wks. Fall session exams 3rd–4th wks.	Spring session begins 1st wk. No classes Presidents' Day.	Spring break last wk.	Classes resume 1st wk.	Exams 2nd–3rd wks.	Summer session begins last wk.
MASSACHUSETTS INSTITUTE OF TECHNOLOGY	Winter session begins 1st wk. and ends last wk. No classes MLK Day.	Spring session begins 1st wk. No classes Presidents' Day.	Break 3rd wk. Classes resume last wk.	Classes resume 1st wk. No classes Patriots' Day and Tues. after.	Exams 3rd wk.	Summer session begins 2nd wk.
MERRIMACK COLLEGE	Spring session begins 3rd wk. No classes MLK Day.	No classes Presidents' Day.	No classes Thurs–Fri. before Easter. Spring break 3rd wk.	Classes resume 1st wk. No classes Thurs.–Fri. before Easter.	Exams 1st–2nd wks. Summer session begins 3rd wk.	Classes continue.
MOUNT HOLYOKE COLLEGE ✔	Winter session begins 1st wk. and ends 4th wk. Spring session begins at end of month.	Classes continue.	Spring break 3rd wk. Classes resume 4th wk.	Classes continue.	Exams 2nd–3rd wks.	No classes.
NORTHEASTERN UNIVERSITY ✔	Spring session begins 2nd wk. No classes MLK Day	Classes continue. No classes Presidents' Day	Break 1st wk.	Exams 3rd wk. No classes Patriot's Day	Summer I session begins 1st wk. No classes Memorial Day	Summer I exams 3rd wk. Summer II begins 4th wk.
SIMMONS COLLEGE ✔	Spring session begins 4th wk. No classes MLK Day.	No classes Presidents' Day.	Spring break 2nd wk. Classes resume 3rd wk.	No classes Patriots' Day.	Exams 2nd wk.	No classes.
SMITH COLLEGE ✔	Winter session lasts 2nd wk. through 4th wk. Spring session begins at end of month.	Classes continue.	Spring break 3rd wk. Classes resume 4th wk.	Classes continue.	Exams 1st–2nd wks.	No classes.

July	August	September	October	November	December	Additional Info
No classes.	Classes begin last Wed. or 1st Wed. of Sept.	Classes begin 1st Wed. (or last Wed. of Aug.).	No classes Columbus Day and Tues. following it.	Break from Wed. before Thanksgiving Day through the following Sun.	Reading period 1st or 2nd wk. Exams 2nd or 3rd wk.	*Campus visits are not discouraged during exams, but tours are unavailable.*
No classes July 4. Summer session ends at end of month.	Summer break all month.	Fall session begins 1st wk.	No classes Columbus Day.	No classes Veterans' Day. Break from Wed. before Thanksgiving Day thru following Sun.	Exams 3rd wk.	*During exams, interviews are available; tours are discouraged.*
First Sum sess ends 1st wk. Second Sum sess begins 2nd wk. No classes July 4.	Second summer session ends 2nd wk.	Fall session begins 2nd wk.	No classes Columbus Day.	No classes Veterans' Day. Break from Wed. before Thanksgiving thru following Sun.	Exams 3rd wk.	*Book campus tours through college websites. Visits are discouraged during breaks and exams.*
No classes.	No classes.	Fall session begins 1st wk.	Break 3rd Mon.–Tues. No classes on Advising/Exam Day during last wk.	No classes Exam Day during 2nd wk. Break from Wed. before Thanksgiving Day to Sun.	Exams 2nd wk.	*Campus visits are not discouraged during exam periods.*
No classes July 4.	Summer session ends after 2nd wk.	Fall session begins 3rd wk.	No classes Columbus Day.	No classes Veterans' Day. Break from Thanksgiving Day through the following Sun.	Break from end of 3rd wk. to 1st wk. after New Year. (Fall exams are 3rd–4th wks. of Jan.)	*Visits are not discouraged during exams; but there are no classes, and overnight visits are not allowed.*
No classes July 4.	Summer session ends 3rd wk. Freshman orientation during last wk.	Fall session begins 1st wk.	No classes Columbus Day.	Break from Thanksgiving Day through the following Sun. No classes Veterans' Day.	Exams 3rd wk.	*Tours Mon. through Fri. except major holidays.*
No classes July 4.	Summer session ends 3rd wk.	Fall session begins 1st wk.	No classes Columbus Day.	Break from Wed. before Thanksgiving Day through the following Sun.	Exams 2nd–3rd wks.	*N/A*
No classes.	No classes.	Fall session begins 1st wk.	Fall break from Sat. before Columbus Day through the following Tues.	Break from Wed. before Thanksgiving Day through the following Sun.	Exams 3rd wk.	*Daytime visits are not discouraged during exams; tours are available, but not overnight dorm visits.*
No classes July 4th.	Summer II exams 3rd wk.	Fall session begins 2nd wk. No classes Labor Day	No classes Columbus Day	Break from Thanksgiving Day through the following Sun. No classes Veterans' Day	Exams 3rd wk. Winter recess 4th wk.	*N/A*
No classes.	Classes being last wk.	No classes Labor Day.	No classes Columbus Day and Tues. following it.	Break from Wed. before Thanksgiving Day through the following Sun.	Exams 2nd–3rd wks.	*N/A*
No classes.	No classes.	Fall session begins 1st wk.	Fall break from Sat. before Columbus Day through the following Tues.	Break from Wed. before Thanksgiving Day through the following Sun.	Reading period end of 2nd–3rd wks. Exams 3rd wk.	*Very few students are on campus during the summer.*

School	January	February	March	April	May	June
Tufts University ✓	Spring session begins 3rd wk. No classes MLK Day.	No classes Presidents' Day.	Spring break 3rd wk. Classes resume 4th wk.	Classes end 4th wk.	Exams 1st–2nd wks. Summer session begins 3rd wk.	Classes continue.
University of Massachusetts—Amherst ✓	Winter session begins 1st wk. and ends 4th wk. Spring session begins last wk.	No classes Presidents' Day.	Spring break 3rd wk. Classes resume 4th wk.	Classes continue.	Exams 3rd wk.	Summer session begins 1st wk.
Wellesley College	Winter session from 2nd wk. to last wk. Spring session begins last wk.	No classes Presidents' Day.	Spring break 4th wk.	No classes Patriots' Day. (3rd Mon.)	Exams 3rd wk.	No classes.
Wheaton College (MA) ✓	Spring session begins last wk.	Classes continue	Spring break 3rd wk. Classes resume 4th wk.	Classes continue.	Exams 2nd wk.	No classes.
Williams College ✓	Winter session begins 1st wk. and ends 4th wk.	No classes Fri., Feb. 20 (Winter Carnival). Spring semester begins.	Spring break last 2 wks. of month.	Classes resume beginning of the month.	Exams 3rd–4th wks.	No classes.
Worcester Polytechnic Institute	Winter session (Term C) begins 2nd wk.	No classes on Advising Day. Winter session (Term C) ends at end of month.	Break 1st–2nd wks. Spring session (Term D) begins 3rd wk.	Classes continue.	Spring session (Term D) ends 1st wk. Summer session (Term E) begins end of month.	Summer Classes continue.
Michigan						
Kalamazoo College ✓	Winter session begins 1st wk.	No classes Fri. of Presidents' Day weekend.	Exams 3rd wk. Winter session ends at end of 3rd wk. Spring break.	Spring session begins 1st wk.	Classes continue. No classes Memorial Day.	Exams 2nd wk. Summer session begins last wk.
Michigan State University	Spring semester Begins. No classes on MLK day.	Classes continue. End of tuition refund middle of month.	Spring break early March.	Classes end for Spring semester end of April.	Final exams and Commencement. Beginning of Summer Semester.	Summer Semester continues
University of Michigan—Ann Arbor ✓	Winter session begins 1st wk. No classes MLK Day.	Spring break last wk.	Classes resume 1st wk.	Reading period and exams last 2 wks. in May.	Spring session begins 1st wk. No classes Memorial Day.	Reading and exams 3rd wk.
Minnesota						
Carleton College ✓	Winter session begins 2nd wk.	Midterm break over 1st or 2nd weekend.	Spring break 3rd or 4th wk. Spring session begins at end of month.	Last weekend break.	Reading and exams 1st–2nd wk. Classes continue.	No classes.
Gustavus Adolphus College ✓	Jan. Term is a month for specific studies. Classes in session and visitors welcome!	Classes in session. Senior Day.	Classes in session. Spring Open House, come see Gustavus on this visit day.	Classes in session. Preview Day.	Classes in session. Final Exams beginning the third wk.	Classes not in session. First-year students register for classes.

July	August	September	October	November	December	Additional Info
No classes July 4.	Summer session ends 1st wk.	Fall session begins 1st wk.	No classes Columbus Day.	Break from Wed. before Thanksgiving Day through the following Sun.	Exams 2nd–3rd wks.	*The summer session offers courses to about 2,000 degree and nondegree students.*
No classes July 4.	Summer session ends 3rd wk.	Fall session begins 2nd wk.	No classes Columbus Day.	Break from Wed. before Thanksgiving Day through the following Sun.	Exams 2nd–3rd wks.	*N/A*
No classes.	No classes.	Fall session begins 1st wk.	Fall break from Sat. before Columbus Day through the following Tues.	Break from Wed. before Thanksgiving Day through the following Sun.	Exams 3rd wk.	*When classes are not in session (including exam periods), tours are subject to the availability of student guides.*
No classes.	No classes.	Fall session begins 1st wk.	Fall break from Sat. before Columbus Day through the following Tues.	Break from Wed. before Thanksgiving Day through the following Sun.	Exams 2nd–3rd wks.	*About 75 students are on campus during the summer. Campus visits are not discouraged during exam periods.*
No classes.	No classes.	Fall session begins 1st full wk.	Break Mon. 11–Tues. 12.	Break from Wed. before Thanksgiving Day through the following Sun.	Exams 2nd–3rd wks.	*About 90 students involved in faculty–sponsored research are on campus for the summer.*
No classes July 3–5. Summer session (Term E) ends 3rd wk.	Fall session (Term A) begins at end of month.	No classes Labor Day.	Term A ends 3rd wk. Break 2nd–4th wks. Term B begins end of 4th wk.	Break from Wed. before Thanksgiving Day through the following Sun.	Second fall session (Term B) ends 3rd wk.	*N/A*
No classes July 4.	Exams last wk.	No classes Labor Day. Summer session ends 1st wk. Fall session begins 2nd wk.	Classes continue.	Break from Thanksgiving Day through the following Sun.	Exams 2nd wk.	*N/A*
4th of July Holiday. Middle of Summer Semester.	Summer Semester ends. Beginning of Fall semester end of Aug.	No classes Labor Day. End of tuition refund around third wk.	Classes continue.	Thanksgiving break.	Fall classes end. Final exams and Fall Commencement	*N/A*
Summer session begins 1st wk. No classes July 4.	Reading period and exams 3rd wk.	Fall session begins 2nd wk.	Classes continue.	Break from Wed. before Thanksgiving Day through the following Sun.	Reading period and exams 3rd wk.	*N/A*
No classes.	Fall session begins 2nd wk.	Midterm break over 2nd weekend.	Reading period and exams wk. before Thanksgiving Day. Winter break	begins Wed. before Thanksgiving Day.	No classes.	*Approximately 125 students are on campus during the summer.*
Summer Open House! Classes not in session	Two Summer Open Houses!	Fall semester classes begin.	Nobel Conference.	Classes in session. Thanksgiving break.	On the first weekend we have Xmas in Christ Chapel a musical concert.	*Observe a class, tour campus, meet with a professor, director, or coach, spend the night, and more! So give us a call!*

School	January	February	March	April	May	June
MACALESTER COLLEGE ✔	No classes.	Spring session begins 1st wk.	Spring break 3rd or 4th wk.	No classes Good Fri.	Exams 2nd wk.	No classes.
SAINT OLAF COLLEGE ✔	Winter (interim) session begins Jan. 3. and ends Jan. 28.	Spring session begins Feb. 7.	Spring break (with Easter) begins March 19 and ends March 27.	Classes resume 1st wk.	Exams 3rd and 4th wks.	First summer session begins June 6.
UNIVERSITY OF MINNESOTA, TWIN CITIES ✔	Winter session begins 1st wk. No classes MLK Day.	Classes continue.	Exams mid–2nd to beginning of 3rd wks. Spring break 3rd wk.	Spring session begins last wk.	Classes continue. No classes Memorial Day.	Exams 2nd wk. Summer session begins 3rd wk.
Mississippi **MILLSAPS COLLEGE**	Second summer school session begins in the 1st full wk. Summer–long session continues.	Summer school exams 1st wk. Fall session begins 4th wk.	Classes continue.	Fall break 3rd wk.	Thanksgiving break from Wed. noon until the following Sun.	Exams held in the 1st full wk.
UNIVERSITY OF MISSISSIPPI	Spring semester classes begin.	May Diploma applications due.	Spring break 2nd wk. Priority registration begins.	No classes on Good Fri.	Final Exams & Commencement.	Summer school in session.
Missouri **SAINT LOUIS UNIVERSITY**	Spring session begins 3rd wk. No classes MLK Day.	Classes continue.	Midterm Exams First Wk. Spring break 2nd wk. Classes resume 3rd wk.	No classes Holy Thurs. and Good Fri.	Final Exams 2nd wk.	Summer session begins 1st wk.
UNIVERSITY OF MISSOURI—COLUMBIA	Winter session begins 2nd wk. No classes MLK Day.	Classes continue.	Spring break 3rd wk. Classes resume 4th wk.	Easter break	Exams 1st–2nd wks.	Summer session begins 3rd wk.
WASHINGTON UNIVERSITY IN SAINT LOUIS	Spring session begins 3rd wk. No classes MLK Day.	Classes continue.	Spring break 2nd wk. Classes resume 3rd wk.	Classes continue.	Exams 1st–2nd wks. Summer session begins 3rd wk. No classes Memorial Day.	Classes continue.
Montana **UNIVERSITY OF MONTANA—MISSOULA**	Spring semester begins 4th wk.	No classes Presidents' Day	Spring break last wk.	Classes continue	Exams 2nd wk., summer school starts 4th wk.	First session Summer School ends 4th wk.
Nebraska **UNIVERSITY OF NEBRASKA—LINCOLN**	Spring session begins 3rd wk.	Classes continue.	Spring break 2nd wk.	Classes continue.	Exams 1st–2nd wks. Summer session begins 3rd or 4th wk. No classes Memorial Day.	Classes continue.
UNIVERSITY OF NEBRASKA—OMAHA	Spring session begins 2nd wk. No classes MLK Day.	Classes continue.	Spring break 3rd wk.	Classes continue.	Exams 1st wk. Summer session begins 2nd wk.	Classes continue.

July	August	September	October	November	December	Additional Info
No classes.	No classes.	Fall session begins 2nd wk.	Break last Thurs. through Sun. at end of month.	Break from Thanksgiving Day through following Sun.	Exams 3rd wk.	*Approximately 100 students conduct funded research and 350 work on campus during the summer.*
First summer session ends July 14. Second summer session begins July 18.	Second summer session ends Aug. 24.	Fall session begins Sept. 9.	Fall break from Oct. 23 through Oct. 26.	Thanksgiving break from Nov. 24 through Nov. 28.	Exams 3rd and 4th wks.	*Approximately 70 regular students are on campus during the summer.*
No classes July 4.	Summer session ends 3rd wk.	Fall session begins 1st wk.	Classes continue.	Break from Thanksgiving Day through the following Sun.	Exams from mid–1st wk. to mid–2nd wk.	*Campus visits are not discouraged during exam periods.*
Spring session begins 2nd wk.	Classes continue.	Spring break 3rd wk. No classes Fri. before Easter.	Exams 4th wk.	No classes.	Summer session begins June 1.	*Individual visits available throughout year. Call for appointment.*
Summer School in session	Fall semester begins	Labor Day holiday (no classes)	Priority Registration begins	No classes during wk. of Thanksgiving	Fall semester final exams	*N/A*
No classes July 4. Summer session ends last wk.	Fall session begins last wk.	No classes Labor Day.	Midterm Exams 3rd wk. Two-day fall break mid month.	Break from Wed. before Thanksgiving Day through following Sun.	Final Exams mid 2nd wk. to mid 3rd wk.	*N/A*
No classes July 4.	Summer session ends 1st wk. Fall session begins last wk.	Classes continue.	Fall break mid–month.	Break from Tues. before Thanksgiving Day through the following Sun.	Exams 3rd wk.	*Campus visits are not discouraged during exam period.*
No classes July 4.	Summer session ends 2nd wk. Fall session begins last wk.	No classes Labor Day.	Fall break mid–month.	Break from Wed. before Thanksgiving Day through the following Sun.	Exams 2nd–3rd wks.	*N/A*
Second session Summer School starts 1st wk. No classes July 4th	Second session Summer School ends 1st wk. Fall classes begin 4th wk.	Labor Day Holiday	Classes continue	Break from Wed. before Thanksgiving until following Sun.	Exams begin 3rd wk.	*N/A*
No classes July 4.	Summer session ends 2nd wk. Fall session begins last wk.	Labor Day holiday.	Mid–month fall break.	Break from Wed. before Thanksgiving Day through the following Sun.	Exams 3rd wk.	*N/A*
No classes July 5.	Summer session ends 2nd wk. Fall session begins 4th wk.	Classes continue. No classes Labor Day.	Fall break on Mon. and Tues. of the 3rd wk.	Break from Wed. before Thanksgiving Day through the following Sun.	Exams 3rd wk.	*Campus visits are not discouraged during exams.*

School	January	February	March	April	May	June
Nevada	N/A	N/A	N/A	N/A	N/A	N/A
UNIVERSITY OF NEVADA—LAS VEGAS						
New Hampshire **DARTMOUTH COLLEGE** ✓	Winter session begins 1st wk.	Classes continue.	Exams 2nd–3rd wks. Spring session begins last wk.	Classes continue.	Exams last wk.–1st wk. of June.	Exams 1st wk. Summer session begins 3rd wk.
UNIVERSITY OF NEW HAMPSHIRE ✓	Spring semester begins 4th wk. No classes MLK Day.	Classes continue.	Spring break 3rd wk. Classes resume 4th wk.	Classes continue.	Exams 3rd wk. Summer session begins last wk.	Classes continue.
New Jersey **DREW UNIVERSITY** ✓	Spring session begins at end of month.	Classes continue.	Spring break 3rd wk. Classes resume 4th wk. No classes Good Fri.	No classes Good Fri.	Exams 2nd–3rd wks. Summer session begins end of month.	Classes continue.
PRINCETON UNIVERSITY ✓	Fall session reading period 2nd–3rd wks. Fall session exams 3rd–4th wks.	Spring session begins 1st wk.	Midterm exams 2nd wk. Spring break 3rd wk. Classes resume 4th wk.	Classes continue.	Reading period 2nd–3rd wks. Exams 3rd wk.–end of the month.	No classes.
RUTGERS UNIVERSITY—NEW BRUNSWICK	Spring session begins 3rd wk.	Classes continue.	Spring break begins end of 2nd wk. Classes resume 4th wk.	Classes continue.	Exams 2nd wk. Summer session begins after Memorial Day.	Classes continue.
New York **ALFRED UNIVERSITY**	Spring session begins Tues. of 3rd wk.	Classes continue.	Spring break 1st or 2nd wk. Classes resume 2nd or 3rd wk.	Classes continue.	Exams 2nd wk. Summer session begins 3rd wk.	First summer session ends 3rd wk. Second summer session begins 4th wk.
BARD COLLEGE ✓	Winter session begins 1st wk. and ends 4th wk. Spring session begins last wk.	Classes continue.	Reading period 3rd wk. Spring break last wk.	Classes resume 1st wk.	Spring session ends 3rd wk.	No classes.
BARNARD COLLEGE ✓	Spring session begins 3rd wk. No classes MLK Day.	Classes continue.	Spring break 2nd wk. Classes resume 4th wk.	Classes continue.	Exams 1st–2nd wks.	No classes.
CLARKSON UNIVERSITY	Classes begin Jan. 8	Classes continue	Spring break from March 12–22	Exams last wk.	Summer session I begins 3rd Wk.	First Summer session ends last Sat. of the Month
COLGATE UNIVERSITY ✓	Spring session begins 3rd wk.	Classes continue.	Spring break 3rd wk. Classes resume 4th wk. No classes Good Fri.	No classes Good Fri.	Exams 2nd wk.	No classes.

July	August	September	October	November	December	Additional Info
N/A	N/A	N/A	N/A	N/A	N/A	N/A
No classes July 4.	Exams 4th wk.	Fall session begins 3rd wk.	Classes continue.	Break from Thanksgiving Day through the following Sun.	Exams 1st wk.	N/A
No classes July 4.	Summer session ends 2nd wk. Fall semester begins last wk.	No classes Labor Day.	Classes continue.	No classes Veterans' Day. Break from Thanksgiving Day through the following Sun.	Exams 3rd wk.	About 4,500 students are on campus during summer. Campus tours not available during exams.
No classes July 4. Summer session ends 4th wk.	No classes.	Fall session begins 1st wk.	No classes the 9th and 10th.	Break from Wed. before Thanksgiving Day through the following Sun.	Exams 2nd–3rd wks.	Visits are not discouraged during exams, but overnight visits are discouraged then.
No classes.	No classes.	Fall session begins 2nd wk.	Midterm Exams 3rd wk. Fall break end of month–1st wk. in Nov..	Classes resume 1st wk. Break from Wed. before Thanksgiving Day through the following Sun.	Winter break from end of 2nd wk. to end of 1st wk. in Jan.	Campus visits are not discouraged during reading and exam wks., but classes cannot be visited during those times.
Classes continue.	Third summer session ends mid–month.	Fall session begins 1st wk.	Classes continue.	Break from Thanksgiving Day through the following Sun.	Exams 3rd wk.	N/A
Classes continue.	Second summer session ends 1st wk. Fall session begins last wk.	Classes continue.	Midsemester break 2nd or 3rd Mon. and Tues.	Break from Wed. before Thanksgiving Day through the following Sun.	Exams 2nd and 3rd wks.	Campus visits are strongly encouraged all year long.
No classes.	Freshman workshop begins 2nd wk. and ends last wk.	Fall session begins 1st wk.	Reading period 3rd wk.	Break from Wed. before Thanksgiving Day through the following Sun.	Fall session ends 3rd wk.	Exams are held the final wk. of each session.
No classes.	No classes.	Fall session begins 1st wk.	Classes continue.	Break from Tues. before Thanksgiving Day through the following Sun.	Exams 3rd wk.	Approximately 200 high school and freshmen students are on campus during the summer.
Summer session II ends last Sat. in July	Fall semester begins 4th wk.	Classes continue. Fall recess from Sept. 24–29.	Classes continue	Break from Tues. before Thanksgiving through the following Sun.	Exams from Dec. 6–10.	Interviews are not discouraged during exams but it can be difficult to get tours during those times.
No classes.	Fall session begins 4th wk.	Classes continue.	Fall break from 3rd or 4th Thurs. through the following Sun.	Break from Wed. before Thanksgiving Day through the following Sun.	Exams 2nd–3rd wks.	Very few students are on campus during the summer.

School	January	February	March	April	May	June
COLUMBIA UNIVERSITY ✓	Spring session begins 3rd wk. No classes MLK Day.	Classes continue.	Spring break 3rd wk. Classes resume 4th wk.	Reading period last wk.–1st wk. in May.	Exams 1st–2nd wks.	No classes.
CORNELL UNIVERSITY ✓	Winter session, Spring session begin 3rd wk.	Classes continue.	Spring break 3rd wk. Classes resume 4th wk.	Classes continue.	Exams 2nd–3rd wks.	Summer session begins 1st wk.
EUGENE LANG COLLEGE ✓	Spring session begins 4th wk. No classes MLK Day.	Classes continue. No classes Presidents' Day.	Spring break 3rd wk.	Classes continue.	Exams 2nd wk.	No classes.
FORDHAM UNIVERSITY ✓	Spring session begins 3rd wk. No classes MLK Day.	No classes Presidents' Day.	Spring break 2nd wk. Classes resume 3rd wk. No classes Holy Thurs. and Good Fri.	No classes Holy Thurs. and Good Fri.	Exams 2nd wk.	Summer session begins 1st wk.
HAMILTON COLLEGE	Spring session begins 3rd wk.	Classes continue.	Spring break 3rd and 4th wks.	Classes continue.	Exams 2nd wk.	No classes.
HARTWICK COLLEGE	Jan. session begins 2nd wk. and ends 4 wks. later.	Spring semester begins 2nd wk.	Spring break last wk.	Classes resume 1st wk.	Exams 3rd– 4th wk.	No classes.
HOBART AND WILLIAM SMITH COLLEGES ✓	Spring semester begins 3rd wk.	Classes continue.	Spring break 3rd wk.	Classes continue.	Exams 2nd wk.	No classes.
HOFSTRA UNIVERSITY	Jan. session begins 1st wk. No classes MLK Day.	Spring session begins 1st wk. No classes Presidents' Day.	Classes continue.	Spring recess 1st wk.	Reading Days and Finals 3rd wk. Summer session I begins last wk.	Summer session I ends last wk.
ITHACA COLLEGE ✓	Spring session begins 3rd wk.	Classes continue.	Spring break 2nd wk. Classes resume 2nd or 3rd wk.	Classes continue.	Exams 1st wk. Summer session begins last wk.	Classes continue. Session I ends last wk. Session II begins last wk.
THE JUILLIARD SCHOOL	Spring semester begins 2nd wk.	Classes continues.	Spring break first two wks.	Only dance and drama classes from last wk. to first wk. in May.	Final exams 2nd wk.	No classes.
MARIST COLLEGE ✓	Winter mini–session first two wks. Spring term begins 3rd wk. No classes MLK Day.	Classes continue.	Spring break 3rd wk. Classes resume 4th wk.	No classes Good Fri. and Easter Mon.	Exams 2nd wk. Summer I begins 4th wk. No classes Memorial Day.	Summer I ends last wk.

July	August	September	October	November	December	Additional Info
No classes.	No classes.	Fall term begins 1st wk.	Classes continue.	No classes Election Day and Mon. preceding. Break from Thanksgiving Day.	Reading period and exams 2nd–3rd wks.	*Summer session offered.*
Classes continue.	Summer session ends 2nd wk. Fall session begins last wk.	Classes continue.	Fall break from Sat. before Columbus Day through the following Tues.	Break from Wed. before Thanksgiving Day through the following Sun.	Exams 2nd–3rd wks.	*Campus visits are not discouraged during exam periods.*
No classes.	No classes.	Fall session begins 1st wk.	Classes continue.	Break from Thanksgiving Day through the following Sun.	Exams 3rd wk.	*N/A*
No classes July 4.	Summer session ends 2nd wk.	No classes Labor Day. Fall session begins 1st wk.	No classes Columbus Day.	Break from Wed. before Thanksgiving Day through the following Sun.	Exams 3rd wk.	*N/A*
No classes.	Fall session begins last wk.	Classes continue.	Fall break from Oct. 1–6.	Break from Tues. before Thanksgiving Day through the following Sun.	Exams 3rd wk.	*Approximately 50 students are on campus during the summer. Campus visits are not discouraged during exam periods.*
No classes.	No classes.	Fall sessions begin 1st wk.	Fall break from 3rd Sat. through the following Tues.	Break Wed. before Thanksgiving day through the following Sun.	Exams 3rd wk.	*During the summer students do research with faculty research advisors on campus.*
No classes.	No classes.	Classes begin 1st wk.	Fall break 2nd weekend.	T–giving Wed–Sun.	N/A	*N/A*
Summer session II begins 1st wk. No classes Independence Day.	Summer session II ends 1st wk. Summer session III begins 2nd wk. and ends last wk.	Fall semester begins 1st wk. No classes Labor Day.	No classes Yom Kippur.	Thanksgiving recess– no classes through Sun.	Fall semester reading days and finals 3rd wk.	*Campus visits are discouraged during exam periods.*
No classes July 4. Session II Classes continue.	Summer session ends 1st wk. Fall session begins last wk.	No classes Labor Day.	Fall break 2nd or 3rd wk.	Break from Sat. before Thanksgiving Day through the following Sun.	Exams 3rd wk.	*N/A*
No classes.	No classes.	No class on Labor Day. Fall semester begins first wk.	Classes continues	Break from Thanksgiving Day through the following Sun.	Exams third wk.	*N/A*
Summer II begins first wk. No classes July 4.	Summer II ends 2nd wk. Fall session begins last wk.	Classes continue. No classes Labor Day.	No classes 3rd Fri.	Break from Wed. before Thanksgiving through the following Sun.	Exams 3rd wk.	*Campus visits are encouraged throughout the year.*

School	January	February	March	April	May	June
NEW YORK UNIVERSITY	Spring session begins 3rd or 4th wk. No classes MLK Day.	No classes Presidents' Day.	Spring break 2nd wk. Classes resume 3rd wk.	Classes continue.	Exams 1st–2nd wks. Summer session begins 3rd wk. No classes Memorial Day.	Classes continue.
RENSSELAER POLYTECHNIC INSTITUTE	Spring session begins 2nd wk. No classes MLK Day.	No classes Presidents' Day.	Spring break 2nd wk. Classes resume 3rd wk.	Classes continue.	Exams 1st wk. First summer session begins 3rd wk. No classes Memorial Day.	First summer session ends last wk.
ROCHESTER INSTITUTE OF TECHNOLOGY	Winter session continues 1st wk.	Exams last wk. Spring break from end of month–1st wk. in March.	Spring break 1st wk. Spring session begins 2nd wk.	Classes continue.	Exams 4th wk.	Summer session begins 1st wk.
SAINT BONAVENTURE UNIVERSITY	Sat. Tour Dates Jan. 17th and 31st	Sat. Tour Dates Feb. 7th, 21st and 28th	Sat. Tour Dates March 27th	Spring Into Bonaventure–Accepted Students Event April 2nd/ Sat. Tour Date April 3rd.	College Planning Day May 2nd	N/A
SAINT JOHN'S UNIVERSITY	Spring session begins 3rd wk. No classes MLK Day.	No classes Presidents' Day.	Spring break 2nd wk.	Easter recess from Holy Thurs. to Easter Mon.	Exams 1st wk.	First summer session begins.
SAINT LAWRENCE UNIVERSITY	Spring session begins 3rd wk.	Classes continue.	Spring break 3rd wk. Classes resume 4th wk.	Classes continue.	Reading period and exams 1st–2nd wks. Summer session begins last wk.	Classes continue.
SARAH LAWRENCE COLLEGE ✔	Spring session begins 3rd or 4th wk.	Classes continue.	Spring break 3rd–4th wks.	Classes continue.	Spring session ends 3rd wk.	No classes.
SKIDMORE COLLEGE ✔	Spring session begins 3rd wk.	Classes continue.	Spring break 2nd–3rd wks. Classes resume 4th wk.	Classes continue.	Exams 2nd–3rd wks.	First summer session begins 1st wk.
SUNY AT BINGHAMTON	Spring session begins Jan. 20. No classes MLK Day.	Classes continue.	Spring break March 11–14.	Classes resume April 13.	Exams May 10–13.	First summer session begins June 1.
SUNY AT BUFFALO	Spring session begins at start of 2nd. full wk.	Classes continue.	Spring break 3rd wk.	Classes continue.	Exams: 1st wk. Summer session begins 3rd wk.	Summer classes continue.
SYRACUSE UNIVERSITY ✔	Spring session begins 2nd wk. No classes MLK Day.	Classes continue.	Spring break 2nd wk.	No classes Good Fri. Exams last week–1st wk. in May.	Exams 1st wk. Summer session begins 2nd or 3rd wk.	Summer break last wk.

July	August	September	October	November	December	Additional Info
No classes July 4.	Summer session ends 2nd wk.	Fall session begins 1st wk. No classes Labor Day.	Classes continue.	Break from Thanksgiving Day through the following Sun.	Exams 2nd–3rd wks.	*Campus visits are discouraged during exam periods if other visiting days are available.*
Second summer session begins 2nd wk.	Second summer session ends 2nd wk. Fall session begins last wk.	No classes Labor Day.	Fall break from Sat. before Columbus Day through the following Tues.	Break from Wed. before Thanksgiving Day through the following Sun.	Exams 3rd wk.	*Campus visits are encouraged and available during breaks.*
No classes July 4.	Summer session ends 2nd wk.	Fall session begins 1st wk.	Classes continue.	Exams 3rd–4th wks. Break after exams through the end of the month.	Winter session begins 1st wk. Break from Sat. before Xmas–Jan. 3.	*A fairly large number of students are on campus for summer session. Campus visits are not discouraged during exam periods.*
N/A	N/A	N/A	N/A	N/A	N/A	*N/A*
Summer session I ends before July 4. Summer session II begins 2nd wk.	Summer session II ends at end of 1st wk.	Fall session begins 1st wk.	No classes Columbus Day.	Break day before Thanksgiving Day through the following Sun. No classes All Saints' Day.	Exams 2nd–3rd wks. No classes Dec. 8, Feast of the Immaculate Conception.	*Campus visits are not discouraged during exam periods.*
Classes continue.	Summer session ends 1st wk. Fall session begins last wk.	Classes continue.	Fall break from 3rd Thurs. through the following Sun.	Break from Sat. before Thanksgiving Day through the following Sun.	Reading period and exams 2nd–3rd wks.	*Campus visits are not discouraged during exam periods.*
No classes.	No classes.	Fall session begins 2nd wk.	Classes continue.	Break from Wed. before Thanksgiving Day through the following Sun.	Fall session ends 2nd wk.	*Only a few students are on campus during the summer.*
First summer session ends 1st wk. Second Summer session begins 2nd wk.	Second summer session ends 2nd wk.	Fall session begins 2nd wk.	No classes 4th Fri. mid–month.	Break from Wed. before Thanksgiving Day through the following Sun.	Exams 3rd–4th wks.	*Campus visits are not discouraged during exams, but visits at other times are preferred.*
First summer session ends July 2. Second summer session begins July 12.	Second summer session ends Aug. 13. Fall session begins Aug. 30.	No classes Labor Day.	No classes Rosh Hashanah and Yom Kippur.	Break from Wed. before Thanksgiving Day through the following Sun.	Exams Dec. 13–17.	*Check with the Admissions Office before visiting during exam periods.*
No classes July 5.	Summer session ends at the end of 1st. wk. Fall session begins last week	No classes Labor Day. No classes Yom Kippur.	Classes continue.	Break from Wed. before Thanksgiving Day through the following Sun.	Exams: start of 2nd full wk. to start of 3rd full wk.	*During exam periods, information sessions and tours are not scheduled, but interviews are available.*
Classes resume 1st wk.	Summer session ends approximately 1st wk. Fall session begins last wk.	No classes Labor Day. No classes Yom Kippur.	No classes Yom Kippur. Fall break mid–month (long weekend).	Break from Wed. before Thanksgiving Day through the following Sun.	Exams 2nd–3rd wks.	*Campus visits are not discouraged during exam periods.*

School	January	February	March	April	May	June
UNION COLLEGE (NY) ✓	Winter session begins 1st wk.	Classes continue.	Exams 2nd–3rd wks. Spring session begins 4th wk.	Spring session begins 1st wk.	Classes continue.	Exams 2nd wk. Optional summer session begins 3rd wk.
UNITED STATES MILITARY ACADEMY	Spring session begins 3rd wk. No classes MLK weekend.	No classes Presidents' weekend.	Spring break 3rd wk. Classes resume 4th wk.	Classes continue.	Exams 3rd wk.	Military training exercises.
UNIVERSITY OF ROCHESTER ✓	Spring session begins 3rd wk.	Classes continue.	Spring break 1st wk. Classes resume 2nd wk.	Classes continue.	Reading period and exams 2nd–3rd wks. Summer session begins last wk.	Classes continue.
VASSAR COLLEGE ✓	Spring session begins 3rd wk.	Classes continue.	Spring break 2nd wk. Classes resume 4th wk.	Classes continue.	Exams 2nd–3rd wks.	No classes.
WELLS COLLEGE	N/A	N/A	N/A	N/A	N/A	N/A
North Carolina **DAVIDSON COLLEGE**	Spring session begins 2nd wk. No classes MLK Day.	Classes continue.	Spring break 1st wk.	Easter break: Mon. & Tues. after Easter	Exams 1st–2nd wks.	No classes.
DUKE UNIVERSITY	Spring semester begins Jan. 7; no classes on MLK Holiday	Classes continue	Spring break begins 7 pm March 5. Spring break.	Exams last wk. through May 1.	Exams end May 1. Summer session begins May 15.	Summer session I ends June 24. Summer session II begins June 28.
GUILFORD COLLEGE	Spring session begins 2nd wk. No classes MLK Day.	Classes continue.	Spring break from 1st weekend through the following weekend.	Exams from end of month–1st wk. of May.	Exams continue 1st wk. Summer session begins mid–month.	Classes continue.
UNIVERSITY OF NORTH CAROLINA—ASHEVILLE	Spring session begins 2nd full wk. No classes MLK Day.	Classes continue.	Spring break 2nd wk. Classes resume 3rd week	Classes continue.	Exams 1st wk. Classes end. Final grades due 2nd Mon.	Summer term 1 begins June 7.
UNIVERSITY OF NORTH CAROLINA—CHAPEL HILL	Spring session begins 2nd wk. No classes MLK Day.	Classes continue.	Spring break begins end of 1st full wk. Classes resume 3rd full wk.	No classes Good Fri. Classes end 4th wk. Exams go through 1st wk. of May.	Exams 1st wk. Summer session begins 3rd full wk. No classes Memorial Day.	Exams 1st wk. Commencement 2nd weekend. First summer session begins 3rd wk.
WAKE FOREST UNIVERSITY	Spring session begins 3rd wk. No classes MLK Day.	Classes continue.	Spring break 2nd wk. Classes resume 3rd wk.	Classes continue.	Exams 1st–2nd wks. Summer session begins last wk.	Classes continue.

July	August	September	October	November	December	Additional Info
No classes July 4.	Summer session ends 1st wk.	Fall session begins 2nd wk.	Classes continue.	Exams just before Thanksgiving Day.	No classes.	*Campus visits are encouraged throughout the year.*
Military training exercises.	Fall session begins 3rd wk.	Classes continue.	Fall break 3rd Sat. through the following Mon.	Break from Thanksgiving Day through the following Sun.	Fall session ends 3rd wk.	*In summer, cadets receive training that does not allow interaction with visitors.*
No classes July 4.	Summer session ends 2nd wk.	No classes Labor Day. Fall session begins 1st wk.	Fall break from Fri. before Columbus Day through the following Tues.	Break from Fri. before Thanksgiving Day through following Sun.	Reading period and exams 2nd–3rd wks.	*N/A*
No classes.	No classes.	Fall session begins 1st wk.	Fall break 3rd or 4th week; classes resume last wk. or 1st wk. in Nov.	Break from Wed. before Thanksgiving Day through the following Sun.	Exams 3rd wk.	*N/A*
N/A	N/A	N/A	N/A	N/A	N/A	*N/A*
No classes.	Fall session begins 3rd wk.	Classes continue.	Break on Mon. and Tues. of 2nd week	Break from Wed. before Thanksgiving Day through following Sun.	Exams 2nd–3rd wks.	*Campus visits are allowed during exams; overnight stays and class visits are not.*
Classes continue	Summer session II ends Aug. 7. Fall semester begins Aug. 23.	Classes continue	Fall Break begins Oct. 8.	Break from Wed. before Thanksgiving Day through following Sun.	Exams Dec. 6.	*N/A*
No classes July 4. Summer session ends at end of 3rd wk.	Fall session begins 4th wk.	Classes continue.	Break from end of 3rd wk. through the following wk.	Break from Wed. before Thanksgiving Day through the following Sun.	Exams 3rd wk.	*Approximately 300 students are on campus for summer session.*
Classes continue. Summer Term 1 ends July 2. Summer term 2 begins July 6.	Summer term 2 ends Aug. 2 (or 1st Mon.). Fall session begins middle of 3rd wk.	Classes continue. Labor Day holiday 1st Mon.	Fall break last three days of 1st wk. Classes resume on 2nd wk.	Thanksgiving holidays last three days of 4th wk. Classes resume on 5th Mon.	Exams 1st full wk. Classes end. Final grades due 2nd Tues.	*N/A*
No classes Mon. following July 4. Second summer session exams during 3rd wk.	Fall session begins 4th wk.	No classes Labor Day.	Break end of 3rd wk. Oct. 12 is University Day.	Break from 1:00 pm Wed. before Thanksgiving Day through the following Sun.	Classes end 1st wk. Exams end 2nd wk. Dec. commencement Dec. 19.	*N/A*
No classes July 4 weekend.	Summer session ends 2nd wk. Fall session begins last wk.	Classes continue.	Classes continue.	Break from Wed. before Thanksgiving Day through the following Sun.	Exams 2nd wk.	*Campus visits are not discouraged during exams, but no tours are available. Instead information sessions can be scheduled.*

School	January	February	March	April	May	June
North Dakota						
UNIVERSITY OF NORTH DAKOTA	Spring session begins Jan. 13. No classes MLK Day.	Classes continue. No classes Presidents Day.	Spring break 3rd wk. Classes resume 4th wk.	Classes continue. No classes Good Fri. through Easter Mon.	Classes continue. Exams 2nd wk. 1st 6 wk. Summer session begins 3rd wk.	Classes continue. Mid 6 wk. Summer session begins.
Ohio						
ANTIOCH COLLEGE	Classes begin 2nd wk.	Classes continue.	Exams during 3rd wk. Spring break last wk.	Classes resume 1st wk.	Classes continue.	Exams during 3rd wk. Summer break begins last wk.
CASE WESTERN ✓ RESERVE UNIVERSITY	Classes begin 3rd wk. MLK holiday.	Classes continue.	Spring break 2nd wk. Classes resume 3rd wk.	Exams begin last wk.	Exams continue 1st wk. Summer break 2nd wk.	Summer session begins.
THE COLLEGE OF WOOSTER	Spring session begins 2nd wk.	Classes continue.	Spring break 2nd wk. Classes resume last wk.	Classes continue.	Exams begin 2nd wk. Summer break 3rd wk.	Summer session; small number of students on campus.
DENISON UNIVERSITY	Spring session begins 3rd wk. MLK holiday.	Classes continue.	Spring break at end of 2nd wk.	Classes continue.	Exams 1st wk. Summer break begins 3rd wk.	No classes.
HIRAM COLLEGE	Spring–12 session begins 2nd wk.	Classes continue.	Spring break at end of 2nd wk.	Spring–12 exams in 2nd wk. Spring–3 classes begin in 3rd wk.	Spring–3 exams in 2nd week, followed by summer break.	Limited summer classes.
KENYON COLLEGE	Spring session starts 3rd wk.	Classes continue.	Spring break 2nd and 3rd wks. Classes resume 4th wk.	Classes continue.	Exams 2nd wk. Summer break begins 3rd wk.	No classes.
MIAMI UNIVERSITY	Spring session begins 2nd wk. No classes MLK Day.	No classes Presidents' Day.	Spring break 3rd wk. Classes resume 4th wk.	Classes continue.	Exams 1st wk. Break 3rd wk. Summer session begins 4th wk.	Classes continue. Only a limited number of students are on campus.
OBERLIN COLLEGE ✓	Winter session begins 1st wk. and ends last wk.	Spring session begins 1st wk.	Spring break last wk.	Classes resume 1st wk.	Reading period and exams 2nd–3rd wks. Summer break begins last wk.	No classes.
OHIO STATE UNIVERSITY— COLUMBUS	Winter session begins 1st wk. No classes MLK Day.	Classes continue.	Exams 3rd wk. Spring break 3rd wk. Spring session begins last wk.	Classes continue.	No classes Memorial Day.	Exams 1st wk. Break 2nd wk. Summer session begins 3rd wk.
OHIO UNIVERSITY— ATHENS	Winter session begins 1st wk. No classes MLK Day; offices are closed.	Classes continue.	Exams 2nd wk. Spring break 3rd wk. Spring session begins 4th wk.	Classes continue.	No classes Memorial Day and offices are closed.	Exams 1st wk. Summer session begins 2nd wk.

July	August	September	October	November	December	Additional Info
Classes continue. Mid 6 wk. session ends. No classes July 4 Holiday.	Classes continue. 2nd 6 wk. session ends. Graduation on Day 6. Fall begins.	Classes continue. No classes Labor Day.	Classes continue.	Break from Thanksgiving Day through the following Sun.	Classes continue. Exams 2nd wk. Graduation Day. Fall semester ends.	*Campus visits are not discouraged during exam periods.*
No students on campus.	No students on campus.	Classes begin during 3rd wk.	Classes continue.	Exams during wk. before Thanksgiving. Classes continue after Thanksgiving.	Winter break begins mid–Dec.	*Antioch discourages visits during first and last wks. of every quarter.*
Summer session ends. July 4th holiday.	No students on campus until last wk. Fall session begins last wk.	Classes continue.	Oct. break from end of 2nd wk. to middle of 3rd wk.	Break from Thanksgiving Day through the following Sun.	Exams middle of 2nd week–3rd wk.	*N/A*
Summer session continue to end of month.	Classes begin last wk.	Fall break begins 4th wk.	Classes continue.	Break from Thanksgiving Day through the following Sun.	Exams 2nd–3rd wks.	*N/A*
No classes.	Classes begin last wk.	Classes continue.	Fall break 3rd wk.	Break from Thanksgiving Day through the following Mon.	Exams 3rd wk.	*N/A*
Limited summer classes.	Fall–12 classes begin last wk.	No classes Labor Day.	Fall break 2nd weekend.	Fall–12 exams wk. before Thanksgiving, followed by session break.	Fall–3 classes.	*Hiram's calendar consists of 2 semesters, each with a 12–wk. and a 3–wk. session.*
No classes.	Classes begin Aug. 30.	Classes continue.	Reading days Oct. 11–12.	Break from Sat. before Thanksgiving Day through the following Sun.	Exams 3rd wk.	*N/A*
Classes continue. Only a limited number of students are on campus.	Summer session ends 3rd wk. Fall session begins 4th wk.	No classes Labor Day.	Break 2nd Fri. through following Sun.	Break from Tues. before Thanksgiving Day through the following Sun.	Exams 3rd wk.	*N/A*
No classes.	No classes.	Classes begin 1st wk. No classes Labor Day.	Break 3rd wk. Classes resume mid–4th wk.	Break from Thanksgiving Day through the following Sun.	Reading period 2nd wk. Exams 3rd wk.	*N/A*
No classes July 4.	Summer session ends last wk.	Fall session begins 3rd wk.	Classes continue.	No classes Veterans' Day. Break from Thanksgiving Day through the following Sun.	Exams 1st wk. Winter break begins 2nd wk.	*The campus is closed on Martin Luther King Day, Memorial Day, July 4, and Veterans' Day.*
No classes July 4 and offices are closed.	Summer break begins 3rd wk.	Fall session begins 2nd wk.	Classes continue.	Exams begin 5 days before Thanksgiving. Winter break begins Thanksgiving Day.	No classes.	*N/A*

School	January	February	March	April	May	June
OHIO WESLEYAN UNIVERSITY	Spring session begins 3rd wk.	Classes continue.	Spring break 2nd wk. Classes resume 3rd wk.	Classes continue.	Exams 1st–2nd wks. Spring session ends 2nd wk.	Summer session begins 1st wk. and ends last wk.
UNIVERSITY OF DAYTON	Winter semester begins 1st wk. No classes MLK Day.	Two–day break 4th wk.	Spring break 4th wk. Classes resume 5th wk.	Exams begin 4th wk.	Exams end 1st wk. 1st summer session begins 3rd wk. No classes Memorial Day.	1st summer session ends 4th wk. 2nd summer session begins 5th wk.
WITTENBERG UNIVERSITY	Winter session begins 2nd wk.	Classes continue.	Exams 1st wk. Break 2nd wk. Spring session begins 4th wk. No classes Good Fri.	Classes continue.	Classes continue.	Exams 1st wk. Summer session begins late June.
Oklahoma **UNIVERSITY OF OKLAHOMA**	Spring session begins 2nd or 3rd wk. No classes MLK Day.	Classes continue.	Spring break 2nd or 3rd wk. Classes resume 3rd or 4th wk.	Classes continue.	Exams 1st or 2nd wk.	Summer session begins 1st wk.
Oregon **LEWIS & CLARK COLLEGE** ✓	Spring session begins 2nd wk.	Classes continue.	Spring break 3rd–4th wks.	Classes continue. Final exams last wk.	Summer sessions begin.	Summer sessions begin.
REED COLLEGE ✓	Spring session begins 3rd or 4th wk.	Classes continue.	Spring break 3rd wk. Classes resume 4th wk.	Reading period last week–1st wk. in May.	Reading period 1st wk. Exams 2nd wk.	Summer vacation. No classes.
WILLAMETTE UNIVERSITY	Spring session begins 3rd wk.	Classes continue.	Spring break 4th wk. Classes resume 5th wk.	Exams last week– 1st wk. in May	Exams 1st week	No classes
Pennsylvania **ALLEGHENY COLLEGE** ✓	Spring session begins 3rd wk.	Classes continue.	Spring break 3rd wk. Classes resume 4th wk.	Classes continue.	Exams 1st–2nd wks.	No classes.
BRYN MAWR COLLEGE	Spring session begins 3rd or 4th Mon.	Classes continue.	Spring break 1st wk. Classes resume 2nd wk.	Classes continue.	Exams 1st–2nd wks.	No classes.
BUCKNELL UNIVERSITY ✓	Spring session begins 3rd wk.	Classes continue.	Spring break 3rd wk.	Classes continue.	Exams 2nd wk.	Summer session begins 3rd wk.
CARNEGIE MELLON UNIVERSITY	Spring session begins 2nd wk.	Classes continue.	No classes 1st Fri. Spring break 2nd wk.	Classes continue.	Exams 1st– 2nd wks. Summer session begins 3rd wk. No classes Memorial Day.	Classes continue.

July	August	September	October	November	December	Additional Info
No classes.	Fall session begins last wk.	Classes continue.	Classes continue.	Break from Sat. before Thanksgiving Day through the following Sun.	Exams begin at end of 2nd wk. Winter break begins at end of 3rd wk.	*Only a small number of students are on campus during the summer session.*
No classes July 4th.	2nd summer session ends 1st wk. Fall semester begins 4th wk.	No classes Labor Day.	Classes continue.	Break from Wed. before Thanksgiving through the following Sun.	No classes Dec. 8. Exams 3rd wk.	*For more information and to request a campus visit, see our website.*
Classes continue.	Fall session begins 4th wk.	Classes continue.	Classes continue.	Exams wk. before Thanksgiving. Winter break begins Thanksgiving.	No classes.	*Wittenberg's academic year consists of 3 trimesters and a summer term.*
No classes July 4. Summer session ends last wk.	Fall session begins last wk.	No classes Labor Day.	Classes continue.	Break from Wed. before Thanksgiving through the following Sun.	Exams 2nd and 3rd wk.	*Tours Mon. through Fri. and Sat. a.m. (except holidays). See www.go2.ou.edu for dates and times.*
Summer sessions end.	No classes.	Fall session begins after Labor Day.	Fall break 2nd wk.	Exams immediately precede Thanksgiving Day.	Classes end Dec. 13. Exams Dec. 15–20.	*Campus visits are not discouraged during exams, but overnight dorm stays and class visits are not possible.*
No classes.	Fall session begins last wk.	No classes Labor Day.	Fall break 3rd wk. Classes resume 4th wk.	Break from Thanksgiving Day through the following Sun.	Reading period 1st wk. Exams 2nd wk.	*Campus visits are not discouraged during exams, but overnight stays are not possible.*
No classes	No classes	Fall session begins 1st wk.	No classes 4th Fri.	Break from Wed. before Thanksgiving Day through the following Sun.	Exams 3rd wk.	*Sat. tours and interviews available mid–Sept. thru mid–Dec. and mid–Jan. thru April.*
No classes.	Fall semester begins 4th wk.	Classes continue.	Classes continue. Fall break 2nd wk.	Break from Wed. before Thanksgiving Day through the following Sun.	Exams 3rd wk.	*Approximately 100 students are on campus during the summer.*
No classes.	No classes.	Fall session begins 1st wk.	Break from end of 2nd wk. to middle of 3rd wk.	Break from Wed. before Thanksgiving Day through the following Sun.	Exams from end of 2nd wk. to end of 3rd wk.	*N/A*
Summer session ends 3rd wk.	Fall session begins 4th wk.	Classes continue.	Fall break from 3rd Sat. through following Tues.	Break from Wed. before Thanksgiving Day through the following Sun.	Exams 2nd and 3rd wks.	*Except for 50 students engaged in research, very few students are on campus during Aug.*
No classes July 4.	Summer session ends at end of 1st wk. Fall session begins last wk.	No classes Labor Day.	No classes 4th Fri.	Break from Wed. before Thanksgiving through following Sun.	Exams 2nd– 3rd wk.	*Dates for summer session are for full summer session.*

School	January	February	March	April	May	June
CHATHAM COLLEGE	Winter session begins 1st full wk. and ends last wk. No class MLK Day.	Spring session begins 1st wk.	Spring break 3rd wk. Class resume 4th wk.	Classes continue.	Exams end of 2nd–3rd wk.	Summer session begins 1st wk.
DICKINSON COLLEGE ✔	Spring session begins 4th wk.	Classes continue.	Spring break from end of 2nd wk. to beginning of 4th wk.	Classes continue.	Exams 2nd–3rd wks.	Summer session begins 1st wk. Classes continue.
DREXEL UNIVERSITY	Winter session begins 2nd wk. No classes MLK Day.	No classes Presidents' Day.	Exams 3rd wk. No classes Good Fri.	Spring session begins 1st wk. No classes Good Fri.	No classes Memorial Day.	Exams 2nd wk. Summer session begins 4th wk.
DUQUESNE UNIVERSITY	Spring semester begins 2nd wk. University Closed MLK Day.	Classes continue.	Spring/ Easter Break March 21–28, 2005. University closed March 24–25, 2005.	Final exams begin last wk.	Summer session begins.	Summer DukeFest June 27, 2004.
FRANKLIN & MARSHALL COLLEGE ✔	Spring session begins 3rd wk.	Classes continue.	Spring break begins at end of 1st wk. Classes resume at start of 3rd wk.	Classes continue.	Reading days and exams 1st and 2nd wks.	Summer session begins 1st week
GETTYSBURG COLLEGE ✔	Spring session begins 4th wk.	Classes continue.	Spring break 3rd wk. Classes resume 4th wk.	Classes continue. Closed Good Fri.	Exams 2nd wk.	No classes.
HAVERFORD COLLEGE	Spring session begins 3rd wk.	Classes continue.	Spring break 2nd full wk.	Classes continue.	Reading period and exams 2nd–3rd wks.	No classes.
LAFAYETTE COLLEGE ✔	Winter session begins 1st wk. and ends 4th wk. Spring session begins last wk.	Classes continue.	Spring break 3rd wk.	Classes continue.	Exams 2nd wk.	Summer session begins 1st wk.
LEHIGH UNIVERSITY ✔	Winter/Spring semester begins mid–Jan.	Break Thurs.–Fri. of Presidents' weekend.	Spring break second wk. in March.	Classes end the last wk. in April.	Final exams first two wks. in May. Summ sess I begins Third wk. in May. Graduation end of May.	Summer session I ends third wk. in June.
PENNSYLVANIA STATE UNIVERSITY PARK	Spring session begins 2nd wk.	Classes continue.	Spring break 1st wk. Classes resume 2nd wk.	Classes continue.	Reading period 1st wk. Exams 2nd wk. Intersession begins 3rd wk.	Intersession ends 1st wk. Summer session begins 2nd wk.
SWARTHMORE COLLEGE	Classes begin 3rd or 4th wk.	Classes continue.	Spring break 2nd wk. Classes resume 3rd wk.	Classes continue.	Exams 1st–2nd wk.	No classes.

July	August	September	October	November	December	Additional Info
Summer session ends 3rd wk.	No classes.	Fall session begins 1st wk.	Break Thu–Fri of 3rd wk.	Break from Wed. before Thanksgiving through the following Sun.	Exams from end of 2nd wk. –beginning of 3rd wk.	*Campus visits are not discouraged during exam period.*
No classes July 4.	Summer session ends on Aug. 6.	Fall session begins 1st wk.	Break 1st half of 3rd wk.	Break from Tues. before Thanksgiving Day through the following Sun.	Exams 3rd wk.	*N/A*
No classes July 4.	Classes continue.	No classes Labor Day. Exams 1st wk. Fall session begins 3rd wk.	No classes Columbus Day.	Break from Wed. before Thanksgiving Day through the following Sun.	Exams 1st wk.	*Campus visits are not discouraged during exam periods.*
University closed July 5, 2004– Independence Day Observed.	New freshman orientation begins Aug 18, classes begin Aug 23, 2004.	University closed Sept 6, 2004– Labor Day.	Classes continue. Fall campus visit day Oct 10, 2004.	University closed Nov 1– Holyday, no classes wk. of Thanksgiving, closed Nov 24–25.	Closed Dec 8– Holyday. Final exams mid Dec. University closed between Xmas and New Years.	*Please visit our website for the most up to date calendar. www.admissions.duq. edu*
Classes continue.	Summer session ends mid– month.	Fall session begins 1st wk.	Break from end of 2nd wk. to middle of the following wk.	Break from Tues. before Thanksgiving Day through the following Sun.	Reading days and exams from end of 1st week– middle of 3rd wk.	*About 250 students are on campus in the summer. Campus visits are not discouraged during exams.*
No classes.	Fall session begins last wk.	Classes continue.	No classes 1st Mon. and Tues. (reading days).	Break from Wed. before Thanksgiving Day through the following Sun.	Exams 3rd wk.	*N/A*
No classes.	No classes.	Fall session begins on Labor Day.	Break Mon.– Tues. of 3rd wk.	Break from Thanksgiving Day through the following Sun.	Reading period and exams 2nd– 3rd wks.	*Approximately 50 students work on campus from June 1 to Aug. 15.*
Classes continue.	Summer session ends last wk. Fall session begins last wk.	Classes continue.	Break 1st Mon. and Tues.	Break from Wed. before Thanksgiving Day through the following Sun.	Exams 2nd–3rd wks.	*N/A*
Summer session II begins second wk. in July.	Summer session II ends second wk. in Aug.	Fall session begins 1st wk. (or end of Aug.).	Break Thurs. and Fri. before Columbus Day.	Break from day before Thanksgiving day through following Sun.	Classes end first wk. Exams end by mid–Dec.. Break until mid Jan.	*Limited campus tour schedule during exams and break. Check visit schedule updated on the web @ Lehigh.edu.*
No classes July 4.	Summer session ends 1st wk. Fall session begins 3rd wk.	No classes Labor Day.	Classes continue.	Break from Thanksgiving Day through the following Sun.	Exams 2nd wk.	*N/A*
No classes.	No classes.	Fall session begins Labor Day.	Break from end of 2nd wk. through end of 3rd wk.	Break from Thanksgiving Day through the following Sun.	Exams from end of 2nd week–end of 3rd wk.	*Interviews can be scheduled during exam periods.*

School	January	February	March	April	May	June
TEMPLE UNIVERSITY	Spring classes begin 3rd wk.	Classes continue.	Spring break 2nd wk.	Classes continue.	Spring classes end 1st wk. 2 study days. Exams 2nd wk. 1st summer session begins 3rd wk.	Classes continue.
UNIVERSITY OF PENNSYLVANIA ✔	Spring session begins 3rd wk.	Classes continue.	Spring break 2nd wk. Classes resume 3rd wk.	Classes continue.	Exams 1st–2nd wks. Summer session begins 4th wk.	Classes continue.
UNIVERSITY OF PITTSBURGH— PITTSBURGH CAMPUS	Spring Term begins first wk. No classes on 3rd Mon. for MLK.	Spring Term Classes continue.	Spring Recess begins the first Sun. and ends the second Sun.	Exam period is 3rd wk. and Spring Term ends.	May through Aug.: seven Summer sessions, of varying lengths, begin and end.	Summer sessions Classes continue.
THE UNIVERSITY OF SCRANTON	Intercession begins on Jan. 5. Spring semester begins Jan. 29	Royal Nights– overnight program for accepted students, Feb. 15 and 22.	Spring break third wk., classes resume 4th wk. Royal Nights Mar. 7 and 28	Preview Day for Accepted Students April 3.	Exams 3rd wk. Commencement is Memorial weekend.	Summer sessions begin 1st wk.
VILLANOVA UNIVERSITY ✔	Spring session begins 3rd wk.	Classes continue.	Break 1st full wk. Break from Thurs. before Easter through the following Mon.	Break Thurs. before Easter thru following Mon. Rdg. days and exams last wk.–1st wk. May.	Exams 1st wk. Summer session begins last wk.	Classes continue.
Rhode Island						
BROWN UNIVERSITY ✔	Spring session begins during 3rd full wk.	Break from Sat. before Presidents' Day through the following Tues.	Spring break last wk.	Classes resume 1st wk. Reading period begins end of month.	Exams 2nd–3rd wks.	No classes.
PROVIDENCE COLLEGE	N/A	N/A	N/A	N/A	N/A	N/A
RHODE ISLAND SCHOOL OF DESIGN ✔	Winter session begins 2nd wk. No classes MLK Day	Winter session ends 2nd wk. Spring session begins 4th wk.	Spring break 5th wk.	Classes resume first full wk.	Exams 3rd– 4th wk.	Summer session begins 3rd wk.
UNIVERSITY OF RHODE ISLAND ✔	Spring session begins 3rd wk. No classes MLK Day.	Classes continue.	Spring break 2nd wk. Classes resume 3rd wk.	Classes continue.	Exams 1st–2nd wks. Summer session begins 4th wk.	Summer session I ends 3rd wk. Summer session II begins 4th wk.
South Carolina						
CLEMSON UNIVERSITY	Spring session begins 2nd wk.	Classes continue.	Spring break 3rd wk. Classes resume 4th wk.	Exams from last wk.–1st wk. in May.	Exams 1st wk. Summer session begins 3rd wk.	Classes continue.
COLLEGE OF CHARLESTON	Spring session begins second wk. No classes MLK Day.	Classes continue.	Spring break begins first or second wk.	Last day of spring classes, end of the month. Exams begin, end of the month.	Spring semester exams end. Commencement, second or third Sun. Maymester begins.	Maymester ends, Summer session I begins.

July	August	September	October	November	December	Additional Info
1st summer session ends 1st wk. 2nd session begins 2nd wk.	2nd summer session ends mid–month.	Fall semester begins 1st wk.	Classes continue	Break from Thanksgiving to following Sun.	Fall classes end second wk. 2 study days. Exams 3rd wk.	*N/A*
Classes continue.	Summer session ends 1st wk.	Fall session begins 1st wk.	Fall break mid–month.	Break from Wed. before Thanksgiving Day through the following Sun.	Exams 2nd–3rd wks.	*N/A*
Independence Day observed– no classes. Summer sessions Classes continue.	Last of the Summer sessions ends 1st wk. Fall term begins fourth wk.	No classes in observance of Labor Day. Fall term Classes continue.	Fall term Classes continue.	Fall term Classes continue. Thanksgiving Recess from Wed. through following Sun.	Exam period is 2nd wk. and Fall term ends.	*N/A*
No class July 5	Summer sessions end 1st wk. and classes begin last wk.	No classes Labor Day.	Open house Oct. 24.	Open house Nov. 7.	N/A	*N/A*
No classes July 4. Summer sessions end last wk.	Fall session begins last wk.	Fall session begins 1st wk. No classes Labor Day.	1–wk. break scheduled 2nd, 3rd, or 4th wk.	Break from Wed. before Thanksgiving Day through the following Sun.	Reading days and exams from end of 2nd–3rd wk.	*Campus visits are not discouraged during exam periods. Refer to www.admission.villanova.edu for current campus visit and date availability.*
No classes.	No classes.	Fall session begins 1st wk.	No classes Columbus Day.	Break from Wed. before Thanksgiving Day through the following Sun.	Reading period begins end of 1st wk. Exams 2nd–3rd wks.	*N/A*
N/A	N/A	N/A	N/A	N/A	N/A	*N/A*
Summer session ends last wk.	No classes	Fall session begins 3rd wk.	No classes Columbus Day	Break from Wed. before Thanksgiving through the following Sun.	Exams 2nd wk.	*The summer session is only for transfer students; no other students are on campus at that time.*
No classes July 4. Summer session II ends 4th wk.	No classes.	Fall session begins 1st wk.	No classes Columbus Day.	Break from Thanksgiving Day through the following Sun.	Exams 2nd–3rd wks.	*N/A*
No classes July 4. Summer session II ends 4th wk.	Classes begin 3rd wk.	Classes continue.	Classes continue.	Fall break 1st wk. Break from Thanksgiving Day through the following Sun.	Exams 2nd wk.	*Campus visits are not discouraged during exam periods.*
No classes, July 4 Holiday. Summer session I ends. Summer session II begins.	Summer session II ends. Fall semester begins end of the month.	Classes continue.	Fall break, middle of month.	Thanksgiving holiday, Wed.–Sun. of Thanksgiving wk.	Classes end first wk., exams begin and end. Mid–year commencement middle of month.	*Please check our website for academic calendar and campus tour and visitation schedule at www.cofc.edu*

School	January	February	March	April	May	June
FURMAN UNIVERSITY	Winter session begins 1st wk.	Exams 3rd–4th wks. Spring break 4th wk.–1st wk. in March.	Spring session begins 1st or 2nd wk. No classes Good Fri. or Mon. after Easter.	No classes Good Fri. or Mon. after Easter.	Exams last wk.	First summer session begins 2nd wk. and lasts 6 wks.
UNIVERSITY OF SOUTH CAROLINA COLUMBIA	Spring session begins 3rd wk.	Classes continue.	Spring break 2nd wk. Classes resume 3rd wk. No classes Easter Mon.	No classes Easter Mon. Exams last wk.–1st wk. in May.	Exams 1st wk.	Summer session begins 1st wk.
Tennessee						
FISK UNIVERSITY	Jan. 5–6, Mon.–Tues. Placement tests for new students; advising and registration Jan. 7.	Feb. 2, Mon. University scholarship application deadline for enrolled students.	March 1, Mon. Scholar's Research Day; March 1–5, Mon.–Fri. Spring recess.	April 1–11, Thurs.–Sun. Spring Arts Festival April 8.	May 3, Mon. Commencement.	N/A
RHODES COLLEGE	Spring session begins 2nd wk. No classes MLK Day.	Classes continue.	Spring break 2nd wk. Easter break from Wed. before Easter to following Mon.	Classes end last wk.	No classes after exams in 1st wk.	No classes.
THE UNIVERSITY OF THE SOUTH	Spring session begins 2nd wk.	Classes continue.	Spring break from mid–2nd month to end of 3rd wk. Classes resume 4th wk.	Classes continue.	Exams 1st–2nd wks.	Summer session begins 2nd wk.
UNIVERSITY OF TENNESSEE— KNOXVILLE	Spring session begins 2nd wk. No classes MLK Day.	Classes continue.	Spring break	No classes Good Fri. Classes end last wk.	Exams first wk. Mini–term starts, no classes Memorial Day.	Summer session begins.
VANDERBILT UNIVERSITY	Spring session begins 2nd wk.	Classes continue.	Spring break 1st wk. Classes resume 2nd wk.	Exams last wk. – 1st wk. in May.	Exams continue 1st wk. May session.	Summer session begins 1st wk.
Texas						
BAYLOR UNIVERSITY ✓	Spring session begins 2nd wk. No classes MLK Day.	Classes continue.	Spring break 2nd wk. Classes resume 3rd wk.	Break from Good Fri. to Easter Mon.	Exams 2nd–3rd wks. Summer session begins after Memorial Day.	Summer classes begin June 1.
RICE UNIVERSITY ✓	Spring session begins 2nd wk.	Classes continue.	Spring break 1st wk. Classes resume 2nd wk. No classes Thurs.–Fri. before Easter.	No classes Thurs.–Fri. before Easter. Reading period 3rd wk. Exams 4th wk.	No classes.	No classes.
SOUTHERN METHODIST UNIVERSITY ✓	Inter–term classes to mid–month. Spring session begins 3rd wk. No classes MLK Day.	Classes continue.	Spring break 2nd wk. Classes resume 3rd wk.	No classes Good Fri.	Exams 1st wk. No classes Memorial Day.	Classes continue. Summer session begins 1st wk.
TCU ✓	Spring session begins 3rd wk.	Classes continue.	Spring break 3rd wk. Classes resume 4th wk. No classes Good Fri.	No classes Good Fri.	Exams 2nd wk. Summer session begins 3rd wk.	Classes continue.

July	August	September	October	November	December	Additional Info
Second summer session begins 4th wk.	Second summer session ends mid–month.	Fall session begins 2nd wk.	Fall weekend variable. No classes Fri.	Break from Sat. before Thanksgiving Day through the following Sun.	Exams 1st–2nd wks.	*Approximately 300 students are on campus for summer sessions.*
Exams 1st wk. No classes July 4. Summer session continues 2nd wk.	Summer session ends 2nd wk. Fall session begins last wk.	No classes Labor Day.	Fall break Mon.–Tues. mid–month.	No classes Election Day. Break from Wed. before Thanksgiving through following Sun.	Exams 2nd–3rd wks.	*Campus visits are not discouraged during exam periods.*
N/A	N/A	N/A	N/A	N/A	N/A	*N/A*
No classes.	Fall session begins last wk.	Classes continue.	Break 3rd Mon.–Tues.	Break from Wed. before Thanksgiving Day through the following Sun.	Exams from end of 2nd–3rd wks.	*Approximately 30 students are on campus during the summer.*
Summer session ends end of 3rd wk.	Fall session begins last wk.	Classes continue.	Break from end of 2nd wk.–middle of 3rd wk.	Break from Wed. before Thanksgiving Day through the following Sun.	Exams 2nd–3rd wks.	*During exams, interviews are available; tours are not.*
First summer session ends. Second summer session begins. No classes July 4	Summer session ends first wk. Classes begin 3rd wk.	No classes Labor Day.	Fall break, mid–month.	Thanksgiving break.	Classes end. Exams 2nd wk.	*N/A*
No classes July 4 (in most cases).	Summer session ends 2nd wk. Fall session begins last wk.	Classes continue.	Classes continue.	Break from Sat. before Thanksgiving Day through the following Sun.	Exams 2nd–3rd wks.	*N/A*
No classes July 4.	Summer session ends 2nd wk. Fall session begins last wk.	Classes continue.	Classes continue. Break (1–day) mid–month.	Break from Wed. before Thanksgiving through the following Sun.	Exams 2nd–3rd wks.	*N/A*
No classes.	Fall session begins last wk.	No classes Labor Day.	No classes Mon.–Fri. mid–month.	Break from Thanksgiving Day through the following Sun.	Reading period 2nd wk. Exams 2nd–3rd wks.	*N/A*
No classes July 5.	Summer session ends 1st wk. Fall session begins last wk.	Classes continue.	Classes continue. Fall break 11–12.	Break from Thanksgiving Day through the following Sun.	Exams 2nd wk.	*N/A*
No classes July 4.	Summer session ends 1st wk. Fall session begins last wk.	Classes continue. No classes Labor Day.	Break (1-day) mid–month.	Break from Thanksgiving Day through the following Sun.	Exams 3rd wk.	*N/A*

School	January	February	March	April	May	June
TEXAS A&M UNIVERSITY— COLLEGE STATION	Spring semester begins 3rd wk. No classes on MLK Day.	Classes Continue	Spring break 3rd wk. Classes resume 4th wk.	Classes Continue	Spring semester Finals 2nd wk. Spring Graduation.	SS I begins 1st wk.
TRINITY UNIVERSITY ✓	Spring session begins 3rd wk.	Classes continue.	Spring break 3rd wk. Classes resume 4th wk.	No classes Good Fri.	Reading period 1st wk. Exams 1st–2nd wks. Summer session begins last wk.	Classes continue.
UNIVERSITY OF DALLAS	Interterm classes to mid month. Spring session begins 3rd wk.	Visit Weekend I (Odyssey). Classes continue.	Spring break 2nd wk. Visit Weekend II (Odyssey).	Break from Good Fri. to Easter Mon.	Exams 2nd wk. May session begins. Closed Memorial Day	Summer session begins 2nd wk.
THE UNIVERSITY OF TEXAS AT AUSTIN ✓	Spring session begins 2nd or 3rd wk. No classes MLK Day.	Classes continue.	Spring break 2nd or 3rd wk. Classes resume 3rd or 4th wk.	Classes continue.	Exams 2nd wk.	Summer session begins 1st wk.
Toronto UNIVERSITY OF TORONTO ✓	Winter session begins first wk.	Classes continue. Reading wk. mid–month.	Classes continue.	University closed Good Fri. Classes end after second wk. Final examinations.	Summer session classes begin. University closed on Victoria Day.	Summer session classes continue. Spring convocation.
Utah BRIGHAM YOUNG UNIVERSITY (UT)	Winter session begins 2nd or 3rd wk. No classes MLK Day.	No classes Presidents' Day.	Classes continue.	Exams 4th wk.	Spring session begins 1st wk.	Exams 3rd wk. Summer session begins 4th wk.
Vermont BENNINGTON COLLEGE	No classes: winter terms is a fieldwork term.	No classes.	Spring session begins 1st wk.	Spring break last weekend.	Exams last wk.– 2nd wk. of June.	Exams continue into 2nd wk.
GODDARD COLLEGE	No classes.	Spring session begins 1st wk.	Spring break 3rd wk.	Classes continue.	Evaluation wk. last wk.	No classes.
MARLBORO COLLEGE	Spring session begins 3rd wk.	Classes continue.	Spring break from end of 2nd wk. to end of month.	Classes resume 1st wk.	Exams end of 2nd–3rd wk.	No classes.
MIDDLEBURY COLLEGE ✓	Winter session begins 2nd wk. and ends last wk.	Spring session begins 2nd wk. No classes from 3rd Wed. through following Sun.	Spring break last wk.	Classes resume 1st wk.	No undergraduate classes.	No undergraduate classes.
UNIVERSITY OF VERMONT ✓	Spring session begins 3rd wk. No classes MLK Day.	No classes Presidents' Day.	Spring break 3rd wk. Classes resume 4th wk.	Classes continue.	Exams 2nd wk. Summer session begins 4th wk.	Classes continue.

July	August	September	October	November	December	Additional Info
SS I Finals. SS II begins. No classes July 4th.	SS II Finals. Summer Graduation 2nd wk.	Fall semester begins 1st wk.	Classes continue.	Classes continue. 2 day Thanksgiving break.	Fall semester Finals 2nd wk. Fall Graduation.	*New freshmen conferences held throughout the summer.*
No classes July 4. Summer session ends 2nd wk.	Fall session begins last wk.	No classes Labor Day.	No classes 3rd Fri.	Break from Thanksgiving Day through the following Sun.	Reading period 1st or 2nd wk. Exams 2nd–3rd wks.	*Campus visits are not discouraged during exam periods.*
No classes July 4.	Summer session ends 2nd wk.	Fall classes begin 1st wk.	No classes 3rd Fri.	Break from Thanksgiving Day through the following Sun.	Exams from end of 2nd wk. through 3rd wk.	*Campus visits available during exam wk.; overnight stays and classes are not.*
No classes July 4.	Exams 2nd–3rd wks. Fall session begins last wk.	No classes Labor Day.	Classes continue.	Break from Thanksgiving Day through the following Sun.	Exams 2nd–3rd wks.	*About 10,000 students are on campus during the summer. Visitors are welcome during exams, but it's best to visit another time.*
University closed on Canada Day. Summer session Classes continue.	University closed on Civic holiday. Summer session classes end. Summer session exams.	University closed Labor Day. Fall term classes begin second wk.	Classes continue. University closed Thanksgiving Day.	Classes continue. Fall Convocation.	Exams 2nd and 3rd wk. University closed over the Xmas holidays.	*Campus visits are encouraged year round except on statutory holidays and over the Xmas holidays.*
No classes July 4.	Summer session ends 2nd wk.	Fall session begins 1st wk.	Classes continue.	Break from Thanksgiving Day through the following Sun.	Exams 3rd wk.	*N/A*
No classes.	No classes.	Fall session begins 1st wk.	Break 3rd–4th wks.	Break from Wed. before Thanksgiving through the following Sun.	Exams 1st and 2nd wks.	*Tours and interviews are available during exam periods.*
No classes.	No classes.	Fall session begins 1st wk.	Classes continue.	Break from Wed. before Thanksgiving through the following Sun.	Evaluation wk. 3rd wk.	*Campus visiting is discouraged during evaluation wks.*
No classes.	No classes.	Fall session begins 1st wk.	Classes continue.	Break from Tues. before Thanksgiving Day through the following Sun.	Exams 2nd wk.	*Campus visits are not discouraged during exams.*
No undergraduate classes.	Fall session begins 2nd wk.	Break 3rd Thurs. and Fri.	Break from Tues. before Thanksgiving Day through the following Sun.	Exams 2nd–3rd wks.	Very few regular college students are on campus during the summer.	*N/A*
No classes July 4.	Summer session ends at end of 1st wk. Fall session begins last wk.	No classes Labor Day.	Classes continue.	Break from Wed. before Thanksgiving Day through the following Sun.	Exams 2nd wk.	*N/A*

School	January	February	March	April	May	June
Virginia						
COLLEGE OF WILLIAM AND MARY ✔	Spring session begins 3rd wk.	Classes continue.	Spring break 2nd full wk. Classes resume 3rd wk.	Classes continue to end of month.	Exams 1st–2nd wks.	Summer session begins 1st wk.
HAMPDEN— SYDNEY COLLEGE	N/A	N/A	N/A	N/A	N/A	N/A
HOLLINS UNIVERSITY ✔	Short–term session begins during 1st wk. and ends at end of month.	Spring session begins 1st wk.	Spring break last full wk.	Classes resume 1st wk.	Exams end of 2nd–3rd wks.	No undergraduate classes.
JAMES MADISON UNIVERSITY ✔	Spring session begins 2nd wk. No classes MLK Day.	Classes continue.	Spring break 2nd wk. Classes resume 3rd wk.	Semester ends last day of month.	Exams 1st wk. Summer session begins 3rd wk. No classes Memorial Day	First summer session ends 2nd wk. Second summer session begins 3rd wk.
MARY WASHINGTON COLLEGE	Classes begin the second wk.	Classes continue.	Spring break the first wk. of the month.	Classes continue; exams begin the last wk. of the month.	No classes.	Summer school session.
RANDOLPH– MACON COLLEGE	Jan. Term begins 1st full wk., end last wk.	Spring session begin 2nd wk.	Spring break last wk.	Classes resume 1st full wk.	Exams 3rd wk. Graduation last wk.	Summer session begins first wk.
RANDOLPH– MACON WOMAN'S COLLEGE	Spring session begins 3rd wk.	Classes continue.	Spring break 2nd wk. Classes resume 2nd full wk.	Exams last Sat.– 1st wk. in May.	Exams 1st wk.	No classes.
SWEET BRIAR COLLEGE ✔	Spring session begins 2nd wk.	Classes continue.	Spring break 1st wk.	Exams last wk.	No classes.	No classes.
UNIVERSITY OF VIRGINIA ✔	Spring session begins 3rd wk.	Classes continue.	Spring break from end of 1st full wk. to Mon. of 3rd wk.	Classes continue to end of month.	Exams end of 1st wk.–2nd wk.	No classes.
WASHINGTON AND LEE UNIVERSITY	Winter term begins 2nd wk.	Break from end of 2nd wk. to beginning of last wk.	Classes continue.	Exams 2nd wk. Break from end of 2nd wk. to beginning of 4th wk. Spring term begins 4th wk.	Classes continue.	Exams and graduation 1st wk.
Washington						
THE EVERGREEN STATE COLLEGE ✔	Winter session begins 2nd wk. No classes MLK Day.	No classes Presidents' Day.	Exams and end of winter session 3rd wk.	Spring session begins 1st wk.	No classes Memorial Day.	Exams 2nd wk. Summer session begins last wk.

July	August	September	October	November	December	Additional Info
Classes continue.	Summer session ends at end of 1st full wk. Fall session begins last wk.	Classes continue.	Break from end of 2nd wk. to Wed. of the following wk.	Break from Wed. before Thanksgiving Day through the following Sun.	Exams from end of 1st wk. through 3rd wk.	*Campus visits are not discouraged during exam periods.*
N/A	N/A	N/A	N/A	N/A	N/A	*N/A*
No undergraduate classes.	No undergraduate classes.	Fall session begins 1st wk.	Two day Fall break during 1st full wk.	Break from Sat. before Thanksgiving Day through the following Sun.	Exams 2nd–3rd wks.	*Summer tours and interviews are offered at 9 am, 11 am, and 2pm, Mon.–Fri.*
No classes July 5. 8–wk. session ends 2nd Fri. 10–wk. session ends 4th Fri.	Fall semester begins 4th wk.	Classes continue.	No classes Oct. 15.	Break from Thanksgiving Day through the following Sun.	Exams begin 2nd wk.	*N/A*
Summer school session.	Classes begin the last wk.	Classes continue.	Classes continue; Fall Break during the middle on the month.	Classes continue; break for Thanksgiving beginning Wed.	Classes during the first wk.; exams begin.	*N/A*
Summer session ends 2nd wk.	No classes.	Fall session begins 1st wk.	Fall break begins end 2nd wk. through following Tues.	Break from Wed. before Thanksgiving through following Sun.	Exams 2nd wk.	*Very few regular students on campus during summer.*
No classes.	Fall session begins last wk.	Classes continue.	Fall break from 3rd Fri. through following Mon.	Break from Tues. before Thanksgiving Day through the following Mon.	Exams 3rd wk.	*N/A*
No classes.	Fall session begins last wk.	Classes continue.	Classes continue.	Break from Sat. before Thanksgiving Day through the following Sun.	Exams 2nd wk.	*N/A*
No classes.	Fall session begins last wk.	Classes continue.	Break from end of 3rd wk. through the following Tues.	Break from Wed. before Thanksgiving Day through the following Sun.	Exams 2nd wk.	*N/A*
No classes.	No classes	Fall term begins 2nd wk.	No classes for 2 reading days mid–month.	Break from Fri. before Thanksgiving Day through the following Sun.	Exams from end of 2nd wk. through 3rd wk.	*N/A*
No classes July 4. Summer session ends last wk.	No classes.	Fall session begins 4th wk.	Classes continue.	Break from Sat. before Thanksgiving Day through the following Sun.	Exams 2nd wk.	*Only limited visits are available during the summer. Make arrangements 2–3 wks. in advance.*

School	January	February	March	April	May	June
GONZAGA UNIVERSITY	Spring semester begins 3rd wk.; no classes MLK Day.	No classes Presidents' Day.	Spring break 2nd wk.; no classes noon on Fri before Easter through Easter Mon.	Break noon on Fri. before Easter through Easter Mon.	Exams 1st wk.; 1st summer session begins 3rd wk.	1st summer session continues until 4th wk.; 2nd summer session begins 5th wk.
SEATTLE UNIVERSITY	N/A	N/A	N/A	N/A	N/A	N/A
UNIVERSITY OF PUGET SOUND ✓	Spring session begins day after MLK Day.	Classes continue.	Spring break 3rd wk. Classes resume 4th wk.	Classes continue.	Exams 2nd wk. Summer session begins 3rd wk.	Classes continue.
UNIVERSITY OF WASHINGTON ✓	Winter session begins 1st wk.	No classes Presidents' Day.	Exams 2nd or 3rd wk. Spring break 3rd or 4th wk. Spring session begins at end of month.	Classes continue.	Classes continue. No classes Memorial Day.	Exams 2nd wk. Summer session begins last wk.
WASHINGTON STATE UNIVERSITY	Winter session begins 2nd wk. No classes MLK day.	No classes President's Day 9th & 23rd 2004– WSU Preview campus visitation	3/8/04– WSU Preview campus visitation 3rd wk.– spring break	End of month– end of instruction for term	1st wk.– final exams 2nd wk.– early summer session begins No classes Memorial Day	Alive! new student orientation 2nd wk.– 8-wk summer session begins Last wk.– late.
WHITMAN COLLEGE ✓	Spring session begins 3rd wk. No classes MLK Day.	No classes Presidents' Day.	Spring break 2nd–3rd wks. Classes resume last wk.	Classes continue.	Exams 2nd wk.	No classes.
West Virginia **WEST VIRGINIA UNIVERSITY**	Spring session begins 2nd wk. No classes MLK Day.	Classes continue.	Spring break 3rd wk. Classes resume 4th wk.	Exams last wk.– 1st wk. in May.	Exams 1st wk. Summer session begins 3rd wk. No classes Memorial Day	Classes continue.
Wisconsin **BELOIT COLLEGE** ✓	Spring session begins 3rd wk.	Classes continue.	Spring break 2nd full wk. Classes resume 3rd wk.	Classes continue.	Exams from end of 1st wk.–2nd wk.	No classes.
LAWRENCE UNIVERSITY ✓	Winter session begins 2nd wk.	No classes 1st Fri.–Sat.	Exams 2nd or 3rd wk., followed by Spring break.	Spring session begins.	No classes Memorial Day.	Exams 1st or 2nd wk.
MARQUETTE UNIVERSITY ✓	Spring session begins 3rd wk.	Classes continue.	Spring break 2nd wk. Classes resume 3rd wk.	No classes from Holy Thurs. through the following Mon. (Easter break).	Exams 2nd wk. Summer session begins 3rd or 4th wk. No classes Memorial Day.	Classes continue.
RIPON COLLEGE ✓	N/A	N/A	N/A	N/A	N/A	N/A

July	August	September	October	November	December	Additional Info
Summer session 2 continues.	2nd summer session ends 1st wk.; New Student Orientation begins last wk.	Labor Day Holiday observed 4th wk.	Founder's Day Holiday Mon 4th wk.; Fall Family Weekend 2nd to last weekend.	Thanksgiving holiday begins Wed before and continues through the following Sun.	Exams 3rd wk.; Holiday begins after exams.	*Campus visits are not discouraged during exam times, but class visits and lunch tours are unavailable.*
N/A	N/A	N/A	N/A	N/A	N/A	*N/A*
Classes continue.	Summer session ends 2nd wk.	Fall session begins 1st wk.	Classes continue.	Break from Thanksgiving Day through the following Sun.	Exams 3rd wk.	*Campus visits are allowed during exams, but class visits and overnight stays are not.*
No classes July 4.	Summer session ends 3rd wk.	No classes Labor Day. Fall session begins last wk.	Classes continue.	No classes Veterans' Day. Break from Thanksgiving Day through the following Sun.	Exams 2nd–3rd wks.	*Approximately 13,000 students are on campus during the summer session.*
Alive! new student orientation No classes July 4th	First wk.– end of summer session 15th 2004– Wk. of Welcome Last wk.– classes begin	No classes Labor Day 3rd wk.– WSU Future Cougar Day visitation program	Classes Continue	1st wk.– WSU Preview campus visitation No classes Veteran's Day No classes Thanksgiving wk.	2nd wk.– end of instruction for term 3rd wk.– final exams	*N/A*
No classes.	No classes.	Fall session begins 1st wk.	No classes Columbus Day.	Break from Sat. before Thanksgiving Day through the following Sun.	Exams 2nd wk.	*N/A*
No classes July 4.	Summer session ends 1st wk. Fall session begins 3rd wk.	Classes continue.	Classes continue.	Break from Sat. before Thanksgiving Day through the following Sun.	Exams 3rd wk.	*About 7,000 students are on campus during the summer session.*
No classes.	Fall session begins last wk.	Classes continue.	Break from end of 2nd wk. to beginning of 4th wk.	Break from Thanksgiving Day through the following Sun.	Exams 3rd wk.	*Campus visits are not permitted during exams.*
No classes.	No classes.	Fall session begins 4th wk.	Classes continue.	Break from Thanksgiving Day through the following Sun.	Exams 1st–2nd wks.	*Visits can be arranged during exams, but no overnight stays or class visits.*
No classes July 4.	Summer session ends 2nd wk. Fall session begins last wk.	No classes Labor Day.	No classes 4th Fri.	No classes Nov. 1. Break from Wed. before Thanksgiving through the following Sun.	Exams 3rd wk.	*N/A*
N/A	N/A	N/A	N/A	N/A	N/A	*N/A*

School	January	February	March	April	May	June
Wisconsin **UNIVERSITY OF** ✓ **WISCONSIN— MADISON**	Spring session begins 3rd wk.	Classes continue.	Spring break 2nd or 3rd wk. No classes Good Fri.	Classes resume 1st wk. No classes Good Fri.	Exams 2nd–3rd wks. Summer session begins last wk.	Classes continue.
Wyoming **UNIVERSITY OF WYOMING**	Spring session begins the Mon. before MLK Day. No classes MLK Day.	Classes continue.	Spring break 2nd wk.	Classes continue.	Exams– first wk. Summer session begins the Mon. after exams. No classes Memorial Day.	Summer session continues.

July	August	September	October	November	December	Additional Info
No classes July 4.	Summer session ends at end of 1st full wk.	Fall session begins 1st wk.	Classes continue.	Break from Thanksgiving Day through the following Sun.	Exams from end of 2nd full wk. to 3rd wk.	N/A
No classes July 4th.	Summer session ends 3rd wk. Fall session begins the last Mon. in Aug.	No classes– Labor Day	Classes continue.	Break from Wed. before Thanksgiving Day through the following Sun.	Exams– 2nd wk.	Campus visits encouraged during Fall & Spring.

ALPHABETICAL SCHOOL INDEX

ALPHABETICAL STATE INDEX

ABOUT THE AUTHORS

JANET SPENCER is a professor of law and the mother of two children with whom she visited 30 schools. She lives in New York City.

SANDRA MALESON is a technical writer and editor and has toured many colleges with her two children. She lives in Elkins Park, PA.

NOTES

NOTES

www.PrincetonReview.com

The Princeton Review
Admissions Services

At The Princeton Review, we care about your ability to get accepted to the best school for you. But, we all know getting accepting involves much more than just doing well on standardized tests. That's why, in addition to our test preparation services, we also offer free admissions services to students looking to enter college or graduate school. You can find these services on our website, *www.PrincetonReview.com*, the best online resource for researching, applying to, and learning how to pay for the right school for you.

No matter what type of program you're applying to—undergraduate, graduate, law, business, or medical—**PrincetonReview.com has the free tools, services, and advice you need to navigate the admissions process.** Read on to learn more about the services we offer.

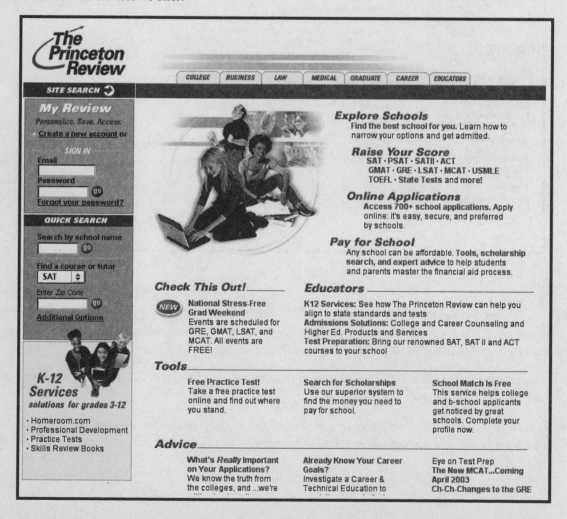

Research Schools
www.PrincetonReview.com/Research

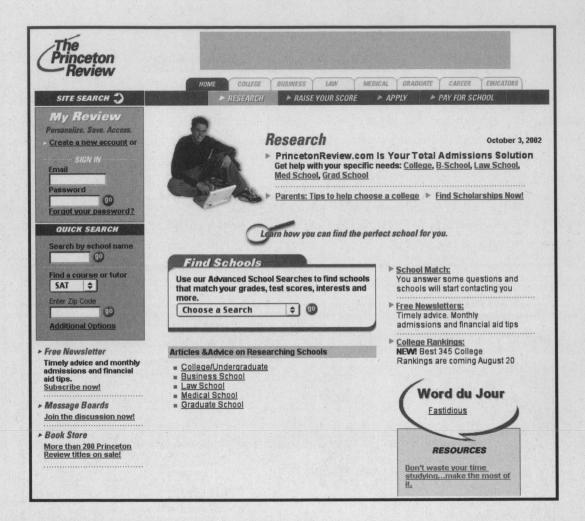

PrincetonReview.com features an interactive tool called **Advanced School Search.** When you use this tool, you enter stats and information about yourself to find a list of schools that fit your needs. From there you can read statistical and editorial information about every accredited business school, law school, medical school, and graduate school.

If you are applying to business school, make sure to use **School Match**. You tell us your scores, interests, and preferences and Princeton Review partner schools will contact you.

No matter what type of school or specialized program you are considering, **PrincetonReview.com has free articles and advice, in addition to our tools, to help you make the right choice.**

Apply to School
www.PrincetonReview.com/Apply

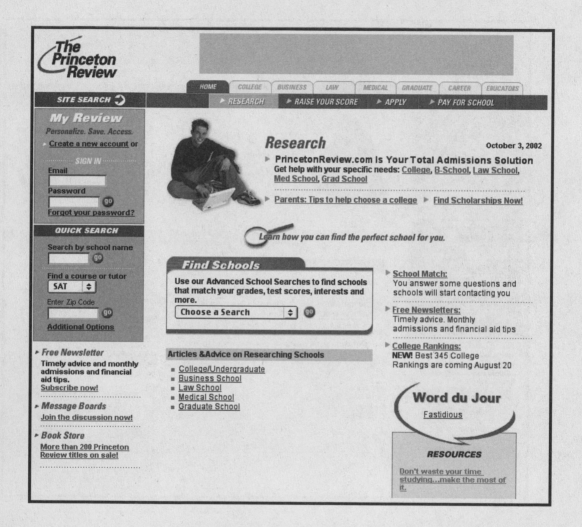

For most students, completing the school application is the most stressful part of the admissions process. PrincetonReview.com's powerful **Online School Application Engine** makes it easy to apply.

Paper applications are mostly a thing of the past. And, our hundreds of partner schools tell us they prefer to receive your applications online.

Using our online application service is simple:

- Enter information once and the common data automatically transfers onto each application.
- Save your applications and access them at any time to edit and perfect.
- Submit electronically or print and mail in.
- Pay your application fee online, using an e-check, or mail the school a check.

Our powerful application engine is built to accommodate all your needs.

Pay for School
www.PrincetonReview.com/Finance

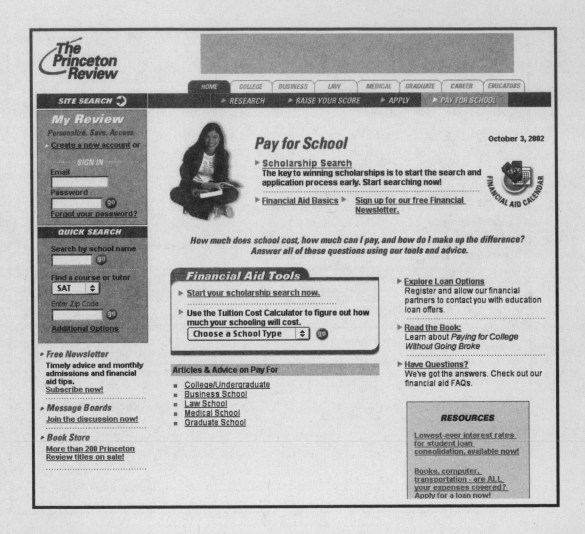

The financial aid process is confusing for everyone. But don't worry. Our free online tools, services, and advice can help you plan for the future and get the money you need to pay for school.

Our **Scholarship Search** engine will help you find free money, although often scholarships alone won't cover the cost of high tuitions. So, we offer other tools and resources to help you navigate the entire process.

Filling out the FAFSA and CSS Profile can be a daunting process, use our **Strategies for both forms** to make sure you answer the questions correctly the first time.

If scholarships and government aid aren't enough to swing the cost of tuition, we'll help you secure student loans. The Princeton Review has partnered with a select group of reputable financial institutions who will help **explore all your loans options**.

If you know how to work the financial aid process, you'll learn you don't have to **eliminate a school based on tuition.**

Be a Part of the PrincetonReview.com Community

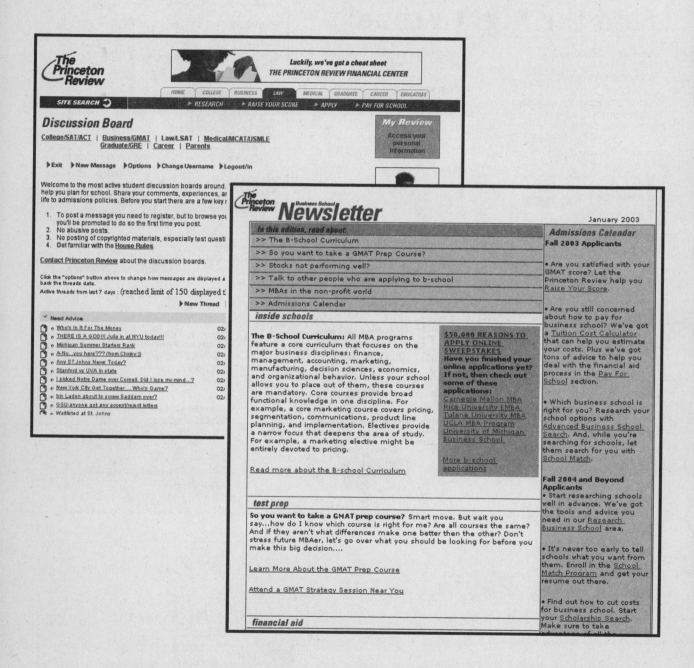

PrincetonReview.com's **Discussion Boards** and **Free Newsletters** are additional services to help you to get information about the admissions process from your peers and from The Princeton Review experts.

Make the Grade with Study Guides for the AP and SAT II Exams

AP Exams

CRACKING THE AP BIOLOGY
2004-2005 EDITION
0-375-76393-7 • $18.00

CRACKING THE AP CALCULUS
AB & BC
2004-2005 EDITION
0-375-76381-3 • $19.00

CRACKING THE AP CHEMISTRY
2004-2005 EDITION
0-375-76382-1• $18.00

CRACKING THE AP COMPUTER SCIENCE
AB & BC
2004-2005 EDITION
0-375-76383-X• $19.00

CRACKING THE AP ECONOMICS
(MACRO & MICRO)
2004-2005 EDITION
0-375-76384-8 • $18.00

CRACKING THE AP ENGLISH
LITERATURE
2004-2005 EDITION
0-375-76385-6 • $18.00

CRACKING THE AP
EUROPEAN HISTORY
2004-2005 EDITION
0-375-76386-4 • $18.00

CRACKING THE AP PHYSICS B & C
2004-2005 EDITION
0-375-76387-2 • $19.00

CRACKING THE AP PSYCHOLOGY
2004-2005 EDITION
0-375-76388-0 • $18.00

CRACKING THE AP SPANISH
2004-2005 EDITION
0-375-76389-9 • $18.00

CRACKING THE AP STATISTICS
2004-2005 EDITION
0-375-76390-2 • $19.00

CRACKING THE AP U.S. GOVERNMENT
AND POLITICS
2004-2005 EDITION
0-375-76391-0 • $18.00

CRACKING THE AP U.S. HISTORY
2004-2005 EDITION
0-375-76392-9 • $18.00

CRACKING THE AP WORLD HISTORY
2004-2005 EDITION
0-375-76380-5 • $18.00

SAT II Exams

CRACKING THE SAT II: BIOLOGY
2003-2004 EDITION
0-375-76294-9 • $18.00

CRACKING THE SAT II: CHEMISTRY
2003-2004 EDITION
0-375-76296-5 • $17.00

CRACKING THE SAT II: FRENCH
2003-2004 EDITION
0-375-76295-7 • $17.00

CRACKING THE SAT II:
WRITING & LITERATURE
2003-2004 EDITION
0-375-76301-5 • $17.00

CRACKING THE SAT II: MATH
2003-2004 EDITION
0-375-76298-1 • $18.00

CRACKING THE SAT II: PHYSICS
2003-2004 EDITION
0-375-76299-X • $18.00

CRACKING THE SAT II: SPANISH
2003-2004 EDITION
0-375-76300-7 • $17.00

CRACKING THE SAT II:
U.S. & WORLD HISTORY
2003-2004 EDITION
0-375-76297-3 • $18.00

Available at Bookstores Everywhere.
www.PrincetonReview.com

Bookstore
www.PrincetonReview.com/college/Bookstore.asp

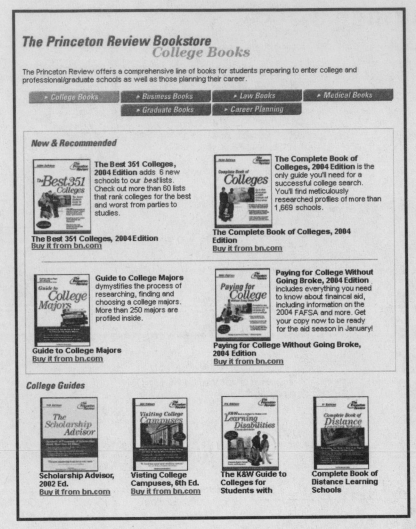

In addition to this book, we publish hundreds of other titles, including guidebooks that highlight life on campus, student opinion, and all the statistical data that you need to know about any school you are considering. Just a few of the titles that we offer are:

- Complete Book of Business Schools
- Complete Book of Law Schools
- Complete Book of Medical Schools
- The Best 351 Colleges
- The K&W Guide to Colleges for Students with Learning Disabilities or Attention Deficit
Disorder
- Guide to College Majors
- Paying for College Without Going Broke

For a complete listing of all of our titles, visit our **online bookstore:**

www.PrincetonReview.com/college/bookstore.asp